Free Speech in the New Media

Edited by

Thomas Gibbons

University of Manchester, UK

ASHGATE

Published by
Ashgate Publishing Limited
Wey Court East
Union Road
Farnham
Surrey GU9 7PT
England

Ashgate Publishing Company
Suite 420
101 Cherry Street
Burlington, VT 05401-4405
USA

Ashgate website: http://www.ashgate.com

British Library Cataloguing in Publication Data
Free speech in the new media. - (Library of essays in media law)
   1. Freedom of speech 2. Telecommunication - Law and legislation
   I. Gibbons, Thomas
   342'.0853

Library of Congress Control Number: 2008939268

ISBN: 978 0 7546 2791 3

Mixed Sources
Product group from well-managed forests and other controlled sources
www.fsc.org Cert no. SGS-COC-2482
© 1996 Forest Stewardship Council
FSC

Printed and bound in Great Britain by
TJ International Ltd, Padstow, Cornwall

Contents

Acknowledgements

The editor and publishers wish to thank the following for permission to use copyright material.

Cardoza Law Review for the essay: Monroe E. Price (2000–2001), 'The Newness of New Technology', *Cardozo Law Review*, **22**, pp. 1885–913.

Colin C. Munro and the Cambridge Law Journal for the essay: Colin R. Munro (2003), 'The Value of Commercial Speech', *The Cambridge Law Journal*, **62**, pp. 134–58.

Jack M. Balkin and New York University Law Review for the essay: Jack M. Balkin (2004), 'Digital Speech and Democratic Culture: A Theory of Freedom of Expression for the Information Society', *New York University Law Review*, **79**, pp. 1–58. Copyright © 2004 by Jack M. Balkin.

Lee C. Bollinger and Michigan Law Review Association for the essay: 'Freedom of the Press and Public Access: Toward a Theory of Partial Regulation of the Mass Media', *Michigan Law Review*, **75**, pp. 1–42. Copyright © 1976 by Lee C. Bollinger and Michigan Law Review.

Oxford University Press for the essay: Rachael Craufurd Smith (2007), 'Media Convergence and the Regulation of Audiovisual Content: Is the European Community's Audiovisual Media Services Directive Fit for Purpose?', *Current Legal Problems*, **60**, pp. 238–77.

Sweet and Maxwell for the essays: Andrew Geddis (2004), 'You Can't Say "God" on the Radio: Freedom of Expression, Religious Advertising and the Broadcast Media after *Murphy* v *Ireland*', *European Human Rights Law Review*, **9**, pp. 181–92; Ian Cram (2002), 'Beyond Madison? The U.S. Supreme Court and the Regulation of Sexually Explicit Expression', *Public Law*, pp. 743–57.

The Texas Law Review Association for the essay: Mark S. Fowler and Daniel L. Brenner (1982), 'A Marketplace Approach to Broadcast Regulation', *Texas Law Review*, **60**, pp. 207–57.

The University of California for the essay: Jonathan Weinberg (1993), 'Broadcasting and Speech', *California Law Review*', **81**, pp. 1103–206. Copyright © 1993 by the California Law Review, Inc.

Wiley-Blackwell for the essays: Jacob Rowbottom (2006), 'Media Freedom and Political Debate in the Digital Era', *Modern Law Review*, **69**, pp. 489–513. Copyright © The Modern Law Review Limited 2006; Georgina Born and Tony Prosser (2001), 'Culture and Consumerism: Citizenship, Public Service Broadcasting and the BBC's Fair Trading Obligations', *Modern Law Review*, **64**, pp. 657–87. Copyright © The Modern Law Review Limited 2001; Andrew

Scott (2003), '"A Monstrous and Unjustifiable Infringement"? Political Expression and the Broadcasting Ban on Advocacy Advertising', *Modern Law Review*, **66**, pp. 224–44. Copyright © The Modern Law Review Limited 2003.

Wolters Kluwer for the essay: Mike Varney (2004), 'European Controls on Member State Promotion and Regulation of Public Service Broadcasting and Broadcasting Standards', *European Public Law*, **10**, pp. 503–30. Copyright © 2004 Kluwer Law International; Berend Jan Drijber (1999), 'The Revised Television Without Frontiers Directive: Is it Fit for the Next Century?', *Common Market Law Review*, **36**, pp. 87–122. Copyright © 1999 Kluwer Law International.

Yale Law Journal Company, Inc. for the essay: Thomas G. Krattenmaker and L.A. Powe, Jr (1995), 'Converging First Amendment Principles for Converging Communications Media', *The Yale Law Journal*, **104**, pp. 1719–41.

Series Preface

Media law issues frequently dominate the news. A libel or privacy action by a politician or celebrity, an investigation into an alleged broadcasting scam, and the use of the Internet for downloading terrorist material or pornography are all stories which attract national, and increasingly international, publicity. Freedom of expression, whether on the traditional press and broadcasting media, or through the new electronic media, remains of fundamental importance to the workings of liberal democracies; indeed, it is impossible to see how a democracy could exist without a free, pluralist media for the dissemination of information and the discussion of political and social affairs. The media also provide us with celebrity gossip and popular entertainment.

But a free media does not entail the complete absence of law and regulation. Far from it. Laws are needed to balance the competing interests of the media, the public whom they inform and entertain and those individuals whose reputation, privacy, or even safety, might be endangered by newspapers, broadcasters and bloggers. All these branches of the media exercise considerable power and they can abuse it to distort the truth and harm individuals. Competition and other laws must be framed to prevent the emergence of media monopolies and oligopolies which are as incompatible with an effective democracy as is the domination of one political party. The Internet has been characterised by little or no regulation, beyond general criminal and civil laws, but it is legitimate to question whether this can remain the case given the ease with which, say, pornographic images can be circulated round the world in a moment. The globalisation of the media exacerbates legal problems, for a communication can be published more or less simultaneously in a number of different jurisdictions; some countries might, for example, protect privacy strongly, while others might not protect it at all because they consider privacy laws inimical to media freedom.

There is now a rich literature on many aspects of media law and regulation. The aim of these four volumes has been to present a sample of this literature, grouped round particular themes. Some of them concern topics which have been explored in legal periodicals for decades: freedom of the press, the balance between this freedom and reputation and privacy rights, media publicity prejudicing fair trials. Others deal with more modern aspects of the law, in particular whether and how the broadcasting and electronic media should be regulated. Inevitably, many essays are drawn from United States periodicals, as that country, with its strong attachment to freedom of speech and its powerful media industries, has produced an immense literature on all areas of media law. But we have also included articles from many Commonwealth countries. We have selected those which discuss issues of media law from a theoretical or comparative perspective. Lawyers in all jurisdictions can learn something from the treatment of common problems in other countries. The globalisation of the media means that knowledge of comparative law in this area is now of importance to practising lawyers.

ERIC BARENDT, *University College London*
THOMAS GIBBONS, *University of Manchester*

Introduction

New media is a term that has come to describe forms of communication which are based on digital technology. It embraces the various kinds of content that are delivered and received across digital broadcasting, digital cable and satellite, mobile telephony and the Internet. Compared to traditional media, the significance of digital technology is that it enables information to flow between creators/producers and users/audiences in radically different ways. The nature of content need no longer determine the way that it is disseminated and the people it can reach, and new markets for new products can more easily be established. In particular, because digital technology allows information to be bundled into discrete elements that can be marketed separately, it allows the flow of information to be controlled more easily by producers and consumers. The resulting phenomenon, of convergence between different forms of media and communications, throws earlier debates about free speech and broadcasting regulation into sharp relief and raises fresh questions about the continued persuasiveness of justifications for government interference with media activity.[1] This volume of essays deals with questions of political and constitutional principle and theory that affect new media. An accompanying volume, *Regulating Audiovisual Services*, examines more closely the issues of regulatory design and technique that convergence raises for the audiovisual sector.

Free Speech and Converged Media

Freedom of expression is a political and constitutional principle of major importance that normally requires governments to provide very strong justifications for interfering with flows of communication.[2] In the case of radio and television broadcasting, however, the presumption against regulation has been more easily overcome. As Barendt (1993, ch. 1) has discussed, there have traditionally been three main arguments offered to justify regulating broadcasting. One is that the electromagnetic spectrum is a public resource. But this may as easily provide a reason for the creation of a property market in spectrum as for the regulation of content transmitted across it. Another argument is that spectrum is scarce, so government has to allocate its use fairly and efficiently, thereby necessarily excluding some speakers from accessing it. Again, a non-regulatory, market-based approach may be equally compelling. Third, it is argued that mass media have an especially powerful impact on public opinion and therefore need to be regulated in the public interest. There are really two strands to this argument: one is that the audience is unable to control the material it receives (the apparent pervasiveness of broadcasting's intrusion into the household and its impact on a general audience including children); the other strand is a mass medium's potential to reduce diversity of expression and

---

1   For a discussion in the United Kingdom context, see Gibbons (2001/2002).
2   See the first volume in this series, *Freedom of the Press*, edited by E. Barendt (2009). See also Barendt (2005).

of content. Here, the acceptability of either point is more dependent on empirical data about media effects than on opposition to possible excesses of power over communication.

Assuming it is granted that some regulation of traditional analogue broadcasting may be justified, what are the implications for new media? The appropriate outcome is not self-evident from the fact of convergence in itself. Convergence does not necessarily require rationalization in the direction of the 'first amendment' approach that has traditionally been applied to print media; it may be that the reasons for intervening in broadcasting are also applicable to new media. What is required is the identification of satisfactory principles for deciding how free speech is to be preserved in the new media.

As a starting point, Chapter 1, a well-known article by Lee Bollinger, discusses what he calls two opposing constitutional traditions in the United States. The print media are given almost complete protection from government interference, whereas the broadcast media may be subject to various forms of control, based on the requirement, under the Communications Act 1934, that the Federal Communications Commission (FCC) exercise its responsibilities with reference to the 'public interest, convenience or necessity'. Although Bollinger's discussion is relevant to other kinds of media regulation, such as measures to control harmful or indecent content, his particular focus is affirmative regulation for the purpose of enabling the public to receive access to a variety of ideas and experiences. That was exemplified by the FCC's 'fairness doctrine', which required broadcasters to provide fair and adequate coverage of opposing views related to controversial issues. Bollinger's aim is to discover whether there is any rational basis for treating one sector of the media differently from the other. He concludes that there is no such basis but, nevertheless, suggests that a dual approach may be justified in order to balance freedom of the media with a way of mitigating 'the serious inequality in speech opportunities' (p. 4) that exist.

Bollinger demonstrates that there are serious flaws in the 'scarcity rationale', mentioned above, both as a basis for regulation in itself and as a reason for distinguishing between print and broadcast media. His observations are all the more pertinent in the light of developments since he was writing, in the shape of cable, satellite and Internet distribution of content. However, one of his main points is to claim that discussion of the scarcity rationale is really concerned with a deeper principle, that 'when only a few interests control a major avenue of communication, those able to speak can be forced by the government to share' (p. 11).[3] The anomaly in US constitutional doctrine is that this principle appears to be applicable only to broadcasting and not to print. Furthermore, it is only permissive and does not require government to intervene and, indeed, since Bollinger wrote, the FCC has abolished the fairness doctrine. Are there other rationales to explain the different approaches to print and broadcasting? Bollinger considers arguments that broadcasting is distinctive because it is a more concentrated industry or because it has a special impact on its audience (especially that of television on viewers), but he does not find them convincing. Nevertheless, he believes that a *'partial* regulatory scheme' (p. 34; original emphasis) may be defended because, however

---

3   For a different understanding, see Lively (1992). Lively agrees that the scarcity rationale has had a major influence in accounting for the press/broadcasting divide, but he regards it as illogical and leading to a unique interpretation of the First Amendment that elevates the rights of viewers and listeners above those of broadcasters (at p. 609).

illogical its historical emergence, it enables competing first amendment values – editorial freedom and exposure to a full range of ideas and opinions – to complement each other.

Bollinger's conclusions, if not his basic analysis, have been criticized as an unsatisfactory compromise (Barendt, 2005).[4] Nevertheless, as Hitchens points out, it may serve to highlight that, 'the issue may really be not why broadcasting is regulated, but why the press is not' (2006, p. 47). As her book shows, the values of pluralism and diversity may justify positive regulatory intervention to enhance interests in freedom of communication. Indeed, this is a view that is not so controversial from a European perspective, where the free speech principle is not regarded solely as a matter of negative liberty.

One reason, then, why Bollinger's conclusion may be insufficient is that his explanation for the contrasting approaches to print and broadcasting regulation requires further elaboration. In Chapter 2 Jonathan Weinberg argues that the explanation is that the free speech philosophy applied to print is the manifestation of a different 'world-view' from that which underlies broadcasting policy. Free speech reflects 'individualism and a sharp public-private distinction' (p. 51), whereas broadcasting emphasizes community interests that may justify some government paternalism. Weinberg notes that each has its advantages and drawbacks. Free speech philosophy is highly sceptical about extending governmental power over communication, but it assumes that a marketplace of ideas will function effectively to encourage expression and to bring a wide range of competing views to public attention. Broadcasting regulation is sensitive to structural inequalities in access to public debate and to the possible effects of different kinds of communication on its audiences, but it proceeds by way of imposing public interest requirements that may be vague, contestable and subject to excessive administrative discretion.

For Weinberg, the point is that, if traditional free speech is regarded as the basic standpoint for judging broadcasting regulation, the process of licensing and enforcing licence requirements may indeed be seen as unjustified interference with editorial independence. But if the adequacy of that free speech standpoint is questioned, a different picture may emerge. In particular, he argues that the 'marketplace metaphor' is flawed because it does not recognize that members of society do not have sufficient meaningful opportunities to speak and to convince others of their views, and it assumes that discourse will be rational and thereby yield some conception of truth or democratic self-determination. At the same time, he is suspicious of governmental intervention to improve the process by way of controlling broadcasters' speech, concerned that it could undermine the benefits of free speech doctrine. His solution to the dilemma is to examine the possibilities of public service broadcasting on the one hand and the potential of the Internet on the other, as means of providing greater exposure for 'unprivileged' viewpoints.

As Bollinger (p. 28) foresaw, new technology forces existing regulatory principles to be reconsidered and modified where appropriate. In Chapter 3 Thomas Krattenmaker and Lucas Powe ask the question, 'How can one reconcile the fact of technological and media convergence with the legal presumption of distinct treatments?' (p. 149). They argue that, in choosing which approach to adopt for converging media technologies, the broadcast model should be discarded in favour of the print model. In their view, not only is special regulation for broadcasting a constitutional anomaly, but new forms of media can be dealt with more

---

4   Barendt (2005) also describes it as incoherent; see also Hitchens (2006, p. 47). The regulation of media ownership is considered in Volume 4 of this series.

appropriately under the traditional first amendment principles that have been applied to print.

In presenting the case for the general application of these first amendment principles, Krattenmaker and Powe are reflecting a broader antipathy to governmental interference in communications. For them, editorial control over speech is a matter for private institutions, because attempts at regulation serve to chill speech or to stifle it. Imposing a public interest standard on programming serves to deny the viewing or listening choices that adults would otherwise make. The marketplace is the appropriate means for ensuring speakers' access to the media and the availability of a diversity of content for audiences.

A merit of their approach is that it does not succumb to technological determinism. There has been a tendency in some policy debates to emphasize technical similarities and differences, in comparing media in order to chart the direction of convergence, and to draw the conclusion that the appropriate approach to regulation will necessarily follow from the way that the medium is characterized.[5] Just prior to the time that Krattenmaker and Powe were advancing their perspective in the United States, the European Commission had issued a Green Paper on convergence which suggested that new, converged media would have more in common with telecommunications than broadcasting and, since telecommunications regulation was more market- and competition-oriented, that would be the best model for future regulation of all communications (see Harrison and Woods, 2007, ch. 5).

Nevertheless, there may still be a case for regulating television, even in the new media environment, as an important essay by Sunstein (2000) demonstrates.[6] Sunstein maintains that there is a public interest in television content and that regulation may be justified, on both economic grounds and its social functions, in order to promote democratic objectives. Furthermore, he argues that the introduction of digital broadcasting does not diminish the case for intervention to support those objectives in new forms of television content. In support of these claims, Sunstein suggests that broadcasting is not an ordinary market commodity. This is because it is characterized by a number of market failures, whereby typical economic relationships between providers and consumers do not exist or function ineffectively, and its particular association with public discussion requires measures to support its democratic significance.

Indeed, implicit in the essays considered so far is the recognition that media activities are inextricably bound up with democracy. However, it may be that earlier debates about the scope of media regulation (including the relationship between print and broadcasting) have been constrained by a particular view of democracy. This is the view of Jack Balkin (Chapter 4), who advances a challenging argument that Internet and digital technologies serve to highlight features of freedom of expression that have hitherto been underemphasized, namely its cultural and participatory dimensions. For Balkin, 'The digital revolution makes possible widespread cultural participation and interaction that previously could not have existed on the same scale ... and makes the production and distribution of information a key source of wealth' (p. 175).

---

5   For criticism of this approach, see Goldberg *et al.* (1998).

6   The essay also contains a valuable discussion of innovative forms of regulation, and is therefore reproduced in Volume 4 of this series.

The first trend is essentially democratic, making it possible for an increasing number of people to take part in the creation and distribution of material. It extends beyond formal representative institutions and public deliberation, encompassing what Balkin describes as a 'democratic culture' (p. 175) in which individuals are closely involved in the processes that give meaning to their lives. A theory of freedom of expression for the digital era requires protection for the ability to participate in the system of culture creation. But the second trend may run counter to those developments. Digital technology enables methods of control over information to be more effective, and that can restrict democratic participation. Balkin argues that media companies deploy free speech arguments both broadly and narrowly, in order to secure their commercial interests in exploiting the wealth potential of digital expression. To resist the regulation of digital networks, they say that intervention will prevent open access to information. To resist the expansion of the public domain in intellectual property rights, they say that free speech implies the ability to protect the manner of expression. Balkin is concerned that these arguments are beginning to dominate and that freedom of speech is in danger of becoming a general right against economic regulation of the information industries.

As Balkin observes, these issues have also been discussed in relation to more traditional media and have prompted initiatives to control media ownership and to ensure greater diversity of content and access for a broader range of viewpoints. He acknowledges that (contrary to what some suppose) the existence of the Internet (with its open and relatively unrestricted nature) will not compensate for the democratic deficiencies of existing media, because the Internet is not independent of traditional media but builds upon them. Nevertheless, he thinks that we no longer live in an age where a few speakers broadcast to a largely inactive audience; Internet speech has made a difference, and free speech theory must accommodate that change. For him, the principal features of Internet speech are its reflection of popular culture, its innovation, its creativity in re-working content and ideas (what he calls 'glomming on', p. 182), its interactivity and participation, and its association with virtual communities.

Balkin's approach to solving the trend to control new, digital speech is to focus on free speech values, rather than constitutional rights, and to build their recognition and respect into the very infrastructure of communications and its regulation. He wants opportunities to be made for individual expression to surface without being subjected to the kinds of constraint that may be imposed on more traditional media. But is he being too optimistic in believing that the Internet will revolutionize communications? He does not believe that it will hasten the demise of traditional media but he does suggest that it will act as a counterbalance which should be protected by free speech theory.

In Chapter 5 Jacob Rowbottom offers a more sceptical response to claims that the Internet will herald a more democratic media. Acknowledging the features of Internet speech (on which Balkin places much emphasis) – the low cost of communication, the relative ease of participation and the greater scope for user control – he argues that online expression is likely to manifest the same problems as traditional media: '[it] can not only perpetuate existing media elites, but also create new ones' (p. 232). His starting point is that media freedom is not the same as individual expression, because control over expression is vested in a relatively small number of people, so there will continue to be a need to regulate to ensure that such expression is exercised in accordance with social and democratic responsibilities. However, he takes issue with the idea that the greater emphasis on individual expression on the Internet has the effect of making such regulation less important and re-orienting the rationales for intervention. Rather, he argues that even the online world is characterized by a small number of speakers or mediators addressing a mass audience and controlling the content that it receives, so existing regulatory approaches will continue to be appropriate for them.

Public Service Broadcasting

Debates about the relationship between free speech and electronic media are predicated on policy assumptions about the nature of that media. Chapter 6, by Georgina Born and Tony Prosser, opens with a question that captures the main issue: 'Is broadcasting [broadly conceived] best conceived as a commercial activity or as an expression of cultural norms and expectations?' (p. 259). Outside the United States, and especially in Europe, the latter – public interest – dimension has dominated from the outset. For decades, but to varying degrees, governments controlled the airwaves and organized broadcasting through public service monopolies which had duties to provide for the public as a whole. This was no longer a general model by the 1980s as new forms of delivery offered competition to broadcasting, the European Convention on Human Rights was invoked to secure greater pluralism in broadcasting provision (Craufurd Smith, 1997) and economic liberalization gained political ascendancy. The trend in Europe has been a gradual deregulation away from total public service programming, but the essential compatibility of its values with free speech doctrine has hardly been challenged. In policy terms, although one effect of the European Community's 'Television without Frontiers' directive was to liberalize many Member States' broadcasting systems, those States have jealously guarded the public service traditions of their national broadcasters (see Amsterdam Treaty, p. 262).

Many of the core principles of public service broadcasting can be attributed to the institution of the UK's British Broadcasting Corporation (the BBC) (see Barendt, 1993; Craufurd Smith, 1997; Curran and Seaton, 2003, chs 8–11). It developed its original 1920s remit, to 'inform, educate and entertain', into an elaborate set of practices that were at once both creatively challenging and universally appealing, yet arguably elitist and paternalistic. Quality programming was funded entirely from a licence fee, without commercial support from advertising or sponsorship. Over the years, the BBC has developed its conception of public service values in a critical and reflexive way and various elements of public service broadcasting have been imposed on commercial providers by regulation in the UK and more widely in Europe. Nevertheless, a number of questions about public service broadcasting continue to be keenly discussed.

One question is the nature of the public service remit. Increasingly, there have been demands for its substance to be explicitly articulated, rather than repose in the broadcasters' culture and practice. Justifications need to be offered for the degree of public expenditure that it involves, and for the level of subsidy that it entails in attracting audiences from commercial competitors. Another question is the extent to which public service providers should produce programme genres similar to those provided by commercial providers, or concentrate on content which the market will not supply. A third question is whether, in the light of media convergence, the public service remit should be extended to new media, including online content. The essay by Born and Prosser discusses these issues in the context of the lengthy and wide-ranging reform process that started in the late 1990s in the UK, and led to new communications regulation, the Communications Act 2003, and a new Charter for the BBC in 2006.[7] They particularly emphasize the democratic or 'citizenship' element of public service, which has always been a rationale for its existence, if sometimes only latently, and takes on added significance as the scarcity rationale diminishes in cogency.

More recently, the UK's regulator, Ofcom, has restated the principles of public service broadcasting in terms of its purpose and key characteristics, rejecting a 'genre' approach to its definition and implicitly accepting its democratic function.[8] The purposes of public service service broadcasting are:

- to inform ourselves and others and to increase our understanding of the world through news, information and analysis of current events and ideas;
- to stimulate our interest in and knowledge of arts, science, history and other topics through content that is accessible and can encourage informal learning;
- to reflect and strengthen our cultural identity through original programming at UK, national and regional level, on occasion bringing audiences together for shared experiences; and
- to make us aware of different cultures and alternative viewpoints, through programmes that reflect the lives of other people and other communities, both within the UK and elsewhere.

The distinctive characteristics of public service programmes are:

- high quality – well funded and well produced;
- original – new UK content, rather than repeats or acquisitions;
- innovative – breaking new ideas or re-inventing exciting approaches, rather than copying old ones;
- challenging – making viewers think;
- engaging – remaining accessible and enjoyed by viewers; and
- widely available – if content is publicly funded, a large majority of citizens need to be given the chance to watch it. (Ofcom, 2005, para. 1.11)[9]

Ofcom has recognized that, in the digital age, public service content and its distribution will change, to reflect new technologies and users' behaviour, but that it will continue to have a major role in the new media.

Nevertheless, the precise role of public service provision, and especially its relationship with commercial providers, is by no means settled. As Born and Prosser indicate, wider developments at the European level are of critical importance for national policies to support public service broadcasting. In particular, European Community law on freedom to provide services within the internal market, and the provisions of its competition law on 'state aid', place limits on the way that public service content can be imposed on national media markets.

---

7   Royal Charter for the Continuance of the BBC, 2006, Cm. 6925, available at: http://www.bbc. co.uk/bbctrust/

8   This reflects Ofcom's duty to promote citizenship, under s.1 of the Communications Act 2003.

9   For documents relating to that first review, together with the second review in 2007/8, visit the Ofcom website at: http://www.ofcom.org.uk/. See also BBC (2005).

In Chapter 7 Mike Varney offers an overview of developments in this area. He discusses how the effect of European Community law is to remove indirect support for public service from the commercial market, and to force the detail of public subsidy to be made more explicit. At the same time, he shows that the European Court of Justice and the European Commission are not unsympathetic to the public service mission and indeed to measures intended to promote free speech through pluralism and diversity (see also Prosser, 2005).

By contrast, in Chapter 8 Mark Fowler and Daniel Brenner make the classic case for wholesale deregulation of broadcasting in favour of a market-based approach. It is particularly interesting and relevant to the public service broadcasting debate because of the way it characterizes its target, the US regime for issuing broadcast licences under the Communications Act 1934, by reference to the public interest standard. Fowler and Brenner describe this as a 'fiduciary' or 'community trustee' approach and they argue that is no longer justified. Instead, they propose that broadcasters should be regarded as marketplace participants and that broadcasting policy should be directed towards maximizing the services that the public desires. For them, normal marketplace mechanisms should be used to determine what the audience wants and the means of supplying it, rather than have the FCC decide it on their behalf: 'The public's interest, then, defines the public interest' (p. 322). The implication is that any regulation of the broadcasting industry, and the content it provides, should be confined to competition measures designed to promote the efficient functioning of the relevant market. To the extent that a liberalized market is consistent with liberty of speech, some of their arguments overlap with the constitutional points discussed in the previous section. But Fowler and Brenner are as much concerned with the economic shape of the broadcasting industry. They see the very existence of licensing as a distortion of market effects, replacing individual choice with costly governmental or regulatory paternalism. By comparison, the marketplace approach would attend to the basic commodity that can be traded in a broadcast market, namely electromagnetic spectrum.

Fowler and Brenner's thinking has had at least indirect policy outcomes. It was reflected in the Peacock review of the BBC's finances, commissioned by the Thatcher government (Peacock Committee, 1986), which prompted wider deregulation of the UK's broadcasting industry in 1990. Various forms of spectrum trading have been introduced in both the USA (in 1994) and the UK (in 1998). However, in the UK, the peculiar economics of broadcasting have been recognized as justifying at least some regulatory intervention.[10]

Content Standards

Beliefs

Part III of the volume deals with problems raised by particular kinds of content restriction. The two essays in this subsection are concerned with the advocacy of beliefs. In Chapter 10 Andrew Scott examines the legality of the UK's prohibition in the electronic media on 'advocacy advertising' – that is, advertising for the purpose of communicating social, political and moral

---

10 The Peacock Committee itself made the case. See also Ofcom (2005). For developments in the United States, see Goodman (2007) and Campbell (2006).

arguments to a wider public.[11] The ban has been a long-standing feature of broadcasting regulation in the UK and was re-enacted in the Communications Act 2003, notwithstanding reservations that it may be incompatible with Art. 10 of the European Convention on Human Rights (protecting freedom of expression). As Scott argues, the ban appears to conflict with the priority that the Convention jurisprudence gives to political expression in the light of its intrinsic connection with democratic practice. He considers four justifications offered for continuing the ban – protecting audiences from intrusive political comment, the existence of alternative outlets for political expression, the need to insulate the public sphere against over-powerful interests, and possible negative implications for the funding of political parties – and finds them all unpersuasive. His view appeared to find support in the European Court of Human Rights[12] but some doubt has arisen in the light of that Court's apparently inconsistent attitude to religious advertising.[13] In Chapter 9 Andrew Geddis explores possible reasons for this, arguing that there are no differences in principle between political and religious expression, but that the Court has wrongly allowed States a greater margin of appreciation in regulating religious content in broadcasting. At the root of this debate are differing views about what measures are needed to safeguard the functioning of a healthy democracy. Recently, the House of Lords has confirmed that the ban on broadcast political advertising is compatible with the Convention, effectively rejecting the criticisms advocated by Scott.[14] Especially noteworthy is its emphasis on the perceived power of the electronic media as a reason for regulating it in the interests of promoting free speech.

Indecency

A second pair of essays deals with the control of indecency. The context is set by Monroe Price's discussion of 'the newness of technology' in Chapter 11. Although his analysis resonates with those of Balkin and of Rowbottom, discussed above, his purpose is not to take sides in predicting whether new technology is likely to be truly revolutionary. Rather, he is interested in the way it is perceived and acted upon by legislators and lawyers. He notes that there is a greater tendency in the United States, as opposed to Europe, to measure new media by reference to the First Amendment issues considered in relation to traditional media. Thus, the Internet is characterized in terms of its similarities to print media and its differences from broadcasting or cable television, in order to determine the constitutionality of regulation. Relevant questions then centre on, for example, user choice, the ability to separate audiences by age (adults and children) in time or space, and the capacity to enforce controls over the new technology. Price shows how these considerations featured in the US Supreme Court's ruling in *Reno*.[15] Policy responses, and judicial reactions to them, may be based on speculation about the threats and opportunities that the Internet brings, rather than on a sense of the underlying principles at stake. In the course of his discussion, Price offers a useful commentary on the work of Lessig, who has written extensively on the relationship between the law and the

---

11 The title of his essay quotes from Barendt's evidence to a Parliamentary scrutiny committee. See also Barendt (2003).

12 *VGT Verein gegen Tierfabriken* v. *Switzerland* (2002) 34 EHRR 4.

13 *Murphy* v. *Ireland* (2003) 38 EHRR 212.

14 *R (Animal Defenders)* v. *Secretary of State for Culture, Media & Sport* [2008] UKHL 15.

15 *US* v. *Reno* 21 U.S. 844 (1997). For subsequent developments, see Chapter 12 in this volume.

architecture of the Internet. Lessig was critical of the *Reno* decision, which treated the Internet as analogous to print media and therefore meriting the least restrictive form of regulatory intervention, because it relied on the potential of technology (such as filtering and encryption) to protect the interests of children, but without appreciating that that technology could pose much greater threats to free speech than a regulatory measure.

As Price implies in his conclusion – 'Something is changing … in the interaction between the staggering symbolic output of the society and the development of its children' (p. 437) – there may be other values than the First Amendment at stake when regulating the new media. In his discussion of sexually explicit expression in Chapter 12, Ian Cram argues that a Madisonian interpretation of the First Amendment, giving primacy to political speech, also implies that the strictest scrutiny of content regulation may not be appropriate for examples of speech lower down the hierarchy. Discussing *Reno* and the later litigation in *Ashcroft*, he makes a case for proportionate intervention to protect children against harmful effects of online content. Such an approach would not be controversial in Europe, and the emphasis there has been on finding effective regulatory techniques to secure protection.[16]

Content Regulation in the European Community

For the European Community, various aspects of content regulation were brought together by the 'Television without Frontiers' directive, first promulgated in 1989,[17] amended in 1997[18] and further revised in 2007 under a new title – the 'Audiovisual Media Services Directive' (AVMSD).[19] The aim of the original directive and its 1997 amendment was to coordinate aspects of television regulation within the Community's internal market. It combines a 'country of origin' principle with one of freedom of transmission and reception, for the purpose of enforcing a minimum set of harmonized standards. This means that responsibility for enforcing those standards on broadcasters or providers is given to the Member State where the media company is established, and other Member States are required to accept material received from that jurisdiction without imposing on it stricter regulation of their own. The revision in 2007 has the same aim but its scope has been extended beyond television to new forms of audiovisual media. In Chapter 13 Berend Drijber discusses the position before 2007 but his essay continues to be relevant, since it examines a range of issues that have not been substantially affected by the AVMSD. Rachael Craufurd Smith, in Chapter 14, discusses the implications of the AVMSD itself, with a particular stress on its attempt to cater for newer media.

By the very nature of the European Community, the framing of the minimum content requirements has been a highly politicized process (see Collins, 1994) and has focused on three main themes. One involves aspects of jurisdiction and potential conflicts between different Member States' own media regulation and their interpretations of the minimum requirements in the Directive. Another theme has been the imposition of positive content requirements

---

16 See the essays in Volume 4 of this series. For general discussion of free speech principles related to the Internet, see Barendt (2005).

17 Directive 89/552/EEC.

18 Directive 97/36/EC.

19 Directive 2007/65/EC. For background information and texts, visit the European Commission's Information Society Portal at: http://ec.europa.eu/information_society/index_en.htm.

in the form of quotas for European content and independent European production, and of protection for free-to-air programming of major events of importance to society. A third theme is a set of negative content requirements, imposing restrictions on advertising and sponsorship, harmful and illegal material that especially affects children, and the violation of some basic human rights. As Collins has noted, the positive and negative elements represent, respectively, 'dirigiste' support for the protection of European culture and media policy on the one hand, and pressure for liberalization of the market on the other.[20]

Drijber's analysis of the problems raised by jurisdiction and the country of origin principle demonstrates the tensions that lie dormant in such an elaborate political compromise. Notably, concerns about the problem of 'circumvention', whereby a media company may avoid being regulated by a strict Member State through the device of establishing in a more lenient regime and transmitting from there, have persisted, and are intended to be addressed in the AVMSD by a new conciliation process to deal with them. Similarly, the arguments for and against quotas in mainstream television have not changed, and they were strongly pursued in negotiations leading to the AVMSD, which has altered the position but only for interactive and on-demand content (now described as 'non-linear' services, and discussed by Craufurd Smith). Again, the provisions for major events of national importance have not been changed by the AVMSD. Drijber's essay has been overtaken by a relaxation of some advertising rules in the AVMSD: detailed requirements about the scheduling of advertising within programmes have been largely removed and, significantly, product placement will now be allowed, except in children's programming. Nevertheless, his general discussion illustrates the complications of seeking to coordinate, at a transnational level, the activities of an industry that combines economic pursuits with strongly held political and cultural objectives.

The complexity is intensified when the implications of new technology are added for consideration. Craufurd Smith's essay poses a question similar to the one in Drijber's title: is the new Audiovisual Media Services Directive 'fit for purpose'? In both essays, there is a sense of scepticism about the ability of regulation to keep pace with the rapid changes in technology that characterize communications. In 1997, it had been appreciated that the concept of broadcasting was becoming outdated as a basis for regulation but it was considered sufficient to make provision for new kinds of advertising (such as teleshopping) without introducing radical change. By the turn of the new century, it was apparent that the Directive would have to be substantially recast in order to respond to media convergence. Although all aspects of its themes – jurisdiction, and positive and negative content – were reviewed, the major debate focused on the scope of the Directive and the implications, a debate that ranged across many of the issues examined in Part I of this volume. On one view, new audiovisual media reflected an online world, for which minimal regulation was desirable. From the opposite perspective, if content regulation was justified in traditional media, the fact of delivery of similar material across a different platform would not alter the rationale. As Craufurd Smith shows, what the AVMSD has done is to attempt to resolve these differences by adopting a technology-neutral approach and directing attention to the user's experience as the foundation for intervention. A basic distinction is made, therefore, between 'linear' and 'non-linear' content, between material that is 'pushed' through mass dissemination and material that is 'pulled' on-demand and interactively.

---

20 For recent comprehensive discussion, see Harrison and Woods (2007).

While this linear/non-linear divide may, in principle, justify different approaches to regulation, it is not easy to implement across new and changing technologies in a consistent way. Craufurd Smith discusses three sets of criteria for differentiating between content on that basis: the amount of control that the user exerts, the impact of the material on the public and the maturity of the relevant industries. Her conclusion is that, because of difficulties in applying the criteria across different categories of content, the AVMSD will not provide a definitive basis for regulating new media. Furthermore, it may be over-ambitious in seeking to harmonize the differing rules of Members States in areas of child protection and hate speech.

Advertising

It may be that one of the most practically significant changes introduced by the AVMSD is the relaxation of the rules on advertising, in the face of commercial pressures to extract value from programming in the light of time shifting and the use of personal video recorders by the audience. Are there implications for freedom of speech? Controls over advertising and sponsorship have traditionally been a major part of broadcasting regulation. They have three broad justifications: the protection of editorial decision-making from commercial pressures, the protection of consumers and the minimizing of unfair competitive advantage. Inevitably, they may conflict with the free speech interests of prospective advertisers, and 'commercial speech' doctrine provides a theoretical framework for examining the principles at stake. In Chapter 15 Colin Munro provides a discussion of both the US and European approaches.[21] In both cases, there is a recognition that the justifications for safeguarding speech may need to be modified when the speakers are commercial entities, to acknowledge that such speech may itself interfere with the democratic functions of free expression, and that such speech may really be a manifestation of property interests that may not merit relatively stronger protection. Product placement is a good example of the conflicts involved. Although the AVMSD allows its use, the accompanying conditions are an indication of its sensitivity. As well as being banned for children's programming, there must be no influence on editorial integrity, no direct encouragement to purchase and no undue prominence. In addition, there must be clear signposting for users. Interestingly, just as the European position is easing in this area, there are strong arguments from the US for the imposition of tighter checks in the interests of editorial integrity.

References

Barendt, E. (1993), *Broadcasting Law: A Comparative Study*, Oxford: Oxford University Press.
Barendt, E. (2003), 'Free Speech and Abortion', *Public Law*, 580–91.
Barendt, E. (2005) 'Freedom of Speech in the Media', in E. Barendt (ed.), *Freedom of Speech* (2nd edn), Oxford: Oxford University Press, pp. 417–50.
Barendt, E. (ed.) (2009), *Freedom of the Press*, Library of Essays in Media Law 1, Farnham: Ashgate.
BBC (2005), *Building Public Value*, available at: http://www.bbc.co.uk

---

21 For a closely argued philosophical and legal analysis of the idea of commercial expression, concluding that it is a 'constitutional fraud', see Shiner (2003). The case of *Kasky* v. *Nike Inc.*, mentioned in Munro's essay, was not actually reviewed by the US Supreme Court and was settled out of court.

Campbell, A. (2006), 'A Public Interest Perspective on the Impact of the Broadcasting Provisions of the 1996 Act', *Federal Communications Law Journal*, **58**, pp. 455–76.

Collins, R. (1994), *Broadcasting and Audio-Visual Policy in the European Single Market*, London: John Libbey.

Craufurd Smith, R. (1997), *Broadcasting and Fundamental Rights*, Oxford: Oxford University Press.

Curran, J. and Seaton, J. (2003), *Power without Responsibility* (6th ed.), London: Routledge.

Gibbons, T. (2001/2002), 'Reforming the Regulation of Communications', in E. Barendt and A. Firth (eds), *Yearbook of Copyright and Media Law*, VI, New York: Oxford University Press, pp. 185–205.

Goldberg, D., Prosser, T. and Verhulst, S. (eds) (1998), *Regulating the Changing Media: A Comparative Study*, Oxford: Clarendon Press.

Goodman, E.P. (2006), 'Stealth Marketing and Editorial Integrity', *Texas Law Review*, **85**, pp. 83–152.

Goodman, E.P. (2007), 'Media Policy and Free Speech: The First Amendment at War with Itself', *Hofstra Law Review*, **35**, pp. 1210–62.

Harrison, J. and Woods, L. (2007), *European Broadcasting Law and Policy*, Cambridge: Cambridge University Press.

Hitchens, L. (2006), *Broadcasting Pluralism and Diversity: A Comparative Study of Policy and Regulation*, Oxford: Hart Publishing.

Lively, D. (1992), 'Modern Media and the First Amendment: Rediscovering Freedom of the Press', *Washington Law Review*, **67**, pp. 599–624.

Ofcom (2005), *Ofcom Review of Public Service Broadcasting – Phase 3, Competition for Quality*, available at: http://www.ofcom.org.uk/consult/condocs/psb3/

Peacock Committee (1986), *Report of the Committee on Financing the BBC*, Cmnd. 9824, London: HMSO.

Prosser, T. (2005), *The Limits of Competition Law: Markets and Public Services*, Oxford: Oxford University Press.

Shiner, R.A. (2003), *Freedom of Commercial Expression*, Oxford: Oxford University Press.

Sunstein, C.R. (2000), 'Television and the Public Interest', *California Law Review*, **88**, (2), pp. 499–564.

Part I
Free Speech and Converged Media

[1]

FREEDOM OF THE PRESS AND PUBLIC ACCESS: TOWARD A THEORY OF PARTIAL REGULATION OF THE MASS MEDIA

Lee C. Bollinger, Jr.*†

During the past half century there have existed in this country two opposing constitutional traditions regarding the press. On the one hand, the Supreme Court has accorded the print media virtually complete constitutional protection from attempts by government to impose affirmative controls such as access regulation. On the other hand, the Court has held affirmative regulation of the broadcast media to be constitutionally permissible, and has even suggested that it may be constitutionally compelled. In interpreting the first amendment, the Court in one context has insisted on the historical right of the editor to be free from government scrutiny, but in the other it has minimized the news director's freedom to engage in "unlimited private censorship"[1] and has exalted the "right of the public to receive suitable access to social, political, aesthetic, moral and other ideas and experiences."[2] The opinions in each area stand apart, carefully preserved through a distinctive core of precedent, analysis and idiom.

The purpose of this article is to examine critically these decisions and to explore whether there is any rational basis for limiting to one sector of the media the legislature's power to impose access regulation.[3] The article takes the position that the Court has pursued the

---

* Associate Professor of Law, University of Michigan. B.S. 1968, University of Oregon; J.D. 1971, Columbia University.—Ed.

† I am grateful to my colleagues Vince Blasi, Richard Lempert, Don Regan, Terry Sandalow and Joe Vining and to Geoffrey Stone of the University of Chicago Law School for their helpful comments and criticisms in the preparation of this article. I am especially indebted to my colleague Joe Sax and to Bo Burt of the Yale Law School for their instruction and guidance.

1. Red Lion Broadcasting Co. v. FCC, 395 U.S. 367, 390 (1969).

2. 395 U.S. at 392.

3. The term "access regulation" encompasses a variety of quite different forms of regulation. It can refer to a legal obligation to cover all points of view on any public issue as well as to a more modest rule that simply forbids discrimination in the acceptance of proffered advertisements. The underlying principle for the regulation can vary along with its scope and impact on the press. It may be designed to protect reputations, to equalize opportunities of citizens to present their points of view on certain issues, or to maximize the amount of information available to the public. *See* B. SCHMIDT, FREEDOM OF THE PRESS VS. PUBLIC ACCESS ch. 2 (1976).

It is certainly not the purpose of this article to assert that all forms of access

2   *Michigan Law Review*   [Vol. 75:1

right path for the wrong reasons. There is a powerful rationality underlying the current decision to restrict regulatory authority to broadcasting, but it is not, as is commonly supposed, that broadcasting is somehow different in principle from the print media and that it therefore is not deserving of equivalent first amendment treatment. As will be discussed in section I, the Court's attempt to distinguish broadcasting on the basis of its dependence on scarce resources (the electromagnetic spectrum) is unpersuasive; moreover, whatever validity the distinction may once have had is now being undercut by the advance of new technology in the form of cable television.[4] Further, other possible points of distinction that may be raised, such as the broadcasting industry's high level of concentration and television's purported special impact on its viewers, do not presently justify the different first amendment treatment. For reasons that will be developed in section II, access regulation has been treated differently in the context of broadcasting than it has in that of the print media largely because we have long *assumed* that in some undefined way broadcasting is, in fact, different. Rather than isolate broadcasting from our constitutional traditions, however, the Court should now acknowledge that for first amendment purposes broadcasting is not fundamentally different from the print media. Such an admission would not compel the Court either to permit access regulation throughout the press or to disallow it entirely. There is, we shall see, an alternative solution.

There has recently been a dramatic outpouring of articles addressing the issues associated with access regulation in the press.[5] This literature demonstrates the dual constitutional nature of regulation: It can be at once a valuable, indeed essential, means of redressing the serious inequality in speech opportunities that exists today within the mass media *and* a dangerous deviation from our historical commitment to a free and unfettered press. The problem, therefore, is formulating a constitutional approach that captures the benefits of access regulation yet still minimizes its potential excesses.

---

regulation are permissible; nor is it to specify which ought to be constitutionally sanctioned and which not. The assumption is made, primarily on the basis of the Court's holding in Red Lion Broadcasting Co. v. FCC, 395 U.S. 367 (1969), *discussed in* text at notes 14-34 *infra*, that access regulation in *some form* is constitutionally acceptable. The purpose of the article is to address the theoretical problems raised by the next question: the extent to which the Constitution ought to be construed as permitting such regulation within the mass media.

4. *See* text at notes 112-15 *infra*.

5. For an exhaustive listing of articles, see Lange, *The Role of the Access Doctrine in the Regulation of the Mass Media: A Critical Review and Assessment*, 52 N.C. L. REV. 1, 2 n.5 (1973).

These first amendment goals, it will be argued, can be achieved by permitting legislative access regulation but sharply restricting it to only one segment of the mass media, leaving the choice of the area of regulation to Congress. Without adequately explaining or perhaps even comprehending its decisions, the Supreme Court has actually reached the constitutionally correct result in refusing to permit government regulation of the print media, but has done this only because Congress had already chosen to regulate the broadcast media.

I. The First Amendment as Portmanteau

In 1974, when the Court considered the constitutionality of access regulation in the print media,[6] it was able to turn to a long-standing constitutional tradition. Our society has generally been committed to the notion that, with a few narrow exceptions, the government should stay out of the business of overseeing editorial discretion in the press.[7] Our historical experience has given rise to a hearty skepticism of the ability of officials to decide, for example, what is "fair" political debate. This skepticism recoguizes the corruptibility of government and its seemingly innate desire to maguify whatever power over the press it might possess at a given time. The longstanding conception of the press as a "fourth branch" of government has seemed antithetical to the idea that the state should have power to affect its content. Even the most ardent advocates of access legislation have never sought to claim historical respectibility for their proposals; theirs is the argument of changed circumstances.[8]

At issue in *Miami Herald Publishing Co. v. Tornillo*[9] was a Florida statute requiring a newspaper in the state to publish without cost the reply of any candidate criticized in its columns.[10] In a rela-

---

6. *See* Miami Herald Publishing Co. v. Tornillo, 418 U.S. 241 (1974).

7. *See, e.g.,* 2 Z. Chafee, Government & Mass Communications 477 (1947).

8. *See, e.g.,* Barron, *Access to the Press—A New First Amendment Right,* 80 Harv. L. Rev. 1641 (1967). *See also* the Court's summary of the access proponents' arguments in Miami Herald Publishing Co. v. Tornillo, 418 U.S. 241, 247-54 (1974).

9. 418 U.S. 241 (1974).

10. The statute provided:

104.38 *Newspaper assailing candidate in an election; space for reply*—If any newspaper in its columns assails the personal character of any candidate for nomination or for election in any election, or charges said candidate with malfeasance or misfeasance in office, or otherwise attacks his official record, or gives to another free space for sueh purpose, such newspaper shall upon request of such candidate immediately publish free of cost any reply he may make thereto in as conspicuous a place and in the same kind of type as the matter that calls for such reply, provided such reply does not take up more space than the matter replied to. Any person or firm failing to comply with the provisions of

tively brief and conclusory opinion, the Court surveyed prior print media cases and found implicit in them the proposition that "any . . . compulsion [by the government on newspapers] to publish that which 'reason' tells them should not be published is unconstitutional."[11] Access regulation violates that principle because it intrudes "into the function of editors"[12] and because, as the Court assumed, although there was no evidence on the point, it also creates an impermissible risk of a chilling effect on news content.[13]

What seems so remarkable about the unanimous *Miami Herald* opinion is the complete absence of any reference to the Court's unanimous decision five years earlier in *Red Lion Broadcasting Co. v. FCC*.[14] In that case, the Court upheld two component regulations of the Federal Communications Commission's "fairness doctrine,"[15]

---

this section shall be guilty of a misdemeanor of the first degree, punishable as provided in § 775.082 or § 775.083.
FLA. STAT. § 104.38 (1973). Enacted in 1913, Law of June 6, 1913, ch. 6470, § 12, 1913 Fla. Laws 274, the statute had slumbered peacefully until the 1970s. In the only other reported case, the statute was held unconstitutional. State v. News-Journal Corp., 36 Fla. Supp. 164 (Volusia County Judge's Court, Fla. 1972). The Supreme Court noted that "in neither of the two suits, the instant action and the 1972 action, has the Florida Attorney General defended the statute's constitutionality." 418 U.S. at 247 n.7.

11. 418 U.S. at 256.

12. 418 U.S. at 258. As the Court said:
The choice of material to go into a newspaper, and the decisions made as to limitations on the size of the paper, and content, and treatment of public issues and public officials—whether fair or unfair—constitutes the exercise of editorial control and judgment. It has yet to be demonstrated how governmental regulation of this crucial process can be exercised consistent with First Amendment guarautees of a free press as they have evolved to this time.
418 U.S. at 258.

13. The chilling effect was described in the following terms:
Faced with the penalties that would accrue to any newspaper that published news or commentary arguably within the reach of the right-of-access statute, editors might well conclude that the safe course is to avoid controversy. Therefore, under the operation of the Florida statute, political and electoral coverage would be blunted or reduced. Government-enforced right of access inescapably "dampens the vigor and limits the variety of public debate," *New York Times Co. v. Sullivan . . . .*
418 U.S. at 257.
Justice Brennan wrote a concurring opinion in *Miami Herald*, in which Justice Rehnquist joined, expressing his understanding that the Court's decision indicated no "view upon the constitutionality of 'retraction' statutes affording plaintiffs able to prove defamatory falsehoods a statutory action to require publication of a retraction," 418 U.S. at 258. Justice White also filed a concurring opinion that stated:
We have learned, and continue to learn, from what we view as the unhappy experiences of other nations where government has been allowed to meddle in the internal editorial affairs of newspapers. Regardless of how beneficient-sounding the purposes of controlling the press might be, we prefer "the power of reason as applied through public discussion" and remain intensely skeptical about those measures that would allow government to insinuate itself into the editorial rooms of this Nation's press.
418 U.S. at 259 (footnotes omitted).

14. 395 U.S. 367 (1969).

15. Developed over the years under the Commission's general power to promul-

one of which, the so-called personal attack rule,[16] is almost identical in substance to the Florida statute declared unconstitutional in *Miami*

gate regulations consistent with the "public interest," 47 U.S.C. §§ 303, 307 (1970), the doctrine requires broadcasters to provide adequate and fair coverage of opposing viewpoints on controversial issues of public importance. The substance of these obligations was set forth in early Commission decisions. *See* Great Lakes Broadcasting Co., 3 F.R.C. Ann. Rep. 32, 33 (1929), *revd. on other grounds*, 37 F.2d 993 (D.C. Cir.), *cert. dismissed*, 281 U.S. 706 (1930); Trinity Methodist Church, South v. FRC, 62 F.2d 850 (D.C. Cir. 1932), *cert. denied*, 288 U.S. 599 (1933). However, the first official policy statement explaining the doctrines in detail was not issued by the Commission until 1949. *See* REPORT ON EDITORIALIZING BY BROADCAST LICENSEES, 13 F.C.C. 1246 (1949). Congressional endorsement of the doctrine followed ten years later. Act of Sept. 14, 1959, Pub. L. No. 86-274, § 1, 73 Stat. 557, *amending* 47 U.S.C. § 315(a) (1958) (codified at 47 U.S.C. § 315(a) (1970)); *see* Red Lion Broadcasting Co. v. FCC, 395 U.S. 367, 380-82 (1969).

Another well-known regulation of this genre is the equal time rule. A feature of the statutory scheme since the beginning, the rule provides that a broadcaster who permits a political candidate to "use" his station must "afford equal opportunities to all other such candidates for that office in the use of such broadcasting station." 47 U.S.C. § 315 (Supp. V 1975).

The broadcast media has, of course, been subject to extensive legal restraints beyond access regulation since the passage of the Radio Act in 1927. Radio Act of 1927, ch. 169, 44 Stat. 1162. Congress acted in that year in response to a massive problem of signal interference, which threatened the life of the new technology, and "under the spur of a widespread fear that in the absence of governmental control the public interest might be subordinated to monopolistic domination in the broadcasting field." FCC v. Pottsville Broadcasting Co., 309 U.S. 134, 137 (1940). Within the space of about a decade, radio had grown in popularity and social importance to such an extent that intervention was necessary to allocate the small number of available frequencies. Congress delegated this responsibility to the Federal Radio Commission, vesting it with authority to issue licenses and promulgate regulations consistent with the public "convenience, interest, or necessity." Radio Act of 1927, ch. 169, § 4, 44 Stat. 1163. The Federal Communications Act was passed in 1934, but aside from renaming the Commission, the essential nature of radio regulation was left unchanged. Communications Act of 1934, Tit. III, ch. 56, 48 Stat. 1081, *as amended by* 47 U.S.C. §§ 301-395 (1970). The professed object of the new enterprise remained to "make available, so far as possible, to all the people of the United States a rapid, efficient, Nation-wide wire and radio communications service." 47 U.S.C. § 151 (1970).

16. The regulation covering personal attacks and political editorials provides as follows:

(a) When, during the presentation of views on a controversial issue of public importance, an attack is made upon the honesty, character, integrity or like personal qualities of an identified person or group, the licensee shall, within a reasonable time and in no event later than one week after the attack, transmit to the person or group attacked (1) notification of the date, time and identification of the broadcast; (2) a script or tape (or an accurate summary if a script or tape is not available) of the attack; and (3) an offer of a reasonable opportunity to respond over the licensee's facilities.

(b) The provisions of paragraph (a) of this section shall not be applicable (1) to attacks on foreign groups or foreign public figures; (2) to personal attacks which are made by legally qualified candidates, their authorized spokesmen, or those associated with the candidates in the campaign; and (3) to bona fide newscasts, bona fide news interviews, and on-the-spot coverage of a bona fide news event (including commentary or analysis contained in the foregoing programs, but the provisions of paragraph (a) of this section shall be applicable to editorials of the licensee).

(c) Where a licensee, in an editorial, (i) endorses or (ii) opposes a legally qualified candidate or candidates, the licensee shall within 24 hours after the editorial, transmit to respectively (i) the other qualified candidate or candidates for

Herald. That omission, however, is no more surprising than the absence of any discussion in *Red Lion* of the cases in which the Court expressed great concern about the risks attending government regulation of the print media.

Instead of scrutinizing government regulation of broadcasting in light of the print media cases and our traditional reservations about government oversight of the press, the Court in *Red Lion* regarded broadcasting as a "unique medium"[17] that needed a distinctive first amendment analysis. Specifically, the Court plunged ahead to assert for the first time the incompatibility of a concentrated medium, which is how it characterized broadcasting, with the first amendment goals expressed in the Holmesian metaphor of the "market-place of ideas."[18] The marketplace theme as developed in *Red Lion* states that when, as now, the channels of communication are effectively controlled by a few interests, there is the risk that many important voices will be excluded and that, as a consequence, the public will be seriously hampered in its efforts to conduct its affairs wisely. Unless the government intervenes to insure the widespread availability of opportunities for expression within the mass media, the objectives of the first amendment may be frustrated. Thus, the Court reasoned in a frequently quoted passage:

> Nor can we say that it is inconsistent with the First Amendment goal of producing an informed public capable of conducting its own affairs to require a broadcaster to permit answers to personal attacks occurring in the course of discussing controversial issues, or to require that the political opponents of those endorsed by the station be given a chance to communicate with the public. Otherwise, station owners and a few networks would have unfettered power to make time available only to the highest bidders, to communicate only their views on public issues, people and candidates, and to· permit on the air only those with whom they agreed. There is no sanctuary in the First Amendment for unlimited private censorship operating in a medium not open to all.[19]

These constitutional principles are an elaboration of the "scarcity

---

the same office or (ii) the candidate opposed in the editorial (1) notification of the date and the time of the editorial; (2) a script or tape of the editorial; and (3) an offer of a reasonable opportunity for a candidate or a spokesman of the candidate to respond over the licensee's facilities: *Provided, however,* That where such editorials are broadcast within 72 hours prior to the day of the election, the licensee shall comply with the provisions of this paragraph sufficiently far in advance of the broadcast to enable the candidate or candidates to have a reasonable opportunity to prepare a response and to present it in a timely fashion.
47 C.F.R. § 73.123 (1973).

17. 395 U.S. at 390.

18. Abrams v. United States, 250 U.S. 616, 630 (1919) (Holmes, J., dissenting).

19. 395 U.S. at 392.

doctrine" first articulated in *National Broadcasting Co. v. United States (NBC)*,[20] in which Justice Frankfurter argued that because radio was "inherently . . . not available to all" it was "unique" and therefore "subject to governmental regulation."[21] Needless to say, the opinion in *Red Lion* reflects a far different attitude toward the relationship between editors and government than that in *Miami Herald*.

---

20. 319 U.S. 190 (1943). The broadcasters in *NBC* challenged on statutory and constitutional grounds the so-called chain broadcasting regulations, designed by the Commission to regulate various aspects of a network's relationship with its affiliated stations. *See* 319 U.S. at 198-209.

21. 319 U.S. at 226. Justice Frankfurter's discussion of the constitutional issues (he disposed of the statutory claims early in the opinion, 319 U.S. at 215-26) was to become the classic statement of the justification for government regulation in broadcasting:

> We come, finally, to an appeal to the First Amendment. The regulations, even if valid in all other respects, must fall because they abridge, say the appellants, their right of free speech. If that be so, it would follow that every person whose application for a license to operate a station is denied by the Commission is thereby denied his constitutional right of free speech. Freedom of utterance is abridged to many who wish to use the limited facilities of radio. Unlike other modes of expression, radio inherently is not available to all. That is its unique characteristic, and that is why, unlike other modes of expression, it is subject to governmental regulation. Because it cannot be used by all, some who wish to use it must be denied.

319 U.S. at 226-27. The focus, ultimately, was to be on the public interest served by licensing:

> The question here is simply whether the Commission, by announcing that it will refuse licenses to persons who engage in specified network practices . . . is thereby denying such persons the constitutional right of free speech. The right of free speech does not include, however, the right to use the facilities of radio without a license. The licensing system established by Congress in the Communications Act of 1934 was a proper exercise of its power over commerce. The standard it provided for the licensing of stations was the "public interest, convenience, or necessity." Denial of a station license on that ground, if valid under the Act, is not a denial of free speech.

319 U.S. at 226-27.

Justice Frankfurter's analysis was hardly satisfying. It addressed the question whether the government could constitutionally deny a license to any applicant, an issue not raised by the broadcasters, and held that the scarcity of a major resource used in broadcasting (the electromagnetic spectrum), which is not sufficiently plentiful to supply all who wish to broadcast, justified a governmental licensing scheme. Justice Frankfurter completely failed to address other crucial questions: Why was the *method* chosen for allocation of licenses constitutional? If the method were constitutional, what limitations did the first amendment impose on its administration? And, why were these regulations not subject to those limitations? Perhaps the kindest comment on Justice Frankfurter's treatment of the constitutional issue was made by Professor Kalven, who observed that the "passage catches a great judge at an unimpressive moment." Kalven, *Broadcasting, Public Policy and the First Amendment*, 10 J. Law & Econ. 15, 43 (1967). *See also* T. Emerson, The System of Freedom of Expression 657 (1970). Nevertheless, the physical scarcity thesis became the principal rationale for distinguishing broadcasting from the print media and the basis for regulation in the "public interest," *see* 2 Z. Chafee, *supra* note 7, at 638, although other rationales occasionally surfaced. *See, e.g.,* Columbia Broadcasting Sys., Inc. v. Democratic Natl. Comm. (CBS), 412 U.S. 94, 101, 126 (1973) (referring to "public domain" thesis that broadcasters could be regulated because they used the "publicly owned" airspace).

A comparison of *Red Lion* and *Miami Herald*, however, reveals more than different first amendment motifs. The tone and attitude manifested in these cases toward the proper limits of governmental intervention are entirely dissimilar. In *Miami Herald*, the Court clearly and firmly opposed any further experimentation with access legislation, while in *Red Lion*, the Court acted as if it were reviewing a decision of an administrative agency where great weight had to be paid to the agency's expertise in dealing with a "new technology of communication." Illustratively, the Court in *Red Lion* responded to the broadcasters' claim that the right-of-reply regulations created an impermissible chilling effect by displaying deference toward the FCC's determination that the possibility of such an effect was "at best speculative."[22] This approach is in sharp contrast to the Court's later assertion in *Miami Herald* that access regulation "inescapably 'dampens the vigor and limits the variety of public debate.' "[23]

An even more significant example of the Court's leniency towards governmental experimentation with access regulation in broadcasting is the Court's response in *Red Lion* to the broadcasters' claim that, although there once might have been technological scarcity, the situation had changed significantly.[24] The broadcasters' argument was hardly frivolous. The development of the UHF (ultra high frequency) portion of the spectrum had greatly expanded the total number of available channels, and when the Court considered the issue, a significant number were (and continue to be) unused.[25]

---

22. *See* 395 U.S. at 393.

23. 418 U.S. at 257, *quoting* New York Times Co. v. Sullivan, 376 U.S. 254, 279 (1964).

24. 395 U.S. at 396.

25. In a footnote, the Court set forth the following table that had been prepared by the Commission as of August 31, 1968:

COMMERCIAL

Market Areas	Channels Allocated		Channels on the Air, Authorized, or Applied for		Available Channels	
	VHF	UHF	VHF	UHF	VHF	UHF
Top 10	40	45	40	44	0	1
Top 50	157	163	157	136	0	27
Top 100	264	297	264	213	0	84

NONCOMMERCIAL

Market Areas	Channels Allocated		Channels on the Air, Authorized, or Applied for		Available Channels	
	VHF	UHF	VHF	UHF	VHF	UHF
Top 10	7	17	7	16	0	1
Top 50	21	79	20	47	1	32
Top 100	35	138	34	69	1	69

1968 FCC Annual Report 132-35.

395 U.S. at 398 n.25.

On several occasions, moreover, the FCC had denied a license to a single applicant for a particular VHF (very high frequency) frequency because the applicant had failed to meet the Commission's programming requirements or because granting the license would have had an adverse *economic* impact on existing stations in the community.[26] In light of these facts, the broadcasters surely might have expected a Court concerned with freedom of the press to limit carefully the government's exercise of regulation to those situations consistent with the constitutional rationale adopted in *NBC*—that is, to instances where there was truly "physical scarcity."

This was not, however, the *Red Lion* Court's focus. Instead, the Court was primarily concerned with society's interest in establishing priorities for use of new technologies and was willing to affirm regulation that may not have been needed at that time to promote traditional first amendment interests:

> The rapidity with which technological advances succeed one another to create more efficient use of spectrum space on the one hand, and to create new uses for that space by ever growing numbers of people on the other, makes it unwise to speculate on the future allocation of that space. It is enough to say that the resource is one of considerable and growing importance whose scarcity impelled its regulation by an agency authorized by Congress. Nothing in this record, or in our own researches, convinces us that the resource is no longer one for which there are more immediate and potential uses than can be accommodated, and for which *wise planning* is essential.[27]

Instability would result, the Court surmised, if the Commission could only intervene when the demand suddenly exceeded the supply of frequencies in a community. In any event, it was thought, existing broadcasters had obtained such "advantages" by virtue of government selection that "[s]ome present possibility for new entry by competing stations is not enough, in itself, to render unconstitutional the Government's effort to assure that a broadcaster's programming ranges widely enough to serve the public interest."[28]

The point of this comparative analysis of *Red Lion* and *Miami Herald* can be clarified by juxtaposing what the Court both articulated and failed to articulate in these decisions. The Court in *Red Lion* introduced a new principle into our first amendment jurisprudence. Essentially, that principle provides that when only a few interests control a major avenue of communication, those able to speak can be forced by the government to share. The initial logic

---

26. *See, e.g.*, Henry v. FCC, 302 F.2d 191 (D.C. Cir. 1962).

27. 395 U.S. at 399 (emphasis added).

28. 395 U.S. at 400.

supporting the principle is clear: If it is accepted that a principal objective of the first amendment is to assure the widespread dissemination of various points of view, then any serious constriction of the available methods of communication would seem to justify some remedial action. Applying this logic to broadcasting, the Court found that concentration there justified action *and* that access regulation is an appropriate legislative response.

Equally important, on the other hand, is what the Court has failed to say in its decisions on access regulation. It is clear that the Court has not made explicit just what is so "unique" about the broadcast media that justifies legislative action impermissible in the newspaper context. It is doubtful that the so-called scarcity rationale articulated in *NBC* and *Red Lion* provides an explanation. Certainly the scarcity rationale explains why Congress was justified in devising an allocation scheme to prevent the overcrowding of broadcasting frequencies. It may also serve to explain in part why the television industry is so concentrated.[29] The scarcity rationale does not, however, explain why what appears to be a similar phenomenon of natural monopolization within the newspaper industry does not constitute an equally appropriate occasion for access regulation.[30] A

---

29. *See* note 30 *infra.*

30. *See, e.g.,* B. SCHMIDT, *supra* note 3, at ch. 4. It is difficult to compare effectively the extent of concentration in the broadcast and newspaper media. There are 8,760 broadcast stations, compared with 1,733 English language daily newspapers. *See* BROADCASTING, YEARBOOK 1975, at A-2; NEWSPAPER ENTERPRISE ASSOCIATION, 1975 WORLD ALMANAC 303 (1974). However, most of the broadcast outlets are radio stations (7,807), leaving 954 television stations (513 Commercial VHF, 198 commercial UHF, 95 noncommercial VHF and 147 noncommercial UHF). BROADCASTING, YEARBOOK 1975, at A-2. Other data, however, complicate the picture. A relatively recent assessment of the effects of media concentration noted:

> From 1945 to 1970, the number of U.S. cities with competitive daily newspapers fell from 117 to 63, while the total number of dailies remained nearly constant. By 1973, only 55 competitive newspaper cities remained, and only the very largest cities such as New York and Chicago supported competitive morning or evening dailies. Moreover, 20 of the 55 cities retain daily newspaper competition only through joint operating agreements by which two newspapers share printing and business operations.

W. BAER, H. GELLER, J. GRUNDFEST, K. POSSNER, CONCENTRATION OF MASS MEDIA OWNERSHIP: ASSESSING THE STATE OF CURRENT KNOWLEDGE 35 (1974) (footnotes omitted). At a later point, the study further compares the national concentration of ownership in television and newspapers: "There are nearly 400 television station owners, but the fifty largest group owners serve 74 percent of the total daily audience. Among the more than 1,000 newspaper publishers, the fifty largest control 58 percent of all circulation." *Id.* at 57-58.

The point here is not to establish a methodology for measuring comparatively the risks of concentration in the electronic and print media but rather to support the less controversial proposition that the evils of concentration—to the extent that they exist—would appear to be a problem within the newspaper context as well as the broadcast media. *See* Robinson, *The FCC and the First Amendment: Observations on 40 Years of Radio and Television Regulation,* 52 MINN. L. REV. 67, 156-59 (1967).

difference in the cause of concentration—the exhaustion of a physical element necessary for communication in broadcasting as contrasted with the economic constraints on the number of possible competitors in the print media—would seem far less relevant from a first amendment standpoint than the fact of concentration itself. Thus, it might be argued that a person "attacked" in the *Washington Post*, or one who holds a different viewpoint than that expressed in that newspaper, is able to publish a pamphlet or his own "newspaper" in response. But does this have any more appeal than a similar argument with respect to the Columbia Broadcasting System?

It is true, of course, that a person with the requisite capital and inclination could, theoretically, always establish his own newspaper if the local print media refused to publish his point of view, whereas it is highly unlikely that he could establish his own broadcast station if the local stations refused to cover his viewpoint. But this seems a slim basis on which to predicate such dramatically different constitutional treatment. Even if we assume greater ease in entering the print media, however, the question remains why the purported openness of the newspaper market should not be considered an important factor in assessing the significance of concentration in the broadcast media. Why, this analysis asks, did the Court in *Red Lion* treat the broadcast media as separate and discrete? Why did the Court, in an exercise similar to defining the "relevant market" in an antitrust case, narrow its focus to a particular segment of the mass media? Why did the Court not say that, so long as people can gain access somewhere within the mass media, there is no need for legislative action in any concentrated branch? The treatment of the broadcast media as discrete constitutes at least implicit acknowledgement that the newspaper and other major print media are also highly restricted. If anyone could set up a major newspaper, would we really care if entry into the broadcast media was physically precluded? Or is the explanation somehow hinged to the nature of the regulatory scheme itself?

The fact is that the Court has never sought to answer the difficult questions relating to the scope of the new constitutional principle.[31]

31. In a concluding footnote to the *Red Lion* opinion, the Court seemed to leave open the question whether the cause of concentration could ever be important:

We need not deal with the argument that even if there is no longer a technological scarcity of frequencies limiting the number of broadcasters, there nevertheless is an economic scarcity in the sense that the Commission could or does limit entry to the broadcasting market on economic grounds and license no more stations than the market will support. Hence, it is said, the fairness doctrine or its equivalent is essential to satisfy the claims of those excluded and of the public generally. A related argument, which we also put aside, is that quite apart from scarcity of frequencies, technological or economic, Congress does not

The Court in *Miami Herald* acknowledged the argument that the increased concentration within the newspaper industry constituted changed circumstances justifying affirmative governmental action but offered little in the way of satisfactory explanation.[32]   Instead of exploring the relevance for the print media of the new principle developed in broadcasting, the Court merely reiterated the opposing, more traditional, principle that the government cannot tell editors what to publish.[33]   It thus created a paradox, leaving the new principle unscathed while preserving tradition.[34]

There thus now exists an unresolved tension between the constitutional themes that have been drawn in the electronic and print media.   As will be shown below, however, this does not mean that the tension cannot be resolved.

II.   TOWARD A FIRST AMENDMENT THEORY

. . . a law of inherent opposites, Of essential unity, is as pleasant as port . . . .[35]

The preceding section has attempted to demonstrate the unpersuasiveness of the scarcity argument: Concentration is not unique to broadcasting and, in any case, the scarcity rationale has no application to the cable technology[36] where questions of access regulation are now brewing.   Thus, even for those who have embraced it, the rationale is at best a short-term answer to what appears to be a long-term problem.   It is, therefore, now important to inquire whether there is any basis other than the scarcity doctrine for denying Con-

---

abridge freedom of speech or press by legislation directly or indirectly multiplying the voices and views presented to the public through time sharing, fairness doctrines, or other devices which limit or dissipate the power of those who sit astride the channels of communication with the general public.
395 U.S. at 401 n.28.

32. 418 U.S. at 249-51.

33. 418 U.S. at 258.

34. One possible key to understanding *Miami Herald* might lie in the fact that the case involved a *state* attempt to impose access regulation on the press. It is possible, in other words, that the Court was moved to reach the result it did because it thought it would be too difficult to supervise regulatory experiments in 50 states or that, for somewhat different reasons, this area of access regulation has become a matter exclusively of federal concern. For reasons that will be developed later, I believe that *Miami Herald* would have—and should have—been decided the same way if the regulations had been of federal origin. *See* text at notes 82-102 *infra.* That is not to say, however, that in circumstances where it is thought to be constitutionally appropriate to impose access regulation, Congress, in contrast to the states, would not have a special role to play in seeking to implement first amendment goals. *Cf.* Katzenbach v. Morgan, 384 U.S. 641 (1966).

35. W. STEVENS, *Connoisseur of Chaos,* in COLLECTED POEMS OF WALLACE STEVENS 167 (1954).

36. *See* note 112 *infra.*

gress the authority to extend access regulation beyond the already-regulated electronic media.

A.   *Comparison of the Electronic and Print Media*

The customary approach to the problem of disparate treatment of the electronic and print media has been to line them up side by side and see whether there are any differences between them that justify the result. It is implicitly assumed that if broadcasting cannot be distinguished from the print media, it must be treated similarly; if it is different, then it can be regulated to the extent that the differences allow. The scarcity analysis, which focuses exclusively on broadcasting without making express comparisons and which argues that this branch of the communications media possesses a "unique" characteristic of concentration, is one such attempt to isolate a difference that would permit separate treatment. Although that difference apparently should fail the test of materiality, there may be more appropriate distinctions, such as a possible qualitative difference of degree in levels of concentration and a reputed special impact of television on its viewers.

Irrespective of the cause of concentration within each branch of the media, television is in some respects more concentrated than any segment of the print media. There are fewer television stations, for example, than daily newpapers,[37] but even more significantly, fewer interests control the content of television broadcasting than is true within the newspaper industry. In television an oligopoly of three networks commands the attention of a vast percentage of the television audience, while in newspapers the concentration is more dispersed, with monopolization on a local, regional, or more limited, national level.[88]

This might not be regarded as very significant if few people watched television, but, of course, the situation is quite the reverse. In many important respects, television is today the most pervasive medium of communications in our society. Not only does virtually everyone have access to a television set, but more people watch it, even for purposes of obtaining news, and for longer periods, than read the publications of the print media.[39] In addition, television is frequently considered to have a "special impact" on its audience. Thus, many

---

37. *See* note 30 *supra.*

38. *See* Barrow, *Program Regulation in Cable TV: Fostering Debate in a Cohesive Audience,* 61 VA. L. REV. 515, 530 (1975).

39. *See* E. EPSTEIN, NEWS FROM NOWHERE 9 (1973); B. SCHMIDT, *supra* note 3, at 120.

14   *Michigan Law Review*   [Vol. 75:1

courts and commentators believe television is today the dominant means of influencing public opinion, not only because more people watch it than read newspapers, but also because it possesses some undefined and unquantifiable, but nevertheless unique, capacity to shape the opinions of the viewers in ways unrelated to the merits of the arguments presented.[40] The television medium, it is also said, offers the opportunity to thrust information and ideas onto the audience. Unlike printed publications, which can be avoided by "averting the eyes,"[41] television provides the opportunity to force extraneous messages onto audiences gathered for other purposes.[42] This medium, in short, may be the preeminant forum for the discussion of ideas and viewpoints in the society and it may offer opportunities to persuade that cannot be matched elsewhere within the system of expression. The greater concentration of power in television, therefore, may arguably represent more serious social and first amendment problems than the situation in the print media.[43]

This line of argument, promising though it may seem, contains several serious problems. First, the analysis fails to explain why the current level of concentration in newspapers, even assuming that it is not as high as that in television, is not sufficiently troublesome by itself to justify governmental intervention. The monopoly status of so many of our community newspapers does not present a happy prospect for the first amendment. Beyond some point, the level of concentration seems to become irrelevant to constitutional doctrine. The question to be asked, therefore, is not whether broadcasting is more concentrated than the print media, but whether both have passed beyond the point of safety for first amendment purposes.

It seems reasonable to believe that, if concentration in broadcasting has passed an acceptable level, concentration in newspapers has also reached a similar level. Are the abuses of journalistic power and one-sidedness more likely in the electronic than in the print media?

---

40. *See, e.g.,* Banzhaf v. FCC, 405 F.2d 1082, 1100-01 n.77 (D.C. Cir. 1968), *cert. denied,* 396 U.S. 842 (1969).

41. Cohen v. California, 403 U.S. 16, 21 (1971).

42. Cohen v. California, 403 U.S. 16, 21 (1971). The Supreme Court has also noted the "captive" nature of the broadcast audience. *See* Columbia Broadcasting Sys., Inc. v. Democratic Natl. Comm., 412 U.S. 94, 127-28 (1973).

43. *Cf.* L. Tribe, Channeling Technology Through Law 29 (1973):

Almost as difficult as conceiving of cumulative trends is imagining the effects of scale. Barely 100,000 television receivers were in use in the United States in 1948. In the next year there were a million. A decade later there were 50 million. The social and psychological consequences of such phenomenal growth are hard even to contemplate, let alone predict. Indeed, in the case of television these effects are still a matter of debate, and apparently adequate research tools for measuring or evaluating them do not yet exist.

Is the access for new ideas more problematical in the broadcast than in the print media?   Certainly there is no empirical evidence supporting affirmative answers to these questions, and their validity as intuitive propositions is subject to doubt.   Television is characterized more by its placidity than by its politicization.[44]   Moreover, newspapers are a primary source of news for television, and the print media may instead prove to be the first line of defense against new ideas.[45]   Further, it is significant that in television there are three independently owned national networks vying for viewers, a potentially important systemic check against distortion that is lacking in communities with only a single newspaper.   Finally, the major networks do control the content of prime-time television, but the major wire services, such as Associated Press and United Press International, similarly control much of the national news reported in newspapers throughout the country, although perhaps to a somewhat lesser degree.

Even more problematical, however, is the alleged special impact of television.   Quite apart from any natural suspicions concerning the validity of the claim, given the frequency with which it seems to confront each new medium of communications,[46] the impact thesis is a dangerously amorphous justification for regulation.   It provides no clear limits to official authority and invites censorship as well as affirmative regulation.   Further, in so far as the thesis rests upon the premise that regulation is more acceptable the greater the audience and the impact, it seems inconsistent with the underlying purpose of the first amendment, which presumably is to protect effective as well as ineffective speech.   A comparison of the gross audience figures is, in any event, a clumsy basis on which to gauge the differing effects of various media on the formation of public opinion or policy.   Use of such data alone completely ignores the insights of political scientists into the complexity of cognition and decision-making.[47]   Finally, there is simply no evidence at the present time to support the proposition that television shapes attitudes and ideas in ways so unprecedented as to require urgent remedial regulation.   Thus, until more evidence exists to support the theory, or perhaps until a much wider consensus is formed in its support, it seems wise to avoid relying on the special impact theory.

---

44. *See generally* E. Epstein, *supra* note 39.

45. *See generally id.*

46. *See, e.g.*, Times Film Corp. v. Chicago, 365 U.S. 43 (1961) (motion pictures).

47. *See generally* R. Dahl, Pluralist Democracy in the United States: Conflict and Consent (1967).

This discussion does not mean to suggest that the line of analysis focusing on the potential differences between television and newspapers and magazines is unworthy of further investigation. On the contrary, the issues raised are highly important and should continue to command attention. On the whole, however, the arguments presently contain too many doubtful underlying assumptions to support a conclusion that the media are fundamentally different. Differences indeed exist, but they are either too insignificant to justify momentous distinctions in treatment under the first amendment or too broad and vacuous to be persuasive. We must, therefore, conclude that they are the same.[48]

It is at this point that conventional thinking about broadcast regulation largely stops. Once it is determined that the broadcast and print media are constitutionally indistinguishable, then it is concluded that the Court's theory of access regulation is without rational foundation and should be discarded at the earliest opportunity.[49] Such a conclusion possesses a certain legalistic appeal, but it also may be an oversimplification. The very weakness of the scarcity rationale suggests that there is something more here than first meets the eye. The dual treatment of the press has been so long accepted, even by persons known for their sensitivity to first amendment values,[50] that the scarcity rationale may in fact be a convenient legal fiction covering more subtle and important considerations.

It is helpful, therefore, to adopt a less formalistic approach to the problem and to probe beyond normal legal analysis to account for this remarkable constitutional development. For even if broadcasting and the printing press are essentially the same, they nevertheless have different origins, have existed for different periods of time, and one has been controlled from its beginnings while the other has been left unrestricted. It is important, in short, that our analysis be sensitive to the historical process through which the present system has developed.

Such an approach reveals two closely interrelated factors that help reconcile the divergent traditions within the press. First, society has long considered broadcasting to be meaningfully different

---

48. The following discussion would still be important even if there existed a serious possibility of a material difference justifying regulation only of the electronic media. If regulation is properly limited on a basis other than the differences suggested above—as is argued in the text below—the Court need not undertake the troublesome and frequently ephemeral task of making comparisons as the bases for their decisions.

49. *See* Lange, *supra* note 5.

50. *See, e.g.,* 2 Z. CHAFEE, *supra* note 7, at 640-41.

from the print media, and this perception has greatly influenced the decision to allow regulation only in the former. Understanding this perception and its effects is necessary for an appreciation of the complex way in which first amendment theory is implemented and developed. Second, broadcast regulation involves only a *part* of the press; this fact provides not only an explanation for past treatment by the courts but also offers the most rational basis for future constitutional adjudication in this area.

B. *Divergent Societal Perceptions of Broadcasting and Print Media*

The phenomenon of broadcast regulation has, in many respects, the qualities of an historical accident. An examination of its origins and development reveals the striking ease with which it slid into our political and constitutional system. One stark fact is apparent: Society obviously has *thought differently* about broadcasting than it has about the print media. Certainly doubts and objections have been raised periodically,[51] but on the whole there have not been the outcries against censorship that would undoubtedly have occurred if regulation had been imposed on newspapers.[52] Broadcasters, although often lamenting what they considered to be public insensitivity to their first amendment rights, have been conspicuously unassertive of their rights.[53] Even the scholarly community has tended to overlook the significance of the constitutional treatment of broadcasting. Major casebooks published as late as 1965, for example, did not even mention either the existence of broadcast regulation or the seminal *NBC* decision.[54] Even after *Red Lion*, major casebooks did not present broadcast regulation as posing a significant constitutional dilemma; broadcast decisions were merely described briefly in a note format.[55] A recently published major casebook continues to describe the broadcast decisions in a long note, does not address the broader first amendment significance of the decision to regulate, and

---

51. *See, e.g.*, Kalven, *supra* note 21; Robinson, *supra* note 30.

52. "In brief, we all take as commonplace a degree of government surveillance for broadcasting which would by instant reflex ignite the fiercest protest were it found in other areas of communication." Kalven, *supra* note 21, at 16. *See also* 2 Z. CHAFEE, *supra* note 7, at 637.

53. Writing before *Red Lion*, Professor Kalven suggested that "the [broadcasting] industry has under-estimated its legal position and given up too soon." Kalven, *supra* note 21, at 24.

54. *See* N. DOWLING & G. GUNTHER, CASES AND MATERIALS ON CONSTITUTIONAL LAW (7th ed. 1965).

55. *See* the two-page note on *Red Lion* in G. GUNTHER & N. DOWLING, CASES AND MATERIALS ON CONSTITUTIONAL LAW 1225-26 (8th ed. 1970).

provides no cross reference to *Miami Herald* in connection with the discussion of libel.[56] If the scholars who formulate and organize for study the most pressing issues under the first amendment fail to find any particular significance in broadcast regulation other than as a minor exception to the general rules, it is not surprising that society generally has apparently failed to recognize the broadcast cases as a major departure from first amendment principles.

Furthermore, one of the more striking pieces of evidence of a general perception that broadcasting is somehow "special" is the fact that, during the past half century of regulation, there have been remarkably few attempts to expand any part of the rather extensive regulatory structure into the print media.[57] Broadcast regulation has been an isolated phenomenon, not a basecamp for incursions into the print media.

A search for explanations as to why the electronic media have been regarded as distinct from the print media should begin with the Supreme Court decisions. After all, the Court in an early case appeared to dismiss the broadcasters' first amendment arguments as being unworthy of serious discussion and officially embraced the physical scarcity rationale.[58] The *Red Lion* opinion, moreover, is written as if the result were inexorable, and gives no hint that the Court is troubled by its earlier analysis in *NBC*. These decisions undoubtedly reinforced the view that regulation in the "public interest" was somehow appropriate in this "unique" medium. Like the

---

56. *See* W. LOCKHART, Y. KAMISAR & J. CHOPER, CONSTITUTIONAL LAW 975-79, 1201-10 (4th ed. 1975). In the ninth edition of the Gunther casebook, published in 1975, *Red Lion* and *CBS* are described in a three-page textual comment and *Tornillo* immediately afterwards in a two-page note. G. GUNTHER, CASES AND MATERIALS ON CONSTITUTIONAL LAW 1230-34 (1975).

57. Although in the past half century there have been numerous proposals advanced for some form of access regulation, *see, e.g.,* 2 Z. CHAFEE, *supra* note 7, at 694-95; Barron *supra* note 8, few seemed to have reached even the stage of serious legislative debate and far fewer have been enacted. A Mississippi right-of-reply statute, MISS. CODE ANN. § 3175 (1942) (now MISS. CODE ANN. § 23-3-35 (1972)), was essentially overturned in Manasco v. Walley, 216 Miss. 614, 63 So.2d 91 (1953). In 1969, Nevada repealed its right-of-reply statute, Law of April 14, 1969, ch. 310, § 10, [1969], repealing NEV. REV. STAT. § 200.570 (1963). As already noted, *see* note 7 *supra*, the Florida statute considered in *Miami Herald* had lain dormant since its enactment in 1913.

In 1970, Congressman Farbstein introduced a bill in the House of Representatives which would have authorized the Federal Communications Commission to apply fairness doctrine concepts to newspapers. H.R. 18927, 91st Cong., 2d Sess. (1970). The bill was never reported out of Committee. In 1973, the Massachusetts Supreme Judicial Court issued an Opinion of the Justices to the Senate, — Mass. —, 298 N.E.2d 829 (1973), in which it advised against the constitutionality of a right-of-reply statute then under consideration in the Massachusetts General Assembly.

58. *See* National Broadcasting Co. v. United States, 319 U.S. 190 (1943), *discussed in* note 21 *supra*.

legerdermain of the pornography decisions to the effect that obscenity is not "speech" and therefore not constitutionally protected,[59] the Court's reliance on the physical scarcity rationale may have provided an intellectual construct that facilitated ignoring the logical ramifications of the decision.

It would be misleading, however, to attribute too much weight to the Court's role. There is considerable evidence of a widespread societal predisposition to broadcast regulation. For example, although no one has ever questioned the government's decision to take some action to alleviate the problems of interference caused by overcrowding of the spectrum, there were several alternative methods of allocation that would have involved far less governmental intervention into traditional journalistic functions, but which were not seriously considered. Illustratively, Congress could have allocated frequencies on a first-come-first-served basis, relying primarily on chance to determine the composition of the medium.[60] Or it could have awarded licenses to the highest bidders in an auction, or to winners in a lottery, following the more traditional laissez-faire path of permitting a mixture of chance and market pressures to determine the shape of the medium.[61] Rather than selecting any of these methods, however, Congress opted for the extraordinary choice of regulating a branch of the communications industry in the "public interest."[62] What is startling about this decision is not the form of public control selected, which was the prevailing response of the time to economic concentration, but the fact that it was adopted so easily in the first amendment context.

Satisfactory explanations for developments such as this are always elusive, but at least several can be suggested. Our society has generally perceived the electronic media as more entertainment-oriented than the print media. Although the Court held in *Joseph Burstyn, Inc. v. Wilson*[63] that the first amendment protected non-political speech, that case was not decided until long after broadcast regulation had been instituted and approved in *NBC*. By the

---

59. *See, e.g.*, Roth v. United States, 354 U.S. 476, 481-85 (1957).

60. *See* 395 U.S. at 390-91.

61. This approach is urged in Coase, *Evaluation of Public Policy Relating to Radio and Television Broadcasting: Social and Economic Issues*, 41 J. LAND & P.U. ECON. 161 (1965). *See also*, Kalven, *supra* note 21, at 30-32.

62. "The Communications Act is not designed primarily as a new code for the adjustment of conflicting private rights through adjudication. Rather it expresses a desire on the part of Congress to maintain, through appropriate administrative control, a grip on the dynamic aspects of radio transmission." FCC v. Pottsville Broadcasting Co., 309 U.S. 134, 138 (1940).

63. 343 U.S. 495, 499-502 (1952).

time *Burstyn* was decided, regulations in broadcasting had received widespread acceptance, so that even after that decision our society may have continued to be less sensitive to restrictions on nonpolitical speech.[64] Further, the different treatment accorded broadcasting may in part be attributable to the unknown nature of the medium at the time regulation was imposed. The features of broadcasting technology have long been embryonic and, consequently, the problems broadcasting *might* present have seemed so unpredictable as to warrant regulation as a precautionary measure. Finally, since the government was virtually compelled to intervene in broadcasting in order to alleviate the problem of signal interference, that justifiable intervention may well have eased the path for more extensive attempts to structure the medium. The brute fact of governmental licensing served to isolate the medium from our tradition of nonregulation. Broadcasting was emphatically *not* the same as the print media, and it may not have been important that the difference did not justify everything done to it.

An explanation for the phenomenon is, however, of secondary importance to the fact of its existence. Crucial here is not that broadcasting is in fact different in principle from the print media, but that it has been believed to be different. This difference in perception goes a long way in explaining the contrasting first amendment protections afforded both branches of the media. In the area of first amendment rights, there has been a perennial concern over the political consequences of oversight, which is reflected in the idea that regulation lets the "camel's nose in the tent."[65] It has rightly been thought necessary to maintain a firm line against governmental intrusion (the camel's nose) into freedom of speech and press in order to avoid continual disputation over the scope of those freedoms, which may itself snuff out the vitality of those rights. Speaking in the late 1940s of proposals to regulate newspapers, Professor Chafee argued:

> The First Amendment embodied a very strong tradition that the government should keep its hands off the press. Every new governmental activity in relation to the communication of news and ideas, however laudable its purpose, tends to undermine this tradition and render further activities easier. "If we do this, why can't we do that?" Appetite grows by what it feeds on. Legal barriers can of course be erected, but it takes constant effort to prevent them from being nibbled away. Therefore, no proposal for governmental action

---

64. *Cf.* Kalven, *supra* note 21, at 30.

65. *See* Columbia Broadcasting Sys., Inc. v. Democratic Natl. Comm., 412 U.S. 94, 154 (Douglas, J., concurring).

should be judged in isolation. It must be considered in relation to other possible state controls over the press, which have not yet been suggested.[66]

Indeed, this prospect of expanding intervention by the state is a troublesome aspect of access regulation, which has many different faces and only a broadly stated purpose that contains no sharp limitations on governmental authority. Even if a decision to allow access regulation would not unleash an irresistible drive for impermissible controls, the substantial public debate that might well be generated over more intrusive regulation could itself serve to chill the independent function of the press.[67]

These concerns have had much greater significance in the context of the print media than in that of the broadcasting industry because of the differences society has perceived in them. It is noteworthy, for example, that Professor Chafee made his argument only in the newspaper context.[68] While it is true that Chafee thought regulation of broadcasting was constitutionally appropriate because of the physical limitations on access, the fact that regulation has merit does not, of course, render the camel's-nose-in-the-tent argument inapposite in that area. Instead, the real reason for not raising the argument in the broadcasting context is suggested by the reference in the quotation to the longstanding "tradition that the government should keep its hands off the press."

Access regulation in the print media would have immediately signified a pronounced break with traditional first amendment theory. If the Court had, for instance, approved the creation of a Federal Newspaper Commission to administer a fairness doctrine, a spontaneous national debate over the wisdom and implications of the decision would almost certainly have erupted. The constitutional law casebooks would have prominently displayed the decision, supplementing it with text asking probing questions about the holding. What before had seemed unthinkable would then have become thinkable; the free, autonomous press long symbolic of the first

---

66. 2 Z. CHAFEE, *supra* note 7, at 683. Chafee added at a later point:
Once government becomes active in the communications field, it can go on indefinitely. Zealous officials will keep thinking up new ways for improving the press according to their own ideals. And there is no bright line between encouragement and repression . . . . If officials can tell newspapers what to put into their editorial pages, as is proposed for the Free Press Authority, it is only a step to tell them what to leave out.
Id. at 709-10.

67. This is a danger that has found frequent expression in the state-aid-to-religion cases, *see, e.g.,* Lemon v. Kurtzman, 403 U.S. 602, 622-24 (1971), but whose relevance is not limited to that branch of the first amendment.

68. *See* note 66 *supra.*

amendment would have been put on a leash.[69] No longer would the Court be seen as merely sanctioning an aberrant regulatory system limited to a distinct, novel technology of communication, but instead would be seen as pursuing a major policy change with respect to the first amendment.

Thus, the way our society has thought about the two branches of the media has deeply affected the issue of whether to permit access regulation in either area.[70] Regulation has been more tolerable in the broadcast sector because circumstances there have confined its implications. This is not, it should be noted, an isolated phenomenon. It is rather typical of a general tendency revealed in the case law to permit the government greater leeway in controlling the development of new technologies of communication. An interesting analogy to the broadcast regulation cases are the Supreme Court decisions involving motion pictures.

Treated as a suspicious newcomer to the system of expression, motion pictures were first assigned an inferior status, almost as if there were a first amendment initiation rite. In 1915, the Supreme Court ruled that the medium was not entitled to any first amendment protection,[71] and, although this anomaly was readily apparent, the

---

69. In his last book, *The Morality of Consent*, the late Alexander Bickel seems to express a similar idea in connection with the *Pentagon Papers* case, New York Times Co. v. United States, 413 U.S. 713 (1971). Part of the significance of that case, as Bickel notes, was that it signified the first instance in our history in which the federal government sought "to censor a newspaper by attempting to impose a restraint prior to publication, directly or in litigation." A. BICKEL, THE MORALITY OF CONSENT 61 (1975). Thus, even though the Supreme Court ultimately vindicated the right of the New York Times to publish the material, the "spell was broken, and in a sense freedom was thus diminished." *Id.* Bickel went on to say: "The conflict and contention by which we extend freedom seem to mark, or at least to threaten, a contraction; and in truth they do, for they endanger an assumed freedom which appeared limitless because its limits were untried. Appearance and reality are nearly one. We extend the legal reality of freedom at some cost in its limitless appearance. And the cost is real." *Id.* Thus, the first perceived break with tradition, and the very fact of having seriously considered the proposition asserted by the government, served to undercut our sense of freedom from this type of governmental activity and to highlight the possibilities for future action for those interested in trying again.

70. This thought may be in part what Professor Emerson had in mind when, after concluding that access regulation in the broadcast media can be justified "out of affirmative concepts of the First Amendment," he stated:

Such a doctrine of First Amendment power and limitation is far-reaching and entails obvious dangers. Applied to the press, for example, it might authorize controls over newspaper coverage that would be highly questionable. In the area of radio and television, however, *the government is already heavily involved with the task of preventing electrical interference and solving similar engineering problems. Thus, the regulations have a different substantive and administrative impact* and would not necessarily constitute an abridgment of free expression in the same way as comparable regulations in other areas not already heavily weighted by government controls.

T. EMERSON, *supra* note 21, at 665 (emphasis added).

71. Mutual Film Corp. v. Industrial Comm., 236 U.S. 230 (1915). Interpreting a

Court did not lift the yoke of censorship until its 1952 decision in *Joseph Burstyn, Inc. v. Wilson.*[72] In that case the Court extended first amendment protections to motion pictures, although it was quick to caution that it did not "follow that motion pictures are necessarily subject to the precise rules governing any other particular method of expression."[73] The constitutional principles that permitted motion pictures to be treated differently were not specified, and the issue of different treatment soon arose in 1961 in *Times Film Corp. v. Chicago*[74] and again, in 1965, in *Freedman v. Maryland.*[75] In those cases, the Court sanctioned local laws permitting blatant prior censorship of motion pictures.[76] Although the Court has never

provision of the Ohio constitution comparable in scope to the first amendment, the Court stated: "It cannot be put out of view that the exhibition of moving pictures is a business pure and simple, originated and conducted for profit, like other spectacles, not to be regarded, nor intended to be regarded by the Ohio constitution, we think, as part of the press of the country or as organs of public opinion." 236 U.S. at 244.

72. 343 U.S. 495 (1952). The Court struck down as an invalid prior restraint a New York statute that authorized the department of education to deny a license to show a film if it was "sacrilegious".

73. 343 U.S. at 503.

74. 365 U.S. 43 (1961).

75. 380 U.S. 51 (1965).

76. At issue in *Times Film* was a Chicago ordinance reqniring that prior to exhibition all films had to be submitted to the commissioner of police, who was authorized to refuse a permit if various standards were not met. Certain punishments were provided for showing a motion picture without a permit. The petitioner had refused to submit its film "Don Juan" for prior screening, and the commissioner of police had accordingly refused to issue a permit. Petitioner then sought injunctive relief against enforcement of the ordinance on the ground that it violated the first and fourteenth amendments.

When the case reached the Supreme Court, the majority interpreted the petitioner's claim as an assertion that the state could never, for any reason, restrain any motion picture prior to exhibition. The Court rejected this position noting that in *Near v. Minnesota*, 283 U.S. 697 (1931), it had specifically listed certain areas (including obscenity) as being legitimately within the reach of prior restraints. But the *Times Film* Court seemed to say more, to extend "its blessing," as Chief Justice Warren noted in dissent, 365 U.S. at 65 (Warren, C.J., dissenting), to the procedure embodied by the Chicago ordinance that required all motion pictures to be submitted to a censor before exhibition so that the city could exclude those that were obscene. Aside from a cryptic reference to the need to consider in each case the "capacity for evil" in determining the "permissible scope of community control," the Court made no attempt to distinguish movies from other forms of expression. 365 U.S. at 49-50. At the very end of the opinion, Justice Clark observed simply: "At this time we say no more than this—that we are dealing only with motion pictures and, even as to them, only in the context of the broadside attack presented on this record." 365 U.S. at 50.

The dissent in *Times Film* attacked the majority on the ground that it had failed to explain "why moving pictures should be treated differently than any other form of expression, why moving pictures should be denied the protection against censorship —'a form of infringement upon freedom of expression to be especially condemned.'" 365 U.S. at 50, 76 (Warren, C.J., dissenting), *quoting Joseph Burstyn, Inc. v. Wilson*, 343 U.S. 495, 502 (1952). As to the suggestion that censorship of movies is appro-

explicitly so held, presumably it would be unconstitutional to require that all *books* be submitted to an official body before publication so that obscene material could be censored.[77] Yet the Court has essentially authorized this procedure for films without, it should be added, articulating why movies are different from books in any important respect.

The film and broadcasting cases seem to demonstrate that new technologies of communication are both new battlegrounds for renewed fighting over old first amendment issues and focal points for reform efforts.[78] As a result, the actual implementation of first

---

priate because movies have a special "impact," the dissent argued that there was no evidence of an extraordinary impact and that, even if there were, the first amendment still forbade such prior censorship. 365 U.S. at 77.

In *Freedman v. Maryland* the Court held that the Constitution required various procedural protections in any censorship system that requires prior submission of films. As to why such a system is constitutional at all, the Court stated simply that "[t]he requirement of prior submission to a censor sustained in *Times Film* is consistent with our recognition that films differ from other forms of expression." 380 U.S. at 60-61. Justice Douglas, with whom Justice Black joined, stated merely that "[i]f censors are banned from the publishing business, from the pulpit, from the public platform—as they are—they should be banned from the theatre." 380 U.S. at 62 (Douglas, J., dissenting).

77. *Cf.* Kingsley Books, Inc. v. Brown, 354 U.S. 436, 441 (1957).

78. The so-called loudspeaker cases constitute another line of decisions that illustrates the Court's efforts to accommodate both the government's regulatory interest in the context of a new technology of communication and traditional first amendment interests. Permeating the cases are issues of access, privacy, and the scope of governmental regulation. In the first such case, Saia v. New York, 334 U.S. 558 (1948), the Court held invalid a city ordinance that prohibited the use of sound amplifying equipment unless the user had first obtained permission from the chief of police. Since the ordinance provided no standards for the issuance of permits, the Court said it constituted an unconstitutional prior restraint. Writing for the majority, Justice Douglas said that, while loudspeakers could be regulated as to time, place and manner, they could not be completely banned simply because they could be abused. 334 U.S. at 562. Justice Frankfurter dissented, arguing that the problem of preserving privacy in the face of new technologies which could greatly amplify the human voice was so important and so intractable that local communities should be afforded considerable latitude in devising solutions. 334 U.S. at 566 (Frankfurter, J., dissenting). Justice Jackson also dissented, stating that "society has the right to control, as to place, time and volume, the use of loud-speaking devices for any purpose, provided its regulations are not unduly arbitrary, capricious or discriminatory." 334 U.S. at 569 (Jackson, J., dissenting).

In Kovacs v. Cooper, 336 U.S. 77 (1949), although no one opinion commanded a majority of the justices, the court upheld a conviction for violation of an ordinance that forbade the use on public streets of a "sound truck" that emits "loud and raucous noises." Three justices held that the ordinance did not completely prohibit sound trucks but only permissibly barred those that emitted "loud and raucous noises." Justice Frankfurter concurred speaking generally of the idea that freedom of speech has a "preferred position" in the Constitution. At the end of his opinion, however, he objected to the argument that all forms of communication must be treated alike. Referring rather vaguely to movies and broadcasting, he asserted that both media had presented special "problems" that permitted their different first amendment treatment. As for loudspeakers, Justice Frankfurter said that "only a disregard of vital differences between natural speech . . . and the noise of sound trucks would give

amendment theory is much more complex than commonly supposed. The traditional areas of communication, generally the primary focus of attention, retain their purity while new technologies of communication are treated as analytically discrete and are subjected to various social controls.

This first amendment development process is not wholly undesirable. For a dynamic social system in which new problems continually arise, this process of juxtaposing innovation in a new technology of communication against tradition may offer a highly effective and useful mode of adaptation. The opportunity to implement change without the appearance of change can, in this respect, be a disguised blessing brought by the new technologies.

As the movie cases illustrate, however, there are significant risks associated with hidden regulation. Improper regulation, for example, may fester longer because it is not subjected to comprehensive analysis. Further, those persons within the regulated medium can, over time, lose an awareness that their constitutional rights are being violated. If courts and political institutions appear to be insensitive to their first amendment freedoms, and if the public and their

---

sound trucks the constitutional rights accorded to the unaided human voice." Since they posed greater dangers to the countervailing right of privacy, it was not for the "Court to devise the terms on which sound trucks should be allowed to operate, if at all:" 336 U.S. at 96-97 (Frankfurter, J., concurring).

Justice Jackson also filed a concurring opinion, in which he indicated that complete prohibition would be permissible. The only limit he would place on state authority is that it not "censor the contents of the broadcasting." He then added:

I do not agree that, if we sustain regulations or prohibitions of sound trucks, they must therefore be valid if applied to other methods of "communication of ideas." The moving picture screen, the radio, the newspaper, the handbill, the sound truck and the street corner orator have differing natures, values, abuses and dangers. Each, in my view, is a law unto itself, and all we are dealing with now is the sound truck.

336 U.S. at 47 (Jackson, J., dissenting).

Interpreting the ordinance as completely enjoining the use of loudspeakers, Justice Black wrote a strongly worded dissent in which Justices Douglas and Rutledge joined. 336 U.S. at 98 (Black, J., dissenting). Justice Black said the decision of the majority "would surely not be reached by this Court if such channels of communication as the press, radio, or moving pictures were similarly attacked." 336 U.S. at 102. He opined that such arbitrary treatment of *means* of communication carried the evil of giving "an overpowering influence to views of owners of legally favored instruments of communication." 336 U.S. at 102. Moreover, he appeared to suggest that, since loudspeakers are often used by persons without the money to operate newspapers or publish books, and since such persons often have different views than those who operate more traditional channels of communication, a restriction on the use of loudspeakers may deprive the public of access to important views. 336 U.S. at 103.

The tendency to treat new means of communication as analytically discrete may contain more than a bald refusal to account for differences between new and traditional methods of expression. It may also reflect an unwillinguess to restrict everywhere within the system of expression the government's interest in regulation. As new media enter the system, the state's interests in regulation may become more legitimate as the effects of the regulation are more limited.

professional counterparts in other branches of the media consistently fail to support them,[79] these persons might well become discouraged and less assertive of their rights against the government.[80] For the Court, therefore, to rely on fictional differences between new and traditional media may ultimately be counterproductive. It serves unnecessarily to isolate important means of communication from our first amendment traditions, and the Court abdicates its important role of instilling in those communicating within the society a full sense of their constitutional rights.

With respect to broadcasting, moreover, the perception of the medium as "different" will eventually fade, as appears to be already happening.[81] When all the communications media finally are perceived as the same in principle, the Court will then be pressed to justify its different treatment. By that time it may be thought appropriate to say what is apparently said about some other anomalies, like the powers of the grand jury or the special status of the insanity defense,[82] that the explanation is to be found in the legitimacy that time itself can give. But in the case of access regulation in the press, the Court can say much more.

C. *The Rationality of Partial Regulation*

Ultimately, the Court's decisions on the question of access regulation exhibit fundamental good sense. The good sense, however, derives not from the Court's treatment of broadcasting as being somehow special, but rather from its apparent desire to limit the

---

79. It is interesting that in none of the Supreme Court's three major decisions on broadcast regulation did any newspaper or newspaper association file an amicus curiae brief.

80. *Cf.* Kalven, *supra* note 21, at 15-17.

81. One of the more interesting aspects of the *Red Lion-CBS* decisions is the shift in idiom used in discussing the first amendment rights of broadcasters. As described previously, *see* text at notes 17-22 *supra*, *Red Lion* placed heavy emphasis on the right of the public to receive different viewpoints and seemingly little weight on the journalistic freedom of the broadcasters. *See* 395 U.S. at 386-90. The focus was on broadcasters *qua* "licensees" and not *qua* "journalists." In contrast, the *CBS* opinion reflects a significant shift in tone. The Court for the first time referred to broadcasters as a part of the "press," as is illustrated by the following excerpt:

Nor can we accept the Court of Appeals' view that every potential speaker is "the best judge" of what the listening public ought to hear or indeed the best judge of the merits of his or her views. All journalistic tradition and experience is to the contrary. For better or worse, editing is what editors are for; and editing is selection and choice of material. That editors—newspapers or broadcast —can and do abuse this power is beyond doubt, but that is no reason to deny the discretion Congress provided. Calculated risks of abuse are taken in order to preserve higher values.

Columbia Broadcasting Sys., Inc. v. Democratic Natl. Comm., 412 U.S. 94, 124-25 (1973).

82. *See* Henkin, *On Drawing Lines*, 82 HARV. L. REV. 63, 72 (1968).

over-all reach of access regulation.   The Court need not, however, isolate the electronic media to achieve this result.   Although
it is uncertain whether the Court in *Miami Herald* saw it as such, the
critical difference between what the Court was asked to do in *Red
Lion* and what it was asked to do in *Miami Herald* involved choosing
between a partial regulatory system and a universal one.   Viewed
from that perspective, the Court reached the correct result in both
cases.

The central problem in this area results from the complexity of
the access issue.   The truth of the matter is, as the Court's opinions
so plainly, if unintentionally, demonstrate, that there are good first
amendment reasons for being both receptive to and wary of access
regulation.   This dual nature of access legislation suggests the need
to limit carefully the intrusiveness of the regulation in order safely
to enjoy its remedial benefits.   Thus, a proper judicial response is one
that will permit the legislature to provide the public with access
somewhere within the mass media, but not throughout the press.
The Court should not, and need not, be forced into an all-or-nothing
position on this matter; there is nothing in the first amendment that
forbids having the best of both worlds.

Access regulation both responds to constitutional traditions and
cuts against them.   On the one hand, it helps to make possible the
realization of first amendment goals.   Unlike attempts to censor
types of speech, an access rule is designed to operate in the service
of the first amendment.   It seeks to neutralize the disparities that
impede the proper functioning of the "market-place of ideas," to
equalize opportunities within our society to command an audience
and thereby to mobilize public opinion, and in that sense to help realize democratic ideals.

That unrestrained private interests can, at times, hamper the free
exchange of ideas as seriously as governmental censorship has been
apparent with painful clarity within the past half century.   Chafee
wrote several decades ago about the need to define a new theoretical structure for governmental involvement in the implementation of
first amendment rights in response to the problems of private
censorship:

> [W]hat is the use of telling an unpopular speaker that he will incur
> no criminal penalties by his proposed address, so long as every hall
> owner in the city declines to rent him space for his meeting and there
> are no vacant lots available?   There should be municipal auditoriums,
> schoolhouses out of school hours, church forums, parks in summer,
> all open to thresh out every question of public importance, with just
> as few restrictions as possible; for otherwise the subjects that most

need to be discussed will be the very subjects that will be ruled out as unsuitable for discussion.

We must do more than remove the discouragements to open discussion. We must exert ourselves to supply active encouragements.[83] Chafee's articulation of the seeds of an "affirmative" theory of freedom of speech constituted an important qualification of the thinking of laissez-faire theorists such as John Stuart Mill and John Milton. Many commentators since Chafee have elaborated on his idea.[84] The debate that has been generated unquestionably involves the most vital first amendment issues of our time.

The Supreme Court has, through its actions, occasionally demonstrated that it recognizes the serious problems posed by unregulated private interests operating in areas that affect the first amendment. In a seminal decision in *Associated Press v. United States*,[85] the Court approved a governmental order directing a national wire service to make its news available on a nondiscriminatory basis, stating that "[f]reedom of the press from governmental interference under the first amendment does not sanction repression of that freedom by private interests."[86] In another well-known line of cases the Court held that a private company town and a shopping center were prohibited under the first amendment from excluding certain speech that the private owners would have preferred to censor.[87] These decisions, together with *Red Lion*, outline a still tentative approach to removing the inequalities in speech opportunities.[88]

Of all the efforts thus far to restructure private arrangements that impinge on the "market-place of ideas," access regulation represents the most direct assault, and, consequently, the most dangerous.[89] Al-

83. Z. CHAFEE, FREE SPEECH IN THE UNITED STATES 559 (1941).

84. *See* T. EMERSON, *supra* note 21, at ch. xvii; Reich, *The Law of the Planned Society*, 75 YALE L.J. 1227 (1966).

85. 326 U.S. 1 (1945).

86. 326 U.S. at 20.

87. *See* Marsh v. Alabama, 326 U.S. 501 (1946); Amalgamated Food Employees v. Logan Valley Plaza, Inc., 391 U.S. 308 (1968). *But see* Hudgens v. NLRB, 424 U.S. 507 (1976); Lloyd Corp. v. Tanner, 407 U.S. 551 (1972).

88. An interesting response to the problem of access in the mass media has been the noticeable solicitude for minor modes of communication. Judicial opinions and scholarly commentary have emphasized the need for protection of these methods of communication precisely because of the restricted nature of the press. *See, e.g.,* Martin v. Struthers, 319 U.S. 141, 146 (1943) ("Door to door distribution of circulars is essential to the poorly financed causes of little people"); Kovacs v. Cooper, 336 U.S. 77, 98 (1949) (Black, J., dissenting). *See also* Kalven, *The Concept of the Public Forum: Cox v. Louisiana*, 1965 SUP. CT. REV. 1, 30; Stone, *Fora Americana: Speech in Public Places*, 1974 SUP. CT. REV. 233, 233-34. Though important, this is hardly an adequate response to the problem of concentration in the mass media.

89. Other major attempts at reform have come primarily in the area of antitrust law. The Newspaper Preservation Act, Pub. L. No. 91-353, 84 Stat. 466 (1970) (co-

though its aims conform to those of the first amendment, the methods of access regulation constitute a significant departure from our traditional constitutional notions concerning the need to maintain a distance between the government and the press, especially on matters directly touching news content.   Access regulation carries the greatest potential for altering the press as we have known it and for exposing us to grave risks.

In general, access regulation may have three adverse consequences for the marketplace of ideas.   The first is a commonly identified cost of access regulation: It may have a depressing effect on journalistic motivation to engage in discourse on social issues.[90] This cost is presumably greater with some forms of access regulation than with others.   The chilling effect associated with the right-of-reply rules is likely much greater than that associated with the requirement that editors publish all advertisements on a nondiscriminatory basis.   Even where the chilling effect is thought to be a problem, however, no data exist as to the extent to which the regulation does, in fact, have an inhibiting effect.   Nevertheless, in those cases where a significant chilling effect may predictably occur, there is cause for concern, given our general commitment to the idea that debate is most likely to be fruitful if it is "uninhibited, robust, and wide-open."[91]   The prospect that some regulated editors will choose to forego coverage of some political discussion because of reply requirements need not necessitate rejection of access regulation; its benefits may still outweigh this cost.   Such a cost, however, remains a matter of concern, and should be minimized as much as possible.

A second general concern associated with access regulation involves the risk that the administrative machinery required to implement it will be used to force the press into some official line and

---

dified at 15 U.S.C. §§ 1801-1804 (1970)), is a recent example of the use of the antitrust laws to foster opportunities for debate within the press.   However, it also represents a recognition that the antitrust laws themselves are not likely to achieve more diversity of outlets since the high economies of scale in the newspaper industry seem to lead to the creation of natural monopolies. *See* B. SCHMIDT, *supra* note 3, at 51-54.

On a private level one might note the recent formation of the National News Council.   The Council is a mediating organization with no powers of enforcement. For a description of its operation and an analysis of the effectiveness of this and other press councils, see Ritter & Leibowitz, *Press Councils: The Answer to Our First Amendment Dilemma,* 1974 DUKE L.J. 845.

90. For an evaluation of the chilling effect of access regulation, see Lange, *supra* note 5, at 70-71; Kalven, *supra* note 21, at 19-23; Robinson, *supra* note 30, at 136-40.   It will be recalled that the Court in *Red Lion* dismissed the broadcaster's chilling effect argument as speculative, while in *Miami Herald* it relied on the argument in striking down the regulation. *See* text at notes 11-19 *supra.*

91. New York Times Co. v. Sullivan, 376 U.S. 254, 270 (1964).

will undermine its role as a critic and antagonist of government. Although neither *Red Lion* nor *Miami Herald* discussed this risk, the possibility of official misbehavior has been a traditional reason for withholding approval of governmental schemes to "improve" the press.[92] It is a consideration that reflects the sum of our experience and should not be lightly disregarded. Evidence that this risk is still vital may, regrettably, be found in an examination of our recent upheaval in presidential politics.

In the course of the revelations about Watergate, it became known that the executive branch, angered by unflattering remarks, criticisms and disclosures of government secrets, embarked on an extensive campaign to harass the press. A substantial part of the attack apparently involved using administrative machinery to apply pressure on journalists.[93] There were also serious allegations that the executive branch had sought to apply pressure directly on the *Washington Post* by creating difficulties for the *Post*'s subsidiary radio stations with the Federal Communications Commission.[94] If there is a Watergate lesson for the first amendment, therefore, it is that we should continue to be extremely wary of making available official

92. *See, e.g.,* 2 Z. CHAFEE, *supra* note 7, at 476-77.

93. One of the impeachment charges leveled by the House Judiciary Committee was that officials of the Nixon administration had induced, or had suggested inducing, tax audits of troublesome members of the media. *See* CONGRESSIONAL INFORMATION SERVICE (1974), H521-34, at 16, 18, 21.

The willingness of the administration to employ federal machinery to silence the press was most vividly reflected in the events surrounding the creation of the "enemy list." John Dean, then the President's legal counsel, stated in one memorandum: "This memorandum addresses the matter of how we can maximize the fact of our incumbency in dealing with persons known to be active in their opposition to our administration. Stated a bit more bluntly—how we can use the available federal machinery to screw our political enemies." CONGRESSIONAL INFORMATION SERVICE (1973), S961-4, at 1689. Dean went on to suggest that "grant availability, federal contracts, litigation, prosecution, etc." should all be considered in determining how most effectively to "screw" opponents. *Id.* The enemy list as compiled contained a total of 57 reporters, editors, columnists and television commentators. *Id.* at 1716-18. The *Washington Post*, the *New York Times* and the *St. Louis Post Dispatch* were among the institutions included. *Id.* at 1716. *See also* Washington Post, Dec. 3, 1973, section A, at 24, col. 4 (documents disclosed by Senator Lowell Weicker); THE WHITE HOUSE TRANSCRIPTS 57-58, 63, 404, 782-84 (Bantam Books, Inc. 1974).

94. In January 1973, the Associated Press and United Press International reported that the broadcast licenses of two Florida television stations, both owned by the *Washington Post*, were being challenged before the Federal Communications Commission by a group which included long-time friends and political associates of President Nixon. N.Y. Times, Jan. 4, 1973, at 21, col. 1; Washington Post, Jan. 3, 1973, section A, at 6, col. 1. It was subsequently revealed that Glenn J. Sedam, Jr., general counsel to the Committee for the Re-Election of the President, had advised some of the Nixon associates involved in the challenges. Washington Post, Jan. 9, 1973, section A, at 6, col. 1. Only the *Post*'s two stations, out of 36 stations in the state, had their licenses contested. It should be noted, however, that the administration and all the principals involved in the challenges denied any political motivation. Washington Post, Jan. 9, 1973, section A, at 6, col. 1.

machinery for the regulation of the press.   Such a regulatory structure would stand as a constant temptation to governmental officials—
a source of leverage with which to compel obedience within the press
and, in more subtle ways, to manipulate the content of public debate.

The third potential adverse consequence of access regulation is
that it may result in an escalation of regulation, the camel's-nose-
in-the-tent phenomena mentioned earlier.[95]   This criticism is one of
those stock arguments that suffers badly from overuse.   It is easy
to dismiss the claim because it is advanced so often in circumstances
where it carries no conviction.   With respect to access regulation,
however, the argument has powerful force and should not go
unheeded.

The problem is not simply that regulation will induce irresistable
pressure for censorship.   The dangers are more subtle and complicated.   Access regulation comes in a variety of shapes and sizes.
Some forms, like a vigorously enforced fairness doctrine, may lead
to utter blandness of content and in this way may permit official
manipulation of the news.   In addition, it is virtually impossible for
the Court to articulate in advance unambiguous standards.   Experience with a particular regulation will often be necessary to judge its
desirability and constitutionality.   It is important to know, for
example, how frequently the government will be drawn into conflict
with the editors,[96] what financial burdens the administrative procedures will impose on those that are regulated, and whether the
administering officials will be prone to misconduct or will exhibit a
healthy respect for first amendment freedoms.[97]

By sanctioning the concept of access regulation, the Court can
expect administrative experimentation with the various types of regulation.   And since clear guidelines cannot be established, there may
be constant pressure to expand the regulatory power into impermissible areas.   The clamour for greater regulation may itself be
used as a weapon to bend the press into line.   If what turns out to
be improper regulation is imposed, irremediable harm may have
already occurred before the Court acts.   Similarly, the difficulties in
assessing the future consequences of the regulation may lead the

---

95. *See* text at note 65 *supra.*

96. Such data has been available with respect to broadcast regulation.   We know,
for example, that in fiscal 1973, the Commission received about 2,400 fairness doctrine complaints and forwarded 94 to broadcasters for comment.   39 Fed. Reg. 26,375
(1974).

97. For an indication that consideration of the type of person likely to assume
the administrative role is relevant here, see Times Film Corp. v. Chicago, 365 U.S.
43, 69-73 (Warren, C.J., dissenting).   *See also* J. Milton, Areopagitica 210 (3 Harvard Classics (1909)).

Court to sanction conduct that is ultimately very harmful.[98] In both instances, it must be remembered that "[l]egal experiments, once started, cannot be stopped the moment they show signs of working badly."[99]

Viewed in its entirety, therefore, access regulation is both desirable and dangerous. That it raises a constitutional problem of enormous difficulty is reflected in the schizophrenic nature of *Red Lion* and *Miami Herald*. In light of the double-edged character of access regulation, the Court's appropriate response is to affirm congressional authority to implement only a *partial* regulatory scheme. Only with this approach, with a major branch of the press remaining free of regulation, will the costs and risks of regulation be held at an acceptable level. Or, put another way, only under such a system can we afford to allow the degree of governmental regulation that is necessary to realize the objectives of public access.

One advantage of a partial regulatory system is that the unregulated sector provides an effective check against each of the costs of regulation. A partial scheme offers some assurance that information that might not be disseminated by the regulated sector of the press will nevertheless be published by the unregulated press. If, for example, a local broadcast station chooses not to cover a debate between two prominent mayoral candidates because of equal time obligations, then the public will still be informed of the event by the local newspaper. Second, a partial scheme offers some assurance that governmental use of the regulatory authority to bludgeon the press into an official line will not suppress the truth. If, for example, the *Washington Post* had curtailed its Watergate investigations to ward off what it might reasonably have perceived to be governmental pressure to have the licenses of its subsidiary radio stations revoked, other newspapers free of governmental entanglements, such as the

---

98. As one commentator has argued:
    Any widespread governmental action is likely to produce unexpected results. England, early in the eighteenth century, sought to strengthen her long-standing alliance with Portugal by admitting Portuguese wines at a very low rate of duty. This encouraged the drinking of port rather than French claret. The result was to afflict two centuries of Englishmen with gout . . . . Similar surprises can take place when the government concerns itself with communications industries.
2 Z. CHAFEE, *supra* note 7, at 475. Perhaps an example of an unforeseen effect of broadcast regulation is the apparent political abuse surrounding the fairness doctrine. *See* F. Friendly, *What's Fair on the Air?* N.Y. Times Magazine, March 30, 1975, at 11. Professor Friendly charges, *inter alia*, that during the early 1960s officers of the Democratic National Committee organized and funded "private" organizations that would demand of radio and television stations an opportunity to reply to any coverage of right-wing positions in order to discourage media coverage of anti-administration viewpoints.

99. 2 Z. CHAFEE, *supra* note 7, at 699-700.

New York Times, would still have continued the investigation. Finally, such a system gives some assurance that the pressures for and effects of harmful regulation will be cushioned. If, for example, a Vice-President were to urge much more vigorous access regulation in order to ward off criticism of the President, and as a result the regulated sector were to tone down its criticism, the unregulated press would remain active.

Restricting regulation to only a part of the press, however, offers more than a check against these costs. It provides, again through the presence of the unregulated media, a beneficial tension within the system. The unregulated sector can operate to minimize the three costs of regulation. Consider, for example, the chilling effect problem. The publication of news in the unregulated press serves as a competitive prod to the regulated press to publish what it might otherwise omit.[100] Thus, broadcasters may initially have been reluctant to cover Watergate events because of fears of official reprisals and access obligations, but a decision not to cover the story would have been impossible once the print media began exploiting it.[101]

The most significant aspect of a partial regulatory scheme, how-ever, is that it preserves a benchmark—an important link with our constitutional traditions as the Court permits experimentation with regulation. The continuing link with traditional first amendment theory conveys the message that old principles have not been abandoned, and it forces every departure to be more carefully scrutinized and justified. The message is one of adjustment rather than wholesale revision.[102]

One of the more interesting features of our experience with broadcast regulation has been the absence of egregious abuses of power by the FCC. The Commission has, on the whole, been extraordinarily circumspect in the exercise of its powers.[103] It is

---

100. *Cf.* E. EPSTEIN, *supra* note 39, at 150.

101. It is also likely that the principles represented by the regulations themselves will have an effect throughout the entire media system. Representing the public's pronouncement of proper journalistic behavior, the principles may over time filter in-to the unregulated sphere, in much the same way that we occasionally see the con-stitutional due process requirements voluntarily adopted by private institutions. Thus, under a partial regulatory system a fruitful symbiotic relationship may be expected to develop.

102. The process resembles that which is observed in other areas of constitutional law, for example, the applicability of criminal procedure rules to the juvenile justice system. *Cf. In re* Winship, 397 U.S. 358 (1970); *In re* Gault, 387 U.S. 1 (1967).

103. 1 Z. CHAFEE, *supra* note 7, at 11-12; 2 *id.* at 476-77; Kalven, *supra* note 21, at 18, 19-20. The only area, it seems, where the Commission can perhaps be charged with having seriously ignored important free speech interests is indecent

reasonable to assume that this self-restraint is explained in large part by the constant juxtaposition of the autonomous print media, representing our continued respect for the ideal of a free press, against the regulated broadcasting media. By preserving the unregulated print media, the benchmark against which the reform must continually be measured, even if not explicitly, the Court has furnished a built-in restraint against excesses in regulation. Those representing the interests of broadcasters have been able to point to the practices of the print media as concrete illustrations of traditional constitutional principles rather than to some abstract principle of freedom of the press, thus making more explicit any departure from nonregulation. The effect of this process can be readily observed in more recent court decisions, where frequent references to the print media demonstrate the force of the newspaper analogy.[104]

In an article on broadcast regulation written in 1967, Professor Kalven observed that "[l]aw . . . is determined by a choice between competing analogies."[105] What had been "sorely needed" in the broadcasting area was "the competing analogy to set against the claims for control."[106] There had never been "a precedent setting the *outer boundaries* of [FCC] control . . . ."[107] The absence of an explicit limit on Commission authority has been unfortunate, but the problem has been less significant than it otherwise would be precisely because the unregulated print media has provided a "competing analogy."

It is from this perspective that the *Miami Herald* decision begins to make some sense. On the surface, the decision seems singularly inattentive to the parallel broadcasting cases, yet in fact it speaks directly to them. *Red Lion* had given the impression that editorial rights were to be subordinated to the "public's right to hear." It spawned a political and legal movement, spearheaded by Professor Jerome Barron,[108] plaintiff's counsel in *Miami Herald*, for more

---

speech. *See, e.g., In re* Pacifica Foundation, 36 F.C.C. 147 (1964); *In re* WUHY-FM Eastern Educ. Radio, 24 F.C.C.2d 408 (1970). *See* Kalven, *supra* note 21, at 18.

104. *See, e.g.,* Columbia Broadcasting Sys., Inc. v. Democratic Natl. Comm., 412 U.S. 94 (1973); National Broadcasting Co. v. FCC, 516 F.2d 1101 (D.C. Cir. 1974), *cert. denied,* 424 U.S. 910 (1976).

105. Kalven, *supra* note 21, at 38.

106. *Id.*

107. *Id.* at 37.

108. *See* Barron, *supra* note 8; Barron, *An Emerging First Amendment Right of Access to the Media?,* 37 GEO. WASH. L. REV. 487 (1969); Barron, *Access—The Only Choice for the Media?,* 48 TEX. L. REV. 766 (1970). Other articles on access are collected in Lange, *supra* note 5, at 2 n.5.

The movement for a first amendment right of access to the broadcast media has

extensive regulation. In its reaffirmation of fundamental first amendment principles, the *Miami Herald* Court's opinion urges caution and restraint, and sharply limits regulatory reform. To be sure, the opinion represents a lowpoint in judicial craftsmanship, but it is nevertheless explicable.

It must be admitted that the proposed partial theory of regulation is unique in its specific formulation. Nowhere else has the Court interpreted the Constitution to allow Congress such a discretionary regulatory role. The theory is, however, no less valid for this reason. It can satisfy the test of legitimacy applied to new constitutional pronouncements. As discussed above, the Court is able to present reasoned arguments for both allowing regulation and restricting it as a way to further the purposes and values underlying the first amendment.

It has long been recognized that the Constitution is not a static instrument. Old constitutional principles are continually being discarded or revised as they are discovered to be ineffective in protecting fundamental values or to hamstring unduly the achievement of legitimate social aims; new principles are continually being devised to meet the exigencies of an ever-changing reality. A part of this process, as the access question demonstrates, involves deciding to what extent new principles are to overtake traditional approaches. It is a major part of the Court's most vital function of carrying forward and reinterpreting constitutional values in light of changed circumstances.

The theory of partial regulation mandates, in effect, a system in which the burdens of regulation will be allocated unequally among the various institutions of the press. Those associated with the institution that Congress chooses to regulate may claim that it is unfair for them to bear the burdens of regulation when their similarly situated counterparts do not. Their claim would be that the scheme of classification is "underinclusive." This claim of unequal treatment may be a factor to be considered in deciding whether to mandate a partial system, but it ought not be determinative for several reasons. First, courts and commentators generally give greater constitutional leeway to an underinclusive rather than an "overinclusive" approach to a general problem, since in underinclusive classifications "all who are included in the class are at least tainted by the mischief at which the law aims . . . while over-inclusive classifications reach out to the innocent bystander, the hapless

---

been arrested by the Court's decision in Columbia Broadcasting Sys., Inc. v. Democratic Natl. Comm., 412 U.S. 94 (1973).

victim of circumstances or association."[109] Second, the trait that defines the class would not be the content of speech and it would not reflect an official animus against a particular group of people because it would be directed at *institutions* and not individuals. That is, the classifying trait would be the neutral factor of technology, and not a suspect factor such as race. This means that those individuals indirectly affected would be able to shift to the unregulated media and escape the burden imposed should they find it offensive, and that the opportunity for government to pursue solely political or discriminatory purposes under the guise of the first amendment is minimized.

In seeking to advance first amendment goals, the Court should not be precluded from deciding on a rational basis to limit congressional powers of regulation. There may be more than one claim to "equality" to be considered. Those persons excluded from public debate because of private ownership also have a claim to "equality" in the sense of obtaining an equal opportunity to speak.[110] If a full restructuring of the press to accommodate those claims is too dangerous, then the Court must balance the interests of those excluded from the media against the interests of those members of the press whom Congress will ultimately select to bear the burden of regulation in a partial system. Phrased somewhat differently, it is the *first amendment itself* that justifies this differential treatment of mass communication technologies.

The analysis of *Red Lion* and *Miami Herald*, therefore, demonstrates the need to maintain a partial regulatory structure *for its own sake*. What the Court has never fully appreciated is that the very similarity of the two major branches of the mass media provides a rationale for treating them differently. By permitting different treatment of the two institutions, the Court can facilitate realization of the benefits of two distinct constitutional values, both of which ought to be fostered: access in a highly concentrated press and minimal governmental intervention. Neither side of the access controversy emerges victorious. The Court has imposed a compromise—a compromise, however, not based on notions of expediency, but rather on a reasoned, and principled, accommodation of competing first amendment values.

There is, it is true, something to be said in favor of limiting legis-

109. *See* Tussman & tenBroek, *The Equal Protection of the Laws*, 37 CALIF. L. REV. 341, 351 (1949).

110. *See* Karst, *Equality as a Central Principle in the First Amendment*, 43 U. CHI. L. REV. 20, 43-52 (1975).

lative experimentation with access to the electronic media and precluding Congress from choosing any segment of the mass media to regulate. This is a product of the different treatment long accorded broadcasting: What seems possible in broadcasting seems unthinkable for newspapers. It is, however, unwise to maintain separate traditions for separate branches of the media; it is, in the end, counterproductive to first amendment interests. Instead, the Court ought to acknowledge broadcasters as full-fledged participants in our first amendment traditions and yet permit Congress to engage in *some* experimentation with press freedom to facilitate public access, allowing Congress to choose the medium to be regulated. This means, of course, that eventually the legislative branch may shift the target of its regulatory scheme to other segments of the media, provided it abandons its earlier target. Thus, it ought theoretically to be possible for Congress to abandon its regulation of the electronic media and choose instead to provide access within the confines of the newspaper industry. The extent to which it ought to be able to regulate the print media is problematical. The answer to that question, however, must ultimately depend on a contemporary evaluation of the factors that justify partial regulation.

III.   A Constitutional Assessment of Cable Technology

Madame Sosotris, famous clairvoyante, had a bad cold . . . .[111]

An interpretation of the first amendment that permits Congress to impose access regulation, but only within a limited segment of the press, has important implications for the emerging technology of cable television. It is frequently argued that, since *Red Lion* predicated its approval of access regulation upon the limited channel space of the electromaguetic spectrum, the shift to the virtually unbounded channel capacity of coaxial cables will eliminate the constitutional justification for regulation.[112] This argument, however,

---

111. T.S. Eliot, *The Waste Land*, The Dial (Nov. 1922).

112. *See, e.g.,* Note, *Cable Television and the First Amendment,* 71 Colum. L. Rev. 1008 (1971); Note, *The Proposed Cable Communications Act of 1975: A Recommendation for Comprehensive Regulation,* 1975 Duke L.J. 93, 112-13.

Similar thinking appears to underlie the 1974 report of the Cabinet Committee on Cable Communications, which recommended the immediate end of access regulation with respect to cablecasting. The Cabinet Committee on Cable Communications, Report to the President 37-38 (1974). The Office of Telecommunications Policy (OTP) has prepared legislation embodying this and other policies for submission to Congress. Section 401 of the Proposed Act provides as follows:

No executive agency of the United States . . . and no State or political subdivision or agency thereof . . . shall:

(a) require or prohibit program originations by a cable operator or channel programmer, or impose upon such operator or programmer any restrictions or

misconceives the scarcity rationale as the true, or at least the only, explanation for the disparate treatment of the electronic media. A theory of partial regulation better explains *Red Lion* and *Miami Herald*, and that thesis would permit access regulation within television even if there were an unlimited number of channels.

That is not to say that the cable technology may not affect the existing structure of the television industry, and hence congressional perception of the urgency of regulation. By increasing the available number of channels, thereby easing the costs of entry into the television market, cable may create a much more atomized system of programming with each channel claiming only a relatively small portion of the viewing audience.[113] It is even possible that the increased competition could result in the breakdown of the presently gargantuan networks.

It is not at all certain that this will be the result. Indeed there are good reasons for thinking that the present structure will remain largely unchanged for the foreseeable future.[114] In any case, it is virtually impossible at this time to predict precisely what transformation, if any, will occur, because it is difficult to determine what economic advantages present broadcasters will have acquired, the extent to which audience tastes will change or remain the same, and the interplay of a host of other factors that will undoubtedly play a role.

The potential of cable television to increase substantially the number of competing television outlets, however, should not change

obligations affecting the content of such program originations, including rights of response by any person, opportunities for appearances by candidates for public office, or requirements for balance and objectivity . . . .
For commentary on the proposed bill, see Note, 1975 DUKE L.J. 93, *supra.* The present status of the bill is uncertain. It has thus far failed to pass the executive clearance process, and the OTP is studying various objections raised against the bill. It is unclear what the change in administration portends for the proposed legislation.

Instead of using the circumscribed electromagnetic spectrum as a means of transmitting television signals, cable television relies on coaxial cables laid underground or strung aboveground like telephone wires. No physical law limits the number of cables that can be connected. Thus, while the available frequencies in the VHF portion of the spectrum permit only 12 channels, cable can carry as many as 80 channels. Through interconnection devices and the use of satellites, the potential exists for a vastly expanded national and local network of television channels. Broadcasting as a mode of transmission could become obsolete. For a detailed discussion of the nature and uses of coaxial cable, see THE SLOAN COMMISSION ON CABLE COMMUNICATIONS, ON THE CABLE: THE TELEVISION OF ABUNDANCE 11-16 (1971) (hereinafter SLOAN REPORT). It is important to realize, however, that cable has not yet developed to this stage. Cable systems presently reach only approximately 12.5 per cent of the nation's television households and offer between 8 and 12 channels. *See* BROADCASTING, CABLE SOURCEBOOK 1975, at 5.

113. *See, e.g.,* R. SMITH, THE WIRED NATION (1972).

114. *See, e.g.,* SLOAN REPORT 78-81, 118, 169; LaPierre, *Cable Television and the Promise of Programming Diversity,* 42 FORDHAM L. REV. 25, 119-24 (1973).

the constitutional determination permitting Congress to impose access regulation on television. Even if eventually there are ten channels more or less evenly dividing the nation's audience, a rather remote possibility, Congress ought still to be permitted to provide that the opportunity to reach the television audience will not depend entirely on private ownership. As is true now, the government should be able in one forum to balance the freedom of press interests of those owning established channels of communication against the interests of those effectively excluded from major avenues of communication.

Nevertheless, cable technology does mean that a *legislative* crossroad has been reached on the matter of access regulation. The emergence of cable makes more possible than ever before reliance on the interplay of private interests to assure an effective marketplace of ideas. As a result, cable offers a new context in which to rethink questions relating to the scope and types of access regulation. It may be thought wiser, for example, to limit regulation to selected mass audience channels than to impose access regulation throughout television. Certain types of access regulation, moreover, may be considered either more or less appropriate than they were previously. Furthermore, the desirability of avoiding certain forms of access regulation that might affect the development of cable may be affirmed. A broad application of the fairness doctrine, for example, could inhibit the entry of programmers who desired to program with a strong ideological bias aimed at a limited and politically homogeneous audience. While this has been a cost of regulation in the past, its dimensions have been much more confined because the number of potential entrants so affected was much smaller.

Cable, therefore, raises important questions for the current regulatory scheme. Currently, it is the FCC that provides answers to these questions. The Commission has chosen to impose access regulation within a cable, although thus far only on channels originating with the cable owner.[115] Whether it will choose to apply access

---

115. In 1972, the Commission after several years of study announced a highly elaborate and intricate body of regulations covering cable television reflecting a shift in Commission attitude from containment of cable to mild encouragement. FCC, CABLE TELEVISION REPORT AND ORDER ON RULES AND REGULATIONS RELATIVE TO CATV SYSTEMS, 36 F.C.C.2d 143 (1972), *stays denied*, 34 F.C.C.2d 165, 170, 172, 174, 176, 178, 180, *reconsideration denied*, 36 F.C.C.2d 326. *See* LaPierre, *supra* note 114, at 87.

The most significant provisions are those that relate to the potential expansion of the total number of television channels available. Under the present regulations, cable systems must have a minimum capacity of 20 channels. 47 C.F.R. § 76.251(a) (1) (1975). For each broadcast signal carried, the operator must make available one channel for nonbroadcast programming. 47 C.F.R. 76.251(a)(2) (1975). Of the

regulation to leased channels operated by independent programmers is still uncertain.

The question likely to confront the Court in the near future is whether the Commission has the statutory authority under the Communications Act of 1934 to impose access regulation on cable television. When that case does arise, the Court ought to rule against the Commission for at least two reasons. First, given the potential of cable technology to alter significantly the television medium, together with the important first amendment interests at stake in the access question, the Court should find that the imposition of access regulation on cable is beyond the scope of the Communications Act. The access problems that brought about the remedial efforts of the 1934 Act are not comparable to those in cable technology. Second, the history of the Commission's treatment of cable does not inspire confidence in its judgments in this area. There is considerable evidence that the Commission has been more concerned with protecting the economic interests of conventional broadcasters than with fully exploiting the resources of cable technology.[116] Thus, the Court ought to require Congress to make the decision on access in the first instance.

This approach to the question of access regulation in cable is not precluded by the Court's decision on two occasions upholding the authority of the Commission under the Communications Act to impose various regulations on cable. The question whether the Commission has the power to regulate cable at all is separate from the question whether it has the authority to issue a particular rule. For our purposes, it is significant that neither of the Court's cable decisions involved an issue as important from a first amendment perspective as that of access regulation. Further, in both cases the Court seemed to recognize the need for congressional reevaluation of the need for regulating cable. In *United States v. Southwestern Cable Co.*,[117] its first cable decision, the Court approved FCC

latter channels, one each must be available for use by the public on a first-come first-served basis, 47 C.F.R. § 76.251(a)(4) (1975), by educational authorities, 47 C.F.R. § 76.251(a)(5) (1975), and by local government, 47 C.F.R. § 76.251(a)(6) (1975), and the remainder must be open for lease on a common carrier basis to independent programmers, 47 C.F.R. § 76.251(a)(7) (1975). The rules further provide that the equal time and fairness doctrine rules are applicable to all origination cablecasts. 47 C.F.R. §§ 76.205, 76.209 (1975). Other limitations relating to lotteries, obscenity, and sponsorship identification, which are regularly imposed on broadcasters, are also extended to cablecasters. 47 C.F.R. §§ 76.213, 76.215, 76.221 (1975).

The Commission's future regulatory role with respect to cable is, apparently, still a matter of considerable doubt within the agency. *See* Price, *Requiem for the Wired Nation: Cable Rulemaking at the F.C.C.*, 61 VA. L. REV. 541, 544 (1975).

116. *See, e.g.,* LaPierre, *supra* note 114.

117. 392 U.S. 157 (1968).

action under the Commission's "local carriage" rule,[118] which forbade certain cable systems from importing broadcast signals without Commission approval, and thereby served to protect the market of local broadcasters. The Court, speaking of a need to provide for the "orderly development" of an appropriate system of local television broadcasting,[119] upheld the rule as "reasonably ancillary to the effective performance of the Commission's responsibilities for the regulation of television broadcasting."[120]

In a subsequent decision in *United States v. Midwest Video Corp.*,[121] the Court considered the Commission's "program origination" rule requiring nonbroadcast programming on some cable systems. The rule provided that "no CATV [cable] system having 3,500 or more subscribers shall carry the signal of any television broadcast station unless the system also operates to a significant extent as a local outlet by cablecasting and has available facilities for local production and presentation of programs other than automated services."[122] The Court was deeply divided on the issue of the statutory validity of the rule. In finding the regulation consistent with the "public interest" and thus within the power of the Commission, Justice Brennan, representing a plurality of four justices, said:

> The effect of the regulation, after all, is to assure that in the retransmission of broadcast signals viewers are provided suitably diversified programming—the same objective underlying regulations sustained in *National Broadcasting Co. v. United States* . . . , as well as the local-carriage rule reviewed in *Southwestern* and subsequently upheld.[123]

A dissenting opinion joined by four justices argued that the regulation was invalid on the ground that the Communications Act nowhere accorded the FCC the power to compel anyone "to enter the broadcasting field."[124] With obvious reluctance, Chief Justice Burger cast the deciding vote for the Commission but observed that the

---

118. The regulation as quoted in the Court's opinion provided that [n]o CATV system operating in a community within the predicted Grade A contour of a television broadcast station in the 100 largest television markets shall extend the signal of a television broadcast station beyond the Grade B contour of that station, except upon a showing approved by the Commission that such extension would be consistent with the public interest, and specifically the establishment and healthy maintenance of television broadcast service in the area. 392 U.S. 157, 159 n.2.

119. 392 U.S. at 177.

120. 392 U.S. at 178.

121. 406 U.S. 649 (1972).

122. 47 C.F.R. § 74.1111(a), revised as 47 C.F.R. § 76.201(a) (1973). This regulation was suspended for most of its life and then abandoned by the Commission in 1974. 39 Fed. Reg. 43,302 (1974).

123. 406 U.S. at 649, 669.

124. 406 U.S. at 677, 679 (Douglas, J., dissenting).

"almost explosive development of CATV suggests the need of a comprehensive re-examination of the statutory scheme as it relates to this new development, so that the basic policies are considered by Congress and not left entirely to the Commission and the courts."[125]

As the Commission seeks to extend its authority over cable television, the Court ought to be sensitive to the need for congressional guidance in an area that so plainly involves first amendment interests.[126] The suggestion of Chief Justice Burger should be the basis for decision. A considered legislative judgment on matters relating to access regulation in cable television is important and overdue, but it should also be recognized that this is an appropriate juncture to pause and reassess the costs and benefits of the entire experiment.

Most importantly, perhaps cable offers the Court an appropriate occasion for discarding the shibboleth of the scarcity rationale. The Court should begin the process of defining a rationale for regulation that recognizes the limited power of Congress to impose access regulation within the mass media. At the same time the Court can openly recognize the link between broadcasting and our constitutional traditions and begin to create a heightened sensitivity to the first amendment rights of broadcasters.

IV. CONCLUSION

What appears on the surface to be the paradox of *Red Lion* and *Miami Herald* turns out on close inspection to be a rationally defensible regime. The different treatment accorded the broadcasting and print media is an especially intriguing illustration of the implementation of new first amendment principles. The substance of the constitutional solution that has been devised, or, more accurately, to which the decisions point, is both acceptable and sound. In the end, it is the first amendment itself that requires different treatment of these institutions, accommodating both the will of the legislature to participate in the realization of first amendment goals and the role of the Court as the ultimate guarantor of those goals. The impact of a new technology like cable is not so much that it alters the accommodation, but that it permits the Court to take a fresh and unblinking view of it.

125. 406 U.S. at 676 (Burger, C.J., coucurring).

126. *Cf.* Bickel & Wellington, *Legislative Purpose and the Judicial Process: The Lincoln Mills Case*, 71 HARV. L. REV. 1 (1957).

[2]

Broadcasting and Speech

Jonathan Weinberg†

It is illegal to speak over the airwaves without a broadcast license. The FCC grants those licenses, and decides whether they will be renewed, on the basis of a vague "public interest" standard. The resulting system of broadcast regulation conflicts, starkly and gratuitously, with ordinary free speech philosophy. In this Article, the author argues that that inconsistency is crucially linked to inadequacies in free speech theory itself. Conventional free speech theory ignores the extent to which imbalances of private power limit freedom of expression. It presupposes that public discourse takes place on a rational plane. The author explores the link between the philosophical failings of broadcast regulation and the empirical failings of free speech theory by identifying competing legal visions that underlie discussions of broadcasting and freedom of speech. The first of these visions, which forms the bases for ordinary free-speech philosophy, emphasizes hard-edged rules, individualism, a belief in overall private autonomy, and a sharp public-private distinction. The second, at the heart of our broadcast regulatory system, emphasizes situationally sensitive standards, altruism, the pervasive role of the government in structuring private ordering, and the pervasiveness of dependence and constraint. These competing visions, the author submits, are fundamentally irreconcilable; our speech regulatory law is driven by the contradiction between them.

INTRODUCTION

The field of broadcast regulation has seemed, of late, to be slipping into constitutional chaos. The Federal Communications Commission (FCC) has repealed the "fairness doctrine"—a regulatory mainstay since before there was an FCC—calling it unconstitutional.[1] The Supreme Court decision upholding the fairness doctrine, the FCC blithely stated, "cannot be reconciled with well-established constitutional precedent."[2] A D.C. Circuit decision a few years ago took the position that the entire

---

† Associate Professor, Wayne State University Law School. A.B. 1980, Harvard College; J.D. 1983, Columbia Law School. I owe thanks to Frederick Schauer, Robert Post, Avery Katz, Jonathan Entin, Jeffrey Rachlinski, William Marshall, Robert Sedler, Leroy Lamborn, and the Research Group on Diversification of Media and Diversification of Regulation for their helpful comments on drafts of this Article. Most of all, though, I owe thanks to Jessica Litman, who read all drafts and—every time—told me things I did not want to hear.

1. *Syracuse Peace Council*, 2 F.C.C.R. 5043 (1987) (concluding that the fairness doctrine, on its face, violates the First Amendment and contravenes the public interest), *aff'd on narrower grounds*, 867 F.2d 654, 656 (D.C. Cir. 1989), *cert. denied*, 493 U.S. 1019 (1990).

2. *Id.* at 5056 (discussing *Red Lion Broadcasting Co. v. FCC*, 395 U.S. 367 (1969)).

basis for our broadcast regulatory scheme is incoherent.[3] Courts have seemed eager to strike down as unconstitutional federal statutes regulating broadcasting;[4] Presidents Reagan and Bush vetoed bills on the same ground.[5] The cable television regulatory scheme has been the subject of especially punishing judicial attack.[6] Academics have joined the

---

3. Telecommunications Research and Action Ctr. v. FCC, 801 F.2d 501, 508-09 (D.C. Cir. 1986) (arguing that the Court's rationale for greater content regulation of broadcast than of print media rests on a "distinction without a difference . . . lead[ing] to strained reasoning and artificial results"), *cert. denied,* 482 U.S. 919 (1987).

4. *See, e.g.,* Beach Communications, Inc. v. FCC, 965 F.2d 1103 (D.C. Cir. 1992) (striking down, as unconstitutional, statutory direction that certain satellite master antenna TV facilities be subject to local cable franchise requirement), *rev'd,* 113 S. Ct. 2096 (1993); Edge Broadcasting Co. v. United States, 20 Media L. Rep. (BNA) 1904 (4th Cir. 1992) (striking down, as unconstitutional, statutory restrictions on broadcast of lottery information and advertisements), *rev'd,* 113 S. Ct. 2696 (1993); Action for Children's Television v. FCC, 932 F.2d 1504 (D.C. Cir. 1991) (striking down, as unconstitutional, legislation mandating that the FCC enforce a ban of all radio and television broadcasts of "indecent" materials), *cert. denied,* 112 S. Ct. 1281 (1992); News Am. Publishing v. FCC, 844 F.2d 800 (D.C. Cir. 1988) (striking down, as unconstitutional, legislation forbidding extension of waivers of newspaper-television cross-ownership rule); Daniels Cablevision, Inc. v. United States, 1993 U.S. Dist. LEXIS 12806 (D.D.C. Sept. 16, 1993) (striking down, as unconstitutional, three provisions of the Cable Television Consumer Protection and Competition Act of 1992); Chesapeake & Potomac Tel. Co. v. United States, No. 92-1751-A, 1993 U.S. Dist. LEXIS 11822 (E.D. Va. Aug. 24, 1993) (striking down, as unconstitutional, legislation prohibiting telephone companies from offering video programming within their service areas); *see also* Preferred Communications v. City of Los Angeles, 754 F.2d 1396, 1411 & n.11 (9th Cir. 1985) (finding that section 621(a)(1) of the Cable Communications Policy Act would be invalid if read, as the legislative history provides, to authorize exclusive cable franchising), *aff'd on narrower grounds,* 476 U.S. 488 (1986).

5. *See* 138 CONG. REC. H11477 (daily ed. Oct. 5, 1992) (President Bush vetoing the Cable Television Consumer Protection and Competition Act of 1992, arguing in part that its "must carry" provisions were unconstitutional); Memorandum of Disapproval for the Children's Television Act of 1988, 24 WEEKLY COMP. PRES. DOC. 1456 (Nov. 5, 1988) (President Reagan vetoing the Children's Television Act of 1988, arguing that it would violate the First Amendment); Veto of the Fairness in Broadcasting Act of 1987, 23 WEEKLY COMP. PRES. DOC. 715 (June 19, 1987) (President Reagan vetoing the Fairness in Broadcasting Act of 1987, arguing that it is "antagonistic to the freedom of expression guaranteed by the First Amendment"). President Bush invoked the First Amendment in withholding his approval from the Children's Television Act of 1990, which became law without his signature. *See* Statement on the Children's Television Act of 1990, 26 WEEKLY COMP. PRES. DOC. 1611-12 (Oct. 17, 1990).

6. *See, e.g.,* Century Communications Corp. v. FCC, 835 F.2d 292 (D.C. Cir. 1987) (striking down FCC "must carry" rules requiring operators to transmit local over-the-air television broadcast signals as violative of the First Amendment), *cert. denied,* 486 U.S. 1032 (1988); Quincy Cable TV, Inc. v. FCC, 768 F.2d 1434 (D.C. Cir. 1985) (same), *cert. denied,* 476 U.S. 1169 (1986); Preferred Communications v. City of Los Angeles, 754 F.2d 1396 (9th Cir. 1985) (holding that the city could not, consistently with the First Amendment, limit access to one region of the city to a single cable television company if public utility facilities in that region were physically capable of accommodating more than one system), *aff'd on narrower grounds,* 476 U.S. 488 (1986); Midwest Video Corp. v. FCC, 571 F.2d 1025 (8th Cir. 1978) (striking down FCC regulations imposing mandatory channel capacity, equipment, and access rules as unauthorized and probably unconstitutional), *aff'd on narrower grounds,* 440 U.S. 689 (1979); Home Box Office, Inc. v. FCC, 567 F.2d 9 (D.C. Cir.) (striking down FCC pay cable rules as unsupported by evidence, unauthorized by law, and unconstitutional), *cert. denied,* 434 U.S. 829 (1977); Daniels Cablevision, Inc. v. United States, 1993 U.S. Dist. LEXIS 12806 (D.D.C. Sept. 16, 1993) (striking down, as unconstitutional, three provisions of the Cable Television Consumer Protection and Competition Act of 1992); Chesapeake & Potomac Tel. Co. v. United States, No. 92-1751-A, 1993 U.S. Dist.

onslaught. Some have attacked specific aspects of the regulatory scheme,[7] while others have suggested that the entire American broadcast regulatory system is hopelessly in conflict with core First Amendment values and should be discarded.[8]

LEXIS 11822 (E.D. Va. Aug. 24, 1993) (striking down, as unconstitutional, legislation prohibiting telephone companies from offering video programming within their service areas); Century Fed., Inc. v. City of Palo Alto, 710 F. Supp. 1552 (N.D. Cal. 1987) (concluding that the city's access channel, universal service, and state-of-the-art requirements violated the First Amendment); Pacific West Cable Co. v. City of Sacramento, 672 F. Supp. 1322 (E.D. Cal. 1987) (holding that exclusive cable franchising scheme violated cable operator's First Amendment rights); Group W Cable, Inc. v. City of Santa Cruz, 669 F. Supp. 954 (N.D. Cal. 1987) (same); Century Fed., Inc. v. City of Palo Alto, 648 F. Supp. 1465 (N.D. Cal. 1986) (holding that exclusive cable franchising scheme violated the First Amendment). *But see* Chicago Cable Communications v. Chicago Cable Comm'n, 879 F.2d 1540 (7th Cir. 1989) (rejecting a constitutional challenge to a cable franchise agreement), *cert. denied,* 493 U.S. 1044 (1990); Central Telecommunications, Inc. v. TCI Cablevision, Inc., 800 F.2d 711 (8th Cir. 1986) (rejecting a constitutional challenge to the city's de facto exclusive franchise), *cert. denied,* 480 U.S. 910 (1987); Omega Satellite Products Co. v. City of Indianapolis, 694 F.2d 119 (7th Cir. 1982) (upholding district court's rejection, on motion for preliminary injunction, of First Amendment challenge to cable regulatory scheme); Community Communications Co. v. City of Boulder, 660 F.2d 1370 (10th Cir. 1981) (reversing preliminary injunction, based on the First Amendment, blocking city's exclusive cable franchising scheme), *cert. dismissed,* 456 U.S. 1001 (1982); Turner Broadcasting Sys. v. FCC, 819 F. Supp. 32 (D.D.C.) (rejecting a constitutional challenge to "must carry" provisions of the 1992 Cable Television Consumer Protection and Competition Act), *cert. granted,* 62 U.S.L.W. 3207 (U.S. Sept. 28, 1993) (No. 93-44); Erie Telecommunications, Inc. v. City of Erie, 659 F. Supp. 580 (W.D. Pa. 1987) (rejecting a First Amendment challenge to city's franchise fee and "public access" requirements), *aff'd on narrower grounds,* 853 F.2d 1084 (3d Cir. 1988); Berkshire Cablevision v. Burke, 571 F. Supp. 976 (D.R.I. 1983) (rejecting a First Amendment challenge to "public access" requirement), *vacated as moot,* 773 F.2d 382 (1st Cir. 1985).

7. *See, e.g.,* Jonathan W. Emord, *The First Amendment Invalidity of FCC Ownership Regulations,* 38 CATH. U. L. REV. 401 (1989) (attacking FCC ownership rules as constitutionally suspect); Thomas G. Krattenmaker & L.A. Powe, Jr., *The Fairness Doctrine Today: A Constitutional Curiosity and an Impossible Dream,* 1985 DUKE L.J. 151 (arguing that the fairness doctrine is incoherent and unworkable).

8. *See, e.g.,* JONATHAN W. EMORD, FREEDOM, TECHNOLOGY, AND THE FIRST AMENDMENT (1991) (arguing that only a property rights model for broadcast regulation can ensure adequate protection for freedom of speech and press); LUCAS A. POWE, JR., AMERICAN BROADCASTING AND THE FIRST AMENDMENT (1987) (contending that broadcast licensing is unjustifiable and has provided a vehicle for blatant content censorship); MATTHEW L. SPITZER, SEVEN DIRTY WORDS AND SIX OTHER STORIES: CONTROLLING THE CONTENT OF PRINT AND BROADCAST (1986) (arguing that neither economic nor psychological rationales support differential treatment of print and broadcast media); Mark S. Fowler & Daniel L. Brenner, *A Marketplace Approach to Broadcast Regulation,* 60 TEX. L. REV. 207, 209 (1982) (urging "that the perception of broadcasters as community trustees . . . be replaced by a view of broadcasters as marketplace participants"); Thomas W. Hazlett, *The Rationality of U.S. Regulation of the Broadcast Spectrum,* 33 J.L. & ECON. 133, 137-38 (1990) (arguing that the interference rationale for broadcast licensing is nonsensical); William T. Mayton, *The Illegitimacy of the Public Interest Standard at the FCC,* 38 EMORY L.J. 715 (1989) (arguing that the current regulatory scheme, under which the FCC exercises broad "public interest" power, is based on a misinterpretation of the Communications Act of 1934); Laurence H. Winer, *The New Media Technologies and the Old Public Interest Standard,* 29 JURIMETRICS J. 377 (1989) (concluding that the public interest standard for broadcast media should be discarded). All of these authors agree that our broadcast regulatory system is fundamentally misguided; they do not all agree on what we should do with it now, sixty-five years after the Radio Act of 1927 set us on this course.

Other academics, by contrast, argue that we should extend the current broadcast regime. *See,*

Our broadcast regulatory scheme is certainly vulnerable to attack. The Federal Communications Commission (FCC) distributes a limited number of broadcast licenses to selected individuals and corporations based on its determination of the "public interest." The FCC has declared it illegal for any unlicensed entity to engage in mass communication over the airwaves. This is all rather odd. Ordinary First Amendment philosophy strongly disfavors government licensing of speakers;[9] the broadcast regulatory system, by contrast, embraces such licensing. The Supreme Court first justified this system with reference to "the problem of interference": because of the danger of competing broadcasters interfering with one another, "if there is to be any effective communication by radio, only a few can be licensed and the rest must be barred from the airwaves."[10] That explanation, though, has been the target of withering attack: "Economists, political scientists and lawyers generally agree" that the interference rationale for public-interest licensing is "nonsensical."[11] It is "simply silly";[12] it "has worn so thin that continuing to refute it would be gratuitous."[13]

As a result, some commentators describe the 1927 decision to create a government agency to regulate broadcasting through public-interest

---

e.g., Cass R. Sunstein, *Free Speech Now,* 59 U. CHI. L. REV. 255, 289 (1992) ("It is worthwhile to consider . . . a compulsory hour of public affairs programming per evening, . . . content review of children's television by nonpartisan experts, or guidelines to encourage attention to public issues and diversity of view."). Substantive proposals for *greater* regulation, however, are less destabilizing than are arguments that our entire broadcast regulatory scheme is fundamentally unconstitutional. They typically can be made within the ruling constitutional paradigm for broadcasting. *See, e.g.,* Enforcement of Prohibitions Against Broadcast Indecency in 18 U.S.C. § 1464, 5 F.C.C.R. 5297 (1990) (concluding that a blanket prohibition of "indecent" radio and television comports with constitutional standards), *vacated sub nom.* Action for Children's Television v. FCC, 932 F.2d 1504 (D.C. Cir. 1991), *cert. denied,* 112 S. Ct. 1281 (1992).

    9. *See generally* Near v. Minnesota, 283 U.S. 697, 713 (1931) (striking down a statute on the ground that it effectively imposed a licensing system on newspaper owners and publishers who charged official misconduct).

    10. Red Lion Broadcasting Co. v. FCC, 395 U.S. 367, 388-89 (1969). It is well-accepted that
    [b]roadcasting is the transmission of electromagnetic waves over the radio spectrum. When more than one station in a particular geographical area simultaneously attempts to use the same piece of spectrum space, the result is chaos. Thus, for the spectrum to have reliable utility, the right to exclusive use of a portion [of the spectrum] must be protected.
BENNO C. SCHMIDT, JR., FREEDOM OF THE PRESS VS. PUBLIC ACCESS 126 (1976). According to proponents of the interference rationale, in light of the physical scarcity of the broadcast spectrum, "[g]overnment allocation and regulation of broadcast frequencies are essential"; and given "the need for such allocation and regulation, . . . nothing in the First Amendment . . . prevent[s] the Commission from allocating licenses so as to promote the 'public interest.' " FCC v. National Citizens Comm. for Broadcasting, 436 U.S. 775, 799 (1978).

    11. Hazlett, *supra* note 8, at 137-38 (footnotes omitted); *see also* LEE C. BOLLINGER, IMAGES OF A FREE PRESS 87-88 (1991) ("It is a decisive fact about broadcast regulation that the primary rationales used to justify that system . . . are illogical.").

    12. L.A. Powe, Jr., *Mass Communications and the First Amendment: An Overview,* 55 LAW & CONTEMP. PROBS. 53, 69 (1992).

    13. Daniel D. Polsby, *Candidate Access to the Air: The Uncertain Future of Broadcaster Discretion,* 1981 SUP. CT. REV. 223, 257-58.

allocation[14] as a mistake.[15] These critics suggest that the right to use the frequency spectrum should have been treated as a simple property right, bought and sold on the market, and subject to common-law property rules.[16] That, after all, is the way we distribute the right to communicate in print. We allow people to *own* the resources of communication, rather than allocating them administratively.[17] Regulating broadcast via a property-rights system, critics say, would have been both consistent with First Amendment values and economically efficient.[18] Our current system, they contend, is neither.[19]

The constitutional attacks on our broadcast regulatory system have force. Ordinary First Amendment jurisprudence insists that if the government must engage in licensing, it may not rely on informal, vague, or discretionary criteria and procedures.[20] Licensing criteria must be sharp-edged and objective.[21] As a general matter, the government may not reg-

---

14. Radio Act of 1927, Pub. L. No. 69-632, 44 Stat. 1162 (superseded 1934). Before 1927, the Secretary of Commerce exercised some supervision over broadcasting but had little real statutory authority. *See generally* POWE, *supra* note 8, at 54-60 (detailing the Secretary's attempts to regulate broadcasting under the Wireless Ship Act of 1910 and the Radio Act of 1912). The 1927 Radio Act was superseded by the Communications Act of 1934, 47 U.S.C. §§ 151-160 (1988).

15. *See, e.g.,* ITHIEL DE SOLA POOL, TECHNOLOGIES OF FREEDOM 108-50 (1983). Others call it a raw power grab. *See, e.g.,* Hazlett, *supra* note 8 at 152-65 (arguing that the Radio Act of 1927 departed from ordinary First Amendment principles in a self-conscious attempt to benefit powerful incumbent radio broadcasters and members of Congress at the expense of weaker broadcasters, would-be broadcasters, consumers, and the U.S. treasury).

16. The leading article supporting this position is Ronald H. Coase, *The Federal Communications Commission,* 2 J.L. & ECON. 1 (1959).

17. If we were to regulate print as we do broadcast, we might establish a Federal Paper Commission, with members appointed by the President, with the job of allocating the right to communicate in print (or perhaps allocating newsprint itself) among the populace without regard to who owns what. *See* Jonathan Weinberg, *Questioning Broadcast Regulation,* 86 MICH. L. REV. 1269, 1271-72 (1988) (book review). Instead, we rely on a property-rights system: in order to write my thoughts on a piece of paper, copy the paper, and distribute the copies to others, I must first own the paper and the copier, or have permission from their owner(s) to use them. These rules structure our mass communications system in far-reaching ways: only those who own paper, photocopiers, printing presses, and the like, and those operating at their sufferance, can engage in mass communications. *See infra* notes 217-25 and accompanying text.

18. On economic efficiency, see Coase, *supra* note 16, at 18:

> Quite apart from the malallocations which are the result of political pressures, an administrative agency which attempts to perform the function normally carried out by the pricing mechanism operates under two handicaps. First of all, it lacks the precise monetary measure of benefit and cost provided by the market. Second, it cannot, by the nature of things, be in possession of all of the relevant information possessed by the managers of every business which uses or might use radio frequencies, to say nothing of the preferences of consumers for the various goods and services in the production of which radio frequencies could be used.

See also id. at 27 ("It is sometimes implied that the aim of regulation in the radio industry should be to minimize interference. But this would be wrong. The aim should be to maximize output.").

19. *See generally* sources cited *supra* note 8.

20. *See infra* notes 51-55 and accompanying text.

21. *See* Forsyth County v. Nationalist Movement, 112 S. Ct. 2395, 2401-02 (1992). Government licensing of speakers in accordance with vague or uncertain standards generally violates the First Amendment because it "makes it difficult to distinguish . . . between a licensor's legitimate denial of a permit and its illegitimate abuse of censorial power," and intimidates would-be speakers

ulate speech on the basis of its content; in the rare cases in which content restrictions are allowed, they must be clear and specific.[22] The broadcast regulatory system, however, is essentially defined by vague and inscrutable standards used to control both the identity of the persons licensed to own stations[23] and the content of what those persons may say.[24] While our First Amendment philosophy decries vagueness and discretion in government regulation of speech, the broadcast regulatory system positively celebrates them. While First Amendment jurisprudence denies government the power to license speakers (or to reward or punish their speech) on the basis of its own views as to what private speech would best serve the "public interest," the broadcast regulatory system places that government power at its core. The interference rationale cannot justify any of this.

The inconsistency of our regulatory scheme with First Amendment philosophy, however, is not the end of the story. In this Article, I take the argument a step further: I believe that while our broadcast regulatory scheme *is* fundamentally flawed, the situation is more complicated than the critics of broadcast regulation have allowed.[25] It is complicated in part because our freedom-of-speech philosophy, which I have described as inconsistent with our broadcast regulatory system, itself conflicts with much of what we know about the world. That philosophy is rooted in the notion that we process speech on a rational level, "that there is on the whole a preponderance among mankind of rational opinions and rational conduct,"[26] and that we can thus properly treat speech as a competition of ideas in a metaphorical marketplace. It further assumes that this rational competition of ideas is substantially unaffected by the huge disparities in economic resources available to various speakers and proponents of different views.

None of these assumptions, however, is completely true. Our public debate is to a large extent "dominated, and thus constrained, by the same

---

into "censoring their own speech." City of Lakewood v. Plain Dealer Publishing Co., 486 U.S. 750, 757-58 (1988).

22. *See, e.g.,* Smith v. Goguen, 415 U.S. 566 (1974) (striking down a state flag-misuse statute as vague).

23. *See* Policy Statement on Comparative Broadcast Hearings, 1 F.C.C.2d 393 (1965) (setting out criteria governing FCC comparative licensing process). *See generally infra* text accompanying notes 66-109.

24. *See, e.g.,* Syracuse Peace Council, 2 F.C.C.R. 5043, 5049 (1987) (stating that the FCC's "fairness doctrine," in effect for over 50 years, "necessarily involves a vague standard, the application and meaning of which is hard to predict"), *aff'd,* 867 F.2d 654 (D.C. Cir. 1989), *cert. denied,* 493 U.S. 1019 (1990). *See generally infra* text accompanying notes 110-32.

25. *Cf.* Lee C. Bollinger, Jr., *Freedom of the Press and Public Access: Toward a Theory of Partial Regulation of the Mass Media,* 75 MICH. L. REV. 1, 16 (1976) ("The very weakness of [the arguments supporting current broadcast regulation] suggests that there is something more here than first meets the eye.").

26. JOHN STUART MILL, ON LIBERTY 24 (Library of Liberal Arts ed. 1956) (1859).

forces that dominate social structure."[27] It is doubtful that the market-place of ideas meaningfully exposes all ideas to scrutiny; the system is too pervasively dominated by large commercial gatekeepers that are unlikely to give time to less-conventional or offensive views.[28] Moreover, individuals' reactions to speech are largely determined by experience, psychological propensities, societal roles, half-submerged prejudices, and socialization.[29] The packaging and frequency of messages may be more persuasive than the rational force of their arguments. The emotive and experiential impact of messages often may be more important than their rational impact.[30]

I propose in this Article that the two problems I have discussed—the inconsistency of our broadcast regulatory system with core First Amendment philosophy, and the fact that that philosophy itself lacks factual mooring—are linked. Broadcast regulation is marked by a crucial procedural failing—it relies on ad hoc, situationally sensitive judgments by regulators seeking to advance a vaguely defined "public interest." Ordinary freedom-of-speech philosophy is marked by a substantive failing—it refuses to recoguize the ubiquity of inequality and private power as a limitation on freedom. Relying on insights developed by authors associated with critical legal studies, I will argue that the respective failings of our broadcast regulatory and First Amendment philosophy are central to the link between them. They are, I suggest, two sides of a single coin.

Our freedom-of-speech philosophy can be seen as reflecting a larger worldview emphasizing individualism and a sharp public-private distinction. In this worldview, the private sphere is the natural home of individual freedom, and the government should not intervene in that sphere except in exceptional circumstances. Values are for each individual to choose; they are neither objective nor communally determined. Paternalism has no place in government decisionmaking. The law should restrain government arbitrariness and bias through clear, black-letter rules.

In contrast, our system of broadcast regulation can be seen as reflecting a competing worldview. That worldview emphasizes the community rather than the individual. It stresses that government plays a

27. Owen M. Fiss, *Why the State?*, 100 HARV. L. REV. 781, 786 (1987); *accord* Catharine A. MacKinnon, *Pornography, Civil Rights, and Speech*, 20 HARV. C.R.-C.L. L. REV. 1, 3-4 (1985); *see also* CHARLES E. LINDBLOM, POLITICS AND MARKETS 201-21 (1977) (arguing that the business elite molds public opinion through the media).

28. *See* TODD GITLIN, INSIDE PRIME TIME 92-93, 189-90, 192, 254-55 (1983) (discussing television networks' reluctance to air controversial programs); EDWARD S. HERMAN & NOAM CHOMSKY, MANUFACTURING CONSENT: THE POLITICAL ECONOMY OF THE MASS MEDIA 16-18 (1988) (emphasizing advertiser influence over broadcast programming).

29. *See infra* notes 266-80 and accompanying text.

30. *See infra* notes 288-91 and accompanying text.

pervasive role in structuring private ordering, and that dependence and constraint characterize the so-called "private" sphere. Because, under this approach, values are objective or communally determined, government paternalism is often appropriate. Government actors should apply the law through individualized, situationally-sensitive decisionmaking.

The contradiction between the two worldviews I have described helps explain why the conflict between ordinary free speech philosophy and our system of broadcast regulation is inescapable: our overall speech law is glaringly schizoid. Both our broadcast regulation rules and our conflicting First Amendment philosophy reflect important but incomplete visions found throughout our legal system. These two visions cannot be reconciled, but neither can they be wholly suppressed. As a result, while calls to "fix" our broadcast system by making broadcast more like print have substantial merit, doing so will not make the broadcast system's problems go away. No change in the law could do that.

In Part I of this Article, I explain the inconsistency of our system of broadcast regulation with ordinary First Amendment philosophy; in Part II, I discuss the inadequacy of that philosophy itself. In Part III, I attempt to situate both our free speech philosophy and our system of broadcast regulation within the larger framework of the competing worldviews I have discussed. In Part IV, I take a look at the doctrinal consequences of all this, asking if there is any way to build a workable regulatory structure for the electronic mass media.

I
PUBLIC-INTEREST LICENSING AND THE FREE SPEECH TRADITION

A. A Quick Tour of Free Speech Philosophy

I will argue in this Part that public-interest licensing of broadcast speakers is inconsistent with usual First Amendment philosophy. To make that point, I will start by setting out a brief and incomplete sketch of that philosophy. I will return to that sketch later;[31] my goal now is simply to introduce a few relevant themes.[32]

Ordinary First Amendment philosophy emphasizes the ability of every citizen to speak freely in the "marketplace of ideas"; government has only a limited prerogative to interfere with that speech. Public debate must incorporate a wide diversity of speakers and views. Government may play no role that allows it the opportunity to limit or skew that diversity. The resulting marketplace of ideas is a forum in which individuals, and society as a whole, can decide what is true and

---

31. *See infra* text accompanying notes 374-81.
32. *See generally* Weinberg, *supra* note 17, at 1282-85 (discussing ideals underlying First Amendment doctrine).

right.[33] Free speech, further, does not merely advance the discovery of truth; it fosters political self-government.[34] Some see it as definitional to the process of self-determination that constitutes democracy.[35] Some see it as arming the people with the information and ideas that they need to govern themselves.[36] Some see it as providing a check on the state apparatus for the benefit of a citizenry not involved in the daily workings of government.[37] In any event, government may not assert any control over the processes of mass communication that would bias those processes, and it may not limit the agenda of public debate: that debate must be "uninhibited, robust, and wide-open."[38]

This view of freedom of speech incorporates a vision of the citizenry as ultimate sovereign, for whose sake open debate must be preserved, and of the government as untrustworthy, insecure, and inclined to suppress criticism in covert or overt ways.[39] That vision has important doctrinal consequences.[40] The government may not, without good and sufficient reason, restrict individuals' ability to speak.[41] Such an action, even if designed to serve legitimate goals and neutral as to the content of the speech, must bear a burden of justification under the First Amendment.[42]

---

33. *See infra* notes 176-92 and accompanying text. For alternative visions of free speech focusing on the right of individual self-expression, see generally C. EDWIN BAKER, HUMAN LIBERTY AND FREEDOM OF SPEECH (1989) (advocating a liberty-based theory of the First Amendment); THOMAS I. EMERSON, TOWARD A GENERAL THEORY OF THE FIRST AMENDMENT 4-7 (1966) (focusing on the right of the individual to self-fulfillment through speech); *infra* note 179 and accompanying text.

34. *See* First Nat'l Bank v. Bellotti, 435 U.S. 765, 771-72, 776-77 (1978); Buckley v. Valeo, 424 U.S. 1, 14 (1976); Monitor Patriot Co. v. Roy, 401 U.S. 265, 271-72 (1971); Mills v. Alabama, 384 U.S. 214, 218 (1966); Garrison v. Louisiana, 379 U.S. 64, 74-75 (1964); Grosjean v. American Press Co., 297 U.S. 233, 249-50 (1936). *See generally* New York Times Co. v. Sullivan, 376 U.S. 254, 266 (1964) (confirming First Amendment protection of paid political advertisements).

35. *See* Robert C. Post, *Racist Speech, Democracy, and the First Amendment,* 32 WM. & MARY L. REV. 267, 279-83 (1991).

36. *See* Letter from James Madison to W.T. Barry (Aug. 4, 1822), *quoted in* Eric G. Olsen, Note, *The Right to Know in First Amendment Analysis,* 57 TEX. L. REV. 505, 506 (1979).

37. *See* Vincent Blasi, *The Checking Value in First Amendment Theory,* 1977 AM. B. FOUND. RES. J. 521; *cf.* New York Times Co. v. United States, 403 U.S. 713, 723-24 (1971) (Douglas, J., concurring) (stating that the "dominant purpose of the First Amendment was to prohibit . . . governmental suppression of embarrassing information").

38. *New York Times Co.,* 376 U.S. at 270.

39. *See* BOLLINGER, *supra* note 11, at 20.

40. *See generally* Jonathan Weinberg, *Broadcasting and the Administrative Process in Japan and the United States,* 39 BUFF. L. REV. 615, 643-45 (1991) (discussing the implications for broadcast regulation of U.S. constitutional philosophy).

41. *See, e.g.,* United States v. Grace, 461 U.S. 171 (1983) (striking down a ban on picketing on the sidewalks in front of the U.S. Supreme Court building).

42. *See, e.g.,* Ward v. Rock Against Racism, 491 U.S. 781 (1989) (upholding city regulation of public music concerts after finding the regulations content-neutral and narrowly tailored to serve a significant government interest); Schneider v. State, 308 U.S. 147 (1939) (striking down content-neutral ordinance prohibiting distribution of handbills). *See generally* Geoffrey R. Stone, *Content-Neutral Restrictions,* 54 U. CHI. L. REV. 46 (1987). The government may preclude individual speech on, or using, government property, assuming that that property is not deemed a "public forum," but even there the government regulation must be substantively reasonable and viewpoint-

Government restrictions of speech on the basis of *content* are particularly disfavored.[43] The government has little power to restrict speech merely because the communicative impact of that speech may be harmful. The government may restrict speech based on its communicative impact when necessary "to further a state interest of the highest order,"[44] but may not do so simply to uphold its own general notion of the public interest or to advance its own values.[45]

Further, the government may not, as a general matter, restrict individuals' speech because of things they have said in the past[46] or things they propose to say in the future.[47] Thus, in 1931 the Supreme Court struck down a law allowing state authorities to secure an injunction against the publication of a "malicious, scandalous, and defamatory" newspaper.[48] The publisher of such a newspaper would have been subject to suit for damages under then-existing constitutional doctrine. Nonetheless, the Court said, to allow the government to seek a court order forbidding further publication would be "the essence of

---

neutral. *See, e.g.,* United States v. Kokinda, 497 U.S. 720 (1990) (upholding, as reasonable, a regulation prohibiting solicitation of funds on Postal Service premises).

43. *See generally* Kenneth L. Karst, *Equality as a Central Principle in the First Amendment,* 43 U. Chi. L. Rev. 20, 29-35 (1975) (arguing for the use of the equality principle to protect against content censorship); Geoffrey R. Stone, *Content Regulation and the First Amendment,* 25 Wm. & Mary L. Rev. 189 (1983) (exploring the content-based/content-neutral distinction under the First Amendment). *But see* Marc A. Franklin, *Constitutional Libel Law: The Role of Content,* 34 UCLA L. Rev. 1657 (1987) (arguing that constitutional libel law should make distinctions based on content).

44. Florida Star v. B.J.F., 491 U.S. 524, 533 (1989) (quoting Smith v. Daily Mail Publishing Co., 443 U.S. 97, 103 (1979)); *see also* Hess v. Indiana, 414 U.S. 105, 109 (1973) (government may punish a speaker for "words . . . intended to produce, and likely to produce, *imminent* disorder").

Modern First Amendment philosophy thus rejects the approach of cases such as Frohwerk v. United States, 249 U.S. 204 (1919), and Debs v. United States, 249 U.S. 211, 216 (1919), that the government may criminalize speech with the "natural tendency and reasonably probable effect" of impeding government objectives. Justice Kennedy has questioned whether even compelling justification and narrow tailoring should be sufficient to save a content-based restriction outside of "historic and traditional categories long familiar to the bar," Simon & Schuster, Inc. v. New York State Crime Victims Bd., 112 S. Ct. 501, 514 (1991) (Kennedy, J., concurring in the judgment), but he had to twist into a pretzel to avoid the consequences of those words in Burson v. Freeman, 112 S. Ct. 1846, 1858-59 (1992) (Kennedy, J., concurring) (upholding ban on electioneering outside polling places).

45. *See, e.g.,* Kingsley Int'l Pictures Corp. v. Regents, 360 U.S. 684, 685 (1959) (striking down a statute that prohibited the exhibition of films portraying "acts of sexual immorality . . . as desirable, acceptable or proper patterns of behavior") (quotation omitted). *But see* City of Renton v. Playtime Theatres, Inc., 475 U.S. 41 (1986) (upholding an ordinance restricting the location of adult theaters); Paris Adult Theatre I v. Slaton, 413 U.S. 49, 57 (1973) (approving an order enjoining the exhibition of "obscene, pornographic films").

46. *See* Near v. Minnesota, 283 U.S. 697 (1931); *see also* Lowe v. SEC, 472 U.S. 181 (1985) (construing a statute to avoid government registration of certain investment advice newsletters).

47. *See* New York Times Co. v. United States, 403 U.S. 713 (1971) (per curiam) (refusing injunction sought by the United States against publication of the Pentagon Papers); *id.* at 714-15 (Black, J., concurring); *id.* at 720 (Douglas, J., concurring); *id.* at 724-25 (Brennan, J., concurring); *id.* at 730 (White, J., concurring).

48. Near v. Minnesota, 283 U.S. at 701-02 (1931) (quotation omitted).

censorship."[49]

Licensing schemes, indeed, are inherently suspect even when they do not incorporate explicit content distinctions. In 1938, the Supreme Court considered a city ordinance forbidding any person to distribute written material without first obtaining permission from a government official. The Court held that the ordinance "strikes at the very foundation of the freedom of the press by subjecting it to license and censorship."[50]

Finally, to the extent that the government can at all limit individuals' ability to speak through a licensing-like process, it must rely on neutral, objective, and mechanical criteria and procedures. Because government "discretion has the potential for becoming a means of suppressing a particular point of view,"[51] any licensing requirement must contain "narrow, objective and definite standards to guide the licensing authority."[52] "If the permit scheme 'involves appraisal of facts, the exercise of judgment, and the formation of an opinion' by the licensing authority, 'the danger of censorship and of abridgement of our precious First Amendment freedoms is too great' to be permitted."[53]

Thus, a few years ago, the Supreme Court struck down a city ordinance giving a government officer discretion, within the bounds of the "necessary and reasonable," to grant or deny permission to place newspaper vending machines on public sidewalks.[54] The Court conceded that there might be circumstances in which the city could legitimately deny a permit: the vending machines might be found to interfere with other uses of the sidewalks. The ordinance was unconstitutional, however, because the city's discretion was not limited by clear-cut rules. The vague regulatory scheme made "*post hoc* rationalizations by the licensing official and the use of shifting or illegitimate criteria . . . far too easy."[55] It could prevent courts from detecting government's "illegitimate abuse of censorial power," and could therefore "intimidate[] parties into cen-

---

49. *Id.* at 713.

50. Lovell v. City of Griffin, 303 U.S. 444, 451 (1938).

51. Forsyth County v. Nationalist Movement, 112 S. Ct. 2395, 2401 (1992) (quoting Heffron v. International Soc'y for Krishna Consciousness, 452 U.S. 640, 649 (1981)).

52. *Id.* (quoting Shuttlesworth v. Birmingham, 394 U.S. 147, 150-51 (1969)).

53. *Id.* at 2401-02 (quoting Cantwell v. Connecticut, 310 U.S. 296, 305 (1940) and Southeastern Promotions v. Conrad, 420 U.S. 546, 553 (1975)).

54. City of Lakewood v. Plain Dealer Publishing Co., 486 U.S. 750 (1988); *see also* Shuttlesworth v. City of Birmingham, 394 U.S. 147 (1969) (invalidating an ordinance giving the city discretionary control over public demonstrations); Staub v. City of Baxley, 355 U.S. 313 (1958) (invalidating an ordinance giving the city discretionary control over solicitation by dues-charging organizations); Kunz v. New York, 340 U.S. 290, 295 (1951) (invalidating an ordinance giving the city the discretionary control over public worship meetings); Saia v. New York, 334 U.S. 558 (1948) (invalidating an ordinance giving the city the discretionary control over use of sound amplification devices).

55. *Lakewood,* 486 U.S. at 758.

soring their own speech."[56] The regulatory scheme was particularly "threatening" because it involved a "multiple or periodic licensing requirement," ensuring that newspapers were "under no illusion regarding the effect of the 'licensed' speech on the ability to continue speaking in the future."[57]

B.   *The Nature of Our Broadcast Regulatory System*

Broadcasting is speech.[58] Indeed, much of broadcasting is political speech, in a quite noncontroversial sense of "political." The innocent or naive, therefore, might expect it to be covered by the rules I have set out above. In fact, though, our broadcast regulatory system takes a path of its own. I shall explore that path at some length in order to make clear how far it wanders from the route of ordinary free speech philosophy.

The central requirement of our broadcast system is set out in the Communications Act of 1934:[59] "No person shall . . . operate any apparatus for the transmission of . . . communications . . . by radio" except with a license granted by the Federal Communications Commission [FCC], a government agency.[60] The FCC is to grant a license to an applicant only "if public convenience, interest, or necessity will be served thereby";[61] the term of that license may not be longer than five to ten years, depending on the medium.[62] The Commission may renew the license only on the basis of a similar finding that renewal would serve the "public interest, convenience, and necessity."[63]

---

56. *Id.* at 757-58.

57. *Id.* at 759-60; *see also* FW/PBS, Inc. v. City of Dallas, 493 U.S. 215 (1990) (invalidating a licensing scheme as enforced against sexually oriented businesses engaged in First Amendment activity).

58. *See* United States v. Paramount Pictures, Inc., 334 U.S. 131, 166 (1948) (noting that "radio [is] included in the press whose freedom is guaranteed by the First Amendment").

59. 47 U.S.C. §§ 151-160 (1988). Under the statute, the FCC exercises regulatory authority over all forms of interstate communication via spectrum or wire, excluding federal governmental uses. *See id.* §§ 152, 305. The FCC succeeded the Federal Radio Commission, which regulated broadcasting under the Radio Act of 1927, ch. 169, 44 Stat. 1162 (superseded 1934). A variety of sources provide useful general background on the law made by the FCC. They include Stanley M. Besen et al., Misregulating Television: Network Dominance and the FCC (1984); T. Barton Carter et al., The First Amendment and the Fifth Estate (3d ed. 1993); Donald M. Gillmor et al., Mass Communication Law 683-904 (5th ed. 1990); Douglas H. Ginsburg et al., Regulation of the Electronic Mass Media (2d ed. 1991); Erwin G. Krasnow et al., The Politics of Broadcast Regulation (3d ed. 1982); Vincent Mosco, Broadcasting in the United States (1979); Lucas A. Powe, Jr., American Broadcasting and the First Amendment (1987).

60. 47 U.S.C. § 301 (1988). "Radio," in this context, refers to the electromagnetic spectrum generally; "communications . . . by radio" thus include television, unknown when the statute was enacted in 1934.

61. *Id.* § 307(a); *see also id.* § 309(a) ("public interest, convenience, and necessity").

62. *Id.* § 307(c). Television licenses are granted for a term of five years; radio licenses for a term of seven years; and nonbroadcast licenses (for dissemination of radio communications to someone other than the general public, as in taxi or ambulance radio services) for a term of ten years.

63. *Id.*

The holder of a broadcast license is required to operate in the public interest. The nature of this requirement, however, has been hazy over the years. Near the beginning of our broadcast regulatory history, the Federal Radio Commission elucidated the public interest as follows:

> Broadcasting stations are licensed to serve the public and not for the purpose of furthering the private or selfish interests of individuals or groups of individuals. . . . In a sense a broadcasting station may be regarded as a sort of mouthpiece on the air for the community it serves, over which its public events of general interest, its political campaigns, its election results, its athletic contests, its orchestras and artists, and discussion of its public issues may be broadcast.[64]

More recently, the FCC has described operation in the public interest as relating to the provision of nonentertainment programming responsive to community needs.[65]

Three key problems arise for the Commission in implementing its public-interest mandate. First, when several applicants seek mutually exclusive broadcast authorizations, how is the agency to decide whose licensure would best serve the "public interest"? Second, when a licensee has completed one or more license terms and is seeking renewal, how is the Commission to evaluate whether that licensee's speech to date has adequately served the "public interest"? Finally, how is the Commission to decide when a licensee's speech during the license term has deviated so far from the "public interest" that it warrants some sort of punishment?

1. Selecting the Licensee

During the FCC's first thirty years, procedures for selecting among competing would-be licensees were unabashedly discretionary and content-sensitive.[66] The FCC exercised particularly broad power in deciding which of two qualified applicants for a broadcast license would better serve the public interest. It saw its role as one of reaching, in each unique instance, "an over-all relative determination upon an evaluation of all factors, conflicting in many cases."[67] In one case, for example, the agency chose an applicant because the Commissioners saw it as more likely to "encourage broadcasts on controversial issues or topics of current interest to the community," to "cooperat[e] with civic interests," and to "provide . . . opportunity for local expression."[68] On appeal, the

---

64. Great Lakes Broadcasting Co., 3 F.R.C. ANN. REP. 32 (1929), *modified on other grounds,* 37 F.2d 993 (D.C. Cir.), *cert. dismissed,* 281 U.S. 706 (1930).

65. *See* Revision of Programming & Commercialization Policies, 98 F.C.C.2d 1076, 1091-92 (1984), *on reconsid.,* 104 F.C.C.2d 357 (1986), *rev'd in part sub nom.* Action for Children's Television v. FCC, 812 F.2d 741 (D.C. Cir. 1987).

66. *See* Weinberg, *supra* note 40, at 655-56.

67. Johnston Broadcasting Co. v. FCC, 175 F.2d 351, 356-57 (D.C. Cir. 1949).

68. *Id.* at 358. Further, the winning applicant's proposed staffing plan seemed to the

D.C. Circuit upheld that emphasis on the applicant's proposed programming: "[I]n a comparative consideration, it is well recognized that comparative service to the listening public is the vital element, and programs are the essence of that service."[69]

Because this process was so highly discretionary, it was susceptible to considerable hidden bias. In the 1950s, the Commission was stung by allegations that Commissioners had solicited and received bribes in licensing proceedings.[70] Moreover, the success or failure of many license applicants appeared to be determined by their Democratic or Republican political leanings.[71] The Commission thereafter sought to inject more formality into the comparative process. Its 1965 *Policy Statement on Comparative Broadcast Hearings* laid out a plan for a more mechanical examination of applications.[72]

Under the current regime, inaugurated by the 1965 *Policy Statement*, the Commission compares competing applicants primarily with reference to three factors: (1) the extent and size of the applicants' holdings in other media outlets;[73] (2) the extent to which the station owners personally would participate in management (with bonuses to be added if they were local residents), had participated in local civic affairs, had experience in the broadcast field, or were members of minority groups;[74] and (3) the size of the audience that the applicants' proposed

---

Commission to promise "a much more effective provision for program preparation and presentation." *Id.* at 358-59.

   69. *Id.* at 359 (footnote omitted). The court, however, ordered that the matter be remanded to the Commission on the ground that certain engineering data attached to the prevailing application had never been sworn to by the applicant. *Id.* at 354-56.

   On the comparative criteria developed by the FCC before 1965, see generally H. Gifford Irion, *FCC Criteria for Evaluating Competing Applicants,* 43 MINN. L. REV. 479 (1959).

   70. *See Investigation of Regulatory Commissions and Agencies: Hearings Before a Subcomm. of the House Comm. on Interstate and Foreign Commerce,* 85th Cong., 2d Sess. 553-1934 (1958) (Miami channel 10 affair); *id.* at 4889-935, 5055-266, 5297-348, 5497-535, 5621-45 (Pittsburgh channel 4 affair); BERNARD SCHWARTZ, THE PROFESSOR AND THE COMMISSIONS 194-203, 252-53 (1959).

   71. Specifically, applicants owning newspapers that had endorsed Eisenhower in the preceding election were more successful in FCC comparative proceedings than applicants owning newspapers that had endorsed Stevenson. *See* Bernard Schwartz, *Comparative Television and the Chancellor's Foot,* 47 GEO. L.J. 655, 689-94 (1959).

   72. 1 F.C.C.2d 393 (1965).

   73. The Commission stated in 1965 that it would disfavor applicants with outside media holdings, in order to promote "a maximum diffusion of control of the media of mass communications." *Id.* at 394. It would consider the significance of an applicant's interests in other media to be a function of the extent of the applicant's stake in the other media; the degree to which the other media were in, or close to, the community being applied for; and the degree to which the other media were significant in terms of size, regional or national coverage, and influence. *Id.* at 394-95.

   74. *See id.* at 395-96; *see also* Metro Broadcasting, Inc. v. FCC, 497 U.S. 547 (1990). Under FM Broadcast Assignments, 101 F.C.C.2d 638, 645-47 (1985), *aff'd sub nom.* National Black Media Coalition v. FCC, 822 F.2d 277 (2d Cir. 1987), the FCC also awards an enhancement credit to operators of daytime-only AM stations seeking FM licenses. In Mid-Florida Television Corp., 69 F.C.C.2d 607, 651-52 (1978), *set aside on other grounds,* 87 F.C.C.2d 203 (1981), the FCC awarded

signals could reach.[75]

This approach, however, has not succeeded in converting the process from a discretionary to a mechanical one. Indeed, it works quite badly.[76] Comparative hearing results are neither consistent nor predictable.[77] The Commission has found no meaningful and fair way to tally up an applicant's strengths and weaknesses, or to compare one applicant to another; it has referred to "slight," "moderate," "substantial," "dis-

---

an enhancement credit for female ownership, but that preference seems to be moribund following Lamprecht v. FCC, 958 F.2d 382 (D.C. Cir. 1992), declaring it unconstitutional.

75. *See, e.g.*, Susan S. Mulkey, 4 F.C.C.R. 5520, 5521 (1989) (granting a slight comparative preference for superior coverage). In the 1965 *Policy Statement*, the Commission stated that it would also consider (1) the applicant's proposed program service, to the extent that the differences between the proposals were "material and substantial," going "beyond ordinary differences in judgment" to demonstrate one applicant's "superior devotion to public service," 1 F.C.C.2d at 397; (2) an applicant's record as licensee of other broadcast outlets, if "unusually good" in the sense of showing "unusual attention to the public's needs and interests, such as special sensitivity to an area's changing needs through flexibility of local programs designed to meet those needs," or "unusually poor," as manifested by "a failure to meet the public's needs and interests," *id.* at 398; and (3) the applicant's character (that is, whether it has been found guilty of criminal or other bad acts), *id.* at 399. An addendum to the 1965 *Policy Statement* added the availability of auxiliary power equipment as an additional comparative factor. *See* Addendum to Policy Statement on Comparative Broadcast Hearings, 2 F.C.C.2d 667 (1966).

Today, however, as a practical matter, the Commission rarely allows proposed program service or past broadcast record to be placed in issue. *See* Random Selection (Lottery), 4 F.C.C.R. 2256, 2266 n.17 (1989) (describing current comparative process). *But see* Simon Geller, 90 F.C.C.2d 250, 273-76 (1982) (granting an applicant substantial preference for proposed programming), *remanded on other grounds sub nom.* Committee for Community Access v. FCC, 737 F.2d 74 (D.C. Cir. 1984). When those factors are put in issue, they are "seldom" or "only in extraordinary cases" dispositive. Reexamination of the Policy Statement on Comparative Broadcast Hearings, 7 F.C.C.R. 2664, 2666 (1992). The Commission has deleted character from the list of comparative criteria; character is now considered only in connection with the minimum qualifications for licensing. *See* Policy Regarding Character Qualifications in Broadcast Licensing, 102 F.C.C.2d 1179 (1986). Auxiliary power, similarly, no longer plays a significant role.

An unrelated factor, not mentioned in the 1965 *Policy Statement*, however, has played a dispositive role in the comparative process. Under 47 U.S.C. § 307(b) (1988), the FCC is required to award licenses so as to provide "fair, efficient, and equitable distribution of radio service." Where applicants are proposing to serve different communities of license, and the Commission determines that one of those communities should be preferred under § 307(b), the Commission eliminates all applicants not proposing to serve that community. *See* FCC v. Allentown Broadcasting Corp., 349 U.S. 358 (1955); WHW Enters., Inc. v. FCC, 753 F.2d 1132, 1134-38 (D.C. Cir. 1985); Random Selection (Lottery), 4 F.C.C.R. at 2258 (notice of proposed rulemaking).

76. The comparative hearing process has been the target of virtually unceasing criticism. The Commission itself recently stated that the process "can be described most charitably as laborious, exceedingly time consuming, expensive and often result[ing] in choices based on, at most, marginal differences." Random Selection (Lottery), 4 F.C.C.R. at 2256. *See generally* STEPHEN R. BARNETT ET AL., LAW OF INTERNATIONAL TELECOMMUNICATIONS IN THE UNITED STATES 107 (1988) (comparative hearing process is "absurd," and has attracted "devastating criticism that is now virtually unanimous"); HENRY J. FRIENDLY, THE FEDERAL ADMINISTRATIVE AGENCIES 53-73 (1962); Robert A. Anthony, *Towards Simplicity and Rationality in Comparative Broadcast Licensing Proceedings*, 24 STAN. L. REV. 1, 39-55 (1971); Glen O. Robinson, *The Federal Communications Commission: An Essay on Regulatory Watchdogs*, 64 VA. L. REV. 169, 237-43 (1978); Weinberg, *supra* note 40, at 657-58.

77. *See* Random Selection (Lottery), 4 F.C.C.R. at 2258-59; BARNETT ET AL., *supra* note 76, at 107; Robinson, *supra* note 76, at 238-40.

tinct," "clear," and "enhanced" "pluses," "merits," "demerits" and "preferences," and has sought to balance them via "administrative 'feel.' "[78] Often, competing applicants for a broadcast license differ only marginally in terms of the criteria the Commission has set out. As a result, the FCC's choices among them are necessarily arbitrary.[79]

The foundational problem is that nobody has devised reliable mechanical criteria for figuring out which broadcast applicants, if licensed, would best serve the "public interest." It is doubtful that the Commission can by any means find the "best" applicant of a group in which all satisfy basic qualifications; but it is certain that the Commission's purportedly uniform, objective standards are not doing the

---

78. *See, e.g.,* Simon Geller, 102 F.C.C.2d 1443, 1452-53 (1985); Cowles Fla. Broadcasting, Inc., 60 F.C.C.2d 372, 411, 414, 416, 422 (1976), *rev'd sub nom.* Central Fla. Enters. v. FCC, 598 F.2d 37 (D.C. Cir. 1978), *cert. dismissed,* 441 U.S. 957 (1979). *Geller* was a comparative hearing upon license renewal treated by the Commission as if it were an initial hearing. *Cowles* was a comparative hearing upon license renewal. Comparative renewal hearings and initial hearings are similar in their inability to balance comparative factors in any meaningful or satisfying way. *See infra* notes 90-109 and accompanying text.

79. *See, e.g.,* Merrimack Valley Broadcasting, Inc., 99 F.C.C.2d 680, 682 (1984); Greater Wichita Telecasting, Inc., 96 F.C.C.2d 984, 994 (1984) (Rivera, Comm'r, concurring); Alexander S. Klein, Jr., 86 F.C.C.2d 423, 424-25 (1981). Commissioner Robinson thus complained in *Cowles* that while it would be "almost invariably . . . insufficient for making the choice" if the Commission were to confine itself to verifying applicants' minimal qualifications, the Commission's efforts to go beyond that verification, and decide which is truly the best applicant, have been "productive of nothing but senseless waste of resources." Cowles Fla. Broadcasting, Inc., 60 F.C.C.2d at 444 (Robinson, Comm'r, dissenting).

The Commission's basic qualifications for licensing are themselves to some extent subjective as well. *See, e.g.,* Henry v. FCC, 302 F.2d 191, 194 (D.C. Cir.) (FCC not required to grant a license to an otherwise qualified sole applicant who has not "demonstrate[d] an earnest interest in serving a local community by evidencing a familiarity with its particular needs and an effort to meet them"), *cert. denied,* 371 U.S. 821 (1962). While the FCC has achieved some uniformity by embodying these judgments in published rules, rather than in ad hoc decisions in individual cases, the rules themselves have changed over time. For example, while the Commission requires broadcast applicants to be of good "character," *see supra* note 75 and accompanying text, it has shifted over time on the issue of how good one's character must be. *Compare* Character Qualifications in Broadcast Licensing, 102 F.C.C.2d 1179, 1196-98 (1986) (limiting the categories of felony convictions which establish bad character for purposes of basic qualifications) *with* Character Qualifications in Broadcast Licensing, 5 F.C.C.R. 3252 (1990) (expanding the range of misconduct relevant to character to include all felony convictions), *on reconsid.,* 6 F.C.C.R. 3448 (1991); *see also* Licensee Participation in Drug Trafficking, 66 Rad. Reg. 2d (P & F) 1617 (1989). *See generally* Character Qualifications in Broadcast Licensing, 87 F.C.C.2d 836 (1981).

The Commission similarly has shifted its views of the point at which the nature and extent of an applicant's media holdings is such that the "public interest" absolutely precludes the applicant from being awarded a given license. *See, e.g.,* Revision of Radio Rules & Policies, 7 F.C.C.R. 2755 (1992) (relaxing limits on multiple ownership). *See generally* GINSBURG ET AL., *supra* note 59, at 180-207. Regulation in this area necessarily involves the drawing of arbitrary lines, and the inquiry has had its own political content. In News Am. Publishing, Inc. v. FCC, 844 F.2d 800 (D.C. Cir. 1988), the court struck down a statute barring extensions of existing waivers of a rule generally prohibiting common ownership of a daily newspaper and a broadcast station in the same market. The only two waivers outstanding when the statute was enacted applied to properties owned by Rupert Murdoch. The law is thought by some to have been passed in part because of Senator Kennedy's frustration with Murdoch's Boston newspaper. *See* Allan R. Gold, *Kennedy vs. Murdoch: Test of Motives,* N.Y. TIMES, Jan. 11, 1988, at A13.

job.[80] The agency thus has had to choose between making subjective determinations, overtly or covertly, in aid of making the best possible selections, or following the mechanical rules at the cost of making selections that do not necessarily serve the statute's larger "public interest" goals.

The Commission itself is dissatisfied with the existing comparative licensing process.[81] The D.C. Circuit recently directed the Commission to reconsider whether its "integration" preference, relating to the participation of owners in management, in fact advances the public interest in any meaningful way.[82] The Commission has proposed to eliminate from the comparative process all of the factors currently considered other than the extent and size of the applicants' holdings in other media outlets (a criterion the FCC proposes to rethink), the size of the audience the applicants' signals would reach, and minority status.[83] It has proposed to add to the list of comparative factors a preference for applicants promising not to sell or otherwise transfer the station for at least three years,[84] and perhaps another for applicants who successfully request the allotment of new broadcast frequencies through rulemaking.[85] It has proposed to tote up the preferences through an "objective and rational" point system rather than the present, more amorphous, approach.[86]

The Commission hopes, through these changes, to be able to reach "swifter, more certain choices," avoiding the need to rely on "subjective and imprecise" factors that emphasize "relatively slight distinctions

---

80. Thus Commissioner Wiley's dissent in *Cowles*:

> I personally cannot believe that the American public derives any benefit out of the existing process by which we attempt to apply objective criteria (for example, integration of ownership and management) to the largely subjective (and, in most cases, unanswerable) question of which applicant will provide the best future service.

Cowles Fla. Broadcasting, Inc., 60 F.C.C.2d at 431 (Wiley, Comm'r, dissenting). *See generally* STEPHEN G. BREYER, REGULATION AND ITS REFORM 72-89 (1982); Lon L. Fuller, *Adjudication and the Rule of Law,* 54 AM. SOC'Y INT'L L. PROC. 1, 7-8 (1960); Matthew L. Spitzer, *Multicriteria Choice Processes: An Application of Public Choice Theory to Bakke, the FCC, and the Courts,* 88 YALE L.J. 717 (1979) (arguing that the FCC cannot choose licensees on a principled basis so long as it seeks to base its decisions on incommensurable criteria).

81. *See* Random Selection (Lottery), 4 F.C.C.R. 2256 (1989) (characterizing comparative process as inefficient, costly, and of doubtful benefit to the public).

82. *See* Bechtel v. FCC, 957 F.2d 873, 881 (D.C. Cir.), *cert. denied,* 113 S. Ct. 57 (1992). The Commission defended the integration preference in Anchor Broadcasting, 8 F.C.C.R. 1674 (1993).

83. *See* Reexamination of the Policy Statement on Comparative Broadcast Hearings, 7 F.C.C.R. 2664 (1992). The agency has also proposed to continue the existing "day-timer" preference, and has left open the question of whether to continue granting a preference based on applicants' past or proposed local residence. *Id.* at 2667-68.

84. *Id.* at 2668. This preference would revive, in large part, the "anti-trafficking" policy discarded in the early years of the Reagan administration. *See* Transfer of Broadcast Facilities, 52 Rad. Reg. 2d (P & F) 1081 (1982).

85. *See* Reexamination of the Policy Statement on Comparative Broadcast Hearings, 7 F.C.C.R. at 2668.

86. *Id.* at 2668-69.

among the applicants."[87] It is hardly clear, though, that the new proposals will avoid the dilemma posed by comparative licensing so far: the agency cannot simultaneously have an objective and nondiscretionary selection process on the one hand, and a process adept at "select[ing] . . . the applicant that will best serve the public interest"[88] on the other. Indeed, it seems likely that the Commission's proposal will cause many (if not most) comparative proceedings to end in ties, with two or more applicants sharing the same number of points. The Commission's proposal leaves open the question of how these ties are to be broken, but appears to favor random selection or a first-to-file preference.[89] Both of these minimize agency discretion, but neither is well-tailored to selecting the "best" applicant as that concept has been conventionally understood.

2. *Renewal*

Discretion and subjectivity play significant roles in the renewal of licenses as well. When a new applicant seeks to be awarded a license in place of the incumbent, the FCC must again hold a comparative hearing.[90] The Commission must consider incumbent and new applicants in a single comparative proceeding, not "unreasonably weighted" in favor of the incumbent licensee. It must decide, on the basis of that comparison, whose licensure would best serve the public interest.[91] In evaluating the incumbent's record, the Commission must look to the station's nonentertainment programming, in particular its local news and public affairs programming, and it must evaluate how the licensee has responded to community needs and problems.[92] It grants the incumbent licensee a "renewal expectancy" preference on a showing that its past record has been "sound, favorable and substantially above . . . mediocre."[93]

---

87. *Id.* at 2664.

88. *Id.* at 2665.

89. *Id.* at 2668-69. The Commission also suggested the possibility of giving the license to the applicant with the greatest broadcast experience, but cautioned that that approach might disadvantage women and minorities—something that would, in the Commission's view, cause the plan to violate statutory law. *See id.* at 2667, 2669.

All this suggests that the Commission's recent proposal may simply be a backhanded way of reviving its 1989 suggestion to award new broadcast licenses through random selection. *See* Random Selection (Lottery), 4 F.C.C.R. 2256 (1989). The FCC abandoned this initiative in the face of nearly unanimous opposition from the industry and the bar. *See FCC Revamping Comparative Hearing Process,* BROADCASTING, May 14, 1990, at 31; *Few Choose to Follow FCC's Bouncing Ball,* BROADCASTING, June 19, 1989, at 50.

90. *See* Citizens Communications Ctr. v. FCC, 447 F.2d 1201 (D.C. Cir. 1971) (interpreting 47 U.S.C. § 309(e)).

91. *Id.* at 1214; *see also* Central Fla. Enters., Inc. v. FCC, 598 F.2d 37, 41 (D.C. Cir. 1978), *cert. dismissed,* 441 U.S. 957 (1979).

92. *See, e.g.,* Radio Station WABZ, Inc., 90 F.C.C.2d 818, 840-42 (1982), *aff'd sub nom.* Victor Broadcasting, Inc. v. FCC, 722 F.2d 756 (D.C. Cir. 1983).

93. Monroe Communications Corp. v. FCC, 900 F.2d 351, 353 (D.C. Cir. 1990) (quoting

The Commission has expressed its unhappiness with the comparative process; evaluation of the incumbent's past service, it has pointed out, is once again subjective, uncertain, and content-sensitive.[94] It has attacked the comparative renewal process in two ways. First, it has urged that the law be changed more nearly to guarantee renewal.[95] Second, notwithstanding its statutory obligation to conduct a comparative hearing when an incumbent is challenged on renewal by a new applicant, the FCC has been reluctant *ever* to find that the "public interest" would be better served by the new applicant.[96] It gives the renewal expectancy "primary weight . . . *vis-à-vis* the other comparative criteria."[97] Indeed, it has sometimes been quite creative in its efforts to "balance" the various comparative factors and still come out with the largely preordained result.[98]

Cowles Broadcasting, Inc., 86 F.C.C.2d at 1006, *aff'd sub nom.* Central Fla. Enters., Inc. v. FCC, 683 F.2d 503 (D.C. Cir. 1982), *cert. denied,* 460 U.S. 1084 (1983)).

94. *See* Formation of Policies & Rules Relating to Broadcast Renewal Applicants, 4 F.C.C.R. 6363, 6363-64 (1989).

95. The Commission, for example, has proposed to grant *all* incumbent broadcasters a presumption of entitlement to renewal expectancy, and thus to renewal, upon compliance with FCC rules requiring each licensee to maintain certain files for public inspection. *Id.* at 6365.

96. The Commission did, in one notorious case, deny renewal to a Boston television station in favor of a new applicant. *See* WHDH, Inc., 16 F.C.C.2d 1 (1969), *aff'd sub nom.* Greater Boston Television Corp. v. FCC, 444 F.2d 841 (D.C. Cir. 1970), *cert. denied,* 403 U.S. 923 (1971). The Commission had decided, because of the unique procedural history of the proceeding, to treat the incumbent as if it too were a new applicant. "To say that *WHDH* shocked the broadcast industry would be an understatement." GINSBURG ET AL., *supra* note 59, at 114; *see also* Simon Geller, 90 F.C.C.2d 250, 270 (1982) (treating a radio broadcaster as if it were a new applicant and denying renewal on that basis).

97. Formation of Policies & Rules Relating to Broadcast Renewal Applicants, 4 F.C.C.R. at 6363 (describing existing process).

98. In 1976, for example, Cowles Florida Broadcasting was the incumbent licensee of WESH-TV, Channel 2, in Daytona Beach, Florida, when a group calling itself Central Florida Enterprises sought to take the license away. Cowles had violated the law by relocating its main studio to the larger city of Orlando; further, its corporate parent had been involved in mail fraud. There was little question that Cowles' was the inferior application when it came to outside media interests, ownership participation in management, and minority ownership. Its record of public service, moreover, was hardly impressive to the unbiased eye. *See* Cowles Fla. Broadcasting, Inc., 60 F.C.C.2d 372, 441-42 (1976) (Robinson, Comm'r, dissenting). The Commission, however, after "weighing" all of these factors, nonetheless granted Cowles the license on the theory that Cowles' record of broadcast service in its three years as the incumbent licensee gave it a decisive edge. *Id.* at 417-22; *see also id.* at 439 (Robinson, Comm'r, dissenting) (comparative renewal proceedings are "not a real contest between two applicants, but a pretend game played between the Commission and the public. The outcome of the game is predetermined; the art (and the sport) is to maintain interest until the inevitable outcome is registered. . . . It rather resembles a professional wrestling match . . . .").

The D.C. Circuit reversed. Central Fla. Enters., Inc. v. FCC, 598 F.2d 37 (D.C. Cir. 1978), *cert. dismissed,* 441 U.S. 957 (1979). On remand, the Commission found for Cowles again, setting out its rationale in a more self-consciously mechanical manner. This time, with some misgivings, the court of appeals affirmed:

> [W]e are still troubled by the fact that the record remains that an incumbent *television* licensee has *never* been denied renewal in a comparative challenge. American television viewers will be reassured, although a trifle baffled, to learn that even the worst television stations—those which are, presumably, the ones picked out as vulnerable to a challenge—

As with initial licensing, the Commission has found conflict between its desire to reduce uncertainty and discretion in the license renewal process on the one hand, and the basic "public interest" structure of the underlying law on the other.[99] In one recent case, for example, the Commission first granted, but then, after a judicial rebuke, was forced to deny renewal to a UHF licensee that had converted to a pay-TV scrambled movie service. The licensee had shut down its local studios and was running conventional programming only between 6:00 and 7:00 in the morning.[100] The Commission, in comparing this licensee to a competing applicant, could hardly give it public-interest credit based on its news, its public affairs programming, or its attention to community affairs—none were in evidence.[101] It ultimately denied the licensee any renewal expectancy, and consequently denied it renewal. The licensee, it held, had engaged in a "wholesale abandonment of public service programming."[102]

One might respond to this story by challenging the legal premise underlying the court's and the Commission's actions: why should news and public-affairs programming be the primary touchstone of the public interest? Aren't movies in the public interest as well? Is it not "the theory of our Constitution"[103] that *all* speech is in the public interest?

The problem is that the Communications Act is generally understood to require the Commission, when choosing among broadcast appli-

---

are so good that they never need replacing. We suspect that somewhere, sometime, somehow, some television licensee *should* fail in a comparative renewal challenge, but the FCC has never discovered such a licensee yet.

Central Fla. Enters., Inc. v. FCC, 683 F.2d 503, 510 (D.C. Cir. 1982) (footnotes omitted), *cert. denied*, 460 U.S. 1084 (1983).

99. The Commission's unhappiness with the comparative process, on the other hand, has not been motivated entirely—or even primarily—by the arcana of legal theory. *See infra* notes 404-05 and accompanying text.

100. *See* Video 44, 4 F.C.C.R. 1209 (1989), *rev'd sub nom.* Monroe Communications Corp. v. FCC, 900 F.2d 351, 354, 356 (D.C. Cir.), *on remand*, 5 F.C.C.R. 6383 (1990).

101. The Commission initially granted renewal anyway, in part by giving the licensee credit for news and public affairs programming it had run *before* converting its format. The agency reasoned further that the licensee had made *some* minimal effort to run nonentertainment programming even after converting, and that subscription TV's commercially risky and uncertain nature excused the station's initial failings. *Id.* at 1211-12.

The D.C. Circuit reversed. The Commission, said the court, had lost sight of the public-interest determination. The point of the renewal expectancy, it prompted, was that a licensee's programming record, as reflected in its news, public affairs and nonentertainment programming, is generally probative of its future responsiveness to community needs. It was unlikely that Video 44's programming record before its drastic and apparently permanent format change would be probative of future behavior. *Monroe Communications Corp.*, 900 F.2d at 355-56. (Another issue in the case was presented by the sexually explicit nature of some of Video 44's programming, which included "adult" films. The Commission had declined to consider this factor in ruling on Video 44's renewal application, *see id.* at 356-59, but it is possible that the issue played an atmospheric role in the court of appeals' treatment of the renewal expectancy issue.)

102. Video 44, 5 F.C.C.R. 6383, 6385 (1990) (quoting Video 44, 102 F.C.C.2d 419, 462 (1985) (ALJ initial decision)).

103. Abrams v. United States, 250 U.S. 616, 630 (1919) (Holmes, J., dissenting).

cants and making renewal decisions, to make the choice that *best* serves the "public interest." If the Commission were to take the view that any and all speech is equally in the public interest, it could not find any applicant superior to any other. It is programming, after all, that is at the heart of the Communications Act's public-interest mandate. Broadcasters have no meaningful impact on our public life *except* through their programming; the government has no significant communications-law interest in regulating the identity of broadcast licensees except insofar as their identity affects the content of broadcast speech.[104]

The Commission initially elevated news and public-affairs reporting precisely so that it could make the statute's "public interest" determination in a more tolerable, more objective, manner. Selecting broadcasters on the basis of their commitment to local public-affairs reporting wasn't necessarily the best course from the perspective of the "public interest" in its largest sense, but it gave the Commission some workable basis on which to make choices. In the case just mentioned, the Commission initially sought to eliminate unpredictability and subjectivity by simply ruling for the incumbent; the D.C. Circuit responded that to do so would be to subordinate the statutory directive that some speakers are more in the "public interest" than others, and that the FCC was to ensure that those *most* in the "public interest" had the licenses. It is unlikely, however, that any "public interest" standard the FCC can capably administer will end up having much to do with the public interest.

What about the renewal process when there is no competing applicant? In theory at least, even when nobody is opposing a license renewal, the broadcaster seeking renewal "must run on his record, and the focus of that record is whether his programming has served the public interest."[105] Before the Reagan administration, the FCC required even uncontested renewal applicants to submit extensive data concerning such matters as their nonentertainment and children's programming, the number of public service announcements they had broadcast, and their compliance with FCC requirements for ascertainment of community needs and interests.[106] In the agency's view, this was the only way it

---

104. *See* Metro Broadcasting, Inc. v. FCC, 497 U.S. 547, 566-84 (1990) (FCC and Congress appropriately concluded that greater minority ownership of broadcast outlets would result in greater diversity of broadcast speech.).

105. Black Citizens for a Fair Media v. FCC, 719 F.2d 407, 411 (D.C. Cir. 1983) (quoting FCC brief), *cert. denied,* 467 U.S. 1255 (1984); *see also Monroe Communications Corp.,* 900 F.2d at 355 (observing that the question on renewal is whether the broadcaster, based on its past record, is likely to perform meritoriously in the future).

106. *See Black Citizens for a Fair Media,* 719 F.2d at 409. As early as 1927, radio stations applying for renewal were asked to set forth the average amount of time they devoted to "entertainment," "religious," "educational," "agricultural," and "fraternal" programs. *See* Public Service Responsibility of Broadcast Licensees (1946), *reprinted in* DOCUMENTS OF AMERICAN BROADCASTING 148, 150 (Frank J. Kahn ed., 4th ed. 1984).

could make the necessary "public interest" determination.[107]

In the early 1980s, the FCC abandoned that approach. It stopped requiring that uncontested renewal applicants submit programming information, and it announced that it would no longer review programming in connection with such applications.[108] While in theory licensees are still required to provide nonentertainment programming responsive to issues of concern to the community, the Commission now makes the necessary public-interest finding in uncontested cases via a "presumption" that the applicant has complied with the statutory requirement.[109] This, of course, again avoids the concern that the "public-interest" determination will introduce ambiguity and subjectivity into the renewal process. Like the Commission's approach in comparative renewal cases, though, its cost is the agency's failure to look to the "public interest" in any individualized way.

---

107. The agency would grant uncontested renewal applications routinely, by staff action, if they appeared to satisfy certain quantitative guidelines relating to such matters as minutes of commercials per hour and overall percentages of local, informational, and nonentertainment programming. Applications that did not satisfy those guidelines were subjected to expensive processing delays.

After World War II, the Commission took an especially aggressive stance in this area: it set a number of renewal applications for hearing because of inadequate balance among program categories, insufficient unsponsored programming, insufficient local live programming, insufficient discussion of public issues, or excessive commercialization. *See* Eugene J. Roth, 12 F.C.C. 102 (1947); Howard W. Davis, 12 F.C.C. 91 (1947); Community Broadcasting Co., 12 F.C.C. 85 (1947). The Commission did not in fact deny any renewals on these grounds, and violent industry opposition, *see, e.g., Hearings on S. 1333 Before a Subcomm. of the Senate Comm. on Interstate and Foreign Commerce*, 80th Cong., 1st Sess. (1947), caused the agency to adopt a more subdued approach.

Under guidelines adopted in 1961, FCC staff would check for compliance with quantitative guidelines in the areas of noncommercial programming, local live programming, nonnetwork programming, and "sustaining" (unsponsored) programming. They would check to see if commercialization limits were being exceeded, and would look for "adequate explanation" if programming were missing in any of the following categories: entertainment, religious, agricultural, educational, news, discussion (forum, panel, or roundtable), and talk. *See* Revision of Programming & Commercialization Policies, 98 F.C.C.2d 1076, 1078 n.3 (1984), *on reconsid.*, 4 F.C.C.2d 357 (1986), *rev'd in part sub nom.* Action for Children's Television v. FCC, 812 F.2d 741 (D.C. Cir. 1987); Lee Roy McCourry, 2 Rad. Reg. 2d (P & F) 895, 896 (1964) (setting UHF application for hearing because applicant had proposed 70% entertainment, 30% education, and no programming in the other categories). *See generally* KRASNOW ET AL., *supra* note 59, at 196-97.

In 1973, the agency published its processing rules for the first time, including commercialization limits and a requirement that stations program a minimum percentage of nonentertainment programming. Amendment to Delegations of Authority, 43 F.C.C.2d 638 (1973). The Commission revised those rules in 1976 to require scrutiny of local and informational programming as well. Amendment to Delegations of Authority, 59 F.C.C.2d 491 (1976).

108. *See, e.g.,* Revision of Programming & Commercialization Policies, 98 F.C.C.2d 1076 (1984); Deregulation of Radio, 84 F.C.C.2d 968 (1981), *aff'd in part sub nom.* Office of Communication of the United Church of Christ v. FCC, 707 F.2d 1413 (D.C. Cir. 1983); Revision of Applications for Renewal of License of Commercial and Noncommercial AM, FM, and Television Licensees, 49 Rad. Reg. 2d (P & F) 740 (1981), *aff'd sub nom.* Black Citizens for a Fair Media v. FCC, 719 F.2d 407 (D.C. Cir. 1983).

109. Revision of Programming & Commercialization Policies, 98 F.C.C.2d at 1093.

3. *Misconduct*

This brings us, finally, to the question of how the Commission treats those incumbent licensees who are accused of serious misconduct, such that renewal, it is argued, would disserve the public interest. How successful has the FCC been at locating the "public interest" in *this* arena? The FCC has denied broadcast renewal applications on a variety of grounds.[110] In several cases, its decision not to renew a license was based at least in part on the content of the licensee's speech.[111]

With regard to its content restrictions, the FCC once again has not

---

110. Grounds for nonrenewal have included misrepresentations to the Commission, unauthorized transfers of control, technical violations (e.g., being unable to stick to the assigned frequency), and "character" failings. *See* John D. Abel et al., *Station License Revocations and Denials of Renewal, 1934-69*, 14 J. BROADCASTING 411 (1970); Fredric A. Weiss et al., *Station License Revocations and Denials of Renewal, 1970-78*, 24 J. BROADCASTING 69 (1980). Commission case law in these areas too has been criticized as subjective. *See* Brian C. Murchison, *Misrepresentation and the FCC*, 37 FED. COMM. L.J. 403, 420 (1985) (characterizing FCC case law regarding nonrenewal as a sanction for the licensee's misrepresentations to the Commission as "drift[ing] on a sea of subjectivity"). Beginning in 1971, the FCC began a crackdown against fraudulent billing practices, and denied or revoked eleven licenses on that basis. Weiss et al., *supra* at 76. The initiative, however, was relatively short-lived; a later Commission eliminated the rules against fraudulent billing. *See* Elimination of Unnecessary Broadcast Regulation, 59 Rad. Reg. 2d (P & F) 1500 (1986).

The single most sweeping denial of renewal ever undertaken by the Commission was Alabama Educ. Television Comm'n, 50 F.C.C.2d 461 (1975), a single decision affecting eight licensees affiliated with the state-run Alabama public television system. The Commission denied renewal to those licensees because the system discriminated racially in programming and in employment; it allowed them, however, to apply for the vacated licenses in competition with other applicants.

111. *See* United Television Co., 55 F.C.C.2d 416, 423 (1975) (FCC denied renewal based on the licensee's broadcast of religious programming offering numbers game picks, "special money-drawing roots," and "spiritual baths" in return for monetary donations), *aff'd sub nom.* United Broadcasting Co. v. FCC, 565 F.2d 699 (D.C. Cir. 1977), *cert. denied*, 434 U.S. 1046 (1978); Star Stations of Ind., Inc., 51 F.C.C.2d 95, 107 (1975) (FCC denied renewal based in part on licensee's use of newscasts "as a vehicle to publicize [his] preferred candidate [in a political race]—not as an exercise of news judgment, but as a deception of the public"); Alabama Educ. Television Comm'n, 50 F.C.C.2d 461 (1975); Brandywine-Main Line Radio, Inc., 24 F.C.C.2d 18 (1970), *on reconsid.*, 27 F.C.C.2d 565 (1971) (FCC denied renewal application of station largely devoted to religious fundamentalism and the views of the political right wing on the ground that the licensee had violated the fairness doctrine, and had, when it acquired the station, deceived the Commission about its intention to broadcast certain religious and political programming), *aff'd on arguably narrower grounds*, 473 F.2d 16 (D.C. Cir. 1972), *cert. denied*, 412 U.S. 922 (1973); Palmetto Broadcasting Co., 33 F.C.C. 250 (1962) (FCC found that the station had broadcast coarse, vulgar, and suggestive material and had not met community needs; it found further that the licensee had exercised inadequate control over the station and had lied to Commission in claiming lack of knowledge of objectionable material), *aff'd sub nom.* Robinson v. FCC, 334 F.2d 534 (D.C. Cir.), *cert. denied*, 379 U.S. 843 (1964); *see also* Trustees of the University of Pennsylvania Radio Station WXPN (FM), 69 F.C.C.2d 1394 (1978) (listeners complained that college radio station broadcast indecent speech; FCC denied renewal on the ground that the licensee had inadequately supervised station operation); Hawaiian Paradise Park Corp., 22 F.C.C.2d 459 (1970) (setting renewal application for hearing on a variety of grounds including fairness doctrine, personal attack, and political broadcasting violations), *reconsid. denied*, 26 F.C.C.2d 329 (1970) (licensee withdrew application); Lamar Life Broadcasting Co., 38 F.C.C. 1143 (1965) (FCC granted short-term renewal to a station that had engaged in discriminatory and one-sided programming regarding racial issues), *rev'd sub nom.* United Church of Christ v. FCC, 359 F.2d 994 (D.C. Cir. 1966) (directing FCC to hold an evidentiary hearing on whether it

avoided subjectivity and vagueness. The agency, for example, has in greater or lesser degree regulated indecency on the air;[112] its efforts in that regard have surely exposed it to charges of subjectivity.[113] Perhaps emblematic are Commissioner James Quello's comments on the annual "Bloomsday" broadcast of readings from James Joyce's *Ulysses* by a Pacifica radio station: Quello was quoted as saying that the readings should not be broadcast because their language was "stuff you deck someone over. I'm amazed it made it as a classic."[114]

The most well known of all of the FCC's essays at content regulation over the years, however, was the "fairness doctrine." Pursuant to the fairness doctrine,[115] the Commission required each licensee not only to devote a reasonable percentage of time to covering "controversial issues of public importance" in its service area, but to cover those issues "fairly," by providing a "reasonable opportunity" for the presentation of opposing points of view.[116]

Fairness enforcement was subjective.[117] In order to enforce the fair-

---

should deny renewal outright); Pacifica Found., 36 F.C.C. 147 (1964) (FCC granted renewal after inquiring into sexually explicit programming and possible Communist affiliations).

112. The Commission regulates "indecent" broadcast speech under 18 U.S.C. § 1464. *See, e.g.,* Enforcement of Prohibitions Against Broadcast Indecency in 18 U.S.C. § 1464, 5 F.C.C.2d 5297 (1990), *vacated sub nom.* FCC v. Pacifica Found., 438 U.S. 726 (1978) (upholding FCC proscription of indecent language against a First Amendment challenge); Action for Children's Television v. FCC, 932 F.2d 1504 (D.C. Cir. 1991), *cert. denied,* 112 S. Ct. 1281 (1992).

113. *See, e.g.,* POWE, *supra* note 8, at 162-90; Lili Levi, *The Hard Case of Broadcast Indecency,* 20 N.Y.U. REV. L. & SOC. CHANGE 49, 112-38 (1992-93).

114. *See* Winer, *supra* note 8, at 379 (quoting *(Bleep) (Bleep) (Bleep) (Bleep) And Yes I Said Yes I Will Yes,* WALL ST. J., May 26, 1987, at 35). The Commission has declined to rule on whether *Ulysses* is in fact indecent under ruling law. *See* GINSBURG ET AL., *supra* note 59, at 547 (citing a letter from FCC Mass Media Bureau to William J. Byrnes, June 5, 1987).

115. The roots of the fairness doctrine can be traced back to Great Lakes Broadcasting Co., 3 F.R.C. ANN. REP. 32, 33 (1929), *rev'd on other grounds,* 37 F.2d 993 (D.C. Cir.), *cert. dismissed,* 281 U.S. 706 (1930); the Commission codified the doctrine in Editorializing by Broadcast Licensees, 13 F.C.C. 1246 (1948). Ten years later, Congress inserted into the Communications Act a reference to "the obligation imposed upon [broadcasters] under this chapter to . . . afford reasonable opportunity for the discussion of conflicting views on issues of public importance." 47 U.S.C. § 315(a) (1988). The D.C. Circuit later ruled, though, that Congress had not adopted the fairness doctrine as a "binding statutory directive"; it had merely recognized the Commission's promulgation of the fairness doctrine as an existing "administrative construction." Telecommunications Research & Action Ctr. v. FCC, 801 F.2d 501, 517 (D.C. Cir. 1986), *cert. denied,* 482 U.S. 919 (1987).

116. *See* Handling of Public Issues Under the Fairness Doctrine, 48 F.C.C.2d 1, 10-17 (1974), *aff'd in part, rev'd in part sub nom.* National Citizens Comm. for Broadcasting v. FCC, 567 F.2d 1095 (D.C. Cir. 1977), *cert. denied,* 436 U.S. 926 (1978).

The doctrine was motivated by the fear that the few station owners lucky enough to receive broadcast licenses would have "unfettered power to make time available only to the highest bidders, to communicate only their own views on public issues, people and candidates, and to permit on the air only those with whom they agreed." Justice White articulated the concern: "There is no sanctuary in the First Amendment for unlimited private censorship operating in a medium not open to all." Red Lion Broadcasting Co. v. FCC, 395 U.S. 367, 392 (1969).

117. *See generally* Krattenmaker & Powe, *supra* note 7, at 169-76 (arguing that the fairness doctrine is inescapably incoherent). *But see* BOLLINGER, *supra* note 11, at 123 (arguing that the fairness doctrine is no more subjective than are other areas of First Amendment jurisprudence).

ness doctrine, the Commission needed some substantive vision of what ground a discussion had to cover in order to be fair; it needed some centerline from which to judge whether a given issue was "controversial" and whether coverage was "balanced." There is, however, no Platonic midpoint of the political spectrum. In one case before the FCC, thus, a conservative group argued that CBS news reporting relating to military and foreign affairs was slanted towards the view that the United States should decrease its national security efforts.[118] One could not think about this claim, though, without first identifying an appropriate baseline: in order to decide whether CBS' views were unbalanced, one needed a standard for comparison. There was no reason why the "unbiased" view had to be that national security efforts remain exactly the same.

As a practical matter, the Commission made those fairness judgments by looking to its understanding of what was politically controversial in the America of the time.[119] This approach was problematic in two ways. First, it meant that whether a licensee violated the fairness doctrine depended on the Commission's perhaps idiosyncratic perceptions of the current political debate. The FCC, for example, throughout the 1960s and 1970s, never considered the appropriateness of illegal drug use a "controversial" issue:[120] it was clear to the Commission that all responsible people considered illegal drug use to be degrading and wrong, and thus that there was no meaningful controversy. Large seg-

---

118. *See* American Sec. Council Educ. Found. v. FCC, 607 F.2d 438 (D.C. Cir. 1979), *cert. denied,* 444 U.S. 1013 (1980). The Commission rejected the claim on the ground that "national security" was too broad an issue for fairness consideration. *See id.* at 448-51.

119. Thus, when an NBC documentary addressed the issue of "the overall performance of the private pension system and the need for governmental regulation of all private pension plans" in a manner the FCC deemed unbalanced, the Commission based its conclusion that pension reform was "controversial" on the fact that proposals then before Congress relating to pension reform "were opposed in whole or in part by 'various groups . . . including the National Association of Manufacturers, several labor unions, the Chamber of Commerce of the United States, and the Nixon administration.'" Accuracy in Media, 44 F.C.C.2d 1027, 1034 n.3, 1039 (1973) (quoting the Broadcast Bureau's decision below), *rev'd sub nom.* NBC v. FCC, 516 F.2d 1101, 1141 (D.C. Cir. 1974), *vacated as moot, id.* at 1180, *cert. denied,* 424 U.S. 910 (1976). NBC did not contest this point.

Actually, while the *details* of pension reform were widely disputed at the time, there was greater consensus regarding the *need* for some pension reform. Even those who argued that pension reform shouldn't "throw out the baby with the wash water" agreed that there were "loopholes that need[ed] closing." *NBC,* 516 F.2d at 1145 (quoting transcript of program). Whether one viewed support for pension-law reform as a "controversial" position thus depended in significant part on one's own position on the political spectrum, which in turn defined whose views one took seriously, and whose one relegated to the fringe.

120. *See* Licensee Responsibility to Review Records Before Their Broadcast, 28 F.C.C.2d 409, 415 (1971) (Johnson, Comm'r, dissenting) (describing the FCC as having "repeal[ed] the applicability of the fairness doctrine to this subject"), *aff'd,* Yale Broadcasting Co. v. FCC, 478 F.2d 594 (D.C. Cir.), *cert. denied,* 414 U.S. 914 (1973).

ments of the American population, however, disagreed.[121] More fundamentally, tying fairness to current political debate was inherently subjective. Under ordinary First Amendment philosophy, no one political view is more "fair" than any other. To identify the "fairness" centerline with the status quo was both arbitrary and politically loaded.

The Commission repealed the fairness doctrine in 1987.[122] Any subjectivity introduced by that doctrine into broadcast law is now gone.[123] This raises an ultimate question: is subjectivity a necessary, inherent aspect of public-interest content regulation, or is it merely a chance

---

121. *See, e.g.,* HUNTER S. THOMPSON, FEAR AND LOATHING IN LAS VEGAS (1971); *infra* notes 124-28 and accompanying text.

On another topic, see Polish Am. Congress v. FCC, 520 F.2d 1248, 1251 (7th Cir. 1975) ("Polish jokes" presented no issue under the fairness doctrine because petitioners did not establish "any controversy in this country concerning the intelligence or other qualities of Polish Americans") (quoting the Broadcast Bureau's decision below), *cert. denied,* 424 U.S. 927 (1976). Petitioners sought a fairness ruling, of course, precisely because they believed that a controversy *did* exist—that many Americans saw Poles as stupid, and that broadcasters should not be allowed to present only one side of that story.

122. *See* Syracuse Peace Council, 2 F.C.C.R. 5043 (1987), *aff'd,* 867 F.2d 654 (D.C. Cir. 1989), *cert. denied,* 493 U.S. 1019 (1990).

The Commission had concluded two years earlier that the doctrine "unnecessarily restrict[ed] the journalistic freedom of broadcasters" and "actually inhibit[ed] the presentation of controversial issues of public importance." Fairness Doctrine Obligations of Broadcast Licensees, 102 F.C.C.2d 145, 147 (1985). Broadcasters, it had stated, were inhibited from presenting controversial material because they feared having to defend their "fairness" in expensive and burdensome FCC proceedings. *Id.* at 161-69. Fairness enforcement worked against the expression of controversial views because its principal targets were those presenting programming that complainants, themselves typically in the mainstream of society, "found to be abhorrent or extreme." *Id.* at 189. Fairness enforcement, the agency had said, involved the government in "evaluating the merits of particular viewpoints" and the "reasonableness of . . . selected program formats," *id.* at 189, 191; it created the opportunity for government intimidation of broadcasters on political grounds, *id.* at 193-94.

Relying on those conclusions, the Commission in 1987 declared that the fairness doctrine "violates the First Amendment and contravenes the public interest." Syracuse Peace Council, 2 F.C.C.R. at 5043. It was unconstitutional because it "reduce[d] . . . the public's access to viewpoint diversity," *id.* at 5052, and was unnecessary to achieve viewpoint diversity. The doctrine therefore constituted gratuitous government interference with speech. *Id.*

The D.C. Circuit affirmed. Syracuse Peace Council v. FCC, 867 F.2d 654 (D.C. Cir. 1989), *cert. denied,* 493 U.S. 1019 (1990). Judge Williams, joined by Judge Wald in relevant part, voted to affirm solely on the basis of the agency's "public interest determination . . . without reaching the constitutional issue"; he was "persuaded that the Commission would have found that the fairness doctrine did not serve the public interest even if it had foregone its ruminations on the constitutional issue." *Id.* at 656, 657. While he found no adequate basis for the Commission's insistence that the *net* effect of the fairness doctrine was to reduce the coverage of controversial issues, he nonetheless concluded that the Commission's decision was legitimate; it rested on the permissible factual finding that the fairness doctrine had substantial deterrent effects on the same scale as its expression-generating ones, and on the permissible normative policy judgment that governmentally deterred speech was a greater evil than governmentally coerced speech was a good. *Id.* at 665.

123. For now, anyway. Congress in 1987 passed a bill reinstating the fairness doctrine; President Reagan vetoed it. Veto of the Fairness in Broadcasting Act of 1987, 23 WEEKLY COMP. PRES. DOC. 715 (June 19, 1987). A similar bill is now pending in Congress. *See* Fairness in Broadcasting Act of 1993, H.R. 1985, 103d Cong., 1st Sess. (1993). Its proponents hope that President Clinton will be more supportive.

aspect of doctrines the Commission happens to have set in place? I believe that it is inherent; one more story may help explain why.

The Commission in the early 1970s received a Department of Defense briefing regarding what it characterized as "a subject of current and pressing concern": "lyrics of records played on broadcasting stations . . . tending to promote or glorify the use of illegal drugs as [sic] marijuana, LSD, 'speed,' etc."[124] The agency responded by issuing a public notice explaining that it would contravene licensee "responsibility" for a broadcaster to play a record without "a management level executive . . . knowing the content of the lyrics," making the judgment whether the record "promotes . . . illegal drug usage," and on that basis making a judgment whether playing the records would promote the public interest.[125] The FCC stressed that "when there is an epidemic of illegal drug use—when thousands of young lives are being destroyed . . . — the licensee should not be indifferent to the question of whether his facilities are being used to promote the illegal use of harmful drugs."[126] Such indifference, inconsistent with the broadcaster's duties as a "public trustee . . . who is fully responsible for . . . operation in the public interest," could "jeopardize" a broadcaster's license.[127] The D.C. Circuit

---

124. Licensee Responsibility to Review Records Before Their Broadcast, 28 F.C.C.2d at 409.

125. *Id.* Commissioner Robert E. Lee expressed the "hope that the action of the Commission . . . will discourage, if not eliminate the playing of records which tend to promote and/or glorify the use of illegal drugs. . . . Obviously . . . the licensee will exercise appropriate judgment in determining whether the broadcasting of such records is in the public interest." *Id.* at 410 (Robert E. Lee, Comm'r, concurring). Commissioner Houser expressly agreed. *Id.* at 411 (Houser, Comm'r, concurring). Commissioner Johnson dissented, although taking pains to state that he personally "happen[ed] to believe in getting high on life—the perpetual high without drugs." *Id.* at 415 (Johnson, Comm'r, dissenting).

The Commission's action was taken under the general public-interest standard; the agency never took any action regarding drug use under the fairness doctrine. *See supra* note 120 and accompanying text.

126. Licensee Responsibility to Review Records Before Their Broadcast, 31 F.C.C.2d 377, 378 (1971), *aff'd sub nom.* Yale Broadcasting Co. v. FCC, 478 F.2d 594 (D.C. Cir.), *cert. denied,* 414 U.S. 914 (1973).

127. *Id.* at 379-80. Several weeks after its initial notice, Commission staff provided broadcasters with a list of 22 songs, supplied by the Department of the Army, "brought to the attention of the FCC in connection with the subject of so-called drug-oriented song lyrics." *Id.* at 379 n.5. Notwithstanding Commissioner Johnson's protest that "many of the song lyrics singled out . . . by the . . . Defense Department . . . have nothing whatsoever to do with drugs," Licensee Responsibility to Review Records Before Their Broadcast, 28 F.C.C.2d at 414-15 (Johnson, Comm'r, dissenting), broadcasters circulated the document as a "do not play" list; some apparently dropped the recordings of any artists thought to be pharmaceutically suspect. Yale Broadcasting Co. v. FCC, 478 F.2d 594, 603 (D.C. Cir.) (statement of Bazelon, J., on motion for rehearing *en banc*), *cert. denied,* 414 U.S. 914 (1973).

On reconsideration, the Commission repudiated the list, and emphasized that it was neither barring "a particular type of record" nor threatening to discipline licensees for the decision to play "a particular record." After all, licensees could reasonably reach differing judgments as to whether a particular song in fact promoted drug use, and the agency was not in a position to review such individual judgments. Licensee Responsibility to Review Records Before Their Broadcast, 31 F.C.C.2d at 378.

found no constitutional infirmity in the agency's not-so-veiled threat.[128]

The FCC's public notice, and the D.C. Circuit's decision upholding it, were reviled by First Amendment commentators[129]—and rightly so. Yet the Commission *is* charged with ensuring that broadcasters conduct themselves in the manner best designed to promote the public interest. Under that standard, it is long-settled law that broadcasters, as public trustees, "must assume responsibility for all material . . . broadcast through their facilities."[130] If the "public interest" requirement is to have meaning, it is only natural that broadcast licensees should have to "assume responsibility" as well for the possibility that certain programming might lead some benighted souls into addiction, or worse.[131] It is true that this conflicts with traditional First Amendment philosophy, under which the government's ideas about whether certain speech promotes the public interest are almost always irrelevant.[132] The Commission's grapplings with the counterculture, though, suggest that the source of that conflict is not individual FCC decisions, but the entire enterprise of "public interest" regulation of speech.

C. Public-Interest Licensing and Free Speech Philosophy

1. The Essential Conflict

It is easy to criticize our broadcast regulatory system. The whole licensee selection process is somewhat silly: whichever person the FCC selects for the license can sell out to a third party shortly afterwards, and the Commission may not block that transaction on the ground that the transferee seems less qualified than the applicants it had recently turned down.[133] In addition, television's organization around local licensees now seems quaint. Most citizens receive their TV news and entertainment programming primarily from *nationally*-based, unlicensed networks and cable programmers, largely without regard to the identity of local broadcast licensees. The identity of local broadcast licensees may

---

128. *Yale Broadcasting Co.*, 478 F.2d at 597-99.

129. *See, e.g.*, POWE, *supra* note 8, at 176-82.

130. Commission En Banc Programming Inquiry (1960), *reprinted in* DOCUMENTS OF AMERICAN BROADCASTING, *supra* note 106, at 191, 199.

131. Indeed, the D.C. Circuit concluded on review, "for the Commission to have been less insistent on licensees discharging their obligations would have verged on an evasion of the Commission's own responsibilities." *Yale Broadcasting Co.*, 478 F.2d at 599.

132. *See supra* notes 43-45 and accompanying text.

133. *See* 47 U.S.C. § 310(d) (1988) (forbidding the Commission, in considering an application for license transfer, to "consider whether the public interest, convenience, and necessity might be served by the transfer . . . of the . . . license to a person other than the proposed transferee"); *see also* Policy Statement on Comparative Broadcast Hearings, 1 F.C.C.2d 393, 405-06 (1965) (Lee, Comm'r, concurring) (arguing that a system in which the Commission's "tortuous and expensive hearing" can be followed by a sale to an entity to whom the FCC would not have awarded the license in the comparative proceeding is one "hell of a way to run a railroad"). *But see supra* text accompanying note 84 (setting out a Commission proposal to grant a preference to applicants who promise not to sell or transfer the station for at least three years).

well help determine the amount and nature of purely local news and public-affairs programming, but that programming seems almost peripheral to the larger world of TV broadcasting.[134]

The characteristic of our broadcast regulatory system relevant to this Article, though, is more basic and should by now be fairly obvious: it is that the system conflicts in almost every respect, and gratuitously so, with conventional freedom-of-speech philosophy. When viewed against the backdrop set out earlier in this Article, the broadcast regulatory system seems nothing short of astonishing. Under ordinary First Amendment philosophy, the decision whether speakers or speech advance the "public interest" is not one for government; government is specifically disabled from making that choice. The government may not impose content restrictions simply to advance its own notions of the public interest, and it surely may not make licensing decisions based on content. Any licensing requirement that the government does impose must incorporate "narrow, objective, and definite standards."[135] Because any such scheme unacceptably threatens censorship and suppression of particular points of view, no licensing scheme can involve "appraisal of facts, the exercise of judgment, and the formation of an opinion . . . by the licensing authority."[136] Such criteria threaten "illegitimate abuse of censorial power,"[137] and encourage self-censorship. Most "threatening" are periodic licensing requirements, which ensure that speakers are "under no illusion regarding the effect of the 'licensed' speech on the ability to continue speaking in the future."[138]

The FCC, by contrast, grants licenses, decides whether those licenses will be renewed, and decides what licensees will be permitted to say, on the basis of a vague "public interest" standard. The agency has not been successful at importing objective content into that criterion. Its licensing decisions are necessarily arbitrary; because they are neither consistent nor easily predictable, they present the opportunity for political bias and are not easily susceptible of useful review. The FCC has explicitly evaluated broadcasters and would-be broadcasters based on the content of their speech, proposed and past. This process has been unavoidable, given a statutory scheme in which the crux of the renewal decision is whether the licensee's programming has served the public

---

134. The approach may have made more sense in an earlier world in which the primary sources of television news and public affairs programming were local rather than national. It was not until the 1960s that the networks extended their flagship news shows from 15 to 30 minutes. Alfred C. Sikes, Remarks on Broadcast Journalism and the Public Interest at the Alfred I. DuPont-Columbia University Awards Ceremony (Jan. 16, 1990), *in* 1990 FCC LEXIS 388.

135. Forsyth County v. Nationalist Movement, 112 S. Ct. 2395, 2401 (1992) (quoting Shuttlesworth v. Birmingham, 394 U.S. 147, 150-51 (1969)).

136. *Id.* at 2401-02 (citation omitted) (quoting Cantwell v. Connecticut, 310 U.S. 296, 305 (1940)).

137. City of Lakewood v. Plain Dealer Publishing Co., 486 U.S. 750, 758 (1988).

138. *Id.* at 759-60.

interest.[139] That scrutiny too, though, has been subjective and highly discretionary.[140]

The broadcast regulatory system, in short, violates all of the rules; it is in sharp conflict with ordinary First Amendment law. To give government the discretionary power to decide who can speak and who cannot, based on what the speakers have already said or propose to say, gives it wholly unacceptable influence over the thought processes of the community. To erect a body of mass communications law under which the government grants some persons, but not others, a "license" to speak, makes it a crime to speak without a license, adopts no neutral or objective standards to govern who will get a license and who will not, considers the content of proposed speech in making the licensing choice, reviews periodically whether it will take away the rights of current licensees, reserves the authority to consider licensees' past speech in making *that* choice, all in the name of encouraging that speech that best serves the "public interest," seems just about as far from the law demanded by conventional freedom-of-speech philosophy as it is possible to get.

2. *The* Red Lion *Rationale*

How can we possibly fit government licensing of broadcasters into the First Amendment model? The traditional explanation for our broadcast regulatory system, adopted by the Supreme Court without dissent in *Red Lion Broadcasting Co. v. FCC,*[141] is that "there are substantially more individuals who want to broadcast than there are frequencies to allocate." In consequence,

it is idle to posit an unabridgeable First Amendment right to

---

139. *See supra* text accompanying notes 103-04.

140. Robert Post has suggested that because the FCC is making judgments based on community standards, its decisionmaking should not be dismissed as subjective; rather, it is intersubjective. The agency is making its determinations not as a matter of mere personal whim, but as a matter of community values. As a result, while those decisions may be controversial, they should not be classed as arbitrary. *See* Robert C. Post, *The Constitutional Concept of Public Discourse: Outrageous Opinion, Democratic Deliberation, and* Hustler Magazine v. Falwell, 103 HARV. L. REV. 601, 624-26 (1990) (discussing Hustler Magazine v. Falwell, 485 U.S. 46 (1988)).

Ordinary First Amendment doctrine, however, typically has treated such decisionmaking as still too dangerous for speech regulation. *Hustler,* thus, exemplifies the Court's usual approach; the Court there found an "outrageousness" standard too uncertain to support the imposition of damages. 485 U.S. at 55. While the determination of obscenity under Miller v. California, 413 U.S. 15 (1973), is indeed dependent in part on community standards, that approach is the exception rather than the rule.

141. 395 U.S. 367 (1969). The Court in *Red Lion* was called upon to decide the validity of a Commission rule requiring broadcasters to offer "a reasonable opportunity to respond" when, "during the [broadcaster's] presentation of views on a controversial issue of public importance, an attack is made on the honesty, character, integrity or like personal qualities of an identified person or group." *Id.* at 373-74 (quoting the then-current version of 47 C.F.R. § 73). The Court upheld the constitutionality and statutory basis of the rule, its specific application in the case before the Court, and the larger "fairness doctrine" from which it had been derived. *See id.* at 375-401. Justice Douglas did not participate. *See id.* at 401.

broadcast comparable to the right of every individual to speak, write, or publish. If 100 persons want broadcast licenses but there are only 10 frequencies to allocate, all of them may have the same "right" to a license; but if there is to be any effective communication by radio, only a few can be licensed and the rest must be barred from the airways.[142]

The need to avoid interference on the airwaves thus calls for a government agency to limit the number of broadcast speakers, and to patrol them to make sure they stay on their assigned frequencies. Further, because the selected licensees have no right to their licenses, the government can require them to speak on behalf of the larger excluded community, acting as trustees or fiduciaries for the "public":

> [A]s far as the First Amendment is concerned those who are licensed stand no better than those to whom licenses are refused. A license permits broadcasting, but the licensee has no constitutional right to be the one who holds the license or to monopolize a radio frequency to the exclusion of his fellow citizens. . . . [T]he Government [may] requir[e] a licensee . . . to conduct himself as a proxy or fiduciary with obligations to present those views and voices which are representative of his community and which would otherwise, by necessity, be barred from the airwaves.[143]

Any other result, the Court warned, might limit access to the means of broadcast communications to a few persons or corporations; that could lead to the "monopolization" of broadcast discourse by a few private licensees, ending any possibility of "an uninhibited marketplace of ideas in which truth will ultimately prevail."[144]

The reasoning set out in *Red Lion*, unfortunately, does not resolve the conflict I have identified. The *Red Lion* rationale requires two logical steps. The first is that the physical fact of broadcast frequency interference necessitates administrative allocation of broadcast rights; the second is that that administrative allocation should take the form of public-interest licensing. Much attention has been given recently to attacks on the first step of this reasoning. As Ronald Coase argued more than forty years ago, the mere fact that 100 persons cannot, using a particular piece of frequency spectrum, all broadcast at power levels of their choosing, does not prove that we need an *administrative agency* to exclude some of them. We might instead use a property-rights system, under which the right to use spectrum is bought and sold like any other resource.[145]

---

142. *Id.* at 388-89.

143. *Id.* at 389.

144. *Id.* at 390.

145. *See* Coase, *supra* note 16, at 25-35; *see also* BOLLINGER, *supra* note 11, at 87-90 (discussing and criticizing broadcast regulation in light of Coase's analysis); SPITZER, *supra* note 8, at 9-27 (same); Harry Kalven, Jr., *Broadcasting, Public Policy and the First Amendment*, 10 J.L. & ECON.

Government would enforce those property rights through the courts, and the system could work, after a fashion, without the need for any administrative mechanism.[146]

I want to focus attention, though, on the *second* step of the traditional rationale: assuming that one concedes the value or usefulness of some form of administrative allocation of broadcast rights, it by no means follows that we therefore must adopt *public-interest licensing.*[147] Almost none of the conflict I have described between conventional First Amendment philosophy and our system of broadcast regulation derives from administrative allocation of broadcast rights as such; it derives, rather, from the peculiar nature of the licensing system we have adopted, which gives the government great discretion over the identity of licensees and the content of their speech.[148]

That discretion is surely not inevitable. Nothing in the nature of administrative allocation requires that the government have the sort of control over the identity of broadcast speakers, and the content of their speech, that our current system gives it. Comparative issues could be resolved by lottery, auction, or other means; there is no need for the government to undertake intrusive inquiry once a license is awarded. From the perspective of conventional free-speech philosophy, the discretionary power that our current system gives the government over speech is simply gratuitous.[149]

15, 30-32 (1967) (same); William W. Van Alstyne, *The Möbius Strip of the First Amendment: Perspectives on* Red Lion, 29 S.C. L. Rev. 539, 553-58 (1978) (same).

> The interference problem is widely recognized as one of defining separate frequency "properties"; it is logically unconnected to the issue of who is to harvest those frequencies. To confuse the *definition* of spectrum rights with the *assignment* of spectrum rights is to believe that, to keep intruders out of (private) backyards, the government must own (or allocate) all the houses.

Hazlett, *supra* note 8, at 138.

146. *But see* Weinberg, *supra* note 17, at 1274-77 (expressing doubt whether a pure market-based system would function efficiently).

147. *See* Kalven, *supra* note 145, at 37-38; *see also* Matthew L. Spitzer, *The Constitutionality of Licensing Broadcasters,* 64 N.Y.U. L. Rev. 990, 1058-59, 1062-66 (1989) (describing a broadcast regulation system in which an administrative body allocates broadcast rights but has no content regulatory role).

148. Take the town meeting which is often thought of as a model of free speech in operation. If the Chairman is keeping order he has problems somewhat like those of broadcasting. Not everyone can talk at once nor can they talk too long since time is scarce nor can they talk far off the point. *The speakers are in effect "licensed" by the chairman,* yet no one has ever said that this spoiled the game. What is understood by us all here is an implicit standard limiting the chairman to [viewpoint-neutral] regulation.

Kalven, *supra* note 145, at 47-48 (footnote omitted); *see also* Cox v. New Hampshire, 312 U.S. 569, 575-76 (1941) (upholding as constitutional a state parade licensing scheme requiring the licensing board to limit itself to content-neutral "considerations of time, place and manner" relating to "the convenience of public use of the highways").

149. This is not to say that the government need not have *some* policy role; any administrative allocation plan will necessarily require the government to make public-policy choices. A regulatory agency must address such questions as where to place each service (such as FM radio, UHF television, and land mobile radio) on the frequency band; how wide a portion of the frequency band

I am not seeking here to argue that the United States should have adopted any particular allocation scheme for broadcasting, whether administrative or market-based.[150] My point, rather, is the philosophical incompatibility of public-interest licensing with the ordinary rules: given what I have described as the vagueness, unpredictability, subjectivity, and content control inherent in our public-interest licensing system, one cannot accept that system without suspending ordinary First Amendment thinking in favor of a different, and inconsistent, philosophy.[151]

Nor can public-interest licensing be reconciled with conventional free-speech philosophy on the basis of *Red Lion*'s concern that public-interest licensing is necessary, in light of the scarcity of spectrum, to avoid an undesirably concentrated marketplace of ideas controlled by the wealthy. Allocating licenses through lotteries would serve that end at least as well; it is by no means clear why we should substitute a system involving profound government discretion over speech. (Indeed, it is doubtful that public-interest licensing *does* much serve the end of avoid-

---

to allocate to each service; how to distribute stations geographically; how much spectrum to allot to each station; and how much power and antenna height to allow each station. Weinberg, *supra* note 40, at 642 n.112.

AM radio allocation in this country, thus, was premised in part on the Federal Radio Commission's General Order 40, which structured the broadcast system by prescribing the power levels available to stations on each frequency, and hence the number of stations that could be accommodated on each frequency, and how far their signals would reach. *See* 1928 F.R.C. ANN. REP. 48 (as found in Supplemental Report for Period from July 1, 1928 to September 30, 1928); Weinberg, *supra* note 40, at 648. That allocation turned out to be flawed: the combination of General Order 40 with early allocation decisions favoring urban applicants and the first-come-first-served approach the FCC relied on after 1939, *see id.* at 653-54, ended up to some extent depriving rural areas of service. *See id.* at 654.

In licensing television stations, the FCC took a completely different tack, promulgating a Table of Assignments that filled up the frequency band by assigning at least one channel to each of 1,274 different communities. In so doing, the Commission again made policy judgments regarding where broadcast licenses should be located, whether to favor large or small communities, and so on. That plan was also flawed. It limited the number of signals available in the major markets because of the Commission's insistence on assigning many small communities their own television stations (which sometimes turned out not to be economically viable) rather than serving those communities through powerful metropolitan stations. *See id.* at 654-55 & 654 n.169; *see also* Robinson, *supra* note 76, at 259-61 (deploring the industry structure produced by the Commission's "misdirected and ineffectual" regulation). The crucial point, though, is that while the government in an administrative allocation scheme has the power to make important policy choices shaping the broadcast structure, it need have no discretionary power over the identity of particular licensees or the content of their speech.

150. For argument that any administrative allocation system would be inferior to a market-based plan, see Spitzer, *supra* note 147, at 1062-65.

151. *See* BOLLINGER, *supra* note 11, at 71-73; *see also* Owen M. Fiss, *Free Speech and Social Structure,* 71 IOWA L. REV. 1405, 1416 (1986); Kalven, *supra* note 145, at 15-18; Van Alstyne, *supra* note 145, at 574. *But see* Omega Satellite Prod. Co. v. City of Indianapolis, 694 F.2d 119, 128-29 (7th Cir. 1982) (cable franchising procedures that were assertedly "political," "devoid of standards," and "create[d] the potential for denying a franchise on invidious grounds" could nonetheless be constitutional; "it is a fair question how far the courts should go in making municipalities rewrite their cable television ordinances to prevent dangers that may be largely hypothetical.").

ing domination by the wealthy, since licenses—once awarded—can be freely sold in the marketplace to the highest bidder.[152]) In short, our broadcast regulatory scheme, emphasizing the government's broad discretion in protecting the citizenry from the media and from concentrations of private wealth, may well be justifiable on its own terms, but it cannot be reconciled with the ideology we apply in other free-speech contexts.[153]

How—and why—did we come to adopt an approach so inconsistent with our ordinary philosophy? A variety of commentators have addressed this question;[154] I will not repeat all of their answers here.[155]

---

152. *See Weinberg, supra* note 40, at 617 n.3; *supra* note 133 and accompanying text. Distributing the right to a commodity on an egalitarian basis but allowing that right to be freely transferred on the market is unlikely to produce an ultimate distribution much different from that which the market would have produced in the first instance. *See* James Tobin, *On Limiting the Domain of Inequality,* 13 J.L. & ECON. 263, 268 (1970). Congress could end the free marketplace in already-awarded licenses by repealing the last sentence of 47 U.S.C. § 310(d), but public-interest licensing would remain a gratuitously intrusive way of avoiding market distortions.

Moreover, if one accepts the notion that the ordinary First Amendment rules should be suspended for broadcasting, because too few persons can participate in broadcasting to generate a working marketplace of ideas, it is difficult to avoid reaching the same conclusion with regard to the print media. Print markets, like broadcast markets, are neither well-populated nor competitive. *See* BOLLINGER, *supra* note 11, at 94. The Supreme Court has declared those facts regarding print markets to be legally irrelevant. *See* Miami Herald Publishing Co. v. Tornillo, 418 U.S. 241, 254 (1974). There is no obvious reason why the scarcity analysis should not be the same for broadcast. Indeed, the argument can surely be made that print outlets are *more* scarce than broadcast outlets. While all but 4% of the public have access to five or more television stations, *see* Syracuse Peace Council, 2 F.C.C.R. 5043, 5054 (1987), *aff'd,* 867 F.2d 654 (D.C. Cir. 1989), *cert. denied,* 493 U.S. 1019 (1990), remarkably few members of the public have access to more than one local daily newspaper, *see id.* ("[O]nly 125 cities have two or more local newspapers."); C. Edwin Baker, *Advertising and a Democratic Press,* 140 U. PA. L. REV. 2097, 2115 (1992) (reporting that in 1986, only 28 cities had separately owned and operated daily newspapers). *But see* Spitzer, *supra* note 147, at 1018 (arguing that neither print nor broadcast is inherently more scarce).

In any event, it is by no means apparent why broadcasting should be regarded as a "marketplace" of its own at all, separate from all other forms of speech, rather than as simply part of a larger marketplace of ideas also encompassing other forms of media. *See* Fairness Doctrine Obligations of Broadcast Licensees, 102 F.C.C.2d 145, 198-202 (1985) (treating traditional broadcast services, new electronic media and print as all part of a larger information services marketplace); L.A. Powe, Jr., *"Or of the [Broadcast] Press,"* 55 TEX. L. REV. 39, 55-56 (1976).

153. Our regulation of cable television further demonstrates the conflict; the regulatory scheme is today finding itself vulnerable to attack on traditional freedom-of-speech grounds precisely to the extent that it has adopted features, such as monopoly franchising and access regulation, typical of public-interest licensing. *See, e.g.,* Preferred Communications, Inc. v. City of Los Angeles, 754 F.2d 1396, 1403-04 (9th Cir. 1985) (refusing to apply broadcast regulation precedents to justify regulation of cable), *aff'd on narrower grounds,* 476 U.S. 488 (1986); Century Fed., Inc. v. City of Palo Alto, 648 F. Supp. 1465, 1470-75 (N.D. Cal. 1986).

154. *See, e.g.,* POOL, *supra* note 15, at 108-29, 136-38; *see also* Hazlett, *supra* note 8; Jora R. Minasian, *The Political Economy of Broadcasting in the 1920s,* 12 J.L. & ECON. 391 (1969) (discussing the history of broadcast regulation).

155. William Mayton has argued that Congress, in passing the Communications Act of 1934, never intended the FCC to have more than modest "traffic cop" powers relating to the assignment of wavelengths and power levels and the control of interference. *See* Mayton, *supra* note 8, at 728-39, 750-54. Professor Mayton's argument is useful but overstated. Congress, in setting out the public-interest standard for licensing in the Radio Act of 1927, may well have had the "traffic cop" role

The most important explanation begins from the fact that our early broadcast law was written *before* the development of contemporary freedom of speech law. The Radio Act was passed in 1927; the Communications Act in 1934. Modern First Amendment philosophy, well-established as it is now, did not begin to take shape until about the same time.[156] *Near v. Minnesota,*[157] one of the first cases in which the Supreme Court ruled in favor of a First Amendment claim,[158] was not decided until 1931, four years after the passage of the Radio Act. When the Radio and Communications Acts were enacted, what we now think of as ordinary First Amendment philosophy was still in embryonic form. The case that Lee Bollinger has termed "the fullest, richest articulation of the central image of freedom of the press"[159]—*New York Times Co. v.*

---

primarily in mind. All influential parties agreed from the start, though, that choosing licensees would require more subjective attention to the public interest; Secretary Hoover referred to licensee selection as "a very large discretionary or a semi-judicial function." *See generally* 1 HARRY P. WARNER, RADIO AND TELEVISION LAW § 92, at 770-71 (1949) (quoting Fourth National Radio Conference 8 (1926)).

As the Federal Radio Commission went about the business of broadcast regulation between 1927 and 1934, it asserted a variety of extensive powers well beyond the "traffic cop" model, basing decisions on the content of applicants' speech. *See, e.g.,* Trinity Methodist Church v. Federal Radio Comm'n, 62 F.2d 850 (D.C. Cir. 1932) (affirming FRC denial of license renewal to a broadcaster who attacked local government officials, the bar association, organized labor, and religious groups), *cert. denied,* 288 U.S. 599 (1933); KFKB Broadcasting Ass'n v. FRC, 47 F.2d 670 (D.C. Cir. 1931) (affirming FRC denial of license renewal to a broadcaster who used his station to prescribe medicines he sold). *See generally* POOL, *supra* note 15, at 122-29. Congress was aware of those facts in 1934, and yet carried over the Radio Act's "public interest" language into the Communications Act. *See* Kalven, *supra* note 145, at 25.

In any event, Professor Mayton focuses his argument on FCC powers *outside* of the comparative arena. Congress in 1934, though, plainly intended the FCC to make a judgment somehow in comparative licensing cases, and one would be hard-pressed to argue, in light of contemporary administrative practice, that Congress saw the agency as making those judgments via lotteries or auctions. The congressional scheme thus called upon the FCC to make policy judgments in comparative cases of the sort ultimately codified in the Policy Statement on Comparative Broadcast Hearings, 1 F.C.C.2d 393 (1965). And if Congress intended the FCC to deny licenses in comparative cases based on such extrastatutory considerations, it is not a powerful argument (nor was it the law under the Radio Act) that the agency should be disabled from making similar policy judgments in noncomparative contexts. Under such a regime, any broadcaster, initially unchallenged, not conforming to the FCC's policies for comparative cases would simply lose its license at the first challenge.

156. *See* MARK A. GRABER, TRANSFORMING FREE SPEECH 4 (1991).

157. 283 U.S. 697 (1931).

158. In Fiske v. Kansas, 274 U.S. 380 (1927), a case with clear First Amendment shadings, the Court had reversed a conviction of an International Workers of the World organizer under the Kansas Criminal Syndicalism Act, on the ground that the sole evidence presented by the state—a copy of the IWW constitution—insufficiently demonstrated that the IWW advocated criminal syndicalism within the meaning of the statute. In Stromberg v. California, 283 U.S. 359, 361 (1931), the Court struck down as vague a state statute prohibiting the public display of a "red flag . . . or device of any color or form" as a "sigu, symbol, or emblem of opposition to organized government." The Court found the statute unclear as to whether it would preclude "peaceful and orderly opposition to government by legal means." *Id.* at 369.

159. BOLLINGER, *supra* note 11, at 2.

Sullivan [160]—would not be decided until 1964. That the drafters of those statutes were not sensitive to later constitutional developments should not be surprising.

On the other hand, it *is* surprising that we paid so little attention to the conflict in the years that followed. The most important First Amendment theorists of this century, including Alexander Meiklejohn and Thomas Emerson, supported public-interest licensing.[161] The opinion in *Red Lion,* upholding public-interest licensing, was approved by all participating members of the Court, including First Amendment "absolutist"[162] Justice Black.[163] Public-interest licensing is still the law of the land, sixty-four years after the Radio Act was enacted. The ACLU, whose very mission is the protection of constitutional rights, maintains its support for the fairness doctrine.[164] If the situation were merely that Congress innocently established in the 1920s and 1930s a system that later turned out to be problematic under contemporary constitutional law, one would think that we would have done something about it by now.

The problem, I believe, is a deeper one. My analysis so far has assumed the completeness and correctness of ordinary freedom-of-speech thinking. The continuing strength of public-interest licensing, however, derives from the fact that ordinary First Amendment philosophy is itself problematic. Broadcast law, I will argue, reflects concerns about the dangers posed by concentrations of private media power, and the degree to which private institutional and economic power can skew the reasoning process of the community. These concerns, which find no place in First Amendment philosophy, are nonetheless real and legitimate. To appreciate this point, it is useful to go back and look at freedom-of-speech law more generally.

II
The Free Speech Tradition Reexamined

In this section of my discussion, I will examine American freedom-of-speech philosophy primarily by focusing on the central image of the "marketplace of ideas." I will first make the argument that the marketplace image is indeed central: it is both historically and doctrinally at the heart of modern First Amendment philosophy. I will next argue that the metaphor is flawed and that those flaws matter. The marketplace meta-

---

160. 376 U.S. 254 (1964).

161. *See* sources cited in Bollinger, *supra* note 11, at 91.

162. *See* Edmond Cahn, *Justice Black and First Amendment "Absolutes": A Public Interview,* 37 N.Y.U. L. Rev. 549, 552-54 (1962).

163. There were, however, dissenting voices among prominent scholars: the losing briefs in *Red Lion* were signed by, among others, Harry Kalven, Herbert Wechsler, and Archibald Cox. *See* Fiss, *supra* note 151, at 1416 & n.28.

164. *See* Norman Dorsen, *Talking Liberties,* Civ. Liberties, Winter 1990-91, at 16.

phor's instrumental vision is that free discussion can best be achieved when government plays no role in the marketplace of ideas (other than the enforcement of property rights in communications resources, and other common-law support for private ordering). Two descriptive premises are implicit in that vision. The first is that enough members of society, in the absence of an active government role, have a meaningful opportunity to speak and to convince others of their views. The second is that our discourse is essentially rational: that people process speech for the most part on a rational level, and choose to adopt one belief rather than another as a result of this reasoning process. Neither of these premises, though, seems true.

The image of the "marketplace of ideas" has played a crucial role in free-speech thinking.[165] Milton, as far back as the seventeenth century, supported his argument against government licensing of speech by invoking the image of truth and falsehood grappling in "free and open encounter." In such a conflict, he asked, "who ever knew Truth put to the wors[t]"?[166] John Stuart Mill articulated the philosophy at length two centuries later.[167] Still later, Justice Holmes conjured up the vision in classic words:

> [W]hen men have realized that time has upset many fighting faiths, they may come to believe even more than they believe the very foundations of their own conduct that the ultimate good desired is better reached by free trade in ideas—that the best test of truth is the power of the thought to get itself accepted in the competition of the market, and that truth is the only ground upon which their wishes safely can be carried out.[168]

The metaphor began to play a major role in American thought after our 1930s rejection of *Lochner*[169] and acceptance of a new judicial phi-

---

165. *See* BAKER, *supra* note 33, at 12 (marketplace theory "dominates [First Amendment thinking] both rhetorically and conceptually"); FREDERICK SCHAUER, FREE SPEECH: A PHILOSOPHICAL ENQUIRY 15 (1982) (the argument that free speech is valuable because it leads to the discovery of truth is "the predominant and most persevering" of all arguments historically employed to justify the free speech principle).

166. JOHN MILTON, AREOPAGITICA (1644), *reprinted in* IV THE WORKS OF JOHN MILTON 293, 347 (Frank A. Patterson et al. eds., 1931).

167. *See* MILL, *supra* note 26, at 19-67.

168. Abrams v. United States, 250 U.S. 616, 630 (1919) (Holmes, J., dissenting). American courts, indeed, have invoked that theme regardless of whether they were upholding or rejecting the free speech claim. *See, e.g.,* Dennis v. United States, 341 U.S. 494, 503 (1951) (stating that "speech can rebut speech, propaganda will answer propaganda, free debate of ideas will result in the wisest government policies," yet upholding convictions of Communist Party leaders); *id.* at 550 (Frankfurter, J., concurring) ("The history of civilization is in considerable measure the displacement of error which once held sway as official truth by beliefs which in turn have yielded to other truths.").

169. Lochner v. New York, 198 U.S. 45 (1905), *overruled by* Day-Bright Lighting, Inc. v. Missouri, 342 U.S. 421 (1952).

losophy hostile to the idea of natural, inherent individual rights.[170] Under progressive views of the judicial role in the early-twentieth century, individual "rights" had value only to the extent that they advanced societal goals in a particular historical context; the legislature was to decide the degree to which recognizing a particular individual claim would benefit society as a whole.[171] This presented a problem for those who would grant judicial protection for free speech rights. On what theory could the courts overrule a legislative determination that the value of punishing certain speech exceeded the value of protecting it?

The solution, advanced by Zechariah Chafee (among others), was that judges should protect speech because of its role as the basis of democratic society, rather than as a discredited natural right.[172] Free speech not only promoted the societal interest in "the attainment and spread of truth . . . as the basis of political and social progress,"[173] but also supported the democratic process, whose results the judges were bound to

---

170. Courts in the late-nineteenth and early-twentieth centuries had commonly seen free speech claims as presenting no issues substantially different from those posed by economic regulation. *See, e.g., In re* Garrabad, 54 N.W. 1104, 1107 (Wis. 1893) (describing the issue raised by a parade permit ordinance as substantially identical to that posed by Yick Wo v. Hopkins, 118 U.S. 356 (1886), because both cases concerned arbitrary executive control over the exercise of a protected right—in the one case parading in the streets and in the other engaging in the laundry business); *see also* Rich v. City of Naperville, 42 Ill. App. 222, 223-24 (1891) (parade permit); Frazee's Case, 403, 30 N.W. 72, 74 (Mich. 1886) (same). Prior to the *Lochner* era, thus, state courts commonly rejected speech claims on the ground that free speech was a "condition[] of civil liberty" subject to regulation under the police power like any other. State v. McKee, 46 A. 409, 413-14 (Conn. 1900); *see, e.g.,* Commonwealth v. Abrahams, 30 N.E. 79, 79 (Mass. 1892) (upholding regulation of public speech, relying in part on Quincy v. Kennard, 24 N.E. 860 (Mass. 1890), a case upholding the city's power to regulate the raising of swine).

The *Lochner* era offered free speech claimants an avenue to expanded legal protection. The petitioner in Gitlow v. New York, 268 U.S. 652 (1925), thus, emphasized that he was not merely raising a free speech claim; he invoked the spirit of *Lochner* by arguing that the legislature had abridged a liberty interest protected by the due process clause. *See* Jonathan Weinberg, *Gitlow v. New York* and "The Fundamental Personal Rights and 'Liberties' Protected by the Due Process Clause of the Fourteenth Amendment" 17-18 (April 1983) (unpublished manuscript, on file with author). The Supreme Court accepted that characterization of the issue. *Gitlow,* 268 U.S. at 664. In Whitney v. California, 274 U.S. 357, 372 (1927), the Court framed the free speech question before it in terms of whether the state statute was "an unreasonable or arbitrary exercise of the police power of the State." Justice Brandeis, arguing in favor of expansive free speech protection in that case, at one point found himself relying on five cases nullifying economic regulation in which he had dissented:

> Prohibitory legislation has repeatedly been held invalid . . . where the denial of liberty involved was that of engaging in a particular business. The power of the courts to strike down an offending law is no less when the interests involved are not property rights, but the fundamental personal rights of free speech and assembly.

Id. at 374 (Brandeis, J., concurring) (footnote omitted). After the demise of *Lochner,* this argument was no longer available.

171. *See generally* GRABER, *supra* note 156, at 69-74 (describing Roscoe Pound's "sociological jurisprudence").

172. *See id.* at 122-59 (chronicling Chafee's contributions to constitutional free speech doctrine).

173. ZECHARIAH CHAFEE JR., FREE SPEECH IN THE UNITED STATES 137 (1941).

respect.[174] The idea that free speech would guarantee a working democratic process made acceptable the courts' withdrawal from the task of protecting individual economic rights.[175] The marketplace metaphor underlay this vision of free speech as valuable because of its role in promoting both the attainment of truth and democratic self-government.

Since that time, the marketplace metaphor has served as the basis for essential First Amendment doctrine.[176] Its faith in the ultimate functioning of the communicative process, for example, is at the heart of Justice Brandeis' injunction that "[i]f there be time to expose through discussion the falsehood and fallacies, to avert the evil by the processes of education, the [proper response to subversive advocacy] is more speech, not enforced silence."[177] The marketplace metaphor is pivotal in our thought.[178] It is not the only vision that has played a role in modern free speech protection; modern First Amendment philosophers have constructed impressive and well-accepted arguments that free speech should be protected because it advances goals connected to individual autonomy, self-realization, and human dignity.[179] These arguments too, how-

---

174. *See id.* at 361.

175. *See id.;* J.M. Balkin, *Some Realism About Pluralism: Legal Realist Approaches to the First Amendment,* 1990 DUKE L.J. 375, 390-92.

176. The exact phrase did not appear in a Supreme Court opinion until Lamont v. Postmaster General, 381 U.S. 301, 308 (1965) (Brennan, J., concurring). For a survey of the development of the metaphor, see David Cole, *Agon at Agora: Creative Misreadings in the First Amendment Tradition,* 95 YALE L.J. 857, 875-904 (1986).

The selection of the "marketplace" as the ruling metaphor here is in one respect curious: it is used to support government withdrawal from the "market for ideas" notwithstanding our nearly complete acceptance of vigorous government involvement in the "market for goods." One commentator has called this incongruity "really quite extraordinary." R.H. Coase, *The Market for Goods and the Market for Ideas,* PAPERS & PROCS. OF THE 86TH ANN. MEETING OF THE AM. ECON. ASS'N 384, 386 (1974); *see also* Aaron Director, *The Parity of the Economic Market Place,* 7 J.L. & ECON. 1 (1964).

177. Whitney v. California, 274 U.S. 357, 377 (1927) (Brandeis, J., concurring). Language can be found iu Justice Brandeis' brilliant concurrence supporting just about every modern theory of the First Amendment. Advoeates of the First Amendment as a path to individual self-fulfillment, thus, can note Brandeis' approving statement that "[t]hose who won our independence believed that the final end of the State was to make men free to develop their faculties"; they "valued liberty both as an end and as a means." *Id.* at 375. Advocates of a "safety valve" theory of the First Amendment can cite Brandeis' exhortation that the Framers knew "that order cannot be secured merely through fear . . . ; that it is hazardous to discourage thought, hope and imagination; that fear breeds repression; that repression breeds hate; that hate menaces stable government; that the path of safety lies in the opportunity to discuss freely supposed grievances and proposed remedies." *Id.* The basic idea that free speech promotes truth and provides its own inoculation against "noxious doctrine," *id.,* however, seems to me particularly central to the opinion.

178. *See generally* BAKER, *supra* note 33, at 7-12 (discussing the central role of marketplace theory in the Court's development of First Amendment law).

179. *See, e.g., id.;* Thomas I. Emerson, *Toward a General Theory of the First Amendment,* 72 YALE L.J. 877, 879-81 (1963) (discussing "self-fulfillment"); Martin H. Redish, *The Value of Free Speech,* 130 U. PA. L. REV. 591, 593 (1982) (arguing that the "true value" of free speech is "individual self-realization"). *See generally* Kent Greenawalt, *Free Speech Justifications,* 89 COLUM. L. REV. 119 (1989) (categorizing consequentialist and nonconsequentialist justifications for a free-speech principle). In addition, while free speech justifications that focus on the role of speech in a

ever, often rely on the core premises of the marketplace metaphor.[180]

The idea that the value of free speech lies in its advancement of such goals as the discovery of truth and democratic self-government is sufficiently at the core of our First Amendment philosophy that it would be troubling to find it seriously flawed.[181] Nonetheless, it is flawed. Others have made this argument before,[182] but the point is usually treated as of little practical relevance. Proof of the weakness of the marketplace metaphor is seen as "an insight more fundamental than we can use."[183] I think, though, that the flaws in the marketplace metaphor are both real and important. In order to examine them, I will discuss the metaphor more closely.

The marketplace metaphor is central to a wide range of First Amendment philosophies. Scholars see the marketplace as important because it yields truth, which is in turn seen as intrinsically or instrumentally valuable.[184] They see it as important because it yields information and ideas useful to the process of democratic self-government;[185] they see it as itself a part of self-government.[186] All of these approaches, though,

---

political democracy in large part present special cases of the truth discovery argument, *see* Greenawalt, *supra* at 145-46, some of those arguments seem independent of the marketplace metaphor. *See* BAKER, *supra* note 33, at 28-30; SCHAUER, *supra* note 165, at 35-46. In particular, Robert Post's focus on public discourse as a necessary constituent of self-determination, and thus democracy, does not require the marketplace metaphor. *See* Robert Post, *Meiklejohn's Mistake: Individual Autonomy and the Reform of Public Discourse,* 64 U. COLO. L. REV. 1109 (1993); Post, *supra* note 35, at 279-83. For Post, an empirical challenge to the factual basis of the marketplace metaphor is almost always irrelevant. The concept of individual autonomy must remain central to First Amendment law in any event, "as a moral ascription that marks the boundaries of our commitment to democratic self-government." 64 U. COLO. L. REV. at 1132.

180. *See infra* note 209.

181. It is standard wisdom that the rich variety of First Amendment theories protects First Amendment doctrine from attack. Even where one theory is insufficient standing alone, the "synergy" between the various theories provides additional strength. *See* L.A. Powe, Jr., *Scholarship and Markets,* 56 GEO. WASH. L. REV. 172, 182 (1987). This does not mean, though, that we should simply ignore the flaws in the marketplace metaphor. The inadequacy of the leading philosophical justification supporting one of the most celebrated provisions of American constitutional law is at best odd. At worst, it is a signal that something somewhere is very wrong.

182. *See, e.g.,* C. Edwin Baker, *Scope of the First Amendment Freedom of Speech,* 25 UCLA L. REV. 964 (1978); Jerome A. Barron, *Access to the Press—A New First Amendment Right,* 80 HARV. L. REV. 1641 (1967); Stanley Ingber, *The Marketplace of Ideas: A Legitimizing Myth,* 1984 DUKE L.J. 1; MacKinnon, *supra* note 27.

183. Kalven, *supra* note 145, at 30 (describing Coase's proof that broadcast licenses could be allocated through the market).

184. See, first and foremost, MILL, *supra* note 26. For a somewhat skeptical perspective, see Frederick Schauer, *Reflections on the Value of Truth,* 41 CASE W. RES. L. REV. 699, 706 (1991) ("So what? Why is it good for a society to have more truth?").

185. *See* ALEXANDER MEIKLEJOHN, FREE SPEECH AND ITS RELATION TO SELF-GOVERNMENT 22-27 (1948).

186. Under such a theory, some see the creation of socially accepted truth in the marketplace as part of the process through which the community, as a community, constructs its world. This view adds the trappings of democracy to the skeptical position, often attributed to Justice Holmes, that we should *define* truth by reference to whatever emerges from the process of open discussion. This approach has appeal as a response to modern claims that truth is inherently subjective, and thus

share a common theme. The desired value—whether truth or democracy—is seen as best emerging from total competition among conflicting ideas and viewpoints. When First Amendment philosophers seek truth, they reason that truth is most likely to emerge when we expand the marketplace, and the scope of ideas expressed, and sweep away all impediments to free discussion.[187] Democracy, similarly, can be most nearly attained only when all can participate in the open process of debate.[188]

How is this full competition among conflicting ideas to be achieved? According to the instrumental vision central to the metaphor, free discussion can best take place when government plays no role in the competition of ideas.[189] Governmental involvement is seen as likely to constrict vital interchange; the ideal model of full and complete exchange of views thus is that of discussion in the "private" sphere.

Two descriptive premises are implicit in this instrumental vision. The first premise is that enough members of society, in the absence of an intrusive government role, have meaningful opportunity to speak and to convince others of their views. If too few members of society had that opportunity, we could not count on a large and diverse population offering "the multitude of ideas that are the fuel of the engine for advancing knowledge."[190] Marketplace theory supposes that powerless sectors of that population are in a meaningful position to offer ideas. It supposes that ideas can be meaningfully evaluated without regard to the level of political, economic, and social resources available to their proponents. Otherwise, there is little reason to believe that the marketplace would yield either truth or democratic self-determination.

The second premise is that our discourse is essentially rational: that people process speech on a rational level, and choose to adopt one belief rather than another as a result of this reasoning process. This, as Kent Greenawalt has noted, seems especially vital to the force of the marketplace metaphor:

> [P]erhaps on deeper questions, people do not make reasoned judgments about competing positions but merely acquire reinforcement of views that conform with social conventions or serve their particular interests or unconscious desires. In that event, the

---

hardly "discoverable" through a Millian marketplace of ideas. It seems particularly vulnerable, though, to the question of why democracy "commits us to the results of a marketplace of ideas rather than, say, the results of democratically determined suppression." Greenawalt, *supra* note 179, at 154.

187. *See, e.g.,* SCHAUER, *supra* note 165, at 16.

188. *Id.*

189. In fact, adherents of the marketplace metaphor do not contemplate that the government will play *no* role in regulating speech; they expect the government to enforce property rights in communications resources, and otherwise to provide common-law-based support for private ordering. Marketplace ideology, though, does not treat this as "real" government regulation. *See generally infra* Part III.

190. SCHAUER, *supra* note 165, at 27.

"marketplace of ideas" . . . gives little promise of yielding truth even in the long run, particularly if the disproportionate influence of a few centers of private power over what gets communicated is likely to be exercised in favor of dominant and comforting views.[191]

The problem is that neither of these premises seems true. Scholars have attacked them as problematic, indeed wholly unjustified.[192] Before I evaluate the strength of these premises, though, I want to take a moment to consider whether their accuracy is as vital to the success of the metaphor as I have assumed. Some scholars argue that marketplace theory is well-founded even though the marketplace does not perfectly promote truth. Even if economic, political, and social inequality distort the marketplace, they argue, and even if the irrationality of discourse cripples it further, the marketplace is a success, and marketplace theory is worth preserving, because it leads us towards truth better than do other approaches.[193] This conclusion is especially secure, they argue, because free speech protects goals such as self-realization that are not usually associated with the marketplace metaphor at all.[194]

A. Do the Premises of Marketplace Theory Matter?

I believe that the flaws of marketplace theory are important. Marketplace philosophy disables the government even from addressing serious distortions of the marketplace resulting from imbalances of private power.[195] It is hardly obvious that truth will always be better served without government intervention than with.

This defense of marketplace theory, moreover, slights the costs that marketplace theory imposes. A philosophy shunning any government involvement in the "open and unregulated market for the trade in

---

191. Greenawalt, *supra* note 179, at 135. Professor Greenawalt continues, though, that "[t]he critical question is . . . how well [truth] will advance in conditions of freedom *as compared with* some alternative set of conditions." *Id.* (emphasis added).

192. *See, e.g.,* sources cited *supra* note 182.

193. *See, e.g.,* BAKER, *supra* note 33, at 17-22 (evaluating the argument).

194. *See supra* note 179 and accompanying text; *see also* L.A. Powe, Jr., *Mass Speech and the Newer First Amendment,* 1982 SUP. CT. REV. 243, 281 (arguing that we cling to conventional First Amendment philosophy not because of "a naive belief that truth is knowable or that the electorate will rationally choose it," but because of "the simple recognition that no theory requiring people to stop speaking (or stop listening) better fits with our traditions than the one we have adopted").

195. *See, e.g.,* Buckley v. Valeo, 424 U.S. 1, 48-49 (1976) (rejecting an argument, in support of campaign finance law, based on an asserted government interest in "equalizing the relative ability of individuals and groups to influence the outcome of elections": "the concept that government may restrict the speech of some . . . in order to enhance the relative voice of others is wholly foreign to the First Amendment"). In the words of Owen Fiss, marketplace theory seeks to protect individuals' speech autonomy by placing a "zone of noninterference . . . around each individual," and prohibiting "the state (and the state alone) . . . from crossing the boundary." Fiss, *supra* note 27, at 785.

ideas"[196] has significant disadvantages. Speech, after all, can do harm;[197] marketplace theory leaves the government largely powerless to protect individuals from such harm. First Amendment theory and doctrine respond to that concern by de-emphasizing the link between speakers and the harms speech can cause.[198] For example, speakers are not held responsible, unless tremendously stringent tests are met, for entirely foreseeable criminal actions they inspire third parties to take; those third parties are seen as independent moral agents, whom the state ought to address directly.[199] This stands in sharp contrast, for example, to product liability cases, in which we hold manufacturers responsible for injuries they should have foreseen and could have prevented, even if those injuries would not have occurred but for someone else's subsequent negligence or criminality.[200]

Similarly, First Amendment doctrine often emphasizes the responsibility of *victims* to avoid or ameliorate any harm that befalls them.[201] Public-figure targets of defamation are expected to exploit their own access to the news media and thus lessen the damage to their reputations.[202] Persons subjected to indecent language in public are admon-

---

196. SCHAUER, *supra* note 165, at 16.

197. "[V]irtually everyone writing today in the first amendment area understands, as their academic elders seemed not to, that speech hurts." L.A. Powe, Jr., *Mass Communications and the First Amendment: An Overview,* 55 LAW & CONTEMP. PROBS. 53, 54 (1992); *see* Frederick Schauer, *The Phenomenology of Speech and Harm,* 103 ETHICS 635 (1993). The Court recently confronted such harm in R.A.V. v. City of St. Paul, 112 S. Ct. 2538, 2549 (1992) (striking down an ordinance addressed to speech that, in the words of the Court, injured "the basic human rights of members of groups that have historically been subjected to discrimination, including the right of such group members to live in peace where they wish").

198. *See* J.M. Balkin, *The Rhetoric of Responsibility,* 76 VA. L. REV. 197, 254-61 (1990); *cf.* Holmes v. Securities Investor Protection Corp., 112 S. Ct. 1311, 1318 (1992) (stating that courts use causation concepts as "judicial tools" to limit and assign responsibility).

199. *See* Brandenburg v. Ohio, 395 U.S. 444, 447 (1969) (holding that the state may not prohibit advocacy of violence or criminal acts except where that advocacy "is directed to inciting or producing imminent lawless action and is likely to incite or produce such action"). The Supreme Court used parallel reasoning some 30 years earlier in holding that a local government may not restrict handbill distribution in order to reduce littering: "There are obvious methods of preventing littering. Amongst these is the punishment of those who actually throw papers on the streets." Schneider v. State, 308 U.S. 147, 162 (1939). *See* Balkin, *supra* note 198, at 258-59 (discussing *Schneider*).

200. *See* Balkin, *supra* note 198, at 259-60 (discussing Larsen v. General Motors Corp., 391 F.2d 495 (8th Cir. 1968), which deals with an automobile manufacturer's responsibility to provide a "crashworthy" vehicle); Frederick Schauer, *Uncoupling Free Speech,* 92 COLUM. L. REV. 1321, 1345 n.76 (1992) (discussing intervening fault by plaintiffs).

201. *See* Schauer, *supra* note 197, at 647-48.

202. Indeed, the law presumes that "public figures have voluntarily exposed themselves to increased risk of injury from defamatory falsehood." Gertz v. Robert Welch, Inc., 418 U.S. 323, 345 (1974). Lee Bollinger has characterized this statement as "an unfair ploy by the Court, an avoidance maneuver by which it tries to minimize the degree to which we should care about the pain inflicted under our rules. . . . [I]t simply is wrong to suppose that the pain inflicted by defamatory statements about public officials and figures is not our responsibility or concern." BOLLINGER, *supra* note 11, at 25.

ished to "avoid further bombardment of their sensibilities . . . by averting their eyes."[203] We are reluctant to find that the targets of speech need government protection; we typically stress their ability to look after their own interests. First Amendment theory is thus hostile to the feminist argument that women are unable adequately to defend themselves against the effects of pornography because they are victims of a sex-based system of subordination and repression smothering their voices.[204] In the employment realm, by contrast, we take for granted that employees may not have complete freedom of action in defending themselves from workplace demands contrary to public policy; we recognize that employers may have economic power that substantially constrains their employees' choices.[205] In product liability cases, similarly, we tend to hold manufacturers responsible for consumers' predicaments; we assume that consumers may lack the information, alternatives, or expertise they need to avoid the danger presented by defective products.[206] Yet the same plaintiff judged "helpless in consumer transactions" is treated as an independent, uncoerced moral actor, "adept and competent," able to look after her own interests in the marketplace of ideas.[207]

---

203. Cohen v. California, 403 U.S. 15, 21 (1971). The government, similarly, is told to ameliorate the harm presented by subversive speech by responding with "more speech." *See, e.g.,* Whitney v. California, 274 U.S. 357, 377 (1927) (Brandeis, J., concurring).

204. *See* Balkin, *supra* note 198, at 260-61. *See generally* Andrea Dworkin, *Against the Male Flood: Censorship, Pornography, and Equality,* 8 HARV. WOMEN'S L.J. 1 (1985); MacKinnon, *supra* note 27.

205. This recognition lies at the heart of much of our employment law, reflected in rules ranging from maximum hours regulation, to workplace safety rules, to the incorporation of a sexual harassment proscription into Title VII.

206. This approach is sufficiently pervasive as to control even "failure to warn" cases, where the manufacturer is held liable for consumer misuse flowing from the manufacturer's failure to supply adequate instructions. *See, e.g.,* Burch v. Amsterdam Corp., 366 A.2d 1079 (D.C. 1976). One might argue that the manufacturer here is being punished for the content of its speech; yet we can find the defendant responsible because we categorize the case as relating to product-liability law rather than to expression.

207. Balkin, *supra* note 198, at 260; *see also* Coase, *supra* note 176, at 384-85; Post, *supra* note 179, at 1130-32 (describing the difference in approach as essential to democracy).

First Amendment doctrine concedes that in particular circumstances individuals may be powerless to avoid the harms of certain speech. The most obvious example is private-figure defamation; while positing that "[t]he first remedy of any victim of defamation is self-help—using available opportunities to contradict the lie or correct the error," Gertz v. Robert Welch, Inc., 418 U.S. 323, 344 (1974), the Supreme Court has recognized that private individuals do not enjoy meaningful "access to the channels of effective communication," and thus may have no "realistic opportunity to counteract false statements." *Id.* On the other hand, this solicitude for the victims of defamation is limited to cases in which the harmful speech was narrowly focused to target a particular individual victim. *See* Collin v. Smith, 578 F.2d 1197 (7th Cir.) (striking down an ordinance designed to prevent a Nazi demonstration notwithstanding arguments that the demonstration would amount to group libel and intentional infliction of emotional distress), *cert. denied,* 439 U.S. 916 (1978). The idea that individuals may be powerless to avoid the harms caused by speech similarly underlies the "captive audience" rationale for upholding speech restrictions. *See, e.g.,* Lehman v. City of Shaker Heights, 418 U.S. 298, 307 (1974) (Douglas, J., concurring) (holding that a city may limit access to advertising space on public transit in order to protect "the right of the commuters to be free from forced intrusions on their privacy"); *see also* FCC v. Pacifica Found., 438

This vision of society helps justify the costs that a libertarian speech theory imposes.[208] Any evil done by speech is laid at the doorstep of those who have failed to disseminate the appropriate counter-speech. The assumptions implicit in this vision, however, amount to a repackaging of the two earlier premises of equality and rationality in the marketplace of ideas. The marketplace of ideas is thought to work, notwithstanding distorting influences, because the individuals participating in it are free and uncoerced, readily able to distribute their own competing messages, which will be considered in the marketplace in accord with their merits. The premises underlying the marketplace metaphor, thus, are even more important than they seem at first glance; we cannot avoid examining them by relying on an escape mechanism that takes them for granted.[209]

Were we to reject the premise that individuals can participate effectively in the marketplace, we would have to give much more serious consideration to the desirability of government involvement in the marketplace designed to counterbalance the distorting influence of private power and wealth.[210] We would have to think hard about the mag-

---

U.S. 726, 748-49 (1978) ("To say that one may avoid further offense by turning off the radio when he hears indecent language is like saying that the remedy for an assault is to run away after the first blow."). In the First Amendment tradition, however, such cases tend to be treated as part of a limited, sharply demarcated exception to the otherwise universal reality of autonomy. There is little reliance, as there is in the economic sphere, on the idea that imbalances of power or information *routinely* limit individuals' ability to avoid or mitigate the harm that speech can do.

208. FRANKLYN S. HAIMAN, SPEECH AND LAW IN A FREE SOCIETY 425-29 (1981) provides a good illustration; for a criticism of that book on essentially this ground, see Frederick Schauer, *Free Speech and the Assumption of Rationality*, 36 VAND. L. REV. 199, 205-09 (1983) (book review).

209. Indeed, because this escape mechanism tends to be implicit even in *non*-marketplace-based theories of free speech, those theories too rest on marketplace premises. Some free speech theorists suggest that speech should be given unique protection from government intrusion because of its role in individual self-development and self-realization, or its connection to individual dignity and equal respect. *See, e.g.*, Redish, *supra* note 179; David A.J. Richards, *Free Speech and Obscenity Law: Toward a Moral Theory of the First Amendment*, 123 U. PA. L. REV. 45 (1974). Those theorists, however, must reconcile special protection for speech with the fact that *conduct* serving the same values is easily regulable. They tend to fall back on the view that the harms caused by speech are not as problematic as those caused by conduct. *See* Schauer, *supra* note 197, at 640-41; HAIMAN, *supra* note 208, at 20-21. That assumption, however, often reaches back to the vision I have just described; it is because the marketplace can "correct" the damage done by speech that we need not take that damage seriously.

210. This is something we almost never do. The Court in Buckley v. Valeo, 424 U.S. 1, 48-49 (1976), rejected the argument that the "governmental interest in equalizing the relative ability of individuals and groups to influence the outcome of elections" justified a statutory limit on independent political campaign expenditures; it declared that "the concept that government may restrict the speech of some elements of our society in order to enhance the relative voice of others is wholly foreign to the First Amendment."

There are isolated exceptions to this rule. Austin v. Michigan Chamber of Commerce, 494 U.S. 652 (1990), may provide one; the Court there upheld a state statute barring political contributions in candidate elections from corporate treasury funds. The Court found legitimate the state's desire to prevent the "distorting effects of immense aggregations of wealth that are accumulated with the help of the corporate form and that have little or no correlation to the public's support for the

nitude of the effects of inequality in the marketplace, the extent to which government action could minimize those effects, and the dangers of such government intervention.[211] We ultimately might conclude that the danger posed by self-interested bureaucrats meddling with public discourse is so great that we are better off with a rule of strict government noninvolvement even in a decidedly unfree marketplace of ideas.[212] But we could not blandly rely on the metaphor of the free and unfettered marketplace, and we would have to question whether such a biased discourse really has the salutary effects that are said to justify highly protective free speech doctrine.

Were we to abandon the premise of rationality, we still might feel that government control of public discourse is so pernicious as to make desirable a rule that speech should be unrestrained by government. But we would have to reevaluate whether the marketplace's limited contribution to the discovery of ultimate Truth justifies our toleration of the harms that unrestrained speech can do and that speech-restrictive laws are often intended to prevent. We would have to question whether we should maintain our current commitment to free speech nearly across the board, or whether—at least in certain contexts—restricting speech might do more good than it is likely to do harm.[213]

B. Are the Premises of Marketplace Theory Correct?

Modern First Amendment philosophy depends heavily on the assumptions of equality and rationality. And yet those assumptions—part of what Jerome Barron referred to as the "romantic view of the first

---

corporation's political ideas." *Id.* at 660. *Red Lion* provides another. *See infra* notes 329-31 and accompanying text.

211. Government action to remedy such inequality would present difficulties. I have already discussed the problems inherent in one attempt—the fairness doctrine—to remedy the inequality of resources available to present different viewpoints. *See supra* notes 115-22 and accompanying text. A wholehearted attempt to ensure all individuals' complete equality of opportunity to advance ideas would require a radical transformation of our media system, effected through "state intervention of tremendous scope." BAKER, *supra* note 33, at 46; *see also* SCHMIDT, *supra* note 10, at 18-22 (contemplating modes of expanded access); Stanley Ingber, *The First Amendment in Modern Garb: Retaining System Legitimacy*, 56 GEO. WASH. L. REV. 187, 216-19 (1987) (book review) (warning of the dangers of extensive government involvement in a system of expanded access). The difficulty of finding solutions, though, ought not to cause us to deny the existence of the problem.

212. *See generally* Blasi, *supra* note 37.

213. These questions ultimately relate to a more general attack on marketplace theory (or on any consequentialist justification for a free speech principle): the argument that an unrestrained marketplace of ideas will best lead us to Truth proves, at best, that free speech has important benefits. It does not provide any way to balance the benefits against the harms of free speech; much less does it provide a blanket rule that, in that balancing, the free speech claim should (almost) always win. *See* SCHAUER, *supra* note 165, at 28-29.

amendment"[214]—are more than problematic.[215] They form a myth structure that corresponds only faintly to reality.[216] I will first discuss the assumption that a genuinely wide range of diverse views compete in the marketplace of ideas, on an essentially even playing field, notwithstanding the differing economic, political and social resources available to the ideas' proponents. I will next discuss the assumption that people rationally process new information and ideas that the marketplace makes available to them.

1. Equality

The first crack in the plaster of the romantic conception is simply this: effective mass communication requires access to communications technology. That technology is expensive; printing presses, teleprompters, broadcast engineers, and satellite transponders cost money. As a result, "virtually every means of communicating ideas in today's mass society requires the expenditure of money."[217] The fact that some have access to these resources, and that others do not, grotesquely skews the balance of effective communication. In the modern marketplace of ideas, those with extensive institutional or financial resources can speak more loudly than those without; the average person has little ability to speak in any but the softest of voices.[218] As A.J. Liebling put it, freedom of the press in this country is guaranteed only to

---

214. Barron, *supra* note 182, at 1642; *see also* JEROME A. BARRON, FREEDOM OF THE PRESS FOR WHOM? at xiv, 320-21 (1973). Professor Barron's "romantic view" should not be confused with the First Amendment "romance" that Steven Shiffrin has championed. Professor Shiffrin argues that the point of the First Amendment is "to protect the romantics— . . . the dissenters, the unorthodox, the outcasts." It is "affirmatively to sponsor the individualism, the rebelliousness, the antiauthoritarianism, the spirit of nonconformity within us all." STEVEN H. SHIFFRIN, THE FIRST AMENDMENT, DEMOCRACY, AND ROMANCE 5 (1990). This is a different notion of romance; Shiffrin's profound and subtle views are far removed from the First Amendment orthodoxy I have been describing.

215. *See generally* BAKER, *supra* note 33, at 12, 15 ("At least within the academic world, the assumptions . . . are almost universally rejected"; the marketplace metaphor's "power and popularity [are] quite curious" in light of the metaphor's "obvious dependence on incorrect assumptions.").

216. *See* Weinberg, *supra* note 17, at 1271.

217. Buckley v. Valeo, 424 U.S. 1, 19 (1976). *See generally* Balkin, *supra* note 175, at 407-10 ("To put it bluntly, the more property one has, the greater one's ability to compete in the marketplace of ideas, just as in the ordinary marketplace. . . . [T]o the extent that one does not own the means of communication, one must bargain with others to obtain access."); Stephen L. Carter, *Technology, Democracy, and the Manipulation of Consent,* 93 YALE L.J. 581, 581-82 (1984) (book review) (considering "the threat posed when access to information is controlled . . . by those private interests able to spend enough money to purchase access for their points of view").

218. *See* Weinberg, *supra* note 17, at 1282-83; *see also* BARRON, *supra* note 214, at 325-26 (tracking the "inequality in capacity to communicate ideas"); J. Skelly Wright, *Money and the Pollution of Politics: Is the First Amendment an Obstacle to Political Equality?,* 82 COLUM. L. REV. 609 (1982) (criticizing the Court's decisions in *Buckley* and First Nat'l Bank v. Belotti, 435 U.S. 765 (1978)). Professor Powe makes this point as well, *see* Powe, *supra* note 194, at 263, although he emphatically disagrees with Judge Wright as to its significance.

those who own one.[219]

This problem flows from our application of marketplace of ideas theory to a society characterized by marked inequalities in economic, social and political power. Access to communications resources mirrors access to other sources of power and resources: those without communications resources have little opportunity to contribute to political or other debate.[220] A rule directing government to enforce property rights but otherwise barring it from interfering with the speech flowing from that skewed distribution of societal resources does not yield substantive equality in ability to influence the public debate. Rather, it guarantees further inequality; debate carried out against that backdrop will be "dominated, and thus constrained, by the same forces that dominate social structure."[221]

There is thus a pervasive skew in the "real world" marketplace of ideas—that is, debate involving words spoken by politicians, would-be politicians, grassroots activists, corporate spokespersons, and other people *not* employees of, or under contract to, media corporations.[222] It would surely be an oversimplification to identify wealth as the single force dominating that ideological marketplace, and it would be palpably incorrect to claim that the side with more money prevails in every public debate.[223] But it would be equally untrue to claim that wealth is only

---

219. A.J. LIEBLING, THE PRESS 32 (1975). The issue of access to the press, in fact, is not quite so simple. A person might have greater control over or access to the means of communication because he owns a press (or a television station, or any other mass communication resource); because he is associated with an institution that owns one; because he is associated with an institution that is otherwise involved, directly or indirectly, with the mass communications industry; or because he has access to specialized nonprofit publishers (such as law reviews). Nonetheless, the number of Americans so blessed is relatively small. The ordinary citizen fits in none of these categories, and when it comes to mass communication, that citizen is out of luck.

220. For a mainstream affirmation of this principle, see BOLLINGER, *supra* note 11, at 137; for a more radical one, see Herbert Marcuse, *Repressive Tolerance [Postscript 1968], in* ROBERT P. WOLFF ET AL., A CRITIQUE OF PURE TOLERANCE 81, 118-19 (1969):

> The chance of influencing [public opinion], in any effective way, . . . is at a price, in dollars, totally out of reach of the radical opposition. . . . [F]ree competition and exchange of ideas have become a farce. The Left has no equal voice, no equal access to the mass media and their public facilities—not because a conspiracy excludes it, but because, in good old capitalist fashion, it does not have the required purchasing power.

221. Fiss, *supra* note 27, at 786; *see also* Fiss, *supra* note 151, at 1412-13; Baker, *supra* note 182, at 980 (noting that the marketplace "reinforces currently dominant views").

The general principle here is the familiar clash between formal and substantive equality; formally equal treatment of people who are differently situated may perpetuate substantive inequality, at least in the short term.

222. That I characterize these speakers, including such modern celebrities as David Duke, as all operating in the real world is perhaps just an example of the absurdity of the modern era.

223. *See* Fiss, *supra* note 151, at 1412. Indeed, not all parts of society reflect the same political influences; it is often charged today that "politically correct" views predominate on college campuses. At least one commentator with conservative leanings, though, does not find this too upsetting, noting that *"the rest of us have them right where we want them."* JOE QUEENAN, IMPERIAL CADDY 132 (1992).

Leftist intellectuals with hare-brained Marxist ideas get to control Stanford, MIT, Yale,

one of many factors exerting power in that marketplace, with an insignificant effect on the overall representation of views. Access to wealth and institutional resources regnlarly plays an important distorting role in the political marketplace.[224] More fundamentally, economic, social, and political power help define the general boundaries of the mainstream within which an idea must fall in order to be taken seriously, rather than merely ignored.[225]

The world I have discussed so far, on the other hand, is only part of the modern marketplace. To a huge degree, effective communication in our society is left in the hands of a specialized set of entities I have not so far discussed—large, for-profit media corporations, with unmatched command of communications resources. These corporations are not obviously and inherently biased, nor are they politically monolithic. On the contrary, precisely because they are profit-oriented, they often put considerable power in the hands of artists and commentators who may be of varying political persuasions.[226] The contribution made by these voices to the marketplace of ideas is large. It includes the voices of the network news, and other major, mass-oriented, advertiser-supported news media; it includes more narrowly tailored political commentary, often found in books and magazines; and it includes entertainment, where the politics may be either implicit or overt.[227]

---

and the American Studies department at the University of Vermont. In return, the right gets IBM, DEC, Honeywell, Disney World, and the New York Stock Exchange. Leftist academics get to try out their stupid ideas on impressionable youths between seventeen and twenty-one who don't have any money or power. The right gets to try out its ideas on North America, South America, Europe, Asia, Australia and parts of Africa, most of which take MasterCard. The left gets Harvard, Oberlin, Twyla Tharp's dance company, and Madison, Wisconsin. The right gets NASDAQ, Boeing, General Motors, Apple, McDonnell Douglas, Washington, D.C., Citicorp, Texas, Coca-Cola, General Electric, Japan, and outer space.

This seems like a fair arrangement.

Id. at 132-33.

224. For one study, see Daniel H. Lowenstein, *Campaign Spending and Ballot Propositions: Recent Experience, Public Choice Theory and the First Amendment,* 29 UCLA L. REV. 505 (1982) ("one-sided" corporate spending generally effective in defeating voter-initiated referenda). For a particularly colorful example of the use of wealth and communications resources in the political process, see GREG MITCHELL, THE CAMPAIGN OF THE CENTURY: UPTON SINCLAIR'S RACE FOR GOVERNOR OF CALIFORNIA AND THE BIRTH OF MEDIA POLITICS (1992).

225. *See* LINDBLOM, *supra* note 27, at 210 (Dissident views are constrained by the "myth of 'balance' in public debate. . . . The 'balance' of views thus presented to the citizen . . . [does] not much challenge the fundamentals of politico-economic organization in market-oriented systems."); *infra* text accompanying notes 292-93. It is unlikely that Ross Perot would have made such a large political splash for his own theories and views absent his unique access to wealth.

226. CNN, thus, offers its podium both to Jesse Jackson and to John Sununu.

227. Some argue that the role of the mass media simply amplifies the role of wealth in society, since media corporations are themselves large concentrations of capital, owned and controlled by the wealthy, and sharing common interests with other major corporations, banks, and government. *See, e.g.,* HERMAN & CHOMSKY, *supra* note 28, at 3-14. This analysis without more, though, is insufficient; it "ignores the observable fact that reporters often initiate stories of their own, that editors rarely meet with publishers, and that most working journalists have no idea who sits on the board of directors of the institutions they work for." Michael Schudson, *The Sociology of News*

One can paint a picture in which, even though all do not participate equally in the marketplace of ideas, the media give us a second-best solution. One might argue that a sufficient diversity of views is relayed by these media corporations to simulate such a market; that numerous and diverse ideas are transmitted by authors and artists through the mass media; and that those ideas compete in the marketplace without substantial skew based on the resources available to their proponents.[228] This argument has surface appeal. The first question one might ask, though, is *why* we should expect the ideas transmitted in this manner to be numerous and diverse. Media professionals themselves, after all, are not particularly numerous[229] or heterogeneous.[230] National journalists tend to be white and "[b]y all the conventional indicators, . . . solidly upper-middle-class";[231] they have been said to operate largely on the basis of a shared matrix of values.[232]

The spectrum of views expressed through the media may seem broad only because it is all we are used to.[233] It may seem broad only to those of us whose opinions are in the same ballpark. Some black scholars, by contrast, argue that mass media images reflect "the racial misconceptions and fantasies of the dominant white culture."[234] A gay legal scholar writes that "[o]ur culture . . . ignores or actively represses information about gay issues."[235] A colleague recently pointed out to me that she has seen her own radical feminist politics reflected in the mass media

---

Production, 11 MEDIA, CULTURE & SOC'Y 263, 267 (1989). In a variety of ways, the media do at least sometimes oppose entrenched power holders. By any stretch of the imagination, President Nixon during Watergate was such a power holder, and American corporations in recent memory have found themselves "aghast" at media coverage of a variety of public issues. *Id.* at 268.

228. Chief Justice Burger seems to have had this in mind when he stated that if the law required broadcasters to accept editorial advertisements, then "the marketplace of 'ideas and experiences' would . . . be . . . heavily weighted in favor of the financially affluent . . . . [Thus,] the views of the affluent could well prevail over those of others." CBS v. Democratic Nat'l Comm., 412 U.S. 94, 123 (1973). His apparent belief was that the mass media currently are unaffected by wealth, and that that insulation saves the marketplace from a wealth-based bias.

229. *Cf.* BOLLINGER, *supra* note 11, at 27 ("As the number of those who control the gateway to public discussion decreases," natural marketplace correctives to bias are lost.).

230. *See* S. ROBERT LICHTER ET AL., THE MEDIA ELITE 20-53 (1986) (surveying the backgrounds and attitudes of journalists at major media organizations). Lichter concludes that "the media elite's perspective is predominantly cosmopolitan and liberal." *Id.* at 32.

231. HERBERT J. GANS, DECIDING WHAT'S NEWS 209 (Vintage Books 1980) (1979).

232. *See infra* text accompanying notes 260-63.

233. *See* Baker, *supra* note 152, at 2242 ("In our understanding of the events of the day, we are largely the products of our press. It is awfully easy to adopt the Whiggish view [that 'it ain't broken, so don't fix it'] precisely because 'it' is largely 'us.' ").

234. Jannette L. Dates & William Barlow, *Conclusion: Split Images and Double Binds, in* SPLIT IMAGE: AFRICAN AMERICANS IN THE MASS MEDIA 455 (Jannette L. Dates & William Barlow eds., 1990).

235. Marc A. Fajer, *Can Two Real Men Eat Quiche Together? Storytelling, Gender-Role Stereotypes, and Legal Protection for Lesbians and Gay Men,* 46 U. MIAMI L. REV. 511, 584 (1992); *see also id.* at 650-51.

not at all.[236]

One might argue that the ideas and views relayed through the media gatekeepers will in general be numerous and diverse, reflecting the ideas that otherwise would be offered by the population at large, and reflecting the reception that the population at large would give those ideas, precisely because the media must respond to the market. Because the media are profit-oriented, the argument runs, they necessarily will articulate those ideas that members of the speech-consuming public wish to buy; the operation of the economic marketplace will thus assure the operation of the marketplace of ideas.[237]

I believe that this argument is flawed. Media speakers[238] are subject to several important biases.[239] The first and most obvious is a wealth-based bias. Any medium dependent on advertising takes as its relevant audience not the citizenry as a whole, but rather that population skewed on demographic and class lines in order to maximize buying power. Newspapers and broadcasters make their money by selling audiences to advertisers, and affluent audiences with the "right" demographics are much more attractive in that marketplace.[240] Advertising pressures thus favor content preferred by audiences with buying power; it is for this reason, perhaps, that newsmagazines "tend . . . to universalize upper-middle-class practices as if they were shared by all Americans."[241] The "marketplace of ideas" the mass media create, in short, is as biased on

---

236. *See also* LINDBLOM, *supra* note 27, at 205 (finding no serious challenge to belief in "private enterprise [and] a high degree of corporate autonomy"); *Political Notes,* DETROIT FREE PRESS, Oct. 12, 1992, at 5A (noting exclusion of Libertarian Party candidates from presidential and vice-presidential debates notwithstanding their being on the ballot in all 50 states).

237. *See* RICHARD A. POSNER, ECONOMIC ANALYSIS OF LAW 546-48 (2d ed. 1977) (arguing that broadcasters wishing to "maximize . . . income will provide the mixture and diversity of ideas deemed optimum by [their] customers").

238. In this context as well, all participants in the marketplace are not equal; those with greater resources have greater ability to serve as gatekeepers screening others who wish to speak. To a profound extent, a top tier of large media entities supplies the news, and, in so doing, helps define the nation's news agenda. In the context of getting a book into the larger public debate, Time Warner has far more influence than Tweedlebottom Press. It is the largest media entities, those most fully integrated into the market, that play the most important role.

239. In using the word "bias," I do not mean to suggest that media speakers are engaged in any sort of conscious conspiracy, worked out in dark basements by men with large cigars and alligator shoes. Media professionals, in my experience, are decent and honorable folk. I *do* mean to suggest that the range of ideas and views presented by the mass communications media is strongly shaped by factors relating primarily to the structure of the media marketplace and the nature of the newsgathering process.

240. *See* Baker, *supra* note 152, at 2126-27, 2164-68. The left-wing British *Daily Herald,* for example, folded notwithstanding a loyal readership of 4.7 million people—"nearly twice as many as the readership of *The Times, Financial Times* and *Guardian* added together"—because its readers, while numerous, did not have enough disposable income to constitute a valuable advertising market. *Id.* at 2110-11 (quoting James Curran, *Capitalism and Control of the Press, 1800-1975, in* MASS COMMUNICATION AND SOCIETY 195, 225 (James Curran et al. eds., 1979)); *see also* GINSBURG ET AL., *supra* note 59, at 593-94 (commenting on television shows canceled while still mass hits because they attracted demographically "wrong" audiences).

241. GANS, *supra* note 231, at 27.

economic lines as is the economic marketplace. It is as democratic as a
political voting system weighted by income.[242]

Another important tilt, in the area of news and public affairs reporting, relates to the source of that news:

> [R]eporters get the largest share of their news from official gov-
> ernment agencies. . . .
>
> One study after another comes up with essentially the same
> observation, and it matters not whether the study is at the
> national, state, or local level—the story of journalism, on a day-
> to-day basis, is the story of the interaction of reporters and
> officials.[243]

This results in part from what Mark Fishman called the "principle of
bureaucratic affinity": given the media's need for a steady, reliable flow
of news information, collected in a cost-effective manner, "only other
bureaucracies can satisfy the input needs of a news bureaucracy."[244]
Observers have characterized this reliance on leading public officials and
other comparably authoritative and efficient sources for news information as the most significant of all the factors helping to determine the

---

242. *See* HERMAN & CHOMSKY, *supra* note 28, at 16. This is not to say that speech attractive to
the poor and largely anathema to the wealthy is wholly excluded from the marketplace. Time
Warner makes money selling the music of Ice-T, whose views are condemned by political, economic,
and media leaders; one song it distributed described the fictional narrator's intention to kill police
officers. That song, however, was withdrawn after extensive protest from law-enforcement groups
and political figures. Sheila Rule, *"Cop Killer" To Be Cut From Ice-T Album,* N.Y. TIMES, July 29,
1992, at C15. Indeed, a variety of record companies are now demanding deletion or rerecording of
controversial songs. Sheila Rule, *After Ice-T,* N.Y. TIMES, Oct. 7, 1992, at C19. My point, more
generally, is that a marketplace in which ideas are exchanged through economic transactions against
the backdrop of the existing distribution of wealth and entitlements is fundamentally different from
the idealized marketplace of ideas, in which that distribution plays no significant role.

243. Schudson, *supra* note 227, at 271; *see also* Baker, *supra* note 152, at 2137 & n.134. *See
generally* GANS, *supra* note 231, at 116-45.

244. MARK FISHMAN, MANUFACTURING THE NEWS 143 (1980) (endnote omitted). Large
news agencies need news information on a steady basis, and must concentrate their reporters and
cameras where important news often takes place, where rumors and leaks are common, and where
regular press conferences are held. *See* HERMAN & CHOMSKY, *supra* note 28, at 18-19. To satisfy
this need for news, government agencies often establish huge public-affairs operations. *See* MARK
YUDOF, WHEN GOVERNMENT SPEAKS 6-8 (1983). The Air Force alone, in a single year not too
long ago, issued 45,000 headquarters and unit news releases and 615,000 hometown news releases,
arranged 6600 interviews with news media, and held 50 meetings with editorial boards. *See*
HERMAN & CHOMSKY, *supra* note 28, at 20. In military contexts in particular, the government has
unusual opportunities to manage the information made available to the news media. *See, e.g.,* JOHN
R. MACARTHUR, SECOND FRONT: CENSORSHIP AND PROPAGANDA IN THE GULF WAR 146 (1992);
John Barry & Roger Charles, *Sea of Lies,* NEWSWEEK, July 13, 1992, at 28, 38-39. The views of
experts supplied by government agencies are taken as authoritative even by the "liberal" media.
During a recently surveyed year, for example, a majority of the guests on the McNeil-Lehrer News
Hour (excluding other journalists) were present or former government officials. HERMAN &
CHOMSKY, *supra* note 28, at 24-25. Large business bureaucracies make it their business to be
similarly helpful. Mobil Oil, for example, had a public-relations budget in 1980 of $21 million and a
public-relations staff of 73, engaged in part in the production of video press releases for television
news. *Id.* at 341 n.72.

content of mass media news.[245] Government officials are "the most easily and quickly available, as well as most reliable and productive, source of news"; they can exert pressure against major media organizations if those organizations fail to treat them as routine and presumptively credible sources.[246] These factors make it more likely that the view of the world that pervades the news is consistent with that of the government and other sources who provide its raw material.[247]

Other forces push the media towards the conventional and mainstream. To the extent that media entities are dependent on advertising, they edit out the "heterodox or the controversial"[248] in order to maximize their advertising reach and to ensure that they do not unsettle advertisers.[249] Broadcast television provides the most obvious example. As Todd Gitlin has explained, advertisers in the aggregate "functionally set the outer limits of permissible television."[250] The point is not that advertisers retaliate or impose pressure in particular cases;[251] rather, because "[n]etwork executives internalize the desires of advertisers as a whole,"[252] they, "without even troubling to think about it, . . . are likely to rule out any show likely to offend a critical mass of advertisers."[253]

Controversy itself is seen as inconsistent with creating a proper environment for advertising, a "buying mood."[254] At least one network limited its coverage of the Persian Gulf War because advertisers did not

---

245. *See* GANS, *supra* note 231, at 281-82.

246. *Id.* at 282; *see also id.* at 144-45.

247. *See* GANS, *supra* note 231, at 145. *See generally* YUDOF, *supra* note 244. The fact that the government controls so much of the raw material of the news introduces a further source of skew: only mainstream publications are given access to that raw material by being credentialed, for example, for presidential press conferences, or for access to the theatre of war. *See* FREDERICK SCHAUER, PARSING THE PENTAGON PAPERS 6-7 (Joan Shorenstein Barone Center on the Press, Politics and Public Policy Research Paper R-3, 1991).

248. Barron, *supra* note 182, at 1646.

249. *See* Baker, *supra* note 152, at 2127-28, 2130-31, 2156-57. As Justice Brennan put it, "[I]n light of the strong interest of broadcasters in maximizing their audience, and therefore their profits, it seems almost naive to expect the majority of broadcasters to produce the variety and controversiality of material necessary to reflect a full spectrum of viewpoints." CBS v. Democratic Nat'l Comm., 412 U.S. 94, 187 (1973) (Brennan, J., dissenting). The dynamics of an advertising-driven industry also make broadcasters uniquely vulnerable to pressure-group boycotts, whose "net effect is systematically to reduce offerings, not to expand them." Baker, *supra* note 152, at 2163; *see id.* at 2158-63.

250. GITLIN, *supra* note 28, at 252.

251. Although there are numerous examples, in the history of American mass media, of advertisers doing exactly that. *See* Baker, *supra* note 152, at 2146-52 (discussing pressures imposed by tobacco, patent medicine, fruit, cosmetics, coffee, auto, and other advertisers); *see also* Bruce Horovitz, *Advertisers Influence Media More, Report Says,* L.A. TIMES, Mar. 12, 1992, at D2 (discussing a study by Ronald K.L. Collins and the Center for the Study of Commercialism).

252. GITLIN, *supra* note 28, at 253.

253. *Id.* at 254; *see also* Baker, *supra* note 152, at 2142 (reporting that "advertisers' concerns result in extensive media 'self-censorship' ").

254. *See* Baker, *supra* note 152, at 2153-56; *see also* GITLIN, *supra* note 28, at 189 (quoting an advertising agency executive who describes the TV movie *Playing for Time* as "honest and frightening as hell, but I just can't see a client who has a selling job to do placing his spots after

consider that programming sufficiently "upbeat" to provide a suitable advertising environment. The network unsuccessfully offered to tailor war coverage so that commercials would run after segments "specially produced with upbeat images or messages about the war, like patriotic views from the home front."[255]

Nor is it merely advertisers who help ensure blandness in television. Network executives also feel a need to keep audiences comfortable, and not to "jar the expectations of the regular TV audience, which they take to be uneducated, distracted, and easily bewildered."[256] Both cable and broadcast television are deeply committed to the familiar and the comfortable, in part because audiences seem to want it that way.[257] Thus, author Bill McKibben describes the 150-channel Fairfax, Virginia cable television system as "like a pleasant tract housing development of the mind: tastefully different colors on some of the houses, and every fourth one with a pair of gabled windows. But no yurts. No caves. No treehouses."[258]

None of this is to say that there are not many persons active in the news and entertainment sectors of the mass media who desire change in the status quo, nor is it to say that those desires are never reflected in their programming. Indeed, my position is consistent with the argument of those who assert that the national news media take politically liberal positions.[259] The media system can favor liberal over conservative views,

---

scenes that consistently end on such a remarkably low point"); HERMAN & CHOMSKY, *supra* note 28, at 17-18.

255. Baker, *supra* note 152, at 2156 (quoting Bill Carter, *Few Sponsors for TV War News*, N.Y. TIMES, Feb. 7, 1991, at D1, D20).

256. GITLIN, *supra* note 28, at 187.

257. Bill McKibben, *TV: Why Even the New Seems Like Déjà Vû*, N.Y. TIMES, Apr. 5, 1992, § 2, at 1. The pressures toward conformity can come from a variety of directions, depending on where the fear of controversy is greatest. Some years ago, ABC required the writers of a movie sympathetically portraying a homosexual father to add lines in which the character suggested that his sexual orientation was a "sickness." GITLIN, *supra* note 28, at 260. A few years later writers complained that it had become politically impossible to write scripts that would "upset the gay-liberation lobby." *Id.* at 260-61 (quoting Earnest Kinoy).

Consistent with their fear of genuine controversy (as opposed to sanitized "issue-of-the-week" programming) the broadcast networks will not run political advocacy advertisements at all. *See* Jan Hoffman, *Picture is Jumbled on Which Abortion Messages Can Get on TV*, N.Y. TIMES, June 11, 1992, at A18. Broadcast policies against running such advertisements, on the other hand, to some extent grew out of fears that running the ads would trigger fairness doctrine obligations. For a discussion of political advocacy advertising, see *infra* note 407.

258. McKibben, *supra* note 257, at 1. *See generally* BILL MCKIBBEN, THE AGE OF MISSING INFORMATION (1992) (ruminating on the author's viewing of one cable system's entire, 93-channel daily programming).

259. The media, and media professionals, have been variously attacked as both irredeemably liberal and incorrigibly conservative. *Compare* LICHTER ET AL., *supra* note 230, at 294 ("[L]eading journalists are politically liberal and alienated from traditional norms and institutions.") *and* L. Brent Bozell III, *Annoy the Media, Elect Bush*, WALL ST. J., Nov. 2, 1992, at A14 ("The liberal bias of the mainstream press almost goes without saying.") *with* HERMAN & CHOMSKY, *supra* note 28, at 298 (The media "inculcate and defend" conservative principles and the status quo.). This incongruity can be explained in part, perhaps, by the "hostile media phenomenon" identified in

within the sphere of acceptable discourse, at the same time as it supports the existing political and economic status quo by shutting out more radical arguments for change. Herbert Gans, in his classic study, wrote that the national news media act within a context of values including "ethnocentrism, altruistic democracy, responsible capitalism, small-town pastoralism, individualism, moderatism, social order, and national leadership";[260] these are among the "unquestioned and generally unnoticed background assumptions" within which their message is framed.[261] The news, according to Gans, reflects an implicit belief that unprincipled or self-serving actions taken by public officials and other powerful individuals create "moral disorder" that must be exposed and condemned, together with an implicit belief in the desirability of controlling and containing "social disorder," viewed from a white, upper-middle-class perspective.[262] Mass media news thus validates our basic social, economic and political structures. It also validates the authority of the elite holders of political and economic power, but only so long as those individuals do not transgress the media's own moderate-reform-oriented norms.[263]

One can argue that these are good and healthy values for the news to reflect; one can surely argue to the contrary. One can argue that Gans has misperceived the situation. But whatever the merits of the values he describes, or of the media system they appear to inform, if we are looking for a freewheeling and wide-open marketplace of ideas, this is not it. There is no reason to believe that the media, either in news or in entertainment, meaningfully present a genuinely wide or diverse spectrum of ideas and information to remedy the failings of the marketplace.

Is all lost? One can take hope from the fact that some ideas and views *are* communicated in the existing marketplace, if perhaps only within a narrow sphere. One might consider the situation tolerable so long as one believed that in the everyday operation of the marketplace those ideas were given the sort of serious, "rational" consideration that the marketplace metaphor seems to contemplate. That assumption too, however, seems doubtful.

2. Rationality

It is appropriate to take statements in the legal literature about cognitive psychology with a grain of salt. Legal scholars engaging in forays

---

Robert P. Vallone et al., *The Hostile Media Phenomenon: Biased Perception and Perceptions of Media Bias in Coverage of the Beirut Massacre*, 49 J. PERSONALITY & SOC. PSYCHOL. 577 (1985) (finding that *both* pro-Israel and pro-Arab partisans, after viewing identical samples of network television programming covering the Beirut massacre, saw the news segments as biased in favor of the other side).

260. GANS, *supra* note 231, at 42.
261. Schudson, *supra* note 227, at 279.
262. GANS, *supra* note 231, at 52-62.
263. *Id.* at 60-62.

into that field are venturing far from their area of expertise; it is reasonable to suspect either that they do not know what they are talking about, or that they are engaging in selective and out-of-context citation of only that literature helpful to their arguments.[264] Notwithstanding that caution, it is useful here to include at least a nod to relevant social-science literature, in particular that literature addressing the ways in which people process new information. In that area, the approach that has attracted the largest following is a cognitive processing model commonly known as schema theory; that approach has important consequences for our current inquiry.[265]

The gist of the cognitive psychology learning, for our purposes, is that in order to handle the endless flow of communication sweeping over them, people necessarily react to each new bit of information by seeking to fit it into a set of preexisting cognitive structures that provide "simplified mental models" of the world.[266] This reliance is well known to trial

---

264. Legal academics' citation of social science literature may have a lot in common with lawyers' citation of legislative history; legislative history research, I was told as a newly minted law clerk, is a matter of "walking into a crowded room and looking around for your friends." *But see* Jessica Litman, *Copyright Legislation and Technological Change,* 68 OR. L. REV. 275 (1989) (encyclopedic discussion of copyright-law legislative history); Jessica D. Litman, *Copyright, Compromise, and Legislative History,* 72 CORNELL L. REV. 857 (1987) (same).

265. *See* SUSAN T. FISKE & SHELLEY E. TAYLOR, SOCIAL COGNITION 96-179 (2d ed. 1991); DORIS A. GRABER, PROCESSING THE NEWS: HOW PEOPLE TAME THE INFORMATION TIDE 31 (2d ed. 1988); Robert P. Abelson, *Psychological Status of the Script Concept,* 36 AM. PSYCHOLOGIST 715 (1981); Robert Axelrod, *Schema Theory: An Information Processing Model of Perception and Cognition,* 67 AM. POL. SCI. REV. 1248 (1973). A variety of studies that do not use the "schema" terminology nonetheless rely on information-processing models that appear to take essentially similar approaches. *See, e.g.,* ROGER C. SCHANK & ROBERT P. ABELSON, SCRIPTS, PLANS, GOALS, AND UNDERSTANDINGS: AN INQUIRY INTO HUMAN KNOWLEDGE STRUCTURES 36-68 (1977) ("scripts"); STRUCTURE OF DECISION: THE COGNITIVE MAPS OF POLITICAL ELITES (Robert Axelrod ed., 1976) ("cognitive maps"); W. Lance Bennett, *Perception and Cognition: An Information-Processing Framework for Politics, in* 1 THE HANDBOOK OF POLITICAL BEHAVIOR 69, 163-72 (Samuel L. Long ed., 1981) ("preliminary cognitive representations"); Nancy Cantor, *A Cognitive-Social Approach to Personality, in* PERSONALITY, COGNITION, AND SOCIAL INTERACTION 23 (Nancy Cantor & John F. Kihlstrom eds., 1981) ("cognitive structure"); David L. Swanson, *A Constructivist Approach, in* HANDBOOK OF POLITICAL COMMUNICATION 169, 176-80 (Dan D. Nimmo & Keith R. Sanders eds., 1981) ("constructs"); *see also* PAUL CHEVIGNY, MORE SPEECH: DIALOGUE RIGHTS AND MODERN LIBERTY 59-66 (1988); Paul Chevigny, *Pornography and Cognition: A Reply to Cass Sunstein,* 1989 DUKE L.J. 420, 425; Fajer, *supra* note 235, at 524-27 ("pre-understanding").

The schema concept has not gained universal acceptance in the world of social psychology; some scholars argue that it does not provide a valuable theoretical structure for research. *See generally* Susan T. Fiske & Patricia W. Linville, *What Does the Schema Concept Buy Us?,* 6 PERSONALITY & SOC. PSYCHOL. BULL. 543 (1980) (concluding that the schema approach is useful and important). I emphasize schema theory in the pages that follow, but could make most of my crucial points without it: even scholars who reject schema theory agree that people's penchant for processing information in a way consistent with their own beliefs tends to defeat "rational" information processing. *See, e.g.,* Charles G. Lord et al., *Biased Assimilation and Attitude Polarization: The Effects of Prior Theories on Subsequently Considered Evidence,* 37 J. PERSONALITY & SOC. PSYCHOL. 2098 (1979).

266. GRABER, *supra* note 265, at 29.

lawyers. It is reflected, for example, in the results of a study in which people were shown a film about a car accident, questioned about it, and asked, a week later, whether they had seen any broken glass in the film. There was none, but because schemas[267] of car accidents usually involve breakage, a substantial number of the subjects reported seeing it anyway.[268]

The approach of processing new ideas and information by fitting them into existing schemas causes problems when people encounter information that they cannot easily deal with in that manner. People commonly reject information that challenges the accuracy of their schemas. They will not always do so; sometimes they may revise a schema to take into account the new information. But they strongly resist such revisions, and undertake them only reluctantly. They are likely instead to deny the validity of the new information, to attempt to reinterpret it so that it conforms to the schema after all, or to process it as an isolated exception to the general rule.[269] To provide a common-place example, a man who believes women to be submissive and stupid, and meets a woman obviously contradicting the stereotype, is likely to

> simply develop a new stereotype such as "castrating female" or "career woman," keeping his original stereotype for most women and considering his new stereotype to be a kind of exception to the rule. Eventually, as his experience increases, the number of stereotypes he has available also increases—mother, princess, bitch, castrating female, showgirl—and any behavior a female

---

267. Psychology and political science academics generally use "schemata" as the plural of "schema," but I suspect that law professors use more than enough Latin already.

268. The subjects were divided into two groups. The first was asked, shortly after seeing the film, how fast the cars were going when they "smashed into" each other; the second, how fast they were going when they "hit" each other. Thirty-two percent of the first group, and 14% of the second, reported broken glass a week later. ELIZABETH F. LOFTUS, EYEWITNESS TESTIMONY 77-78 (1979); *see also* Amos Tversky & Daniel Kahneman, *Judgment Under Uncertainty: Heuristics and Biases, in* JUDGMENT UNDER UNCERTAINTY: HEURISTICS AND BIASES 3-20 (Daniel Kahneman et al. eds., 1982) (discussing studies in which the subjects' schema-driven reasoning led them to biased or irrational conclusions).

In an earlier and scarier study, researchers showed white subjects a picture of a subway scene including a white man carrying a straight razor and confronting a black man. Subjects were then told to describe the picture to each other, as in the game of "telephone." By the sixth retelling, in the majority of cases, the final description placed the razor in the hands of the black man, and several times he was reported as "brandishing it wildly" or "threatening" the white man with it. *See* Gordon W. Allport & Leo J. Postman, The Basic Psychology of Rumor (Nov. 19, 1945), *in* 8 TRANSACTIONS OF THE NEW YORK ACADEMY OF SCIENCES 61, 66, 78-79 (2d ser., 1946). *But see* Molly Treadway & Michael McCloskey, *Cite Unseen: Distortions of the Allport and Postman Rumor Study in the Eyewitness Testimony Literature,* 11 LAW & HUM. BEHAV. 19, 22 n.1 (1987) (noting that the Allport and Postman study used no control group, and concluding that the errors could reflect simple memory failure rather than racial bias).

269. *See* GRABER, *supra* note 265, at 174-77, 199; *see also* William J. McGuire, *Attitudes and Attitude Change, in* 2 HANDBOOK OF SOCIAL PSYCHOLOGY 233, 275-76 (Gardner Lindzey & Elliot Aronson eds., 3d ed. 1985); Mark Peffley et al., *Economic Conditions and Party Competence: Processes of Belief Revision,* 49 J. POLITICS 100, 101 (1987).

performs can fit within at least one of these stereotypic conceptions without disconfirming the overarching stereotype.[270]
Because people interpret ambiguous reality in accordance with their
schemas, those schemas are self-reinforcing; they become more powerful
as they are repeatedly "tested" but never disconfirmed.[271]

This helps explain the oft-noted point that the mass media are more
effective in reinforcing people's existing attitudes than in changing
them.[272] People have some tendency to ignore information not relevant
to their existing schemas.[273] Once they have made up their minds and
"reached closure" on a particular issue, they are more likely to reject any
new information, whether supportive of or undermining their views.[274]
Indeed, because people seek out and resonate to information consistent
with their schemas,[275] they will support programming that reinforces
their biases. Economic pressures thus lead broadcasters to create such
programming, further reinforcing the status quo. What Walter
Lippmann called "the pictures in our heads" crowd out the outside
world.[276]

Culturally supplied schemas provide perspectives from which people
view social problems. They provide a "metaphysics, an ethics, an episte-
mology, and a value scheme" that provide context and explanation into
which people can seek to fit new information and ideas.[277] They "bear
the imprint of the particular culture in which learning takes place."[278]
To a great extent, they are internalized early in life through socialization
in home, at school, by religious institutions, and through the media.[279]

---

270. Shelley E. Taylor & Jennifer Crocker, *Schematic Bases of Social Information Processing, in*
1 SOCIAL COGNITION: THE ONTARIO SYMPOSIUM 89, 120 (E. Tory Higgins et al. eds., 1981).

271. *See* Daniel Goleman, *Your Unconscious Mind May Be Smarter Than You,* N.Y. TIMES,
June 23, 1992, at C1, C11; *see also* Fajer, *supra* note 235, at 525. Fajer argues that "[t]his
background set of 'knowledge' " powerfully and resiliently shapes the law. *Id.* at 513.

272. Louis L. Jaffe, *The Editorial Responsibility of the Broadcaster: Reflections on Fairness and
Access,* 85 HARV. L. REV. 768, 769-70 (1972). This is not to say that the media are powerless in
affecting attitudes: for the media selectively to reinforce some of a person's attitudes but not others
may well lead to changes in the person's overall complex of beliefs.

273. GRABER, *supra* note 265, at 186.

274. *See id.* at 125-26, 130; David L. Protess et al., *Uncovering Rape: The Watchdog Press and
the Limits of Agenda Setting,* 49 PUB. OPINION Q. 19, 31 (1985) (speculating that the media have
more influence on subjects that have not "already reached a 'saturation' level in the public's mind").

275. *See* FISKE & TAYLOR, *supra* note 265, at 218-20.

276. WALTER LIPPMANN, PUBLIC OPINION 3 (1922).

277. ROBERT E. LANE, POLITICAL IDEOLOGY: WHY THE AMERICAN COMMON MAN
BELIEVES WHAT HE DOES 418 (1962).

278. LIPPMANN, *supra* note 276, at 185; *see also* LANE, *supra* note 277, at 417-18 (stating that
members of society interpret observations and experiences through cultural premises); Bennett,
supra note 265, at 122-24.

279. *See* GRABER, *supra* note 265, at 184-86. The schools make an especially important
contribution to the socialization process: attendance is compulsory; the audience is unsophisticated;
and children's well-being and future success are made contingent on their learning and internalizing
what is taught to them. *See* Ingber, *supra* note 182, at 28-30. Schools thus are successful at
"promoting respect for authority and traditional values be they social, moral, or political." Board of

In the United States, these cognitive structures underlie the substantial political consensus—the shared generalized norms about market-based liberal democracy and the "American way"—that characterizes our heterogeneous society.[280]

This explanation provides grounding for a feminist critique of First Amendment law. Catharine MacKinnon and others have argued that pornography reinforces—indeed creates—scripts and schemas of women as wanting to be taken and used, to be subjected, violated, and possessed. Pornography "constructs what a woman is" by reference to men's desires and fantasies.[281] Perhaps more fundamentally, it is argued, pornography reinforces a fundamental schema of sex itself as about dominance and submission; in that picture, "[s]ubjection itself with self-determination ecstatically relinquished is the content of women's sexual desire and desirability."[282] Pornography "tells men what sex means, what a real woman is, and codes them together in a way that is behaviorally reinforcing."[283]

The results of the schematic coding, according to feminist theory, are profound. Because the schema objectifies women, it strips them of credibility in the eyes of those for whom the schema is powerful.[284] When women complain of sexual assault and violence, a complaint at odds with a cognitive structure in which violence and domination are appropriate and welcome sexual interplay, their voices are not heard or believed.[285] Men for whom that schema has been cued by pornography, according to some studies, are more likely to condone sexual assault, to predict that they would force sex on a woman if they knew they would not get caught, and to view rape victims as less seriously injured.[286] To

---

Educ. v. Pico, 457 U.S. 853, 864 (1982) (plurality opinion) (quoting Brief for Petitioner); *see also* Brown v. Board of Educ., 347 U.S. 483, 493 (1954).

Other socializing influences include mass media entertainment, which "inculcates the predominant cultural values and socializes individuals to execute certain roles," reaffirming the "basic . . . stories that structure [our] experience." OFFICE OF TECHNOLOGY ASSESSMENT, U.S. CONGRESS, CRITICAL CONNECTIONS: COMMUNICATION FOR THE FUTURE 203 (1990). *See generally* CLIFFORD GEERTZ, THE INTERPRETATION OF CULTURES 214-18 (1973) (cultural templates).

280. *See* GRABER, *supra* note 265, at 66, 210-11, 254; *see also* Carter, *supra* note 217, at 588.

281. MacKinnon, *supra* note 27, at 17.

282. *Id.*

283. *Id.* at 59.

284. Consider
   the credibility problems Linda Marchiano encounters when she says that . . . in "Deep Throat" . . . she . . . did not feel or enjoy what the character she was forced to portray felt and enjoyed. . . . [B]efore "Linda Lovelace" was seen performing deep throat, no one had ever seen it being done in that way, largely because it cannot be done without hypnosis to repress the natural gag response. *Yet it was believed.* . . . Yet when Linda Marchiano now tells that it took kidnapping and death threats and hypnosis to put her there, that is found *difficult to believe.*

Id. at 35-36.

285. *See id.* at 14, 34-36, 63. *See generally* Dworkin, *supra* note 204, at 15-19.

286. *See* MacKinnon, *supra* note 27, at 52-55. *But cf.* Powe, *supra* note 12, at 64 & n.80.

1162   *CALIFORNIA LAW REVIEW*   [Vol. 81:1101

the extent that such a cognitive structure pervades our society, socialized through entertainment and otherwise, it becomes more nearly imperceptible, part of the general cultural background.[287]

All this has distressing implications for marketplace theory. To the extent that our schemas constrain our reactions to new ideas and information, our thinking is not characterized by "reason," in the Cartesian sense. Hobbled by our adherence to long-established mental patterns, we can hardly create a collective marketplace of ideas that is a place of unfettered discourse and discovery.[288] It is the packaging of an argument, not its content, that determines how it will be received:[289] the manner in which an argument or news story is focused will influence listeners' unconscious choice as to which schema they will fit it into, and thus may drastically change their response.[290] Because their schemas influence what new ideas and information they are willing to accept, "people's social location . . . control[s] the manner in which they perceive or understand the world."[291] To the extent that our most basic views and values are relatively immune to rational argument, the marketplace metaphor seems pointless.

When one considers the cumulative impact of the economic and psychological attacks on the marketplace metaphor, it seems almost willfully blind to excuse the costs that free-speech doctrine imposes by answering that government may not deny speech its fair opportunity to prevail in the marketplace. We do not seem to have a working "marketplace" outside a fairly narrowly bounded range of socially acceptable ideas and values. Debate seems to be possible only within a "community agenda of alternatives";[292] it withers outside those borders.[293]

Empirical studies such as these, unfortunately, are even more of a morass for the unwary and inexpert than is the theoretical material I set out earlier. On the difficulties in interpreting such empirical work, see, e.g., Weinberg, *supra* note 17, at 1290 n.64.

287. *See* MacKinnon, *supra* note 27, at 7-8, 20.

288. *See* Ingber, *supra* note 182, at 25-27, 34-36.

289. *See* Baker, *supra* note 182, at 976-77 (arguing that form and frequency of message presentation, as well as personal interests and experiences, determine how debate will affect individuals' understandings).

290. This phenomenon is clearest in the area of opinion surveys. *See* GRABER, *supra* note 265, at 158-60, 261; *see also supra* note 268. In one recent nationwide survey, 44% of those polled responded that we spend too much money on "welfare," and only 23% that we spend too little. Only 13%, though, answered that we spend too much on "assistance to the poor"; on the contrary, 64% told the pollsters that we should spend more. Robin Toner, *New Politics of Welfare Focuses on Its Flaws,* N.Y. TIMES, July 5, 1992, § 1, at 1.

291. Baker, *supra* note 182, at 967 ; *see id.* at 976. The differences in schemas caused by social location may be submerged to the extent that "[p]eople exposed to the same media sources are prone to tap into similar schemata in response to their shared media cues," GRABER, *supra* note 265, at 159, but that is hardly an improvement from the perspective of the marketplace metaphor.

292. NELSON W. POLSBY, COMMUNITY POWER AND POLITICAL THEORY 135 (2d ed. 1980); *see also* Ingber, *supra* note 182, at 73-74.

293. Political and policy ideas, thus, that are considered quite conventional in European countries (not to mention in countries whose political systems differ more radically from our own)

All of the criticisms of the marketplace model discussed here have been raised before,[294] yet First Amendment doctrine rolls right along as if none of them posed a problem. First Amendment jurisprudence acknowledges their existence—and sometimes concedes their validity— only to hold that they must be deemed irrelevant to actual law.[295] This is especially true when it comes to concerns about the nonrational effects of speech, which rarely bear fruit except in obscenity law.[296] They are tolerated in that domain because of the notion that the speech in question isn't really "speech" at all.[297] In the vast majority of contexts, we suppress even thinking about these issues.

Our inattention to these arguments seems even more odd when one

---

are not seriously debated in this country at all. This is not to say that people cannot come to accept ideas opposed by important socializing influences and by politically and economically powerful institutions. Recent events in the former Soviet Union and Eastern Europe demonstrate that they can. But the obstacles to that process seem sufficiently daunting as to make the marketplace quite doubtful as a model or a metaphor.

294. *See, e.g.,* BARRON, *supra* note 214; Allan C. Hutchinson, *Talking the Good Life: From Free Speech to Democratic Dialogue,* 1 YALE J.L. & LIB. 17 (1989); MacKinnon, *supra* note 27.

295. Chief Justice Burger, writing for a unanimous Court in Miami Herald Publishing Co. v. Tornillo, 418 U.S. 241 (1974), explained that even if one conceded that "the public has lost any ability to . . . contribute in a meaningful way to the debate on [public] issues," that "economic factors . . . have made entry into the marketplace of ideas . . . almost impossible," and that accordingly "the 'marketplace of ideas' is today a monopoly controlled by the owners of the market," those concerns were simply irrelevant to analysis of a state right-of-reply statute. The statute was unconstitutional, without more, because it "[c]ompell[ed] editors . . . to publish that which ' "reason" tells them should not be published.' " *Id.* at 250, 251, 256.

Judge Easterbrook, similarly, writing in American Booksellers Ass'n v. Hudnut, 771 F.2d 323 (7th Cir. 1985), *aff'd mem.,* 475 U.S. 1001 (1986), agreed that "[e]ven the truth has little chance unless a statement fits within the framework of beliefs that may never have been subjected to rational study," for "[p]eople may be conditioned in subtle ways." *Id.* at 329, 330. Nevertheless, he stated, "the Constitution does not make the dominance of truth a necessary condition of freedom of speech"; that the marketplace metaphor fails should have no effect on established doctrine forbidding the creation of "an approved point of view." *Id.* at 330, 332.

Campaign finance jurisprudence, finally, has similarly rejected almost all statutory attacks on the use of private economic power to skew the marketplace of ideas. *See* Buckley v. Valeo, 424 U.S. 1, 39-59 (1976); *see also* First Nat'l Bank v. Bellotti, 435 U.S. 765, 790-92 (1978). *But see* Austin v. Michigan State Chamber of Commerce, 494 U.S. 652, 660 (1990) (upholding a statute designed to ameliorate "the corrosive and distorting effects of immense aggregations of wealth that are accumulated with the help of the corporate form and that have little or no correlation to the public's support for the corporation's political ideas," by prohibiting corporate treasury expenditures in support of or opposition to candidates).

296. *See* Paris Adult Theatre I v. Slaton, 413 U.S. 49, 63 (1973) (emphasizing the "corrupting and debasing" impact of obscene speech). Concerns about the nonrational effects of speech occasionally emerge in other contexts as well. *See, e.g.,* NLRB v. Retail Store Employees Union, Local 1001, 447 U.S. 607, 619 (1980) (Stevens, J., concurring) (peaceful labor picketing invites "an automatic response to a signal, rather than a reasoned response to an idea"); Mark D. Schneider, Note, *Peaceful Labor Picketing and the First Amendment,* 82 COLUM. L. REV. 1469, 1490-93 (1982) (criticizing assertions that labor picketing invites "emotive" responses and therefore does not warrant First Amendment protection).

297. *But see* R.A.V. v. City of St. Paul, 112 S. Ct. 2538, 2543 (1992) (characterizing obscenity and fighting words as not "entirely invisible to the Constitution," and explaining that "the occasionally repeated shorthand characterizing obscenity as 'not being speech at all' " is not "literally trne").

notices that they are of the sort that we *accepted* in the economic context almost seventy-five years ago.[298] They rest on the same foundations as did the arguments used by the legal realists in the 1920s and 1930s to attack *Lochner v. New York.*[299] That a regime of formal freedom and equal rights may in fact be unfree and unequal because of gross preexisting inequality in economic or other power is not a new argument, and surely was not invented by Jerome Barron or Catharine MacKinnon. It was at the heart of our rejection of *Lochner.* We long ago accepted these arguments in the economic context, even while refusing to acknowledge them in the area of speech.[300]

Why have these claims gotten so little acceptance with respect to freedom of speech? Different authors have offered different explanations. Some suggest that we have been unwilling to accept Realist attacks on formalism in speech law, because doing so would require us to acknowledge the failure of the theory underlying *Carolene Products*[301] and our rejection of *Lochner:* that courts' enforcement of the value-neutral rules of the democratic process disposes of any need for them to second-guess substantive legislative choices.[302] Others argue that the socially dominant accept the marketplace metaphor because it validates their own socially dominant views.[303] One might argue that legal decisionmakers are resistant to these arguments because they are wary of breaching the theoretical integrity of First Amendment philosophy, worried that the entire structure will be threatened; they are not so unhappy with the status quo as to be willing to think thoughts that might endanger or compromise the theoretical framework.[304] All of these answers, though, seem to me still insufficient; in the remainder of this Article I shall attempt to provide yet another explanation.

III
PUTTING IT TOGETHER

We find ourselves faced with not one but two dilemmas. The first relates to the failure of broadcast regulation to conform to ordinary free-

---

298. *See* Balkin, *supra* note 175, at 379-82; Sunstein, *supra* note 8, at 264-66.

299. 198 U.S. 45 (1905).

300. *See supra* notes 205-07 and accompanying text.

301. United States v. Carolene Prods. Co., 304 U.S. 144, 152 n.4 (1938).

302. *See* GRABER, *supra* note 156, at 160; Balkin, *supra* note 175, at 387-97.

303. *See, e.g.,* BAKER, *supra* note 33, at 16; CATHARINE A. MACKINNON, FEMINISM UNMODIFIED 206-13 (1987).

304. *Cf.* Frederick Schauer, *The Calculus of Distrust,* 77 VA. L. REV. 653, 666-67 (1991) (discussing constitutional theory generally).

Still others offer quite different reasons. Legal academics and legal decisionmakers, some point out, are intellectuals who traffic in ideas; "self-interest combines with self-esteem" to lead them to the view that others should be regulated while they should be exempt. Coase, *supra* note 176, at 386. Others offer different answers still. *See, e.g.,* BOLLINGER, *supra* note 11, at 59-60; Ingber, *supra* note 182, at 71-85.

dom-of-speech philosophy; the second relates to the failure of ordinary freedom-of-speech philosophy to conform to the world we live in. I believe that these two problems are linked.

A key lesson of Part I is that broadcast regulation is inconsistent with conventional freedom-of-speech philosophy because broadcast law gratuitously gives government officials the job of restraining speech *not* on the basis of hard-edged, easy-to-apply, nondiscretionary bright-line rules, but on the basis of subjective and ambiguous standards. Government officials thus can exercise great discretion as to who can speak over the air and what those speakers can say. That problem, in large part, is one of *form;* the transgression of broadcast law is that it takes the form of vague directions to government officials to advance vague values. The key lesson of Part II, by contrast, is that First Amendment ideology seems incomplete along a *substantive* dimension; it is based on a substantively inaccurate picture of what the world looks like.

In order to bring these two lessons together, I have relied on some insights developed by authors associated with critical legal studies (CLS). I have not adopted the entire weave of CLS thinking;[305] I have taken selected points that seem to me helpful in understanding the problems that this Article raises.[306] I rely heavily on the technique, common in CLS writing, of "analysis of paired oppositions": that is, identifying opposed philosophical tendencies, or procedural forms, that seem pervasive in legal decisionmaking.[307] CLS writers sometimes use the tech-

---

305. If any such thing as "CLS thinking" can be identified. Mark Tushnet, one of the movement's most prolific authors, writes:

> As I read articles by and about critical legal studies, I not infrequently find myself puzzled. The authors of the articles provoking this reaction describe what they believe critical legal studies to be, and yet the descriptions do not resonate strongly with what I think about the law. . . . [I find] people whom I regard as co-participants in the enterprise of critical legal studies . . . taking as central to their understanding of cls propositions that I find extremely problematic, or dismissing as unimportant propositions that I find central . . . .

Mark Tushnet, *Critical Legal Studies: A Political History,* 100 YALE L.J. 1515, 1516 (1991). Tushnet concludes that "the project of critical legal studies does not have any essential intellectual component" but is instead a "political location." *Id.*

306. My attitude towards those insights is somewhat tentative and ambiguous. With regard to some of them, I am uncertain whether the insight is completely right, or whether it is but "partial and incomplete truth," MILL, *supra* note 26, at 56: accurate in some contexts but not in others, perhaps, or illuminating only some facets of a complex reality. For the most part, I have not stopped to explore those concerns and doubts in the context of this Article. A key point of this Article, after all, is that a theory drawn from CLS insights *does work*—where other approaches do not—in explaining the particular puzzle of speech law. To spend too much time on the validity of the insights in areas unrelated to broadcasting would detract from that main point.

307. *See* Tushnet, *supra* note 305, at 1524. Examples include Jay M. Feinman, *Critical Approaches to Contract Law,* 30 UCLA L. REV. 829 (1983); Frances E. Olsen, *The Family and the Market: A Study of Ideology and Legal Reform,* 96 HARV. L. REV. 1497 (1983); Pierre Schlag, *Rules and Standards,* 33 UCLA L. REV. 379 (1985); Joseph W. Singer, *The Legal Rights Debate in Analytical Jurisprudence from Bentham to Hohfeld,* 1982 WIS. L. REV. 975, 980-84; Betty Mensch, *Freedom of Contract as Ideology,* 33 STAN. L. REV. 753, 759-64 (1981) (book review); *see also*

nique of identifying fundamental dichotomies to argue that the body of law being discussed is incapable of reasoned justification, and, indeed, incoherent.[308] I will look to these oppositions, in my own analysis, first to consider the extent to which ordinary free speech philosophy and broadcast regulation can be understood as reflecting such opposing poles. I will later, in the next Part of this Article, consider the extent to which the oppositions reflected in our speech law are irreconcilable: is there a way to get the best of both worlds?

I will begin this Part by examining the opposition between the two procedural options for resolving legal issues known as "rules" and "standards." Core free-speech philosophy maintains a strong commitment to rules; broadcast regulation relies heavily on standards. I will next examine the substantive opposition embodied in Part II of this Article. That dichotomy opposes a worldview focusing on the freedom and autonomy inherent in the "private" sphere, unregulated by government, to a worldview focusing on the pervasiveness of inequality and constraint throughout the world of private ordering. I will note Duncan Kennedy's suggestion of a link between rules and the philosophy he refers to as individualism, and between standards and the philosophy he refers to as altruism. The opposition of individualism and altruism, I will suggest, is in turn linked to the opposition of autonomy and constraint. I will then note the opposition of value subjectivity and value objectivity, as well as paternalism and nonpaternalism. All of these, I will suggest, can be pulled together into two, more nearly comprehensive, opposing worldviews. The first links rules, individualism, a belief in overall private autonomy, a sharp public-private distinction, value subjectivity, and nonpaternalism; the other links standards, altruism, a belief in the pervasiveness of constraint, a denial of the public-private distinction, value objectivity (or a belief in the communal nature of values), and paternalism. I will suggest, finally, that in important ways the first of these worldviews is privileged in our law.

Balkin, *supra* note 198. Some authors have followed Derrida into deconstructionism, seeking to establish that the twin poles of such dichotomies are each dependent on the other—that while "rational" thought seeks hierarchically to privilege one pole, each in fact supplements and signifies the other. *See, e.g.,* J.M. Balkin, *Deconstructive Practice and Legal Theory,* 96 YALE L.J. 743, 746-61 (1987); Clare Dalton, *An Essay in the Deconstruction of Contract Doctrine,* 94 YALE L.J. 997, 1007-08 (1985).

Nor need one be associated with CLS to undertake similar analysis. Some of the oppositions I find in this Article are reminiscent of the distinctions between "democracy" and "community" drawn in the work of Robert Post, who finds CLS unhelpful. Post rejects the notion that democracy and community are inherently irreconcilable; rather, they are "distinct and antagonistic but reciprocally interdependent." Robert C. Post, *Between Democracy and Community: The Legal Constitution of Social Form, in* DEMOCRATIC COMMUNITY: NOMOS XXXV 163, 163 (John W. Chapman & Ian Shapiro eds., 1993).

308. Because there are legitimate opposing themes and techniques available to resolve any issue, no resolution has any special claim to correctness, and no resolution is consistent with all underlying themes.

With that background, the missing pieces of the speech law puzzle fall into place. Core freedom-of-speech thinking looks like a straightforward exposition of the privileged position; our system of broadcast regulation has much more in common with the nonprivileged pole. The distinction is not quite so neat as all that; we have reintroduced some privileged-position law into the broadcast regulatory structure. Still, the glaring inconsistency of the two bodies of law stems from their roots in the two opposing worldviews. I suggest, at the end of this Part, that the basic nature of speech law makes accommodation between the two competing visions much more problematic than in other doctrinal areas. Individualist free speech philosophy has no point other than protecting the private citizen from public tyranny. As a result, it raises the public-private distinction to a level of sacred inviolability. Free speech philosophy plays that role because of the privileged position's roots in mainstream liberal political philosophy. That philosophy is centrally about the problem of political despotism. A theory of free speech is in turn central to that concern. As a result, privileged-position thinking assumes its most severe form when we start talking about speech.

A. An Initial Framework

It has often been noted that legal issues can be resolved by using either (1) simple, hard-edged, black-letter rules, causing results to turn mechanically on a limited number of fairly easily ascertainable facts, or (2) more nearly ad hoc, informal, situationally sensitive application of general policy directives.[309] I will adopt a terminology popularized by Duncan Kennedy, referring to the first approach as that of "rules" and the second as that of "standards."[310]

The choice between rules and standards seems ubiquitous in legal

---

309. *See* Schlag, *supra* note 307, at 379-80, 383-98; Kathleen M. Sullivan, *The Supreme Court, 1991 Term—Forward: The Justices of Rules and Standards*, 106 HARV. L. REV. 22, 58-59 (1992). Indeed, the argument has been made that *all* legal issues can be resolved in each of these two ways. One might object to this formulation on the ground that all legal solutions are not self-evidently in one or the other of the two categories; rather, one might argue, it is more appropriate to order legal solutions along a continuum with polar black-letter and situationally sensitive models at each end. Because ruleness and standardness exist only along a continuum, according to one commentator, "to claim that a law is [exclusively] either a rule or a standard is to deny its fundamental reality." David G. Carlson, *Contradiction and Critical Legal Studies*, 10 CARDOZO L. REV. 1833, 1838 (1989) (book review). For immediate purposes, though, my core argument is simply that it is meaningful and potentially useful to rely on the two polar models in discussing legal solutions. The fact that so many legal disputes can so easily be framed in terms of rules versus standards suggests that there is something to the distinction.

310. Duncan Kennedy, *Form and Substance in Private Law Adjudication*, 89 HARV. L. REV. 1685, 1685, 1687-89 (1976); *see also* ROBERTO M. UNGER, KNOWLEDGE & POLITICS 91 (1975) (approaching the same dichotomy using the terminology of "legal justice" and "substantive justice"). The terminology of rules and standards can be traced at least as far back as Roscoe Pound. *See* Roscoe Pound, *Hierarchy of Sources and Forms in Different Systems of Law*, 7 TUL. L. REV. 475, 482-86 (1933) (also discussing "principles," "conceptions," and "doctrines").

1168   *CALIFORNIA LAW REVIEW*   [Vol. 81:1101

decisionmaking. In the area of contract law, for example, using a rule-like approach, we might seek to enforce *all* contracts supported by formal consideration, subject to sharply and clearly bounded exceptions for fraud, duress, and lack of capacity. On the other hand, we might take the view that an element of "fraud" or "duress" is present in greater or lesser degree in *every* case, and thus cannot form the basis for a sharply bounded exception. We therefore might use a standard-like approach to invalidate contracts if, based on a situationally sensitive analysis, the parties seem to have had markedly unequal bargaining power, or if the contracts simply seem too unfair.[311] The rule-like approach promotes certainty and ease of application, but subordinates concerns about real-life inequalities in contracting.

In the area of criminal law, similarly, we can constrain the discretion of capital juries in the penalty phase by requiring legislatures sharply to define the circumstances calling for death in clear, rule-like, nondiscretionary terms.[312] We can empower juries to exercise situationally sensitive judgment by requiring that they always be allowed to hear any conceivably mitigating evidence, and acquit if they so choose.[313] The Supreme Court, in fact, over the past fifteen years has sought to do both at once, yielding spectacularly incoherent results.[314]

What are the consequences of relying on rules rather than standards, or vice versa? Because no rule exhibits a perfect "fit" with the

---

311. *See* MARK KELMAN, A GUIDE TO CRITICAL LEGAL STUDIES 18-19 (1987).

312. *See* Gregg v. Georgia, 428 U.S. 153, 155, 188-95 (1976).

313. *See* Lockett v. Ohio, 438 U.S. 586, 604-05 (1978); Woodson v. North Carolina, 428 U.S. 280, 303-05 (1976).

314. *See generally* Walton v. Arizona, 497 U.S. 639, 656-74 (1990) (Scalia, J., concurring); Robert Weisberg, *Deregulating Death*, 1983 SUP. CT. REV. 305.

Other examples abound. In the administrative law realm, the Occupational Safety and Health Administration (OSHA) can on the one hand prescribe exactly how many feet wide scaffolding must be; it can on the other hand simply ban scaffolding that poses "unreasonable" danger. The former, rulelike approach may ignore a variety of relevant distinctions among work settings, and may be ill-suited to coping with industry changes. It may, however, be easier and surer of administration than the latter, standard-like approach, especially where workers have little power. *See* KELMAN, *supra* note 311, at 33-34. On rule-bounded legality versus situationally sensitive bargaining in administrative regulation, see generally Weinberg, *supra* note 40, at 623-40.

AFDC benefits law can focus on the "rights" of recipients to benefits based on certain verifiable factual predicates (rule), or it can grant extensive, situationally-sensitive power to the welfare caseworker based on her professional judgment (standard). *See* William H. Simon, *Legality, Bureaucracy, and Class in the Welfare System*, 92 YALE L.J. 1198, 1223-24 (1983). Welfare law over the last 30 years has moved almost completely from the latter to the former vision. *See* Goldberg v. Kelly, 397 U.S. 254, 271 (1970). Neither system, however, has worked particularly well. *See generally* THEODORE R. MARMOR ET AL., AMERICA'S MISUNDERSTOOD WELFARE STATE (1990).

In the area of private conflict of laws, we can select the appropriate jurisdiction through clear, hard-edged rules emphasizing uniformity and certainty of result, such as the traditional rule of *lex loci delicti*, which refers all conflicts involving any substantive issue in a tort case to the law of the place of injury. We can, on the other hand, abandon the old rules and rely instead on a more standard-like, ad hoc, "interest analysis." *See generally* Alfred Hill, *The Judicial Function in Choice of Law*, 85 COLUM. L. REV. 1585, 1623-25 (1985); Harold L. Korn, *The Choice-of-Law Revolution: A Critique*, 83 COLUM. L. REV. 772, 787-99 (1983); Willis L.M. Reese, *Choice of Law: Rules or*

policies underlying it, application of a rule will on some occasions lead to results contrary to those policies. Setting eighteen years as the age of majority for voting purposes excludes from the franchise some who are quite capable and mature, yet includes many who might be deemed, on a closer inspection, childish, inexperienced, and immature.[315] Standards, because they merely restate underlying policies, do not exhibit that problem. On the other hand, the great advantage of rules (as opposed to standards) in conventional thought is that rules are said to increase certainty, predictability, and ease of administration in law application, and decrease arbitrariness and the possibility of biased enforcement.[316] Few of us, after all, would welcome the creation of a government office charged with the task of examining each of us individually, regardless of age, and determining whether we were sufficiently experienced and mature to be allowed to vote.[317]

The divergent choices we have made in our conventional free speech philosophy and in our system of broadcast regulation replicate the rules-standards opposition. Core free-speech philosophy manifests a strong commitment to rules; it emphasizes at every turn that the law should be expressed in hard-edged, nondiscretionary terms so as to minimize the possibility of government discretion, arbitrariness, and bias.[318] Situationally sensitive judgment by government officials is forbidden; government may not make legal results in this area turn on "appraisal of facts, the exercise of judgment, and the formation of an opinion."[319] The

---

Approach, 57 CORNELL L. REV. 315 (1972); Robert A. Sedler, *Rules of Choice of Law Versus Choice-of-Law Rules: Judicial Method in Conflicts Torts Cases,* 44 TENN. L. REV. 975 (1977).

For examples drawn from constitutional law, see Sullivan, *supra* note 309, at 76-95. For other examples of the choice between rules and standards in specific doctrinal areas, see Schlag, *supra* note 307, at 383 n.19.

315. The *point* of rules, indeed, is that they "screen[] off from a decisionmaker factors that a sensitive decisionmaker would otherwise take into account," Frederick Schauer, *Formalism,* 97 YALE L.J. 509, 510 (1988), and thus may require results ill-serving the reasons behind the rules. *See id.* at 534-37.

316. *See* Kennedy, *supra* note 310, at 1688; Sullivan, *supra* note 309, at 62-63.

317. For a careful defense of rules, see Schauer, *supra* note 315, at 538-44. For a recent judicial discussion of the value of rules in constitutional law, see Quill Corp. v. North Dakota, 112 S. Ct. 1904, 1914-16 (1992); for an attack on the rule thus justified, see *id.* at 1921-22 (White, J., concurring in part and dissenting in part).

318. The reader should not confuse the rules-standards issue in regulating citizens' *primary conduct* (where First Amendment philosophy insists that speech regulation be cast in the form of rules), with the issue, one level up, whether rules or standards are most appropriate for determining *whether a regulation is constitutional.* One can adopt a rules (categorical or absolutist) or standards (balancing) approach for determining whether a regulation substantively goes too far in suppressing speech; one can adopt a rule-like or standard-like approach for determining what sort of speech is worthy of what level of protection. *See* LAURENCE H. TRIBE, AMERICAN CONSTITUTIONAL LAW § 12-2, at 792-94 (2d ed. 1988); Schlag, *supra* note 307, at 394-98. Whatever the result of those determinations, though, the law on the books is supposed to consist solely of rules. *See generally* Frederick Schauer, *The Second-Best First Amendment,* 31 WM. & MARY L. REV. 1, 14-15 (1989).

319. Forsyth County v. Nationalist Movement, 112 S. Ct. 2395, 2401-02 (1992) (quoting Cantwell v. Connecticut, 310 U.S. 296, 305 (1940)).

state may not enact vaguely worded restrictions on speech; those are deemed to inhibit expression by causing people, unsure how the restrictions will be applied, to "steer [wide] of the unlawful zone."[320] Consistently with the ideology of rule-bounded legality, First Amendment law insists that only clear and hard-edged rules operate with sufficient predictability and adequately minimize the possibility of hidden arbitrariness or bias.

By contrast, our broadcast regulatory system foundationally relies on the situationally sensitive standard: the FCC is told only that it should take those steps that advance the "public interest, convenience, and necessity." This is the opposite of the hard-edged rule. The "vaguish, penumbral bounds expressed by the standard of the 'public interest' "[321] leave the administrator discretion to advance the legislator's values, and hold no promise of predictability or protection against bias. "The statutory standard . . . leaves wide discretion and calls for imaginative interpretation."[322] As originally enunciated and applied by the FCC, the Communications Act public-interest standard aspired to intuitive, sensitive judgment, largely unconstrained, and closely attuned to the dilemmas of each individual case.[323] The agency was to "bring[] the deposit of its experience, the disciplined feel of the expert, to bear on applications for licenses in the public interest."[324]

Standards are also prominent when it comes to regulating broadcast conduct. Indecency law calls upon the licensee to avoid "patently offensive" programming; the FCC has insisted that offensiveness can only be gauged through "judgment" and careful consideration of "the many variables that make up a work's 'context.' "[325] The recently enacted Children's Television Act of 1990 calls upon the Commission in vague terms to "consider," in reviewing a television renewal application, "the extent to which the licensee . . . has served the educational and informational needs of children."[326] The Commission has not promulgated regulations bounding that inquiry with hard-edged rules.[327] The fairness

---

320. Grayned v. City of Rockford, 408 U.S. 104, 109 (1972) (quoting Baggett v. Bullitt, 377 U.S. 372 (1964)).

321. FCC v. RCA Communications, Inc., 346 U.S. 86, 91 (1953).

322. *Id.* at 90.

323. *See* Weinberg, *supra* note 40, at 655-56; *supra* notes 66-69 and accompanying text.

324. *RCA Communications,* 346 U.S. at 91. The FCC later departed from this glorification of unbounded discretion. *See infra* text accompanying notes 395-405.

325. Infinity Broadcasting Corp., 3 F.C.C.R. 930, 932 (1987), *aff'd in relevant part sub nom.* Action for Children's Television v. FCC, 852 F.2d 1332 (D.C. Cir. 1988).

326. 47 U.S.C. § 303b (a) (Supp. II 1990).

327. In part because the Commission has not promulgated limiting rules, it has received extensive filings asserting that broadcasters have served "the educational and informational needs of children" through "GI Joe," "The Jetsons," "Super Mario Brothers," and similar programming. *See* Edmund L. Andrews, *Broadcasters, to Satisfy Law, Define Cartoons as Education,* N.Y. TIMES, Sept. 30, 1992, at A1; Joe Flint, *Study Slams Broadcasters' Kids Act Compliance,* BROADCASTING, Oct. 5, 1992, at 40. The Commission has since sought comment as to whether and in what manner it

doctrine, although repealed in the late 1980s, remained situationally sensitive to the last. Thus, the formal dichotomy embodied in Part I of this Article is procedural: ordinary free-speech philosophy is committed to rules, while broadcast regulation is built around the situationally sensitive standard.

In contrast, in Part II, the distinction is substantive; it relates to a vision of how the world operates. Conventional free-speech philosophy is characterized by its image of an atomistic "marketplace" of ideas akin to the economic marketplace, marked by individual autonomy, competition, and separateness.[328] It assumes that individuals can participate meaningfully as individuals in the marketplace of ideas, autonomously able to speak and to convince others of their views, unaffected by the skewing or coercive effects of inequalities of wealth and power in the private sphere. It assumes that people react to speech in rational ways, choosing to adopt one belief rather than another as part of a willed, chosen reasoning process; it rejects the position that people's views are largely determined by their schemas, their socialization, their social position, or other factors irrelevant to "reason" in the Cartesian sense. The only meaningful source of constraint in the marketplace of ideas in this vision is government intervention. Government intervention forces silence where there would otherwise be speech, limiting the free play of ideas that would otherwise prevail.

I argued in Part II that the vision of ordinary free-speech philosophy is inaccurate, that its assumptions badly describe reality. Broadcast regulation reflects that critique. Broadcast regulation is rooted in the concern that inequality of private power and resources undermines citizens' free interaction. Absent administrative allocation, according to *Red Lion,* a few private licensees might "monopoliz[e]" broadcast discourse, making impossible "an uninhibited marketplace of ideas."[329] If government does not enforce a fairness doctrine, in the world of *Red Lion,* private holders of media power will be able to exercise "unlimited private censorship."[330] Broadcast regulation incorporates the concern that viewers' tastes and wants are themselves determined, shaped by general socioeconomic forces and by the mass media itself: that what viewers get from the mass media may help determine what they want.[331] It

---

might "exemplify and define the [statute's] programming requirements." Revision of Programming Policies for Television Broadcast Stations, 1993 FCC LEXIS 987 (March 2, 1993), at 8.

328. *Cf.* Post, *supra* note 35, at 284, 293-94 (not relying on the marketplace metaphor, but nonetheless describing individualism as central to First Amendment philosophy and the democratic project).

329. Red Lion Broadcasting Co. v. FCC, 395 U.S. 367, 390 (1969); *see also* BOLLINGER, *supra* note 11, at 63.

330. *Red Lion Broadcasting Co.,* 395 U.S. at 392.

331. *See* Balkin, *supra* note 175, at 379; Sunstein, *supra* note 8, at 288 ("[P]rivate broadcasting selections are a product of preferences that are themselves a result of the broadcasting status quo, and not independent of it.").

therefore insists that government *not* simply leave broadcasting to the control of the marketplace; rather, government must supervise broadcasting in the "public interest." All this stems from a worldview in which the unregulated private sphere is marked not by freedom and autonomy, but—at least to some degree—by domination and constraint.

Just as the procedural differences between free-speech philosophy and broadcast law are mirrored in the larger legal context, this substantive conflict finds reflections in the larger world as well. A CLS-minded observer would point out that the interplay between a worldview focusing on the autonomy of actors in the "private sphere" and one emphasizing the ubiquity of dependence and constraint is not limited to the narrow confines of speech and broadcast law. Rather, it looks a lot like an opposition observable in the world of law at large.

Contract law, for example, faces the same choice between ideologies as does speech law. How ought contract law to approach the issues of duress and fraud? It might follow mainstream freedom of speech philosophy by treating private ordering in the marketplace as completely free and autonomous; it would limit its response to concerns of duress, fraud, and unconscionability by confining those concerns to exceptional, supplementary, sharply bounded doctrinal areas.[332]

Alternatively, contract law might seek to follow broadcast regulation, and the critique of mainstream free-speech philosophy, by developing a body of doctrine treating dependence, duress, and constraint as more nearly pervasive.[333] This approach would not treat "private" contract as something presumptively to be left free from "public" intrusion. Rather, it would incorporate the view that the pervasiveness of unequal

---

332. This approach incorporates a strong opposition between private and public spheres. The private sphere is seen as the realm of intentionalism and free choice; the public sphere, by contrast, as the necessary-evil realm of collective coercion. Constitutional lawyers will recognize this in its most extreme form as the philosophy of Lochner v. New York, 198 U.S. 45 (1905). For a useful summary, see Olsen, *supra* note 307, at 1502-03.

The approach has its problems. All private contracts, after all, take place against a background of state-created and state-enforced rights and entitlements; every bargain is thus a function of a legal system that is not "natural" but political. *See* Mensch, *supra* note 307, at 764; *see also* Sunstein, *supra* note 8, at 264-65; Weinberg, *supra* note 17, at 1273-74. There is no sharp-edged way to distinguish between agreements entered into as a matter of uncoerced choice, and those that are a product of impermissible duress; as the Realists pointed out, all choices in this world are constrained. We make our arrangements only within the existing legal framework and the existing (significantly publicly determined) distribution of rights and privileges. *See* John P. Dawson, *Economic Duress—An Essay in Perspective,* 45 MICH. L. REV. 253, 287-88 (1947); Robert L. Hale, *Bargaining, Duress, and Economic Liberty,* 43 COLUM. L. REV. 603, 605 (1943). On the attempt of the Second Restatement of Contracts to define "duress" and "unconscionability," see Dalton, *supra* note 307, at 1032-39. *See generally* Cass R. Sunstein, *Lochner's Legacy,* 87 COLUM. L. REV. 873, 903-10 (1987) (discussing and criticizing the position that any understanding of government neutrality must depend on assumptions about the "natural" distribution of rights and entitlements).

333. This seems a better description of social reality. "[T]he whole economic structure quite obviously depend[s] on the law accepting as legitimate countless deals imposed by one party on another." Dalton, *supra* note 307, at 1027.

bargaining power calls for routine public involvement in so-called private activity. The very existence of that unequal bargaining power would be seen as resulting from entitlements conferred by law—which is to say, by government.[334]

I will refer to the substantive conflict reflected in ordinary free-speech philosophy and broadcast law, as well as other areas of the law, as the opposition of autonomy and constraint. The worldview oriented to autonomy, in which individuals are seen as acting freely and independently to advance their own values, treats human action as the product of free choice. The worldview oriented to constraint, by contrast, emphasizing that our choices are rarely either independent or free, treats human action as importantly determined by chains of earlier events.[335]

---

334. *See* Hale, *supra* note 332, at 627-28. *See generally* Robert W. Gordon, *Critical Legal Histories,* 36 STAN. L. REV. 57, 102-10 (1984) (arguing that legal rules fundamentally constitute and define private relationships); Olsen, *supra* note 307, at 1508-09 (attacking the image of the state as a "noncoercive, neutral arbiter" in the market); Sunstein, *supra* note 8, at 264-65 (discussing New Deal reformers' view that government not only "acts" when it disturbs existing distributions, but is responsible for those distributions in the first instance). On the other hand, the approach is itself problematic: how can we develop a coherent body of contract doctrine that treats ordinary contracts as unfree?

335. The conflict of autonomy and constraint is in this sense found in the criminal law. *See generally* Meir Dan-Cohen, *Responsibility and the Boundaries of the Self,* 105 HARV. L. REV. 959, 959-60, 990-99 (1992). The concept of blame plays an important role in our criminal law. Most of us believe that it would be wrong to punish someone who was not blameworthy, even if that punishment in fact deterred the commission of crimes. This belief assumes that we can meaningfully describe some people as more blameworthy than others. It is obvious, though, that "circumstances clearly beyond the control of the actor have, at a minimum, a strong bearing on the possibility that he will commit wrongful acts." KELMAN, *supra* note 311, at 89. Drug-related violence, for example, is significantly more common among those living in an environment of urban poverty, unemployment, and educational deprivation than among those living in better conditions. Since we only sometimes recognize such circumstances in assessing blame, we tend to waver between approaches.

On the doctrinal level, this opposition can be seen in a variety of contexts. To what extent should we impose criminal liability for negligent behavior? A traditional view, now out of fashion, was that negligence was "natural" to some people, determined, and thus not an appropriate subject for criminal punishment. Is it appropriate to punish drug addicts for being addicted? Is drug addiction a "status offense," the punishment of which is unfair because the activity is involuntary? Or is punishing the addict a reasonable moral response to the initial decision to take the drugs that led to addiction? In what circumstances should we downgrade murder to manslaughter because the defendant was "provoked," that is, because his action was a partly determined response to external circumstances? *See id.* at 93-94, 95-96. A predisposition toward rules and the salvation of a refuge in "science" leads us to refuse to find at all blameworthy those who fall within the exceptional, purportedly hard-edged and sharply bounded category of "insanity." It seems questionable, though, whether legal insanity coincides with any genuine hard-science medical category. We tend to sweep under the rug murkier questions of the determinants of human action, in part because we simply have no good way of dealing with them within the criminal-justice system. *See id.* at 91, 277-78.

Nor is this conflict limited to the criminal law. In reforming a trust or interpreting a statute or constitutional provision (say, the Equal Protection Clause), to what extent should we consider the drafters' views (say, that segregated schools were permissible and appropriate) to be self-created, chosen, and worthy of respect, and to what extent should we consider them a mere product of their times, which the drafters would not reaffirm were they to revisit the matter today? The latter course allows us to disregard their views by treating them as merely socially determined. *See id.* at 99-101.

As a result, the concepts of autonomy and constraint are connected to the philosophical concepts of intentionalism and determinism.[336]

The opposition of autonomy and constraint is also linked to a conflict between political philosophies some have referred to as individualism and altruism. Individualism emphasizes separateness, autonomy, and self-reliance: one's own ends are viewed as normatively primary, entitling one to pursue them so long as one respects the basic rights of others. Altruism, by contrast, emphasizes sharing and sacrifice. Within the context provided by "the degree of communal involvement or solidarity or intimacy," one seeks to help others regardless of their "rights."[337]

Individualism assumes autonomy by presupposing that people interact freely as individuals, that they choose their contracts and relationships by consulting their own values and are responsible for the choices they make. It makes sense only with an intentionalist foundation: the idea that one is entitled to treat one's own ends as normatively primary presupposes that one's ends are in fact one's own, meaningfully and intentionally chosen. Its philosophical dilemma is the need to maximize liberty—individual freedom of action—while maintaining order.[338] That task is incoherent unless it is possible to conceive of meaningful freedom of action. Similarly, altruism makes more sense in a world characterized by mutual dependence. It has as a premise that the responsibility for each of our individual situations is significantly communal, rather than individual. That premise is unmoored from its foundation if we in fact are free, individually, to make our own choices, to choose our own lives. It makes more sense if we live in a world where our lives and circumstances are the product of socially determined forces.

Duncan Kennedy suggested, some fifteen years ago, that rules are linked to individualism, and standards to altruism.[339] The connection is surely not straightforward; law motivated by altruistic concerns may well be cast in rule-like form.[340] Concerns about discretion and adminis-

---

336. *See* KELMAN, *supra* note 311, at 86-113. The terminology, however, is misleading. The determinist philosophy that human agents have *no* free will, and thus that all actions are *fully* causally determined, is not implicated here. *See* Phillip E. Johnson, *Do You Sincerely Want to Be Radical?*, 36 STAN L. REV. 247, 263 n.53 (1984); John Stick, *Charting the Development of Critical Legal Studies*, 88 COLUM. L. REV. 407, 414 (1988) (book review).

337. Kennedy, *supra* note 310, at 1718; *see id.* at 1713-18. *But see* Peter Gabel & Duncan Kennedy, *Roll Over Beethoven*, 36 STAN. L. REV. 1, 15-16 (1984) (recanting "the whole idea of individualism and altruism," explaining that "these things are absolutely classic examples of 'philosophical' abstractions which you can manipulate into little structures").

338. *See* UNGER, *supra* note 310, at 66-67; *see also* Mark V. Tushnet, *Following the Rules Laid Down: A Critique of Interpretivism and Neutral Principles*, 96 HARV. L. REV. 781, 783-84 (1983).

339. *See* Kennedy, *supra* note 310, at 1737-66.

340. Redistributive taxation provides an obvious example; labor and public benefits law provide others. 17 U.S.C. § 203, providing for the termination of certain transfers of copyright, plants a nearly impenetrable thicket of rules in order to protect authors and their beneficiaries from pervasive inequality in the marketplace.

trability may arise regardless of the lawmaker's individualistic or altruistic perspective.[341] Indeed, whether law seems individualistic or altruistic may depend entirely on the perspective from which one views it.[342]

The suggestion is important for purposes of this Article, though, because it implies a link between the procedural and the substantive elements of our competing approaches to speech regulation. Is there a link between mainstream free-speech philosophy's adherence to rules, and a worldview of individualism, autonomy and intentionalism? Between the broadcast regulatory system's reliance on standards, and a worldview of altruism, dependence and determinism?

Perhaps there is. Rules, according to Mark Kelman, are linked to "stereotypical individualism" because they are designed for "the person who lives by the rules," who "wants to know just what is expected of him: even if a lot is expected, he can do it, as long as there are no surprises, as long as he can plan his life anticipating and controlling all obligations that he will ultimately be asked to meet." He "does not beg for fairness or a second look at transactions when things go wrong; consequences are accepted, allowed to fall where they may so long as no one has explicitly cheated." He is confident of his abilities, going by the book, to take care of his interests or to live with his failure to do so.[343]

By contrast, Kelman contends, a legal regime emphasizing standards—and thus the need for fact-specific determinations in every case—rejects the easy assumption that we will all be okay so long as we follow the rules. It rejects the assurance that formal equality, in the face of substantive inequality, is the measure of justice. Rather, formal equality under the rules merely "forbids rich and poor alike to sleep under bridges."[344] We cannot simply assume autonomy in the private sphere. The ubiquity of dependence and constraint requires the decisionmaker to look to the barriers to freedom that may be inherent in a specific situation. "[O]ne has to see whether one's trading partners can *actually* take care of themselves; one can't simply presume that their formal legal capacity is the same as actual capacity." This fact-specific inquiry calls for "sensitivity and awareness to others, even to others one hasn't voluntarily chosen to be sensitive to."[345]

---

341. *See* Schlag, *supra* note 307, at 420 (arguing that "[b]oth altruism and individualism can generate arguments for both rules and standards"); Sullivan, *supra* note 309, at 96-100.

342. Recognition of a tort cause of action, thus, can be seen as altruistic because it emphasizes the responsibility of the tortfeasor to look out for the interests of others; it can be seen as individualistic because it ignores any responsibility of the injured to subordinate his own interests so that others might benefit. *Cf.* Balkin, *supra* note 198, at 208-11 (any legal rule can be seen as either "individualist" or "communalist").

343. KELMAN, *supra* note 311, at 59-60.

344. ANATOLE FRANCE, THE RED LILY 75 (The Modern Library 1917) (1894).

345. KELMAN, *supra* note 311, at 60. "Rules," Kelman concludes, "respect strong, individually chosen distinctions in relations .... Standards assert that simply living in a community establishes a relationship of some trust and care ...." *Id.*

In sum, relying on Kelman's approach, we can draw a connection between the rule-boundedness of conventional First Amendment thinking and a philosophy of individualism, autonomy, and intentionalism; between broadcast regulation's reliance on standards and a philosophy of altruism, dependence, and determinism. Can we take this further?

Consider the opposition between value subjectivity and value objectivity. Mainstream Western political thought,[346] beginning with Hobbes and Locke, has taken as foundational the belief that values—theories of the good—are individual, subjective, and arbitrary.[347] While individuals' values and goals may happen for a time to coincide, that coincidence is temporary and precarious.[348] The state is appropriately seen as "facilitative," seeking not "that particular good lives be led but simply allow[ing] persons to achieve their own vision of the good."[349] That, though, is not the only way to imagine the world; alternatively, one can see values as objective or as communally determined.

Rules appeal to the aesthetics of precision, to the psychology of denial or skeptical pragmatism (or, alternatively, of blinding ourselves to imprecision and mistakes or believing it is girlishly utopian to hope for perfection); standards appeal to the aesthetics of romantic absolutism, to the psychology of painful involvement in each situation, to the pragmatism that rejects the need for highfalutin generalities.

Id. at 61.

Kelman's description of rules leads to his ultimate endorsement of an "antirights, antilegalist approach." "Rules," he concludes, "are the opiate of the masses." *Id.* at 63, 275. I have serious doubts whether a move from rules to standards, and from rights to empathy, would in fact advance freedom. It seems to me that such an approach would tend to suppress minorities of any stripe. While rule-bound legalism, like any legal system, privileges those already socially dominant, I worry that communitarian approaches, for dissidents or minorities, may be still worse. *See* PATRICIA J. WILLIAMS, THE ALCHEMY OF RACE AND RIGHTS 146-48 (1991) (observing that minority-group members can find formal legality empowering by using it to create a legally respected social self, even as financially comfortable white males can find it alienating and distancing); Kimberlé W. Crenshaw, *Race, Reform, and Retrenchment: Transformation and Legitimation in Antidiscrimination Law,* 101 HARV. L. REV. 1331, 1356-69, 1381-87 (1988) (arguing that CLS analysis fails to recognize the realities of the racially oppressed); Richard Delgado, *The Ethereal Scholar: Does Critical Legal Studies Have What Minorities Want?,* 22 HARV. C.R.-C.L. L. REV. 301, 303-07, 314-19 (1987); Deborah L. Rhode, *Feminist Critical Theories,* 42 STAN. L. REV. 617, 635 (1990) ("[C]ritical feminism's central objective should be not to delegitimate [rights-based] frameworks but rather to recast their content and recognize their constraints."); *see also* Rebecca L. Brown, *A Tribute to Justice Thurgood Marshall: Or: How I Learned to Stop Worrying and Love Formalism,* 1 TEMP. POL. & CIV. RTS. L. REV. 7, 16-17 (1992). In Frances Olsen's study of the family and the market, thus, the form of social ordering associated with the altruistic ethic is not community but hierarchy. *See* Olsen, *supra* note 307, at 1529-30.

I rely here on Kelman's approach, therefore, not for its normative content but for its descriptive and explanatory power.

346. I refer here to the body of thought commonly referred to as "liberal" thought, encompassing the work of such disparate thinkers as Hobbes, Locke, Hume, Kant, Bentham, Posner, Nozick, Tribe, and Rawls.

347. *See* UNGER, *supra* note 310, at 76; *see generally* BRUCE A. ACKERMAN, SOCIAL JUSTICE IN THE LIBERAL STATE (1980). The text is perhaps oversimplified; some modern liberal writers reject the position that the liberal state must be strictly neutral between conceptions of the good. *See* Stick, *supra* note 336, at 417.

348. *See* UNGER, *supra* note 310, at 81.

349. KELMAN, *supra* note 311, at 66.

Both rules and the philosophy of individualism can be seen as linked to the belief that values are individual, subjective and arbitrary; standards and altruism, to the belief that values are communal or objective.[350] If we are to decide disputes by reference to standards of "reasonable" actions or "fair" dealing, after all, we must be able to reach some sort of shared conception of what it means to be "reasonable" or "fair."[351] Rules require no such moral dialogue for their application; they can be applied, as standards cannot, in a world in which values are individually, even randomly, chosen, shared only by chance.[352] Value subjectivity, in turn, is linked to individualism: where there exists no objective or meaningfully shared understanding of the Good, there is no justification for collective attempts to run individual lives.[353] By contrast, altruism can see the state not as a means to facilitate the exogenous, pre-existing goals of its individual members, but as a means to the collective development of shared ends.[354]

Consider the opposition between a philosophy embracing paternalism and one rejecting it.[355] Value subjectivity and individualism seem to forbid paternalism. If values are entirely subjective, there is no basis for any conclusion that an individual's choice is the "wrong" one for her; it may in fact accord with her own subjectively chosen preferences. Not to respect it is not to respect the boundaries between people that individualism demands.

Once again, though, it is possible to imagine an alternative philosophy. That philosophy might take one of two forms. First, it might attack the notion that people's choices in fact reflect their desires.[356] The fact that all choices are constrained by circumstance causes people routinely to make choices they view as unsatisfying. The "choice" to take an unsafe job may maximize utility under the circumstances, but may have little to do with the chooser's desires in a more general sense. Moreover, on a psychological level our desires are marked by profound ambivalence. Mechanically identifying them with our choices oversimplifies

---

350. *See* UNGER, *supra* note 310, at 76-81; Kennedy, *supra* note 310, at 1766-71.

351. *See* KELMAN, *supra* note 311, at 61. The belief that we cannot, Kelman suggests, is crucial to the void-for-vagueness doctrine: "The law 'Don't do *bad*' is the paradigm of vagueness precisely because people's accounts of what is bad are unshared, subjective." *Id.* at 78; *see also* Schauer, *supra* note 315, at 512 n.8.

352. *See* Kennedy, *supra* note 310, at 1768-69.

353. *See id.* at 1770-71; KELMAN, *supra* note 311, at 61-62.

354. *See* Kennedy, *supra* note 310, at 1771-72.

355. *See* Duncan Kennedy, *Distributive and Paternalist Motives in Contract and Tort Law, with Special Reference to Compulsory Terms and Unequal Bargaining Power,* 41 MD. L. REV. 563, 572-73 (1982); *see also* KELMAN, *supra* note 311, at 137-41.

356. More basically, it might attack the notion that people *have* independent, exogenous desires; an alternative view might stress that the "very structure of individual perception, belief and desire, and thus the terms of individual choice, are already shaped by culture and ideology even before the individual begins to choose." J.M. Balkin, *Ideology as Constraint,* 43 STAN. L. REV. 1133, 1137 (1991) (book review).

them to the point of parody.[357]

Second, an alternative philosophy might challenge head-on the basic theme of nonpaternalism that government should be structured so as uncritically to facilitate the effectuation of people's desires. In ordinary life, Kennedy has argued, we often act to influence people's choices in order to cause them to do things we believe to be in their own interest. Paternalism in that sphere, he has suggested, reflects a moral imperative *not* simply and mindlessly to defer to others' decisions, but rather to help them make important judgments, difficult as that may be, because we care about them. We are responsible for them, because we share in a community.[358]

We can link up all of these oppositions into a comprehensive expression of two antagonistic worldviews. One worldview links rules, individualism, a belief in overall private autonomy, a sharp public-private distinction, value subjectivity, and nonpaternalism; the other links standards, altruism, determinism, a belief in the pervasiveness of constraint, value objectivity (or a belief in the communal nature of values), and paternalism.[359]

I have so far presented each of these oppositions as relating two evenly balanced positions. Is that appropriate, or are some poles more equal than others? I would argue that the opposing worldviews I have hypothesized do not occupy equal places in American law. Consider first the opposition of rules and standards. Rules have the decided advantage. The whole notion of the Rule of Law places at the center of our legal thinking the idea that judges should be applying hard-edged rules that leave little room for interpretation or discretion. In that way we have a government of "laws, not men."[360] The fact that law application sometimes works best as a nuanced, nonrule-bound, discretionary process seems like a necessary evil, an exception to the way that legal reasoning—that is, rule application—is supposed to work. Standards give the judge or agency independent power that we then scurry about trying to figure out how to constrain. A well-stocked law library contains scores

---

357. *See* KELMAN, *supra* note 311, at 126-33; *cf.* Sunstein, *supra* note 8, at 287-88 (contrasting "democratic aspirations" and "consumption choices"). *See generally* FLANNERY O'CONNOR, WISE BLOOD, *reprinted in* THREE BY FLANNERY O'CONNOR 8 (2d ed. 1964) ("[F]ree will does not mean one will, but many wills conflicting in one man. Freedom cannot be conceived simply. It is a mystery . . . .").

358. *See* Kennedy, *supra* note 355, at 631-49.

359. This vision is developed in KELMAN, *supra* note 311, at 15-150.

360. *See* F.A. HAYEK, THE CONSTITUTION OF LIBERTY 153 (1960) ("The conception of freedom under the law . . . rests on the contention that when we obey laws, in the sense of general abstract rules laid down irrespective of their application to us, we are not subject to another man's will and are therefore free."); *see also* Youngstown Sheet & Tube Co. v. Sawyer, 343 U.S. 579, 646 (1952) (Jackson, J., concurring) ("[O]urs is a government of laws, not of men, and . . . we submit ourselves to rulers only if under rules."); Antonin Scalia, *The Rule of Law as a Law of Rules,* 56 U. CHI. L. REV. 1175 (1989) (arguing that courts should, to the extent possible, announce clear rules and avoid situationally sensitive analysis).

of books about the "problem of discretion"; there are no books, however, about the "problem of rules."[361] Rules are what law is about. Standards, as a result, are what we use in the cases when it seems that rules won't work.

Consider next the question of individualism and altruism. It is hard even to think about altruism as part of a *legal* structure; the very word "altruism" suggests action beyond that which is legally required.[362] The structure of the law we know is Hohfeldian; its core is a nucleus of legal freedom equated with autonomy, rights, and obligations. It is therefore individualistic. Altruistic concerns enter only as a supplement, an "after-the-fact adjustment[] to a pre-existing legal structure that has its own, individualist, logical coherence."[363] Altruistic notions provide "a periphery of exceptions to the core doctrines."[364]

As one considers the remaining oppositions, though, things begin to seem more complicated. In the legal vision of the turn of the century, the individualistic autonomy of actors in the private sphere was paramount, both as a normative good—indeed, as the definition of freedom—and as the only legally cognizable reality.[365] In this post-Realist age, though, the boundaries are muddier. *Lochner* is no longer good law. We premise much of the modern administrative state on the recognition that the economic sphere *is* in important degree marked by domination and constraint, that government refusal to intervene is not necessarily empowering. The government plays an unabashed public-law role in labor relations, the relation between manufacturer and consumer, and in a host of other formerly "private" interactions.[366]

In some respects the old approach still applies; the criminal law, for example, appears still to be built on what Meir Dan-Cohen calls the "free will paradigm."[367] While the criminal law does not always adhere to the intentionalist position, affirming individual autonomy and moral responsibility in the sphere of private ordering, we tend to view departures

---

361. KELMAN, *supra* note 311, at 292.

362. *See* Kennedy, *supra* note 310, at 1717.

363. *Id.* at 1719.

364. *Id.* at 1737. In classical legal thought, thus, individualism was the ethic of the marketplace, which was in turn the domain of law. Altruism was the ethic of the family, which was "delegalized." *See* Olsen, *supra* note 307, at 1520-22.

365. *See* Kennedy, *supra* note 310, at 1728-31; Elizabeth Mensch, *The History of Mainstream Legal Thought*, *in* THE POLITICS OF LAW 13, 23-26 (David Kairys ed., rev. ed. 1990). Mensch emphasizes that legal thinkers of the time did not deny the existence of inequality and coercion in the private economy; rather, they deemed those factors simply not cognizable within the logical structure of the law. (Even at the time, on the other hand, the law was not free from opposing concerns; consider, for example, the paternalistic motivations underlying the anti-lottery statute upheld in Champion v. Ames, 188 U.S. 321 (1903)).

366. This shift is manifest in private law as well as public. *See, e.g.*, Balkin, *supra* note 198, at 259-60 (describing nonprivileged assumptions in modern product liability law).

367. Dan-Cohen, *supra* note 335, at 959.

"somewhat apologetically, as exceptions to the free will idea."[368] Once again, "the picture of responsibility is that of a core and a periphery."[369]

Yet the ubiquity of paternalist concerns (for example, in government safety and health regulation) demonstrates the importance of such concerns in our law. Paternalism has a particularly bad image in our legal culture. We associate it both with Stalinist notions of how the "vanguard class" will teach the rest of us where our true interests lie, and with racist and sexist depictions of blacks and women as children, not really understanding their own interests or competent to protect them.[370] Notwithstanding widespread condemnation, though, its role is undeniable.

Where does this leave us? Some scholars take the view that with respect to *all* of the paired visions I have discussed—rules vs. standards, individualism vs. altruism, value subjectivity vs. value objectivity, intentionalism vs. determinism, nonpaternalism vs. paternalism—mainstream legal thought still treats the former term as privileged, the latter as nonprivileged.[371] Privileged legal discourse presents a vision of the world in which people presumptively are free, independent, "self-determined subjects,"[372] interacting in a world free of coercion or meaningful inequality, choosing their own values and their own destinies. The privileged term is assumed to provide the presumptively appropriate way to resolve disputes; the nonprivileged approach (although it may be frequently resorted to) is seen as extraordinary, in need of special justification, illegitimate except in the context of sharply bounded exceptions to the general rule. The privileged approach, moreover, is seen as accurately *describing* the world in all but exceptional cases.

As a result, while both privileged and nonprivileged attitudes are present in the law, it is the privileged position that shapes our thinking about the law, and about the world upon which the law acts. We tend to downplay the nonprivileged description of reality; we treat nonprivileged thinking as applicable only within exceptional, sharply bounded spheres. In part, we accept the privileged vision because of doubt that we could workably, consistently with freedom, structure the legal system to take into account the nonprivileged realities—say, that people's actions are in

---

368. *Id.* at 960.

369. *Id.*

370. *See* KELMAN, *supra* note 311, at 138; Kennedy, *supra* note 355, at 588-90; *see also* Bradwell v. Illinois, 83 U.S. (16 Wall.) 130, 141-42 (1873) (Bradley, J., concurring) (justifying exclusion of women from the bar in part on the ground that women should be "protected and defended" by men).

371. *See* KELMAN, *supra* note 311, at 290-95. All this is reminiscent of the deconstructionist position that any definition necessarily involves a hierarchical opposition. Deconstructive practice, though, calls for a demonstration that the hierarchy is false: that whenever *A* can be termed the rule and *B* the exception, the same sort of reasoning can be used to term *B* the rule and *A* the exception. *See* Balkin, *supra* note 307, at 747 (arguing that "[a]ny hierarchical opposition of ideas, no matter how trivial, can be deconstructed" to show that the privileged status is an illusion).

372. KELMAN, *supra* note 311, at 290.

important part not "chosen" but socially determined, or that people might sometimes be better off if they did not get what they choose—and we respond by denying that the nonprivileged realities are real at all.[373]

I will assume the validity of this position, by using the terms "privileged" and "nonprivileged," throughout the rest of this discussion. I don't think that in its strongest form it is crucial to my reasoning, though. Most of the analysis that follows relies only on my central argument that we can find two overarching worldviews reflected in the law, each incorporating normative and descriptive elements, and each incorporating one pole of the various paired oppositions I have discussed.

B. *Explaining Speech Law*

This background places free-speech philosophy and broadcast regulatory doctrine in a new light. Core First Amendment philosophy looks like a straightforward exposition of the "rules" position. As discussed earlier, it reflects the individualistic ideology of rule-bounded legality; it is fundamentally rationalist and intentionalist. It reflects an essential commitment to the view that we are each masters of our fate and captains of our soul, that the law need not concern itself with the determining effects of either social or psychological reality.

Core freedom-of-speech thinking seems grounded at its root in a thoroughgoing commitment to value subjectivity. Its guiding principle is that government cannot seek to suppress speech advocating disfavored values, for we cannot meaningfully say in this context that any values are wrong or should be disfavored. Under the Constitution "there is no such thing as a false idea."[374] Rather, "[i]f there is any fixed star in our constitutional constellation," it is that we cannot use the mechanism of government to "prescribe what shall be orthodox in politics, nationalism, religion, or other matters of opinion."[375] Indeed, this is the ideological root of the marketplace metaphor: it is *because* there is no way for us to fasten on objective truth or justice that we must let all ideas compete—that we can never say "enough," that we know what the truth is, and that the good done by free competition of ideas in a given case is outweighed by the harm done through the propagation of a false idea.[376]

Core freedom-of-speech thinking rejects paternalism, the notion that

---

373. *See id.* at 275-79, 283-84 (arguing that we tend to deny the existence of problems for which there is no ready legal solution).

374. Gertz v. Robert Welch, Inc., 418 U.S. 323, 339 (1974).

375. Board of Educ. v. Barnette, 319 U.S. 624, 642 (1943).

376. *See* American Booksellers Ass'n v. Hudnut, 771 F.2d 323, 330-31 (7th Cir. 1985), *aff'd mem.*, 475 U.S. 1001 (1986). The matter is not in fact quite so simple. A person who believes in the existence of objective truth may follow core freedom-of-speech thinking on the theory that free competition in ideas is the best way to arrive at that truth. I believe that theory to be problematic, as I explained *supra* Part II. More important, though, is the fact that such a person is constrained by the marketplace metaphor to behave *as if* truth were subjective.

the community can regulate speech because it fears that the choices citizens could make in response to speech might not be in their own interests.[377] Such regulation is inconsistent with the individualism I have discussed; it is seen as denying each person's fundamental autonomy to decide what to believe and what to reject.[378] Given the foundational assumptions that our choices in response to speech are free and rational, and that each of us has an equal right to select his or her own values, with no way to characterize any value as right or wrong, there is simply no room for government second-guessing of citizens' reactions to speech. Outside of the exceptional case, *all* beliefs, by hypothesis, are rational elaborations of valid (although arbitrary) values. There is no basis for government to make the judgment that people would be better off holding other views or making other choices.

Core freedom-of-speech thinking rests on a strong public-private distinction, coupled with a rejection of government regulation except in sharply bounded, exceptional cases.[379] It does not wholly close its eyes to the possibility that private coercion could impermissibly threaten the marketplace of ideas, so that government should appropriately act to protect that marketplace; it recognizes, for example, that police must act to protect the speech of a speaker physically threatened by an angry mob.[380] What is crucial, though, is that such challenges to the model are not seen as endemic; rather, they are recognized only as limited, confined

---

377. *But see* Posadas de Puerto Rico Assocs. v. Tourism Co., 478 U.S. 328 (1986) (upholding paternalistic regulation of truthful advertising for lawful casino gambling). *Posadas* fell within a "commercial speech" area in which conventional First Amendment thinking applies at best incompletely; Philip Kurland nonetheless characterized that opinion as reminiscent of *Alice in Wonderland* and Kafka's *The Castle*, in which "words take on new meanings and bureaucracy triumphs over the rule of law." Philip B. Kurland, Posadas de Puerto Rico v. Tourism Company: *" 'Twas Strange, 'Twas Passing Strange; 'Twas Pitiful, 'Twas Wondrous Pitiful,"* 1986 SUP. CT. REV. 1, 2.

378. *See* Thomas Scanlon, *A Theory of Freedom of Expression,* 1 PHIL. & PUB. AFF. 204, 213-14 (1972) (arguing that "harms to . . . individuals which consist in their coming to have false beliefs as a result of . . . expression" cannot justify legal restrictions on speech because such restrictions would be inconsistent with treating citizens as "equal, autonomous, rational agents"). *But cf.* T.M. Scanlon, Jr., *Freedom of Expression and Categories of Expression,* 40 U. PITT. L. REV. 519, 532-34 (1979) (noting that considerations of "justified paternalism" and of costs associated with unregulated expression militate against too-sweeping a condemnation of such regulation).

379. Indeed, First Amendment thinking can coherently reject government regulation precisely because it maintains a strong public-private distinction. It views the property-based market mechanism as essentially private, not "regulation" at all, and ignores the governmental hand necessary to make it go. *See* Weinberg, *supra* note 17, at 1273-74. Robert Post explains that the public-private distinction is essential to First Amendment thinking without regard to its empirical basis; even without such basis, he argues, the distinction is needed as a matter of "moral and political ascription" if we are to retain democratic self-determination. Post, *supra* note 179, at 1128.

380. This is the doctrine of the "heckler's veto." *See* Fiss, *supra* note 151, at 1416-17 (describing the doctrine as an "established part" of the free speech tradition). *But see* Feiner v. New York, 340 U.S. 315 (1951) (sustaining the conviction of a street corner speaker arrested after ignoring police orders to stop speaking because of the restlessness of the crowd).

exceptions to the overall rule of private ordering.[381]

Broadcast law, by contrast, has much more in common with the opposing pole. It is built around the situationally sensitive standard, the procedural mode of the nonprivileged pole.[382] It reflects a profound fear that inequality of private power and resources undermines citizens' free interaction. It reflects a belief that viewers' tastes and wants are not endogenous, but are themselves shaped by outside forces. There is no room in the ideology of autonomy, after all, for a fear of "private censorship"; in that vision, all citizens can participate freely in the marketplace of ideas so long as government does not interfere. The fear of private censorship makes perfect sense, though, from the vantage point of the nonprivileged concern with substantive inequality in the marketplace.

Consistently with the nonprivileged position's fear of the distorting effects of economic inequality, broadcast law directs the government to regulate private broadcasters, through the "public interest" standard, with the goal that they speak *as if* they were freed from market pressures. Consistently with the nonprivileged position's rejection of the public-private distinction, FCC regulations relating to broadcast industry structure (as well as the now-defunct fairness doctrine) reflect the desire to create and reorient "private" institutional structures in the interest of promoting greater equality in the speech forum.[383]

Broadcast regulation incorporates the paternalist concern that what viewers choose through the marketplace ("American Gladiators," say, or "America's Funniest Home Videos") may not be what is best for them. Our broadcast regulatory system insists that stations carry public-affairs programming whether viewers want to watch it or not. We subsidize public broadcasting stations at least in part on the theory that viewers' tastes may be improved through exposure to more highbrow programming.

The broadcast-law requirement that the government scrutinize broadcast licensees for their service to the public interest is revealing in its identification of both problem and solution. As for the problem, the law reflects the nonprivileged (determinist, paternalistic) concern that

---

381. *See supra* note 207.

382. *See supra* notes 321-27 and accompanying text. *But see infra* notes 395-405 and accompanying text.

383. *See, e.g.,* 47 C.F.R. § 73.3555 (1992). The FCC has put in place national multiple ownership rules, limiting the number of stations a licensee can own or control nationwide in a given service, *id.* § 73.3555 (d); rules limiting the number of broadcast stations a licensee can own or control in a single market, *id.* § 73.3555 (a), (b); and rules limiting joint ownership of a newspaper and broadcast station in a single community, *id.* § 73.3555 (c), (e). Other relevant regulation of industry structure includes the preference in licensing for applicants with smaller and less extensive holdings in other media outlets, *see supra* note 73 and accompanying text, and a variety of preferences given to minority license applicants and licensees, *see generally* Metro Broadcasting, Inc. v. FCC, 497 U.S. 547 (1990) (upholding FCC policies on minority ownership against equal protection challenge).

because the market is skewed and viewers' tastes are themselves shaped by the market, viewers are imperfect decisionmakers as to what is in their own interests. The solution offered is for the government to regulate programming in the "public interest": this reflects the nonprivileged (altruistic, not individualistic) worldview in assuming that there *is* such a thing as the "public interest," distinct from the mere sum of individual interests, which the government can be empowered to seek.[384] It reflects the nonprivileged belief that government action can promote freedom, rather than restrain it.

Red Lion reflects the nonprivileged pole as well in its understanding of the role of broadcast licensees. Licensees are not classic, individualistic, First Amendment speakers; rather, they are formed in the altruistic mold. A broadcast licensee is a "proxy or fiduciary," with the function of "present[ing] those views and voices which are representative of his community."[385] Much the same can be seen in *Red Lion's* description of First Amendment rights; there too, the Court seemed to diverge sharply from the individualist tradition, speaking of the "collective right" of the "people as a whole" to have the broadcast system function consistently with First Amendment values.[386]

In a variety of ways, broadcast law appears to depart from the pure nonprivileged model. First, it can be argued that a broadcast law hewing unreservedly to the nonprivileged pole would place greater emphasis on direct content regulation. The privileged-position model, emphasizing the autonomy of the private sphere, requires some "sufficiently close nexus"[387] before the state can be held responsible for its mere failure to *prevent* private action. Thus, for example, there is no violation of the Equal Protection Clause if the government stands idly by while a person engages in racial discrimination in her private life or workplace. But the view of the state more nearly consistent with the nonprivileged pole rejects that distinction. It contends that governmental ordering is pervasive throughout the nominally private sphere, and that the government is

---

384. *Cf.* UNGER, *supra* note 310, at 81-82 (arguing that in individualist philosophy, groups have no values apart from the individual and subjective goals of their individual members). Laurence Winer thus invokes Ayn Rand in arguing that broadcasting ought to be regulated in accord with core First Amendment principles; he denies that there exists any "such thing as the 'public interest' (other than the sum of the individual interests of individual citizens)." Winer, *supra* note 8, at 379 (quoting AYN RAND, CAPITALISM: THE UNKNOWN IDEAL 123, 126 (1967)).

385. Red Lion Broadcasting Co. v. FCC, 395 U.S. 367, 389 (1969). For the Court's later apparent departure from that view, *see infra* notes 406-14 and accompanying text.

386. 395 U.S. at 390. As then-Commissioner Robinson pointed out, the apparent position of the *Red Lion* Court that "the *First Amendment* gives positive rights to listeners/viewers to dictate what speakers shall tell them" is incoherent as a statement of individualist Hohfeldian relations; understood in that manner, it "makes nonsense of the First Amendment; in fact, it stands it on its head." The Handling of Public Issues Under the Fairness Doctrine, 58 F.C.C.2d 691, 706-07 (1976) (Robinson, Comm'r, dissenting), *aff'd in part, rev'd in part sub nom.* National Citizens Comm. for Broadcasting v. FCC, 567 F.2d 1095 (D.C. Cir. 1977), *cert. denied,* 436 U.S. 926 (1978).

387. Jackson v. Metropolitan Edison Co., 419 U.S. 345, 351 (1974).

responsible for those actions it merely allows and facilitates as well as those it requires. Thus, "when the government grants access to racist groups to use streets and parks for racist speech, it is to that extent subsidizing racist speech. . . . [When it] declines to allow suits for intentional infliction of emotional distress or other forms of racial harassment, it is permitting racists to harm minorities."[388] On that understanding, government bears responsibility for the effects of all speech it allows to be broadcast. A broadcast regulatory system truly adhering to the nonprivileged model might seek to use situationally sensitive means to ban private broadcast speech disserving equality in the world at large.

A Commission that took seriously these implications of its public interest mandate might see its own role as an activist one, directed at removing broadcasters whose speech was *less* in the public interest from the air, to be replaced by those whose programming would be *more* in the public interest. It might look harder at programming (and proposed programming) in ruling on license and transfer applications, taking a closer look at whether the broadcast of racial or religious invective, say, really furthered the public interest.[389]

The FCC has not played such a role. It has almost never denied renewal to a television licensee in a comparative challenge.[390] While it has occasionally denied television license renewals in other contexts—

---

388. Balkin, *supra* note 175, at 377. While Professor Balkin was merely setting out the argument and not endorsing it, other scholars have argued along just these lines. *See, e.g.,* Charles R. Lawrence III, *If He Hollers Let Him Go: Regulating Racist Speech on Campus,* 1990 DUKE L.J. 431, 444-49 (arguing that the state action rule exculpates private racism by "immuniz[ing] private discriminators from constitutional scrutiny"); Mari J. Matsuda, *Public Response to Racist Speech: Considering the Victim's Story,* 87 MICH. L. REV. 2320, 2374-80 (1989) (describing government's tolerance and protection of hate group activities as a form of state action that legitimates and supports racist speech); *see also* Sunstein, *supra* note 8, at 266-77.

389. *But cf.* Anti-Defamation League of B'nai B'rith v. FCC, 403 F.2d 169, 171 (D.C. Cir. 1968) (holding that "recurrent bigoted appeals to anti-Semitic prejudice" were not grounds for nonrenewal of broadcasting company's license where the company had offered free time for response (quotation omitted)), *cert. denied,* 394 U.S. 930 (1969).

This story may be less simple than it appears. Duncan Kennedy has indicated that even the altruist position encompasses "the necessity and desirability of a sphere of autonomy or liberty or freedom or privacy within which one is free to ignore both the plights of others and the consequences of one's own acts for their welfare." Kennedy, *supra* note 310, at 1718. I think the approach I take in text, though, is true to altruism as a "direction[] or orientation[] of policy argument." Balkin, *supra* note 356, at 1158.

390. The Commission in the notorious *WHDH* case denied renewal to a Boston television station in favor of a challenger. In that case, though, the unique procedural history of the proceeding had led the agency to treat the incumbent as if it were merely another applicant. *See* WHDH, Inc., 16 F.C.C.2d 1 (1969), *aff'd sub nom.* Greater Boston Television Corp. v. FCC, 444 F.2d 841 (D.C. Cir. 1970), *cert. denied,* 403 U.S. 923 (1971); *see also supra* note 96. The *Video 44* case is a more recent one in which the Commission denied renewal in a comparative proceeding. *See* Video 44, 5 F.C.C.R. 6383 (1990). The agency, however, refused to do so until prodded by the court of appeals. *See* Video 44, 4 F.C.C.R. 1209 (1989), *rev'd sub nom.* Monroe Communications Corp. v. FCC, 900 F.2d 351 (D.C. Cir. 1990); *see also supra* notes 100-02 and accompanying text. I am aware of no cases in which a conventional broadcast license genuinely was won by a challenger, rather than lost by the incumbent.

even, on very rare occasions, on grounds implicating broadcast content—
it has not done so in any systematic way. Rather, its actions have been
sporadic exceptions to a norm of unbroken renewal.[391] Similarly, even
when the fairness doctrine was in force, the Commission found actual
fairness doctrine violations only in the rarest of cases.[392] While the
Commission issued a warning in the drug-oriented songs controversy,[393]
it took no further steps against offending licensees. Indeed, for the FCC
to have actively imposed on private speakers an official government view
of what speech was in the "public interest" would have been wholly
unacceptable to the Commissioners, steeped in privileged-position law,
and to the dominant legal culture. It would have made the contradiction
between competing legal modes too stark and inescapable. Even in an
area marked by nonprivileged concerns, ordinary First Amendment values—encapsulated in the Communication Act's formal denial to the
Commission of "the power of censorship"[394]—preclude so great a governmental assertion of power over speakers and speech.

There are other ways in which broadcast law arguably departs from
the pure nonprivileged model. The FCC over the past thirty years has
responded to pressures to abandon the procedural mode of situationally
sensitive adjudication.[395] The history of FCC control over market entry,
for example, reflects a continual move *away* from situationally sensitive
standards in search of more hard-edged rules. In the initial years of FCC
decisionmaking, the agency decided whether to grant uncontested license
applications in a quintessentially situationally sensitive, subjective, and
ad hoc manner. Addressing whether there was "need" for the proposed
new service, the Commission went so far as to consider whether a station
provided relatively less valuable public service because its programming
was already available to the public on phonograph records. Judicial hostility, however, eventually put a stop to the practice. The Commission

---

391. *See supra* notes 105-11 and accompanying text.

392. In one two-year period at the height of fairness enforcement, the FCC received 4280
fairness complaints; it made findings adverse to the licensee in nineteen (4/10 of 1%) and took
tangible punitive action (a fine in each case) in eight of the nineteen. Seven of those eight, in turn,
related to violations of a fairly hard-edged FCC rule requiring broadcasters to give political
candidates an opportunity to respond to editorials opposing them or endorsing a competing
candidate. The eighth related to a violation of the personal attack rule. *See* The Handling of Public
Issues Under the Fairness Doctrine, 58 F.C.C.2d 691, 709, 710 n.17 (1976) (Robinson, Comm'r,
dissenting), *aff'd in part, rev'd in part sub nom.* National Citizens Comm. for Broadcasting v. FCC,
567 F.2d 1095 (D.C. Cir. 1977), *cert. denied,* 436 U.S. 926 (1978).

393. *See supra* notes 124-32 and accompanying text.

394. 47 U.S.C. § 326 (1988) ("Nothing in this chapter shall be understood or construed to give
the Commission the power of censorship . . . , and no regulation or condition shall be promulgated
or fixed by the Commission which shall interfere with the right of free speech . . . .").

395. Some forms of FCC regulation remain situationally sensitive to this day. *See* CBS v.
Democratic Nat'l Comm., 412 U.S. 94, 118 (1973) ("[T]he difficulty and delicacy of administering
the Communications Act . . . call[] for flexibility and the capacity to adjust and readjust the
regulatory mechanism . . . ."); *supra* notes 321-27 and accompanying text.

ultimately moved to an approach giving it much less discretion in individual, noncomparative licensing decisions.[396]

The problem of selecting among competing would-be applicants saw a similar evolution. The Commission began with a discretionary, content-sensitive process.[397] A number of events, however, including allegations that Commissioners had solicited and received bribes in licensing proceedings, contributed to the demise of that approach.[398] The agency then shifted to the more nearly rule-bound approach of the 1965 *Policy Statement,*[399] notwithstanding dissenters' protests that "the significance to be given in each decision to each . . . criterion must . . . necessarily be considered in context with the other facts of the individual cases."[400] The history of the FCC comparative hearing process ever since has been one of attempts to move still further from standards to rules.[401] A large part of the silliness of the current process has resulted from that attempt to capture the "public interest" determination in hard-edged rules. The Commission has explained that in its continuing efforts to reform the comparative hearing process it seeks further to minimize "subjective and imprecise" criteria, in favor of "swifter, more certain choices."[402]

The Commission's approach to license renewal reinforces the same theme. The Commission has sought to reduce uncertainty by more nearly guaranteeing renewal for incumbent licensees. In connection with uncontested renewal applications, it went from a purely subjective "public interest" determination, to one informed by the applicant's compliance with quantitative, but informal "processing guidelines," to a rule under which all applications are granted virtually automatically.[403] Once again, the nonprivileged approach of ad hoc, informal, situationally sensitive standards yielded, over time, in favor of an approach more nearly consonant with the larger legal regime.

---

396. *See* Weinberg, *supra* note 40, at 651-55.

397. *See supra* notes 66-69 and accompanying text.

398. *See supra* notes 70-71 and accompanying text.

399. 1 F.C.C.2d 393 (1965); *see supra* notes 72-80 and accompanying text.

400. 1 F.C.C.2d at 401 (Hyde, Comm'r, dissenting); *see also id.* at 404 (Bartley, Comm'r, dissenting) ("There are so many varying circumstances in each case that a factor in one may be more important than the same factor in another."). Commissioner Hyde complained:

> The proposed fiat as to the weight which will be given to the various criteria—without sound predication of accepted data and when considered only in a vacuum and in the abstract—must necessarily result in . . . unfairness to some applicants and in the fashioning of an unnecessary straitjacket for the Commission in its decisional process. How can we decide in advance and in a vacuum that a specific broadcaster with a satisfactory record in one community will be less likely to serve the broadcasting needs of a second community than a specific long-time resident of that second community who doesn't have broadcast experience? How can we make this decision without knowing more about each applicant?

Id. at 402.

401. *See supra* notes 81-89 and accompanying text.

402. Reexamination of the Policy Statement on Comparative Broadcast Hearings, 7 F.C.C.R. 2664, 2664 (1992); *see supra* text accompanying note 87.

403. *See supra* notes 105-09 and accompanying text.

1188　　　　　　　　*CALIFORNIA LAW REVIEW*　　　　　　[Vol. 81:1101

This point is an important one; broadcast regulation has been unable to survive as an inviolate, situationally sensitive island in a rule-bound legal sea. Some of the reasons for the shift, though, have only attenuated links to privileged-position ideology. At least when it comes to renewal, for example, the Commission's actions can be traced to the facts that broadcast licenses are worth large sums of money, and licensees invest large sums in their stations. Both Congress and the Commission have tended to respond favorably to the urgings of industry members that renewal be made more nearly certain in order to encourage and protect those investments.[404] The Commission's partial shift from standards to rules thus reflects both the ideological pressures of a dominant legal culture elevating rule-bound decisionmaking as a procedural model, and the practical need to adopt predictable procedures so as more reliably to foster and protect agency clients.[405]

A final way in which FCC regulation can be said to incorporate elements of the preferred position relates to the role of licensees in the broadcast system. The Supreme Court in *CBS v. Democratic National Committee*[406] moved significantly away from the philosophy of *Red Lion* to a more individualistic view of broadcast regulation, reinforcing the public-private distinction in broadcast law. *CBS* involved an attack on broadcasters' policies of refusing to run paid political advocacy advertisements.[407] According to plaintiffs,[408] such policies disserved the "public interest" by narrowing the spectrum of public debate, and thus violated the Communications Act.[409] Moreover, the government's failure to insist that broadcasters run such advertisements undermined the market-

---

404. *See, e.g.,* Formulation of Policy & Rules Relating to Broadcast Renewal Applicants, 4 F.C.C.R. 6363, 6365 (1989) (proposing to grant all incumbents a presumption of entitlement to renewal expectancy, and thus to renewal, upon compliance with FCC rules requiring each licensee to maintain certain files for public inspection); Policy Statement Concerning Comparative Hearings Involving Regular Renewal Applicants, 22 F.C.C.2d 424, 425 (1970) (providing, in response to S. 2004, 91st Cong., 1st. Sess. (1969), that a licensee that has provided "substantial service to the public" is entitled to renewal without regard to competing applicants' qualifications), *vacated sub nom.* Citizens Communications Ctr. v. FCC, 447 F.2d 1201 (D.C. Cir. 1971).

405. These two sets of pressures, on the other hand, may not be wholly unrelated; Kennedy's insight is that such procedural and substantive concerns can be linked. *See* Kennedy, *supra* note 310.

406. 412 U.S. 94 (1973).

407. Political advocacy advertisements seek to promote a position on a political issue or issues, but do not relate to races for elective office. Because they do not relate to races for elective office, broadcasters are under no obligation to carry them; they do not fall within 47 U.S.C. § 312(a)(7), which requires broadcasters to carry advertisements by candidates for federal elective office on behalf of their candidacies. *See generally id.;* CBS v. FCC, 453 U.S. 367 (1981) (upholding an FCC ruling that the three major networks violated 47 U.S.C. § 312(a)(7) by refusing to provide time for a documentary on the record of presidential candidate Jimmy Carter).

408. Plaintiffs included an antiwar group called Business Executives' Move for Vietnam Peace, which had been rebuffed in its attempt to buy radio air time to espouse its views, and the Democratic National Committee, which anticipated similar difficulty in buying time. *CBS,* 412 U.S. at 97-99.

409. *Id.* at 98-101.

place of ideas, and thus violated the First Amendment.[410] The Supreme Court rejected both claims.

Chief Justice Burger's opinion in *CBS* is most notable for its view of the function of licensees in the broadcast system. Gone is the idea that broadcasters are mere "fiduciaries" for the community, vessels of a larger will; instead, a plurality of the Court emphasized that licensees were to play, to the extent "consistent with necessary regulation, a traditional journalistic role."[411] Broadcasters were to be treated, to the extent possible, like ordinary First Amendment speakers, "journalistic 'free agent[s]' "; that the government was simultaneously "an 'overseer' and ultimate arbiter and guardian of the public interest" called for a "delicate balancing" act.[412] Far from being mere altruistic voices of a larger community, broadcasters were individualistic, autonomous speakers.[413] The plurality, moreover, rejected the claim that the government's failure to insist that broadcasters run advocacy advertisements amounted to "state action" implicating the First Amendment at all. Broadcasters were private entities, they insisted; the government had no responsibility for their policies.[414]

It is thus an oversimplification to view our system of broadcast regulation as an unsullied and pure embodiment of nonprivileged thought. This point, on the other hand, should not be overplayed. FCC regulation by "raised eyebrow" is powerful. For the Commission even on rare occasions to condition its renewal of valuable licenses on content acceptability goes a long way towards ensuring that broadcasters will internalize the Commission's wishes in other cases. That our system of broadcast regulation gives the government the *authority* to regulate content (even if the government usually refrains from exercising that authority) unmistakably demonstrates the system's affinity with the nonprivileged position. The contrary shifts I have described in broadcast law amount to the construction of some privileged-position walls on an essentially nonprivileged foundation.

---

410. *Id.* Plaintiffs did not state their second argument in the clearest of terms. As Justice Brennan recapitulated the argument, though, "the public nature of the airwaves, the governmentally created preferred status of broadcasters, the extensive Government regulation of broadcast programming, and the specific governmental approval of the challenged policy" led him to conclude that the government had " 'so far insinuated itself into a position' of participation in this policy" as to subject the policy to First Amendment constraints. *Id.* at 180-81 (Brennan, J., dissenting) (footnote omitted). He then concluded that the ban violated the First Amendment's guarantee of full and free discussion in the marketplace of ideas. *Id.* at 196.

411. *Id.* at 116. The opinion repeatedly uses language referring to broadcasters' "public trustee" role, but the Chief Justice appears to mean something different by those words than the vision embraced by *Red Lion.* In the context of *CBS,* a "public trustee" is simply a First Amendment speaker who happens to be subject to the fairness doctrine.

412. *Id.* at 117.

413. *See* Blasi, *supra* note 37, at 613-14.

414. *See CBS,* 412 U.S. at 117-21; *see also id.* at 148, 154 (Douglas, J., concurring in the judgment) (concluding that *Red Lion* was wrongly decided).

C. A House Divided

With this understanding of speech law, it is useful to revisit the criticisms of free-speech philosophy in Part II of this Article. The reality of speech is that economic inequality distorts the marketplace of ideas; cognitive structure undermines it; power relationships pervert it. In Part II, I described it as surprising that ordinary freedom-of-speech thinking represses those arguments.[415] With the background I have set out, though, repression begins to seem quite predictable and unexceptional; it is a simple reflection of the privileged-position assumption that the privileged arguments accurately describe the world outside of exceptional cases.

I explained earlier that while both privileged and nonprivileged attitudes are present in the law, it is the privileged position that shapes our thinking about the law, and about the world upon which the law acts. We tend to downplay the nonprivileged description of reality, and to treat nonprivileged thinking as applicable only within exceptional, sharply bounded spheres. In part, we accept the privileged vision because we doubt that we could build a workable legal system that takes into account the nonprivileged version of reality. We respond by ignoring the nonprivileged realities altogether.

We ignore the nonprivileged arguments about speech because they threaten the theoretical integrity of First Amendment philosophy, and we are afraid to tear that system down. We see no way to incorporate our concerns about the prevailing model into a workable legal structure.[416] Rather than recognizing the contradictions (while feeling incapable of doing anything about them), we ignore them. We first conclude that the marketplace model is preferable to a regime in which the government is wholly free to suppress speech (as if those were the only two choices), and then make law as if the model were unflawed.[417]

At the same time, though, we believe in the nonprivileged concerns; we find them real and legitimate. We have built a system of broadcast regulation embodying them. That system adopts the procedural modes and the substantive values associated with that unprivileged side of our law. We are staggered when asked to explain that nonprivileged system of regulation in terms that make sense in a privileged-position world.

That, then, is the explanation that this discussion provides; everything seems very neat. There remains a mystery, though: why does the explanation work so well? Put another way, why has this area of law

---

415. *See supra* notes 294-300 and accompanying text.

416. Robert Post thus argues that, in constructing First Amendment law, we cannot take into account the extent to which public discourse is determined by economic and social factors, because treating citizens as less than fully autonomous in this respect is "deeply incompatible with the very premise of democratic self-government." Post, *supra* note 179, at 1130.

417. *See supra* note 295.

evolved in such a starkly dichotomized form? In private-law areas such as torts and contracts, we have managed to incorporate nonprivileged concerns into the law without needing to create two wholly separate bodies of law, one privileged and one nonprivileged. There are some who argue that all modern law is incoherent because privileged and nonprivileged concerns are contradictory and cannot meaningfully coexist in the same legal space.[418] I think, though, that even a vigorous proponent of that view would have to concede that contract and tort law are paragons of oneness and peace when compared with the open warfare between conventional free-speech philosophy and broadcast regulation. We have two starkly different—indeed, contradictory—bodies of law in ordinary free speech doctrine and broadcast regulation. Why have we not found even a muddled and incoherent middle ground?

I can think of two answers to this question.[419] The first looks to history.[420] Nonprivileged regulation of broadcasting was already in place by the time we had fully adopted the privileged position for regulation of speech generally.[421] As we developed that First Amendment philosophy, it was by no means obvious that the new broadcast entertainment should be subject to the same sort of analysis as were older forms of speech.[422] Each area of regulation developed its own momentum, and each was able to rest on its historical credentials. Some of the momentum of the nonprivileged model may have derived from the "natural tendency to positive government of an administrative agency";[423] some, perhaps, from fear of the unique power, pervasiveness and influence of the electronic media.[424] The electronic media, after all, help

---

418. *See, e.g.,* Kennedy, *supra* note 310, at 1774-78.

419. The question, as I pose it, is a descriptive one: what historical or structural factors have led us to our current dual system? In Part IV, I discuss whether a dual system of regulations is desirable from a policy standpoint.

420. *See generally* BOLLINGER, *supra* note 11, at 17-26.

421. *See supra* notes 156-60 and accompanying text.

422. The Supreme Court did not hold that motion pictures, for example, were subject to First Amendment protection until 1952. *See* Joseph Burstyn, Inc. v. Wilson, 343 U.S. 495, 501-02 (1952); *cf.* United States v. Paramount Pictures, 334 U.S. 131, 166 (1948) (indicating, in dictum, that "moving pictures . . . are included in the press whose freedom is guaranteed by the First Amendment"). Indeed, it is questionable whether movies to this day receive the same degree of protection as do books; consider, for example, Freedman v. Maryland, 380 U.S. 51 (1965) (upholding prior screening of movies by censors, subject to certain safeguards).

423. SCHMIDT, *supra* note 10, at 119-20; *see also* Mayton, *supra* note 8, at 739-47 (describing the FCC's development as reflecting an administrative tendency to "aggrandize power"). As Glen Robinson put it, "Regulation is, or quickly becomes, a life-style of the regulatory bureaucrat." Robinson, *supra* note 76, at 192 n.55.

424. *See* Lee C. Bollinger, *Elitism, the Masses and the Idea of Self-Government: Ambivalence About the "Central Meaning of the First Amendment," in* CONSTITUTIONAL GOVERNMENT IN AMERICA 99, 103-04 (Ronald K.L. Collins ed., 1980) (observing that "no other technology of communication has raised more concerns over the problem of manipulation than the electronic media"); *see also* SCHMIDT, *supra* note 10, at 120 ("Television . . . is the focus of late twentieth-century anxieties about the adequacy of an eighteenth-century First Amendment to govern the

define who we are as a society in a way that nothing else does. Once ensconced as an "exception" to ordinary First Amendment law,[425] the broadcast regulatory system could live on without interference.

A second way of looking at this question, though, suggests that speech law is more glaringly schizoid than tort or contract law because the basic nature of speech law leaves less room for accommodation between the two visions. That speech law is painted in primary colors seems incontestable. Individualist free-speech philosophy does not merely treat rules as appropriate or preferable; it treats them as indispensable. Government intrusions on autonomy are not a necessary evil; they are unconstitutional. In contrast, say, to contract law, oriented to promoting economic exchange, individualist free speech philosophy has the primary and explicit goal of protecting the private citizen from public tyranny. As a result, the public-private distinction is raised to a level of sacred inviolability, to a degree little seen elsewhere. All of this means that the privileged position, in speech law, has no room for compromise, no leeway in which, even in an incoherent or muddled manner, one could try to incorporate opposing positions. The only way that nonprivileged positions can find legal recognition is in a full-blown world of their own.

This raises the question, though, why speech law should have these characteristics and goals. Scholars taking a more nearly altruistic approach might wonder why American constitutional law has treated the problem of governmental (as opposed to private) power as speech law's crucial organizing principle. They might wonder why we have erected the public-private dichotomy as the distinction around which all else in speech law revolves.

The ultimate answer may lie in the privileged position's roots in mainstream liberal political theory.[426] The classic problem to which that political philosophy addresses itself is the dilemma of freedom and security: how can we achieve political order without risking governmental tyranny?[427] The philosophy is thus fundamentally a response to the problem of political despotism. Speech plays a central role; free speech is tied to self-determination and the avoidance of governmental tyranny in a way that freedom from state control in the making of contracts, say, is

---

relationship between government and the media, not only because of its technical novelty, but also because its social force is vastly greater than that of any other communications medium in history.").

425. Other doctrinal "exceptions"—difficult to square with First Amendment philosophy on close analysis, and in consequence not subjected to such analysis—include copyright, *see* Jessica Litman, *Copyright and Information Policy*, 55 LAW & CONTEMP. PROBS. 185, 204-06 (1992) (arguing that copyright "received wisdom" conceals the damage that expansive copyright protection does to First Amendment values), and labor picketing, *see* Schneider, *supra* note 296, at 1469 (arguing that courts have removed picketing from First Amendment protection through a series of rationalizations designed to protect business property interests).

426. *See supra* note 346.

427. *See* UNGER, *supra* note 310, at 64-67 (describing order and freedom as the fundamental problems of politics).

not.[428] The result is that when we start talking about speech, privileged-position thinking assumes its most severe form. Within the four corners of the individualist model, government can to some extent impose limited restrictions on contracting without the world coming to an end; we can tolerate a certain amount of compromise (or incoherence). We cannot, though, as easily countenance a challenge to the individualist model's vision of the autonomy of speakers in the private sphere and governmental restriction of that autonomy. That challenge strikes at the heart of the liberal political state.

IV
WHERE DO WE GO FROM HERE?

Our system of broadcast regulation works badly. The overlay of a rule-bound decisional calculus on the situationally sensitive, public-interest licensing determination has yielded incoherence. Indeed, the broadcast regulatory system can be described as "the worst of both worlds."[429] The regulatory structure displays some of the least attractive characteristics of standard-driven systems: the Commission's indecency law, for example, is characterized by vagueness and arbitrariness.[430] It displays some of the least attractive characteristics of rule-bound systems: would-be licensees file applications featuring " 'strange and unnatural' business arrangements" designed to fit within the Commission's rules.[431]

---

428. A would-be tyrant could, of course, seek to amass power through restrictions on private contracts. *See generally* BERNARD H. SIEGAN, ECONOMIC LIBERTIES AND THE CONSTITUTION 83 (1980) ("A free society cannot exist unless government is prohibited from confiscating private property. . . . As Hamilton stated, a power over a man's subsistence amounts to a power over his will."). I think, though, that the relationship of speech to the political realm is more direct.

429. STEVEN H. SHIFFRIN & JESSE H. CHOPER, THE FIRST AMENDMENT 477 (1991). The authors do not fully endorse that language; they present it as "hypothetical commentary."

430. The Commission has emphasized that indecency cannot be evaluated except with an eye to "the host of variables that ordinarily comprise [a work's] context." Infinity Broadcasting Corp., 3 F.C.C.R. 930, 932 (1987), *aff'd in relevant part sub nom.* Action for Children's Television v. FCC, 852 F.2d 1332 (D.C. Cir. 1988). This is a recipe for both vagueness and arbitrariness, since the agency has not given clear signals explaining which elements of context are relevant to prove what. In Guy Gannett Publishing Co., 5 F.C.C.R. 7688 (1990), for example, the Commission imposed a forfeiture on a radio station for playing the feminist song "Penis Envy" by the folk group Uncle Bonsai. The singers, in clear soprano voices, begin with the words "If I had a penis, I'd wear it outside / In cafes and car lots, with pomp and with pride," and conclude, "If I had a penis, I'd still be a girl / But I'd make much more money and conquer the world." *Id.* at 7689-90.

Was the fact that the song was played on the crude and puerile Neil Rogers Show part of the "context" that led to liability? Or someone at the Commission particularly sensitive about songs referring to penises? The letter opinion provides no useful answer. *Cf.* Suzanna Andrews, *She's Bare. He's Covered. Is There a Problem?*, N.Y. TIMES, Nov. 1, 1992, § 2, at 13 (observing that full frontal female nudity is common in movies while a film with a visible penis draws a near-automatic NC-17 rating).

431. Bechtel v. FCC, 957 F.2d 873, 880 (D.C. Cir.), *cert. denied*, 113 S. Ct. 57 (1992). Among the disadvantages of rules is that they encourage "walking the line," that is, tailoring one's conduct in order to take advantage of the imperfect fit, to fall within the letter but not the spirit of the law. *See* Kennedy, *supra* note 310, at 1695-96. The rules may then become more complex as courts

Is there a better way? The nonprivileged model, in general, seems to work badly in the speech context. We are not wholly comfortable with substituting public authority for private power over scarce speech resources, because as a practical matter that means giving government officials supervisory control over a segment of public debate. We have stepped back from giving government officials the sort of hidden censorial power that they can gain through the untrammelled use of situationally-sensitive standards in awarding and renewing "licenses" to speak. We are unwilling to abandon some form of value subjectivity as the foundation stone of our free-speech thinking. Rather, for many of us, the crucial *point* of free speech law is that we cannot, for purposes of suppressing speech, authoritatively declare some values "right" and others wrong. Even slavery and genocide must be treated as legitimate contenders in the marketplace of ideas. Our adherence to that value subjectivity, however, has made our commitment to the "public interest" as the touchstone of broadcast regulation increasingly incoherent.

To the extent that we are worried about self-interested government control of public debate—and we should be—the nonprivileged model's emphasis on the dangers posed by great concentrations of private media power has obvious flaws. In some circumstances, at least, the largest, most powerful private media organs are the ones best able to resist coercive state power. Drawing on the experience of the military-bureaucratic takeover of the Japanese press before World War II, Gregory Kasza concluded that "liberal resistance to state encroachment," where democracy is threatened by a government bent on radical mobilization, is best served by the "civil tyranny" of a few dominant, private speakers.[432] Smaller private speakers are less effective in resisting such governmental attack; quasi-public speakers are less effective still.[433] A regulatory approach aimed at fostering small and medium-sized media outlets while reining in

---

develop exceptions in order to achieve the purposes of the drafters. They may be perceived as unfair, riddled with loopholes for the benefit of the legally sophisticated; and they may, as a result, attract less willing compliance. *See* KELMAN, *supra* note 311, at 44-45. In part for that reason, scholars have argued that the power of rules to minimize uncertainty and arbitrariness is overstated. As courts grapple with the task of applying an apparently simple and straightforward rule in a host of differing fact-situations, they have to promulgate new sub-rules to handle problematic variations (and, indeed, may have to choose among a variety of different potentially applicable rules). The law's former simplicity is lost, so that people can no longer easily predict legal results. To the extent that the courts seek to maximize predictability and minimize complexity and situationally sensitive discretion, the new sub-rules necessarily turn on what, at least some of the time, are meaningless factual distinctions, and thus yield arbitrary results. The fact that the decisionmaker applying these rules has only limited discretion and cannot import a different sort of arbitrariness into the process is of little consolation. *See id.* at 46-47.

The FCC's attempts to lay down rules to govern initial comparative broadcast hearings provide a perfect illustration of all of this.

432. GREGORY J. KASZA, THE STATE AND THE MASS MEDIA IN JAPAN, 1918-1945, at 268 (1988); *see generally id.* at 266-73.

433. *See id.* at 268-70.

huge concentrations of private media power, or establishing a strong quasi-public media voice in opposition to private Big Media, thus, is ill-suited to the creation of a media system that can resist state violation.

Even without regard to the dangers of government control, informal, situationally sensitive speech regulation seems problematic. Such regulation will likely privilege those already dominant in society, and thus suppress dissent. An informal broadcast regulation system, marked by an abhorrence of formal rules and formal processes and a near-total reliance on situationally sensitive standards, may assure that the greatest influence in the broadcast licensing process is exercised by the economically, politically, and socially dominant.[434] Without a system of hard-edged rules, the regulatory body itself may be more susceptible to external political pressures.[435] Without a structure of formal rights, would-be dissenters may have no entree into the regulatory process and may be unable to secure licenses to speak.[436]

Moreover, any vision of an active governmental role in supervising the speech marketplace founders on the significant likelihood that administrative planning will be incompetent, misguided, arbitrary, or political.[437] FCC decisions have repeatedly revealed themselves in hindsight

---

434. Once again, Japan provides a useful example. The effect of that country's informal broadcast regulatory system "has been to place media power squarely within the establishment consensus of the socially and politically acceptable, and to diffuse it through shared authority within . . . power-structure groups." Weinberg, *supra* note 40, at 692.

435. *See id.* at 689-91 (describing susceptibility of Japanese regulatory scheme to political pressures); *see also* Mayton, *supra* note 8, at 760-61 (describing susceptibility of FCC to political pressures).

436. *See, e.g.,* Weinberg, *supra* note 40, at 661-92 (arguing that the restrictive Japanese licensing process "confine[s] media power almost completely within the structure of the socially acceptable and politically influential mainstream"). My point here is simply that informal, situationally-sensitive speech regulation is highly problematic. Is it *more* problematic (that is, more nearly controlled by the economically, politically, and socially dominant) than is marketplace regulation? In order to answer this question, one must consider whether control by the economically, politically, and socially dominant is likely to be more pervasive in the "captured" government agency or in the private sphere. Public choice theory suggests that such control will often be more pervasive in the agency context; interest groups seek statutes granting regulatory authority to agencies precisely because they think (or hope) that they will fare better under that regime than in the unregulated marketplace. *See generally* Peter H. Aranson et al., *A Theory of Legislative Delegation,* 68 CORNELL L. REV. 1, 46-47 (1982).

437. Administrative allocation of broadcast rights is hampered by "the agency's lack of knowledge, inflexibility, and exposure to political pressure," all factors of less concern in connection with market allocation. Coase, *supra* note 16, at 18; *see also* Mayton, *supra* note 8, at 761-62. *See generally* Jonathan Weinberg, Limiting Access to the Broadcast Marketplace, 44 BULL. INST. JOURNALISM & COMM. STUD. 2 (1991) (University of Tokyo). This is not to deny that administrative decisionmaking can be economically superior in certain contexts. The FCC erred, for example, in leaving technical standards for AM stereo to the market rather than imposing them administratively. *See* AM Stereophonic Broadcasting, 64 Rad. Reg. 2d (P & F) 516 (1988) (perpetuating the error). The Commission has not made the same mistake in connection with high-definition TV. *See, e.g.,* Advanced Television Systems, 68 Rad. Reg. 2d (P & F) 167 (1990).

as bad policy.[438] FCC "anti-siphoning" rules, for example, were designed to protect broadcasting from the perceived threat presented by early cable television but ended up stifling cable's development for no good reason.[439] The FCC's comparative hearing process, intended to allow everyone a fair chance to secure a broadcast license on a level playing field,[440] has in fact effectively excluded those without economic means. Only the wealthy can afford to pay large legal fees for the mere opportunity to *compete* for a license, in an essentially random process, without any assurance of success.[441] FCC decisionmaking has at times been overtly political.[442] None of this is encouraging to the proponents of greater involvement by the organs of popular government.

At the same time, we cannot simply conform our law to the privileged pole and ignore nonprivileged concerns. Those concerns are both legitimate and real. Our freedom-of-speech philosophy rests on assumptions about the functioning of the marketplace of ideas that are, ultimately, unsupportable. Their failure means more than that marketplace theory is intellectually unsatisfying. A speech regulatory system based wholly on classic free-speech philosophy underestimates the degree to which private institutional and economic power can skew the reasoning processes of the community. It underestimates the dangers posed by concentrations of private media power. It ignores the benefits potentially available from such public institutions as PBS or the BBC, and it facilitates and disregards socially dominant groups' influence over the public agenda and their ascendancy in public debate.

Can we mediate the two models, taking the best aspects of each?[443] Some scholars have argued that it is impossible to bring together the privileged and nonprivileged approaches in that manner. The two

---

438. *See* Henry Geller, *Communications Law—A Half Century Later,* 37 FED. COMM. L.J. 73, 73-78 (1984) (listing FCC failures).

439. The rules prohibited cable systems from carrying certain movies and sports programming in order to ensure that attractive programming was not "siphoned" away from broadcast TV. *See* Home Box Office v. FCC, 567 F.2d 9 (D.C. Cir.) (striking down the rules), *cert. denied,* 434 U.S. 829 (1977). *See generally* Weinberg, *supra* note 40, at 696-700 (describing the FCC's "anti-siphoning" rules as undercutting the FCC's earlier vision for cable).

440. *See* Ashbacker Radio Corp. v. FCC, 326 U.S. 327, 333 (1945) (holding that the FCC must schedule mutually exclusive broadcast applications for a single comparative hearing, so as to give each applicant the full benefit of the "hearing . . . which Congress chose to give him").

441. *See* Robinson, *supra* note 76, at 242-43 (noting that the difficulties in raising the capital necessary to engage in the uncertain venture of applying and competing for a license effectively excludes the poor from the licensing system).

442. *See* Weinberg, *supra* note 40, at 690; *supra* note 71 and accompanying text. Thomas Hazlett has characterized the political nature of our broadcast regulatory structure as "inherent." It rests, he states, on an FCC-established "off-budget auction, in which the rents associated with licensure are appropriated to competitive constituencies as merited by the political pressure they effect." Hazlett, *supra* note 8, at 169.

443. For an eloquent—if controversial—appeal that we find that middle path, see Fiss, *supra* note 151, at 1415-21. *But see* Powe, *supra* note 181, at 180-86 (attacking Fiss); Hutchinson, *supra* note 294, at 19-23 (same).

approaches, they say, are not made up of " 'competing concerns' [to be] artfully balanced until a wise equilibrium is reached"; rather, they are wholly contradictory, in fundamental, "irreducible, irremediable, irresolvable conflict."[444] This is a difficult issue: it is hard to think clearly about contradiction.[445] Without regard to the accuracy of broad statements about contradiction elsewhere in the law, though, the two approaches do seem irreconcilable in the area of speech regulation.

How, for example, shall we define the scope of permissible government intervention in the speech marketplace? *Some* government involvement (beyond merely maintaining the property-rights system) seems appropriate under any analysis. Almost all of us agree, for example, that the government should enforce the antitrust laws in media markets: anticompetitive behavior and private concentrations of media power can injure the media marketplace.[446] Monopoly-controlled markets, brought about through antitrust violations, injure that "widest possible dissemination of information from diverse and antagonistic sources [that] is essential to . . . a free society."[447]

Yet having accepted the conclusion that *some* government restrictions on speech are legitimate, we are faced with the problem of identifying appropriate restrictions. The privileged position responds to that concern by deeming freedom the norm, and carving out a sharply defined, exceptional zone in which the government is allowed to intervene because the market is deemed no longer "free." That approach is essential to the privileged position; without sharp lines to constrain governmental power, we lose the protection for individual autonomy that is the keystone of rule-bounded legality. The central and contradictory insight of the nonprivileged position, however, is that the failures of the marketplace of ideas are not narrowly confined, but are pervasive. They exist in greater or lesser degree throughout the system. No sharp lines between the realm of freedom and the realm of duress can be drawn; no

---

444. KELMAN, *supra* note 311, at 3; *see also* Kennedy, *supra* note 310, at 1774-78.

445. *See* J.M. Balkin, *Nested Oppositions*, 99 YALE L.J. 1669, 1674-75 (1990) (book review) ("A recurring problem in theoretical argument is the confusion of conceptual opposition with logical contradiction."); *cf.* F. SCOTT FITZGERALD, *The Crack-up, in* THE CRACK-UP 69 (Edmund Wilson ed., 1945) ("[T]he test of a first-rate intelligence is the ability to hold two opposed ideas in the mind at the same time, and still retain the ability to function.").

446. *See* FCC v. National Citizens Comm. for Broadcasting, 436 U.S. 775, 795-96, 800 n.18 (1978) (stating that the FCC can and should apply antitrust considerations in regulating the electronic media). The desire for competitive markets, on the other hand, is not the only goal of our regulatory scheme. *See* FCC v. RCA Communications, Inc., 346 U.S. 86, 91-95 (1953) (holding that the public interest may require the FCC to deny a common-carrier authorization even though granting it would increase competition); *see also* Newspaper Preservation Act, 15 U.S.C. §§ 1801-1804 (1988) (exempting joint newspaper operating arrangements from antitrust scrutiny); *National Citizens Comm. for Broadcasting*, 436 U.S. at 803-14 (affirming the Commission's decision not to order sweeping divestiture of newspaper-broadcast combinations).

447. Associated Press v. United States, 326 U.S. 1, 20 (1945) (rejecting First Amendment challenge to enforcement of the Sherman Act against the Associated Press).

easily applied, black-letter rules can identify the appropriate scope of government intervention; no reasoned justification can be given for drawing the lines in one place rather than another.[448] I can imagine no way to integrate these two opposing positions.

Moreover, any meaningful attempt to remedy the flaws of the individualistic approach requires a substantive, rather than a process-oriented, set of goals. How can we set about to correct the flaws of the marketplace? How will we know a properly working marketplace when we see one? It obviously does no good to declare that we will know a properly working marketplace of ideas because it will lead citizens to adopt "correct" views. That approach would not mediate the two models, but rather would wholly reject traditional First Amendment thinking. Yet in the absence of such a test, how are we to know whether the success of some views and the failure of others in the marketplace are the result of inherent merit or of market flaws?[449] At the very least, we would have to develop some vision of what community debate and discussion ideally ought to look like.[450] Yet such a vision is inevitably substantive. It is impossible to identify "balanced" debate except with reference to a substantive baseline.[451]

Indeed, it is central to the nonprivileged vision that it rejects the public-private distinction; that it sees the state as responsible for the consequences of "private" speech. Yet once we make that leap, all of our choices regarding the circumstances under which we will allow, say, racial hate speech, become political ones; we cannot decide them on the basis of neutral principles. Rather, we must look to our substantive

---

448. It is but a short step from classical antitrust remedies to current FCC restrictions on the nature and number of other media outlets that a broadcaster may own. It is but a short step from there to the position that we should limit political campaign spending in order to "remedy the systematic ways in which inequalities of wealth distort the political process." Paul Brest, *Further Beyond the Republican Revival: Toward Radical Republicanism*, 97 YALE L.J. 1623, 1627 (1988); *see also* J. Skelly Wright, *Politics and the Constitution: Is Money Speech?*, 85 YALE L.J. 1001, 1005 (1976). The Supreme Court has rejected that last stride. *See* Buckley v. Valeo, 424 U.S. 1, 48-49 (1976) (striking down limits on political campaign expenditures). Yet each of these government actions directly restricts the autonomy of the speakers who are its target, in the interest of increasing freedom in the rest of the marketplace. Can we justify the particular line at which we stop opposing governmental to private power?

449. *See* MARK TUSHNET, RED, WHITE AND BLUE: A CRITICAL ANALYSIS OF CONSTITUTIONAL LAW 283 (1988). The problem is reminiscent of the difficulty, in representation-reinforcement theory, of distinguishing between groups that are unfairly treated in the political process and those that, for good and legitimate reasons, simply lose their legislative battles. "[A] judge must have some *substantive* vision of what results the process should have yielded. Otherwise he has no way to know that the process was unfair." Lewis F. Powell, Jr., Carolene Products *Revisited*, 82 COLUM. L. REV. 1087, 1091 (1982).

450. *See* Lillian R. BeVier, *Money and Politics: A Perspective on the First Amendment and Campaign Finance Reform*, 73 CALIF. L. REV. 1045, 1067-74 (1985) (arguing against the constitutionality of active campaign finance law on the grounds that any justification for such laws requires an arbitrary, unworkable image of the "ideally operating political system").

451. *See supra* notes 117-21 and accompanying text.

image of what constitutes the good society. This is impossible so long as we hold on to ordinary free-speech philosophy's insistence that it makes no substantive choices—that it defines no authoritative truth and treats all values and ideas as equally legitimate.[452] Once again, there appears to be no common ground on which the two models can meet and negotiate.

Lee Bollinger once suggested that we have in fact mediated our "opposing constitutional traditions regarding the press" simply by placing them side by side—by allowing one to govern print, and the other broadcast.[453] Instead of a unified scheme of regulation, we have a system where "access"-based regulation of broadcasting is coupled with a hands-off approach to print. This allows our system to "capture[] the benefits of access regulation yet . . . minimize[] its potential excesses."[454]

In the end, I think, Bollinger's attempted solution is insufficient.[455] By attempting to take both privileged and nonprivileged concerns into account, our speech law has become both unstable and incoherent. As I have shown, the contradiction between the two poles has made our broadcast law incoherent even when viewed *in isolation.* We will not accept a wholly nonprivileged broadcast scheme, but we cannot combine privileged and nonprivileged elements in a broadcast regulatory system in a way that makes any sense.[456] Nor, in practice, do the strengths and weaknesses of the two systems in fact complement each other. All we have is a mess.

Bollinger's approach, though, raises a more general question: can we build second-best solutions for speech regulation by creating nonprivileged enclaves within a larger privileged-position world? Ultimately, I believe, such solutions are unsatisfactory in important ways. An ideal nonprivileged approach would seek to disconnect speech from the pressures of the private sphere, so that the economic resources of the speaker or of potential individual listeners would play no role in the speech's success. Establishing a quasi-governmental institution to disseminate speech on the basis of its own view of the public interest might point in that direction; so might distributing speech through some publicly-sup-

---

452. For an illustration of the difficulty, see Sunstein, *supra* note 8, at 277, 290 (simultaneously attacking the concept of viewpoint neutrality as unacceptably contingent on "existing distributions of resources and opportunities as the baseline for decision" and arguing that constitutionally appropriate speech regulation must be viewpoint-neutral).

453. Bollinger, *supra* note 25, at 1.

454. *Id.* at 2.

455. *See* Lili Levi, *Challenging the Autonomous Press,* 78 CORNELL L. REV. 665, 685-90 (1993) (book review).

456. The structure of the print marketplace is nothing to write home about either. *Cf.* Paul Bator, *The First Amendment Applied to Broadcasting: A Few Misgivings,* 10 HARV. J.L. & PUB. POL'Y 75, 75 (1987) (asking the questions " 'Do I like the content of that regime?' Should that regime be extended to another industry?" in response to "the proposal . . . that the First Amendment regime applicable to the press . . . simply be transferred to broadcasting," and concluding that the answer is "no").

ported mechanism available to all. The first of these approaches looks like the public broadcasting system; the second like some sort of common-carrier scheme. I will discuss each of them briefly.

The public broadcasting system is premised on the conviction that an "alternative telecommunications service[]," freed from the strictures of the economic marketplace, can provide "an expression of diversity and excellence" not available from commercially motivated speakers.[457] Television freed from the constraints of the marketplace, we imagined in establishing the system, could "arouse our dreams, satisfy our hunger for beauty, take us on journeys, enable us to participate in events, present great drama and music, explore the sea and the sky and the woods and the hills." It was to be "our Lyceum, our Chautauqua, our Minsky's, and our Camelot."[458]

The public broadcasting concept relies to significant extent on the nonprivileged model. Under an individualist approach, one might legitimately ask whether the fact that the commercial marketplace fails to provide certain programming does not itself demonstrate that that programming is not worth providing. Public broadcasting takes the opposite approach, revealing a more paternalistic, value-objective, communitarian bent. In its purest form, it rests on the position of Lord Reith, first Director-General of the BBC, that it is misguided to seek to satisfy the desires of self-contained, atomistic consumers: "few [members of the listening public] know what they want, and very few what they need."[459] Broadcasting can be used as an instrument of community: "to inculcate citizenship, to pay proper attention to public affairs, . . . to widen as far as possible the range of debate over the whole field of human interest" and "to raise standards."[460]

As a solution to our dilemma, though, public broadcasting is problematic. How should public broadcasters seek to fulfill their responsibility to the "public?" Commissioner Benjamin Hooks once characterized public broadcasting, as practiced by New York City's WNET, as "an electronic Harvard liberal arts course" focusing solely on "cultured,

---

457. 47 U.S.C. § 396(a)(5) (1988); *see also* H.R. Rep. No. 572, 90th Cong., 1st Sess. (1967), *reprinted in* 1967 U.S.C.C.A.N. 1772, 1801 (stating that only noncommercial stations can engage in widespread production and distribution of educational and cultural programs without mass audience appeal).

458. Carnegie Comm'n on Educ. Television, Public Television: A Program for Action 13 (1967) (quoting E.B. White). The Carnegie Commission report was the "intellectual foundation" for the Public Broadcasting Act of 1967, which in turn established the Corporation for Public Broadcasting and our current system of noncommercial TV. Bollinger, *supra* note 11, at 107.

459. R.H. Coase, British Broadcasting: A Study in Monopoly 47 (1950) (quoting Lord Reith).

460. *Id.* at 175 (quoting Sir William Haley). To that end, public broadcasting should be run by those of "the highest quality of character and intellect," unaffected by political or commercial considerations. Michael Tracey, *Japan: Broadcasting in a New Democracy, in* The Politics of Broadcasting 264, 265 (Raymond Kuhn ed., 1985) (quoting Sir Ian Jacob).

white cosmopolites"—"the caucasian intellectual's home entertainment game."[461] He lambasted it as disserving the needs of the poor and minorities. Part of the reason for public television's focus on "British drama, German music, French cuisine, and Russian Ballet,"[462] of course, is that so-called "noncommercial" broadcasting is intimately tied into the commercial marketplace. It depends for its survival on corporate sponsors who enjoy being associated with classy programming.[463] But merely loosening the link between public broadcasting and corporate sponsors would not answer Hooks's complaint. The broader difficulty is that the publishers of public broadcasting are not themselves the "public." Rather, they are a professional elite responding to their own values and institutional agenda.[464] While speech in that enclave is not limited by the constraints of the economic marketplace, it is hardly "free" in the utopian sense. It is merely subject to a different set of institutional constraints.

An alternative, nonprivileged enclave for speech might grow out of new technology. Science fiction writers have imagined a world in which citizens could produce and electronically disseminate speech without regard to their fame or resources, to be retrieved by members of the public through some sort of index or search mechanism.[465] In those visions, anyone can engage in mass speech. All one has to do is produce a work and upload it into the network, and the network takes care of transmission and distribution. Indeed, the beginnings of such systems are in place now. They range from the tens of thousands of small noncommercial computer bulletin boards to the huge but arcane Internet.[466] Today's systems fall short of the vision I have described, though, in two principal ways. First, current systems tend to be limited to small groups of technically sophisticated users with access to relatively expensive equipment.[467]

---

461. Puerto Rican Media Action & Educ. Council, Inc., 51 F.C.C.2d 1178, 1195, 1199 (1975) (Hooks, Comm'r, dissenting).

462. *Id.* at 1199.

463. Over the years, public broadcasting has moved ever further away from the noncommercial ideal. *See, e.g.*, Commission Policy Concerning the Noncommercial Nature of Educ. Broadcasting Stations, 97 F.C.C.2d 255 (1984) (stating that donor acknowledgements may include a description of the donor's product line or service, its location, and its slogan, so long as the slogan merely identifies but does not promote).

464. Indeed, the courts have stressed that public broadcasters are autonomous, and must not be constrained, in making editorial and programming decisions, by the views or objections of members of the public. Muir v. Alabama Educ. Television Comm'n, 688 F.2d 1033, 1041, 1044 (5th Cir. 1982) (en banc), *cert. denied*, 460 U.S. 1023 (1983).

465. *See, e.g.*, KEVIN O'DONNELL, JR., ORA:CLE (1983).

466. *See generally* Mitchell Kapor, Building the Open Road: Policies for the National Public Network 2 (Apr. 29, 1991) (unpublished manuscript, on file with author).

467. While some mass-market commercial networks, such as Sears Prodigy, are designed and operated for the nontechnical user, I think it is fair to characterize the networks as a whole as requiring a level of technical sophistication beyond the grasp of the average U.S. citizen—certainly far beyond the grasp of the average noncomputer user. *See id.* at 15. While personal computer prices drop with each passing day, so that today one can buy an entry-level machine for $1000 or

Second, it can be paralyzingly hard to get information out of the systems. The index and search mechanisms I airily referred to above have not been developed. Internet thus resembles "a gigantic library with no card catalog."[468] Trying to "read" the Usenet, a decentralized conferencing system running over the Internet, "is like drinking from a firehose."[469]

Systems that carry the speech of all users on a common-carriage basis nonetheless might provide the foundation for a new approach.[470] The key to a computer network-based strategy would be that the costs of transmitting and distributing a communication, whether in print or in video, would be quite low, and would not rise with the number of persons receiving the communication. Capacity, further, would be essentially unlimited. Through such an approach, some imagine, we could move toward a mass communication system in which it would be easy and cheap to become an information provider. Many could participate, both as speakers and as listeners.[471]

That vision too, though, must be approached with caution. After all, we already have a pervasive, government-subsidized, common-carrier distribution system for speech. That system is second-class mail, which provides a subsidy for the distribution of most newspapers and periodicals.[472] Here too, the government has provided a transmission and distribution system for speech, subsidized by the taxpayers, on a common-carrier basis.[473] The second-class postal subsidy has contributed greatly

---

less, that price still isn't chicken feed. Computers have a long way to go before they become as inexpensive as telephones or televisions.

468. *Id.* at 5.

469. Tom Maddox, *Reports from the Electronic Frontier,* LOCUS, Sept. 1992, at 11 (quoting Steve Steinberg, editor of *Intertek* magazine).

470. It would not be the first time we have tried a common-carrier approach to mass communications. AT&T made the first bid to do so back in 1922, on its WEAF radio station. In an experiment it called "toll broadcasting," it proposed to "provide no program of its own, but provide the channels through which anyone with whom it makes a contract can send out their own programs." ERIK BARNOUW, TUBE OF PLENTY: THE EVOLUTION OF AMERICAN TELEVISION 44 (rev. ed. 1982) (quoting AT&T announcement). The approach was ultimately a blazing success for AT&T: advertising agencies were glad to buy up its time for programs they sponsored. *Id.* at 44-48. AT&T itself later got out of the broadcasting business, selling WEAF for $1,000,000 to the newly formed National Broadcasting Company, which in turn agreed to lease AT&T long-distance lines to connect its stations. WEAF was ultimately renamed WNBC. *Id.* at 52-53.

AT&T's "toll broadcasting" plan hardly could be said to have promoted the communitarian vision I have described. Its high tariff for broadcast time effectively precluded any noncommercial uses.

471. *See* Kapor, *supra* note 466, at 8-9, 13.

472. Fourth-class (book rate) mail is similarly subsidized. *See* Robert Posch, *Price Censorship is Real and Growing,* COMM. LAW., Fall 1990, at 15, 16-17.

473. The system differs in several crucial respects from the vision I have drawn of the computer networks. First, even with the subsidy, distribution charges are still substantial, and they rise with each additional recipient. Next, second-class mail status is available only to publications that distribute at least half of their circulated copies to paying subscribers or to people who have specifically requested that the periodical be sent to them. *See* Elizabeth Gorman, *The First Amendment and the Postal Service's Subscriber Requirement: Constitutional Problems with Denying Equal Access to the Postal System,* 21 U. RICH. L. REV. 541 (1987) (citing the U.S. Postal Service's

to the vibrancy and diversity of America's magazine market. In some ways, the system works remarkably well. Tens of thousands of periodicals are said to move through the mails, "the little magazines, the special magazines, the cranky magazines, . . . the serious magazines."[474] Yet, even though all sorts of speech flourishes on the fringes of the magazine market, it is still the case that there are a few market leaders, in particular the weekly newsmagazines, exerting huge media power. The speakers exercising by far the greatest might in this marketplace are wealthy, mass-market, taste-creating media conglomerates, led by such pillars of the corporate community as Time Warner.[475] These speakers can expend the greatest resources on production values and on marketing. Indeed, mass-circulation, second-class mailers that can afford segmentation or trucking techniques qualifying them for "work-sharing discounts" get a larger subsidy from the postal service. Those techniques are as a practical matter not available to fringe publishers.[476] All is not joyful anarchy, thus, in the core of the magazine market.

In the computer networks of the future, similarly, all information providers will not be equal, no matter how user-friendly the network is. Wealth will play a role in publicizing the availability and merits of documents or programs. It will play a role in producing speech in an attractive form.[477] The networks, thus, may not provide a nonprivileged enclave after all. They may simply provide a (kinder, gentler?) version of the ordinary marketplace.

Where, then, do we go from here? I present in this Article no policy

---

Domestic Mail Manual). Also, the would-be recipient of information has no way of getting access to information not specifically addressed to her. A speaker, therefore, cannot simply dispatch her communication, unaddressed, to the postal system, and without further thought rely on the distribution network to carry it to the world at large. She must first develop a subscription list, and limit her mailing within the confines of that list. Still, the conclusions we draw about the operation of second-class mail service may have some applicability to our thinking about computer networks.

474. POOL, *supra* note 15, at 150. According to one observer, "[s]ome 37,000 periodicals regularly move through the U.S. mails." EDWIN DIAMOND, SIGN OFF: THE LAST DAYS OF TELEVISION 229 (1982). A random sampling might include such periodicals as *Jason Underground's Notes From the Trash Compactor,* with a "unique Christian anarchist slant"; *Counter Culture,* devoted to "diner appreciation"; *Dendron News,* devoted to "people who have been through the psychiatric system (or who are still enmeshed in it) [and] try to find more humanitarian alternatives"; *Corpus Christi Mariner News,* "for Merchant Marine folks in the Corpus Christi area"; and *The Black Flame,* examining "the use of Satanism as a practical philosophy for surviving a cold, uncaring world." MIKE GUNDERLOY & CARI G. JANICE, THE WORLD OF ZINES: A GUIDE TO THE INDEPENDENT MAGAZINE REVOLUTION 31, 69, 93, 110, 122 (1992). [Editor's note: A random sampling of the "far outer shores of the special interest magazine world," POOL, *supra* note 15, at 150, might also, of course, include the *California Law Review.*]

475. In 1981, twenty corporations accounted for 50.7% of all U.S. magazine sales. BEN H. BAGDIKIAN, THE MEDIA MONOPOLY 10-14 (1983).

476. Posch, *supra* note 472, at back page.

477. In this medium as in (almost) all others, a mass audience will not tune in unless production values are high enough. *See* Ingber, *supra* note 182, at 70-71 (finding something "bittersweet funny" in the attempts of cable public-access programming to compete with the professional presentations of commercial television). *But see* THE RAMONES, ROCKET TO RUSSIA (Sire Records 1977).

solution that will solve all of the problems of the broadcasting system. Rather, my ultimate argument in this Article is that no such policy solution can exist. There is nothing we *can* do in broadcast regulation that will not leave us grappling with further contradictions and unresolved issues. In considering how to revise broadcast law, we do badly to look for sweeping, ideologically pure, universal solutions. The better course may be to look for second-best solutions:

We must recognize that we want contradictory things. We want protection against government arbitrariness, bias, and "censorial power."[478] We want protection against government control of (or influence over) the agenda of public debate. We want to be protected against government attempts to influence what we think and believe. We want to choose, ourselves, what we will say and what we will hear. Yet we want as well a First Amendment theory that reflects the real world, that recognizes the negative effects of real-life inequality and private economic power, and doesn't explain them away through unrealistic assumptions. In choosing what we will say and what we will hear, we want protection, too, against the distorting effects of private power and private censorship. We want, perhaps, programming that reflects something more than what the corporate shills have conditioned us to swallow.

There does not appear to be any way to get all of that. The doctrines and procedural forms that will help us towards one set of goals help us away from the other. As a result, it should not be surprising that our broadcast regulation law is blazingly inconsistent with the rest of our First Amendment philosophy. If we recast our broadcast law to eliminate that contradiction, we will ameliorate one set of doctrinal and practical problems, but we will not "solve" the problems of speech law. We will only rearrange them.

CONCLUSION

Our broadcast regulatory system centers on the "public interest" standard of the Communications Act. The FCC, in deciding whom it will allow to speak using broadcast media, is required to make the choices that will best serve the "public interest." It is the FCC's job, ultimately, to ensure that its licensed broadcasters serve the "public interest." This standard is vague. Notwithstanding the best of intentions, the FCC's application of the standard has been unpredictable and subjective, and its decisions have incorporated hidden content biases. To the extent that the Commission has been able to announce hard-edged, easy-to-apply rules in pursuance of the public interest standard, those rules have had little to do with individualized attention to the "public

---

478. City of Lakewood v. Plain Dealer Publishing Co., 486 U.S. 750, 758 (1988).

interest." This is not the agency's fault: the standard, inherently vague and subjective, cannot be applied as if it were black-letter law.

This system conflicts, starkly and gratuitously, with conventional free-speech philosophy. Conventional free-speech philosophy rejects the content regulation that the Commission routinely engages in. It rejects the broad, subjective, situationally sensitive standards the Commission seeks to apply in ruling whether it will allow citizens to engage in speech. It rejects the whole notion that it is the job of government to decide what speech is and is not in the public interest. The idea of spectrum scarcity is not enough to reconcile this system with ordinary free-speech philosophy. Even if the unique characteristics of broadcasting justify administrative allocation of the broadcast spectrum, there is no way within the four corners of conventional free speech thinking to justify allocating that spectrum on the basis of a government agency's subjective conception of a vaguely defined public interest.

Ordinary free-speech philosophy, on the other hand, itself is flawed; it presents an inaccurate picture of reality. It is crucially based on the metaphor of the marketplace of ideas. That metaphor in turn relies on questionable assumptions about individual autonomy in the private sphere. It assumes that in a society where government enforces common-law ordering but otherwise plays no active role in regulating speech, individuals do indeed have meaningful opportunities to speak and convince others of their views. It assumes that people process speech for the most part on a rational level, and choose to adopt one belief rather than another as a result of this reasoning process. Neither of those assumptions seems well founded. Inequality in economic, social, and political power in our society leads to marked inequalities in the ability to communicate. The institutional mass media do not even the scales. Nor, in any event, do individuals tend to process new information in a "rational" manner; our thinking is significantly constrained by our existing mindset. It seems unlikely that we have a working marketplace of ideas outside of a narrowly bounded range of socially acceptable ideas and values.

The inconsistency of our broadcast regulatory system with ordinary free speech thinking, and the inconsistency of ordinary free speech thinking with reality, make sense if one imagines ordinary free speech thinking and broadcast regulatory thinking as reflecting two conflicting worldviews. The first worldview, more nearly predominant in our legal culture, links the procedural mode of black-letter rules, individualism, a belief in overall private autonomy, a sharp public-private distinction, value subjectivity, and nonpaternalism. The other links the procedural mode of situationally sensitive standards, altruism, determinism, a belief in the pervasiveness of constraint, value objectivity (or a belief in the communal nature of values), and paternalism. These philosophies, each incomplete, can be seen as pervasive in our law. Each reflects legitimate and important impulses.

Conventional free-speech philosophy neatly reflects the former philosophy. It passionately relies on black-letter rules; it reflects individualistic ideology, fundamentally rationalist and intentionalist. It is grounded at its root in a thoroughgoing commitment to value subjectivity and a rejection of paternalism; it maintains a strong public-private distinction. Broadcast law, by contrast, more nearly reflects the latter. It is built around the situationally sensitive standard; it is concerned with substantive inequality, domination, and constraint. It significantly rejects individualistic thinking in favor of an approach more in the altruistic mold. In important respects, it is not a pure evocation of a single worldview. It is too significantly influenced by ordinary free speech values and by the rule-bound mores of the prevailing legal culture. It nonetheless stands as a somewhat muddled island of dissident thinking in the sea of free-speech philosophy.

The approach of our broadcast regulatory scheme works badly when it comes to regulating speech. It is insufficient, though, simply to ignore that approach, and to conform our law to ordinary free-speech philosophy. Free-speech philosophy systematically underestimates the degree to which private institutional and economic power can skew the reasoning processes of the community. It underestimates the dangers posed by concentrations of private power. The philosophy on which our broadcast law is based grows out of concerns that are both legitimate and real.

The two worldviews are not easily reconcilable. There does not seem to be any perfect solution that would mediate the two approaches, and take the best aspects of each. Ultimately, we can do no better than a second-best solution. We have, as a society, legitimate and contradictory goals in regulating speech. The doctrines that move us toward one set of goals move us away from the other. This means that recasting our broadcast regulation to conform to ordinary free-speech philosophy, as some suggest, will not solve our problems. We want things that no coherent philosophy can supply.

[3]

Converging First Amendment Principles for Converging Communications Media

Thomas G. Krattenmaker[†] and L. A. Powe, Jr.[††]

For students of telecommunications law and technology, it has become a trivial ritual to observe that telecommunications technologies and media are converging. Neither producers nor purchasers of audio or video information should find much use, in the near future, for such terms as "television," "computer," "telephone," or "radio." These objects are no longer distinct devices and we believe that any differences among them are ephemeral.

For students of constitutional law and the Supreme Court's jurisprudence of the First Amendment guarantee of freedom of speech, these observations are likely to trigger a different ritual incantation: "Different communications media are treated differently for First Amendment purposes."[1] How can one reconcile the fact of technological and media convergence with the legal presumption of distinct treatments?

We argue in this Essay that this dilemma should not be resolved by permitting the First Amendment to be used as a sword to prevent communications convergence or as a shield to permit government agencies to force these technologies into distinct, procrustean categories. Rather, the latest advances in telecommunications provide federal courts the opportunity to discard the inherently silly notion that freedom of speech depends on the configuration of the speaker's voicebox or mouthpiece.

---

† Dean and Professor of Law, William and Mary Law School. I wish to thank Eric Bernthal and Gary Epstein for cajoling me into putting these thoughts together and to the participants in the William and Mary Law School faculty workshop for helping me to refine them, and to Julie Patterson for helpful research assistance.

†† Anne Green Regents Chair, The University of Texas.

Portions of this Essay derive from a larger work by the authors, THOMAS G. KRATTENMAKER & LUCAS A. POWE, JR., REGULATING BROADCAST PROGRAMMING, published by the MIT Press, copyright © 1994 by MIT and the American Enterprise Institute for Public Policy Research. Passages that are unchanged are reprinted with the permission of the American Enterprise Institute for Public Policy Research, Washington, D.C. We thank J. Gregory Sidak for his encouragement in writing this Essay. Mark Gergen and Richard Markovits each made especially helpful editing suggestions, and Jack Balkin, Doug Laycock, and Mike Seidman provided trenchant and helpful criticism.

1. City of Los Angeles v. Preferred Communications, Inc., 476 U.S. 488, 496 (1986) (Blackmun, J., concurring) (cable television) (comparing Miami Herald Publishing Co. v. Tornillo, 418 U.S. 241 (1974) (newspaper) and FCC v. League of Women Voters, 468 U.S. 364 (1984) (broadcast television)); see also infra note 4.

1720   The Yale Law Journal   [Vol. 104: 1719

Further, reflection will show that this step would not be a radical jurisprudential leap. In truth, among all mass communication technologies, only broadcast radio and television have been afforded distinctive treatment. History reveals that the unusual jurisprudence of broadcasting rests on the slimmest foundations. The Supreme Court crafted these rules not so much because the Justices believed broadcasting was distinct, but more because the Court's major free speech cases concerning broadcasting arose when the Justices were deeply conflicted over the relationships between rights of speech and of property[2] or were deeply divided among themselves over the issue of "obscene" or "indecent" speech.[3]

Moreover, to achieve the rational goals of those who prefer to tame the broadcast industry, it is not necessary to retain a separate First Amendment jurisprudence for broadcasters. If we look behind the facade of broadcast free speech law, we can discern established, durable, fundamental principles that govern regulation of mass communications without regard to the technology employed, that protect freedom of speech while leaving ample room for sober regulation, and that apply equally well to all mass communication media. We believe that the growing telecommunications convergence should lead the Court to embrace these principles explicitly while discarding the false notion that "broadcasting" (whatever that is) requires or deserves a separate First Amendment jurisprudence.

This Essay proceeds in four steps. We first explain, briefly, the well-known dualism in mass media law today: one rule for broadcasters, another for printers. We then describe the kinds of objections made to broadcast programming today, confident that similar criticisms will be voiced about the program fare offered by emerging video, audio, and data technologies. In step three, we explain how the "print" model is in fact a coherent and complete system of regulatory ideals, built on four well-established and sensible principles, reflecting current regulation of all nonbroadcast mass media. Finally, we conclude that this more general model will adequately serve the goals of the sober broadcast regulator while providing a sound basis for judging regulation of emerging technologies as well. The progressive congruence of telecommunications technologies, then, ought to be the catalyst for two jurisprudential developments: (1) discarding the broadcast model and (2) realizing that traditional First Amendment principles—not yet another set of unique rules—are quite well suited to guide and constrain public regulation of these new technologies.

---

2. THOMAS G. KRATTENMAKER & LUCAS A. POWE, JR., REGULATING BROADCAST PROGRAMMING 182–89 (1994) [hereinafter REGULATING BROADCAST PROGRAMMING].
   3. *Id.* at 196–202.

I. Two Models

No matter how often one repeats the statement, it cannot be true that "[d]ifferent communications media are treated differently for First Amendment purposes."[4] Should everything we knew about regulation of books have been discarded once talking motion pictures were invented? Did discovery of the personal computer (or was it the monitor screen?) render obsolete everything the courts said about the First Amendment and broadcasting, or cable, or telephones? Once a free speech jurisprudence is written for computers, must we refuse to employ those rules for a later technology, such as satellites, lest we treat different communications media identically for First Amendment purposes?

Fortunately, it never has been true that each communications medium gets its own free speech rules. Except broadcasting. It is only because of the special status of broadcasting that we can accurately report that constitutional law today reflects two distinct, well-developed models for assessing government regulation of mass communications. The first, and dominant, model is typically referred to as the "print" model but in fact applies to most mass communications media in the United States.

This so-called print model is most neatly encapsulated in *Miami Herald Publishing Co. v. Tornillo*,[5] with its emphasis on the value of editorial autonomy and the dangers of official censorship. If *The Miami Herald* wished to throw the full weight of its dominant position in the Miami market to preclude the election of a union leader for state representative,[6] then the First Amendment authorized its action. The media owner decides what is said and how it will be said. As A.J. Liebling quipped: "Freedom of the press is guaranteed only to those who own one."[7] Or, as the Court more delicately put it: "For better or worse, editing is what editors are for; and editing is selection and choice of material."[8]

A second, competing model is aptly termed the "broadcast" model. It stems from six decades of regulation and is most thoroughly elucidated in *Red Lion Broadcasting*,[9] with its celebration of the values of access and diversity and concomitant fear of private censorship. This model allows governments to intervene to promote First Amendment values by mandating a more diverse programming fare than broadcasters might otherwise choose. Ideas and speakers are thereby afforded access to listeners and viewers.

---

4. 476 U.S. at 496. The statement has its origins in Kovacs v. Cooper, 336 U.S 77, 97 (1949) (Jackson, J., concurring) (sound trucks); its strongest statement is in Chief Justice Burger's dissent in Metromedia, Inc. v. City of San Diego, 453 U.S. 490, 555 (1981) (Burger, C.J., dissenting) (billboards).

5. 418 U.S. 241 (1974) (invalidating right-of-reply statute).

6. L.A. Powe, Jr., *Tornillo*, 1987 SUP. CT. REV. 345, 351–62.

7. A.J. LIEBLING, THE PRESS 32 (Pantheon Books 1981) (1975).

8. CBS v. Democratic Nat'l Comm., 412 U.S. 94, 124 (1973).

9. Red Lion Broadcasting Co. v. FCC, 395 U.S. 367 (1969).

Red Lion permits—indeed, virtually exhorts—government to override broadcasters' programming preferences to effectuate the right of listeners and viewers "to receive suitable access to social, political, esthetic, moral, and other ideas and experiences."[10] Possessed of this authority, federal regulators have wondered (as they need not with print) how to "measure the conflicting claims of grand opera and religious services, of market reports and direct advertising, of jazz orchestras and lectures on the diseases of hogs."[11] And a more recent regulator, reflecting on a massive tornado that hit Wichita Falls, Texas, rejoiced that "'[y]oung people listening to a rock station'" received warnings that they might not have had "'if we didn't require the licensee to provide a minimum of news.'"[12] But, lest broadcasting become too diverse, the model is supplemented by a related power of government to enforce a level of conformity when issues of community morality are implicated.[13] The extent of this authorization to censor "indecent" broadcasting is largely undefined, although as stated it clearly exceeds the censorship power permitted by the print model.

While the print model has been criticized,[14] none of the critics has suggested that its deficiencies result in any way from a failure to consider fully the text, history, traditions, and constitutional structure of the First Amendment. The deficiencies in the model are deemed to arise, not from misguided constitutional interpretation, but from the increasing power of the press and the diminishing quality of news and information produced by those exercising their First Amendment rights. By contrast, critics of the broadcast model have noted that it does not conform to the text, history, traditions, or constitutional structure of the First Amendment and that the results of allowing government to regulate so intrusively create just the abuses that the print model postulates would occur in a system of government supervision: favoritism, censorship, and political influence.[15]

Both the print and the broadcast models have attractive features. The appeal of the print model stems from its congruence with the canons of

---

10. *Id.* at 390.

11. 1 FED. RADIO COMM'N, ANN. REP. 6 (1927).

12. Lionel Van Deerling, *The Regulators and Broadcast News, in* BROADCAST JOURNALISM 204, 206 (Marvin Barrett ed., 1982) (quoting Commissioner Abbott Washburn).

13. *See* FCC v. Pacifica Found., 438 U.S. 726 (1978) (allowing FCC to channel "indecent" broadcasts to hours in which risk of children listening would be minimized). We do not discuss this censorship power at length in this Essay. One reason is that reflection will show, as subsequent cases are revealing, that *Pacifica* is not really a case about broadcasting. Rather, it is about the problem of semiobscene speech in more-than-ordinarily intrusive media from which children are not easily excluded. REGULATING BROADCAST PROGRAMMING, *supra* note 2, at 199–202, 221.

14. *See, e.g.*, CASS R. SUNSTEIN, DEMOCRACY AND THE PROBLEM OF FREE SPEECH (1993); Jerome A. Barron, *Access to the Press—A New First Amendment Right*, 80 HARV. L. REV. 1641 (1967); Owen M. Fiss, *Free Speech and Social Structure*, 71 IOWA L. REV. 1405 (1986); Owen M. Fiss, *Why the State?*, 100 HARV. L. REV. 781 (1987); Judith Lichtenberg, *Foundations and Limits of Freedom of the Press*, 16 PHIL. & PUB. AFF. 329 (1987).

15. *See* LUCAS A. POWE, JR., AMERICAN BROADCASTING AND THE FIRST AMENDMENT (1987); REGULATING BROADCAST PROGRAMMING, *supra* note 2, at 294–96.

constitutional interpretation: text, history, structure, traditions. The broadcast model is attractive because it recognizes the relationship between speech and the distribution of economic resources, because it encourages a worthy journalistic ethic, and because it posits, as the print model does not, that the freedom of the press (like any other provision of the Constitution[16]) may change with the times.[17]

The print model strictly confines governmental ability to regulate programming. If applied to new technologies, the practical effect would be an unfettered discretion to program virtually anything except obscenity. By contrast, the broadcast model grants governments ample leeway to affect programming decisions, whether to expand access and diversity or to exact conformity. Indeed, no other area of First Amendment jurisprudence is so deferential to government intervention, and we are aware of no one who has suggested that the government needs more power to regulate the media than this model authorizes.

Those wishing to eschew an either/or choice between a jurisprudence that permits too much or one that allows too little program autonomy (or government power) can easily envision a third model splitting some of the differences. Encased in appropriate formulaic language,[18] a third model could give the government some flexibility, when necessary, to regulate programming, but nothing more. This intermediate model could incorporate the insights of the broadcast model while cutting back on its intrusiveness into areas of programming. Essentially such a third model would attempt to fashion rules appropriate for the technologies regulated that are no more intrusive than necessary to accomplish the government's objectives. Because each technology is perceived as creating its own problems, government is allowed some, but not necessarily complete, leeway to remedy those problems. A bare majority of the Supreme Court has tentatively and uneasily accepted this middle approach in a case concerning freedom of speech and cable television, *Turner Broadcasting*.[19]

As communications technologies converge, it will be impossible for the Supreme Court to continue to rely on its bipolar (or tripolar) print-broadcasting models. Which of these models "fits" pictures transmitted through cable TV lines, telephone lines, satellites, microwave? (In fact, today some television

---

16. New York Times Co. v. United States, 403 U.S. 713, 761 (1971) (Blackmun, J., dissenting) ("The First Amendment, after all, is only one part of an entire Constitution.").

17. LEE C. BOLLINGER, IMAGES OF A FREE PRESS (1991).

18. ROBERT F. NAGEL, CONSTITUTIONAL CULTURES 122–55 (1989).

19. Turner Broadcasting Sys., Inc. v. FCC, 114 S. Ct. 2445, 2449–51 (1994) (requiring government to prove necessity of requirement that all cable systems carry all locally received over-the-air broadcast signals if broadcasters so demand). We believe "tentatively and uneasily" is an apt description of a 5–4 decision where one of the five Justices (Blackmun) retires immediately and there is every reason to believe the Justices in the majority have no idea how little evidence supports the "necessity" of the must-carry rules.

1724   The Yale Law Journal   [Vol. 104: 1719

viewers watch programs that, in traveling from producer to the home, have traveled part of that distance on each of these media.) And which of these models fits a scholarly journal that is electronically created and transmitted and only placed on the printed page if some recipient so chooses? Would newspapers and magazines suddenly come within a broader scope of content regulation if they were electronically transmitted to their subscribers?

The two (or three) models would yield different outcomes when applied to program content regulation, but none hinders government in regulating the structure or commercial practices of the industry to foster and protect competition. *Associated Press v. United States*[20] held that the antitrust laws fully apply to the print media, and more generally appears to permit government to define and limit ownership rights and commercial contractual relationships in ways perceived to better the functioning of new technologies.[21] Thus the battle over the appropriate First Amendment model for new technologies is about government's latitude to control what is created and consumed, not about its authority to control the structure or commercial practices of the industry.

II. Traditional Rationales for Regulation

How will the emerging communications industry be structured and what will it deliver? Frankly, we do not know. Twenty-five years ago many of the same predictions we hear today for the infobahn—the interconnected grid of emerging telecommunication technologies—were made for cable television. Americans were told to ready themselves for a communications revolution.[22] Network television had been homogenizing the country; cable would decentralize it. Network economics required mass audiences; cable could "affirmatively pinpoint differentiated audiences and serve them economically."[23] There would now be a means to reach "unrecognizable broadcast interests, financing opera, a different kind of news, or other specialized programming."[24] This glorious future has yet to materialize, as Bruce Springsteen's song, "57 Channels and Nothing On," laments. The cable

---

20. 326 U.S. 1 (1945).

21. FCC v. National Citizens Comm. for Broadcasting, 436 U.S. 775 (1978) (unanimously sustaining rules prohibiting future newspaper-broadcast co-ownership in same community).

22. There were numerous reports, but the most quoted was that of the Alfred P. Sloan Foundation, which, "feeling that a politically-appointed Commission might not reach the wisest results, assembled a distinguished group of more or less elder statesmen, asking them to deliberate for a year and then to formulate a set of resolutions that could aid the [Federal Communications] Commission, Congress or any other relevant decisionmaking body." Monroe E. Price, *Requiem for the Wired Nation*, 61 VA. L. REV. 541, 553 (1975). The end product was SLOAN COMM'N ON CABLE COMMUNICATIONS, ON THE CABLE: THE TELEVISION OF ABUNDANCE (1971). Price's wonderful article provides a superbly ironical summary of cable's era of hope: "All those channels, all those hopes, the chance for a wholly new communications system—it was a little intoxicating." Price, *supra*, at 541 (footnote omitted).

23. Price, *supra* note 22, at 547.

24. *Id.* at 548.

experience cautions us to avoid technological predictions. We leave to others descriptions of what new communications technology will look like or what programs and information it will deliver.[25]

We disagree, however, with the Supreme Court that understanding the regulation of an older communications media can offer no guidance to understanding a newer one. We believe that past complaints will be prologue for future complaints about what creators place on, and users receive from, the infobahn.[26] Some will complain that an insufficient amount of the appropriate type or quality of information is available, probably supplemented by a further concern that when the right information is available not enough users are tuning in. Others, by contrast, will complain that users may be accessing information they ought not have. These views generated a virtual panoply of FCC regulations of broadcast content in the past six decades, regulations that we have chronicled elsewhere.[27]

We have noticed that all regulations of broadcast programming share certain features and assumptions. When regulators conclude that viewers and listeners are not tuning in to what the consumers need, regulators tend to counter by attempting to make the merit programming[28] available everywhere. In this fashion, all viewers and listeners, even those who will not change channels, should, at least occasionally, encounter and benefit from good programming. Conversely, bad programming commonly seems too popular. Therefore it must be banned, reduced in quantity, or shunted to periods of infrequent broadcast usage lest viewers and listeners change channels and find the disfavored programming somewhere else.

The former type of regulation—diversity or merit regulation—posits helpless or obstinate viewers. The other type—straightforward censorship—posits enterprising viewers. These apparently contrasting views of broadcast consumers as both paralyzed and enterprising are just two convenient interpretations of a simple fact: It is impossible to regulate viewers and listeners. Both types of regulations also rest on a common perspective: Viewers and listeners are incapable of wise choice. Indeed, when given the option of seeing exactly what a regulator or a critic prefers, viewers often watch something else.

We are quite certain that the new electronic technologies will not alter these facts of life. In the new era, viewers will watch or read what critics and regulators like with insufficient frequency and will enjoy too often what

---

25. *See, e.g.*, Eugene Volokh, *Cheap Speech and What It Will Do*, 104 YALE L.J. 1805 (1995).

26. What follows are criticisms drawn from a much lengthier work. We urge skeptics to read that work before rejecting these conclusions. *See* REGULATING BROADCAST PROGRAMMING, *supra* note 2, at 59–141, 297–315.

27. *Id.* at 59–141.

28. Merit programming is programming deemed so valuable that broadcasters were required to air it, even if few (if any) viewers or listeners wished to tune it in. *See id.* at 145–46.

1726   The Yale Law Journal   [Vol. 104: 1719

commissioners and columnists abhor. It seems all but inevitable that such behavior by viewers, listeners, and readers will generate calls for government action. At this point the search for appropriate guiding principles begins.

III. THE APPROPRIATE SCOPE OF REGULATION

In our recently published book, *Regulating Broadcast Programming*,[29] we articulated guiding principles for regulating the mass media that are well established, yet often not recognized for what they are—the cornerstones of a rather consistent pattern of American regulation of the nonbroadcast mass media.[30] These bedrock legal principles, as applied to such diverse communications media as books, films, magazines, theater, newspapers, recordings, and speech in public forums, function so well that they are often taken for granted.

As computers, satellites, and telephone lines become readily available alternatives to VHF, UHF, cable, and microwave transmission of radio and television, it should become simpler even for the Supreme Court Justices to realize that only a unitary First Amendment for all media will do. In the remainder of this Essay, we explain these ground rules of constitutional law and regulatory policy, show how and why they shape government's basic stance toward all nonbroadcast media, and demonstrate how these principles encompass emerging technologies.

A. *Basic Principles*

Four principles collectively establish the proper responsibilities of government in regulating the structure and performance of the mass media and in supervising access to, and diversity within, those media. They are the principles that, shaped by carefully considered First Amendment values, govern the legal regulation of virtually all other mass media in the United States. These principles provide government with ample authority to regulate the media in ways that can improve their performance, while assuring that government is responsive to, rather than responsible for, American culture, information, and politics. These ground rules of constitutional law and regulatory policy regarding the nonbroadcast media also help to ensure that laws governing the media are targeted at issues government can manage, while avoiding regulations that are simply naive or directed at foisting particular preferences on a pluralist society.[31]

---

29. *Id.*
30. *Id.* at 316–22.
31. The principles set out below are not, under current law, fully applicable where government itself is the speaker or where the speech is properly classified as "commercial speech." Consequently, the analysis does not necessarily apply to cases in which the government is the programmer or the information

1. *First Principle*

Editorial control over what is said and how it is said should be lodged in private, not governmental, institutions. Two basic rationales underlie this principle. They are well stated in *Miami Herald Publishing Co. v. Tornillo*,[32] and so we only summarize them here.

In the first place, both history and theory clearly teach that the imposition by law of "good journalism" or "fair representation" requirements on speakers operates to chill speech, not to liberate, broaden, or protect it.[33] Telling speakers "if you discuss x, you must do (or discuss) y" has the principal effect of inhibiting discussion of x. Further, such government intervention cannot add more speech; at its very best, that intervention can only substitute speech on one topic for speech on another.

In the second place, editorial control, because it is invariably content-based, is an inherently impermissible government function.[34] When government edits, it does so for debatable purposes and with questionable means; that editing necessarily stifles unpopular viewpoints.[35] To mention just two well-known examples: *Red Lion* was part of a John Kennedy–Lyndon Johnson Democratic National Committee effort to silence right-wing radio stations that might oppose the Democrats in 1964,[36] and the stripping of the Reverend Carl McIntire's WXUR of its license because of fairness doctrine violations reduced both the amount of controversial programming and the range of available viewpoints in the Philadelphia area.[37]

The competing principle is drawn from broadcasting: It is regulation in the public interest. As stated by *Red Lion*, government supervision of broadcasters' programming is essential because "[i]t is the right of the viewers and listeners, not the right of the broadcasters, which is paramount."[38] If broadcasters were left to their own discretion (or insufficiently controlled), they would pander to the lowest common denominator, decreasing the quality of important information while simultaneously increasing commercialization.[39] Such programming is not in the public interest and neglects the need to create an

---

constitutes solely commercial speech. We shall turn, in part, to government speech in our discussion of the fourth principle, *see infra* text accompanying notes 63–66.

32. 418 U.S. 241 (1974); *see also* REGULATING BROADCAST PROGRAMMING, *supra* note 2, at 176–77.

33. It is for these reasons that no one would dream of imposing a "balanced coverage" rule on Barbra Streisand, Steven Spielberg, Tom Clancy, or William F. Buckley, Jr.

34. For an extensive demonstration of this point as applied to the fairness doctrine, equal-time provisions, and indecency regulation, see POWE, *supra* note 15, at 108–90.

35. *See* THOMAS I. EMERSON, TOWARDS A GENERAL THEORY OF THE FIRST AMENDMENT 16–25 (1966).

36. POWE, *supra* note 15, at 112–16.

37. REGULATING BROADCAST PROGRAMMING, *supra* note 2, at 266–68.

38. Red Lion Broadcasting Co. v. FCC, 395 U.S. 367, 390 (1969) (citation omitted).

39. Tracy Westin, among others, argues that this has occurred. *Public Interest in Broadcasting: Hearings Before the Subcomm. on Communications and Finance of the House Comm. on Energy and Commerce*, 102d Cong., 1st Sess. 117–18 (1991).

1728   The Yale Law Journal   [Vol. 104: 1719

intelligent, civicly active community where all citizens have access to the full range of information that they need for self-government.

Under the public interest model, government and citizens attentive to civic issues have a role in promoting and improving the community's common values. It is not an adequate response to contend that those who choose to watch, hear, or read information or entertainment that does not further civic values must prefer or enjoy what they choose.

> Preferences that have adapted to an objectionable system cannot justify that system. If better options are put more regularly in view, it might well be expected that at least some people would be educated as a result. They might be more favorably disposed toward programming dealing with public issues in a serious way.[40]

Accordingly, for adherents to the public interest model, government may, indeed should, regulate access to the media (whether new or old) so as to improve and inform those among its citizens who are not already attuned to the public interest. From this perspective the Supreme Court's observation that "no one has a right to press even 'good' ideas on an unwilling recipient"[41] is simply wrong.[42]

Such a public interest rationale for broadcast regulation resulted in FCC rules (or guidelines) designed to create local programming (at the expense of national programming),[43] to produce minimum amounts of news and public affairs,[44] to require balanced presentation of important and controversial issues,[45] to guarantee access to candidates for federal elective office,[46] to suppress music that glorified drug use,[47] to suppress dirty words and discussions of sex,[48] to limit commercials,[49] and to increase educational programming that children should watch.[50] Currently there are advocates who claim that the public interest would also require limiting violence[51] and reducing stereotypes[52] and maybe increasing the numbers of Hispanics and

---

40. CASS R. SUNSTEIN, THE PARTIAL CONSTITUTION 221 (1993). Those who have raised children with specific goals in mind, and lots of one-on-one time over the years to educate and instruct, can only wish that the transmission of preferences was so easy.

41. Rowan v. United States Post Office Dep't, 397 U.S. 728, 738 (1970).

42. One may search SUNSTEIN, *supra* note 14, as well as his contribution to this Symposium, Cass R. Sunstein, *The First Amendment in Cyberspace*, 104 YALE L.J. 1757 (1995), without finding a single mention of *Rowan*.

43. REGULATING BROADCAST PROGRAMMING, *supra* note 2, at 44.

44. *Id.* at 77–79.

45. *Id.* at 61–65.

46. *Id.* at 66–69.

47. *Id.* at 115–18.

48. *Id.* at 104–14.

49. *Id.* at 135–36.

50. *Id.* at 81–84. The FCC has defined children's programming as that which is educational first and entertainment second, thereby seemingly excluding programming watched by the whole family. *Id.* at 84.

51. *Id.* at 120–34.

52. *Id.* at 304–05.

overweight people on the air.[53] Unless the public interest is a fixed concept, presumably other programs that the public needs could be added to this list.

The less attractive results of the public interest model are those regulations that smack of overt censorship. A programmer is forbidden to create, stations are forbidden to air, and adults are forbidden to view and hear programming that would otherwise be available in the market because either Congress or a few commissioners believe that adults are incapable of evaluating what they wish to view. It does not matter whether the banning institution represents a permanent majority of Americans, a transient majority, or a minority that has captured the institution (as appears to have been the case with the 1987 FCC indecency decisions).[54] It does not matter whether the purpose of the regulation is to entrench or change the status quo. In each case, government fiat substitutes for the choices that adult Americans would otherwise make.[55]

While censorship is wrong, mandating a more diverse fare often seems right. Thus a newcomer to this area might be tempted to conclude, for example, that a rule requiring television stations to broadcast more children's programming would be a good thing. Ultimately this rests on the view that any "children's program," no matter how bad, is more likely than not to be better than the alternatives (no matter what the audience may think). Unfortunately, however, true quality comes from a program's substance, not its topic,[56] and FCC efforts to create quality programs that broadcasters do not wish to air, while sporadic, have been unsuccessful.[57]

There are basic reasons why regulatory efforts to mandate quality are ineffective. First, even with television there is too much time to fill and too few truly imaginative people to fill it.[58] Second, audiences appear to know what they like and will resist attempts to re-program their tastes. As Jeff Greenfield notes, "when you no longer need the skills of a safecracker to find PBS in most markets, you have to realize that the reason people aren't watching is that they don't want to."[59]

---

53. *Id.*

54. *See* John Crigler & William J. Byrnes, *Decency Redux: The Curious History of the New FCC Broadcast Indecency Policy,* 38 CATH. U. L. REV. 329, 344–47 (1989).

55. Contrast Justice Robert Jackson: "If there is any fixed star in our constitutional constellation, it is that no official, high or petty, can prescribe what shall be orthodox in politics, nationalism, religion, or other matters of opinion." West Virginia State Bd. of Educ. v. Barnette, 319 U.S. 624, 642 (1943) (Jackson, J.).

56. Henry J. Friendly, *The Federal Administrative Agencies,* 75 HARV. L. REV. 1055, 1071 (1962) (doubting whether "the Commission is really wise enough to determine that live telecasts . . . e.g., of local cooking lessons, are always 'better' than a tape of Shakespeare's Histories").

57. *See* REGULATING BROADCAST PROGRAMMING, *supra* note 2, at 70–74, 99–100.

58. *See* Louis L. Jaffe, *The Role of Government, in* FREEDOM AND RESPONSIBILITY IN BROADCASTING 35, 39 (John Coons ed., 1961). Eric Sevareid put the point succinctly: "Considering the number of hours you had to fill, it's surprising that there's even enough mediocrity to go around." *Quoted in* REGULATING BROADCAST PROGRAMMING, *supra* note 2, at 312.

59. *Quoted in* REGULATING BROADCAST PROGRAMMING, *supra* note 2, at 314.

With newer technologies offering users many more options to watch, hear, or read many more programs and sources of information, these problems will be exacerbated geometrically. Much of the information on the infobahn will be dreck. But users, rather than regulators, will hold the trump cards, because only users can decide how they will spend their time perusing the increased options. Information will have to appeal to users, not government bureaucrats or academic critics, if it is to have a substantial audience. In other words, future users of the infobahn will behave very much like current purchasers of magazines, books, or recordings—and they should be permitted to do so.

2. *Second Principle*

As a matter of policy, government should foster access by speakers to media. Clearly, government has an important role to play in ensuring that the media are not monopolized and in expanding the opportunities of citizens to speak and to be heard. People who own instrumentalities of communication have incentives to reduce their use in order to charge monopoly prices and equally strong incentives to prevent or retard the development of competing instrumentalities. We cannot assume that those efforts will always fail of their own accord. Further, government funding of basic research is often an efficient way of uncovering new communications technologies or new uses for established vehicles, both of which can widen access by increasing the number of available communication channels.

That government should foster speakers' access to the mass media is not a controversial proposition. What has proved quite contestable, however, although usually only with respect to broadcast regulation, is the meaning of access. In broadcasting, access is often defined as replacing the broadcaster's choice of programming with programming chosen by someone not associated with the station.[60] By contrast, when we examine government's relations to other mass media, it seems reasonably clear that, for purposes of the access principle, access means the ability to reach any willing recipient by any speaker willing to pay the economic costs[61] of doing so (and does not mean that government must or should require others to subsidize the would-be communicator). For example, in book publishing we do not assume that access to book publishers is inadequate if an author is not published because publishers believe her book will not sell enough copies to pay for printing costs.

---

60. *Id.* at 243, 244–45.
61. Economic costs are the costs (including opportunity costs) of resources employed in communicating, not necessarily the prices charged by (perhaps monopolistic) owners of those resources.

3. *Third Principle*

Government policies should foster diversity in the media marketplace. If government adheres to the first and second principles, this third principle will follow automatically because it is the opposite side of the coin. Properly understood, the quest for diversity does not require government to provide people speech that they do not value as much as its costs of production and distribution. And, quite obviously, the quest for diversity does not justify censoring some programming upon a theory that the censorship will necessarily generate some different programming.

Instead, diversity is achieved when people are allowed to bid for any information or entertainment they desire—no censorship—and to receive what they seek, so long as they are willing to pay the economic costs of receiving it. That is, the diversity principle dictates that there be no artificial government-imposed barriers to transmission or reception of speech.

This principle, too, is evident in our settled expectations regarding legal control of the nonbroadcast mass media. For example, the magazine market is regarded as diverse because people are free to subscribe to magazines on any or all topics. We do not regard diversity in the magazine market as incomplete if some topics or formats that might lend themselves to magazine treatment are not published because to do so would cost more than subscribers (or advertisers) are willing to pay.[62]

4. *Fourth Principle*

Government is not permitted to sacrifice any of the three foregoing principles to further goals associated with either or both of the others. Where such sacrifice is not needed, however, government may extend the goals associated with any of those principles. Put another way, the Constitution does not mandate subsidies for those seeking access to, or diversity from, the mass communications media;[63] neither does the Constitution prohibit such subsidies.

---

62. One might make precisely the same points about the theatrical film market as well. Movies provide diversity in the sense that people are free to make, to exhibit, and to attend any movie whose costs of production can be covered by expected box office (and tape rental, cable licensing, and other) receipts. We do not regard the movie market as nondiverse, and in need of further government intervention, even though we can easily imagine films that we might like to see but whose costs of production cannot be recaptured by the expected income from selling tickets, and other sources.

63. *See* CBS v. Democratic Nat'l Comm., 412 U.S. 94 (1973) (holding First Amendment does not mandate citizen access to airwaves); Cox v. New Hampshire, 312 U.S. 569, 577 (1941) (sustaining exaction of fee "incident to the administration of the [licensing] Act and to the maintenance of public order in the matter licensed"). We recognize that there is a subsidy inherent in the mandate that government allow speakers to use the public streets and parks to communicate. We are aware of nothing comparable in the area of mass communications.

One of the newest technologies traces its rapid growth to the application of this principle. The federal government has borne most of the costs of establishing the infrastructure that is the Internet, thereby increasing the diversity of the fare available and the accessibility of this medium without favoring any speaker or viewpoint.[64] Antecedent similar examples abound. During the era before cable, we were all the richer for the decision to create and subsidize PBS. Perhaps the benefits of PBS did not exceed its economic costs, but government financing of PBS did no damage to the system of freedom of expression. We cannot know how many magazines have been created and continue to exist because of second-class mailing privileges, but, again, we are better for their existence, because more information is better than less.

Indeed, to the extent the marketplace is perceived as impoverished, subsidies may be an effective way of correcting its inadequacies, so long as these are true subsidies rather than extractions from media competitors.[65] Furthermore, as Mark Yudof's seminal, award-winning work, *When Government Speaks*,[66] explains, the policy issues, while rich and complex, are largely freed from the restraints that the First Amendment otherwise imposes on government actions.

B. *Sources of the Basic Principles*

For those familiar with basic First Amendment law and general American regulatory policy toward the mass media, reflection will reveal that virtually all First Amendment rules and regulatory policies toward the mass media—other than broadcasting—rest on the four principles set out above. Consider the print media. With little or no controversy, we recognize (or tolerate) the following four propositions. First, a regulation that provides, "If you write about *x*, you must behave according to specified journalistic norms," puts a chill on writing about *x*. Second, print media are "accessible" platforms to speakers, even if no one gets published at no cost. Third, the print media provide "diversity," even if we are not assured that every worthwhile view will be offered for sale. Fourth, the First Amendment divested government of power over, or responsibility for, the behavior of editors. Indeed, we might well say that these are the premises underlying *Tornillo*.

We believe American citizens and policymakers embrace those propositions not because they slavishly agree to anything the Supreme Court says, but because of our society's shared belief in the following three empirical

---

64. *See* Ralph Vartabedian, *Colleges Fear Research Cuts by Pentagon*, L.A. TIMES, July 22, 1994, at A1, A20; Aaron Zitner, *A Quiet Leap Forward in Cyberspace*, BOSTON GLOBE, Sept. 11, 1994, at A85.

65. To be a subsidy the costs must be spread generally. The earlier principles preclude taking from *A* to *B* or silencing *A* to let *B* speak.

66. MARK G. YUDOF, WHEN GOVERNMENT SPEAKS (1983).

assumptions. First, governmental control over editorial policies typically will be exercised in a discriminatory fashion, privileging that which is in vogue, mainstream, and safe while handicapping that which is not. Second, recipients—readers, listeners, viewers—are capable of judging the quality of a speaker's presentation and abandoning those speakers who do not measure up to the recipients' standards. Third, speakers compete within and across media for potential recipients, so that the public is constantly presented with a variety of viewpoints from which to choose. Further, it is only because we believe that markets for ideas and values operate in this fashion that we have chosen to place constitutional constraints on government's authority to regulate speech.

We do not blush to admit that we believe these empirical assumptions are true.[67] Another reason we treat these beliefs about politics, markets, speakers, and listeners as a sound basis for erecting principles to govern legal regulation of the media is "the belief that no other approach would comport with the premise of individual dignity and choice upon which our political system rests."[68] If, for example, we build legal rules on the assumption that recipients can discriminate among speakers and speeches, this should tend to become a self-fulfilling prophecy. Recipients will need to develop the ability to discriminate.

Of course, we cannot prove that those empirical assumptions are generally truthful reflections of reality, and we know that they are not always so. But, for purposes of our argument, it is quite important to note a fact that is not contestable. That fact is that these assumptions about politics, markets, speakers, and listeners underlie virtually every facet of First Amendment law and nonconstitutional regulatory policy toward the (nonbroadcast) mass media. Constitutional and statutory rules aimed at not only the print media, but all mass media other than broadcasting, are premised on the notion that, although government has important duties or opportunities to expand access and diversity through content-neutral actions, the goals of an open, stable democracy are best advanced by relying on recipients to choose from among competing speakers unconstrained by government. "To many this is, and always will be, folly; but we have staked upon it our all."[69]

IV. APPLICATION TO CONVERGING TECHNOLOGIES

As we noted at the outset, emerging technologies erase any tenable line delineating that which is broadcasting and exempt from these principles and

---

67. Especially if we add "for the most part and in the long run," which are the conditions that really matter.

68. Cohen v. California, 403 U.S. 15, 24 (1971).

69. United States v. Associated Press, 52 F. Supp. 362, 372 (S.D.N.Y. 1943) (L. Hand, J.); *see* REGULATING BROADCAST PROGRAMMING, *supra* note 2, at 175-79.

that which is not. The principles just discussed offer broadcasters and those employing emerging media technologies the full protection of general media law while leaving ample room for progressive and helpful regulation.

What specific forms of regulation should be considered for the era of technological convergence? Three central points emerge: Content control should be forbidden; entry barriers should be reduced and eliminated whenever possible; and common carrier status must be carefully evaluated.

A. *No Content Controls*

This regulatory strategy flows automatically from our first principle stated earlier. It applies equally to emerging technologies, which must, after all, compete for users' attention, in the same manner that magazines, newspapers, and books seek readers.

B. *Reduce Entry Barriers*

To help assure that new communications technologies are user friendly rather than centrally controlled—whether by government or by industry—the most important policy government could adopt is a commitment to foster as much competition as possible among would-be speakers for audience attention. This obligation, rooted in free speech concerns, mandates reducing barriers to entry that confront potential speakers. This includes those who wish to employ established technologies, such as television stations broadcasting in the VHF spectrum. For example, long ago the FCC made many decisions that substantially constrict the number of VHF stations that can now be licensed.[70] Those decisions can be reversed.[71] The obligation should extend also to potential speakers desiring to employ new technologies—such as communications networks that link up portable computers. Federal regulation has effectively delayed the entry of, first, portable cellular telephones and, later, portable interactive minicomputers, by failing to establish fluid mechanisms for allocating and reallocating spectrum in response to emerging technologies and consumer demand. That omission can and should be remedied.

Reducing entry barriers and extending the spectrum available for communication of information and entertainment serve the goals of both access and diversity by lowering the costs of communicating and expanding the

---

70. Several of these choices are detailed in Thomas L. Schuessler, *Structural Barriers to the Entry of Additional Television Networks: The Federal Communications Commission's Spectrum Management Policies*, 54 S. CAL. L. REV. 875 (1981).

71. This might, however, be a second-best solution today. It might be preferable to free up VHF spectrum for other communications uses and move television to cable and satellite transmission, where it would not block so many other valuable uses.

opportunities for doing so. In this fashion, readers, listeners, and viewers are empowered, without governmental censorship to control what is offered and what is consumed. By simply determining what (if any) materials to access, users of the infobahn can force programmers to serve their interests and desires.[72] To the sober media critic who understands the modest possibilities of achieving real change through regulation, such a program ought to be vastly more appealing than the kinds of clumsy and usually ineffective content controls that were at the center of the fairness doctrine[73] and that underlie present regulation of children's television.[74]

Perhaps the point seems so obvious that to emphasize it is to belabor it. We emphasize it because history teaches a consistent lesson regarding the introduction of new communications technologies: Government should be wary of private barriers to communication and equally wary of public barriers. Indeed, if the past is prologue, entrenched private interests will use public policy to achieve their goals of limiting competition.

Surely, the FCC has known that erecting or maintaining entry barriers is counterproductive. Even Congress has realized this. A key section of the Communications Act of 1934 directs the Commission "to encourage the larger and more effective use of radio in the public interest."[75] Yet, although the FCC has always had available the option to reduce barriers to entry and thereby expand the number of broadcast outlets accessible to the public, Commission policy from the agency's inception through at least the next fifty years was to retard the growth of broadcasting.

A principal reason Congress created the Federal Radio Commission (FRC) was to reduce competition among existing stations.[76] One of the first decisions the FRC made was not to follow the European example of broadening the broadcast band.[77] Listeners would thus not be troubled by having to choose between retaining their old sets limited to stations already

---

72. Pulitzer Prize–winning playwright Robert E. Sherwood, in a remarkably prescient article written in 1929, stated:

I can state, on the best authority, that all television sets will be equipped, as all radio sets are now equipped, with control switches. Thus, when any one decides that he has been fed to the teeth . . . he has only to turn the little switch and shut the damned thing off

Robert E. Sherwood, *Beyond the Talkies—Television*, SCRIBNER'S MAG., July 1929, at 1, 8. All too often the on-off switch is forgotten in discussions.

Similarly, government regulation fosters diversity when it helps people make and enforce choices. Thus, no basic principle is violated if government requires that consumers be offered computers or receivers that are engineered so that channels can be permanently or selectively blocked or so that a very wide range of channels can be received. (Where, however, government mandates that only such receivers be offered, it risks reducing access and diversity by increasing the costs of the receivers beyond the willingness of low-income viewers to pay for the sets.)

73. REGULATING BROADCAST PROGRAMMING, *supra* note 2, at 237–75.

74. *Id.* at 81–84.

75. 47 U.S.C. § 303(g) (1988).

76. REGULATING BROADCAST PROGRAMMING, *supra* note 2, at 21–22; Thomas W. Hazlett, *The Rationality of U.S. Regulation of the Broadcast Spectrum*, 33 J.L. & ECON. 133, 170 (1990)

77. Hazlett, *supra* note 76, at 155.

available on them or purchasing newer ones that could receive added stations made available by broadening the band.

Following World War II, the Commission set about to structure the nascent television industry. After a lengthy hiatus, the FCC adopted a comprehensive station allocation plan that put relatively little weight on affording most Americans a large number of television signals.[78] Instead, the plan gave great weight to factors such as placing at least one transmitter in as many communities (and, therefore, congressional districts) as possible. Consequently, the plan did not even attempt to maximize the number of television stations available to American households and for almost forty years guaranteed that there would be but three national networks.[79] The allocation plan sacrificed viewer interests in access and diversity to narrow political concerns and entrenched industry goals.

More recently, as soon as cable television became more than a device to expand the reach of existing broadcasters, the FCC took actions to stop it dead in its tracks.[80] When the Commission finally decided to let cable grow somewhat, it shackled the new medium with programming requirements that it never dreamed of imposing on broadcasters.[81] To execute both maneuvers the FCC adopted, with the ready assent of reviewing federal courts, a very broad reading of its jurisdictional reach.[82] In a like vein, before telephone companies even dreamed of expanding into offering television services, the Commission prohibited them from doing so.[83]

Finally, at present, cable operators assert that telephone companies are employing state regulations to prevent cable systems from offering audio services that compete with telephony.[84] Meanwhile, telephone companies assert that they are handicapped by federal law from offering wired television services that would compete with cable.[85]

Proliferating electronic communications technologies make even more compelling a regulatory approach that, resting on the four basic principles, relies on competition rather than direct governmental oversight to discipline firms and to force them to respond to consumer desires. Expanding technologies bring lower access costs and wider opportunities for diversity, thus diminishing the appeal of most proposals to expand government oversight.

---

78. REGULATING BROADCAST PROGRAMMING, *supra* note 2, at 87–88.

79. *Id.* at 88, 283–84.

80. *See* POWE, *supra* note 15, at 220–23; Stanley M. Besen & Robert W. Crandall, *The Deregulation of Cable Television*, 44 LAW & CONTEMP. PROBS. 77, 85–91 (1981).

81. *See* POWE, *supra* note 15, at 223–26; Besen & Crandall, *supra* note 80, at 92–98.

82. *See* Thomas G. Krattenmaker & A. Richard Metzger, Jr., *FCC Regulatory Authority over Commercial Television Networks: The Role of Ancillary Jurisdiction*, 77 NW. U. L. REV. 403, 435–40 (1982).

83. In the Matter of Telephone Company-Cable Television Cross-Ownership Rules, 3 F.C.C.R. 5849 ¶¶ 3–4 (1988).

84. Ted Hearn, *NCTA Takes Up Battle with States*, MULTICHANNEL NEWS, Oct. 17, 1994, at 1.

85. *"Equal Protection" Sought*, COMM. DAILY, Sept. 12, 1994, at 4.

More recent government actions suggest reason to hope. Broadcast satellites have been launched with comparatively little governmental control. The federal government constructed the infrastructure of the Internet, a communications technology that permits rather easy and nondiscriminatory access.

C. *Common Carrier Regulation?*

At some point in the evolution of any new communications technology, some important group is sure to argue that the industry should be conducted on a common carrier basis. For example, when cable was in its infancy, a much-debated question was whether cable systems should be required to act as common carriers.[86] The tendency of analysis to gravitate toward the common carrier approach is not surprising. Common carriage is likely to appeal to one who grasps the point of *Tornillo* that editorial control should be left in private hands, but also appreciates the premise of *Red Lion* that a powerful unregulated medium may exclude valuable information and entertainment.

Reflection reveals that nothing in the basic principles of mass media regulation specifies who must exercise the editorial function. Our traditions, as well as the specific language of the First Amendment, only tell us who must not be the editor. Editing is not government's job. Speakers edit free of governmental control or interference, but they need not own the facilities over which they speak. Printing presses, sound stages, recording studios, cable systems, and broadcast stations could all be operated as common carriers.[87] They would behave like existing communications common carriers, that is, for example, like local telephone exchange carriers and mobile radio service producers and most long-distance microwave services and satellite carriers.

We should make clear that the common carriage discussed here must be consistent with our four principles outlined above. In particular, the regulation must be content-neutral, not targeted at particular viewpoints or ideologies. For example, imposing common carrier requirements on all Democrats who own electronic communications facilities would violate the free speech guarantees of the First Amendment. Similarly, randomly choosing one in ten of all AM radio stations for common-carriage status would, at least presumptively, lack the rational basis required by the Fifth Amendment.[88]

---

86. For example, the ACLU unsuccessfully argued, in ACLU v. FCC, 523 F.2d 1344 (9th Cir. 1975), that certain Commission rules were flawed because they did not impose sufficient common carrier obligations on cable systems.

87. Indeed, there exist markets for renting each of these facilities in the United States today.

88. One might understand our first principle to suggest that imposing common carrier status necessarily violates that principle because government thereby denies someone the right to be an editor. That is, for example, if a telephone company is told to operate as a common carrier it loses its right to be an editor. This argument is incorrect for two reasons. First, no principle of mass communications law holds that one has a right to be an editor simply because one owns or controls a communications facility. Our principle of content neutrality simply holds, as illustrated in the text, that one cannot be punished because of the

1738   The Yale Law Journal   [Vol. 104: 1719

In some instances, imposing common carrier obligations can be an effective way to ensure that all speakers receive nondiscriminatory access to platforms. Where this occurs, diversity, as we have defined it, is also enhanced. In simple terms, the appeal of common carrier regulation is that it seems directly responsive to sober claims for content regulation. If, for example, the claim is that we need a fairness doctrine for radio to permit access by speakers whose views are antithetical to advertisers and so would not be carried by advertiser-funded radio stations, one might offer the common carrier alternative. Under such a regime, any speech by a speaker willing to pay the costs of speaking should be carried (access) and can be received by anyone willing to pay any additional costs of receiving it (diversity).

Common-carriage regulation, however, should not be viewed as a panacea. Just because it can be implemented lawfully does not mean it will work well. Indeed, we suspect that, for most media, a thoughtful policy analyst will reject the common carrier model.

First, such regulation is not costless. At a minimum, government resources must be devoted to defining and enforcing the rules. To assure that common carrier prices reflect only the true costs of access may require extensive (and expensive) public-utility-type regulation.

Further, especially as applied to mass communications media, common carrier obligations can prevent the achievement of substantial efficiencies. Magazine publishers and broadcasters do not simply publish articles or air programs. They package groups of articles or programs into a coherent whole. This whole package is often more valuable than the sum of its parts because the package itself communicates. It describes the mix and quality of data or entertainment that the recipient will receive.

To illustrate, a newsmagazine run on a common carrier basis might, in a given week, contain ten stories on health care policy and none on foreign policy, depending on which authors showed up first or bid the highest amounts for available space. Moreover, the stories may reflect very different standards of care in research and writing. Readers might (indeed, probably do) prefer a magazine edited by a single publisher because this tends to ensure a greater variety of topics, balanced coverage, and a uniform level of quality. The single publisher can also provide an overarching point of view, which recipients may prefer to obtain as well.

---

content of one's speech. Second, imposition of common carrier status cannot entail denial of the right to speak. Telephone common carriers, for example, retain the same right to freedom of speech, on their or anyone else's facilities, as all communications corporations. The ability to impose common carrier obligations on a telephone company does not carry with it the ability to prevent that company from transmitting its own messages over its own facilities (although, in extraordinary circumstances, such a requirement might be justified by antitrust principles rooted in a legitimate concern for protecting equal access rights).

Finally, it is not self-evident that common carriers will provide greater access opportunities or diversity of style or viewpoint than will publisher-editors. Where an editor—whether of a newspaper, a broadcast station, or a cable system—has the capacity to add a speaker whom audiences wish to receive, it is usually in that editor's best interests to provide that speech so long as the audiences are willing to pay the (marginal) costs of transmitting it.[89] If a cable system can add a channel at the cost of $5 per month, we expect it will do so for anyone willing to pay that amount.

If the problem is lack of capacity, the preferred government response, as outlined above, is clear: help to increase capacity, to reduce entry barriers. If the cable system cannot or will not add a channel, the better response is to be rid of any rules that constrain cable channel expansion and to provide alternative means—e.g., by microwave or satellite—of transmitting multiple video signals. If the problem is incompatible ideology, the preferred response is the same. By reducing entry barriers and preventing monopolization, government facilitates competition among editors of diverse ideologies, and thus, fosters access to competing viewpoints.

Common carriage, then, should not be viewed as the preferred basis for organizing or regulating the mass media in the United States. In most cases, its costs will exceed its benefits. But, in the unusual case, common carrier regulation can be a cost-effective means of attaining access and diversity goals without engaging in content regulation. For those reasons, a common carrier regime that comports with the four principles described above cannot be said, on *a priori* or philosophical grounds, to impose a threat to civil liberties comparable to that created by empowering government to displace the decisions of private editors.

Common carrier regulation appears to have been a wise choice for common, interactive, wireline audio communication (telephony). With telephones, people largely wish to communicate directly with each other and so little is lost by denying the phone company an editorial voice over these communications. Further, giving telephone companies an editorial discretion would be quite risky. The local telephone loop may well be a natural monopoly; so one would not expect a rival phone company to come into existence to carry messages that the entrenched phone company refused to carry. This suggests, additionally, that a common carrier approach toward the Internet is equally sensible, for the same reasons. People who use the Internet to establish data bases or accessible bulletin boards, however, should not be required to carry all comers, because it is possible to establish many such data bases or bulletin boards along the Internet.

---

89. STANLEY M. BESEN & LELAND L. JOHNSON, AN ECONOMIC ANALYSIS OF MANDATORY LEASED CHANNEL ACCESS FOR CABLE TELEVISION (1982).

V. CONCLUDING OBSERVATIONS

In this Essay, we make explicit two points that were implicit in our larger work, *Regulating Broadcast Programming*.[90] We wrote the book against a jurisprudential backdrop that is centered around the view that broadcasting through the electromagnetic spectrum was a means of communication so different from any medium yet employed that preexisting rules could not be safely applied to broadcasting.[91] We intended the book to prove just the opposite: that the general principles of law and regulation underlying all nonbroadcast mass media would be just as workable, and should be fully applied, to the broadcast media. To make that point unmistakably clear, we intentionally excluded consideration of newer technologies (even cable) from our discussion and analysis. In this sense, the book is backward looking and deliberately so.

Implicit in our argument, however, were two points that ought to be made explicit on the occasion of this Symposium, with its emphasis on the future. First, the advent of new telecommunications technologies, and their convergence with the now traditional electronic media of AM, FM, VHF, and UHF broadcasting, make even less tenable the view that these traditional media require or justify a distinct regulatory jurisprudence. Second, the general principles underlying regnlation of the nonbroadcast mass media should apply fully to the new as well as the old electronic communications media.

Most proponents of increased government control of broadcast-program content have not responded to the arguments advanced in this Essay because they have never considered them. That failure may continue with newer technologies. In the past, critics rushing to impose their value system on broadcasters, listeners, and viewers, have not paused seriously to consider whether the faults they perceive in broadcasting could be remedied by means fully consistent with the regulatory policies we employ toward all other mass media. With those critics, we agree that it is too expensive to get on television, and that television offers fare that is both too bland and too vexatious. And we agree that similar problems may arise on the infobahn and other newer means of mass communications. But we should all be equally able to agree that those problems do not require that government employees metaphorically sit as gatekeepers on the infobahn. Rather, those government officials ought to be reducing entry barriers and expanding access opportunities for programmers and viewers.

For other critics, our arguments must seem hopelessly naive. These are the new brand of media critics, the ones who believe that the arguments we have just advanced cannot make sense in a world where the distribution of wealth

---

90. REGULATING BROADCAST PROGRAMMING, *supra* note 2.
91. *See* Red Lion Broadcasting Co. v. FCC, 395 U.S. 367, 386–87 (1969).

and resources is badly skewed.[92] How can we talk of programmer choice, competition among media, or the sovereignty of the listener-viewer when very few people have the wealth to create visually appealing programs, when outlets have traditionally been restricted in number and reach, and when so many telecommunications consumers are too poorly educated to make wise choices, too impoverished to be able to make their choices count, or lack the resources to access the expanding new technologies?

To be quite honest about it, we find it rather easy to continue to talk about these things. Even if these problems are not alleviated by emerging communications technologies,[93] what other choice do we have? A society in which one governmental entity dictates standards of taste and value lest thousands of unrestricted, competing programmers or Internet gophers "dictate" those same things? A medium with only one definition of "children's programming" rather than the same medium operating with several such definitions? Mass media journalism or computer bulletin boards governed by the White House's view of balance and fairness rather than the views of several networks or hundreds of bulletin board operators competing for viewers' and readers' attention?[94] A federal agency that agonizes over "measur[ing] the conflicting claims . . . of jazz orchestras and lectures on the diseases of hogs"?[95]

We are not persuaded that the "public interest" rephrased in the rhetoric of civic republicanism reduces the force of these questions. We have witnessed and documented over six decades of public interest regulation of broadcasting[96] and do not believe that a newer group of concerned regulators, animated by civic republicanism, can outperform their forebears.[97] Nor, for the reasons discussed above, do we see any need for them to try.

To be sure, our commitment to the bedrock principles of media regulation described in this Essay rests on assumptions that are not always true about the capacities of recipients of speech and of the speechmakers themselves. Interestingly, however, those principles are directly responsive to such inadequacies, wherever they occur. The principles teach that government can and should play important roles in regulating access and fostering diversity. Those techniques, not the methods of the censor, are the appropriate response to the imperfect world of electronic communications, no less than to the imperfect worlds of book and law review publishing.

---

92. *See* sources cited *supra* note 14.

93. As it appears they should be. *See* Volokh, *supra* note 25.

94. *See* POWE, *supra* note 15, at 121–42; *see also* REGULATING BROADCAST PROGRAMMING, *supra* note 2, at 294–96.

95. *See* 1 FED. RADIO COMM., *supra* note 11, at 6.

96. *See generally* REGULATING BROADCAST PROGRAMMING, *supra* note 2.

97. Despite the record of regulatory failures, those forebears are not an undistinguished group by any standards. They include James Lawrence Fly, Clifford Durr, Paul Porter, Newton Minow, Kenneth Cox, Nicholas Johnson, and Richard Wiley.

[4]

DIGITAL SPEECH AND DEMOCRATIC CULTURE: A THEORY OF FREEDOM OF EXPRESSION FOR THE INFORMATION SOCIETY

JACK M. BALKIN*

In this essay, Professor Balkin argues that digital technologies alter the social conditions of speech and therefore should change the focus of free speech theory, from a Meiklejohnian or republican concern with protecting democratic process and democratic deliberation, to a larger concern with protecting and promoting a democratic culture. A democratic culture is a culture in which individuals have a fair opportunity to participate in the forms of meaning-making that constitute them as individuals. Democratic culture is about individual liberty as well as collective self-governance; it concerns each individual's ability to participate in the production and distribution of culture. Balkin argues that Meiklejohn and his followers were influenced by the social conditions of speech produced by the rise of mass media in the twentieth century, in which only a relative few could broadcast to large numbers of people. Republican or progressivist theories of free speech also tend to downplay the importance of nonpolitical expression, popular culture, and individual liberty. The limitations of this approach have become increasingly apparent in the age of the Internet.

By changing the social conditions of speech, digital technologies lead to new social conflicts over the ownership and control of informational capital. The free speech principle is the battleground over many of these conflicts. For example, media companies have interpreted the free speech principle broadly to combat regulation of digital networks and narrowly in order to protect and extend their intellectual property rights. The digital age greatly expands the possibilities for individual participation in the growth and spread of culture, and thus greatly expands the pos-

---

* Copyright © 2004 by Jack M. Balkin. Knight Professor of Constitutional Law and the First Amendment, Yale Law School. My thanks to Bruce Ackerman, Yochai Benkler, Owen Fiss, Eddan Katz, Nimrod Kozlovski, Orly Lobel, Guy Pessach, Robert Post, Reva Siegel, Gunther Teubner, Rebecca Tushnet, Tal Zarsky, and Jonathan Zittrain for their comments on previous drafts.

sibilities for the realization of a truly democratic culture. But the same technologies also produce new methods of control that can limit democratic cultural participation. Therefore, free speech values—interactivity, mass participation, and the ability to modify and transform culture—must be protected through technological design and through administrative and legislative regulation of technology, as well as through the more traditional method of judicial creation and recognition of constitutional rights. Increasingly, freedom of speech will depend on the design of the technological infrastructure that supports the system of free expression and secures widespread democratic participation. Institutional limitations of courts will prevent them from reaching the most important questions about how that infrastructure is designed and implemented. Safeguarding freedom of speech will thus increasingly fall to legislatures, administrative agencies, and technologists.

Introduction: Novelty and Salience

What do digital technologies teach us about the nature of freedom of speech? How should our theories of freedom of expression change to take these technologies into account? In this essay, I argue that the Internet and digital technologies help us look at freedom of speech from a different perspective. That is not because digital technologies fundamentally change what freedom of speech is. Rather, it is because digital technologies change the social conditions in which people speak, and by changing the social conditions of speech, they bring to light features of freedom of speech that have always existed in the background but now become foregrounded.

This effect—making more central and visible what was already always present to some degree—is important in any study of the Internet and digital technologies. In studying the Internet, to ask "What is genuinely new here?" is to ask the wrong question. If we assume that a technological development is important to law only if it creates something utterly new, and we can find analogues in the past—as we always can—we are likely to conclude that because the development is not new, it changes nothing important.[1] That is the wrong way to think about technological change and public policy, and in particular, it is the wrong way to think about the Internet and digital technologies.

Instead of focusing on novelty, we should focus on salience. What elements of the social world does a new technology make particularly salient that went relatively unnoticed before? What features of human activity or of the human condition does a technological change

---

[1] *See, e.g.,* Frank H. Easterbrook, *Cyberspace and the Law of the Horse,* 1996 U. Chi. Legal F. 207, 216 (arguing that clear rules, property rights, and facilitating bargains will resolve regulatory problems in cyberspace much as they do in real space); Joseph H. Sommer, *Against Cyberlaw,* 15 Berkeley Tech. L.J. 1145, 1148 (2000) ("[F]ew of the *legal* issues posed by the new informatics technologies are novel.").

foreground, emphasize, or problematize? And what are the consequences for human freedom of making this aspect more important, more pervasive, or more central than it was before?

The digital revolution places freedom of speech in a new light, just as the development of broadcast technologies of radio and television did before it. The digital revolution brings features of the system of free expression to the forefront of our concern, reminding us of things about freedom of expression that were always the case, but now have become more central and thus more relevant to the policy issues we currently face. The digital revolution makes possible widespread cultural participation and interaction that previously could not have existed on the same scale. At the same time, it creates new opportunities for limiting and controlling those forms of cultural participation and interaction. The digital age makes the production and distribution of information a key source of wealth. Therefore it creates a new set of conflicts over capital and property rights that concern who has the right to distribute and gain access to information. Not surprisingly, the free speech principle sits at the center of these conflicts. Freedom of speech is rapidly becoming the key site for struggles over the legal and constitutional protection of capital in the information age, and these conflicts will shape the legal definition of freedom of speech. The digital revolution offers unprecedented opportunities for creating a vibrant system of free expression. But it also presents new dangers for freedom of speech, dangers that will be realized unless we accommodate ourselves properly to the changes the digital age brings in its wake. The emerging conflicts over capital and property are very real. If they are resolved in the wrong way, they will greatly erode the system of free expression and undermine much of the promise of the digital age for the realization of a truly participatory culture.

Digital technologies highlight the cultural and participatory features of freedom of expression. In this essay, I offer a theory of freedom of speech that takes these features into account. The purpose of freedom of speech, I shall argue, is to promote a democratic culture. A democratic culture is more than representative institutions of democracy, and it is more than deliberation about public issues. Rather, a democratic culture is a culture in which individuals have a fair opportunity to participate in the forms of meaning making that constitute them as individuals.[2] Democratic culture is about individual liberty as well as collective self-governance; it is about each

---

[2] *See* J.M. Balkin, *Populism and Progressivism as Constitutional Categories*, 104 YALE L.J. 1935, 1948–49 (1995) (reviewing CASS R. SUNSTEIN, DEMOCRACY AND THE PROBLEM OF FREE SPEECH (1993), and defining democratic culture as popular participation in culture).

4   *NEW YORK UNIVERSITY LAW REVIEW*   [Vol. 79:1

individual's ability to participate in the production and distribution of culture.

Freedom of speech allows ordinary people to participate freely in the spread of ideas and in the creation of meanings that, in turn, help constitute them as persons. A democratic culture is democratic in the sense that everyone—not just political, economic, or cultural elites—has a fair chance to participate in the production of culture, and in the development of the ideas and meanings that constitute them and the communities and subcommunities to which they belong.[3] People have a say in the development of these ideas and meanings because they are able to participate in their creation, growth, and spread.

Like democracy itself, democratic culture exists in different societies in varying degrees; it is also an ideal toward which a society might strive. Freedom of expression protects the ability of individuals to participate in the culture in which they live and promotes the development of a culture that is more democratic and participatory.

Freedom of speech is *interactive* and *appropriative*. It is interactive because speech is about speakers and listeners, who in turn become speakers themselves. Speech occurs between people or groups of people; individual speech acts are part of a larger, continuous circulation. People participate in culture by interacting with others and influencing and affecting them through communication. This is obvious in the case of speech directed at persuasion, but is true of all speech. Even when we dislike what someone else is saying, we are often affected and influenced by it. Our exposure to speech, our attempt to understand it, to bring it within our understanding, continually reshapes us. Our continuous participation in cultural communication, our agreement with and reaction to what we experience, our assimilation and rejection of what culture offers us, makes us the sort of people that we are.

Freedom of speech is appropriative because it draws on existing cultural resources; it builds on cultural materials that lay to hand. Dissenters draw on what they dislike in order to criticize it; artists borrow from previous examples and build on artistic conventions; even casual conversation draws on common topics and expressions. People par-

---

Media and popular culture theorist John Fiske has coined the term "semiotic democracy" to describe popular participation in the creation of meanings, often by turning existing forms of mass culture to different uses. JOHN FISKE, TELEVISION CULTURE 236–39 (1987); *see also* Michael Madow, *Private Ownership of Public Image: Popular Culture and Publicity Rights*, 81 CAL. L. REV. 125, 146 (1993) (defining semiotic democracy as "a society in which all persons are free and able to participate actively, if not equally, in the generation and circulation of meanings and values"). Fiske's idea has become particularly important in the intellectual property literature. *See infra* note 56.

[3] Balkin, *supra* note 2, at 1948–49.

ticipate in culture through building on what they find in culture and innovating with it, modifying it, and turning it to their purposes. Freedom of speech is the ability to do that. In a democratic culture people are free to appropriate elements of culture that lay to hand, criticize them, build upon them, and create something new that is added to the mix of culture and its resources.

The idea of a democratic culture captures the inherent duality of freedom of speech: Although freedom of speech is deeply individual, it is at the same time deeply collective because it is deeply cultural. Freedom of speech is, in Thomas Emerson's words, a system.[4] It is a cultural system as well as a political system. It is a network of people interacting with each other, agreeing and disagreeing, gossiping and shaming, criticizing and parodying, imitating and innovating, supporting and praising. People exercise their freedom by participating in this system: They participate by interacting with others and by making new meanings and new ideas out of old ones. Even when people repeat what others have said, their reiteration often carries an alteration in meaning or context.[5] As people express themselves, make music, create works of art, sing, gossip, converse, accuse, deny, complain, celebrate, enthuse, boast, and parody, they continually add something to the cultural mixture in which they live. They reshape, however imperceptibly, cultural conventions about what things mean, what is proper and improper, what is important and less important, how things are done and how they are not done. Through communicative interaction, through expression, through exchange, individual people become the architects of their culture, building on what others did before them and shaping the world that will shape them and those who follow them. And through this practice of interaction and appropriation, they exercise their freedom.

Freedom of speech is thus both individual and cultural. It is the ability to participate in an ongoing system of culture creation through the various methods and technologies of expression that exist at any

---

[4] THOMAS I. EMERSON, THE SYSTEM OF FREEDOM OF EXPRESSION 3 (1970).

[5] *Cf.* Jacques Derrida, *Limited Inc a b c . . .*, in 2 GLYPH 162, 200 (1977) ("Iterability alters[.]"). Jed Rubenfeld expresses a similar idea through the metaphor of imagination. He argues that freedom of speech protects the rights of both authors and readers because acts of imagination are inevitably transformative, both for producers and receivers of cultural objects. Jed Rubenfeld, *The Freedom of Imagination: Copyright's Constitutionality*, 112 YALE L.J. 1, 37–38 (2002). Rebecca Tushnet points out that repetition of ideas or social scripts can be a way of expressing solidarity with others, support for a favored cause, or one's own sense of propriety as a member of a religious, political, or social group. Rebecca Tushnet, *Copyright as a Model for Free Speech Law: What Copyright Has in Common with Anti-Pornography Laws, Campaign Finance Reform, and Telecommunications Regulation*, 42 B.C. L. REV. 1, 16–17 (2001).

6 NEW YORK UNIVERSITY LAW REVIEW [Vol. 79:1

particular point in time. Freedom of speech is valuable because it protects important aspects of our ability to participate in the system of culture creation. Participation in culture is important because we are made of culture; the right to participate in culture is valuable because it lets us have a say in the forces that shape the world we live in and make us who we are.

The digital age provides a technological infrastructure that greatly expands the possibilities for individual participation in the growth and spread of culture and thus greatly expands the possibilities for the realization of a truly democratic culture. But the same technologies also can produce new methods of control that can limit democratic cultural participation. Therefore, free speech values—interactivity, mass participation, and the ability to modify and transform culture—must be protected through technological design and through administrative and legislative regulation of technology, as well as through the more traditional method of judicial creation and recognition of constitutional rights. Increasingly, freedom of speech will depend on the design of the technological infrastructure that supports the system of free expression and secures widespread democratic participation. Institutional limitations of courts will prevent them from reaching the most important questions about how that infrastructure is designed and implemented. Safeguarding freedom of speech will increasingly fall to legislatures, administrative agencies, and technologists. Protecting freedom of speech in the digital age will require a new class of cyberlawyers, who understand the impact of technological design on free speech values and can help shape regulatory solutions that promote technologies that, in turn, will help secure the values of free expression.

I

HOW THE DIGITAL AGE CHANGES THE CONDITIONS
OF SPEECH

The next Part of this essay describes how the digital revolution alters our perspective on freedom of speech and leads to a series of disputes about what the free speech principle means. By the "digital revolution," I mean the creation and widespread availability of technologies that make it easy to copy, modify, annotate, collate, transmit, and distribute content by storing it in digital form. These technologies also include the development of vast communication networks that connect every part of the world for the purpose of distributing digital content. The digital revolution changes the factual assumptions underlying the social organization and social practices of freedom of speech in four important ways.

First, the digital revolution drastically lowers the costs of copying and distributing information. Large numbers of people can broadcast and publish their views cheaply and widely. Websites, for example, are easy to construct and easy to access. We do not yet know how low the costs of information transfer will become. For example, the development of weblogs (or blogs) allows people to publish content to the Internet with the press of a button, lowering the costs of publication and distribution even further.

Before the Internet, free speech theorists worried about the scarcity of bandwidth for broadcast media. Frequencies were limited, so only a relatively few people could broadcast to a large number of people. The digital revolution made a different kind of scarcity salient. It is not the scarcity of bandwidth but the scarcity of audiences, and, in particular, scarcity of audience attention. My speech has always competed with yours; as the costs of distribution of speech are lowered, and more and more people can reach each other easily and cheaply, the competition for audience attention has grown ever more fervent.[6] An interesting side effect of lowering the costs of distribution and transmission is that it can alter the relative costs of receiving versus sending information. Although receiving information is easier, sending information can become even less costly. The classic example is spam e-mail, which shifts the costs of distribution from speakers to audiences. Because so many people are producing content and sending it everywhere, audiences are pummeled with vast amounts of information which they must collate, sort, filter, and block. Hence, the digital revolution brings to the forefront the importance of organizing, sorting, filtering, and limiting access to information, as well as the cultural power of those who organize, sort, filter, and limit access.[7]

Second, the digital revolution makes it easier for content to cross cultural and geographical borders. Not only can speakers reach more people in the country in which they live, they can also interact with

---

[6] *See* Jack M. Balkin, Free Speech From a Meme's Point of View 8, 13 (Apr. 4, 2003) (unpublished manuscript, on file with *New York University Law Review*) (explaining rapid growth of expression on Internet in terms of lowered costs of production and distribution of information).

[7] *See* J.M. Balkin, *Media Filters, the V-Chip, and the Foundations of Broadcast Regulation*, 45 DUKE L.J. 1131, 1145 (1996) ("In the Information Age, the informational filter, not information itself, is king."); James Boyle, *Foucault in Cyberspace: Surveillance, Sovereignty, and Hardwired Censors*, 66 U. CIN. L. REV. 177, 194 (1997) (noting that filtering technologies supply state with "a different arsenal of methods with which to regulate content").

and form new communities of interest with people around the globe. It has long been possible to send information globally, but the cost and effort were comparatively great. The Internet gives people abilities that were previously enjoyed only by large commercial enterprises; it offers them access to an infrastructure for sending information worldwide.[8]

Third, the digital revolution lowers the costs of innovating with existing information, commenting on it, and building upon it. An important feature of the digital revolution is the development of common standards for storing and encoding information digitally. Common standards are absolutely crucial to lowering the costs of transmission and distribution. (We might make a rough analogy to the role of standardization that accompanied the Industrial Revolution.) However, the same features of content that make it possible for people to transmit and distribute information cheaply and easily also make it possible to manipulate, copy, and alter information cheaply and easily. In the past it was always possible to copy a text or a drawing by hand, but such copying was comparatively expensive and time-consuming. Once people have a common metric for storing images, music, and text, they can copy, cut, and paste information and send it to others. Common standards for encoding images, music, and text not only make it easy to copy and distribute content, they also make it easier to appropriate, manipulate, and edit content.

The link between the ability to copy and the ability to modify information is central to understanding the possibilities created by the digital revolution. Consumers of digital media products[9] are not simply empowered to copy digital content; they are also empowered to alter it, annotate it, combine it, and mix it with other content and produce something new. Software allows people to innovate with and comment on other digital media products, including not only text, but also sounds, photographs, and movies. The standard example is the well-known story of *The Phantom Edit*, in which an individual reedited George Lucas's *Star Wars* movie *The Phantom Menace* to eliminate as much as possible of the screen time devoted to a particularly obnoxious character, Jar Jar Binks.[10] *The Phantom Edit* exempli-

---

[8] Lowering the costs of distribution also allows more speakers to reach across existing cultural, geographical, and disciplinary boundaries. It allows information to get past previously closed communities, it enables new communities to form based on existing interests, and it helps create new interests around which communities can form.

[9] I borrow this term from C. EDWIN BAKER, MEDIA, MARKETS, AND DEMOCRACY 7–14 (2002) (noting important differences between media products and typical non-information goods).

[10] On *The Phantom Edit*, see Richard Fausset, *A Phantom Menace?*, L.A. TIMES, June 1, 2002, at F1.

fies what the digital age makes possible. It is not simply piracy; it is also innovation, although certainly not the sort of innovation that LucasFilms was interested in promoting.[11] This innovation goes hand in hand with the possibility of digital piracy; both are forms of appropriation made possible by digital technologies and digital communications networks. Lowering the costs of both distribution and appropriation are central features of the digital age. Digital media, in short, invite not only simple copying but also annotation, innovation, and collage.[12]

Fourth, and most important, lowering the costs of transmission, distribution, appropriation, and alteration of information democratizes speech. Speech becomes democratized because technologies of distribution and transmission are put in the hands of an increasing number of people and increasingly diverse segments of society throughout the planet. More and more people can publish content using digital technologies and send it worldwide; conversely, more and more people can receive digital content, and receive it from more and more people. Equally important, speech becomes democratized because technologies of innovation are available to a wider range of people. In the digital age, distribution and innovation go hand in hand.

II
ROUTING AROUND AND GLOMMING ON

In the early days of the Internet, many people assumed that the Internet would displace the mass media and publishing houses as traditional gatekeepers of content and quality. This has not occurred. Rather, the Internet has provided an additional layer of communica-

---

[11] Asked about the phenomenon by an interviewer, Lucas explained,
[E]verybody wants to be a filmmaker. Part of what I was hoping for with making movies in the first place was to inspire people to be creative. *The Phantom Edit* was fine as long as they didn't start selling it. Once they started selling it, it became a piracy issue. I'm on the Artist Rights Foundation board, and the issue of non-creators of a movie going in and changing things and then selling it as something else is wrong.
Gavin Smith, *The Genius of the System: George Lucas Talks to Gavin Smith About Painting by Numbers, Mind-Numbing Minutiae, and Final Cuts*, FILM COMMENT, July-Aug. 2002, at 31, 32.

[12] James Boyle argues that a characteristic feature of the information society is that an increasing proportion of product cost goes to content creation rather than to distribution, and to message rather than medium. James Boyle, *A Politics of Intellectual Property: Environmentalism for the Net?*, 47 DUKE L.J. 87, 93–94 (1997). That is not necessarily inconsistent with my argument that digital technologies lower costs of innovation: Both content creation and distribution costs are lowered, but distribution costs decline much more rapidly. In the meantime, digital technologies spur new forms of content creation that would have been prohibitively expensive (or impossible) in the past.

tion that rests atop the mass media, draws from it, and in turn influences it.

Mass media are asymmetrical and unidirectional. The ability to broadcast widely is held in relatively few hands; what is broadcast is sent out to a large number of people with very little opportunity for people to talk back. Access to mass media is comparatively limited. Mass media create a technological bottleneck, and the people who control mass media are gatekeepers controlling its use. As a result, in a world dominated by mass media, the recurring problem for people who want to speak effectively and reach large numbers of people is how to gain access to an effective podium. People can purchase access if they own a significant amount of property; in the alternative, they can stage media events to draw the mass media's attention. In the latter case, however, speakers cannot easily control their message.

The Internet offers two different strategies for dealing with the mass media: *routing around* and *glomming on*. Routing around means reaching audiences directly, without going through a gatekeeper or an intermediary. For example, you can publish content on your own website or distribute copies of your band's music on the Internet. Routing around relieves the bottleneck problem to some extent, but it does not eliminate it. Mass media are still quite important, because they are still comparatively few and individual speakers are many. Mass media provide a focal point for audience attention: Most people still pay much more attention to the relatively small number of traditional mass media speakers than they do to almost any particular website. That should not be surprising, for two reasons. First, traditional mass media have a head start in achieving a sizeable and stable audience because culture has been organized around them for so long. Second, the large number of speakers on the Internet dilutes audience share and fragments audience attention for any single website, depriving the vast majority of Internet speakers of mass audiences of the same size as the traditional mass media have enjoyed.

Therefore, although the Internet allows people to shape public opinion by routing around traditional mass media, the latter still play a crucial role in setting agendas because they still provide the lion's share of news and information to most people. Mass media remain dominant sources of entertainment, and are likely to be so for the foreseeable future. Because of economies of scale in production costs, mass media can also provide much more impressive and entertaining content than most individuals can.

The second strategy for dealing with mass media responds to this fact. It is the strategy of glomming on. To "glom on" means to appropriate and use something as a platform for innovation. "Glomming on" as a strategy means appropriating things from mass media, commenting on them, criticizing them, and above all, producing and constructing things with them: using them as building blocks or raw materials for innovation and commentary.

The word "appropriate" means to make something one's property. It is sometimes defined as making something one's *exclusive* property, as in appropriating a common benefit. But the glomming on characteristic of the digital age is precisely the opposite—it is *nonexclusive* appropriation. One appropriates something for one's own use, but others are free to appropriate it as well. This is especially the case with information goods, which are nonrivalrous and can be copied repeatedly at minimal cost.

Glomming on, then, is nonexclusive appropriation of media content for the purpose of commentary, annotation, and innovation. Here are four examples. The first is the use and development of weblogs, or blogs. Blogs grab quotes and information from other sources, including the websites run by mass media like the *New York Times* and the *Washington Post*, and use them as launching pads for commentary. Although a few blogs do original reporting, most of the blogosphere is devoted to commentary.[13] A second example is the website Television Without Pity, run by a group of Canadian and American viewers.[14] The site offers detailed scene-by-scene accounts of popular television shows in North America, laced with humorous and often biting commentary. Television Without Pity has grabbed the attention of television companies, which are eager to know how their shows are being received by their audiences.[15] The strategy of glomming on allows at least some television viewers to talk back to television producers. Fan fiction sites, which are devoted to the creation of stories about particular movies, books, and television shows, are a third example of glomming on.[16] *The Phantom Edit*, which I

---

[13] For a list of some of the most popular blogs, see The Truth Laid Bear's Blogosphere Ecosystem, *at* http://www.truthlaidbear.com/ecosystem.php (last visited Nov. 17, 2003).

[14] *See* http://www.televisionwithoutpity.com (last visited Oct. 27, 2003).

[15] Marshall Sella, *The Remote Controllers*, N.Y. TIMES, Oct. 20, 2002, (Magazine), at 70 (noting that "[i]t is now standard Hollywood practice for executive producers . . . to scurry into Web groups moments after an episode is shown on the East Coast," hoping to discover what core viewers like and dislike).

[16] For examples of fan fiction, see generally http://www.fanfiction.net (last visited July 10, 2003). On the clash between fan fiction and copyright law, see Rebecca Tushnet, *Legal Fictions: Copyright, Fan Fiction, and a New Common Law*, 17 LOY. L.A. ENT. L.J. 651 (1997); Ariana Eunjung Cha, *Harry Potter and the Copyright Lawyer*, WASH. POST, June 18, 2003, at A1; Tracy Mayor, *Taking Liberties with Harry Potter*, BOSTON GLOBE, June 29, 2003, (Magazine), at 14. The practice predates the Internet, *see* HENRY JENKINS, TEXTUAL POACHERS: TELEVISION FANS & PARTICIPATORY CULTURE 152–62 (1992), but the Internet has helped spur the formation of new communities of fan fiction writers, whose

12   *NEW YORK UNIVERSITY LAW REVIEW*   [Vol. 79:1

mentioned earlier, is a fourth example of glomming on; it uses a traditional mass media product as an artistic platform for innovation.

Glomming onto the work of others has always existed. It is a standard form of cultural transmission and evolution. The digital revolution enhances opportunities for glomming on to the work of traditional mass media and distributing these innovations and commentary worldwide. The point is not that more glomming on is occurring, although that may be the case, but that more people are able to glom on with greater effect. In theory, at least, digital technology allows glomming on to be broadcast as widely as the media product itself. People used to talk about last night's television programs at the water cooler the next morning; now they can publish their thoughts and distribute them to a global and anonymous audience. People have long written stories about their favorite literary characters, created parodies of familiar stories and songs, and gossiped about their favorite artists. These cultural appropriations were commonplace but moved in relatively constricted circles. They existed everywhere but were not distributed everywhere. All this has changed. The very technologies that make transmission and distribution of digital information relatively costless have made glomming on a force to be reckoned with.

What I have called glomming on—the creative and opportunistic use of trademarks, cultural icons, and bits of media products to create, innovate, reedit, alter, and form pastiches and collage—is a standard technique of speech in the digital world. Glomming on is cultural bricolage using cultural materials that lay to hand. Precisely because of the astounding success of mass media in capturing the public imagination during the twentieth century, the products of mass media, now everywhere present, are central features of everyday life and thought. Mass media products—popular movies, popular music, trademarks, commercial slogans, and commercial iconography—have become the common reference points of popular culture. Hence, it is not surprising that they have become the raw materials of the bricolage that characterizes the Internet.

Indeed, as they were originally developed, significant aspects of the Internet and digital technology facilitate glomming on. I have already mentioned the creation of common standards for encoding digital content. HTML and its successors also encourage glomming on, because they facilitate copying of source material and allow documents to point to each other. This, in turn, allows people to move

---

collective efforts have drawn the attention (and occasionally the ire) of television producers.

seamlessly between documents and blurs the lines between them. To be sure, these features of the digital revolution need not remain untouched: As I shall now describe, businesses have tried to erect technological and legal barriers to glomming on. My point, however, is that what gives rise to these reactions by businesses are the characteristics of digital media that facilitate the cheap and widespread appropriation, manipulation, distribution, and exchange of digital information. Those very characteristics lead to attempts to undermine, limit, and cabin the facility that digital media provide.

Indeed, routing around and glomming on are not merely specific responses to mass media; they are basic characteristics of Internet speech generally. Unless the Internet's architecture has been specifically modified to prevent it,[17] it is usually possible to route around any existing channel or site of discourse and start a conversation elsewhere. Similarly, unless there are technological devices put in place to avoid it, the Internet lends itself to the nonexclusive appropriation of existing content and its subsequent modification, annotation, and parody.

III
The Social Contradictions of the Digital Revolution

Digital technology lowers the costs of distribution and production of content, both locally and worldwide. It makes it easier for people to innovate using existing information and copy and distribute what they produce to others. It makes it possible for more and more people to participate in the creation and distribution of new forms of public discourse, new forms of art, and new expressions of creativity.

The very same features of the digital age that empower ordinary individuals—low costs of distribution and ease of copying and transformation—empower businesses as well. Because it is easier and cheaper to copy and distribute media products worldwide, the digital age opens new markets for media products in digital formats, like compact discs, DVDs, and streaming media.

The digital revolution, after all, is an economic revolution as well as a technological one. Because more types of media and information products can be sold to more people in more places, media products and, more generally, information itself, become increasingly impor-

---

[17] This is the major concern of Lawrence Lessig, Code and Other Laws of Cyberspace (1999) [hereinafter Lessig, Code and Other Laws of Cyberspace], and Lawrence Lessig, The Future of Ideas: The Fate of the Commons in a Connected World (2001) [hereinafter Lessig, The Future of Ideas].

tant sources of wealth. In the same fashion, the infrastructure necessary to communicate and distribute information widely becomes an
important source of wealth. As happened in the first age of industrialization, businesses discover economies of scale in the creation and distribution of information and media products. They become larger and
more powerful; media and information industries become increasingly
concentrated.

So the digital age produces two crucial trends: the democratization of digital content and the increasing importance of digital content
as a source of wealth and economic power. These trends quickly come
into conflict. That conflict, and its consequences for freedom of
speech, is the central problem of the digital age.

The irony is this: The very same features of the digital age that
empower ordinary individuals also lead businesses continually to
expand markets for intellectual property and digital content. Yet as
businesses do so, they must deal with features of the digital age that
empower consumers and give them new abilities to copy, distribute,
and manipulate digital content. Businesses wish to use the new technologies to deliver more and more content to more and more consumers, providing ever new services, ever new opportunities to
purchase, and ever new forms of customization. But the technologies
that allow the penetration and expansion of markets also allow consumers to route around existing media and glom on to digital
content.[18]

It is obvious that businesses are worried about digital piracy—
and, more generally, forms of digital appropriation—made possible by
digital technologies. That is why conflicts between freedom of speech
and intellectual property have come to the forefront of concern. But

---

[18] The basic conflict between centralized control of information production and distribution and routing around and glomming on that I have identified here has many different
aspects. Yochai Benkler views the conflict in terms of contrasting methods of information
production—a conflict between, on the one hand, an industrial model of protection that
produces mass culture prepackaged for consumption, and, on the other, various models of
nonproprietary and peer production. Yochai Benkler, *Through the Looking Glass: Alice
and the Constitutional Foundations of the Public Domain*, 66 LAW AND CONTEMP. PROBS.
173, 181 (2003) [hereinafter Benkler, *The Public Domain*]; *see also* Yochai Benkler, *From
Consumers to Users: Shifting the Deeper Structures of Regulation Toward Sustainable Commons and User Access*, 52 FED. COMM. L.J. 561, 562 (2000). The same technologies that
allow the industrialization of the goods of the mind also make possible new forms of peer
production and collaboration. *See* J.M. Balkin, *What Is a Postmodern Constitutionalism*, 90
MICH. L. REV. 1966, 1974, 1983 (1992) (defining postmodern era as era of industrialization
of products of mind); *see also* Yochai Benkler, *Coase's Penguin, or, Linux and* The Nature
of the Firm, 112 YALE L.J. 369, 375–90 (2002) (describing rise of collaborative methods for
commons-based peer production). The struggle between these models of production, which
is waged both in politics and in law, will determine the "institutional ecology" of information production in the next century. Benkler, *The Public Domain*, *supra*, at 181.

businesses are also concerned about the ability of consumers to alter or even refuse the conditions under which digital content is delivered and offered. Businesses would like to offer goods and services under conditions that encourage consumers to buy them. They want to facilitate advertising that supports their ventures. They want consumers to experience digital products in ways that will encourage consumption and increase profits, and they want to structure the digital environment accordingly. But digital technologies allow consumers the ability to route around these conditions. Thus, the conflict produced by the digital age is not simply a conflict about copying and piracy. It is also a conflict about control.

In a sense, this conflict was inevitable: Once intellectual property, information exchange, and media products become important sources of wealth, it is only natural that businesses will seek to maintain their profits through increasingly aggressive forms of legal and technological control. Thus, at the very moment when ordinary people are empowered to use digital technologies to speak, to create, to participate in the creation of culture, and to distribute their ideas and innovations around the world, businesses are working as hard as possible to limit and shut down forms of participation and innovation that are inconsistent with their economic interests.

We face, in other words, what Marx would have called a contradiction in social relations produced by technological innovation.[19] By "contradiction," I don't mean a logical contradiction, but rather an important and pervasive social conflict brought about by technological change, a conflict that gets fought out in culture, in politics, and, perhaps equally importantly, in law. The social contradiction of the digital age is that the new information technologies simultaneously create new forms of freedom and cultural participation on the one hand, and, on the other hand, new opportunities for profits and property accumulation that can only be achieved through shutting down or circumscribing the exercise of that freedom and participation.

The social conflict produced by technological change is both a conflict of interests and a conflict of values. It produces opposed ideas of what freedom of speech means. The social contradictions of the digital age lead to opposing views about the scope and purposes of the free speech principle. This conflict appears in a number of different areas. Here I will mention only two of them: intellectual property and telecommunications policy.

---

[19] Karl Marx, *A Contribution to the Critique of Political Economy*, *in* THE MARX-ENGELS READER 4, 4–5 (Robert C. Tucker ed., 1978).

16   *NEW YORK UNIVERSITY LAW REVIEW*   [Vol. 79:1

A. Intellectual Property

The first example is the growing tension between intellectual property and freedom of speech. That conflict has always existed, but new digital technologies have made it more salient and important.[20] In hindsight, the conflict between intellectual property and freedom of speech is obvious: The whole point of intellectual property law is to bestow monopoly rights in certain forms of expression, subject to safety valves like fair use and limited times. In fact, in the United States one can even get injunctive relief against prospective copyright infringement, which flies directly in the face of the basic presumption against prior restraints on speech.[21]

In the past, the conflict was often avoided through benign neglect. People engaged in technical violations of intellectual property rights all the time, but their activities were not widespread and distribution was relatively limited. It didn't matter much to IP owners if a few people wrote fan fiction on their typewriters, made jokes about trademarked elements in casual conversation or in limited geographic areas, or made the occasional copy of a record on their cassette tape recorder. However, once digital content could be produced and distributed at relatively low cost and broadcast around the world, owners of intellectual property became much more worried about digital copying and trademark infringement on a massive scale, even as they became increasingly interested in exploiting derivative rights in works they already owned.

Digital content produced by isolated individuals now competes more easily with existing media products, and more easily undermines or tarnishes existing trademarks. Conversely, lower costs of distribution of digital content encourage businesses to promote their rights ever more aggressively because they can expand into new geographical markets and achieve greater market penetration. Technological change exacerbates a tension that was always present but remained dormant until low-cost methods of distribution arrived on the scene. Indeed, the digital revolution is merely the latest episode in a much longer series of technological innovations that have led to the current

---

[20] On the emerging conflict between freedom of speech and intellectual property, see Yochai Benkler, *Constitutional Bounds of Database Protection: The Role of Judicial Review in the Creation and Definition of Private Rights in Information*, 15 BERKELEY TECH. L.J. 535, 587–600 (2000) (suggesting conflict between free speech rights and database protection); Yochai Benkler, *Free as the Air to Common Use: First Amendment Constraints on Enclosure of the Public Domain*, 74 N.Y.U. L. REV. 354, 393–401, 412–14 (1999) (arguing that given emerging methods of production of digital information, copyright promotes neither diversity of information nor free expression).

[21] *See generally* Mark Lemley & Eugene Volokh, *Freedom of Speech and Injunctions in Intellectual Property Cases*, 48 DUKE L.J. 147 (1998).

conflict between freedom of speech and intellectual property rights. Throughout the twentieth century, mass media have become increasingly pervasive in cultural life. Print media spread more widely through technological innovation. The motion picture industry took off in the early part of the twentieth century, followed by radio, television, cable, and satellite broadcasting. All of these technologies changed how widely and cheaply one could distribute content. Each of them, in their own way, lowered distribution costs, even if they also raised the costs of content creation.

As these forms of mass media became increasingly pervasive parts of our life, the industries that create content—Hollywood, the publishing industry, and the advertising industry to name only three examples—began to push for increased protections of intellectual property rights. The reason is simple. Being able to distribute media products to more and more people justifies greater and greater investments in content creation, including, among other things, the assembly of vast teams of people to create movies, television shows, advertising campaigns, and the like. To recoup these costs, producers sought to squeeze as much profit as they could out of their media products, and one way to do that was to make their rights more valuable by pushing aggressively for additional legal protections.

Thus, during the twentieth century intellectual property rights have expanded both horizontally and vertically.[22] Examples of horizontal expansion include increasing the scope of derivative rights that apply to a work at a particular point in time—the right to plot, characters, sequels, design features, orchestration, and so forth. Other examples are the development of process patents and the creation of trademark dilution law. Intellectual property rights have also expanded vertically, as the length of copyright terms has been repeatedly extended forward, and previous works have been retroactively given extensions to keep them in parity with newer works. A recent example in the United States is the Sonny Bono Copyright Term Extension Act of 1998,[23] named after the former pop singer and Congressman. It extended copyrights in the United States from the life of the author plus 50 years to life plus 70 years; it also extended copyright terms to 95 years after publication for works created by corporate or anonymous authors (or 120 years after creation, whichever is shorter).

---

[22] For a summary of the expansion in copyright law, particularly since 1970, see Neil Netanel, *Locating Copyright in the First Amendment Skein*, 54 STAN. L. REV. 1, 18–26 (2001).

[23] Pub. L. No. 105-298, 112 Stat. 2827 (1998) (codified at 17 U.S.C. § 302 (2000)).

18   NEW YORK UNIVERSITY LAW REVIEW   [Vol. 79:1

Media companies, however, have not limited themselves to legal devices. They have also attempted to use technology to protect their interests in intellectual property. An increasingly important form of intellectual property protection involves digital rights management schemes, technological devices that prevent copying of and control access to digital content. The Digital Millennium Copyright Act of 1998[24] created a new species of legal rights, sometimes called "paracopyright," that make it unlawful to circumvent these technological devices or distribute circumvention devices to others. Although digital rights management is often justified as a means of preventing unauthorized copying, it actually goes much further. It is part of a general strategy of control over access to digital content, including digital content that has been purchased by the end user.[25] Digital rights management schemes, for example, can make digital content unreadable after a certain number of uses; they can control the geographical places where content can be viewed; they can require that content be viewed in a particular order; they can keep viewers from skipping through commercials; and so on. Paracopyright creates legal rights against consumers and others who wish to modify or route around these forms of technological control. Once again we see how technological innovation produces social conflict: Because digital technologies make it easier to manipulate digital content in ever new ways, both businesses and consumers want increased control over how digital content is experienced.

Matters have come to a head as copying and modification of digital content have become widespread, and media companies have sought in increasingly aggressive ways to protect their existing rights and expand them further. The problem is that these legal and technological strategies are seriously curtailing freedom of expression. Not surprisingly, media companies have generally resisted the idea that freedom of speech limits the expansion of intellectual property rights. Nevertheless, at the same time that media corporations have resisted free speech objections to the expansion of intellectual property rights, they have avidly pushed for constitutional limits on telecommunications regulation on the ground that these regulations violate their own First Amendment rights.

---

[24] Pub. L. No. 105-304, 112 Stat. 2860 (1998) (codified at 17 U.S.C. §1201 (2000)).

[25] *See generally* LESSIG, THE FUTURE OF IDEAS, *supra* note 17, at 180–217; Niva Elkin-Koren, *It's All About Control: Rethinking Copyright in the New Information Landscape*, *in* THE COMMODIFICATION OF INFORMATION 79 (Niva Elkin-Koren & Neil W. Netanel eds., 2002).

B.   Telecommunications Policy

This brings us to the second great battleground over freedom of speech: telecommunications policy. Mass media communication delivers content through some medium of transmission, whether it be spectrum, networks, telephone wires, or cables. Technologies of distribution are the "pipes" through which content travels. The key question in the digital age is who will control these "pipes."

Historically, telecommunications policy in the United States has developed through several different models. Telephone companies have been viewed as conduits for the speech of others, exercising no independent editorial function. They are regarded as common carriers required to provide access to all. Broadcasters, cable companies, and satellite companies, by contrast, have been treated as hybrid enterprises. Because they provide programming and exercise editorial judgment, they have been treated as speakers with free speech rights. However, because they control key communications networks that are not freely available to all,[26] they have also been subject to structural public-interest regulation. Broadcasters were at one point required to cover public issues and cover both sides of these issues fairly; they are still required to provide equal time to political candidates and to sell advertising time to federal candidates for office; cable companies have been required to make room for public, educational and government channels, to carry signals from spectrum broadcasters, and to provide cable access to low-income areas; satellite companies have been required to set aside space for educational purposes, and so on.[27]

---

[26] *Cf.* Turner Broad. v. FCC (*Turner I*), 512 U.S. 622, 656 (1994) (arguing that monopoly power and cable architecture create bottlenecks and exclude others from speaking); Red Lion Broad. Co. v. FCC, 395 U.S. 367, 388–392, 392 (1969) ("There is no sanctuary in the First Amendment for unlimited private censorship operating in a medium not open to all.").

[27] *See* 47 U.S.C. § 312(a)(7) (2000) (requiring broadcasters to "allow reasonable access to or . . . permit purchase of reasonable amounts of time" to "legally qualified candidate[s] for Federal elective office"); 47 U.S.C. § 315(a) (2000) (establishing "equal opportunities" rule requiring broadcasters who permit one candidate to "use" station to permit candidate's opponents to "use" station as well); 47 U.S.C. § 315(b) (2000) (requiring broadcasters to sell time at lowest unit charge to political candidates); 47 U.S.C. § 531(b) (2000) (authorizing franchise authorities to require cable companies to set aside space for public access, educational and government channels); 47 U.S.C. § 532(b)(1) (2000) (establishing "leased access" provisions which require cable operators to set aside channel capacity for use by commercial programmers unaffiliated with cable franchise operator); 47 U.S.C. § 541(a)(3) (2000) (requiring assurances in awarding cable franchises that cable access "is not denied to any group of potential residential cable subscribers because of the income of the residents of the local area in which such group resides"); 47 U.S.C. § 335(b)(1) (2000) (requiring direct broadcast satellite operators to set aside portion of "channel capacity, equal to not less than 4 percent nor more than 7 percent, exclusively for noncommercial

20   *NEW YORK UNIVERSITY LAW REVIEW*   [Vol. 79:1

The digital revolution has undermined one of the traditional justifications for structural regulation of the mass media—scarcity of bandwidth. Cable can accommodate hundreds of channels, as can satellite broadcasting. The number of speakers on the Internet seems limitless. Broadcast media now compete with cable, satellite, and the Internet for viewer attention. In theory, at least, digital technologies offer everyone the potential to become broadcasters.

Telecommunications companies have pointed to these changes as reasons to loosen or eliminate structural regulations of broadcast, cable, satellite, and Internet access. Businesses have argued that must-carry requirements for cable, open access requirements for broadband companies, limitations on how many media outlets a single business entity can own, and other structural and public interest obligations interfere with media companies' rights to convey the content they wish to as large an audience as possible. They have argued that these regulations, and others like them, violate their First Amendment rights as speakers and editors, and courts in the United States have increasingly begun to agree with them.[28]

Implicit in these arguments is a controversial capitalist theory of freedom of speech. The theory is controversial not because it accepts capitalism as a basic economic ordering principle, but because it subordinates freedom of expression to the protection and defense of capital accumulation in the information economy. The capitalist theory identifies the right to free speech with ownership of distribution networks for digital content. Although distribution networks are "public" in the sense that lots of different people use them and rely on them for communication, their hardware and software are privately owned. Hence, businesses argue, regulation of the distribution network is a regulation of the freedom of speech of the network owner, because the network owner "speaks" through its decisions about which content to favor and disfavor. Must-carry rules interfere with the editorial judgment of cable companies; open access requirements

---

programming of an educational or informational nature"); *Red Lion*, 395 U.S. at 373–75 (describing fairness doctrine).

[28] *See, e.g.*, Time Warner Entm't Co. v. FCC, 240 F.3d 1126, 1136, 1139 (D.C. Cir. 2001) (invalidating FCC's limits on vertical and horizontal integration of cable carriers); Comcast Cablevision, Inc. v. Broward County, 124 F. Supp. 2d 685, 694 (S.D. Fla. 2000) (holding that open access requirements for broadband cable violate First Amendment rights of cable system owners; *see also* U.S. West, Inc. v. United States, 48 F.3d 1092, 1095 (9th Cir. 1994) (striking down ban on telephone companies also selling video content to the public), *vacated as moot*, 516 U.S. 1155 (1996); Chesapeake & Potomac Tel. Co. v. United States, 42 F.3d 181, 202 (4th Cir. 1994) (same), *vacated as moot*, 516 U.S. 415 (1996). The last two cases were held moot by the Supreme Court in light of the Telecommunications Act of 1996, Pub. L. No. 104-104, 110 Stat. 56 (codified in scattered sections of 42 U.S.C. (2000)), which repealed the statutory ban on cross-ownership.

interfere with the programming choices of broadband companies; restrictions on the amount and geographical scope of media owner-ship interfere with the ability of media companies to send their con-tent to as many people as possible.

The capitalist theory is controversial precisely because telecom-munication enterprises are hybrids of content providers and conduits for the speech of others. This is especially true for broadband, cable, and satellite transmission. Recent telecommunications mergers have further exacerbated this hybridization by forming a small number of large, vertically integrated media conglomerates with interests in broadcast media, cable, satellite, book publishing, movie production, telephone and Internet services.

The argument that structural regulation of telecommunications networks restricts the First Amendment rights of telecommunications companies ties the right to speak ever more closely to ownership of capital. Arguing by analogy to print media, the capitalist theory of free speech identifies the right to produce and control digital content with ownership of a communications network. Nevertheless, con-flating the right to speak with the right to control a communication network is problematic for two reasons. First, because they are con-duits and networks, digital communications networks are designed to provide access to multiple voices. However, under the capitalist theory, these conduits exist primarily to promote the speech of the owner of the conduit, just as newspapers exist to promote the speech of the newspaper's owner. The second problem follows from the first: Content providers who also act as conduits have incentives to favor their content over the content of others. For example, cable compa-nies may be tempted to favor streaming media and digital music coming from the company's content providers and advertising part-ners, while slowing down or refusing content coming from competi-tors, or, for that matter, from subscribers who want to be their own broadcasters.[29] Broadband companies may seek to provide "walled gardens" or "managed content areas" which limit consumer access to that of the company's proprietary network and its approved content partners.[30] Broadband companies may attempt to control the end

---

[29] *See* LESSIG, THE FUTURE OF IDEAS, *supra* note 17, at 156–58 (quoting Jerome Saltzer, "Open Access" is Just the Tip of the Iceberg (Oct. 22, 1999), *at* http://web.mit.edu/Saltzer/www/publications/openaccess.html (last visited Oct. 20, 2003) (offering examples of gatekeeping by cable networks)).

[30] *See* Hernan Galperin & Francois Bar, *The Regulation of Interactive Television in the United States and the European Union*, 55 FED. COMM. L.J. 61, 62–64, 69–72 (2002) (dis-cussing strategy of walled gardens in interactive television services); Daniel L. Rubinfeld & Hal J. Singer, *Open Access to Broadband Networks: A Case Study of the AOL/Time*

22   *NEW YORK UNIVERSITY LAW REVIEW*   [Vol. 79:1

user's Internet experience by creating what Cisco Systems has called "captive portals," which, in the company's own words, give a cable system owner "the ability to advertise services, build its brand, and own the user experience."[31] The purpose of these innovations is to guide the end user into a continuous series of offers to consume goods and services from which the Internet access provider will glean profits. Through skillful control of the distribution network, access providers can determine who gets to see what programming and under what terms. The goal is not simple ideological censorship but diversion of end users into ever new consumption possibilities. Access providers seek to cocoon their customers, offering continuous promotion of brands and shopping possibilities while the end user surfs the Internet.

Here we can see a second aspect of the social conflict brought about by technological innovation. New telecommunications networks allow ordinary people to communicate with vast numbers of fellow human beings, routing around existing media gatekeepers and offering competing content. People are no longer simply consumers of prepackaged content from mass media companies that are controlled by a limited number of speakers. Instead, people can use the new telecommunications networks to become active participants in the production of public culture. But the very same technologies that offer these possibilities also offer media companies ever new ways to advertise, sell products, and push their favored content. Thus, just as in the case of intellectual property, businesses that control telecommunications networks will seek to limit forms of participation and cultural innovation that are inconsistent with their economic interests. Once again, the goal is not necessarily censorship of unpopular ideas but rather diversion and co-optation of audience attention. Businesses want to direct the Internet user toward increased consumption of their own goods and services as well as the products of their advertising partners. Recognizing that there is money to be made in advertising, sales, and delivery of content, telecommunications companies do not want to be pure conduits for the speech of others, and they do not want too much content competition from their customers. Instead, they want to use the architecture of the Internet to nudge their customers into planned communities of consumerist experience,

---

Warner Merger, 16 Berkeley Tech. L.J. 631, 656 (2001) (noting dangers of conduit discrimination as well as content discrimination).

[31] Data Sheet, Cisco 6400 Service Selection Gateway, *at* http://www.cisco.com/warp/public/cc/pd/as/6400/prodlit/c6510_ds.htm (last visited Oct. 20, 2003); *see also* Jeffrey A. Chester, *Web Behind Walls*, Tech. Rev., June 2001, at 94, 94, *available at* http://www.democraticmedia.org/resources/articles/webbehindwalls.html (last visited Oct. 20, 2003).

to shelter end users into a world that combines everyday activities of communication seamlessly with consumption and entertainment. In some respects, businesses seek to push consumers back into their pre-Internet roles as relatively passive recipients of mass media content. In other respects, however, they openly encourage interactivity, but interactivity on their terms—the sort of interactivity that facilitates or encourages the purchase of goods and services.

Another way of seeing the social "contradiction" created by the Internet is through the concept of "public" space. Is the Internet a private space or a public space? Digital communications networks are held in private hands, increasingly by large media conglomerates who also hold interests in digital content production and who wish to sell their own goods and services and advertise the goods and services of others. From their perspective, the "publicness" of digital communications networks is merely a side effect of the use of private property by private actors. Because digital communications networks are privately owned, those who own them have the right to structure entry to and use of the network by other private actors. Rather than vindicating free speech values, regulating digital communications networks violates the free speech rights of telecommunications companies.

On the other hand, digital communications networks are "public" in the sense that the public uses them as a space for general interaction. The information superhighway is a public highway used by the public for public communication, debate, gossip, and every possible form of exchange of information. Digital communications networks are also "public" in the sense that their value as networks arises from public participation that produces network effects: Communications networks are valuable to individuals because the public in general uses them, and the larger share of the public that uses the network, the more valuable the network becomes. In other words, a key source of value of the communications network is its publicness, the fact that its inhabitants and its users are the public at large. Because digital communications networks serve a public function and because they gain their value from public participation, the argument goes, digital communications networks should be regulated to serve the public interest and to allow members of the public to use them as public spaces for communication, cultural innovation and public participation. Without such regulation, powerful private interests will trample on free speech values in the relentless pursuit of profits.

IV
FREEDOM OF SPEECH IN THE SECOND GILDED AGE

Let me summarize the argument so far: Technological innovations in the digital age have produced conflicts about the meaning of
free expression in two different locations. The first is the scope of
intellectual property; the second is the regulation of telecommunications networks. The conflict over freedom of speech looks quite different in these two areas. In intellectual property, media corporations
have pushed for ever-greater protection of intellectual property
through both legal and technological means. They have rejected complaints that ever-expanding intellectual property rights and digital
rights management schemes inhibit freedom of expression because
they eliminate fair use and shrink the public domain. In telecommunications regulation, by contrast, media corporations have aggressively
pushed for expansion of free speech rights, arguing that the right to
free speech includes the right to control communications networks.
Invoking a property-based theory of free expression, they have
rejected arguments that public regulation is necessary to keep conduits open and freely available to a wide variety of speakers.

Thus, in the digital age, media corporations have interpreted the
free speech principle broadly to combat regulation of digital networks
and narrowly in order to protect and expand their intellectual property rights. What is more, courts increasingly have begun to agree
with these two positions.[32]

These positions seem inconsistent on their face. In fact, they are
not. They reflect a more basic agenda: It is not the promotion and
protection of freedom of speech per se, but the promotion and protection of the property rights of media corporations. Both intellectual
property and freedom of speech have been reconceptualized to
defend capital investments by media corporations. Intellectual property rights, paracopyright, and digital rights management are justified
as necessary to protect property rights and maintain a fair return on
investment. Freedom of speech increasingly is being reinterpreted as
the right to be free from economic regulation of digital communications networks. This is part of a larger trend of the past twenty-five

---

[32] *See* Eldred v. Reno, 239 F.3d 372, 380 (D.C. Cir. 2000), *aff'd sub nom.* Eldred v.
Ashcroft, 537 U.S. 186, 222 (2003) (holding that First Amendment poses no obstacle to
Congressional extension of copyright terms that shrink scope of public domain, even when
extension is retroactive); Universal City Studios, Inc. v. Reimerdes, 111 F. Supp. 2d 294
(S.D.N.Y. 2000) (upholding constitutionality of application of Digital Millenium Copyright
Act to DeCSS and enjoining linking to websites from which DeCSS might be obtained),
aff'd sub nom. Universal City Studios, Inc. v. Corley, 273 F.3d 429 (2001); *supra* note 26
(citing additional cases).

years, in which businesses have also used the First Amendment to attack restrictions on advertising and campaign finance.[33] We are just beginning to see the First Amendment invoked to defend the accumulation and sale of consumer data against government regulation.[34] One of the most important developments of the past quarter century is the emergence of the First Amendment and the free speech principle as anti-regulatory tools for corporate counsel.[35] At the same time, intellectual property, paracopyright, and digital rights management are being invoked not only to restrict cultural experimentation and innovation, but to control how ordinary individuals experience the Internet.[36] What these positions have in common is not a libertarian impulse, but a desire for greater control over how individuals will be permitted to use digital networks and digital content; which is to say, it is a desire for control over the very technologies that had created new possibilities for individual freedom and cultural innovation in the digital age.

In a sense, this development was inevitable. In the world in which we live, intellectual property and control of digital communications networks are increasingly important sources of wealth. The defense of those forms of wealth must find a legal manifestation. Intellectual property and freedom of speech serve these functions admirably.

We have been through this before. Jacksonian and abolitionist ideas before the Civil War produced a constitutional vision of free labor and free contract. This constitutional vision celebrated the right of ordinary individuals to own their labor. Laissez-faire was defended as a means of keeping government from giving special benefits to the wealthy. As America industrialized, corporations took up these Jacksonian and abolitionist ideas and reinterpreted them, transforming them into defenses of corporate property rights and constitutional attacks on government regulation of employment conditions.

---

[33] *See* J.M. Balkin, *Some Realism About Pluralism: Legal Realist Approaches to the First Amendment*, 1990 DUKE L.J. 375, 375–87 (noting "ideological drift" of free speech principle to protect propertied and corporate interests).

[34] *See, e.g.,* U.S. West, Inc. v. FCC, 182 F.3d 1224, 1235, 1239 (10th Cir. 1999) (invalidating, on First Amendment grounds, FCC regulations protecting privacy and sale of telephone customers' personal information). On some of the problems faced in squaring consumer privacy with a libertarian conception of freedom of speech, see Eugene Volokh, *Freedom of Speech and Information Privacy: The Troubling Implications of a Right to Stop People from Speaking About You*, 52 STAN. L. REV. 1049 (2000).

[35] Balkin, *supra* note 33, at 384; Mark Tushnet, *Corporations and Free Speech, in* THE POLITICS OF LAW: A PROGRESSIVE CRITIQUE 253 (David Kairys ed., 1982); Mark Tushnet, *An Essay on Rights*, 62 TEX. L. REV. 1363, 1386–92 (1984).

[36] LESSIG, THE FUTURE OF IDEAS, *supra* note 17, at 196–202; Elkin-Koren, *supra* note 25, at 84–85, 88–98.

Courts issued labor injunctions against union organizing on the grounds that allowing workers to form unions undermined the value of employer investments in capital.[37] Courts turned the ideology of free labor into a constitutional principle of liberty of contract that prevented governments from regulating wages and working conditions.[38]

In what Clinton Rossiter called the "Great Train Robbery of Intellectual History,"[39] laissez-faire conservatives appropriated the words and symbols of early nineteenth-century liberalism—liberty, opportunity, progress, and individualism—and gave them an economic reinterpretation that served corporate interests.[40] They massaged and refitted the existing rhetoric of free labor and the right of ordinary citizens to pursue a calling into a sophisticated defense of corporate power and privilege that smashed labor unions, protected sweatshops, and eviscerated health and safety laws.[41] By the turn of the twentieth century, the best legal minds that money could buy had reshaped the liberal rights rhetoric of the 1830s into a powerful conservative defense of property that they claimed was the rightful heir to the best American traditions of individualism and personal freedom.

A similar transvaluation of values is overtaking the free speech principle today.[42] The right to speak has been recast as a right to be free from business regulation. Copyright is slowly being converted to property simpliciter with virtually perpetual terms; trademark and patent have steadily grown in scope; and database protection, already

---

[37] *Cf.* Truax v. Corrigan, 257 U.S. 312, 328 (1921) (holding that attempt to ban labor injunctions violated property rights of business owner).

[38] A substantial literature has developed explaining how Gilded Age ideas of freedom of contract were created out of Jacksonian and free labor ideals. *See, e.g.*, Michael Les Benedict, *Laissez-Faire and Liberty: A Re-Evaluation of the Meaning and Origins of Laissez-Faire Constitutionalism*, 3 LAW & HIST. REV. 293 (1985); William E. Forbath, *The Ambiguities of Free Labor: Labor and the Law in the Gilded Age*, 1985 WIS. L. REV. 767, 798–99 (1985); Charles W. McCurdy, *The Roots of "Liberty of Contract" Reconsidered: Major Premises in the Law of Employment, 1867–1937*, 1984 YEARBOOK OF THE SUPREME COURT HISTORICAL SOCIETY 20. Revisions of this view have suggested that other influences were also at work, *see* Stephen A. Siegel, *The Revision Thickens*, 20 LAW & HIST. REV. 631 (2002), but have not undermined the basic point that corporate interests made ample use of these rhetorical resources.

[39] CLINTON ROSSITER, CONSERVATISM IN AMERICA 128 (2d ed. rev. 1962).

[40] *Id.* at 128–62; *see* Balkin, *supra* note 33, at 383–87.

[41] *See generally* ARNOLD M. PAUL, CONSERVATIVE CRISIS AND THE RULE OF LAW: ATTITUDES OF BAR AND BENCH, 1887–1895 (1960); BENJAMIN R. TWISS, LAWYERS AND THE CONSTITUTION: HOW LAISSEZ FAIRE CAME TO THE SUPREME COURT (1942).

[42] The comparison between the ideological drift of the principles of freedom of contract and freedom of speech is explored in Balkin, *supra* note 33, at 375–87, and J.M. Balkin, *Ideological Drift and the Struggle over Meaning*, 25 CONN. L. REV. 869 (1993).

extant in the European Union,[43] is on the horizon in the United States.[44] Indeed, in some respects, digital rights management and paracopyright offer copyrighted works even greater protection than ordinary property receives.[45] Intellectual property, which was originally viewed as a limited government monopoly designed to encourage innovation, has been transformed into a bulwark against innovation, facilitating control over digital content and limiting the speech of others.

We are living through a Second Gilded Age, which, like the first Gilded Age, comes complete with its own reconstruction of the meaning of liberty and property.[46] Freedom of speech is becoming a

---

[43] Council Directive 96/9, 1996 O.J. (L 77/20) (providing for legal protection of databases which, "by reason of the selection or arrangements of their contents, constitute[ ] the author's own intellectual creation").

[44] For a discussion of recent attempts, see Dov S. Greenbaum, *The Database Debate: In Support of an Inequitable Solution*, 13 ALB. L.J. SCI. & TECH. 431, 468–78 (2003).

[45] *Cf.* Randal C. Picker, *From Edison to the Broadcast Flag: Mechanisms of Consent and Refusal and the Propertization of Copyright*, 70 U. CHI. L. REV. 281, 293–96 (2003) (noting that digital rights management permits perfection of continuing control over use of intellectual property in digital content even after media product has been purchased).

[46] Or, in Julie Cohen's memorable phrase, we are entering the era of "*Lochner* in Cyberspace." Julie Cohen, Lochner *in Cyberspace: The New Economic Orthodoxy of "Rights Management,"* 97 MICH. L. REV. 462 (1998).

Paul Schwartz and William Treanor argue, by contrast, that calls for constitutional limitations on the expansion of intellectual property are the best analogy to the laissez-faire constitutional conservatism of the Gilded Age; they compare arguments for constitutional protection of the public domain to *Lochner v. New York*, 198 U.S. 45 (1905). Paul M. Schwartz & William Michael Treanor, Eldred *and* Lochner*: Copyright Term Extension and Intellectual Property as Constitutional Property*, 112 YALE L.J. 2331, 2334–35, 2394–95, 2411 (2003). They fail to consider the social and economic context in which the debate over laissez-faire conservatism occurred. In effect, Schwartz and Treanor argue that small-scale artists, software programmers, Internet end users, and consumers who seek a robust public domain are the functional equivalent of the Robber Barons and concentrated economic interests of the Gilded Age, while today's media corporations like Microsoft, Disney and Viacom are the functional equivalent of immigrant laborers in sweatshops at the turn of the century.

Because they focus exclusively on arguments about the scope of the Copyright Clause, and pay no attention to telecommunications law, Schwartz and Treanor do not recognize that the free speech principle is the key battleground for the legal protection of capital in the information economy. Opposition to the Copyright Term Extension Act turned precisely on the fact that the political economy of the information age blurs distinctions between regulations of speech and regulations of business practices in media corporations, and that ever-expanding property rights in patent, trademark, and copyright adversely affect freedom of expression. *See* Brief of Jack M. Balkin et al. as Amici Curiae in Support of the Petition at 15–21, Eldred v. Ashcroft, 537 U.S. 186 (2003) (No. 01-618), *available at* 2002 WL 1041899.

Much more troubling than the Court's conclusions about the Copyright Clause in *Eldred* is its cavalier dismissal of the important free speech interests in limited copyright terms. *See Eldred*, 537 U.S. at 218–22. From this perspective, *Eldred* most closely resembles not *Lochner v. New York*, but the early twentieth-century cases *Schenck v. United States*, 249 U.S. 47 (1919), *Abrams v. United States*, 250 U.S. 616 (1919), and *Gitlow v. New*

28   NEW YORK UNIVERSITY LAW REVIEW   [Vol. 79:1

generalized right against economic regulation of the information industries. Property is becoming the right of the information industries to control how ordinary people use digital content. We can no more capitulate to the Second Gilded Age's construction of these ideas than to the constructions offered in the first Gilded Age. We must offer a critical alternative to this construction, much as progressive thinkers did a century ago.

V

THE PROGRESSIVIST THEORY AND ITS LIMITATIONS

So far, I have explained how digital technologies have changed the social conditions in which speech is produced, and I have described the way that the information industries have attempted to reinterpret freedom of speech. These reinterpretations reflect the interests of businesses attempting to secure certain privileges in a changing economy. They are by no means necessary or inevitable, and indeed, I think that they are in many respects mistaken.

There is a better way to understand the free speech principle in the digital era. The alternative is a theory of freedom of speech based on the idea of a democratic culture. In order to explain this alternative, I would like to retrace my steps and think about how free speech theory dealt with the last great technological change, the rise of broadcast media.

Probably the most important theoretical approach to freedom of speech in the twentieth century has argued that freedom of speech is valuable because it preserves and promotes democracy and democratic self-government. The notion that there is an important connection between freedom of speech and democracy is hardly new— people have understood the connection for as long as democracies have been around. But the twentieth century produced a special

---

York, 268 U.S. 652 (1925), in which the Court rejected free speech claims and exercised judicial restraint. The danger is that an unrestrained legislature beholden to media interests will continually ramp up intellectual property protections at the expense of the free speech interests of others.

Schwartz and Treanor note the argument that the expansion of intellectual property arises from rent-seeking by media corporations that have corrupted the political process. Schwartz & Treanor, *supra*, at 2406. However, failing to recognize the First Amendment interests involved, they assume that the only issue is the adjustment of property rights between competing stakeholders. They argue that the defects of political process, even if serious, cannot justify heightened judicial review, *see* United States v. Carolene Prods. Co., 304 U.S. 144, 152 n.4 (1938), because the theory of process protection should not apply to ordinary economic and social legislation but only to "the representation of minorities." Schwartz & Treanor, *supra*, at 2407. Perhaps tellingly, they omit the *Carolene Products* Court's argument that the theory of process protection is equally concerned with securing freedom of speech.

emphasis on that connection, and during the course of the twentieth century, many thinkers claimed that the very purpose of freedom of speech was not so much to promote individual autonomy or personal fulfillment as to promote democratic deliberation about public issues. We can find the beginnings of this idea in Progressive Era thinkers in the first two decades of the twentieth century.[47] The most famous statement is by the philosopher of education Alexander Meiklejohn,[48] and his approach has greatly influenced later theorists.[49]

As a shorthand, I will call the democracy-based approach of Meiklejohn and his followers the "republican" or "progressivist" approach. That is because a focus on democratic deliberation rather than individual autonomy is characteristic of republican political theory, and it is also characteristic of much thinking in the Progressive Era in the United States.[50] Progressivism is a sensibility, an attitude about what democracy is and what wise government can do. The progressive has faith in government's ability to promote the public

---

[47] *See* MARK A. GRABER, TRANSFORMING FREE SPEECH: THE AMBIGUOUS LEGACY OF CIVIL LIBERTARIANISM 92–93, 122–26 (1991) (noting rise of democratic conception in Progressive period and discussing democratic elements in Zechariah Chafee, Jr.'s theory of free expression); David M. Rabban, *Free Speech in Progressive Social Thought*, 74 TEX. L. REV. 951, 954–88 (1996) (discussing free speech theories of early twentieth-century progressive thinkers, including John Dewey and Herbert Croly).

[48] *See generally* ALEXANDER MEIKLEJOHN, POLITICAL FREEDOM: THE CONSTITUTIONAL POWERS OF THE PEOPLE (1960) [hereinafter MEIKLEJOHN, POLITICAL FREEDOM]; Alexander Meiklejohn, *The First Amendment is an Absolute*, 1961 SUP. CT. REV. 245 [hereinafter Meiklejohn, *First Amendment*].

[49] *See, e.g.*, OWEN M. FISS, THE IRONY OF FREE SPEECH (1996) [hereinafter FISS, THE IRONY OF FREE SPEECH]; CASS R. SUNSTEIN, DEMOCRACY AND THE PROBLEM OF FREE SPEECH (1993); Owen M. Fiss, *Free Speech and Social Structure*, 71 IOWA L. REV. 1405 (1986) [hereinafter Fiss, *Free Speech and Social Structure*]; Owen M. Fiss, *Why the State?*, 100 HARV. L. REV. 781 (1987) [hereinafter Fiss, *Why the State?*]; Harry Kalven, *The New York Times Case: A Note on "The Central Meaning of the First Amendment,"* 1964 SUP. CT. REV. 191. Fiss well describes the centrality of this theory in twentieth-century legal thought:

> The theory that animates this protection [of the speaker's autonomy], and that inspired Kalven, and before him Meiklejohn, and that now dominates the field, casts the underlying purpose of the first amendment in social or political terms: The purpose of free speech is not individual self-actualization, but rather the preservation of democracy, and the right of a people, as a people, to decide what kind of life it wishes to live. Autonomy is protected not because of its intrinsic value, as a Kantian might insist, but rather as a means or instrument of collective self-determination. We allow people to speak so others can vote. Speech allows people to vote intelligently and freely, aware of all the options and in possession of all the relevant information.

Fiss, *Free Speech and Social Structure, supra*, at 1409–10.

[50] On the connections between democratic free speech theory and republicanism, see BAKER, *supra* note 9, at 126–27, 138–43, 152–53, 170–76. On the connection to the thought of the Progressive Era, see GRABER, *supra* note 47, at 75–121; Balkin, *supra* note 2, at 1947–48, 1956–58; Rabban, *supra* note 47.

interest through rational deliberation, works to structure government and public decisionmaking to promote deliberation and consensus about important public policy issues, worships expertise, and views popular attitudes and popular culture with suspicion because they tend to be emotional, parochial, irrational, untutored, and in need of channeling, refinement, and education.[51]

I think it is no accident that the progressivist/republican approach to free speech arose in the twentieth century, for this was also the century of mass media. People who endorse democratic theories of free speech understand that although mass media can greatly benefit democracy, there is also a serious potential conflict between mass media and democratic self-governance. The reason is that mass media are held by a comparatively few people, and their ownership gives this relatively small group enormous power to shape public discourse and public debate. The danger is that they will use their dominant position in three equally worrisome ways.

The first worry is that the people who control mass media will skew coverage of public issues to promote views that they support. In a world where ownership of mass media is concentrated in the hands of a relatively few very wealthy individuals and corporate conglomerates, the agendas and concerns of the wealthy will prevail, constricting discussion of serious issues and serious alternatives to the status quo. As a result, people will get disinformation or a skewed picture of the world around them, and this will be harmful for democracy.

The second worry is that mass media will omit important information, issues, and positions that the public should take into account. As a result, people will be exposed to only a limited set of issues to deliberate about, and to only a limited number of ways of thinking about and dealing with this limited set of issues.

The third worry is that mass media will reduce the quality of public discourse in the drive for higher ratings and the advertising revenues and other profits that come with them. Mass media will oversimplify and dumb down discussions of public issues, substitute sensationalism and amusement for deliberation about public questions, and transform news and politics into forms of entertainment and spectacle. The endless drive for advertising revenues and profits tends to drive out serious discourse and replaces it with mind-numbing entertainment. This demobilizes the public, leaving them less and less interested in focusing on important public issues of the day.

For these three reasons, democracy-based theorists of free speech in the twentieth century have argued that government must regulate

---

[51] Balkin, *supra* note 2, at 1947–48, 1956–58.

the mass media in a number of different ways: (1) by restricting and preventing media concentration; (2) by imposing public-interest obligations that require the broadcast media to include programming that covers public issues and covers them fairly; and (3) by requiring the broadcast media to grant access to a more diverse and wide-ranging group of speakers in order to expand the agenda of public discussion.

The progressivist/republican approach is an important counterweight to a market-oriented approach to freedom of speech that ties speech rights closely to ownership of property. I mentioned this approach in my discussion of telecommunications policy in the digital age, but of course, the argument that people who own telecommunications media should be free of government regulation predates the Internet. Indeed, the new market-based arguments are simply logical continuations of arguments for deregulation of the broadcast media that have been going on for many years.[52] The Internet has simply given media corporations a new justification for using the free speech principle as an anti-regulatory tool: Because people do not need access to the mass media to speak, governments have lost their greatest justification for mass media regulation.

However, we cannot expect that the Internet will adequately compensate for any loss in media diversity that might come from deregulation, elimination of public interest obligations, and increased media concentration. First, market concentration in mass media is not unrelated to market concentration in cable and broadband ownership. Many of the same companies that have gobbled up an increasingly large share of mass media markets also have control over cable companies and broadband companies. As we have seen, these companies have interests in eliminating competition and controlling the Internet experience of end users. So increased media concentration may actually exacerbate or dovetail with loss of end-user autonomy on the Internet. Second, the quality and diversity of information that flows over the Internet is inevitably shaped by the quality and diversity of information available in broadcast media and cable, because that is where a very large number of people still get most of their news and information. If more traditional mass media provide disinformation, constrict agendas of public discussion, displace discussion of public issues, and demobilize audiences, Internet speech can only partially compensate. We cannot view the Internet as a complete substitute for mass media. Instead, Internet speech is layered on top of the forms of

---

[52] *See, e.g.*, Mark S. Fowler & David L. Brenner, *A Marketplace Approach to Broadcast Regulation*, 60 Tex. L. Rev. 207 (1982) (arguing for repeal of most forms of broadcast regulation).

public discourse and discussion that cable and broadcast media provide. This follows from my argument that speech on the Internet routes around and gloms onto the products of the mass media. The mass media remain a central substrate on which Internet speech builds.

Nevertheless, the Internet does make a difference to freedom of speech. The digital age exposes weaknesses and limitations in democracy-based theories of free speech, just not the ones with which the capitalist approach is concerned.

Progressivist and republican approaches arose in response to the challenge to democracy posed by mass media. And their limitations arise from the same set of concerns. The progressivist/republican approach is limited in three important respects. First, it emphasizes political questions and deliberation about public issues over other forms of speech. It tends to value other kinds of speech to the extent that they contribute to public discussion of political questions rather than for their own sake. Second, for the same reason, the progressivist/republican approach tends to downplay the importance of popular culture, too often seeing it as ill-informed and a distraction from serious issues. Third, because its paradigmatic concern is broadcast media held by a relatively small number of people, who may misuse their power to control the public agenda or demobilize the citizenry, the progressivist/republican approach tends to downplay the centrality of liberty and personal autonomy to freedom of speech.[53] It focuses instead on equality and on the production of a suitable agenda for public discussion. In Meiklejohn's famous phrase, the point of freedom of speech is not that everyone shall speak, but that "everything worth saying shall be said."[54]

The progressivist/republican argument that we should not tie the right of free speech too closely to the right of private property remains valid, particularly in an age of increasing media concentration. That is because the liberty of speech and the liberties involved in property ownership are two different kinds of freedom. Although property rights often assist free expression—think of the right to use the

---

[53] Meiklejohn was perhaps most overt about this, arguing that the First Amendment "has no concern about the 'needs of many men to express their opinions'" but rather is concerned with "the common needs of all the members of the body politic." MEIKLEJOHN, POLITICAL FREEDOM, *supra* note 48, at 55; *see also id.* at 56–57, 61 (criticizing Zechariah Chafee, Jr. for being "misled by his inclusion of an individual interest within the scope of the First Amendment," and Justice Oliver Wendell Holmes for his "excessive individualism"). Owen Fiss, likewise, has emphasized that the First Amendment's concern with autonomy is primarily instrumental: "Autonomy may be protected, but only when it enriches public debate." Fiss, *Why the State?*, *supra* note 49, at 786.

[54] MEIKLEJOHN, POLITICAL FREEDOM, *supra* note 48, at 26.

software and the computer that one owns—they can also undermine it, as suggested by the examples of content discrimination in telecommunications networks and the use of digital rights management to control the end user's experience.

Nevertheless, the paradigm case that motivates the progressivist agenda—the case of few speakers broadcasting to a largely inactive mass audience—no longer describes the world we live in. Even if, as I have argued, the new digital technologies do not displace mass media, they exist alongside it and build on top of it. Digital technologies give lots of people, more than ever before, a chance to participate in the creation and development of public culture. Technological changes in how speech is transmitted, and in who gets to participate in that transmission, change the focus of free speech theory.

VI
THE IDEA OF A DEMOCRATIC CULTURE

Let me begin by pointing to five characteristics of Internet speech that I believe are exemplary of freedom of speech generally. These characteristics are hardly new to the Internet; rather, my point is that the Internet makes them particularly salient. That salience, I shall argue, reshapes our conception of the free speech principle.

First, speech on the Internet ranges over every possible subject and mode of expression, including the serious, the frivolous, the gossipy, the erotic, the scatological, and the profound. The Internet reflects popular tastes, popular culture, and popular enthusiasms.

Second, the Internet, taken as a whole, is full of innovation. The tremendous growth of the Internet in a relatively short period of time shows how enormously creative ordinary people can be if given the chance to express themselves. And it demonstrates what ordinary people can do when they are allowed to be active producers rather than passive recipients of their cultural world.

Third, much of the source of that creativity is the ability to build on something else. This is particularly true of the World Wide Web. As originally conceived, the very structure of HTML code encourages copying, imitation, and linking. The continual innovation and transformation we see in digital media stems directly from their ability to use the old to make the new. Digital media allow lots of people to comment, absorb, appropriate, and innovate—to add a wrinkle here, a criticism there. Internet speech continually develops through linkage, collage, annotation, mixture, and through what I have called routing around and glomming on. Internet speech, like all speech, appropriates and transforms. It imitates, copies, builds upon and mixes.

34 *NEW YORK UNIVERSITY LAW REVIEW* [Vol. 79:1

Fourth, Internet speech is participatory and interactive. People don't merely watch (or listen to) the Internet as if it were television or radio. Rather, they surf through it, they program on it, they publish to it, they write comments and continually add things to it. Internet speech is a social activity that involves exchange, give and take. The roles of reader and writer, producer and consumer of information are blurred and often effectively merge.

Fifth, and finally, because Internet speech is a social activity, a matter of interactivity, of give and take, it is not surprising that Internet speech creates new communities, cultures and subcultures. In this way, it exemplifies an important general feature of freedom of speech: Freedom of speech allows us, each of us, to participate in the growth and development of the cultures and subcultures that, in turn, help constitute us as individuals. Freedom of speech is part of an interactive cycle of social exchange, social participation, and self-formation. We speak and we listen, we send out and we take in. As we do this, we change, we grow, we become something other than we were before, and we make something new out of what existed before.

To sum up, the Internet makes particularly salient five facts about free speech: Speech ranges over a wide variety of subjects, including not only politics but also popular culture. The speech of ordinary people is full of innovation and creativity. That creativity comes from building on what has come before. Speech is participatory and interactive as opposed to mere receipt of information. It merges the activities of reading and writing, of production and consumption. Finally, speech involves cultural participation and self-formation. The Internet reminds us how central and important these features are to speech generally. It reveals to us in a new way what has always been the case.

And this brings me to a central point: The populist nature of freedom of speech, its creativity, its interactivity, its importance for community and self-formation, all suggest that a theory of freedom of speech centered around government and democratic deliberation about public issues is far too limited. The free speech principle has always been about something larger than democracy in the narrow sense of voting and elections, something larger even than democracy in the sense of public deliberation about issues of public concern. If free speech is about democracy, it is about democracy in the widest possible sense, not merely at the level of governance, or at the level of deliberation, but at the level of culture. The Internet teaches us that the free speech principle is about, and always has been about, the promotion and development of a democratic culture.

Democracy is far more than a set of procedures for resolving disputes. It is a feature of social life and a form of social organization. Democratic ideals require a further commitment to democratic forms of social structure and social organization, a commitment to social as well as political equality.[55] And the forces of democratization operate not only through regular elections, but through changes in institutions, practices, customs, mannerisms, speech, and dress. A "democratic" culture, then, means much more than democracy as a form of self-governance. It means democracy as a form of social life in which unjust barriers of rank and privilege are dissolved, and in which ordinary people gain a greater say over the institutions and practices that shape them and their futures.

What makes a culture democratic, then, is not democratic *governance* but democratic *participation*. A democratic culture includes the institutions of representative democracy, but it also exists beyond them, and, indeed undergirds them. A democratic culture is the culture of a democratized society; a democratic culture is a participatory culture.

If the purpose of freedom of speech is to realize a democratic culture, why is democratic cultural participation important? First, culture is a source of the self. Human beings are made out of culture. A democratic culture is valuable because it gives ordinary people a fair opportunity to participate in the creation and evolution of the processes of meaning-making that shape them and become part of them; a democratic culture is valuable because it gives ordinary people a say in the progress and development of the cultural forces that in turn produce them.

Second, participation in culture has a constitutive or performative value: When people are creative, when they make new things out of old things, when they become producers of their culture, they exercise and perform their freedom and become the sort of people who are free. That freedom is something more than just choosing which cultural products to purchase and consume; the freedom to create is an active engagement with the world.[56]

---

[55] On the social features of democracy implicit in the idea of a democratic culture, see J.M. Balkin, *The Constitution of Status*, 106 YALE L.J. 2313, 2314 (1997); J.M. Balkin, *The Declaration and the Promise of a Democratic Culture*, 4 WIDENER L. SYMP. J. 167 (1999).

[56] Legal scholars influenced by John Fiske have argued that intellectual property law should also serve the goals of promoting popular participation in culture, or what Fiske called "semiotic democracy." *See, e.g.*, William W. Fisher III, *Property and Contract on the Internet*, 73 CHI.-KENT L. REV. 1203, 1217 (1998) ("In an attractive society, all persons would be able to participate in the process of meaning-making. Instead of being merely passive consumers of cultural artifacts produced by others, they would be producers, helping to shape the world of ideas and symbols in which they live."); *see also* Kenneth

By "culture" I mean the collective processes of meaning-making in a society. The realm of culture, however, is much broader than the concern of the First Amendment or the free speech principle. Armaments and shampoo are part of culture; so too are murder and robbery. And all of these things can affect people's lives and shape who they are. The realm of culture for purposes of the free speech principle is a subset of what anthropologists study as forms of culture. It refers to a set of historically contingent and historically produced social practices and media that human beings employ to exchange ideas and share opinions.[57] These are the methods, practices, and technologies through which dialogue occurs and public opinion is formed. For example, today people generally regard art as a social

Karst, *Local Discourse and the Social Issues*, 12 CARDOZO STUD. L. & LIT. 1, 27 (2000) (defining cultural democracy as "the broadest possible participation in the cultural processes that define and redefine the sort of society we shall be"). Larry Lessig's recent call for "free culture," *see* LESSIG, THE FUTURE OF IDEAS, *supra* note 17, at 9–10, also has important connections to the principles of semiotic democracy and democratic culture, as does David Lange's notion of free appropriation as a right of citizenship exercised in the public domain, *see* David Lange, *Reimagining the Public Domain*, 66 LAW & CONTEMP. PROBS. 463, 475–83 (2003).

Important examples of this trend in intellectual property scholarship include Rosemary J. Coombe, *Author/izing the Celebrity: Publicity Rights, Postmodern Politics, and Unauthorized Genders*, 10 CARDOZO ARTS & ENT. L.J. 365 (1992); Rosemary J. Coombe, *Objects of Property and Subjects of Politics: Intellectual Property Laws and Democratic Dialogue*, 69 TEX. L. REV. 1853 (1991); Rosemary J. Coombe, *Publicity Rights and Political Aspiration: Mass Culture, Gender Identity, and Democracy*, 26 NEW ENG. L. REV. 1221 (1992); Rochelle Cooper Dreyfuss, *Expressive Genericity: Trademarks as Language in the Pepsi Generation*, 65 NOTRE DAME L. REV. 397 (1990); Niva Elkin-Koren, *Cyberlaw and Social Change: A Democratic Approach to Copyright Law in Cyberspace*, 14 CARDOZO ARTS & ENT. L.J. 215, 272–73 (1996); David Lange, *At Play in the Fields of the Word: Copyright and the Construction of Authorship in the Post-Literate Millennium*, 55 LAW & CONTEMP. PROBS. 139 (1992); Jessica Litman, *The Public Domain*, 39 EMORY L.J. 965 (1990); Madow, *supra* note 2; William Fisher, Theories of Intellectual Property, *at* http://www.law.harvard.edu/Academic_Affairs/coursepages/tfisher/iptheory.html (last visited Dec. 3, 2003).

Other scholars have sought to connect the proper scope of copyright, fair use and the public domain to the promotion of democracy in the sense of public discussion of public issues. *See* Neil Weinstock Netanel, *Copyright and a Democratic Civil Society*, 106 YALE L.J. 283, 347–65 (1996) [hereinafter Netanel, *Copyright and a Democratic Civil Society*] (arguing that copyright promotes democracy by funding independent sectors of creativity); Neil Weinstock Netanel, *Market Hierarchy and Copyright in Our System of Free Expression*, 53 VAND. L. REV. 1879 (2000). This strand of intellectual property scholarship is somewhat closer to the republican or progressivist model; it emphasizes the importance of democratic public discourse and views popular culture as valuable to the extent that it contributes to a democratic civil society. *See* Netanel, *Copyright and a Democratic Civil Society*, *supra*, at 351 n.310.

[57] For a helpful discussion, see Robert Post, *Recuperating First Amendment Doctrine*, 47 STAN. L. REV. 1249, 1253–55 (1995). Post argues that social practices and media for the communication of ideas are central to the formation of public opinion. Robert Post, *Reconciling Theory and Doctrine in First Amendment Jurisprudence*, 88 CAL. L. REV. 2353, 2367–69 (2000); Post, *Recuperating First Amendment Doctrine*, *supra*, at 1275–77.

practice for the exchange of ideas, and they regard motion pictures as a medium of expression.[58] These practices and media of social communication construct the realm that we regard as "speech" for purposes of the free speech principle.[59] We cannot give an exhaustive list of these practices and media precisely because the social conventions and technologies that define them are always evolving; even so, it seems clear enough that the Internet and other digital technologies are media for the communication of ideas, and an increasingly important way for people to express their ideas and form their opinions.[60] They are central—and I would say crucial—media for the realization of a democratic culture.

Culture has always been produced through popular participation. Digital technology simply makes this aspect of democratic life more obvious, more salient. Radio and television are technologies of mass cultural reception, where a few speakers can reach audiences of indefinite size. But the Internet is a technology of mass cultural participation in which audiences can give as well as receive, broadcast as well as absorb, create and contribute as well as consume. Digital technology makes the values of a democratic culture salient to us because it offers the technological possibility of widespread cultural participation.

What is the difference between grounding freedom of speech on the promotion of democracy and grounding it on the promotion of a democratic culture? What is at stake in the move to culture?

There are three important differences, I think, and each stems from the weaknesses of the progressivist/republican model: They con-

---

[58] It was not always thus. *See* Post, *Recuperating First Amendment Doctrine, supra* note 57, at 1252–53 (discussing *Mutual Film Corp. v. Industrial Comm.*, 236 U.S. 230, 243–45 (1915), in which Supreme Court originally held that motion pictures were not "organs of public opinion"). By 1952, the Supreme Court had come around, stating that "it cannot be doubted that motion pictures are a significant medium for the communication of ideas." *Joseph Burstyn, Inc. v. Wilson*, 343 U.S. 495, 501 (1952). The difference between the Court's statements in 1915 and 1952 reflects important changes in American society to which the Court's First Amendment doctrines eventually responded. The scope of the free speech principle always grows out of a normatively inflected recognition of sociological realities.

[59] The free speech principle also applies to regulations of conduct that do not involve a generally recognized medium for the communication of ideas when the government regulates conduct because it disagrees with or desires to suppress the ideas it believes the conduct expresses. *See United States v. O'Brien*, 391 U.S. 367, 377–78 (1968) (holding that reasons for regulation of conduct must be unrelated to suppression of free expression). Thus, when government effectively treats conduct as a medium for the communication of ideas and punishes it on that basis, the free speech principle is also implicated.

[60] *See, e.g.*, Reno v. ACLU, 521 U.S. 844, 850 (1997) ("The Internet is 'a unique and wholly new medium of worldwide human communication.'" (quoting *ACLU v. Reno*, 929 F. Supp. 824, 844 (E.D. Pa. 1996))).

38   *NEW YORK UNIVERSITY LAW REVIEW*   [Vol. 79:1

cern the status of nonpolitical expression, the role of popular culture, and the importance of individual participation and individual liberty.

A. *Nonpolitical Expression*

A serious difficulty with the progressivist/republican model has always been that a wide variety of activities, of which art and social commentary are only the most salient examples, have always fit poorly into a democratic theory of free expression. Lots of speech is not overtly political. Nevertheless, it gets protected under the progressivist/republican model because it is useful for political discussion, because it may become enmeshed in political controversies (and thus threatened or suppressed for political reasons), or because it is very hard to draw lines separating what is political from what is not.[61] In like fashion, lots of activities cannot easily be classified as deliberation—like singing, shouting, protesting, gossiping, making fun of people, or just annoying them or getting them angry. Nevertheless, these activities are protected because we can think of them as raw materials for further democratic deliberation or because we cannot easily draw lines separating them from the social practice of deliberation.[62] In both cases, then, we have kinds of speech that are at the periphery rather than the core; we protect them in aid of something more central and precious. In short, the progressivist vision sees democratic deliberation about public issues at the core of constitutional concern and other subjects and other forms of expression as peripheral or supplementary.

---

[61] Meiklejohn himself argued that works of art were protected speech because they promoted knowledge, sharpened intelligence, and developed sensitivity to human values, thus helping people to make political decisions. Meiklejohn, *First Amendment, supra* note 48, at 255–57. Other scholars have recognized that not all artistic expression equally promotes democratic self-government. *See, e.g.,* SUNSTEIN, *supra* note 49, at 153–59 (1993) (suggesting that nonpolitical art should be relegated to lower tier of First Amendment protection). And of course Robert Bork, who also had a democracy-based theory of the First Amendment, famously argued that art should receive no First Amendment protection if it was not political speech. Robert H. Bork, *Neutral Principles and Some First Amendment Problems*, 47 IND. L.J. 1, 26–28 (1971).

Owen Fiss believes, to the contrary, that art, particularly unorthodox art and art underappreciated by market forces, furthers the goals of collective self-determination and democratic deliberation. He argues that government programs like the National Endowment for the Arts (NEA) that subsidize art should look to art that is concerned with issues on the public agenda or that should be on the public agenda of discussion and comment. Thus, government subsidy of art should be designed to promote discussion of important public issues. FISS, THE IRONY OF FREE SPEECH, *supra* note 49, at 40–45.

[62] *Cf.* Owen M. Fiss, *The Unruly Character of Politics*, 29 McGEORGE L. REV. 1, 2–7 (1997) (noting limitations of Meiklejohnian metaphor of town meeting as applied to confrontational politics).

I have never been satisfied with this approach. I think something is missing here, and the notion of democratic culture helps us understand why. The point of democracy, as its name implies, is to put power in the hands of the people, to give ordinary people some measure of control over the forces that shape their lives and some degree of say about how the world around them develops. But law and governance are only parts of this world. Culture is an even larger part, and in some ways it has an even more capacious role in structuring our lives. The various processes of communication and cultural exchange are the sources of the self and its development over time. Our ideas, our habits, our thoughts, our very selves are produced through constant communication and exchange with others.[63] The influence is reciprocal: Through this continuous communication and exchange, we shape culture and are shaped by it in turn. We absorb it, we inhabit it, we make it new. We send it out into the world, we make it part of us.

Culture is more than governance, more than politics, more than law. And if democracy is giving power to the people, then true democracy means allowing people not only to have a say about who represents them in a legislature, or what laws are passed, but also to have a say about the shape and growth of the culture that they live in and that is inevitably part of them. Power to the people—democracy—in its broadest, thickest sense, must include our relationship not simply to the state but to culture as a whole, to the processes of meaning-making that constitute us as individuals. Those processes of meaning-making include both the ability to distribute those meanings and the ability to receive them.[64]

Culture is an essential ingredient of the self, and so freedom of speech means participation in the forces of culture that shape the self. We participate in the growth and development of culture through interaction, through communicating to others and receiving ideas from others. Cultural democracy is memetic democracy, the continuous distribution, circulation, and exchange of bits of culture from mind to mind.[65] This vision of culture is not democratic because

---

[63] On the formation of self through cultural transmission, see JACK M. BALKIN, CULTURAL SOFTWARE: A THEORY OF IDEOLOGY 269–85 (1998).

[64] As Julie Cohen reminds us, digital technologies tend to blur the boundaries between production and reception, speaking and reading, or even between viewing and copying. *See* Julie E. Cohen, *A Right to Read Anonymously: A Closer Look at "Copyright Management" in Cyberspace*, 28 CONN. L. REV. 981, 1004–09 (1996); *see also* Rubenfeld, *supra* note 5, at 34–36 (arguing that theories of freedom of expression based in autonomy and self expression do not sufficiently account for First Amendment right to read as well as to express one's self).

[65] Memetics is an evolutionary theory that attempts to explain the development of culture through the transmission of bits of culture, or memes, which replicate themselves in

40   NEW YORK UNIVERSITY LAW REVIEW   [Vol. 79:1

people are voting on what is in their culture. It is democratic because they get to participate in the meaning-making processes that form and reproduce culture. They do this through communicating with and interacting with others. Moreover, democratic culture is not democratic because people are participating in processes of deliberation about governance, or even public issues. Rather it is democratic because it is participation in the creation and shaping of culture, which is, at the same time, participation in the growth and development of the self.

B. *Popular Culture*

The second basic problem with the work of Meiklejohn and his heirs has been its relative neglect and suspicion of popular culture. Popular culture is often seen as mass culture controlled by corporations, which demobilizes the citizenry; as sensationalism or dumbed-down speech, which adds little of importance to democratic deliberation; or as mere entertainment, which distracts people from serious discussion of public issues.[66] But from the perspective of democratic culture, popular culture and entertainment should not be merely

---

human minds. The term "meme" was coined by the zoologist Richard Dawkins. *See* RICHARD DAWKINS, THE SELFISH GENE 189–94 (1977). Memetic theory often tends to undermine agency and selfhood, *see, e.g.,* SUSAN BLACKMORE, THE MEME MACHINE (1999), and thus would seem an odd choice for a theory of self expression. But memetics can also be employed to explain concepts central to agency and selfhood like freedom, *see* DANIEL C. DENNETT, FREEDOM EVOLVES 175–92, 266 (2003), or the growth of human belief systems and human innovation, *see* BALKIN, *supra* note 63, at 42–97, 173–75.

The idea of memetic democracy emphasizes the deep connections between self and agency on the one hand, and cultural evolution and the shaping of the self through cultural exchange on the other. Memetic democracy means that everyone gets to participate in the distribution and dissemination of memes, which are the building blocks of the cultural software that constitutes individuals as individuals.

[66] *See, e.g.,* LEE C. BOLLINGER, IMAGES OF A FREE PRESS 138–41 (1991) (contrasting burdens of education for civic life with pleasantness of entertainment); SUNSTEIN, *supra* note 49, at 84–91 (decrying "low quality" programming that appeals to tastes of uneducated); Fiss, *Free Speech and Social Structure, supra* note 49, at 1413 ("From the perspective of a free and open debate, the choice between *Love Boat* and *Fantasy Island* is trivial."); Fiss, *Why the State?, supra* note 49, at 788 (contrasting reruns of "I Love Lucy" and MTV with "the information [members of the electorate] need to make free and intelligent choices about government policy, the structure of government, or the nature of society."). Once again, this familiar progressivist theme is already present in Meiklejohn. *See* MEIKLEJOHN, POLITICAL FREEDOM, *supra* note 48, at 87 (attacking commercial radio for "corrupt[ing] both our morals and our intelligence"). Even Justice Louis Brandeis fell prey to this sort of cultural elitism, which pervades his famous call for protecting the right of privacy from a particular form of speech. *See* Samuel Warren & Louis Brandeis, *The Right to Privacy*, 4 HARV. L. REV. 193, 196 (1890) (arguing that "personal gossip," "[e]asy of comprehension [and] appealing to that weak side of human nature," "crowds the space available for matters of real interest to the community," and "destroys at once robustness of thought and delicacy of feeling").

peripheral or a distraction. They should be a central part of what freedom of speech is about.

In an age of unidirectional mass media, popular culture was, to a very large extent, mass culture—a set of commodities manufactured and sent out to be consumed by a mass audience. But the Internet allows mass culture to be appropriated by ordinary citizens and become, more than ever before, a truly popular culture, because it allows what I have called routing around and glomming on.[67]

We can understand the controversies over intellectual property in this light. Media corporations are turning to digital rights management to avoid digital piracy. But much of what traditional mass media most fears and resents is not piracy but cultural appropriation—individual riffs on mass media digital products shared with others—and the ability of consumers to route around a controlled advertising and marketing environment. Shifting our focus from democracy to democratic culture helps us see that the problem in the digital age is not just deliberation about public issues. It is also the importance of letting ordinary people engage in appropriation and innovation rather than mere consumption; it is the value of ordinary people being able to "rip, mix, and burn,"[68] to route around traditional media gatekeepers and glom onto existing media products.

In a democratic culture, we are interested in protecting not only speech about public issues, but also speech that concerns popular expression in art, as well as cultural concerns such as gossip, mores, fashions, and popular music. The progressivist/republican approach has tended to valorize high culture and high quality programming as aids to democratic deliberation (often conflating the two in the pro-

---

[67] In this sense the Internet simply empowers the popular appropriation and transformation of mass culture that already existed:

> Much of mass culture involves programming, advertisements, architecture, and artwork produced by corporations and designed to sell products and make money. Many critiques of mass culture warn of the deleterious consequences of consumerism and mass consumption. . . . But a populist view [of democratic culture] also emphasizes that ordinary people are not mere passive receptors of the messages offered in advertising, television programming, and other elements of contemporary mass culture. Such assumptions are just another way of denigrating the intelligence and abilities of ordinary people. People do not uncritically absorb and assimilate the images they see on the television screen—they process, discuss, and appropriate them. People are active interpreters and rearrangers of what they find in mass culture. They use the raw materials of mass culture to articulate and express their values. Through this process, they produce and reproduce popular culture.

Balkin, *supra* note 2, at 1948–49 (footnotes omitted).

[68] The reference is to Apple's famous commercial instructing users of its iPod to "[R]ip, mix, and burn. . . . After all, it's your music." Larry Lessig uses the slogan as a metaphor for a free culture. Lessig, The Future of Ideas, *supra* note 17, at 9–11.

cess), with "low" culture protected only as a peripheral concern.[69] But if freedom of speech is concerned with the promotion of a truly democratic culture, popular culture is every bit as important as so-called high culture.[70] In fact, in a democratic culture, the distinction between high culture and low culture begins to blur and the difference between them becomes increasingly difficult to maintain. High culture continually borrows from popular culture; moreover, as culture becomes increasingly democratized, the popular culture of today often turns out to be the high culture of tomorrow.

C. *Individual Participation*

A third problem with the progressivist/republican model has been its tendency to seek to manage discourse and structure public debate.[71] This desire is hardly surprising: In a world dominated by mass media controlled by a relative handful of very wealthy corporations, it seems important to make sure that dissenting views get a word in edgewise, that serious issues are not driven out by the media's never-ending quest for profits, and that audiences are not stultified and demobilized by an endless stream of increasingly vapid entertainment. As a result, the progressivist model has downplayed individual liberty and instead played up the protection of democratic processes, including robust debate on public issues and the creation of an informed citizenry. Earlier, I noted Meiklejohn's famous statement that the point of freedom of speech is not that everyone shall speak, but that everything worth saying shall be said. Meiklejohn even analogized the system of free expression to a town meeting.[72] The purpose of the town meeting was to shape a public agenda for discussion

---

[69] *See* SUNSTEIN, *supra* note 49, at 87–91; *see also* Cass R. Sunstein, *Television and the Public Interest*, 88 CAL. L. REV. 499, 518 (2000) (arguing that goal of television regulation is to promote deliberative democracy).

[70] *See* Balkin, *supra* note 2, at 1948 ("[P]opular culture is neither a debilitated version of democratic culture nor a mere diversion from the sober processes of deliberation imagined by progressivism. It is not a sideshow or distraction from democratic culture but the main event. Moreover, [a] populis[t] [approach to free expression] accepts, as progressivism does not, that popular culture—which is also democratic culture—is by nature unkempt and unruly, occasionally raucous and even vulgar. It is by turns both eloquent and mawkish, noble and embarrassing, wise and foolish, resistant to blandishments and gullible in the extreme. It is imperfect in precisely the same sense that democracy itself is imperfect.").

[71] Robert Post has emphasized this limitation of the Meiklejohn model, arguing that the autonomy of public discourse, necessary for democratic self-government, is undermined by imposing managerial methods to cabin its scope and agendas. *See generally* Robert Post, *Managing Deliberation: The Quandary of Democratic Dialogue*, 103 ETHICS 654 (1993); Robert Post, *Meiklejohn's Mistake: Individual Autonomy and the Reform of Public Discourse*, 64 U. COLO. L. REV. 1109 (1993).

[72] MEIKLEJOHN, POLITICAL FREEDOM, *supra* note 48, at 24–27.

of serious issues; there would be time for only some people to speak. The important point was that the participants in the meeting be informed and stick to the agenda because everyone would decide what to do on the basis of the information presented. Although Meiklejohn's town meeting seems quite distant from the electronic mass media, it had many of the same features: scarcity of time, the need for a public agenda, and the importance of an informed citizenry. Hence the need for regulation was very much the same.

Democratic culture, by contrast, is not solely concerned with people's ability to be informed about a particular agenda. It is concerned with participation, interaction, and the ability of people to create, to innovate, to borrow ideas and make new ones. Meiklejohn remarked that his ideal town meeting was "self-government," not a "dialectical free-for-all."[73] That opposition may hold true for a particular form of democracy. But in a democratic culture, and especially the culture of the Internet, freedom of expression *is* a dialectical free-for-all, a continuous process of interactivity and innovation, in which culture and discussion move and grow in any number of different directions.

Here again a shift in focus from democracy to democratic culture responds to the sorts of freedoms that digital technologies make possible. Digital technologies and telecommunications networks mean that people are no longer forced into the role of mere spectators and consumers; they can be active participants, creating, commenting, and broadcasting their own ideas to a larger public. And in a world in which active participation in the creation and distribution of culture becomes possible for so many, liberty is an important good to be prized, valued, and nourished.

The progressivist/republican conception of free speech arose in the twentieth century because ordinary people were shut out of the most pervasive and important forms of speech and were reduced to the roles of spectators, consumers, and recipients. In that world, protecting the liberty of a favored few who owned the means of communication from regulation was less important than producing discussion on public issues and promoting a robust agenda of diverse and antagonistic sources so that the citizenry could be well-informed and engaged with the great public issues of the day. But new technologies make it possible for vast numbers of people to participate, innovate, and create, to route around and glom on to the traditional mass media and their products. This has increased enormously the practical liberty of the ordinary citizen to speak, and to reach a vast audience.

---

[73] *Id.* at 25.

44   *NEW YORK UNIVERSITY LAW REVIEW*   [Vol. 79:1

When technology makes liberty possible, liberty once again must return to the forefront of concern.[74]

The twentieth-century concern with speech as a method of democratic deliberation privileges the delivery of information about issues of public concern to the public, who receive this information through asymmetric and unidirectional mass media. I do not wish to deny the

---

[74] Indeed, the standard progressivist/republican arguments for regulation of broadcast, cable, and satellite can and should be rearticulated in terms of the more populist perspective of promoting democratic culture. The key point is that the United States has adopted a hybrid system: Instead of separating the functions of editor and distributor, and treating all distribution networks as common carriers like telephone companies, it has allowed a small number of editors/speakers to own powerful distribution networks not open to all in return for accepting various public service obligations and regulations. Thus the hybrid system is based on the model of a contract or a quid pro quo.

Although the hybrid system denies the vast majority of people free access to key distribution networks, it may nevertheless have been justified in the past by its economic advantages. Arguably it offers necessary incentives for broadcasters, cable companies, and owners of satellite systems to invest in, produce, and deliver a wide variety of diverse programming for viewers and listeners that will enrich public debate and public culture. Thus, it provides considerable grist for the mill of a democratic culture.

Nevertheless, a hybrid system is hardly perfect. Heavy reliance on advertising tends to create a significant mismatch between what broadcasters deliver and what viewers want, in part because advertisers seek content that appeals to the common tastes of certain valued demographic groups (whose preferences may otherwise be quite heterogenous) rather than content that cross-cuts demographic groups or appeals to groups with comparatively little disposable income or comparatively unmanipulable consumption patterns. *See* BAKER, *supra* note 9, at 13, 24–26, 88–91, 182–90. Advertisers will also tend to push for content that helps induce greater consumption instead of content that appeals to and fulfils other values that viewers might have. For example, viewers may value many kinds of content that are not strongly tied to shopping, purchasing, and consumption. They may value content that educates them or inspires them to change their lives, rethink their values, or make use of their creative powers. Finally, market forces also will, almost by definition, underproduce content that has high positive externalities (like educational content, or balanced and informative coverage of news) because the value of that content to society cannot be captured by market forces, and, all other things being equal, the greater the positive externalities, the more underproduction there will be. *Id.* at 41–62, 114–18.

The hybrid model of media regulation is not constitutionally required. Rather, it is a quid pro quo or contractual arrangement, and it is constitutional to the extent that it promotes the values of a democratic culture. To be sure, regulatory quid pro quos can violate free speech rights if they impose an unconstitutional condition on free speech. However, structural regulations of the mass media that seek to counteract the limitations of mass media markets should be constitutional if there is a clear nexus between the goals of the regulation and the purposes behind the choice of a hybrid system. To the extent that structural regulations and public interest obligations of mass media compensate for the limitations of a hybrid model, they are tied to the very justifications for issuing broadcast licenses and cable franchises in the first place: They help further the goal of promoting a rich public sphere and a vibrant, participatory, and democratic culture. If government can make a sufficiently good case that the regulations will have this effect, the regulations should not be regarded as unconstitutional conditions on a media company's First Amendment rights. Likewise, public broadcasting that supplements existing markets with content that government reasonably believes to be valuable (like children's programming) should also be constitutionally permissible.

importance of that conception; I merely want to insist that it is only a partial conception, inadequate to deal with the features of speech that the new digital technologies bring to the foreground of our concern. The values behind freedom of speech are about production as much as reception, about creativity as much as deliberation, about the work of ordinary individuals as much as the mass media.

Freedom of speech is more than the freedom of elites and concentrated economic enterprises to funnel media products for passive reception by docile audiences. Freedom of speech is more than the choice of which media products to consume. Freedom of speech means giving everyone—not just a small number of people who own dominant modes of mass communication, but ordinary people, too—the chance to use technology to participate in their culture, to interact, to create, to build, to route around and glom on, to take from the old and produce the new, and to talk about whatever they want to talk about, whether it be politics, public issues, or popular culture.

VII
DIGITAL LIBERTY

Shifting our focus from democracy to democratic culture helps us better understand the idea of freedom of speech in the digital age. Indeed, I would go even further. Digital technologies change our understanding of what liberty of speech is. They make salient features of freedom of speech that have always been present. Digital technologies offer people the liberty to participate in culture through application of existing cultural materials, the ability to appropriate and innovate using tools freely available to all. Digital technology offers a possibility, not yet fully realized (and conceivably one that will never be fully realized), of what democratic culture might be.

A democratic culture is the culture of widespread "rip[ping], mix[ing], and burn[ing],"[75] of nonexclusive appropriation, innovation, and combination. It is the culture of routing around and glomming on, the culture of annotation, innovation, and bricolage. Democratic culture is not the same thing as mass culture. It makes use of the instrumentalities of mass culture, but transforms them, individualizes them, and sends what it produces back into the cultural stream. In democratic culture, individuals are not mere consumers and recipients of mass culture but active appropriators. Culture has always had opportunities for popular participation. The Internet and digital technologies merely increase the number of opportunities for widespread distribution, their scope, and their power; and, in the process, make

---

[75] *See supra* note 68.

46   NEW YORK UNIVERSITY LAW REVIEW   [Vol. 79:1

them more obvious to us. Digital speech places these features of liberty—and the possibility of democratic culture—more clearly and centrally before us.

What is the liberty of expression, viewed from the perspective of the ideal of democratic culture? I would say that it has four important components that have been made more salient by digital technology: (1) the right to publish, distribute to, and reach an audience; (2) the right to interact with others and exchange ideas with them, which includes the right to influence and to be influenced, to transmit culture and absorb it; (3) the right to appropriate from cultural materials that lay at hand, to innovate, annotate, combine, and then share the results with others; and (4) the right to participate in and produce culture, and thus the right to have a say in the development of the cultural and communicative forces that shape the self.

What these facets of liberty have in common is that they are not self-regarding. Communication is interaction, sharing, influencing, and being influenced in turn. Creation is not creation ex nihilo, but building on the work of others; appropriation is not exclusive appropriation but making use of tools that lay to hand that are part of a common pool of resources. Distribution is not isolated but occurs through public pathways and networks that many can travel on. Finally, development of the self is a project that one shares with others.

In short, what the Internet makes salient to us is that freedom of expression, that most individualistic of liberties, that most personal of activities, is at the very same time deeply communal, because it is interactive, because it is participatory, because it builds on the work of what others have done, and because it makes use of public networks and pathways of distribution. I do not mean by this that liberty exists merely for the purposes of the state, or that individual liberty is an illusion. Far from it. I mean precisely the opposite—that the realization of individuality, the expression of one's individual self, the promotion of one's individual dignity, comes out of and through culture, a shared feature of life. Culture is the substrate, the raw materials of individual freedom, from which individual liberty emerges and within which individual liberty operates and innovates.[76]

The concept of a democratic culture restores freedom to its central place in free speech theory, but in the process, offers a particular conception of what that freedom is:

Freedom is participation. Freedom is distribution. Freedom is interaction. Freedom is the ability to influence and be influenced in

---

[76] *See* BALKIN, *supra* note 63, at 17–19.

turn. Freedom is the ability to change others and to be changed as well. Freedom is the ability to glom on and route around. Freedom is appropriation, transformation, promulgation, subversion, the creation of the new out of the old. Freedom is mixing, fusing, separating, conflating, and uniting. Freedom is the discovery of synergies, the reshuffling of associations and connections, the combination of influences and materials.

Freedom is bricolage.

Dissent is central to this conception of free speech, for dissent is cultural as well as political.[77] Just as the progressivist/republican critique has too narrow a focus on why speech is valuable, it has too limited a conception of dissent. People may disagree with what the government is doing, and they may express themselves in politics, in music, or in art. But they can also disagree with the aesthetics and mores of others, and they can dissent by borrowing from and subverting what they borrow. And just as democratic culture undergirds democracy in the narrow sense without being identical to it, cultural dissent is an important source of political dissent without being subsumed by it.

Perhaps equally important, dissent involves all of the features of liberty I have just described: interaction, appropriation, and transformation. Dissent reacts to, borrows from, and builds on what it disagrees with. Dissent, whether in culture or in politics, is not mere negation. Rather, dissent is creative and cumulative. It appropriates elements of what it objects to and uses them in the process of critique, often through subverting or parodying them.[78] The nature and focus of dissent is shaped by what the dissenter disagrees with, and the form of response is shaped by the way the problem appears to the critic. Thus, dissent exists in an interactive and interdependent relationship to the object of its criticism, appropriating elements of what it rebukes in order to make its claims. Dissent makes use of the raw materials that inspire its disagreement and resistance. In this way, dissent, and responses to dissent, are not mere repudiations of what has come

---

[77] *See* Madhavi Sunder, *Cultural Dissent*, 54 STAN. L. REV. 495, 498 (2001) (noting ubiquitous disputes within cultural groups about values of group and terms of membership).

[78] *See, e.g.*, JUDITH P. BUTLER, GENDER TROUBLE: FEMINISM AND THE SUBVERSION OF IDENTITY 141–49 (1990) (noting possibilities for subversion of existing sexual roles and creation of new ones through repetition and through performance); Amy M. Adler, *What's Left?*, 84 CAL. L. REV. 1499, 1529–31 (1996) (describing how pornography has been appropriated for feminist purposes); Judith P. Butler, *The Force of Fantasy: Feminism, Mapplethorpe, and Discursive Excess*, 2 DIFFERENCES 105, 119–20 (1990) (arguing that "discursive excess" offers opportunities for subversion and parody).

before, but have a cumulative effect, building on existing materials and practices, and propelling and transforming culture forward.

I have emphasized that the ability of ordinary individuals to produce their own culture is a central aspect of the liberty of free expression. What justifies this populist focus? Why shouldn't we organize telecommunications and intellectual property law to maximize the ability of large business enterprises to make large investments in cultural products (e.g., blockbuster movies) while allowing consumers to choose which ones they prefer to consume in the marketplace? Why isn't this cultural division of labor an equally good protection of freedom of speech?

One answer is that the ability to participate in culture and produce one's own meanings can offer people greater self-realization and self-fulfillment than perpetually being relegated to the docile consumption of mass media products. But even if we remain agnostic on that point, being an active producer/creator is at least as good a way of living as being a passive consumer/recipient, and it is an equally important part of the liberty of expression.

Market forces are likely to underprotect the right of ordinary individuals to be active cultural producers, because media companies are likely to make more money from consumption of the media products they advertise and sell. From the standpoint of these companies, individual cultural production has no independent value except to the extent that it involves or leads to the consumption of media goods. And to the extent that active cultural participation diverts end users from greater consumption of media products, interferes with the companies' expansive definition of intellectual property rights, or challenges corporate technologies of control, it is less valuable than passive consumption; indeed it is positively harmful and must be cabined in.

One might object that media companies will invest in products and services that facilitate individual cultural appropriation and production if consumers want them badly enough. To some extent this is true: We have already seen the beginnings of this in multi-user online games. But individual cultural production often has high positive externalities; it provides benefits and satisfactions that are not easily captured by markets.[79] So media companies may have insufficient incentives to facilitate individual cultural appropriation and production. Conversely, they will tend to over-invest in products that relegate individuals to a position of relatively passive consumers.

---

[79] *See* BAKER, *supra* note 9, at 41–55.

Choosing what products to consume is a kind of liberty, but it does not exhaust the liberty of free expression. The ability to produce, create, and innovate is just as important. These two forms of liberty are not fungible, and markets do not adequately measure the difference between them.[80] To protect freedom of expression, then, we must make a space for individual cultural appropriation and production. We should not choose a form of political economy that gives greater incentives to be a passive recipient than an active creator of culture.

Democratic culture is a regulative ideal. It offers a picture of what the world could look like given the technology we now have. It offers a picture of what freedom of speech could be in a digital world. Nevertheless, digital technology does not guarantee the production of a democratic culture. As I noted previously, businesses are now using the new technologies to attempt to constrain and channel democratic participation. They are doing so both through laws and through technological solutions, including packet discrimination and digital rights management. And they are justifying these innovations through an interpretation of freedom of speech that ties speech to property rights. This capitalist conception is important both for its explanation of what freedom of speech is (freedom from business regulation) and what it is not (an enforceable limit on the expansion of intellectual property rights).

The ideal of democratic culture is important precisely as a critical perspective that allows us to criticize this emerging interpretation of free speech and intellectual property. The developing capitalist conception of freedom of speech (and its accompanying denial of free speech limitations on the growth of intellectual property) is inconsistent with the promotion of a democratic culture. The same technological changes that suggested what a democratic culture might become have produced a very different interpretation of the free speech principle that ties it ever more closely to the ownership of the forms of capital characteristic of the information age—intellectual property and control over distribution networks. The idea of a democratic culture stands as a critique of this emerging property-based conception. That critique is crucial, because the architecture of the digital age and the law that governs distribution networks are up for grabs. They can develop in many different ways, and the point is to ensure that they develop in the right ways.

---

[80] Purchasing media products is a kind of liberty, because it involves choice. It is also a kind of creativity, because an agreement between a willing buyer and a willing seller creates wealth. But it does not exhaust the forms of choice and creativity with which freedom of speech is concerned.

VIII

THE JUDICIAL MODEL AND ITS LIMITATIONS

To protect freedom of speech in the digital age, we will have to reinterpret and refashion both telecommunications policy and intellectual property law to serve the values of freedom of speech, which is to say, we will have to fashion and interpret them with the goals of a democratic culture in mind.

How is this to be done? I have argued that the digital age subtly alters our understanding of liberty of expression. I believe it also changes how that liberty might be protected.

Throughout the twentieth century, the most familiar method of protecting freedom of speech was through the judicial creation and protection of individual legal rights, and in particular, constitutional rights. Of course, when we look more closely, we will also discover many other features of public policy that promoted free speech values. They include, among other things, free public education, the creation and maintenance of public libraries, a nationwide public mail system, subsidies for postage for books and publications by nonprofit organizations, the use of common carrier models for telephony, and national telecommunications policies that attempted to lower costs and increase access to radio and television. For the most part, however, these policies have been regarded as largely peripheral to the main event—the judicial recognition and creation of doctrines that protect free speech rights from government censorship or other forms of government regulation.

Indeed, the very success of the program of expanding individual free speech rights protected by courts made it an article of faith that this was how freedom of speech should be secured—through the judicial creation and protection of individual rights of free expression enforceable against state actors. This notion has two important and distinct assumptions. First, it assumes that one protects freedom of expression through protecting individual rights of free speech, rather than through creating systems of communication and information-sharing used by lots of people that facilitate free expression. Put differently, it views the system of free expression as no more than the sum of all of the individual rights of free expression. Second, the model assumes that these individual rights will be created and protected primarily by courts, rather than by legislatures or administrative agencies, or, for that matter, by engineers, software designers, and technology companies.

Nevertheless, the examples I mentioned earlier—free public education, free public libraries, common carrier rules in telephony, public interest rules in telecommunications, a public mail system, government subsidies for books and nonprofit publications, and so on—do not match these assumptions. They are policies and institutions that promote a healthy and democratic system of free expression, but they are not composed of individual free speech rights. Rather, they combine lots of different private rights with various government programs and entitlements, and in the case of telecommunications regulations, they may even include requirements for technological design. Second, these features of the system of free expression are not always primarily created or protected by courts. Rather, they are created by a number of parties, including legislatures and administrative agencies.

The model of judicial protection of individual rights remains crucially important in the digital age. But it will not be able to protect freedom of speech fully. The digital age makes increasingly apparent what has always been the case—that the system of free expression relies on something more than the sum of all individual free speech rights. It relies on a technological and regulatory infrastructure. That infrastructure is produced through government regulation, through government subsidies and entitlement programs, and through technological design. Freedom of speech is, and always has been, a cultural phenomenon as well as a legal or political one. A healthy and well-functioning system of free expression depends on technologies of communication and a public ready and able to use those technologies to participate in the growth and development of culture.

In the digital age, the technological and regulatory infrastructure that undergirds the system of free expression has become increasingly important. Elements of the system of free expression that were backgrounded in the twentieth century will become foregrounded in the twenty-first. They will be foregrounded, I argue, because the guarantee of a pure formal liberty to speak will increasingly be less valuable if technologies of communication and information storage are biased against widespread individual participation and toward the protection of property rights of media corporations. If we place too much emphasis on judicial doctrine at the expense of infrastructure, we will be left with formal guarantees of speech embedded in technologies of control that frustrate their practical exercise.

The system of free expression is produced through the synergy of (1) government policies that promote popular participation in technologies of communication, (2) technological designs that facilitate decentralized control and popular participation rather than hinder them, and (3) the traditional recognition and enforcement of judicially created rights against government censorship. The last of these—judicial creation and enforcement of rights of free speech against government abridgement—is the great achievement of the twentieth century. Nevertheless, I believe that in the long run it will be recognized as only one leg of a three-legged stool that supports the system of free expression. The other elements will increasingly move to the foreground of concern as it becomes clear that they are necessary to the promotion of a democratic culture.

IX

THE INFRASTRUCTURE OF FREE EXPRESSION: FROM FREE SPEECH RIGHTS TO FREE SPEECH VALUES

As the focus shifts from an exclusive concern with judicially protected individual constitutional rights to an additional concern with infrastructure, we must also shift our concern from free speech *rights* narrowly considered to free speech *values*. Free speech rights are rights of individuals enforceable by courts. Free speech values are values that we seek to promote through legislative and administrative regulation and through technological design.

Protecting freedom of speech in the digital age means promoting a core set of values in legislation, administrative regulation, and the design of technology. What are those values? They are interactivity, broad popular participation, equality of access to information and communications technology, promotion of democratic control in technological design, and the practical ability of ordinary people to route around, glom on, and transform. Free speech values include those aspects of liberty of expression that the digital age makes most salient: popular participation, interactivity, and the encouragement and protection of cultural creativity and cultural transformation.

Both technological architectures and legal regimes of regulation must be structured to make possible full and robust participation by individuals. Free speech values must enter both into the content of laws and the design of architectures of communication. That is because the key forms of capital in the digital era—intellectual property and telecommunications networks—can serve both as conduits for increased democratic cultural participation or as chokepoints and bottlenecks, centralizing control in the hands of a relatively few persons and organizations. What form informational capital will take, how it will be used, how it will be shared or if it will be shared at all, are the crucial questions of the digital age.

At stake in both intellectual property and telecommunications regulation is the question of democratic participation versus centralized control. This is most obvious in the context of distribution networks: The capitalist theory of free speech asserts the right of the owner of a communications network to control the flow of digital content through the network. But the capitalist theory also seeks to expand intellectual property rights so that rights holders can control the distribution, use, and transformation of media products even after these products are distributed and sold to a mass audience. The theory of free speech as democratic culture, by contrast, argues that both communications networks and intellectual property rights must facilitate broad cultural participation. Communications networks are public in nature even if their technological infrastructure is privately owned. Therefore they must grant fair access to their networks, they must not act as chokepoints or bottlenecks, and they must not unfairly discriminate against content from other sources. Intellectual property rights must also serve democratic ends: They exist to promote the spread of culture and possibilities for cultural innovation and transformation.

To make intellectual property consistent with the idea of free speech as democratic culture, there must be a robust and ever expanding public domain with generous fair use rights. Intellectual property also must not be permitted to create chokepoints or bottlenecks in the spread of knowledge and the distribution of culture.

Judicial creation and protection of individual rights is ill equipped to deal with many of the most important problems of freedom of speech in the digital era. Free speech values are often either promoted or hindered by the ways that technologies are designed and the ways that technological standards are set. Technological designs and standards can let private parties become gatekeepers and bottlenecks controlling the flow of information and the scope of permissible innovation; or, conversely, they can promote widespread participation and innovation.

Law has an important role to play here. Laws affect how technology is designed, the degree of legal protection that a certain technology will enjoy, and whether still other technologies that modify or route around existing technological forms of distribution and control will be limited or forbidden. But increasingly, these sorts of decisions will be made by legislatures and administrative agencies in consultation with private parties. Generally speaking, courts come to free speech controversies after technologies are already in place and deals between stakeholders have already been struck. Courts can construe existing statutes to protect free speech values. But in most cases they cannot easily order that particular new technologies or new standards be implemented. They cannot easily hold, for example, that a certain technological design must be adopted. They cannot insist that private companies refrain from using certain digital rights management tech-

54   NEW YORK UNIVERSITY LAW REVIEW   [Vol. 79:1

nologies in return for a congressional statute that sets up a compulsory licensing scheme. Courts can remand lower court and administrative agency decisions, but they cannot easily remand technologies to their designers and ask them to make the technology more free speech friendly. Nor can they order or oversee the sort of comprehensive bargains that contemporary intellectual property regulation increasingly requires. Those tasks will fall to other actors, with courts enforcing the legal bargains that are produced consistent with free speech values.

The free speech values I have identified—participation, access, interactivity, democratic control, and the ability to route around and glom on—won't necessarily be protected and enforced through judicial creation of constitutional rights. Rather, they will be protected and enforced through the design of technological systems—code—and through legislative and administrative schemes of regulation, for example, through open access requirements or the development of compulsory license schemes in copyright law.

This transforms the study of freedom of speech to the study of the design of architectures and regulatory systems. It is no accident, I think, that many of the people who are at the forefront of the push for freedom in cyberspace are computer scientists, engineers, and software programmers, and it is no accident that lawyers who do cyberlaw spend an increasing amount of time thinking about technological and administrative solutions to civil rights issues. That is because, as I have argued, free speech values are embedded both in administrative regulations and in technological design. To protect free speech in the digital age, lawyers have to become cyberlawyers,[81] not simply lawyers who study cyberlaw, but lawyers who think about how technology can best be structured and how public policies can best be achieved through wise technological design.[82]

Conclusion: Rights Dynamism

I return to the question I posed at the beginning of this essay: How should the theoretical justifications for freedom of speech change given the change in social conditions produced by the digital age?

We can now offer an answer to this question. Technological change presents new possibilities for freedom of expression, shows the value of free speech in a different light, and makes particular features

---

[81] *See* Beth Simone Noveck, *Designing Deliberative Democracy in Cyberspace: The Role of the Cyber-Lawyer*, 9 B.U. J. Sci. & Tech. L. 1, 5, 8–10 (2003).

[82] *See, e.g.*, Lessig, Code and Other Laws of Cyberspace, *supra* note 17, at 3–8.

of freedom of speech particularly salient. These features include interactivity, mass participation, nonexclusive appropriation, and creative transformation. This in turn leads us to a new conception of the purposes of freedom of speech, which I have called the promotion of a democratic culture.

However, these same technological changes also create new forms of social conflict, as business interests try to protect new forms of capital investment. This leads, in turn, to attempts to protect and expand rights in intellectual property and in the control of telecommunications networks. These rights claims clash with freedom of speech values in ever new ways; and the attempt to protect property rights in capital investment leads to competing visions of what freedom of speech is and what it is not.

Finally, as technological innovation alters the social conditions of speech, the technological and legal infrastructure that supports the system of free expression becomes foregrounded. As a result, free speech values must be articulated and protected in new ways, in particular, through the design of technology and through legislative and administrative regulation of technology, in addition to the traditional focus on judicial doctrines that protect constitutional rights.

As the world changes around us, as the possibilities and problems of new technologies are revealed, our conception of the free speech principle begins to change with them. Our sense of what freedom of speech is, why we value it, and how best to preserve that which we value, reframes itself in the changing milieu. And as we respond to these changes, retracing our steps and rethinking our goals, we eventually come to understand what the free speech principle is about, and more importantly, what it always was about but only now can be adequately expressed. That experience is not the experience of making something new. It is the experience of finding something old, of recognizing principles and commitments already dimly understood, which suddenly are thrown into sharper focus by the alteration in our circumstances.

The arguments in this essay are an outgrowth of a more general way of thinking about rights and fundamental liberties. Call it a dynamic theory of rights, or *rights dynamism*. Rights dynamism is the claim that the nature, scope, and boundaries of rights, and in particular fundamental rights like speech, are continually shifting with historical, political, economic, and technological changes in the world.[83]

---

[83] For a more general account of legal historicism, of which dynamism is a special case, see Jack M. Balkin & Sanford Levinson, *Legal Historicism and Legal Academics: The Roles of Law Professors in the Wake of Bush v. Gore*, 90 Geo. L.J. 173, 174–75 (2001) (defining legal historicism as claim that legal conventions and forms of legal argument

56   *NEW YORK UNIVERSITY LAW REVIEW*   [Vol. 79:1

The content and scope of those rights, the interests they protect and the interests they leave unprotected, change as the language of rights and the enforcement of rights are placed in new contexts, and are invoked by different actors and different economic and social interests. Hence it is necessary for those who believe in the language of rights—and in the recognition and protection of basic and fundamental rights such as the liberty of expression—to rethink the premises of rights as the discourse of rights is invoked in emerging social contexts. For only through constant rethinking, in the face of changed circumstances, can we recall and rediscover what our deepest commitments truly are. What appears to be change is actually continuity; what appears to be revision is actually the deepest form of remembrance.

Most people, I suspect, will be wary of such historicism for an obvious reason. If rights are truly fundamental, and therefore worth protecting and fighting for, their content should be relatively fixed over time. We should not alter what is protected and what is not protected every time we come across a result we do not like, for if the content and scope of basic liberties can change, and if they must be retheorized and reconceptualized in each generation, who is to say that they will not be eroded, undermined, or effectively destroyed? Even if we only set out to change our attitudes about these basic rights at the margins, jettisoning some elements and adding others, who is to say that we will not throw out the baby with the bathwater? What security do we have in rights that can change as history changes?

I do not underestimate these worries, or the force of these concerns. They describe a great danger for liberty. They articulate the threat that all historicism (and all relativism) present to principle and to principled argument. But here is the catch. If we do not, from time to time, rethink the scope and extension of our basic liberties, their scope and extension will change anyway, whether we like it or not. For faced as we are with social, technological, and economic change, other people will be busily rewriting rights and turning them to their own advantage. And if we do nothing to contest their work in an

---

gradually change in response to political and social struggles that are waged through them). *See also* PAUL BREST, SANFORD LEVINSON, J.M. BALKIN & AKHIL REED AMAR, PROCESSES OF CONSTITUTIONAL DECISIONMAKING, at xxxi–xxxii (4th ed. 2000) (articulating theory of constitutional historicism). I am using the term "dynamism" rather than historicism in order to emphasize two separate points: First, rights dynamism is internal to participants in the practice of rights discourse rather than a stance that merely studies the discourse from the outside with no particular stake in its outcome. Second, rights dynamism is forward-looking, concerned with the future of a practice whose full contours cannot be known in advance, rather than a backward-looking historicism that attempts to articulate and comprehend changes that occurred in the distant past.

altered environment, we will soon find ourselves living with a set of fundamental rights framed and shaped according to their interests and their agendas.

Rights are a form of discourse, a way of thinking about the needs of social order and human liberty in the context of a changing world. Rights are also a source of power—first, because they are a powerful form of rhetorical appeal, and second, because the enforcement of rights recognized by the state is backed up the power of the state. Because of this, rights and rights discourse are continually invoked by people and by groups to further their ideals, interests, and agendas: For the discourse of rights is the discourse of power, the restructuring of rights is the restructuring of power, and the securing of rights is the securing of power.

⊍ As people face new problems and altered circumstances, they naturally invoke elements of existing rights discourses, hoping to extend them in preferred directions in order to articulate their moral and political ends and further their favored policies. They call upon the struggles and victories of the past and the legal concepts of the present in order to shape the future. This is as true of groups and interests we like as those we oppose.

Rights are not simply a fixed set of protections that the state affords or fails to afford. Rights are a terrain of struggle in a world of continuous change—a site of ongoing controversies, a battleground where the shape and contours of the terrain are remade with each victory. Rights, and particularly fundamental rights, far from being fixed and immovable, are moving targets. They are worth fighting over because the discourse of rights has power and because that discourse can be reshaped and is reshaped through intellectual debate and political struggle.

This feature of rights discourse is a special case of what I have called "ideological drift." The liberty of expression has no special security from such drift. To the contrary, it is subject to the pushing and pulling, the reconceptualizations and transvaluations to which all other rights are heir. The capitalist theory of rights that I have described previously is only the most recent example.

⊰ If one loves liberty, and believes that there are basic liberties that every decent society should recognize and protect, one must also recognize that the rhetorical reconstruction of rights will be ongoing whether we or others perform it. What we do not do for ourselves will surely be done to us.

Eternal vigilance, it is often said, is the price of liberty. But that vigilance is of two forms. The first kind of vigilance is the vigilance of the guardian, who attempts to ensure that every feature and aspect of liberty is preserved today just as it was in ages past. But the second and far more important form of vigilance is the vigilance of the guide or explorer, who helps others make the transition from the world they knew to the one that awaits them.

People are continually thrown into new circumstances and they must articulate the meaning of liberty in those new circumstances. The task of such a guide or explorer is to find the meaning of the old in the new, and to prevent the rhetoric of liberty from becoming liberty's prison. Such vigilance is every bit as important as the vigilance of the guardian. And this vigilance, too, is eternal, and its exercise, too, is the ineluctable price of liberty. The world will not stand still and let us enjoy our freedoms. It will continually make itself anew, and as it does, we must consider the ever-changing predicament of liberty, and the ever new methods by which it may be augmented or curtailed.

The digital revolution is a revolution, and like all revolutions, it is a time of confusion, a time of transition, and a time of opportunity for reshaping the structures of the economy and the sources of power. As a time of opportunity it is also a time of opportunism, a period in which the meaning of liberty of expression will be determined for good or for ill, just as the meaning of economic liberty was determined in an earlier age. Make no mistake: The digital age will change the meaning of freedom of expression. The only question is how it will change. If we do not reconsider the basis of liberty in this age, if we do not possess the vigilance of the guide as well as the guard, we shall end up like every person who travels through the wilderness without a compass, or through the forest without the forester. We shall end up lost.

[5]

Media Freedom and Political Debate in the Digital Era

Jacob Rowbottom*

This article examines the impact of online expression on theories of media freedom. While media freedom has generally been justified instrumentally, the opportunities for expression via the Internet may require greater emphasis on the interests of the individual speaker. Despite this development, this article shows how a small number of speakers will still command a much wider audience and have greater influence over political debate. For such speakers the approach to media freedom devised in the mass media era will remain applicable.

Since its inception, the new media has been predicted to revolutionise political communications.[1] While it is still early days and the technology continues to develop, many predictions have been partially realised. In the 2004 US elections, the weblog (blog), which allows individuals to keep a log of their comments and views online and to update them regularly, was the most talked about development. The blogs produced by individual citizens were seen to act as a watchdog on both politicians and the established media. While this was the big story of 2004, there is no reason to assume the blog will be the dominant format in the future. Already there is talk of podcasting and videoblogging superseding the text-based blog. The new technology is said to be breaking down the barrier between citizen and journalist. An indication of this process was apparent in the wake of the July 2005 bombings in London. Pictures of the immediate aftermath and videos of police raids taken with mobile phones helped to tell the story to the rest of the world. Developments in technology are not restricted to individuals; the established media are also adapting their services. The BBC, for example, already makes a number of its television programmes available for viewing online and many media providers are looking for ways to allow the audience to interact with and comment upon their content. A number of established media entities are buying up companies associated with new media, for example BSkyB has acquired the broadband supplier Easynet;[2] ITV has bought Friends Reunited

---

*King's College, Cambridge. With thanks to Michael Birnhack, the participants of the Cambridge University Public Law Discussion Group and the anonymous referees for comments on earlier drafts.

1 New media is used to describe a wide range of media based on information technology, such as the Internet, World Wide Web, video games and instant messaging. The focus of this article will be online expression, referring to communications on the Internet.

2 *The Times*, 17 October 2005.

490   Media Freedom and Political Debate

and News Corp has bought the owners of myspace.com, Intermix.[3] Such moves reflect the established media's goal to increase their use of digital technologies to distribute content.

These developments raise the question of whether online content should be subject to the same regulations as other types of media or be relatively free of any restraints. If a website features political advocacy in an election campaign, should it carry the name and address of the publisher as is required for printed posters supporting candidates?[4] Should some online content providers be subject to right of reply laws or a duty to cover certain types of content? A heavy-handed approach to regulation may discourage innovation by individual users, as seen in the blogs and many individual websites. However, a hands-off approach carries the danger of undermining the public duties of the media and allowing political debate to become skewed. Such issues are heightened if online technologies become the dominant mode of political communication.

This article does not seek to answer these specific questions, but will address two preliminary issues. First, whether the normative approach to dealing with media freedom should be modified in the light of these changes and place greater emphasis on the individual speaker. The second issue is whether these changes lead to a new paradigm in which regulations to promote the public service element of media activity are inappropriate. In addressing these issues, this article will consider arguments that online expression requires a different approach from that accorded to the traditional mass media. The main grounds for a new approach are premised upon the low cost of communications; the relative ease of participation; the greater emphasis on user control and consequent demise of mediators and controlling elites. While accepting the many beneficial changes brought about through online communications, this article will argue that rather than generating a level playing field, online expression can not only perpetuate existing media elites, but also create new ones. Consequently, online expression operates at different tiers, as found in the offline world. The regulatory approach may therefore require different methods depending on the tier of expression.

In making this argument, the article will be divided into five sections. The first will look at the traditional approaches to regulating the mass media and the relationship between expression rights and media freedom. The second section will examine some of the academic responses to the Internet and its impact on the media and freedom of expression. The third section will consider the increased opportunities for individual participation on the Internet, which differentiate it from traditional forms of mass media. The fourth section will then show how certain media organisations/speakers maintain an elite status online that gives disproportionate influence over public debate. Finally, possible strategies of regulation and the various pitfalls will be outlined. While this raises a range of important issues for different categories of expression, the central focus of this article will be the coverage of politics and political debate, an issue that lies at the heart of the democratic and public service functions of the media.

---

3 *The Daily Telegraph*, 7 December 2005.
4 See the discussion in The Electoral Commission, *Online Election Campaigns: Report and Recommendations* [2003] at paras [4.10–4.16].

Underlying this argument is a view that the regulation of the media and the protection of its freedom must be understood in the context of how people communicate. A system designed with pamphleteers in mind would surely be inappropriate in an age where television is the dominant form of mass communication. Similarly it is necessary to ask whether the development of online expression, such as the Internet, changes why and how we should protect media freedom.[5] This is not to adopt a position of technological determinism. Law does not take a secondary role; it takes an active role in shaping how the technology develops and how it will be used. The current media practices are in part a product and reflection of the regulatory environment. However, the regulatory environment may need to be adapted to respond to these practices. Such changes in the regulation may help ensure that the technology and its use continue to develop in ways that reflect democratic and public service values.

MEDIA FREEDOM AND MODELS OF MEDIA REGULATION

The model of media regulation must be considered in light of rights of expression and media freedom. The relationship between the right of expression and media freedom is complex.[6] Starting with freedom of expression, three well-known justifications are often advanced.[7] The first view is that freedom of expression is essential to a person's autonomy and self-fulfilment. The second is the marketplace of ideas, that minimal government regulation will allow robust debate between citizens that is most likely to lead to the truth. The third justification is that freedom of expression is a necessary component of democratic government. There is an overlap between these justifications and all have been subject to extensive criticisms.[8] Instrumental justifications are often invoked to support media freedom, for example as providing a public function in disseminating information, viewpoints and ideas.[9] As Lord Bingham explained in *McCartan Turkington Breen v Times Newspapers*:

> the majority cannot participate in the public life of their society . . . if they are not alerted to and informed about matters which call or may call for consideration and action. It is very largely through the media . . . that they will be so alerted and informed. The proper functioning of modern participatory democracy requires that the media be free, active, professional and enquiring.[10]

---

5 O. Fiss, 'In Search of a New Paradigm' (1995) 104 *Yale Law Journal* 1613.
6 For a discussion see G. Marshall, 'Press Freedom and Free Speech Theory' [1992] *Public Law* 40; E. Barendt, *Freedom of Speech* (Oxford: Oxford University Press, 2005) 419–424.
7 See Barendt, *ibid*, ch 1 for a discussion of the justifications.
8 For a recent contribution, see L. Alexander, *Is There a Right of Freedom of Expression?* (Cambridge: Cambridge University Press, 2005) ch 7.
9 Barendt, n 6 above, 417–418; J. Litchenberg, 'Foundations and Limits of Freedom of the Press' in J. Litchenberg (ed), *Democracy in the Mass Media* (Cambridge: Cambridge University Press, 1990). Professor Edwin Baker stresses the liberty theory rationale for individual expression, but relies on instrumental justifications in relation to media freedom, E. Baker, *Human Liberty and Freedom of Speech* (New York: OUP, 1989) ch 10.
10 *McCartan Turkington Breen v Times Newspapers* [2001] 2 AC 277, 290–291.

It is harder to maintain that media freedom is valuable because it contributes to the self-fulfilment of the speaker. Only a limited number of people can air their views on television or write their own newspaper column. A barrier exists between the journalist or reporter, and the audience. Even if speakers are granted access to the mass media, this right can only be engaged by a small number of groups or individuals.[11] The value of media freedom comes from the way it serves the interests of the public and audience.[12]

That media freedom is instrumentally justified tells us little about how this freedom is best protected. For example, in the US Justice Stewart argued for the autonomy of select media institutions, distinct from other speech rights, to secure independence from the government.[13] This has not been the approach adopted by the courts in the US, under the European Convention on Human Rights (ECHR) or in UK law. A contrasting view is reflected in Sir John Donaldson's statement that the media's 'right to know and their right to publish is neither more nor less than that of the general public'.[14] However, equating media freedom with that of individual speakers is not always helpful given that the way the media exercise their freedom will be different from that of individual speakers, given the scale and influence of their operations. Furthermore, the two freedoms may conflict. Those controlling the mass media may use their freedom to undermine the expression rights of others, for example excluding particular points of view. While the same point may be made about other institutions that control forums for expression,[15] the point is particularly pressing for the media given its reach and influence over public debate. Consequently, Professor Judith Litchenberg writes:

> Unlike freedom of speech, to which certain aspects of which our commitment must be virtually unconditional, freedom of the press should be contingent on the degree to which it promotes certain values at the core of our interest in freedom of expression generally.[16]

This approach can be seen in the European Court of Human Rights' jurisprudence under Article 10 where special protection is granted to the media when performing its 'public watchdog' role 'to impart information and ideas of public interest'.[17] This protection is granted to the media not as an institution, but rather

---

11   For example, party election broadcasts give political parties direct access to the broadcast media, but this opportunity is limited only to a small number of speakers that contest over a sixth of all seats contested at a general election.
12   In the US precedent giving strongest support for the regulation of the broadcast media, *Red Lion* v *FCC* (1969) 395 US 367, Justice White stated at 390: 'It is the right of the viewers and listeners, not the right of the broadcasters, which is paramount'. In the UK in *R* v *Radio Authority, ex p Bull* [1998] QB 294 and *Prolife Alliance* v *BBC* [2003] UKHL 23 restrictions on media freedom were upheld, taking into account the impact on the audience. However, even if the interests of the audience are taken into account, such an approach rarely gives individual audience members enforceable rights against the media, see E. Barendt, *Broadcasting Law* (Oxford: Clarendon Press, 1995) 47–49.
13   P. Stewart, 'Or of the Press' (1975) 26 *Hastings Law Journal* 631.
14   *Attorney General* v *Guardian Newspapers (No 2)* [1990] 1 AC 109, 183.
15   For example where protestors are excluded from private land that is widely used by the public, such as shopping malls, see *Appleby* v *UK* (2003) 37 EHRR 38.
16   J. Litchenberg, n 9 above, 104.
17   *Jersild* v *Denmark* (1995) 19 EHRR 1.

to the product of the speaker and its capacity to serve debate on matters in the public interest.

The view that media freedom should be protected in so far as it serves that value of freedom of expression helps to explain why some regulations of media activities are consistent with Article 10.[18] The point should not be overstated, as the ECtHR's support for media regulation is limited to merely finding it consistent with Article 10 as a necessary limit on the media expression, rather than finding it to be a necessary component of expression rights. Craufurd Smith argues that the regulation of the media need not be seen in this way as a necessary limitation of expression rights, but can be seen as a way of promoting the conditions for free expression.[19] Even though the ECtHR has not gone this far, the recognition that some regulation is necessary in a democratic society is still important, as if media freedom is an unqualified guarantee against state interference, then the media may simply become an outlet for a self-interested point of view, such as the views of the owners of private media. Such a scenario raises the danger that media freedom will be asserted simply to protect the economic interests of the media company or other property owner, rather than to serve democratic goals or the public interest.[20] The mass media, with the high costs of access and control in the hands of an elite, requires some oversight to prevent its important social and democratic functions being skewed in the interests of a small number of speakers or gatekeepers.

None of this is to say that all regulation of the media is justified, it must be shown that the regulation will serve democratic needs. What type of media regime best serves these needs depends on the model of democracy to be applied.[21] While consideration of the various different models is beyond the scope of this paper, most models of democracy will require some level of news coverage, the presentation of information and analysis, and the provision of diverse viewpoints. Different regimes of regulation have traditionally applied to different types of media. The print media is subject to public interest regulation governing ownership and to those regulations applying to all types of expression, but is not subject to content regulations seeking to promote pluralism, for example it is under no duty of balance or fairness in political coverage. By contrast, the broadcast media in the UK are subject to stricter regulations. All licensed broadcasters are subject to a basic tier of regulation imposing requirements of accuracy and impartiality, and taste and decency.[22] Advertisements on the broadcast media are subject to controls on timing and content, and no political advertisements are permitted on television or radio. Those designated as public service broadcasters

---

18 *Groppera Radio AG v Switzerland* (1990) 12 EHRR 321; *Informationsverein Lentia v Austria* (1994) 17 EHRR 93; *Ediciones Tiempo v Spain* (1989) 62 D & R 247. It has been assumed in the UK that laws regulating media ownership to promote media pluralism are consistent with expression rights.

19 R. Craufurd Smith, *Broadcasting Law and Fundamental Rights* (Oxford: Clarendon Press, 1997) 179–180.

20 See O. Fiss, *Liberalism Divided: Freedom of Speech and the Many Uses of State Power* (New York: Westview Press, 1996) ch 1 and C. Sunstein, *Democracy and the Problem of Free Speech* (New York: The Free Press, 1995) ch 3.

21 For an outline of how the different theories of democracy point to different media roles, see E. Baker, *Media Markets and Democracy* (Cambridge: Cambridge University Press, 2002) ch 6.

22 See the OFCOM Broadcasting Code (2005) and BBC Royal Charter (1996–2006).

are subject to extra tiers of regulation, for example requiring a certain level of educational and cultural programmes to be broadcast. The distinction is reflected in the Article 10 jurisprudence that permits more intensive regulations on the broadcast media.[23] Why the distinct regulatory regimes have developed has been the subject of much debate,[24] and the difference is presented as social and historical rather than theoretical.[25] Consequently, many of the regulations applied to the broadcast media may justifiably be imposed on the press, and vice versa, if it serves democratic needs such as pluralism and diversity.

The precise model of regulation appropriate for online expression is still being worked out.[26] It has been argued that online expression should fit the print model,[27] or is at least closer to that model, rather than the broadcast regulatory regime.[28] The White Paper that formed the basis of the UK Communications Act explained that Internet material should be subject to regulation a tier below the most relaxed standards applied to broadcasters.[29] Online content is exempt from the regulations applied to broadcasters[30] and is subject to general regulations imposed on expression, such as public order laws, defamation, confidentiality and intellectual property. However, the European Commission has proposed extending the Television Without Frontiers Directive to some types of audio-visual content distributed online, suggesting that some online content is similar to the broadcast media.[31] Many of the services provided online have qualities analogous to either type of media. For example, more news providers ranging from the BBC to *The Sun* provide text based and video services on their websites. While online expression has been subject to less regulation than other types of established media, this position needs to be reassessed as more of its services move closer to the current output of broadcasters.

A further point to be noted at the outset is that the level of invasiveness is sometimes used to differentiate types of media. The broadcast media is seen to *push* its content onto the audience without request. By contrast, other types of media,

---

23 Article 10(1) provides that it 'shall not prevent States from requiring the licensing of broadcasting, television or cinema enterprises'. The degree of autonomy this grants to states to regulate the broadcast media is uncertain, see *Informationsverein Lentia*, n 18 above; Groppera, n 18 above; *Autronic AG v Switzerland* (1990) 12 EHRR 485. In the UK, see *Prolife Alliance*, n 12 above at [20]–[21].

24 Barendt, *Broadcasting Law*, n 12 above, 3–10. For a recent criticism see C. S. Yoo, 'The Rise and Demise of the Technology-Specific Approach to the First Amendment' (2003) 91 *Georgetown Law Journal* 245.

25 J. Seaton and J. Curran, *Power Without Responsibility: The Press and Broadcasting in Britain* (London: Routledge, 2003) ch 23.

26 See A. van Loon, 'The end of the broadcasting era' 9 *Communications Law* 172 [2004].

27 See *Reno v ACLU* (1997) 521 U.S. 844. 868–870; T. Krattenmaker and L. Powe, 'Converging First Amendment Principles for Converging Communications Media' (1995) 104 *Yale Law Journal* 1719.

28 Barendt (2005), n 6 above, 456.

29 *Communications White Paper: A New Future for Communications* (December 2004) para 5.9.

30 Communications Act 2003, s 361. See T. Ballard, 'Television Over the Internet: The Boundaries of Content Regulation' [2004] CTLR 58.

31 The European Commission, *Legislative Proposal for the Revision of the 'Television Without Frontiers' Directive*, 13 December 2005. The Television Without Frontiers Directive does not cover public service regulations, which are left to national law. The Commission proposes a two-tier system in which basic rules apply to all audiovisual services, whereas the more onerous Television Without Frontiers Directive will apply only to linear audiovisual services. Non-commercial and private mass and individual communications are excluded from the proposals.

such as newspapers, require active steps by the audience to receive content, the user *pulls* the material from the source. The extent to which this distinction accurately describes the different types of media has been questioned, as it may exaggerate the passivity associated with television. The television viewer still can choose whether he or she wants to watch the television and what channel he or she wishes to view.[32] This level of control increases as more channels become available. Viewers of television are not only getting more choice in the numbers of programmes to watch, but also greater choice when to watch. For example, digital video recorders such as TiVo allow individuals to view programmes at their chosen time, filter advertisements and rewind live TV while watching. Many TV programmes also offer greater interactivity through participation in the form of SMS voting and the selection of additional content using the 'red button' on digital formats. The level of control given to the audience in the *pull* media can also be exaggerated given that a newspaper reader may be able to select a particular title, but beyond that cannot determine which issues are to be covered and in what depth. While the role of the audience varies according to the type of media, it is important not to exaggerate these differences.

Where the online media fits in this framework has been the subject of debate, and will vary according to the application.[33] In *ACLU v Reno*, Justice Stevens argued that 'the Internet is not as "invasive" as radio or television', given that it does not appear on a computer screen unbidden and that users are unlikely to encounter content online by accident.[34] Under this view, receiving content from an Internet webpage requires active steps in which an individual seeks out the particular source by either typing in a URL or choosing a particular link. While the digital media does provide greater opportunities for audience control and participation, this article will consider the limits to this argument. When an individual uses a search engine, he or she will not always be looking for a specific source or item of information, but is hoping to be told which sources will be most helpful or relevant. When a link is selected, it will normally be due to another source recommending that particular webpage. Furthermore, many users will simply return to the same sources or sites for particular types of content, or subscribe to direct feeds from that source. While the technology permits much greater participation for users, the social habits that shape the use of this media and the need for some guidance in navigating the mass of information will enable some online speakers to be able to *push* some of their content to a wide audience.

To summarise, many of the criticisms of the media lie in the fact that control lies in the hands of a few, whether this is through a state appointed broadcaster or through economic power in the private media. Consequently, media freedom cannot be equated with other forms of individual expression given that only a small group of people or institutions will be able to exercise media freedom. One goal of regulating the media is to ensure that media institutions perform their important social functions and exercise their power in conformity with

---

32 A. Briggs and P. Burke, *A Social History of the Media* (Cambridge: Polity, 2002) 322–323.

33 For example, email communications may be sent to the recipient without request, whereas viewing a webpage requires some active steps from the viewer.

34 *Reno v ACLU* (1997) 521 US 844, 869.

their democratic and social responsibilities.[35] Whether this concern applies to online expression is the question addressed in the remainder of this article.

HOPES AND FEARS FOR ONLINE EXPRESSION AND MEDIA FREEDOM

In the early days of the Internet it was hoped that the new media would remove many of the barriers that have traditionally excluded groups from public debate. In an optimistic vision, Professor Eugene Volokh argued in 1995 that online expression would promote 'cheap speech' which, while not eliminating inequalities, would transfer much power to users and speakers:

> the new technologies will make it much easier for all ideas, whether backed by the rich or poor, to participate in the marketplace. Even if many individuals still can't afford to counterspeak effectively, there'll be many more organizations able to speak out on all sides of an issue.[36]

The implication being that online speakers do not require regulation to ensure coverage of particular points of view or types of content. If there is demand for such coverage, there is nothing to stand in the way of its provision. Many of the economic barriers imposed on expression have been reduced, thereby alleviating some of the major complaints against the media. Furthermore, under this view the opportunities for private censorship are also reduced.[37] The marketplace of ideas is seen to function more fairly. While such optimism seems characteristic of the early response to the Internet, such sentiments have been revived with recent popular uses such as blogging.[38]

At the other end of the spectrum, Professor Cass Sunstein, in *Republic.com*, argues that while the Internet may help make expression less expensive and unmediated, it allows users to select information that conforms to their pre-existing views and to exclude opposing arguments through filtering technology.[39] In other words, the user can now, or will be able to, use the media to avoid being confronted with opposing points of view. The lack of an intermediary and decentralised nature of the Internet means that citizens will no longer share the same agenda, and people can retreat into their own virtual worlds. Given Sunstein's model of civic republicanism and deliberative democracy, he is concerned that individuals will use new media to satisfy their private preferences rather than in the service of civic duty. The point highlighted by Sunstein is distinct from the issue in this paper, in that he is concerned with the disappearance of intermediaries that help facilitate shared experience and promote deliberation. However, it is

---

35 Craufurd Smith, n 19 above, 57. Such a view can also be seen in OFCOM's justification of public service broadcasting regulation as serving the needs of citizenship, as opposed to merely correcting market failures, *OFCOM Review of Public Service Broadcasting, Phase 3* (2005) 26.

36 E. Volokh, 'Cheap Speech and What It Will Do' (1995) 104 *Yale Law Journal* 1805, 1847.

37 *ibid*, 1836.

38 For example, in March 2006 Rupert Murdoch stated that '[p]ower is moving away from the old elite in our industry' as a result of such uses of the developing technology, *The Independent*, 20 March 2006.

39 C. Sunstein, *Republic.com* (Princeton NJ: Princeton University Press, 2001).

important in that he does not believe unregulated online expression will serve the need for democratic debate.

Sunstein proposes a series of reforms that attempt to apply principles similar to the broadcast model to online expression, such as creating websites dedicated to public discourse, disclosure of the resources allocated to public interest issues by media companies, subsidies to sites promoting public discussion, and finally he proposes a scheme whereby conflicting viewpoints can access particular sites, by imposing must carry rules, link or hyperlink requirements. Supporting these measures, Sunstein deploys the arguments used in his earlier work on freedom of expression,[40] drawing analogies with the public forum[41] and pointing to the central role of state regulation in creating the Internet and protecting its commercial uses, for example by protecting the rights of those who register domain names.[42] As the regulation of digital speech is therefore unavoidable, the question moves from whether or not to regulate to become a question of what type of regulation will promote our collective goals. Sunstein's work is concerned with promoting the deliberative ideals that he believes underlie the protection of free speech guaranteed in the US Constitution. Sunstein believes that placing too much control in the hands of users may undermine the exchange and deliberation of ideas that is necessary in a democracy.

Sunstein's approach has been met with a number of criticisms. Firstly, those who were critical of his earlier work and reject his arguments in relation to the broadcast media will reject the arguments set out in *Republic.com*. Those who are generally sceptical of government intervention and believe that individuals should be trusted to make their own choices are no more likely to accept the regulation of online expression. A second set of objections is that there is something distinctive about online expression that makes the regulations inappropriate. Professor Dan Hunter argues that there is no need for state subsidies to promote deliberative websites as such websites are being established in any event.[43] Regulating for diversity is also misguided as being extremely wealthy is not a prerequisite for the setting up of a website. The Internet already covers a great deal of diverse information, allowing the democratic need for pluralism to be served without such onerous regulation. Furthermore, it is doubted whether the level of user selection envisaged by Sunstein will be technologically possible, and if it were then the proposed regulations would be easily evaded. This line of argument is that if these regulations were appropriate in an age of the mass media, online expression need not invoke the same concern. This approach does not depart from justification for media freedom outlined above, but rather suggests that such regulations are unnecessary to create a democratic media.

---

40 Sunstein, n 20 above.
41 Public forum is a term used in US First Amendment jurisprudence to describe areas to be used for public debate. Individuals may claim a right of access to public forums for the purpose of expressive activities. Traditionally this concept has been applied to publicly owned lands such as parks and open spaces, for a discussion of the concept see J. Rowbottom, 'Property and Participation: A Right of Access for Expressive Activities' [2005] EHRLR 186, 192–193 and 196. For a discussion of the concept in relation to the Internet see Barendt n 6 above, 456–458.
42 Sunstein, n 39 above, 132–134.
43 D. Hunter, 'Philippic.com' (2002) 90 Calif L Rev 611, 664.

Professor Jack Balkin's approach to online expression has elements of both lines of criticism.[44] He has criticised the policies advocated by Sunstein in relation to the broadcast media on the grounds they put too little weight on popular choices.[45] Balkin's argument also falls into the second school of thought that online expression is fundamentally distinct from other types of communication. He argues that the salient features of online expression undermine the theory of expression on which civic republican and deliberative models are based. In particular, he argues that theories of expression closely associated by civic republicanism have become limited and were devised in response to the specific issues raised by mass media:

> the paradigm case that motivates the progressivist agenda – the case of few speakers broadcasting to a largely inactive mass audience – no longer describes the world we live in.[46]

Whether the mass media audience were ever as passive as the statement suggests is questionable, but online expression offers more overt opportunities for interaction. Professor Balkin does not argue for deregulation of the media, but rather that participation should become a more central concern for this type of expression. Digital technologies facilitate greater participation in politics and culture, neither of which should be in the hands of an elite. Instead, people can participate in shaping culture in a way that was not possible before. It is therefore possible to emphasise freedom of expression from the point of view of the speaker without reinforcing the commercial interests of the media owner. Online expression is not just about the expression of a select number of individuals or institutions that control the media. Instead, the line between media freedom and individual expression becomes blurred, and greater emphasis on the interest of the speaker rather than the audience may be possible. The assumptions underlying the argument that there has been a paradigm shift will now be considered.

SELF-EXPRESSION AND PARTICIPATION ONLINE

As stated above, while traditional media freedom is hard to justify in terms of the interest of the speaker, there is less reason to overlook the needs of individual online speakers given the ease with which a person can create a blog, post a message or create a website. The shift from looking at expression from the point of view of the public or recipient to the point of view of speaker can be illustrated by various types of online expression, such as the blog. While the blog has been most prominent in the US, it has yet to have similar impact in the UK.[47] The blog is nevertheless worth examining as it represents the closest thing to realising the

---

44   J. Balkin, 'Digital Speech and Democratic Culture: A Theory of Freedom of Expression for the Information Society' (2004) 79 *New York University Law Review* 1.
45   J. Balkin, 'Populism and Progressivism as Constitutional Categories' (1995) 104 Yale LJ 1935.
46   Balkin, n 44 above, 31.
47   Although a Guardian/ICM poll found that 31% of 14–21 year olds with a web connection at home had launched their own website or blog, *The Guardian*, 7 October 2005.

democratised media sector predicted in the early days of the Internet.[48] Even if blogs never take off in the same way in the UK, other forms of popular media are likely to share similar characteristics.

Blogs give people a chance to express themselves on any topic and update the content with new posts on a daily basis. Individuals can advance their own views directly to the outside world in a way that is unmediated and not reliant on others to represent their views. Given the vast volume of blogs and the frequency with which they are updated, only a small number can reach a potentially wide audience. As the majority do not attain this potential, they cannot be considered analogous to the established mass media. The value of the blog lies more in the benefit to the authors as an outlet for their views, or potentially to converse, or exchange thoughts with a small network of people.[49] Writing in the mid twentieth century at a time when the mass media was becoming the dominant form of communication, Alexander Meiklejohn wrote:

> What is essential is not that everyone shall speak, but that everything worth saying shall be said. . . the vital point, as stated negatively, is that no suggestion of policy shall be denied a hearing because it is on one side of the issue rather than another.[50]

The view of blog given above appears to turn Meiklejohn's statement on its head. Given the varying quality and reliability of blog content, it matters not that every idea is heard, but that everyone has a chance to speak.

The approach given above moves away from expression serving the public interest and needs of the audience, to a form a self-presentation. As a Hansard Society report explained:

> To blog is declare your presence; to disclose to the world that you exist and what its like to be you; to affirm that your thoughts are at least as worth hearing as anyone else's; to emerge from the spectating audience as a player and maker of meanings.[51]

Freedom of expression in this context cannot be seen as a top down process, but as a two-way process of participation. The greater emphasis given to role of the speaker can be justified from both the self-fulfilment justification of protecting expression, or within the instrumental democratic role for the expression. Under the latter justification, the blog is seen to supplement the formal channels of representation. If a number of blogs create a collective buzz, it will signal to elected representatives and other institutions what issues are of greatest concern. Such involvement by the individual can be compared to the protest, where people

---

48 See M. Froomkin, 'Habermas@discourse.net: Toward a Critical Theory of Cyberspace' (2003) 116 Harv L Rev 749, 859–860.

49 See A. Reed, '"My Blog is Me": Texts and Persons in UK Online Journal Culture (and Anthropology)' (2005) 70 *Ethnos* 220. Although Reed does note that knowing someone else reads the posts is an important part of blogging and many bloggers seek a wider audience.

50 A. Meiklejohn, *Political Freedom* (New York: Harper, 1960) 26–27. For discussion in relation to the Internet, see Balkin, n 44 above.

51 R. Ferguson and M. Howell, *Political Blogs – Craze or Convention?* (London: Hansard Society, 2004) 26.

assemble in prominent places or write letters to well known newspapers, to get a sense of engagement from the system and perhaps have a real impact, rather than state their opinions to a few friends. Like the protest, the influence can also come about through large numbers of people coordinating their activities.

In this way, online expression can be a place for associative activities. This may take place in traditional formats such as interest group websites. While there is little new about this given that such groups have always produced newsletters and other forms of media, it may allow the interest group to reach a wider audience and allow more groups to use a wider range of media, such as audio-visual content or online discussions. The associative activities can take place in less formal ways, for example through a collectively produced website, or through websites or bloggers providing links to sites they closely identify with and discuss one another's content. Online expression may therefore warrant greater emphasis on individual and group participation, a modification of media freedom that can take place within the instrumental justifications for expression or through the self-fulfilment justification, and overlap with the protection of freedom of association.

The blog can change the way we think about media communication in other ways. The author can write from a private space, such as their home and often write about personal experiences, blurring the distinction between private and public expression.[52] The ideas may be incomplete or undeveloped. Just as when people speak in a private setting where they are comfortable, the blogger may use the blog to test ideas and try out arguments, without feeling that they must be committed to the principles in the future. Such blurring contrasts with the way the traditional media content is produced to appeal to a wide audience. Online expression also allows speakers to mix personal experiences with public issues. It gives individuals greater creativity in expressing their views, by allowing content to be copied and modified. Such examples can be seen in the 2005 UK general election where some web sites allowed users to 'remix' election messages, for example changing the wording of election posters.[53] As technology continues to make the use of sound files, video and graphics easier and less expensive, greater movement away from purely text-based services is likely to contribute to this trend. Already podcasting and video blogging enable users to regularly express themselves through sound and video files. The need to mix politics with entertainment may be necessary to reach the desired audience, especially as more and more sources compete for audience attention.

This section has illustrated how it is possible for individuals to participate in media activities as never before, not only in the ease of publishing their thoughts, but also broadening the scope of what can be done. Such a development modifies the thinking about media freedom to give greater emphasis on the perspective of the speaker, an emphasis that was not so central to traditional forms of mass communication. Such expression can also help create networks where influence arises through association. Consequently, such associative or small-scale expressive activity should not be subject to the type of public interest regulations found in the broadcast model. While this is an important development, it does not

---

52 S. Coleman, 'Blogs and the New Politics of Listening' [2005] *Political Quarterly* 273.
53 S. Coleman and S. Ward (eds), *Spinning the Web* (London: Hansard Society, 2005) 8.

completely change the paradigm. As argued in the next section, a handful of speakers or mediators will have disproportionate impact on political debate. Consequently, the elite speaking to the mass audience is still a central feature of the media, for which existing regulatory models may be appropriate. Cheap speech online is important, just as inexpensive expressive activities such as marches or demonstrations are important in the offline world, but there should not be illusions that this creates a level playing field in expression.

MEDIA ELITES AND ONLINE EXPRESSION

The traditional model of public interest media regulation is both suspicious of elites and the central control of the media, yet dependent on them. If control of the media rests in the hands of the few, then the danger exists that it will be used to promote a small number of limited viewpoints, to allow the views of the owner to have disproportionate influence on public discussion or simply ignore public affairs altogether. Yet some form of central control facilitates public interest regulation by providing a clear target for its provisions. The addition of so many online speakers comes at the expense of this order and control that was a necessary part of the mass media model. However, in this section it will be argued that the dominance of media elites will not become a thing of the past and even with the relatively low costs of distribution, a small number of speakers, often with substantial economic resources behind them, will consistently command a mass audience. Consequently, there will be certain types of online speaker that are appropriate targets for mass media regulations.

The established media in the offline world will continue to have a strong influence over public debate. Statistics from the 2005 general election show that while the number of people seeking information about the election online is increasing, the traditional sources such as television and newspapers are dominant.[54] While Internet use in political expression is more developed in the US, research from the Pew Center has shown a similar dominance of television as a source of political information.[55] Consequently, the Internet supplements the traditional media and provides an alternative source of information, rather than replacing traditional outlets. Taking the media as a whole, a level playing field for participants is still not in sight, and those elites controlling the traditional media have much greater influence over political debate than online sources. However, this point suggests that at present online expression does not support arguments for deregulating other sectors, but says little about the regulatory regime that should apply online. Even if this situation changes and the Internet becomes the dominant source of media content, the existing media elites will nonetheless remain. With such a wide range of material available online, people have to be selective about what they read and also need to know where to find the best material. The established and trusted media sites provide a convenient point to receive accurate news, so

---

54 *ibid*, 14.
55 J. Horrigan, K. Garrett, and P. Resnick, *The Internet And Democratic Debate* (Washington: Pew Internet and American Life Project, 2004) 4.

people will continue to visit the familiar names.[56] According to a Hansard Society report, the BBC was the most prevalent source of online political information in the 2005 UK general election, whereas candidates, lobby groups, blogs and tactical voting sites were 'virtually ignored'.[57]

A similar point can be made in relation to blogs. While much has been made of the rise of blogs in democratising the media, a small number receive a very high number of hits each day as well as links from other blogs and websites. Five 'star' bloggers based in the US average over a hundred thousand hits per day, whereas the vast majority of blogs receive much less traffic or links.[58] The reason for the 'star' blogger's success may partly be due to the talents of its author, the content and the frequency with which it is updated. However, even if a blog does have quality content, it takes time for this to become established and known. One way to get to know which websites and online sources are most reliable is through references in trusted sources. Blogs may gain audiences through word of mouth and links from other blogs and websites. If a blog has a significant audience, more people will be able to tell their friends about it or link it to their own website. This can lead to a snowballing effect, where the most popular websites become even more popular as the interest in blogs grows. Once the name and reputation is secured, the advantages can be self-reinforcing.[59] Consequently, getting the right links that can trigger a wider audience can be crucial to the blogger's success.

As this trend develops, the 'star' blogger plays a gatekeeping role, deciding which other sites to link to their blog. Many bloggers would resent being referred to as gatekeepers and argue that they merely lend their support to bloggers or campaigns that already have built up their own following.[60] Whatever basis on which the blogger chooses which views or stories to promote, and which campaigns to support, that choice made by the 'star' blogger will expose those views to a wide audience. The traditional media can have a similar effect, as providing coverage in the press or on television will bring the blog to a wider audience, as occurred with Salam Pax's blogs from Baghdad.[61] The offline media therefore acts as gatekeeper and helps to consolidate the 'star' blog or website. The high number of visitors that follow as a result of the publicity will help the blog gain more links and word of mouth visitors. The popularity of the site can bring about other advantages, for example, the revenues generated by advertising from a highly

---

56 Coleman, n 52 above, 278; R. Klotz, *The Politics of Internet Communication* (Maryland: Rowman and Littlefield, 2004),129.

57 Coleman and Ward, n 53 above, 7.

58 See rankings by traffic, www.truthlaidbear.com (last accessed 9 August 2005). Three of those five sites were also listed in the top ten most linked sites.

59 The extent to which this trend restricts the opportunities for less well known sites to gain a larger number of links is unclear and subject to debate, see D. Drezner and H. Farrell, 'The Power and Politics of Blogs' presented to the American Political Science Association 2004. (http://www. danieldrezner.com/research/blogpaperfinal.pdf, (last accessed 5 September 2005)).

60 *Daily Kos* posting 'I'm not a gatekeeper' 10 August 2005 (http://www.dailykos.com/story/2005/8/10/194917/041 (last accessed 15 December 2005)).

61 'Life in Baghdad via the web' BBC Online, 25 March 2003. The best known blogs also crossover to the traditional media. For example, Markos Moulitsas, the author of the Daily Kos, has written for the Guardian Unlimited website, giving his blog a new UK audience and Salam Pax has written for newspapers and published a book based on his blogs.

visited site may help the author(s) dedicate greater time and resources to it, which will help produce the content that maintains the higher audience. A small number of very popular blogs will therefore occupy a position quite distinct from the vast number of individual websites and blogs.

None of this is to express any conclusion about the fairness of this hierarchy in online expression. The influence and popularity of the successful blogger may be well deserved, but their value is no longer rooted in the self-fulfilment of the speaker outlined above. They serve a role that can help expose viewpoints to a wide audience and to influential opinion formers.[62] Their expression has much greater opportunity to persuade people or influence politics than the expression of most other individuals. The 'star' blogger that reaches a wide audience begins to blur with some characteristics of the established media. While the blog may offer many opportunities for the audience to post comments, it is still the blogger that sets the agenda and decides which postings are most prominent. The 'star' blog or website, due to the wide audience cannot possibly respond to the messages and comments sent in by users, and starts to resemble the top down flow of information of the traditional media, rather than conversation referred to above.[63] The point is not to undermine the important work and developments going on, or suggest such sites be subject to content regulation. Instead, the contribution of the small number of widely visited sites and blogs should be valued to the extent the needs of the mass audience and public are served, as is the case with the traditional mass media. The paradigm of the source speaking to a mass audience may not describe blogging completely, but is still applicable to some elements of online expression.

In addition to this, a new range of gatekeepers exists, whether through search engines, such as Google or services that aggregate blogs, such as Technorati. If the searcher is looking for a very specific piece of information, such as a particular posting by a specific author, the engine merely provides the user with what they are seeking. The user will already have knowledge of the content from some other source and formed his or her preference. However, where the user's search is more generic, the engine will return a larger number of results, which requires some method of prioritisation. In these circumstances users may not know precisely what they want, and the value placed by the user on the content may be dependent on the level of priority given to it by the search engine.[64] The success of an online speaker in reaching a wide audience will depend on if and where these facilities list the site, which in turn depends on method the search engine uses to aggregate the information.[65]

---

62 The influence of the blog is not just down to the size of the audience, but also due to the fact that many opinion formers, such as established journalists are among its readership, see Dryzner and Farrell, n 59 above.

63 C. Shirky, *Power Laws, Weblogs, and Inequality* http://www.shirky.com/writings/powerlaw.weblog.html (first published 8 February 2003, last accessed 8 August 2005).

64 N. Elkin-Koren, 'Let the Crawlers Crawl: On Virtual Gatekeepers and the Right to Exclude Indexing' (2001) 26 *Dayton L Rev* 179, 185.

65 See discussion in The Electoral Commission Consultation Paper, *The implications of online campaigns* (2002) [4.26]–[4.31].

If the search engine operates a business model of aggregation, then priority of place may be given to those who pay, rather than those with quality or reliable content. However, some sites place the sponsored results in a separate category to make this clear to the user. According to information on their own website, Google rank pages according to relevance and reliability.[66] The ranking system looks not only at the page content and how many links a page receives from other sites, but also the importance of the sites providing the link. While such an approach limits the possibility of editorial judgement on the part of Google, it could replicate the inequalities discussed above in relation to blogs.[67] Sites that have many links or have links from influential sites are already more likely to gain a wider audience, and are also more likely to rank highly in a Google search. This perpetuates the high readership and increases the chances of gaining more links from other sites.[68] It may be that this system is more likely to give the reader what they want and preferable to the alternatives, but nevertheless does impact on the chances of gaining a wider readership. Similar points can be made about other methods of distribution such as RSS[69] and the types of aggregation that are being developed for the next generation of search engines, for example looking at the previous choices of the user.[70] The user will have a fixed preference of content or source, or the aggregator has to make some choice of what material is most relevant or important.

Some of the new gatekeepers also provide access to news sources on their sites, so the user can view the latest headlines. At present, Google, for example, ranks news items according to the relevance of the text and places the most recent articles first. However, Google are reportedly seeking to rank news postings not just according to topicality but also based on reliability and accuracy of the news source.[71] How the reliability and accuracy of the news source is determined under the proposed system of prioritisation is a key question, and will be based on a combination of factors including the amount of content produced by the source, the traffic attracted by that source, the number of staff employed and global

---

66   http://www.google.co.uk/corporate/tech.html (last accessed 6 September 2005). See J. Battelle, *The Search* (London: Nicholas Brealey, 2005) ch 4.

67   M. Hindman, K. Tsioutsiouliklis and J. Johnson, '"Googlearchy": How a Few Heavily Linked Sites Dominate Politics Online', a paper presented to the Annual Meeting of the Midwest Political Science Association, Chicago, 2003 (http://cct.georgetown.edu/apsa/papers/Hindman.pdf# search='googlearchy' last accessed 6 September 2005). See also, J. Cho and S. Roy, 'Impact of search engines on page popularity' *Proceedings of the 13th international conference on World Wide Web* (New York, ACM Press, 2004) 20.

68   A recent study has suggested that search engines help to mitigate the dominance of a small number of sites, see S. Fortunato, A. Flammini, F. Menczer and A. Vespignani, 'The egalitarian effect of search engines' 1 November 2005 (http://arxiv.org/abs/cs.CY/0511005 (last accessed 16 December 2005)). However, even if the search engine does bring a wider range of material to the users' attention, this will tend to arise where the search is particularly specific and the page matches that specific interest. While computer scientists continue to debate which methods are most effective in bringing new voices to attention, the point in this article is more basic. The search engine will still perpetuate the overall dominance of the well-known media provider, even if it does bring some attention to other sites at the same time.

69   RSS allows content or summaries of content of websites to be sent directly to the user. This enables users to be alerted to new content without visiting that website.

70   For a discussion of the future of search engines, see Battelle, n 66 above, ch 11.

71   *The Guardian*, 18 June 2005.

operations of the source.[72] Emphasising these factors is likely to reinforce the
position of the large established media companies that can afford to employ a
large number of people globally and update content frequently. Consequently,
the views that will be most prominent and reach the widest possible audience will
still be those selected by a small set of dominant media organisations. This may
give the user what they want and distribute the best quality content, but again it
shows that the paradigm of the mass media is not outdated. Users may have more
control, but a small number of content providers will have the dominant voices
in public discourse.

There will always be ways around the gatekeeper's choices. If the website itself
is newsworthy it will be hard to keep the online speaker out. This may occur
when the website or blog has some scoop or breaks a story the other sources miss,
or features some technological innovation. However, this will only improve the
traffic to those sites in the short-term while that story is of interest. To maintain
the audience, it will need an established name or continuous routing through the
gatekeepers mentioned above. As there are more and more websites and blogs
appearing the need for the gatekeeper will increase. Given the global nature of
the Internet, it is likely the elite or gatekeepers will become more powerful. In
the mass media era, the elites generally operated at a national level, whereas companies such as Microsoft, Google and Yahoo perform this task internationally.
While it may be argued that the competition between search engines ensures that
users will always have alternatives, a small number of search engines are
likely to remain dominant. First, the users often lack the information to
assess the performance of the particular search engine and the basis of its listings.[73]
The user is more likely to stick with the convenience of their known and established search engine, with whom they may already have links, such as an email
account. Secondly, the established names will use their resources to ensure their
product maintains its popularity, by investing their funds into development,
buying up smaller more innovative search engines,[74] or adding new services to
their sites.[75]

Despite the high hopes for the new media, it is important not to overstate its
potential impact. Even those most enthusiastic about online expression do not
suggest blogs and individual sites will topple the established media's power in
shaping political discussion. The reason why the playing field of online speech is
not level is much the same as for other forms of media. Even if licensing were not
an issue, most people could not start a TV station. Although online expression
cuts the costs of printing and distribution of the traditional media, there are still
other substantial costs. To produce original high quality content still requires

---

72 *Ibid.*
73 L. Introna and H. Nissenbaum, 'Shaping the Web: Why the politics of search engines matters'
(2000) 16 *The Information Society* 169.
74 For example in early 2004 Yahoo bought rival search engines Inktomi and Overture, *The Times*, 20
February 2004; and in 2005 bought the photo-sharing site Flickr and bookmarking site Delicious,
which are seen as part of a strategy to develop social networks as the basis for searches, *The Guardian*, 15 December 2005.
75 For example, Google recently launched a free Internet telephony service GoogleTalk.

either the employment of a wide number of reporters and journalists, or the purchase of content elsewhere.[76] Furthermore the nature of online speech may work to increase costs. As there is an expectation that online news sources will always be up to date, the services of reporters, writers and external news providers are required more frequently. Improvements in the technology increase audience expectations of content, for example for more news sites to provide video clips. This and other future developments may make the cost of online content similar to that of the broadcast media.[77] If this is the case, economies of scale could lead to established media and elite online content providers becoming more dominant in the market.

While the small websites may not compete with the established media outlets directly, they do have a significant impact on the media and political communications. For example, the blog may act as a source for the established media, sometimes due to the expertise of the writer or due to the proximity of the blogger to the events.[78] The online media also provides content that is not available elsewhere, as happens when journalists put unpublished stories on the Internet. A famous example is the reporting of US Senator Trent Lott's remarks at Senator Strom Thurmond's 100th birthday online, which were interpreted as expressing support for Thurmond's earlier segregationist policies and led to Lott's resignation. While the established media initially reported his remarks sporadically, a number of influential blogs gave the story sustained coverage, which eventually forced the story to become a major headline. While it is debatable exactly how much credit should lie with the blogs and the established media for this episode, it does suggest that some bloggers can make it harder for a story to be suppressed.[79] Similarly, the work of online reporters and bloggers brought to public attention evidence of the US forces' use of white phosphorous in Fallujah, which had not been reported by other media outlets.[80] A further function is for the online speakers to check the content of the established media. An example of this occurred in the 2004 US elections when claims that President Bush received preferential treatment while serving in the Texas Air National Guard were broadcast on the CBS programme *60 Minutes*. Immediately after the broadcast, the authen-

---

76 R. McChesney, *The Problem of the Media: US Communication Policies in the 21ˢᵗ Century* (New York: Monthly Review Press, 2004) 220: 'Those who believe that all they need is a website and protection from the government censorship to leapfrog the commercial media are dreaming'.
77 N. Netanel, 'Cyberspace Self-Governance: A Skeptical View from Liberal Democratic Theory' (2000) 88 Calif L Rev 395, 463:
     Economies of scale, network effects, intense competition for user attention, and emerging Internet technology for the dissemination of high-quality, star-studded, expensive video content will radically transform cyberspace's expressive matrix. Far from its pluralist 'cheap speech' origins, cyberspace will reverberate to the tune of Time Warner, Viacom, and Disney.
78 For example, photographs of the aftermath of the July 2005 bombings in London were posted on blogs and sent into the established media.
79 E. Scott, ' "Big Media" Meets the "Bloggers": Coverage of Trent Lott's Remarks at Strom Thurmond's Birthday Party' Kennedy School of Government Case Study (2004). http://www.ksg.harvard.edu/presspol/Research.Publications/CaseStudies/1731.0.pdf (last accessed 30 June 2005).
80 J. Pilger, 'John Pilger – recommends the world wide web' *The New Statesman*, 28 November 2005; G. Monbiot, 'The US used chemical weapons in Iraq - and then lied about it' *The Guardian*, 15 November 2005.

ticity of the documents supporting the allegations was questioned in a number of blogs, and then followed by coverage in the mainstream media. The controversy led to CBS anchor Dan Rather's early retirement and the resignation of four CBS employees. The episode has been cited as illustrating the role of online speakers providing not just an additional check on government power, but a check on the media itself, forming a 'fifth estate'.

As with the Trent Lott incident, the CBS episode shows how the blogs worked in tandem with the established media. Furthermore, it was not just a single influential blog that made the story, but a number of bloggers that created a 'buzz' that helped to feed the story. According to research by the Pew Center, blogs often create the buzz, but also follow the agenda set by the established media or political institutions. The situations where a blog can create such an influential buzz are dependent on a range of other factors.[81] This may include the behaviour of the traditional media, and also the type of issue and its timing. For example, the CBS controversy was suited to the online discussion, given that it occurred in the context of an election where there was high interest and high stakes; that one of the key players Dan Rather was already defined in the minds of the bloggers and the subject of much discussion; and that the primary materials at the centre of this issue were available online.[82] Consequently, the story was particularly open to scrutiny in the blogosphere in a way that may not be possible with many other political stories.

Even if the bloggers really are influencing public debate and opinion, their role is still subordinate to the established media. As the above examples show, their work gains significance by influencing the established media. Some reports from the US have suggested that those blogs that express views shared by the established media are more likely to gain widespread coverage and influence.[83] The blogs are also dependent on the established media for their own content. Blogs tend to contain commentary and opinion, as opposed to facts. The established media are required for the primary reporting, photos and information that they comment on. In many ways, the heavily opinionated slant of the online expression means that the established media may become more influential than ever. With so much being disputed and debated, the need for an authoritative voice to provide primary content will be in demand.[84] The online expression may lead to changes where the established media provide content that turns up in different places and websites. However, the role for the mass media elite remains.

---

81 M. Cornfield, J. Carson, A. Kalis and E. Simon, 'Buzz, Blogs, and Beyond: The Internet and the National Discourse in the Fall of 2004' (Washington: Pew Internet and American Life Project, 2005).

82 *ibid.*

83 'Conservatives, Blogs are More Effective' *The New York Times* 11 December 2005.

84 As Tom Curley, President and CEO, The Associated Press told the Online News Association Conference, 12 November 2004:

>   We believe the world needs AP's primary content more than ever, that authoritative voice that we – and you – provide, precisely because there are so many new voices and free-flowing content 'atoms' out there on the network.

For a discussion of the implications on the accuracy of the online news, see Klotz, n 56 above, 127–131.

508   Media Freedom and Political Debate

The above discussion has highlighted the way in which new media elites and the established media will remain the dominant forces in political expression. It has been shown that this is likely to be the case even as the Internet grows as a source of information. The online audience no longer receives content fixed by a channel to a particular schedule, and the user has greater control in selecting what content to view and when to view it. However, as explained above, these choices will be shaped by media elites and some content will still reach a wide or even wider audience than before. Consequently, the mass media paradigm is unlikely to change in the foreseeable future. Questions about how these elites use their power and how they influence politics are as relevant today as they were in the era of the mass media. This is not to overlook the greater opportunities for participation in online expression, but rather to acknowledge that online expression can take many forms, just as its offline counterpart can. Consequently, the next section will argue that the approach to regulating online expression should be tiered, with elites and established media organisations operating at one level and smaller sites and individual users operating at a different level. As stated in a recent Institute for Public Policy Research report, the challenge in media policy is to 'handle the balance between the potentially global, all encompassing forms of expression, and very small-scale, virtually private forms of expression'.[85] The goal is therefore to balance the need for diverse political coverage reaching a wide audience with a range of different viewpoints, while at the same time protecting the self-expression and participation of individuals. The existing approach to regulating the media may be applicable to certain elite content providers and gatekeepers, but should not be so widely applied or onerous as to snuff out the positive developments currently taking place online.

MEDIA REGULATION AND DEMOCRATIC VALUES

This article has focused on the way the established media, influential websites and search engines help determine the success of online expression in reaching a wide audience. A range of other private actors also impact on the opportunities for online expression, including software companies that produce user-friendly applications, ISPs and non-state regulators such as ICANN.[86] Instead of eliminating the chance of private barriers to expression, digital technologies can increase the range of potential barriers. Regulation should not be ruled out, if it can help facilitate democratic expression by controlling the private power and should not automatically be prohibited by the courts. The stricter regulations associated with the broadcast model of regulation need not be rejected, but may require adaptation to some online communications if it would serve the values of freedom of expression. The difficulty is defining the boundaries between the tier of mass media entities and the tier of smaller speakers and forums outlined above.

---

85 W. Davies, *Modernising with Purpose: a manifesto for a Digital Britain* (London: IPPR, 2005) 52.
86 The Internet Corporation for Assigned Names and Numbers (ICANN) oversees domain name registration.

One approach may be to find that those entities already subject to media regulations offline be subject to similar regulations online. Under this approach, the current terrestrial broadcasters would be subject to their public service duties on online, and other licensed broadcasters would have to meet the basic tier of broadcast regulations online. Such a strategy reflects the current approach and is only likely to be workable in the short-term. As the media technologies converge and more people watch programmes online it will be possible for companies and groups to distribute audio-visual programmes solely through online channels. If such newcomers gain a significant share of the audience, then it may undermine the purpose of the current regulations, as a wide range of online content similar to that found on the broadcast media will command a mass audience but remain exempt from the regulations. Furthermore, as is currently the case with cable television, the licensed broadcaster will argue that they need to be less regulated to compete with the other unregulated outlets.[87] If such a relaxation of the regulations is not possible, then the regulated broadcaster may find that it is in their long term interests to distribute their content through the lesser-regulated online channels, in otherwords to opt-out of the broadcast sector. An alternative strategy could be to subject certain types of content to a particular regulatory regime. For example, the regulations applied to broadcasters could apply solely to audio-visual content. Initially this may seem appealing as it fits with current audience expectations, but it does beg the question why audio-visual content should be subject to stricter controls. Given the relative inexpense of video and audio equipment and software, audio-visual content will be used by many individuals, such as videobloggers, and not solely by media elites.

The boundary could be drawn instead between commercial and amateur entities. This could still cause difficulties, for example, a company website or content produced by an interest group should not be equated with mass media, nor should a small scale website that makes a small amount of income on advertising. It may be necessary to target those online speakers that are commercial and whose primary content is the provision of media, whether as an aggregator or provider, and which has a particular share of the market or turnover. Distinguishing the sphere of regulated mass media from other types of communication has parallels in existing law. For example, in media merger rules, newspapers are distinguished from other types of communication by reference to the frequency and content of the publication.[88] Similarly elections laws distinguish newspaper and broadcaster reports from the communications of political campaigners, exempting the former from third party expenditure limits.[89] Distinguishing online media outlets that are the equivalent of modern day mass media may not be a clear cut task, but has a precedent in the UK.

A further difficulty with regulating online media entities is the global nature of the Internet. The requirements of UK democracy should not be imposed on media outlets based abroad and targeting a different country, yet Internet users are still free to access this content. This raises a situation similar to that of cable

---

87 See *OFCOM review of public service broadcasting, Phase 2* (2004) 31.
88 Enterprises Act 2002, s 44(10). See Department of Trade and Industry Guidance Document, *Public Interest Intervention in Media Mergers* (May 2004), 13.
89 Political Parties, Elections and Referendums Act 2000, s 87.

television where foreign broadcasts, such as Fox News and Al-Jazeera, are thought to be straining the regulations applied to licensed broadcasts. Furthermore, European Union law imposes restraints on the capacity to regulate media providers based outside jurisdiction.[90] Given the global environment of the media, traditional rules of impartiality and accuracy are being increasingly questioned,[91] a trend that is likely to increase in relation to the online media. However, it would still be possible to single out those media entities whose content is targeted at an audience within jurisdiction, especially in relation to the coverage of news and politics. Those outlets focusing on UK based news are most likely to command a broad audience in the UK, and are unlikely to face greater competition from outlets covering the news and politics of a different country. In any event, as outlined below, some more partisan media content from abroad may be unproblematic, but simply should not represent the whole media landscape. The global context also raises issues of enforcement and the possibility of evasion. However, it is likely that those sites that are the equivalent of mass media would want to maintain a base in the UK, for example for its reporters or advertising, and are likely to conform to such national rules. Furthermore, the development of geographical location technology may also make it possible to limit the dissemination of material to and from foreign countries.[92] A full consideration of the problem of jurisdiction and enforcement is beyond the scope of this paper. The point is merely that the global nature of online expression does not eliminate the role for the regulation of certain media entities to serve the broader needs of democracy.

If it can be established that such media entities may be the subject of regulation, it still raises the question of what regulations are necessary to serve democratic needs. So far reference has been made to broadcast media regulations for impartiality and balance in political coverage, but such regulations are not imposed on the print press. It may be argued that partisan online content serves democratic needs in the same way the partisan press does. This need will probably be found with many speakers on the new media, such as bloggers or interest group sites. While it is important, such partisan content associated with the print model need not be the norm for all online content. Rather than reflecting one model of democratic expression, the regulated tier of online expression could be designed to permit different regulatory regimes. Prior to the prominence of the Internet, Lee Bollinger argued that the different regulatory regimes for print and broadcast media are justified by balancing one another.[93] Similarly, James Curran has advocated different media sectors serving separate democratic needs.[94] The regulation

---

90 For example under the Television Without Frontiers Directive (89/552/EEC) and the E-Commerce Directive (2000/31/EC). While an examination of the impact EU law on public service regulations is beyond the scope of this paper, see M. Varney, 'European Controls on Member State Promotion and Regulation of Public Service Broadcasting and Broadcasting Standards' (2004) 10 *European Public Law* 503.

91 For example, D. Tambini and J. Cowling, *New News: Impartial Broadcasting in the Digital Age* (London: IPPR, 2002).

92 See Barendt, n 6 above, 474.

93 L. Bollinger, 'The Rationale of Public Regulation of the Media' in J. Litchenberg (ed), n 9 above.

94 J. Curran, *Media and Power* (London: Routledge, 2002) ch 8.

of the new media could be designed to promote the various different functions of the media in a democracy, with different elements of the print and broadcast model to be found in different media sectors. Some areas of the web, such as original news reporting and the largest gatekeeper sites, could reflect the republican concern with balance, impartiality, and differing viewpoints, while some elements of a partisan media reflecting the liberal pluralist approach could be permitted in commentary sites such as blogs. However, even in a sector that recognises the importance of partisan content, different points of view need to be accessed and the various gatekeepers referred to above may need to act to promote access to diverse opinions. It would be unsatisfactory if the only partisan sites that could easily be found online all supported the same perspective, whether left or right.

If regulations to promote impartiality, balance, accuracy, and quality content associated with the public service function of the media are applicable to some online media, then a further question arises as to how best to achieve these aims. One method has been to propose state funded websites to act as civic forums.[95] This approach represents an attempt by the state to set up an elite site of its own that will promote democratic values and reflect a public service rationale, rather than constraining private entities. The danger with setting up such a website purely for political debate is that it may draw few visitors. With such a wide range of options, people are more likely to go to the sites that are most entertaining.[96] Possibly the most successful example of this type of site is the BBC, which has regularly been praised for its online services. It attracts many visitors, not just because of its well-known name, but also its wide range of content, such as entertainment or sports pages. However, dangers exist in placing all public interest requirements on one media entity.[97] A variation of the public service site is the proposal by Blumler and Coleman of a public agency to promote and publicise online deliberation.[98] The agency would act as a gatekeeper to some online expression, be the moderator of discussion and help facilitate the interaction of civic networks online. Such a role could be allocated to the Public Service Publisher that has been proposed by OFCOM to promote and distribute content on digital television and through broadband that fulfils public service requirements.[99] As above, the danger with such an agency is that its success would be dependent on regular use and interest from the public.

For as long as the BBC remains the most popular website in the UK, the public service model will partly define political expression online by shaping user expectations. For example, current broadcast regulations on news coverage create an expectation, so that a blatantly partisan audio-visual news bulletin would have

---

95 Such a scheme may raise state aid issues under Article 87 of the EC Treaty, see Varney, n 90 above, 520.

96 For a discussion of this trend in the US, see M. Prior, 'News vs. Entertainment: How Increasing Media Choice Widens Gaps in Political Knowledge and Turnout' (2005) 49 *American Journal of Political Science* 577.

97 For a discussion in relation to digital television, see *OFCOM Review, Phase 2*, n 87 above.

98 J. Blumler and S. Coleman, *Realising Democracy Online: A Civic Commons in Cyberspace* (London, IPPR, 2001).

99 *OFCOM Review Phase 3*, n 35 above, ch 5.

little credibility with those accustomed to the norms of impartiality and balance. However, as greater convergence with the technologies occurs and significant developments in what can be done continue, the BBC site may face greater competition in future years and may lose its share of the market. As, and if, this occurs, then some regulation of privately run sites may be necessary to ensure the system of expression and media reflects our democratic values. This may include the types of proposal such as rights to reply or must carry rules, as outlined by Sunstein. Rules could be introduced to require some content providers to provide balance and impartial political coverage, as well as access for political parties at election times. In addition incentives could be designed to promote the production of educational and cultural content. The search engines and other gatekeepers could be encouraged to give priority to the impartial/balanced news providers and ensure that the access to partisan content does not give disproportionate emphasis to one slant or viewpoint. These goals could be achieved not only through legal direction in some cases, but through codes of practice, possibly drawn up by OFCOM, or through subsidy and tax relief for those fulfilling these goals.

The approaches outlined above seek to regulate the use of existing technology to ensure the provision of particular types of expression, rather than determine what it is possible to do online. However, there may be other areas of online technology that can promote democratic goals. As Balkin points out, the design and architecture of the digital technology must also be considered as a possible area of regulation.[100] This area of regulation could be used to benefit the small scale speakers discussed above. An important element of free expression is the development of user-friendly applications that make media production possible for those with minimal technical expertise and fewer resources. Promoting such applications could serve the goal of public service regulations to encourage widespread participation in politics and media production. An approach to media regulation that also considers issues of design and architecture will help to promote expression at all the different tiers described above.

CONCLUSION

Many of the issues discussed in this article may not seem urgent or pressing. The Internet has not created an immediate crisis or change in political coverage in the UK. The dominant outlet for political news is still the broadcast media, which is subject to public service duties and regulations. Online expression just adds another outlet. However, this article has attempted to take a long-term view where the changes in technology and audience habits may outdate the current regulations. These changes may alter the way media freedom is justified, placing some emphasis on individual participation, and include regulation to enhance this role. However, this modifies the paradigm rather than marking a complete break with the past. Online there will still remain media elites that command mass audiences, and have greater influence over the provision of information, reporting and political debate. Even if they are acting in accordance with public service

---

100 Balkin, n 44 above, 52.

values at present, there is no reason to assume this will continue, as online expression becomes more dominant the situation could change. What has been sketched in this article is a basis from which certain media entities could be regulated in a way that is consistent with expression rights and media freedom and would ensure that democratic and public service values continue and develop into the digital era.

Part II
Public Service Broadcasting

[6]

Culture and Consumerism: Citizenship, Public Service Broadcasting and the BBC's Fair Trading Obligations

Georgina Born* and Tony Prosser**

The authors examine the future of public service broadcasting in the context of current debates about, and commercial pressures on, the BBC. They describe the European Community constraints on public service broadcasting and the need for a clearer definition of such broadcasting, noting that such a definition is not currently provided in UK law. The BBC is also under increasing pressure from fair trading rules derived from competition law, some of which may weaken its ability to deliver its public service mission. Original research undertaken within the BBC suggests that external and internal pressures have undermined the conditions for a distinctive public service output, although there remains the basis for such an output within the culture of programme-making. The authors develop theoretical bases for a redefinition of public service broadcasting centred on the principles of citizenship, universality and quality in relation to services and output, and examine the implications for the structure of channels in the digital era. Finally, the authors discuss the legal and regulatory implications of their analysis in the context of the Government's Communications White Paper, arguing that the social and cultural purposes of public service broadcasting must not be made subordinate to competition-based concerns.

Is broadcasting best conceived as a commercial activity or as an expression of cultural norms and expectations? The obvious answer is that it is both. Nevertheless, we shall argue that the tension between these different conceptions of the nature of broadcasting has been a major source of uncertainties in broadcasting law (including both European and domestic law) and in the self-image of broadcasters at a number of levels, and that it is far from being resolved. In particular, the two conceptions imply radically different visions of the nature of the television viewer, as sovereign consumer making a choice from a range of services offered by the marketplace, or as a citizen participating in a culture serving the purpose of his or her self-development as well as that of the society of which the citizen is a member.

* Faculty of Social and Political Sciences, University of Cambridge, and Emmanuel College, Cambridge;
** School of Law, University of Glasgow.
This work draws heavily on research projects funded by the ESRC's Media Economics and Media Culture Research Programme: T. Prosser, D. Goldberg and S. Verhulst, *Legal Responses to Regulating the Changing Media*, award no. L126251021, and G. Born, *Redefining Public Service Broadcasting: An Ethnography of the BBC*, award no. L126251041. We are grateful for the ESRC support and would also like to thank a number of people for comments: Andrew Barry, Jay Blumler, Richard Collins, John Corner, Rachael Craufurd-Smith, Mike Feintuck, Tom Gibbons, John Hill, Trine Syvertsen, Damian Tambini and Charlotte Villiers. The usual disclaimer applies.

658   *The Modern Law Review*   [Vol. 64

In this article we shall bring out the implications of this tension in relation to public service broadcasting and the BBC's fair trading obligations, and in doing so we attempt to provide a renewed normative definition of public service broadcasting (PSB).[1] At the outset, our working definition of PSB is broadcasting the content of which is not shaped simply by market signals from advertisers or (in subscription services) from viewers, but by an appeal to principles of citizenship, universality and quality, concepts that we will develop in detail below.[2] We confine our discussion to the BBC; this is not to suggest that the Corporation is, or should be, the only purveyor of PSB, but rather to claim that the problems are particularly acute in view of the expectations it carries and the defects in its structure of governance.

At first sight it might appear that the forces of commercialisation are leading to the rout of broadcasting as culture or public service. The profusion of new services made possible by digitalisation would appear to remove earlier justifications for PSB based on spectrum shortage, and the development of pay-per-view services (should these ever prove popular on a mass scale) will make broadcasting appear closer than ever before to a marketplace in which services are provided to meet the preferences of the sovereign consumer.[3] As a result, we have seen strong pressures exerted by private sector broadcasters to loosen the requirements on them for PSB, while the special position of the BBC has been increasingly questioned as unnecessary, elitist and anti-competitive.[4]

A dominant criticism of the BBC in public and policy debate in the last decade has been for lacking compliance with fair trading norms. Indeed fair trading arguments have become the major means by which the BBC's competitors have attempted to erode the legitimacy of the Corporation; while government has also limited the BBC's opportunities to innovate on these grounds. In responding to these criticisms, the BBC has been caught between a rock and a hard place. On the one hand, if it avoids commercial activities and runs down popular and mainstream programming on its channels, it can be accused of marginality and of taking the route of 'market failure' provision, simply filling the gaps left by its commercial rivals. On the other hand, if the BBC does compete with commercial operators, it makes itself vulnerable to accusations of unfair trading and the abuse of its privileged position. The crescendo of criticisms of the BBC in relation to fair trading issues must be seen in the context of a growing crisis in the legitimacy of the Corporation's governance arrangements.[5] Specifically, the criticism has been made that the governors are constitutionally ill-positioned to take the wider view and promote the interests of the broadcasting sector as a whole, and thus of this important sector of the British economy. Dissatisfaction with the regulation of

---

1 The basis of the article is collaborative and interdisciplinary. It combines comparative research on the regulatory bases and constitutional status of public service broadcasting (Prosser) with the results of a two-year ethnographic study inside the BBC carried out in the late 1990s which is set within an ongoing analysis of the wider broadcasting environment (Born).

2 For earlier discussion of citizenship and PSB see M. Feintuck, *Media Regulation, Public Interest and the Law* (Edinburgh: Edinburgh University Press, 1999).

3 The literature on these developments is legion; for an attempt to consider them in the UK context, see the Select Committee on Culture, Media and Sport, *The Multi-Media Revolution* HC 520 (1997–98).

4 See eg R. Craufurd-Smith, *Broadcasting Law and Fundamental Rights* (Oxford: Clarendon Press, 1997) 49–52. For some recent examples of criticism of the role of the BBC in the developing broadcasting market see the Select Committee on Culture, Media and Sport, *The Funding of the BBC*, HC 25 (1999–2000), and evidence thereto.

5 The Culture, Media and Sport Committee has been a major source of criticism; see notably *The Multi-Media Revolution*, HC 520 (1997–8), paras 141–59.

broadcasting in general has led government to propose major reforms in its Communications White Paper, with a Communications Bill in the new Parliament.[6] We shall address these proposals at the end of this paper.

Our proposal will be that the argument that broadcasting is becoming an essentially commercial activity determined by consumer preferences is, even should it be sustainable, seriously undesirable. A key element of our case will be to criticise the appropriateness of the concept of consumer sovereignty to broadcasting. Our argument will be that the cultural and citizenship purposes usually taken to characterise the normative basis for PSB should be primary, and not subordinate to economic and commercial criteria in determining the future of such broadcasting. However, they have suffered from a lack of adequate legal definition in the UK at least, and so these 'soft' values have easily been subordinated to the apparently 'hard' values of competition law and fair trading obligations. As a result, there is a danger that a public service broadcaster such as the BBC will lose its distinctive mission. We will argue that the public interest served socially and culturally via our conception of PSB is more important than assisting the commercial interests of competitors, the latter being the inevitable result of the application of what is in form neutral competition law to an organisation with cultural obligations not applying to its competitors.

Tensions of public service broadcasting

Perhaps the most celebrated example of the tension between broadcasting seen as essentially a matter of trade and as a key element in the expression and preservation of international cultures was in the recent disputes involving the World Trade Organisation during the Uruguay Round.[7] However, the position of the European Union has itself been torn by similar tensions between broadcasting as commerce and broadcasting as culture. This is itself only part of a wider tension about the role of competition law as applied to public services.[8] To summarise briefly a complex area of law and policy, a strong theme of Community policy has been support for liberalisation through removing barriers to freedom of transmission and reception within the Union, and applying the ordinary principles of competition law to create and maintain open markets within which consumers can exercise their sovereignty. At the same time there has been a recognition that the media are not like other commercial services such as banking. They play a major part in creating shared frameworks of information and entertainment, and thus in the formation of national and regional cultures. They are perceived as having moral implications, are associated with concepts of public service and are the object of important rights set out in national and international instruments. A second theme of policy has thus been that broadcasting has a significant cultural

---

6 *A New Future for Communications*, Cm 5010 (2000), hereafter simply 'White Paper'.

7 See M.E. Footer and C. Beat Graber, 'Trade Liberalization and Cultural Policy' (2000) *J of Economic Law* 115, and P. Schlesinger, 'From Cultural Defence to Political Culture: Media, Politics and Collective Identity in the European Union' (1997) 19 *Media, Culture and Society* 360.

8 For discussion see T. Prosser, 'Public Service Law: Privatization's Unexpected Offspring' 63 *Law and Contemporary Problems* (2000) 63; for a statement of the Commission's views before the Amsterdam Treaty, *Communication on Services of General Interest in Europe*, COM 96/443 final and, more recently, *Communication from the Commission Services of Public Interest in Europe*, COM 2000/850 final. For the particular situation of broadcasting see G. Mather, 'Competition and Public Purpose: A European Approach' in A. Graham et al, *Public Purposes in Broadcasting* (Luton: University of Luton Press, 1999) 99–111.

660 *The Modern Law Review* [Vol. 64

dimension which has underlain the assumption that one goal of the Community should be to protect European (especially French) culture and language against the all-conquering US cultural world, for example in the WTO negotiations mentioned above. Its most important legislative expression has been in the provisions of the Television Without Frontiers Directive requiring, in a weak form, quotas for European works.[9]

The issue arose in the *Eurovision* case before the Court of First Instance.[10] The Commission had granted the European Broadcasting Union (EBU), comprising European public service broadcasters, exemption from the application of Article 81 of the Treaty to its operation of the Eurovision system for the joint buying of television rights to sports events. Membership was only open to broadcasters providing a service of national character, producing a substantial proportion of their own programmes and being required to provide balanced programming catering for minority interests and covering all or most of the population of their states. The exemption was successfully challenged by excluded broadcasters in the Court of First Instance. Amongst several grounds for the decision was the finding that the Commission was under a duty to examine whether the EBU's membership rules were objective and sufficiently determinate to enable them to be applied uniformly and in a non-discriminatory manner. The Commission had failed to do so, and according to the Court the content of the conditions, in the absence of further specification, could not be applied in a uniform and non-discriminatory way.[11] Nor had there been an adequate explanation of why these obligations made exclusive purchasing indispensable, and so the EBU could not benefit from an exemption from the general competition rules under Article 81(3) of the Treaty.

The appeal in this case to the European Court of Justice has been abandoned as the Commission agreed to grant a new exemption after the EBU had agreed new sublicensing rules.[12] However, the message is clear from the decision of the Court. If PSB is to form a ground for an exception to be made to the general rules relating to competition, there must be a clearly defined conception of such broadcasting. Otherwise, the apparently concrete and well-defined concepts of competition law will prevail. Steps have been taken since to provide further protection for PSB through the protocol on PSB adopted as part of the Amsterdam Treaty amendments. This states

> [t]he provisions of this Treaty ... shall be without prejudice to the competence of Member States to provide for the funding of public service broadcasting insofar as such funding is granted to broadcasting organisations for the fulfilment of the public service remit as conferred, defined and organised by each Member State, and insofar as such funding does not affect trading conditions and competition in the Community to an extent which would be contrary to the common interest, while the realisation of the remit of that public service shall be taken into account.[13]

9 Directive 89/552/EEC of 3 October 1989, OJ 1989 L 298/23, arts 4-6 and see D. Goldberg, T. Prosser and S. Verhulst, *EC Media Law and Policy* (London: Longman, 1998) 61–3.
10 *Métropole Télévision SA and others* v *EC Commission*, [1996] 5 CMLR 386, joined cases T-528/93, T-542/93, T-543/92 and T-546/93. For discussion see R. Craufurd-Smith, 'Getting the Measure of Public Services: Community Competition Rules and Public Service Broadcasting' (1997–98) III *Yearbook of Media and Entertainment Law* 147, 151–66.
11 At para 97.
12 See Commission Decision of 10 May 2000 OJ L 151/18, 24.6.2000 and A. Font Galarza, 'The Commission's Assessment of the Eurovision System Pursuant to Article 81 EC' [2000] 2 *EC Competition Policy Newsletter* 28, available at <http://europa.eu.int/comm/competition/publications/cpn/cpn2000_2.pdf>.
13 European Union, *Treaty of Amsterdam*, Protocol on the System of Public Broadcasting in the Member States (1997).

Apart from reflecting the French-led cultural concern, this amendment was also inspired by pressure from the European Parliament for stronger recognition of the importance of PSB within the European Union.[14] However, it is of course far from precise and, as is the way of such international agreements, merely sends the problem one step further for resolution by member states or by the Court.

A particularly important decision was made by the Commission applying the protocol in rejecting a complaint by BSkyB against the UK Government and the BBC relating to the launch of BBC News 24 as a public service funded by the licence fee in competition with Sky News.[15] The Commission, whilst appearing to regret the lack of a clear definition of PSB in UK law, stressed that there was considerable discretion for member states to define the public service remit, the role of the Commission being only to ensure that this discretion was not abused; 'it is not for the Commission to pronounce on the concept used in national legislation to define the provision of such services, nor to discuss the concepts of ... public service ... as defined in the Charter'.[16] The decision was also based on the fact that the new service was free of advertising and so clearly different from services provided by private operators. Nevertheless, the point is again that a clearer definition of PSB is important to protect the ability of member states to ensure that such broadcasting is provided. As we shall now describe, this is currently lacking in the UK.

Public service broadcasting and UK law

The tension between broadcasting as culture and as commerce also exists in the UK. It is reinforced by the currently unsatisfactory legal framework for PSB, unsatisfactory both in terms of its content and its legal status.[17] The BBC stands outside most legal structures for broadcasting regulation in the UK. It was founded not by statute but by a Royal Charter as a Corporation of twelve governors appointed by the Queen in Council for a period of five years. The governors are trustees for the public interest through ensuring that the terms of the Charter and other obligations are fulfilled whilst the management of the Corporation is in principle left to the Director General and Board of Management.[18] This has given rise to a number of problems, for example how a largely non-representative Board appointed by government can effectively represent any definable public interest apart from that of the government of the day, and the uncertain division of responsibilities between governors and managers. This structure contrasts with the need to separate operational and regulatory functions, a key theme in European Union liberalisation policies in other areas such as telecommunications.

---

14 See notably the 'Tongue Report' appended to the European Parliament Resolution on the Role of Public Service Television in the Multi-Media Society, 19 September 1996, A4-0243/96 and also Communication from the Commission: Principles and Guidelines for the Community's Audiovisual Policy in the Digital Age, COM 657 (1999) 12–13.

15 Commission decision of 29.9.1999 in case NN 88/98, *BBC News 24*, OJ 2000 C 78/6. See also R. Craufurd-Smith, 'State Support for Public Service Broadcasting: The Position Under European Community Law' (2000) 28(1) *Legal Issues of European Integration* 3–22.

16 *ibid* para 46, cf paras 69–71.

17 For accounts of the legal structure of broadcasting in the UK see T. Gibbons, *Regulating the Media* (London: Sweet and Maxwell, 2nd ed, 1998) esp chs 3 and 6; Craufurd-Smith, n 15 above, 45–7, 68–78.

18 For details see Gibbons, *ibid* 35–46.

662   *The Modern Law Review*   [Vol. 64

The Charter requires the BBC to provide broadcasting services 'as public services' and programmes of information, education and entertainment; ancillary services such as licence-fee funded online services must also be provided 'as public services'. As a partial response to earlier criticism the revised version of the BBC Agreement with the Secretary of State issued in 1996 requires the Corporation to observe requirements closer to those applied by statute to private broadcasters.[19] The Corporation

> undertakes to provide and keep under review the Home Services with a view to the maintenance of high general standards in all respects (and in particular in respect of their content, quality and editorial integrity) and to their offering a wide range of subject matter (having regard both to the programmes as a whole and also to the days of the week on which, and the times of the day at which, the programmes are shown) meeting the needs and interests of audiences ...[20]

Other requirements are that programmes 'are provided as a public service for disseminating information, education and entertainment' and that they 'stimulate, support and reflect, in drama, comedy, music and the visual and performing arts, the diversity of cultural activity in the United Kingdom'.[21] The requirement of a wide range of subject matter is re-emphasised later in the agreement in the context of programme standards, and due accuracy and impartiality are required in relation to controversial subjects, as well as the customary prohibition on offending good taste and decency.[22] The requirements in the agreement are backed by producers' guidelines published by the BBC; however these deal with the content of individual programmes rather than the overall balance of services.[23] External accountability is now enforced through multiple routes, including reports on progress against promises made by the governors and extensive audit requirements, which will be further described in our discussion of the fair trading rules.

There is considerable doubt as to whether the content of the 1996 Agreement represents an adequate conception of PSB, and of the BBC's role, in modern conditions.[24] A further problem is that, due to the peculiar legal device of using an agreement rather than statute, there has been legal doubt about the enforceability of the undertakings on the part of anyone other than the government and the availability of judicial review.[25] The strengthening of the agreement from 1996 and the developing doctrine of legitimate expectation make it highly likely that the BBC is now subject to enforceable obligations. Nevertheless, for the Corporation public service is required by 'soft' rather than 'hard' law,[26] and, especially in the absence of any independent regulator, this suggests that observance of the requirements is a matter between the Corporation and the government rather than a question of citizenship rights positively conceived and owed to the viewing public.

Both the content and form of current PSB requirements thus display the sort of uncertainty which we mentioned earlier in the context of European Union law.

---

19 Department of National Heritage, *Copy of the Agreement Dated the 25th Day of January 1996 Between Her Majesty's Secretary of State for National Heritage and the British Broadcasting Corporation*, Cm 3152 (1996).
20 *ibid* clause 3.1.
21 *ibid* clause 3.2.
22 *ibid* clause 5.1.
23 BBC, *Producers' Guidelines*, available at <http://www.bbc.co.uk/info/editorial/prodgl/index.shtml>.
24 See eg the Culture, Media and Sport Committee, n 4 above, para 17.
25 See Craufurd-Smith, n 4 above, 73–78 and *Houston v British Broadcasting Corporation* 1995 SLT 1305, which does not provide a definitive answer either way.
26 For the origins of the distinction see K. Wellens and G. Borchard, 'Soft Law in European Community Law' (1989) 14:5 *European Law Review* 267.

This has led the Davies panel, undertaking the crucial task of examining BBC funding, to note that 'we may not be able to offer a tight new definition of PSB, but we nevertheless each felt we knew it when we saw it'.[27] Such a vague conception might be acceptable where there was a broad cultural consensus on the nature of such broadcasting, as there was, effectively, for much of the history of the BBC. But as we noted at the start of this article it is precisely such agreement which has been called into question since the later 1980s by the changing technology and economics of broadcasting, and by increasing commercialism and intensifying competition. The vagueness must itself derive in part from the lack of legal and constitutional status for PSB and its embodiment only in concrete institutions, which has both given it a practical strength and rendered it vulnerable to changing economic and political forces. In this context, we show later that the pressures of political criticism since the 1980s combined with the lack of legal protection for PSB's social and cultural purposes has had deleterious effects within the BBC, eroding the BBC's ability to fulfil those purposes. It has encouraged the dominance of 'hard' managerial techniques within the Corporation which undermine the realisation of its cultural aims by eroding the well-being and autonomy of its production cultures.

In other European nations the concept of public service, especially that of PSB, has entered fully into constitutional culture and expectations. In Germany and Italy decisions of constitutional courts have played a fundamental role in defining the requirements for such broadcasting, and in France, as well as the *Conseil Constitutionnel* having had a role in relation to broadcasting, the concept of public service is a basic component of administrative law.[28] As one of the leading writers has summed up the position:

> [t]he primary achievement of constitutional courts throughout Europe has been to give a clear signal that the audiovisual media should not be treated as just another commodity: radio and television have become central mechanisms through which we gain an understanding of ourselves and others ... state regulation to ensure the provision of reliable and diverse audiovisual services is considered to be legitimate, even essential.[29]

This has meant that the meaning of public service has entered into constitutional discourse.[30] It does not mean, of course, that there is a core and universally agreed conception of public service; this continues to be the subject of heated debate, like many other constitutional concepts. It does mean, however, that there is a definitive source of principle to which appeal can be made in the search for the meaning of the concept, and one that stands above everyday politics.

By contrast, in the UK the key characteristic has been the constitutional and judicial exclusion of the audio-visual field.[31] Despite this the BBC has been the leading European model of PSB, but this has been due to institutional and cultural historical supports which are now threatened by economic, technological and cultural changes. This exclusion has meant that there is neither a source of constitutional principle nor resort to judicial decisions to resolve the problems of the meaning of public service in the face of the BBC's increasing vulnerability. As a result the problem of definition faced by the Davies panel and referred to above is

---

27 Department for Culture, Media and Sport, *The Future Funding of the BBC: Report of the Independent Review Panel, Chairman Gavyn Davies* (1999) 10 (hereafter 'Davies report').
28 See Craufurd-Smith, n 4 above, and E. Barendt, *Broadcasting Law and Fundamantal Rights* (Oxford: Clarendon, 1995). For the potential role of public service law see Prosser, n 8 above.
29 Craufurd-Smith, *ibid* 241–242.
30 See Gibbons, n 17 above, 61.
31 Craufurd-Smith, n 4 above, 68.

insoluble except at the level of examining concrete definitions of each aspect of public service contained in particular legal and organisational norms or particular services. Yet as we have seen such norms are historically changing, fragmentary and of uncertain legal status. If the constitutional base for PSB and an associated legal culture are lacking in the UK, there are also problems within the culture of broadcasting itself, as we show later for the BBC.

Despite this uncertainty and lack of precision about the meaning of PSB, this does not mean that the concept is ripe for jettisoning. The Communications White Paper stresses the critical future role of PSB: '[p]ublic service broadcasting will continue to have a key role to play in the digital future, potentially an even more important role than it has now'. It emphasises also the democratic, educational and cultural significance of PSB.[32] Nevertheless, the White Paper still lacks an adequate definition and, as we shall describe later, the proposed governance and regulatory arrangements do not amount to an adequate basis for the successful protection of the values which the government professes. Before suggesting ways in which it may be possible to develop a more satisfactory concept of PSB, we shall discuss broadcasting as commerce and the BBC fair trading obligations. The latter are little discussed in the White Paper but are of fundamental importance in shaping the culture of PSB through imposing a model of broadcasting based on the competition law principles which apply to markets for ordinary commodities.[33]

The BBC and fair trading

As in European law, it is recognised in principle that PSB may require exemptions from ordinary competition law. Thus the Competition Act 1998, whilst containing no explicit exclusion for the BBC, does include a provision echoing Article 86(2) of the EC Treaty by limiting the application of the prohibitions contained in the Act to services of general economic interest where they would obstruct the performance of the particular tasks assigned to an undertaking.[34] This provision has not been used, and otherwise, the commercial activities of the BBC are subject to ordinary competition law, domestic and European. More important is the body of internal rules regarding fair trading from the BBC, which go much further than the requirements of ordinary competition law, being required because of the special position of the Corporation as publicly funded.[35] Their essential purpose is two-fold: to ensure that commercial activities do not conflict with the values of public service, and to ensure that there is no use of public funds to support commercial activities resulting in unfair competition. As such the two purposes are radically different. The first seeks to protect the principle of PSB through ensuring that, for example, the public service 'brand' is not sullied by inappropriate commercial content, and that funds to support public service are not put at risk by ill-judged commercial ventures. The second is essentially to protect the BBC's competitors from what is perceived as unfair competition.

---

32 White Paper, paras 5.1, 5.3.6, 5.3.8-9, 5.3.11–12.
33 Cf White Paper paras 2.8.1, 5.8.7.
34 Sched 3, para 4. The wording is not identical, however, to that in Article 86(2) which may create future uncertainties.
35 For an excellent summary see D. Currie and M. Siner, 'The BBC: Balancing Public and Commercial Purpose' in Graham et al, n 8 above, 73–97.

The Agreement with the Secretary of State requires the annual reporting of compliance with fair trading requirements including the arrangements for avoiding cross-subsidies between public service and commercial services.[36] However, the detail is to be found in the BBC's Commercial Policy Guidelines.[37] The guidelines prescribe what are appropriate commercial activities and lay down more details on fair trading, for example stating that there should be clear separation between publicly-funded and commercial activities in terms of their operation and accounting, that BBC commercial subsidiaries or operations must pay fair charges for any goods or services received from the BBC, that prices charged by BBC commercial activities to their customers should be a fair reflection of costs incurred and market practice, and that no public funds must be put at risk by commercial activities, for example as start-up capital or to cover initial operating losses of commercial ventures. Implementation is monitored by a standing committee of the Board of Governors, the Fair Trading Compliance Committee, and there is annual external audit by private accountants, currently KPMG. In addition, new commercial activities are subject to specific ministerial approval, and, as we shall see in a moment, the grounds on which approval will be given have recently been codified.

The bulk of the BBC's commercial activities are undertaken through BBC Worldwide, a wholly-owned subsidiary which exploits the secondary commercial value of rights and has established jointly-owned channels and joint ventures to develop global channels. BBC Resources, another wholly-owned subsidiary supplying facilities and allied services, is also allowed to trade externally. BBC public service directorates must deal with them at arm's length. Overall a substantial increase in commercial business is expected; BBC Worldwide aims to quadruple its returns by 2006.[38]

The Davies Panel was critical of these arrangements. It noted considerable concern from rival broadcasters that the procedures for introducing clear separation and transparency between the BBC's public and commercial activities were inadequate, and that commercial activities were unfairly subsidised from the licence fee.[39] The Secretary of State required that independent scrutinies be undertaken of the BBC's fair trading policies and its financial reporting, and that in future fair trading and financial audits would be carried out by different auditors. Independent consultants would be required to carry out periodic review of the systems and controls.[40] In February 2001 Richard Whish, the eminent competition lawyer, was asked to undertake a review of fair trading policies, finding that they compare favourably with those of other undertakings. Further competition-based reviews were also established by the Minister into BBC Online, its internet operation, and BBC News 24, the rolling news operation.

The Secretary of State also issued new, highly restrictive tests for the provision of new public services by the BBC. Apart from requiring consultation with the public, the broadcasting industry, regulators and consumer groups before new services are launched, the Secretary of State will ask whether 'the value to the

---

36 See n 19 above, clause 4(4)f.
37 BBC, *Commercial Policy Guidelines*, (revised 1999), available at <www.bbc.co.uk/info/commercial/index.shtml>.
38 Davies report, n 27 above, 95.
39 Davies report, n 27 above, 96–109, 147.
40 Secretary of State for Culture, Media and Sport, HC Deb col 1239 21 February 2000, and see Department for Culture, Media and Sport, *The Funding of the BBC: Government Response to the Third Report from the Culture, Media and Sport Committee, Session 1999–2000*, Cm 4674 (2000).

666 The Modern Law Review [Vol. 64

public of the service is proportionate to the likely impact on the market' including examining its impact on existing and future commercial services.[41] These procedures were used for the review of proposals for four new digital television and five new national digital radio services during 2001.[42]

This flurry of investigations into the BBC's fair trading rules and new services might appear unobjectionable; after all, one of the expressed objectives of the fair trading rules is to protect the values of public service. However, the fair trading rules and criteria for the approval of new services are relatively well-defined and measurable compared to the norms of PSB, are backed up by 'hard' competition law and the enforcement arrangements described earlier, and have strong ministerial support. The danger is that as a result the values of PSB become subordinated to the creation of an apparently 'level playing field' with commercial competitors, to the disadvantage of the distinct public service missions of the BBC which its competitors do not share. Moreover, in the BBC's internal culture the fair trading norms appear to have prevailed over and eroded the 'soft' PSB norms which they are in part designed to support, as we shall describe in the following section.

Inside the BBC: the subordination of creativity

Perhaps the gravest effects of the state of affairs outlined, in particular the constitutional and definitional uncertainties surrounding British PSB, are shown by the internal state of the BBC in recent years, the last years of the stewardship of the former Director General, Lord Birt.[43] In this section we discuss briefly the character of the BBC's internal culture, and the state of its fair trading arrangements and governance. Thus far we have proceeded on the assumption that there still exist British organisations dedicated to and effectively providing PSB in different guises. Here we show that the changes in the broadcasting sector in the last two decades have bequeathed a complex sociological reality, and that the state of the BBC gives cause for concern. However, we suggest that there remain sufficient foundations for its central purposes where it matters most – in the culture of programme-making – and thus, given necessary policy reforms, for the revivification of its public service orientation.[44]

With the growth of cable and satellite television in the UK from the later 1980s, competition and commercialism greatly intensified in British broadcasting. Since the legitimacy of the BBC licence fee depends partly on the BBC's popularity, pressure on the BBC to compete on ratings grew, and BBC1 was faring poorly by comparison with ITV. In response the BBC focused on two challenges. It improved popular output, fuelling competition between BBC1 and ITV, BBC2 and Channel 4 and resulting by the mid 1990s in a near-parity of audience share. It also

---

41 Department for Culture, Media and Sport, *BBC Public Services: Approvals* (2000). The requirements were revised in January 2001.

42 At the time of writing, the result of the ministerial review of the BBC's proposed new digital services is not known.

43 Despite claims for major reforms by the management regime of the new Director General, Greg Dyke, the BBC is in a transitional period and it is unclear as yet to what extent the underlying changes of the Birt period have been reversed.

44 The basis of this analysis is Born's ethnographic and contextual research: G. Born, *Redefining Public Service Broadcasting: An Ethnography of the BBC* (unpubl. 1999), report submitted to the BBC, the Department of Culture, Media and Sport and the Downing Street Policy Unit.

developed managerial policies aimed at assuaging political criticism. By the late 1990s, three prospective technological shifts promised radical change in the broadcasting sector: the advent of multichannel television, digitalisation, and digital convergence between broadcasting, the internet and telecommunications. While these technological shifts appear inevitable and imminent, they are highly uncertain. In the context of these multiple changes, the BBC's senior management has been under pressure to redefine the role and purposes of the BBC.

Yet for all these pressures, during the late Birt years there was a lack of sustained response among senior management and the governors to the need to redefine the cultural dimensions of the BBC's public service ethos for contemporary conditions. New services were initiated to meet putative new markets, for example in pay television and, with striking success, the internet; and there has been a new stress on the democratic potential of consulting audiences through audience research in order to achieve a popular and diverse range of provision. But beyond these, and despite high-profile statements by senior management, inside the Corporation the search for a redefinition of the public service ethos had the air of an incomplete, ineffectual and semi-conscious process. By contrast, management has been preoccupied with responding to political and economic pressures through a series of other managerial initiatives, in particular marketisation, efficiency and competition policies, and auditing and accountability processes. These have been the dominant concerns of senior management in both its internal and external communications and actions. While BBC senior management's adoption of the central techniques and tenets of neo-liberal governance reflects the pressures on the Corporation during the Thatcher governments and responded to the need to fend off governmental hostility and the threat of privatisation, yet the techniques have outlived that period. Indeed, the Labour administration evidences a renewed concern with the same issues. Recently, under the new Director General, Greg Dyke, there have been two initiatives that suggest the beginnings of a genuine reflection by senior management on the BBC's public service ethos for the digital age. The first is Dyke's emphasis on a greatly expanded educational role for the BBC across all its platforms;[45] and the second, the plan first floated in a speech by the BBC's Director of Television for a shift, in multichannel conditions, from universal to more generic channels.[46] We return to discuss this later.

The value vacuum of the Birt period – in which senior management largely failed to redefine the public service remit culturally and socially, except in the displaced terms of efficiency and markets, accountability and auditing – in conjunction with growing commercialism and competition in the industry had extremely serious consequences. Enormous effort and expenditure went into the tasks of installing quasi-market processes both within the BBC (in the policy of Producer Choice) and between the BBC and the independent production sector, as well as auditing and new accountancy systems, broadcast analysis and audience research sections. For each development, new bureaucracies grew to manage them. Restructuring occurred to make the BBC's various parts transact in apparently more rational and efficient, market-based ways. This in turn led to increased centralisation of decision-making in the planning and commissioning of

---

45 Greg Dyke, 1999 Spectator Lecture, 18 November 1999. The BBC launched a public consultation process on a range of new educational services in September 2000.
46 Mark Thompson, 'Zapped: Why public service TV has to change' speech to the Banff Television Conference, 12 June 2000, available at <http://www.bbc.co.uk/info/news/news245.htm>. Similar plans were proposed in Dyke's McTaggart Lecture, Edinburgh International Television Festival, 25 August 2000, available at <www.bbc.co.uk/info/news/news264.htm>.

programmes, as well as centralisation and reduced diversity in production and editorial cultures.[47] The combined effect of these changes has been to undermine the creative autonomy, the confidence and animation of the BBC's production base. Production departments differ in their ability to withstand these conditions; but overall, they have been placed in a relatively powerless position of supplying programming to templates issued from the centre, rather than having some autonomy in the initiation and development of ideas, and of tutelage to an excessive and disciplinary managerialism.

The voracious competition unleashed throughout the broadcasting sector from the early 1990s had powerful effects. It led to a massive inflation in the value of sports and talent rights, making costs rise sharply in entertainment and sports broadcasting.[48] It caused a pronounced trend towards populist and generic programming in many genres, including documentary, news and current affairs, drama and leisure, and a crowding of suppliers in the centre-ground of programming,[49] including, in some of its output, the BBC. It is essential to realise that, in moving in this populist direction, the BBC was acting in imitation of its main competitors, who were locked into mutual imitation, and this because of the conditioning of audience tastes by prevailing fare and the BBC's problem of maintaining its popularity and legitimacy. The BBC, in this sense, cannot buck prevailing popular trends, unless it has sufficient market power to exert considerable influence rather than simply to compete as one among many similar suppliers.

At the same time, within the BBC, the stoking of market-like processes and of internal and external competition has generated a pronounced entrepreneurialism within production departments, which must now compete to sell ideas and programming to BBC channel commissioners in order to justify overheads and staffing. To ensure continuity of staffing and resources, the pressure to offer certain hits and populist fare is great. Moreover, as prestige, promotion and higher earnings become linked to 'performance' and the delivery of ratings, entrepreneurialism has become a value in itself among BBC programme-makers, tending to drive out less fashionable commitments to risk-taking, innovation, experimentation and minority programming. While these pressures naturally operate in commercial broadcasting, the result of the Birt period was to bring similar pressures to bear *within* the BBC and intensify the BBC's tendency, in some of its operations, to mimic the commercial sector. The effect has been to encourage unproductive self-competition between rival BBC departments, and with the BBC also heading in this direction, to exacerbate even further the imitative populism sweeping across British broadcasting as a whole.

Yet for all this, the anticipated reconception of public service values for contemporary conditions within the BBC does exist on the ground, inside production departments among some programme executives and producers. It

---

47 For the development of an internal market in the BBC see S. Deakin and S. Pratten, 'Reinventing the Market? Competition and Regulatory Change in Broadcasting' (1999) 26 *Journal of Law and Society* 323; V. Wegg Prosser, *BBC Producer Choice and the Management of Organisational Change*, PhD thesis, Management Studies, Brunel University (1998).

48 On the market for sports rights and its wider effects, see D. Booth and G. Doyle, 'UK television warms up for the biggest game yet: pay-per-view' (1997) 19 *Media, Culture and Society* 2; and C. Cowie and M. Williams, 'The economics of sports rights' (1997) 21 *Telecommunications Policy* 7.

49 For a perspective from economics on the phenomenon of crowding in the centre-ground of programming, termed the 'hotelling' effect, see D. Tambini with L. Forgan, S. Verhulst and C. Hall, *Communications: Revolution and Reform* (London: Institute for Public Policy Research, 2001) 31.

takes the form of spaces of reflection and practice in these departments regarding the character, the ethics and aesthetics, of different genres and areas of programming. In each programme sector a culture of attempted quality, innovation and diversity of provision, and a genuine and collective reflection on these issues, forms *some* part of the whole – even if they meet with variable success, or have but a small role within that sector. Among some creative and production staff there thus remains a vital commitment, lived out in everyday practice, to certain core values in a direct line of descent from Reith: values of serving and stimulating the audience, justifying the licence fee, and quality and integrity of output. These values inform production practices and are integrated with reflections on the ongoing evolution of programme genres and the advent of new services. It is, then, in producers' ethical and practical reflections on, and invention in relation to, the changing cultural purposes of the BBC that the clearest expressions exist within the Corporation of a reconception of its public service ethos. This is a hopeful finding, for it is in the cultures of production and in the resulting output and services that any redefinition of public service values must finally impact and be judged.

When we examine the implementation of fair trading rules inside the BBC, a striking inversion of values is evident, echoing the wider legal and political arena. Rather than fair trading issues being subordinate to the task of expediting the BBC's cultural aims, in recent years they have often taken precedence under the external threat of accusations of unfair trading. As we have seen, the BBC's internal rules necessitate a set of complex arrangements for market testing, 'brand' and quality protection, and the separation of public and commercial parts, including arm's-length dealings between public service sectors, for example the production departments, and the commercial arm, BBC Worldwide. While we will argue below that certain of the fair trading rules are necessary, the current arrangements are over complex and in some respects unconvincing. They focus defensively on ensuring that potential criticisms of unfair trading will have little leverage. But in doing so, major structural problems that impact on the BBC's capacity to develop quality cultural products can be sidelined.

To exemplify, consider problems that arose following Birt's 1996 restructuring between BBC Production, the division containing all the production departments, BBC Broadcast, the division containing the channels, and BBC Worldwide. In combination with the fair trading rules, the restructuring greatly disempowered BBC Production vis-à-vis BBC Broadcast and BBC Worldwide in several ways. It forced BBC Production to compete with independent production companies to sell programming to BBC Broadcast. Yet this was a markedly unequal market: independents were free to sell programmes to any broadcaster, but for BBC Production, BBC Broadcast was a monopoly buyer. This enabled Broadcast to offer Production budgets for expensive commissions that were lower than their actual cost to Production, forcing Production to seek co-financing or co-production funds to make up budget shortfalls. This in turn caused Production departments to engage in unofficial entrepreneurial activities, against the BBC's official commercial policy, and to develop programming ideas to attract international commercial co-producers as well as national public service channels, inevitably diluting their commitment to risky or innovative projects as well as those oriented solely to national or minority audiences. Thus steps taken ostensibly to create a level playing field between independent producers and BBC Production had the effect both of radically disadvantaging Production and of undermining its public service purposes.

A further problem follows. It is the practical impossibility of effecting total separation between publicly funded and commercial activities in central areas of BBC operations, namely programme development and programme-making. Observation of the early discussions of programme ideas being developed both for national public service channels and with an eye to potential co-production – increasingly the norm for higher-cost genres – shows that there is little separation at this crucial planning stage. Both markets have to be taken simultaneously into account, and a symbiotic fit or compromise found, usually to the detriment of the more 'autonomous' potential of the national free-to-air channels. This does not necessarily mean that programming developed under these conditions will not be of high quality; but it will bear the marks of its 'two masters' and is likely to be developed according to the templates dictated by co-production partners. Later we will argue that, whatever the practical viability, in the larger normative scheme there is little justification or necessity for this separation in relation to the BBC's main public service activities, those that produce what we will identify as its essential public service goods.[50] If the lack of total separation is a reality which increasingly underwrites the BBC's public service productions by ensuring necessary commercial income, rather than fair-trading issues prevailing, the primary concern should be to ascertain whether high-quality output is being supported or eroded through such pervasive commercial influence – something that is far from predictable. The key issue, then, is how best to organise internal transactions so as to maximise incentives and income flows back to BBC Production, the effect being to free Production from dependence on BBC Broadcast and thus enhance autonomy and boost risk-taking and innovation in programme-making, as opposed to current pressures to offer imitative programming so as to secure safe commissions. From this perspective fair-trading rules and internal market arrangements should be subordinate to the BBC's cultural purposes as embodied by the creative potential of BBC Production.

Towards a redefinition of public service broadcasting

In light of the preceding discussion of the danger that public service norms can in practice be subordinated to fair trading and market processes, we turn now to the necessity of developing effective principles for PSB. A survey[51] of recent

50 Currie and Siner, n 35 above, 87, stress the problem of separation in their discussion of arm's-length trading relationships, noting that 'where commercial and public service activities co-exist in the same directorate, as in BBC News, it is not easy to allocate costs precisely between the two', and that there can be a 'high degree of arbitrariness in the allocation of costs to products produced jointly'. While cautioning that 'inefficiencies could arise' from excessively zealous monitoring of such problematic boundaries, they nonetheless continue to write as though effective boundaries exist.

51 M. Raboy, 'Introduction: public service broadcasting in the context of globalization' in M. Raboy (ed), *Public Broadcasting for the 21st Century* (Luton: John Libbey Media, 1997); Broadcasting Research Unit, *The Public Service Idea in British Broadcasting: Main Principles* (London: BRU, 1985/1988); S. Barnett and D. Docherty, 'Purity or pragmatism? Principles of public service broadcasting' in J. Blumler and T. Nossiter (eds), *Broadcasting Finance in Transition* (New York: Oxford University Press, 1991); Council of Europe, *The Media in a Democratic Society: Draft Resolutions and Draft Political Declaration* (Strasbourg, 1994); R. Collins and J. Purnell, *Commerce, Competition and Governance: the Future of the BBC* (London: Institute for Public Policy Research, 1995); The Tongue report, n 14 above; R. Woldt, *Perspectives of Public Service Television in Europe* (Dusseldorf: European Institute for the Media, 1998); R. Collins, 'Public service broadcasting: an agenda for reform' (1998) 26 *Intermedia* 1; V. Porter, 'Public service broadcasting and the new global information order' (1999) 27 *Intermedia* 4; McKinsey and Co, *Public Service Broadcasters Around the World* (May 1999); Independent Television Commission, *ITC Consultation on Public Service Broadcasting* (London: ITC, 2000).

sociological and policy studies reveals an overlapping consensus on certain core normative criteria for PSB.[52] The criteria can be distilled into three central principles, of which the second and third can largely be derived from the first in which they find their ultimate justification:

a) *Citizenship*: enhancing, developing and serving social, political and cultural citizenship,
b) *Universality*, and
c) *Quality* of services and of output.

Our argument will be that these three principles can provide the basis for new public service requirements in law. In themselves the principles sound almost banal; all three have long been accepted as key elements in any definition of PSB, although they have often been imperfectly realised in practice. We propose in what follows that substance can be given to the principles which is far from banal, and which provides normative foundations for a distinctive contemporary role for PSB.

a) The citizenship principle

Three broad changes in recent democratic theory are relevant to our purposes. The first is a renewed stress on citizenship, the driving motive for which is a concern to transcend the individualistic and rationalistic presuppositions of liberal democratic theory. As one writer puts it, 'The notions of citizenship and community have been stripped of much of their content by liberal individualism'. The challenge for democratic theory is this: 'How can the maximum of pluralism be defended – in order to respect the rights of the widest possible groups – without destroying the very framework of the political community as constituted by the institutions and practices that construe modern democracy and define our identities as citizens?'[53] The criticism made earlier in this article of the conceptual reduction of the broadcast audience to an aggregate of individual consumers is clearly in tune with this reframing of democratic theory. In the context of contemporary multi-cultural societies, the citizenship perspective requires a focus equally on commonality – on people as participants in political, social and cultural communities – and on plurality – on the irreducible complexity of such societies, and the need to allow both the expression of different identities, and dialogue and interaction between them. This double function, and the need to provide a forum in which 'the emerging culture of multiple identities can negotiate its antagonisms',[54] poses new challenges for public service broadcasters such as the BBC. As Raboy suggests, their mandate should not be to 'cater to accentuating difference, as commercial multichannel broadcasting has a tendency to do. Exploring new possibilities for

---

52 Although not all writers specify or agree with every one, there are twelve such criteria. In summary they are: universal access or availability; mixed programming or universality of genres; high quality programming in each genre, including innovation, originality and risk-taking; a mission to inform, educate and entertain; programming to support social integration and national identity; diverse programming catering to minorities and special interest groups, to foster belonging and counteract segregation and discrimination; programming reflecting regional identities; provision of independent and impartial news and fora for public debate and plurality of opinion; commitment to national and regional production, and to local talent; a mission to complement other broadcasters to enrich the broadcasting ecology; affordability; and limited, if any, advertising.

53 Both C. Mouffe, 'Democratic politics today' in Mouffe (ed), *Dimensions of Radical Democracy: Pluralism, Citizenship, Community* (London: Verso, 1992) 3.

54 J. Ellis, 'Public service broadcasting: beyond consensus' (1994), quoted in Raboy, n 51 above, 8.

672 *The Modern Law Review* [Vol. 64

consensus rather than imposing it' is the new role for public service broadcasting.[55]

The second change concerns concepts of pluralism, and here we outline three refinements. The first addresses whether a rights-based foundation is sufficient for achieving the communicative ideals of democratic pluralism. In her discussion of ethical conceptions of democratic communication suited to the plural social conditions of the present, O'Neill substitutes an ethics of obligation for one based on rights. She argues that '[t]oleration of *expression* may need only non-interference; toleration of *communication* must also sustain *conditions* of communication ... An adequate view [of communicative obligations in democratic societies] would have to identify *practices of toleration* that sustain the pre-suppositions of public communication, in forms from which nobody is excluded.'[56] O'Neill thus stresses the purposive cultivation of a diversity of voices in public communication, and the protection of 'positions and voices that are in danger of being silenced or marginalised'.[57]

A second, related refinement concerns what Phillips calls a 'politics of presence' as opposed to a 'politics of ideas' in writing of the challenge issued to democratic practice by social and cultural differences and specifically by excluded and marginalised groups. Against the view that, for example, 'the interests of pensioners or the long-term unemployed can be championed by those who are neither retired nor out of work', she poses the importance of ensuring the presence within the political process of those who are most dispossessed from it. 'Political exclusion is increasingly ... viewed in terms that can be met only by political presence'.[58] This has important implications, by analogy, for the democratic institutional status of public service broadcasters such as the BBC, suggesting that it is not enough to represent on screen a diversity of viewpoints or cultures (the politics of ideas) without also attending to the need for greater social diversity in the population of the BBC and its programme-makers – in other words, in who gets to make programmes and programming decisions (the politics of presence).[59]

A third refinement addresses the 'paradoxes of pluralism', among them the tendency for pluralism to drift into either relativism or into monism, its philosophical opposite. 'It is ... a mistake to believe that pluralism and consensus are antinomic concepts. What pluralism requires is the right to choose, the right to affirm and to affirm oneself. And this right applies to individuals and groups, as well as to collectivities ... when [they] engage in debate about values'.[60] The rationale for a public service broadcaster that serves pluralism by both displaying plural perspectives and allowing them to be implicitly and explicitly in dialogue is

---

55 Raboy, n 51 above.
56 Both from O. O'Neill, 'Practices of toleration' in J. Lichtenberg (ed), *Democracy and the Mass Media* (Cambridge: Cambridge University Press, 1990) 167, emphases added
57 O'Neill, *ibid* 173.
58 A. Phillips, 'Dealing with difference: a politics of ideas, or a politics of presence?' in S. Benhabib (ed), *Democracy and Difference* (Princeton, NJ: Princeton University Press, 1996).
59 There are signs that both the BBC under Greg Dyke and the British television industry as a whole, under ministerial guidance, are increasingly aware of these issues. See Greg Dyke, 'The BBC: Leading cultural change for a rich and diverse UK', speech to the Commission for Racial Equality Race in the Media Awards, 7 April 2000, available at <www.bbc.co.uk/info/news/news233.htm>; see also White Paper, para 4.4.7 on the Cultural Diversity Network set up by television broadcasters in February 2000 'in response to concerns raised by the Secretary of State for Culture, Media and Sport and others about the adequacy of the representation of our multicultural society on and behind the screen'.
60 M. Marcil-Lacoste, 'Paradoxes of pluralism' in Mouffe, n 53 above, 136.

well made here. Commonality or consensus and plurality, in other words, must be understood dialectically in terms both of the display of difference, and of the dialogue between different perspectives that may or may not achieve consensus. The achievement of consensus is here conceived as provisional, marking a departure from the Habermasian public-sphere theory based on a consensus-seeking discourse ethics that is often invoked in discussion of democratic functions of the media.[61]

The philosophies outlined here, then, suggest revised normative foundations for the contemporary communicative functions provided by PSB in conditions of social and cultural pluralism. In this view PSB has the key democratic function of staging for a society communicative and cultural (intersubjective) encounters between its plural communities and minority identities; communicative tolerance is central. But we would emphasise that, as well as mediating social and cultural differences, PSB must continue to offer, as *part of the mix*, 'universalising' modes of address that invoke commonality. Three forms of such commonality can be discerned: standard authoritative discourses of impartiality, facticity and commentary;[62] rituals of social solidarity and national unity,[63] including mainstream popular entertainment programming on national channels; and the forms of global identification evoked by American and other kinds of global television.[64] And yet, in contemporary conditions, they must co-exist without moving to closure or the dominance of one discourse over others. Surveying BBC output in this light, and the prevalence of authoritative consensus over animating diversity, it is striking that the balance between these functions needs redressing. In line with the politics of presence, a critical factor in ensuring this redress and countering the imbalance will be attention to the continued exclusion of minorities from the social population of the BBC, especially its higher echelons – a continuing source of bitter criticism.[65]

A further major change in recent theories of citizenship is recognition of the fundamental importance of culture and identity to the concept in the present. Where Marshall's influential account of citizenship traced it through three stages of emergence and expansion – civil citizenship in the eighteenth century, political citizenship in the nineteenth century, and social citizenship in the twentieth century[66] – we would add a fourth stage: the centrality of cultural citizenship for the late twentieth and twenty-first centuries.[67] The concept of cultural citizenship

---

61 See eg N. Garnham, 'The media and the public sphere' in P. Golding et al (eds), *Communicating Politics* (Leicester: Leceister University Press, 1986), J. Keane, *The Media and Democracy* (Cambridge: Polity, 1991), J. Thompson, *The Media and Modernity* (Cambridge: Polity, 1995).

62 As in the public service tradition of news and current affairs; a seminal analysis is P. Schlesinger, *Putting 'Reality' Together* (London: Methuen, 1978).

63 As in live broadcasts of major national and international 'events' which attract massive audiences, for example, coverage of wars and revolutions (eg Kosovo, the fall of the Berlin Wall), of royal events (eg the funeral of Princess Diana) and sporting events (eg the Olympics). The classic study of these ritual functions of broadcasting is D. Dayan and E. Katz, *Media Events* (London: Harvard University Press, 1992).

64 On the forms of audience identification and pleasure invited by global mass media products, eliciting what might be termed a global cultural imaginary, see G. Born, 'Against negation, for a politics of cultural production' (1993) 34 *Screen* 3.

65 Exactly this criticism and this link were made by B. Bernard, Deputy Chair of the Commission for Racial Equality, in a speech to the BBC Governors' Seminar, *The BBC: Reflecting the Cultural Richness of the UK*, 12 July 2000 (transcript available from the BBC).

66 T.H. Marshall, *Sociology at the Crossroads* (London: Heinemann, 1963).

67 See B. Turner, 'Outline of a theory of citizenship' in Mouffe, n 53 above, 37; and N Stevenson (ed), *Culture and Citizenship* (London: Sage, 2001).

requires clarification. A first, common usage refers to the necessary provision, in the age of mass mediated politics, of news and information on current events and politics such that there exists an informed citizenry able to engage in public debate concerning private and political powers, and thus fulfil its democratic responsibilities. This is the function to which Habermasian public-sphere theory points. Public service broadcasting's role in the provision of news and information, subject to requirements of impartiality and pluralism, is therefore central to the democratic process, although, as we have said, present debate might question the balance between impartiality and pluralism of opinion.

A second usage introduces culture and identity into this view, arguing that the media play a critical role in civil society, but that the space produced by the media should not be conceived as an 'informational space' but as a 'cultural space' in which media are 'involved in the construction of common identities and universalistic solidarities, in multiple publics'.[68] In this perspective broadcasting has an increasingly major function of mediating the identities of both individuals and collectivities, and so in influencing the cultural and identity frameworks of citizenship. Scannell takes this view summarising the historical role of the BBC as 'a task of democratic representation on the terrain of culture rather than politics. The task was to create a common culture that speaks to the whole society and can be shared by people of widely different backgrounds, with different tastes and interests'.[69] This is no doubt an overly sanguine portrayal given that, as Scannell himself shows, throughout its history the BBC has harboured powerful elitist and centralist tendencies. More generally, as Stuart Hall has argued, '[a]ll communities are symbolic communities, all communities are imagined'.[70] Discussing the imperative of pluralising citizenship in contemporary Britain, he continues:

> Broadcasting now has a major role ... to play in ... 're-imagining ... the nation': not by seeking to reimpose a unity and homogeneity which has long since departed, but by becoming the ... 'theatre', in which [Britain's] cultural diversity is produced, displayed and represented ... This ... remains broadcasting's key 'public cultural' role – and one which cannot be sustained unless there is a public service idea and a system shaped in part by public service objectives to sustain it.[71]

A third cultural dimension of mediated citizenship stems from a critique of the excessively cognitivist and rationalistic presuppositions of earlier public-sphere theory which focused on the informational and educational contributions of media. Instead, recent writers have augmented the theory by reference to the imaginative, expressive and affective dimensions of broadcasting, dimensions with major implications for the character of public knowledge and for the formation of identities.[72] The important recognition here is the necessity, in understanding how broadcasting mediates public knowledge, of attending to the intense symbiosis between the public and the popular, reflection and pleasure. This, in turn, enables a recognition of the critical role of high-quality drama and entertainment in providing

---

68 J. Alexander and R. Jacobs, 'Mass communication, ritual and civil society' in T. Liebes and J. Curran (eds), *Media, Ritual and Identity* (London: Routledge, 1998) 23.

69 P. Scannell, 'Britain: public service broadcasting, from national culture to multiculturalism' in Raboy, n 51 above, 26

70 S. Hall, 'Which public, whose service?' in W. Stevenson (ed), *All Our Futures: The Changing Role and Purpose of the BBC* (London: British Film Institute, 1993) 36, citing B. Anderson, *Imagined Communities* (London: Verso, 1983) 15.

71 Hall, *ibid* 36–37.

72 P. Dahlgren, *Television and the Public Sphere* (London: Sage, 1995); J. Hermes, 'Gender and media studies' in J. Corner et al (eds), *International Media Research: A Critical Survey* (London: Routledge, 1997).

a framework for collective imagination and expressive enjoyment for society and its component collectivities. In this light, the staging of communicative dialogues between diverse groups that is central to PSB's democratic role must take the form not just of exchanges of information or opinion, but exchanges involving imaginative cultural forms – the kinds of narratives, myths, parodies and self-reflections contained in comedy, drama and documentary. At the same time, to enhance social integration and boost its popularity and legitimacy, PSB has rightly had recourse to the kinds of mainstream entertainment – popular drama, sports and light entertainment – that have the capacity to unify otherwise disparate social groups.

A final aspect of cultural citizenship follows on: what we would term the *cultural formation* of citizenship. If we take seriously the role of media culture in forming audience tastes and conditioning the wider public culture, then, by analogy with the concern in democratic theory for the formation of an educated and informed citizenry, we would add the importance for contemporary plural societies of a concern with the formation of a *culturally* aware and mature, culturally pluralistic citizenry. In light of the preceding points, this is an essential dimension of cultural citizenship properly conceived; and it should be a core function of PSB to provide such diversity of cultural experience.[73]

In sum, in the contemporary era, PSB can play a central role as an instrument of the processes of social and cultural development that underlie the general condition of citizenship. It does this partly through the encouragement of individual self-development and learning, generating what Curran has termed a 'culture of mutuality'. At a societal level, it makes available widely different understandings of society, permitting communication between them and facilitating agreement and compromise between different opinions, perspectives and values.[74] The implication is that PSB is not merely responsible for filling gaps left in the market place, but for aiding in the very definition and negotiation of social identities that are a core dimension of citizenship and, thereby, for establishing conditions of communication without which markets cannot work. In all the senses outlined, the constitutional role and the communicative functions of PSB are prior to the market, not simply part of it. Market failure is therefore not the most appropriate language to use in its justification, for, as we have stressed, we are concerned with the cultural formation of identities prior to choice, not with the operation of pre-formed choices within markets.[75] As another UK broadcaster put it, 'public service broadcasting is about an approach to broadcasting and not simply a requirement imposed on one or two broadcasters to address specific issues of market failure.'[76]

b) The universality principle

We would distinguish three different senses of universality as it has been deployed in the history of the BBC and of British PSB more generally, as it was initially by Reith.[77] They are:

---

73 There seems to be an implicit recognition of this point in the White Paper, n 6 above, para 4.4.8.
74 J. Curran, 'Mass Media and Democracy Revisited' in J. Curran and M. Gurevitch (eds), *Mass Media and Society* (London: Arnold, 2nd edition, 1996) 105. See also A. Graham, 'Broadcasting Policy in the Multi-Media Age' in Graham et al, n 8 above, 17–46 at 19, 27, 31–33, 34–37, 39.
75 Cf the Davies report, n 27 above, 137.
76 Channel 4, *Response to the Invitation to Submit Comments on the Communications Reform White Paper* (2000), available at <www.culture.gov.uk/creative/dti-dcms_ch4.htm>. See also Raboy, n 51 above, 9.
77 On the historical roots of the BBC philosophy and practice of universality, see P. Scannell and D. Cardiff, *A Social History of British Broadcasting, Vol. One: 1922–1939* (Oxford: Blackwell, 1991).

676   *The Modern Law Review*   [Vol. 64

(i)   technical and geographical universality: the provision of infrastructure
       whereby all members of the population who wish to can receive a high
       quality broadcast signal for all free-to-air BBC services, regardless of
       geographical or social location;
(ii)   social and cultural universality: the provision of programming that caters for
       and reflects the interests of the full social and cultural diversity of Britain and
       its minorities, as well as the aim of enhancing social unity through the
       creation of a 'common culture';
(iii) universality of genre and mode of address: the provision of mixed pro-
       gramming, that is, programming that includes the entire range of broadcast
       genres, thereby meeting a wide range of needs and purposes through the
       trinity of information, education and entertainment. The aim here is that the
       BBC should be truly popular, both as a value in itself – given the social
       importance of entertainment and leisure – and, more instrumentally, in order
       to draw audiences across different and unforeseen kinds of programming,
       whether less known, less popular or new content.

The first sense has evolved into what is the main theme of much current regulatory
and normative debate: that of universality of access given rapid technological
changes and the potential of powerful private interests to create barriers to access, a
matter extensively covered in the Communications White Paper.[78] We return to
these issues shortly.

It is striking that the second and third senses of universality are unhelpfully
elided in the 1996 Agreement. In it the Corporation undertakes to offer 'a
wide range of subject matter (having regard both to the programmes as a
whole and also to the days of the week on which, and the times of the day at
which, the programmes are shown) meeting the needs and interests of
audiences'.[79] The second is the sense that is currently most to the fore, but we
suggest that its concerns can properly be subsumed within the general
principle of cultural citizenship. It features in this White Paper commitment
by the government: '[w]e will ensure that public service broadcasters continue
to celebrate and reflect our culturally diverse communities, and broadcast
programmes which appeal to a wide range of tastes and interests, as well as
to people of different ages and backgrounds'.[80] In present conditions, then,
the second sense of the universality principle is well accepted. Indeed the
advent of digital services has augmented the consensus concerning its
importance, and there is great pressure on the BBC to meet expectations of
greater diversity of both cultural representations on screen, and social
representation within its population. The idea is widespread that digital has
the potential massively to augment regional, minority and specialised services
and thus to enhance the BBC's diversity of provision,[81] although to what
extent this will be achieved by the BBC's digital plans remains to be seen.

If acceptance of the principle of universality in a sense broader than the technical
and geographical is widespread, two contemporary implications of it seem less
well understood. The first implication is that the traditional concept of mixed
programming is superior to the concept of niche channels according to which, for

---

78 White Paper, n 6 above, ch 3.
79 1996 Agreement, n 19 above, clause 3.1.
80 White Paper, n 6 above, para 4.4.8.
81 For the wider argument see M. Horsman, 'Time for digital to deliver' *Media Guardian*, 16 August
    1999, 5.

example, the more demanding programmes on current affairs or the arts would be concentrated in specialist channels rather than being routinely available to all as part of a mixed schedule on mass-appeal channels. In this respect the White Paper has an encouraging reference to the continued importance of 'mixed schedule networks, free at the point of use'.[82] Our concerns are nonetheless raised because the BBC's commitment to mixed programming appears to be seriously undermined. Since mid-2000 the Corporation has announced plans to develop additional digital channels for television and radio, with the effect in television of reorientating the character of the national channels, BBC1 and BBC2. The expansion will bring eight television services, all of which will be more niched than the current national channels. The precise design of the new look BBC1 and BBC2 has not been made clear but, instead of both offering fully mixed schedules, BBC1 will be more focused on entertainment, drama and factual programmes and the character of BBC2 will, in the words of the Director General, 'increasingly focus on intelligent specialist factual programmes'.[83] In short, the range of genres on each channel will be much reduced, although there will remain a range. Public response to the proposals has been mixed. Alarm has been sounded by those, including the Secretary of State and the Culture Committee, who are fearful that what is being signalled is the BBC's retreat from the public service concept – a concept easily ridiculed by reference to crude notions of paternalism and elitism – of taking seriously the responsibility of forming and widening viewer tastes. We share those concerns for the following reasons.

The niche channel model appears attractive if one adopts a consumer choice view of broadcasting; consumers can exercise that choice through the remote control, or in the near future through the sophisticated electronic programme guide or a computerised video recorder. Schedule-based viewing of single channels, in this perspective, will become a thing of the past. However, there are several reasons to query this prediction – a prediction that will, of course, speedily be realised if the major terrestrial broadcasters adopt the niche model. Firstly, some scholars doubt that, even in the digital context, mass-broadcast channels will in fact wane in popular appeal.[84] More importantly, the niche model involves a series of threats to PSB. It brings the danger that programming appealing to non-mainstream consumers will become ghettoised, defeating the pluralist principle that diverse and minority programming should be available not only to the audience immediately envisaged but to the wider audience. Such ghettoisation would have the added effect of making it hard to justify the financing of these programmes through a universal licence fee. It would risk accentuating the very social and cultural divisions which the linked communicative and citizenship functions of PSB in a pluralist age should have as its core aim to diminish. An important role for PSB, signalled earlier as the cultural formation of citizenship, is to make us aware of, and develop our capacity for, tastes and interests we did not previously recognise we might have; to foster the formation of tastes and interests. The model of mixed programming on mass channels is inherently more suited to accomplishing these processes.

The second implication of universality in the age of digital convergence returns to questions of access, in terms of both technological infrastructure and content.

---

82 White Paper, n 6 above, para 5.3.8.
83 Dyke, n 46 above.
84 J. Gripsrud, 'Broadcast television: the chances of its survival in a digital age' paper to the conference *Approaches to Television Studies*, Stockholm 1999; J. Ellis, *Seeing Things: Television in the Age of Uncertainty* (London: I.B. Tauris, 2000) esp ch 11.

678   *The Modern Law Review*   [Vol. 64

Infrastructurally, the technical and political problem of assuring universal social access across the 'digital divide' poses serious challenges, as encapsulated in the debate concerning the timing, the benefits and the likelihood of 'analogue switch-off'.[85] It is a problem that finds little response from some critics of the BBC and commercial players who, using arguments of unfair trading, attack the BBC's entry into new services and its claims for space on new technological platforms. The BBC's presence on new platforms, particularly its provision of digital services, has therefore been controversial. As the Davies panel noted:

> a particular problem arises with the launch of entirely new public services by the BBC in the UK market. These services will typically be free-to-air, and therefore do not directly impact on the BBC's commercial revenues. Nevertheless, precisely because they are free-to-air, they are often seen as grossly unfair competition by private broadcasters. Indeed, the launch of such services by the BBC can call into question the economic viability of similar services which have already been launched by the private sector. The risk that this may happen could be a disincentive to the future development of private sector broadcasting services.[86]

The panel recommended that new criteria should be published by the Secretary of State for the launching of such services, and as we saw earlier these have been extremely restrictive in effect.

But while they may reflect real concerns, the arguments based on competition and unfair trading risk subordinating universal access to the consolidation of technological monopolies and the principles of public service provision to the pursuit of private profit. The BBC has a strong justification for the provision of digital and other new services on the basis of the universality principle. The justification was summarised by the Culture Committee:

> [t]he BBC considers that 35 per cent of the population will not adopt any form of pay television and accordingly views its own development of free-to-air digital services as crucial to the Government's strategy for analogue switch-off. By the time of analogue switch-off, the BBC expects to have five or six free-to-air channels in every home and attaches importance to developing 'the right portfolio of channels'.[87]

The Corporation has thus stressed that after the switch to digital the population needs to be offered 'something other than the opportunity to buy new pay channels: they need to be offered the ability to access a wider range of high quality *free-to-air* services.'[88] Obviously we would not wish to support expensive and speculative ventures with no long-term audience. Nevertheless, the provision of a range of free-to-air services on new delivery platforms that would otherwise be dominated by subscription and pay-per-view programming is exactly what is required by the universality principle of PSB updated for digital conditions.[89] There is, moreover, a further case for the BBC entering new services: the argument that the BBC is likely to 'raise the game' of those markets in which it is a major competitor, which we shall consider more fully in later pages.

---

85 See on this the Secretary of State for Culture Media and Sport, n 40 above.
86 Davies report, n 27 above, 102.
87 Culture, Media and Sport Committee, *Report and Accounts of the BBC for 1999-2000*, HC 719 (1999–2000) para 23.
88 BBC, *Initial Submission to the Government's Communications Review* (London: BBC, 2000) 11 (emphasis retained); see also 15–16, 28.
89 See also the Culture, Media and Sport Committee, n 87 above, para 27.

c) The quality principle

The term 'quality' is much used in broadcasting debates, often with little attempt at definition. Here we aim to clarify the quality principle by giving it some distinctive and normative substance. A problematic feature of recent discussions of quality is relativism expressed in an unwillingness to adjudicate between consumer and producer conceptions of quality in relation to broadcast output.[90] In contrast, we propose that there is a strong case for giving primary normative attention to producer judgements of quality rather than consumer perceptions, since producer intentionality in combination with the conditions bearing on production together determine the character of the output, and in this way condition and set the limits to consumption. This ecological model of the priority of production and its role in conditioning consumption clearly contradicts the consumer sovereignty model, which rests on a notion of pre-existing and autonomous consumer tastes which broadcasters are then enjoined simply to serve. Whereas in the sovereign consumer model the issue is the adequacy of broadcasters' response to putatively pre-existing audience tastes, in the ecological model proposed here the critical issue is the quality and diversity of the programming available to audiences, programming that will in turn cumulatively condition the future direction both of audience tastes, and through them wider currents of public opinion and sensibility, and of broadcasting markets.[91]

In short, production is ontologically prior to consumption. For these reasons – even given the democratic importance of attending to the degree to which broadcast output fulfils consumer desires and needs, something that affects also the legitimacy and profitability of broadcasters – any normative framework concerned with quality of output must attend first and foremost to the conditions of production affecting that output. Similar reasoning has led some writers to suggest that the main indicator for quality of output is producer intentionality, and in particular the ethical stance characterising the culture of production. Mepham argues that there is a general rule for assessing television quality, and that is 'whether or not [its production] is governed by an ethic of truth-telling'.[92] Blumler takes the more general stance that 'the system as a whole should regard the pursuit and elevation of programme quality as a priority goal'. In addition, both writers stress that such intentionalities will necessarily find plural expressions according to different programme genres. They thereby avoid the universalising fallacy that for an inherently plural communications medium such as television, 'some particular criterion of quality should prevail over all others'.[93] It must be emphasised here that these are not elitist arguments. They do not rest on the assumption that producer judgements of quality are necessarily superior to consumer judgements, but on an ontological argument for production's temporal and sequential priority over consumption and hence the necessity of attending to production. Nor do they assume a hierarchical ranking of value between different television genres, but allow for a plural conception of value relative to different genres, including popular and mainstream genres.

---

90 See G. Mulgan, 'Television's holy grail: seven types of quality' in G. Mulgan (ed), *The Question of Quality* (London: British Film Institute, 1990); C. Murroni and N. Irvine (eds), *Quality in Broadcasting* (London: IPPR, 1997).

91 A version of this argument is given by Paddy Scannell, who proposes that BBC broadcasting in its early decades ushered into being for the first time a national culture and a 'radically new kind of public, one commensurate with the whole of society': Scannell, n 69 above, 26.

92 J. Mepham, 'The ethics of quality in television' in Mulgan, n 90 above, 69.

93 J. Blumler, 'Vulnerable values at stake' in Blumler (ed), *Television and the Public Interest* (London: Sage, 1992), both quotations at 31.

While these writers' focus on production cultures is welcome, there remain some problems with their stance. Neither writer is able to say how such high-level intentionalities are played out on the ground in everyday practices of programme-making, nor how quality judgements are operationalised in relation to different genres. A rhetoric of truth-telling is common among television professionals; but this tells us little about the extent to which, or how, it is translated into practice.[94] Moreover, they have little to say regarding the contemporary conditions that constrain and mould producer intentionality; for example the complex structures of control and dependence embodied in the commissioning process which, in the contemporary BBC, delivers strict templates within which producers must work and to which programmes must conform. Producer intentionality is, then, highly constrained; and it follows that an account of quality as embodied in production must attend also to the conditions that impact on production. Normatively, we might say, institutional and industry conditions should exist that foster the creative well-being of production cultures and that influence in positive ways producers' capacities to fulfil the other normative principles of PSB, including innovation, diversity, and programming that fosters social cohesion. An adequate evaluation thus requires analysis of the conditions bearing on production, which influence the orientation and the capacity for quality of a given production culture. For instance, as we have shown, it would be impossible to understand the increasingly populist tendencies exhibited by the BBC channels in recent years, and the erosion of quality in much output, without linking this very directly to the pressures created by the drift downmarket in rival channels, themselves responding to excesses of competition. These are pressures that, within the BBC, *override the integrity and the creative potential* that still exist inside the BBC's production cultures.

It is therefore the nexus of conditions bearing on production that must take logical priority in normative terms. Any future regulator will need the capacity to undertake analysis of such conditions as part of a process of normative judgement – a capacity that the BBC governors have notably lacked in the recent past. In contrast to both the negative regulation concerned with transgression of impartiality, taste and decency standards, and the currently minimalist character of positive content regulation through quotas for certain genres, this would yield a more dynamic and qualitative positive regulation focused on links between output and production, and aimed at strengthening the institutional conditions for quality programme-making.[95]

A final stipulation here concerns the need to distinguish three levels of output in discussions of quality and standards:

1) individual programmes or strands,
2) channel schedules, and the identities and positioning of channels as a whole,
3) the total portfolio of services (channels, internet, ecommerce and other new media services) offered by a broadcaster.

This approach is necessitated by the expanding number of channels and services offered by broadcasters in the digital age. It gives analytical and evaluative purchase on output at levels of increasing integration. Each level has a certain autonomy, so

---

94 This is brutally illustrated by one of the gravest professional crises to hit British broadcasting, namely the revelations of fakery in the production of television documentaries and daytime talk shows in recent years.

95 On the concepts of positive regulation and negative regulation, the strengths of the former and the limits of the latter, see R. Collins and C. Murroni, *New Media, New Policies* (Cambridge: Polity, 1996) 144.

that, as in previous discussions of quality, it remains necessary to consider the quality of individual programmes (1) offered by broadcasters; and until schedule-based viewing is shown to be superseded, similar concerns should exist for the quality of schedules (2). But the three levels are also interrelated, and in this era of centralised strategy and commissioning there is a chain of influence from each higher level down. As niche channels move to the fore and broadcasters increasingly conceive of their services in terms of a portfolio of such niche and other new media offerings, the quality of that portfolio (3) deserves scrutiny, for only in this way will it be possible to assess in relation to citizenship and universality principles its potential benefits and synergies as well as gaps and imbalances. Indeed, where debates until this point have centred on individual programmes, in the digital future the quality of schedules and portfolios will become increasingly critical to evaluate against normative principles; and at these levels, evaluating quality requires attention also to issues of citizenship and universality.

The utility of this approach can be shown by considering the BBC's present plans for digital expansion, which focus primarily on schedules and portfolio. As described earlier, the BBC's portfolio strategy is to expand the number of television and radio channels, at the same time moderating the character of some existing channels so as to increase their complementarity and produce overall an increase in the projected range of social and cultural interests being served. Clearly, this is in some ways a convincing and beneficial use of digital potential to enhance the diversity and thus the citizenship functions of PSB. However, innovation in the portfolio (3) is played off against changes to schedules (2) that are potentially negative, through an erosion of the commitment to mixed schedules and its accompanying values, and thus the changes are likely to cause a decline in quality. The BBC's case is to pose such schedule changes (2) against its claims for greater diversity and viewer-responsiveness in the new portfolio of niched channels (3). But for the reasons given earlier, innovation in the portfolio need not necessitate an abandonment of fully mixed schedules at least in some national channels; changes in portfolio need not dictate these changes in schedules. A further issue is illustrated by the BBC's plans for a much-expanded portfolio of educational and childrens' services, which would appear greatly to enhance its public service value by responding to an urgent need for high quality services to counterbalance an avalanche of commercial channels and fare. However, this must be weighed against the conditions within which the new educational services will operate: the closure of the BBC's dedicated education department and the dispersal of its expertise, the impact of which on the quality of educational programmes remains to be judged.[96] The implication here for quality is to point to the danger that changes and indeed innovation at the levels of portfolio and schedules may be taken erroneously to compensate or even substitute for quality at the still-critical level of individual programmes themselves. We suggest that such changes can *not* substitute in this way, and that the quality principle requires a specific concern both with the conditions bearing on the production of programmes, and with the quality of output at each of the three levels identified – individual programmes, schedules and channels identities, and portfolio of services.

---

96 See Martin Bright, 'BBC staff to vote on strike over "dumbing down" ' *The Observer*, 8 October 2000.

682   *The Modern Law Review*   [Vol. 64

Legal and regulatory implications

In this section we shall draw together the implications of our arguments and make some policy proposals relating to the translation of the normative principles proposed above into law, largely in the form of a response to the Communications White Paper. Our first proposal, however, concerns the legal form of public service obligations. We consider it highly unsatisfactory that the current principles of the BBC's mission are contained not in statute but in the Charter and Agreement. Apart from the somewhat feudal status of a Royal Charter in the context of modern media, the impression is given that PSB is a deal between government and the broadcaster rather than, as we have suggested, a key element of citizenship, and thus both a statement of relations between broadcaster and the public and part of the democratic structure of modern society and so subject to proper democratic scrutiny. We would thus see it as a prerequisite of the future support and protection of the BBC's PSB remit that it be given a statutory basis, as is already the case with the special remit of Channel 4 and the public service requirements applying to other broadcasters. This would have other advantages too. It would satisfy European Community law requirements for a clear definition of PSB, and would reinforce the fact that public service is not merely a set of principles subordinate to hard competition law but a prerequisite for the formation of mature cultural identities and cultural citizenship and thus in principle is prior to the interests protected by competition law.

Clearly, not all the changes we propose can be implemented through legal change; we have stressed, for example, the importance of the well-being of the production cultures within the BBC and the negative effects of an over-enthusiastic adoption of market processes and of the fair-trading rules. Nor could we create overnight something resembling the constitutional concept of public service encountered in some Continental jurisdictions, although the Human Rights Act will go a considerable way towards creating the necessary basis for such constitutionalisation in areas of individual rights and may have a substantial effect on some aspects of broadcasting. Our first proposal for specific legal change would be to unpack the current concept of universality which is contained in the 1996 Agreement, and which, as we noted above, unhelpfully elides different forms of universality, that is, technical and geographical universality, social universality and mixed programming. A redrafted provision would explicitly require all of these. It could be reinforced further through other legal requirements, for example through effective 'must carry' requirements for the transmission of public service channels on other platforms, including digital cable and satellite; it is encouraging to find explicit support for this in the White Paper.[97] The conditions on which new services are permitted by the Secretary of State also need to be redrafted to stress the importance of increased access to PSB, even if this may have detrimental effects on competitors.[98] Finally, we would require the BBC to develop its own principles of PSB as a basis for self-regulation. This would ensure that the detailed conditions were in place for the achievement of the purposes we have suggested and would correct the balance between the current 'hard' fair trading rules and 'soft' PSB requirements; monitoring would take place through the new regulatory

---

97 White Paper, n 6 above, sections 3.4-3.5.
98 For an interesting German comparison see the *Sixth Television Case*, 83 BverfGE 238 (1991); 87 BvergFE 181 (1992), discussed in Barendt, n 28 above, 58–9.

arrangements we discuss below. Once more, this is in line with the stress in the White Paper on a greater role for self-regulation.[99]

These changes would secure that the BBC has a presence in the broadcasting and new media sectors which enables it to impact very substantially on the conditioning of public tastes. This is essential in order to avoid the BBC following its commercial rivals down-market and to enable it to withstand and counteract the drift to increasing populism and sensationalism. Such benign competitive pressure will work only if the BBC continues to have a major presence across all genres and all platforms.[100] Critically, in this way the BBC will be empowered not only to influence the wider industry in a benign direction towards higher-quality programming and richer cultural goals, but also to influence, through its substantial market presence, the conditioning of public tastes. It is this important latter function which is commonly overlooked in discussions of the market role of the BBC in the multichannel future. Without this essential function, the combined populism, sensationalism and lower-quality programming issuing from many commercial providers will meet no resistance in conditioning public tastes and establishing the public's framework of expectations; and in these circumstances the BBC's offerings will be seen as increasingly marginal and exceptional in the public mind, signalling the end of its universality. The overall result is likely to be a general degradation of the quality of Britain's media ecology.

We now need to consider the crucial question of the regulation and governance of the BBC to ensure that the public service remit is fulfilled. There have been repeated proposals from the Culture, Media and Sport Committee that a single Communications Regulatory Commission be established that would undertake both economic and content regulation.[101] It would cover the BBC as well as commercial broadcasters. This has found partial support in the Communications White Paper, which has proposed the creation of a new unified regulator, OFCOM, responsible for the communications sector, including broadcasting content as well as policing competition.[102] However, this would not apply fully to the BBC, where the Paper notes that:

> [w]e are not proposing to change the BBC's role and remit ... We are maintaining the link between the legal responsibility and authority of the BBC governors for delivering the BBC's remit and will preserve their following core responsibilities inside the BBC:
>
> - interpreting the Charter and setting the strategy to deliver the BBC's remit and responsibilities;
> - upholding and protecting the BBC's political and editorial independence;
> - assessing the BBC's performance against remit and objectives;
> - calling management to account.[103]

There are a number of different issues that need to be disentangled in the White Paper proposals. The first is OFCOM's proposed combination of economic and content regulation. Clearly there will be a major role for an economic regulator in the developing media world, for example in providing specialist competition regulation in relation to the bottlenecks that will develop in the form of conditional access, electronic programme guides and other developments.[104] However, we see

---

99 White Paper, n 6 above, sections 5.8, 8.11; cf Tambini et al, n 49 above, 13–15.
100 A similar argument is given in A. Graham and G. Davies, *Broadcasting, Society and Policy in the Multimedia Age* (Luton: University of Luton Press, 1997), and Collins, n 51 above.
101 Culture Committee, n 3 above, paras 158–9.
102 White Paper, n 6 above, ch 8.
103 *ibid* para 5.6.7.
104 See eg D. Goldberg, T. Prosser and S. Verhulst (eds), *Regulating the Changing Media* (Oxford: Clarendon, 1998) 303-14.

dangers in combining this with content regulation in that competition regulation is designed to create open markets and in doing so will treat market participants as identical. Our theme has been that a public service mission and the resulting provision of essential public service goods are sufficient grounds for distinguishing public service broadcasters from other market participants, and that the market rules of the game need to respect this. The danger is that the citizenship, universality and quality principles of broadcasting could be marginalised in such economic regulation, as we have argued has already happened in relation to the BBC. This would justify separating the two types of regulation, either in separate regulatory bodies, or at a minimum in separate branches of the same organisation with equal authority and considerable institutional separation between them, as proposed by Channel 4 and envisaged in the Culture Committee's recommendation. In the words of Channel 4:

> the role of content regulation must not be allowed to be overwhelmed by the more immediately obvious and powerful pressures of economic regulation. A new and integrated regulatory structure would be dealing with issues that go to the heart of our values as a democratic society and which are as much about the interaction of the citizen with society as they are about the relationship between producer and consumer.[105]

We are not persuaded that OFCOM will be in a position adequately to promote the values of PSB rather than those of competition regulation, especially if current suggestions that it will have a predominantly competition-based remit are correct.[106] In terms of content regulation, there is a lesson to be learnt from the BBC governors' failure to perceive the conditions causing a decline in quality. That is, the new content regulator should be full-time, independently informed, and should combine professional and executive expertise from broadcasting with periodic public consultations. In particular, given the centrality of the production sector to the delivery of PSB, producers should be well represented in the content regulatory body. One of its tasks would be, periodically and on the basis of research, to report on the debates and values concerning output that circulate in the industry, to evaluate their results in the output, and to consider what contextual forces are helping or hindering the achievement of PSB goals, goals that we propose would have the status of law. Such an institutionalised process of reflexivity may seem demanding; but without attending to this critical nexus, regulatory attention will be superficial. In the present regulatory regime there is a tendency to be blinded by the detail of broadcasters' individual transgressions in relation to issues of violence, sex or bad language, and to measure PSB by quotas of specific genres in primetime with little attention to the quality of that programming. Our suggestion is to roll back the relatively trivial concern with transgressions and the limitations of quota-based thinking. Rather, some regulatory attention should be given to the bigger picture and to the causal dynamics that profoundly affect the state of PSB. Only in this way will the content regulator be equipped for dialogues with the economic regulator concerning revisions to the structure of the industry, through awareness of the effects of context on output.

The second issue is whether the BBC should fall within the same regulatory structures as other broadcasters. The Corporation has strongly opposed this, defending the role of the Board of Governors as the BBC's 'trustees of the public

---

105 Channel 4, n 76 above. See also Tambini et al, n 49 above, 84–85.
106 Cf White Paper, n 6 above, para 8.5.1, but see the Culture, Media and Sport Committee, *The Communications White Paper*, HC 161 (1999–2000), paras 24–27 and I. Hargreaves, 'Why is the Sun hot for Tony?', *Financial Times Creative Business*, 20 March 2001.

interest' and as ensuring that the Corporation remains independent and able to focus on its unique public service remit. It has pointed also to the specific responsibilities of the governors in consulting audiences, accounting for performance and ensuring compliance with external regulatory requirements.[107] As mentioned above, the White Paper has accepted much of this argument through excluding much (though not all) of the BBC's regulation from the powers of the proposed OFCOM. The latter responsibilities are however tasks which have to be carried out by the management of any organisation, and the existing system of regulation based around the Board of Governors seems to us to be anomalous and problematic in four respects.

First, the combination of regulatory and management responsibilities of the governors contradicts recent trends towards the separation of regulatory from operational functions, a trend by no means limited to broadcasting.[108] Secondly, we have been at pains to emphasise the importance of quality in broadcasting in this paper; not all broadcast production is of equivalent cultural merit. However, the 'great and the good' overtones in the appointment and role of the governors does give an unfortunately elitist slant to the culture of the BBC. Although the governors have been more open and more prepared to debate their role in recent years, this is no substitute for an independent regulatory authority properly informed about and partly representative of those parties engaged in public service provision, and able to act as the focus for wide debate of a full range of issues.[109] The existence of a single authority applying to all broadcasters would also underline the point that, whilst in this article we have stressed the public service mission of the BBC, other broadcasters such as Channel 4 and, less so, Channels 3 and 5 also have a distinctive public service role. Indeed, a specialist content regulator would be free to concentrate on the special content requirements for public service broadcasters, whilst the minimal 'consumer protection requirements' for purely commercial broadcasters could either be left to the economic regulator or form a relatively limited part of the content regulator's role.

Thirdly, existing regulatory arrangements through the BBC governors address separately what are intensely interrelated services. Regulatory integration would enable the new regulator to consider and operate across the public service sector in Britain as a whole. Given the likely increasing importance in this sector of assessing the *complementarity* of services provided by different broadcasters – currently BBC1 and ITV serving integrated, mass audiences, Channel 4 and BBC2 minorities and niches – a complementarity that is set to become more complex and central to public service delivery in the digital era, integration into a single regulator for public service broadcasting will become increasingly productive and important.

Fourthly, because of the erosion of the authority and legitimacy of the BBC's governance arrangements in recent years, independent regulation of the BBC is likely to have the paradoxical and beneficial effects of increasing both the independence of the BBC and the authority of its regulator, providing important insulation from direct governmental pressures. It is also likely to make the playing field more level with regard to the expectations placed on the BBC in comparison with other public service broadcasters by regulator and public alike. In the BBC,

---

107 *Initial Submission to the Government's Communications Review*, n 88 above, 30.
108 See Goldberg, Prosser and Verhulst, n 104 above, 310–314.
109 For the experience of other regulatory bodies see T. Prosser, *Law and the Regulators* (Oxford: Clarendon Press, 1997).

this is not to say that no role would remain for the Board of Governors, for it could remain responsible for overseeing compliance but also for the development of more detailed regulatory requirement through a process of co-regulation or limited self-regulation, a major theme in the White Paper and in recent European Union proposals for the regulatory future.[110] By contrast to the governors, however, the new regulator would be independent from management and possess real professional expertise in broadcasting and production, as well as an independent research base.

Thus on issues of regulation and governance, we would reject the White Paper proposals on the BBC as unlikely to achieve the government's professed aim of protecting public service broadcasting in the digital future. The thrust of this paper is that the merger of competition-based regulation and PSB-based content regulation in a single authority is likely to lead to the neglect of the latter through the dominance of 'hard' competition law values over the 'soft' values of PSB. However, retaining responsibility for the PSB remit with the BBC governors is equally unsatisfactory. We advocate instead a separate content regulator to ensure that the values of PSB are respected within the broadcasting ecology. This will not be a matter only for the BBC, but, given its historic role and expertise, the BBC will clearly play a major role in putting such values into practice.

Finally, we need to return to the BBC's commercial activities. Apart from the fact that our universality argument clearly requires that the BBC provides general entertainment in mixed-schedule channels, we suggest that the BBC acts responsibly when it adds value for the licence-fee paying public by commercially exploiting its unmatched rights and archives. When the BBC's commercial practices serve rather than drive its public service activities, the benefits are great: expanding sales and foreign revenues, the incomes from which flow back into and therefore enhance national, free-to-air services; and in addition, enhanced national and international influence through such exposure, leading to greater prestige or 'brand recognition' for the BBC both nationally and internationally. Moreover, as the national broadcast audience is increasingly confronted by global products, it is essential that the BBC engages in commercial activities that expand its international markets and influence. Without these, the BBC risks being marginalised both in the globalising media economy and at home – an effect of the way that audience tastes are being conditioned by the globalisation of media.[111] The BBC's engagement in limited commercial activities therefore generates a 'virtuous circle' of benign effects. However beyond a certain scale, commercial activities risk overwhelming the BBC's public service orientation and thus also the legitimacy of its distinctive status. It follows that the BBC should engage in commercial activities which are only a limited proportion of its total operations, so that they do not threaten to overwhelm its public service orientation, although these commercial activities may nonetheless be substantial in themselves.

Here we consider it necessary to draw a critical new normative distinction between the BBC's provision of *essential* and *non-essential* public service goods.[112] The BBC's non-essential public service goods would include merchandising, branded goods, publishing and other 'add-ons' or extensions to its core

---

110 See White Paper, n 6 above, sections 5.8, 8.11 and, for example, *Conclusion of the Experts' Seminar on Media Self-Regulation Held at Saarbrucken, 19–21 April 1999*, available at <http://www.eu-seminar.de/>.

111 See Born, n 64 above.

112 In contrast to the normal economists' definition of a public good, we emphasise here the cultural citizenship dimensions of what we are terming public *service* goods in broadcasting and new media.

services. In relation to these activities we see no objection to the rigorous application of competition law and the general principles underlying the current fair trading rules. The BBC's essential public service goods are those pertaining to its central cultural and informational functions in markets where the BBC's role and presence is, or should be, highly significant and includes the setting of standards. These would include new public service channels for digital delivery, for example childrens' channels which are free from advertising.[113] The BBC may even be dominant because of its benign functions of setting quality benchmarks, minority provision and relative autonomy from commercial pressures. We noted earlier that the normal rules of both European Community and domestic competition law are subject to exceptions where full application of the rules would obstruct the performance of a service of general economic interest.[114] This can be justified in relation to the core BBC public services on the ground of its special public service mission; the Corporation should not be treated equivalently to other broadcasters in the market place without such a mission.

Conclusion

The BBC cannot be treated simply as an ordinary object of competition law, particularly when, as in recent years, fair trading rules are used by commercial actors to attack the BBC's legitimate commercial activities and its presence in new markets. This attack ignores the BBC's unique status and its function in the wider broadcasting ecology. It elevates commercial interests over public interests and should be rigorously rebuffed. We are unconvinced that the use of the current fair-trading rules and the conditions for the approval of new services adequately reflect these public interests, which we have attempted to specify in our redefinition of PSB above. Nor are we satisfied that the proposals in the Communications White Paper are an adequate response.

We would underline that the BBC's standard-setting role has enormous importance for the media ecology not only culturally but economically. There is a series of recursive effects. The BBC's standard-setting function affects not only its public service but its commercial activities, and in this way is likely to raise standards in purely commercial sectors in which the BBC is competitive. By setting standards through a substantial scale of operations not only nationally but in certain areas of international media activity, on existing and new platforms, the BBC will progressively influence the markets in which it operates. And by raising the game of commercial British operators, it will aid them in achieving international influence. This is not a zero sum game, as it is often conceived. Rather, through the qualities of the BBC's activities, and through the influence thus exerted on the rest of the British media ecology, the British media industry as a whole is more likely to achieve international influence and market power. The beneficial effects of the BBC being enabled to pursue its higher cultural ambitions accrue not only to the BBC but, through the BBC's impact on the British media ecology, to the entire British broadcasting sector.

---

113 For the legality of this under Community law, see Commission Decision of 24 February 1999 in case NN70/98 *Kindercanal and Phoenix*, OJ 1999 C 238/3. The provision of such children's programming is precisely the purpose of two of the proposed new BBC digital channels currently under review.
114 For a restatement of policy see European Commission (2000), n 8 above.

[7]

European Controls on Member State Promotion and Regulation of Public Service Broadcasting and Broadcasting Standards

Mike Varney*

Public service broadcasting is still widely supported in the European Union, despite technological developments which are now offering a challenge to many of the traditional justifications offered for the support of the concept. This article aims to demonstrate that public service broadcasting, along with associated measures designed to support high standards of quality in other broadcasting services, are still very important in the modern context due to the media's pivotal role in society. An analysis of the impact of 'European public law' which, in this context, is primarily restricted to the law on the freedom to provide services and the associated effects of the 'Television Without Frontiers' Directive and the law relating to state aids, aims to highlight the impact which European Public Law has had on media regulation. Some of the more recent developments, such as the European Court of Justice's decision in *Ferring* and *Altmark*, along with the Commission's corresponding change in attitude to state funding of public service broadcasting, are welcomed. The Court's more recent decisions taken under the freedom to provide services are questioned more closely, as it appears that these measures can be said to have had a more significant impact upon the traditions of media regulation within Member State constitutions.

* Lecturer in Law and Member, Institute of European Public Law, Law School, The University of Hull. I would like to thank Patrick Birkinshaw, Mike Feintuck and Eliza Pop and the anonymous referee for constructive comments on an earlier draft of this article. Any errors and omissions are, of course, my own.

I. Introduction

The tradition of public service broadcasting is still strong in many states within the European Union.[1] This tradition is being placed under considerable strain by the recent technological developments in the digitalisation of the media. The wider range of delivery mechanisms available for the delivery of audiovisual content, along with the explosion of bandwidth for the carriage of channels, present fresh opportunities and challenges for public service broadcasting.[2] Providers are generally seeking carriage on a range of broadcast delivery systems and are also seeking to become a presence on the internet in many cases.

The need for an expansive remit for public service broadcasters, going beyond traditional analogue broadcasting with a limited range of commercial competitors which were also often imbued with public service obligations of some sort, is recognised by commentators[3] and the European institutions[4] alike. Although these positive statements of support are welcome to those who support public service broadcasting, it seems likely that the actual approach of the law to state measures which are aimed at the support of broadcasters is likely to be decisive in the future development of the public service tradition in broadcasting. If the developing law on control of regulatory intervention in the EU takes a negative view on such measures by Member States, then it seems likely that this will have negative implications for the further developments of the public service broadcasting sector.

The primary aim of this article will be to assess the impact of two key areas of European Union law on state measures which are aimed to support public service broadcasters. These areas comprise the law on free movement of service providers as espoused by Article 49 EC and the law on state aid, under Article 87 EC, which is becoming increasingly important as most public service broadcasters use public funds to expand the range of services that they offer. Particular issues of controversy are the launch of specific themed channels[5] and the development of a presence on the

---

[1]   See e.g. Hoffmann-Riem, W., *Regulating Media: The Licensing and Supervision of Broadcasting in Six Countries* (New York: Guilford Press, 1996), Barendt, E.M., *Broadcasting Law: A Comparative Study* (Oxford: Clarendon Press, 1995) and Humphreys, P.J., *Mass Media and Media Policy in Western Europe* (Manchester: Manchester University Press, 1996).

[2]   Hereafter PSB and PSBs.

[3]   See e.g. Feintuck, M.J., *Media Regulation, Public Interest and the Law* (Edinburgh: Edinburgh University Press, 1999), chapter 7 and Harrison, J. and Woods, L.M. 'Defining European Public Service Broadcasting' (2001) 16 *European Journal of Communication* 477.

[4]   There is a wide range of intent on this subject within the EU. See *e.g.* the Protocol on Public Broadcasting in the Member States annexed to the Treaty establishing the European Community which was enacted under the Treaty of Amsterdam and also the *Council Resolution on the Development of the Audiovisual Sector* (21 January 2002) [2002] OJ C 32/04.

[5]   See the Commission's decision in Aid NN 88/98 *BBC News 24* [2000] OJ C 78/06.

internet.[6] Although these services cannot necessarily be considered to be elements of the traditional public service mission, they clearly add vitality to the sector and allow for greater promotion and public involvement with developing technologies. The response of the law to state promotion and funding of these activities by PSBs will be crucial in framing the future development of the public service mission.

II. Why Public Service Broadcasting?

Public service broadcasters, which may be either public or private companies, tend to have specific goals which differ from those pursued by those broadcasters in the market which have purely commercial aims. The PSBs tend to have a wide range of obligations to provide programming for a diverse range of cultural and social groups and to devote a significant amount of their broadcasting time to those programmes which will satisfy the interests of smaller, rather than larger, groups of viewers.[7] This distinctive mission on the part of the public service broadcaster tends to render their objectives somewhat different than that of the independent, commercial, broadcaster. Member States have generally supported such PSBs for a range of reasons, a primary one being an effort to maintain pluralism and diversity in the media, which may not be achieved so successfully by purely market based, commercially driven, broadcasting.[8]

The PSB mission can therefore be seen to have two key strands in the era of digital media. The first aim, as described above, is to produce output that appeals to a range of groups, many of which could be termed to have minority interests. The second key aim of the public service broadcaster is to ensure that such output is available to all citizens either free at the point of use or for a minimal fee that is affordable to the vast majority. The importance of the public service mission has been asserted recently by the Commission, where it stated that

> The broadcast media play a central role in the functioning of modern democratic societies, in particular in the development and transmission of social values. Therefore, the broadcasting sector has, since its inception, been subject to specific regulation in the general interest. This regulation has centred on common values,

---

[6] See the *Communication from the Commission on the Application of State Aid rules to Public Service Broadcasting* [2001] OJ C 320/05 at para. 34.

[7] The public service mandate can be illustrated by the requirements in the BBC's Agreement with the government, see parts 2, 3, 4 and 5 of the Agreement available at: http://www.bbc.co.uk/info/policies/charter/pdf/agreement.pdf (last accessed 17 July 2003).

[8] See *e.g.* Pratten, S. 'Coase on Broadcasting, Advertising and Policy' (2001) *Cambridge Journal of Economics* 617 for an economic analysis and the more polemical work of McChesney, R.W., *Rich Media, Poor Democracy: Communications Politics in Dubious Times* (New York: The Free Press, 2000).

such as freedom of expression and the right of reply, pluralism ... [and] promotion of cultural and linguistic diversity ...[9]

The Council has reached similar conclusions on the issue, when it

Stresses the importance of public broadcasting and encourages it to continue making its significant contribution to the audiovisual sector, amongst other things by taking an active part in the development of new digital services which afford all citizens easier access to the information society.[10]

The approach of the institutions is undoubtedly welcome news for public service broadcasters, which are faced with increasing competition in the market. The digitalisation of media delivery networks and the corresponding increase in the number of delivery mechanisms[11] that are actually available place public service broadcasters in the position of having to make their product available via a wide range of means. Competition in the markets for broadcasting content[12] and the market for viewers is also increasing rapidly due to the considerable increase in the number of private undertakings which are operating in the media sector. The development of digital technologies has generally led to an increase in the costs which PSBs incur, as they have to negotiate carriage on a wider range of delivery networks[13] and also will generally need to expand their provision of content to new technologies, such as the internet.

The need for such development in the PSB sector is illustrated by Keane when he argues that

For their part, public service broadcasters routinely perceive that the repertoire of programmes channelled through existing public service media cannot satisfy

---

[9] COM(2000) 580 *Communication from the Commission: Services of General Interest in Europe* (Brussels: Commission of the European Communities) at page 35.

[10] *Council Resolution on the Development of the Audiovisual Sector* above, note 4 at para. 9.

[11] By delivery mechanisms I mean here the actual means by which the broadcasts are carried to the viewer. Traditionally this would be via an analogue signal to individual television sets, although now there is a greater trend toward delivery via satellite, cable or even delivery via telephony through internet based ADSL services.

[12] One particular area of controversy is the issue of right to broadcast sporting events and other events of major public interest. Article 3a of the *Television Without Frontiers Directive* (89/552) [1989] OJ L 298/23 as amended by Directive 97/36 [1997] OJ L 202/60 deals with this issue, permitting Member States to prevent exclusive rights to certain sporting events being acquired by pay TV operators. See Drijber, B.J. 'The Revised Television Without Frontiers Directive: Is it Fit for the Next Century?', (1999) 36 *Common Market Law Review* 87, at pp. 117-122 and Craufurd, Smith, R. and Böttcher, R. 'Football and Fundamental Rights: Regulating Access to Major Sporting Events on Television', (2002) 8 *European Public Law* 107.

[13] For more on this issue see the discussion of 'must carry' requirements below.

the multitude of opinions in a complex (if not fully pluralist) civil society in motion.[14]

If one takes the case of the BBC, a bulwark of the PSB tradition, there is a clear demonstration of the general response of a PSB when the development of the digital media has allowed greater capacity. The BBC has moved to launch a range of new channels on digital TV[15] and digital radio,[16] along with an expansive presence on the World Wide Web.[17] This range of services is entirely funded via the licence fee levied on most households in the UK which are in possession of equipment capable of receiving television broadcasts.

PSB is therefore attempting to answer its critics in a number of countries by expanding the range of services that are offered in an effort to meet the increasing competition presented by a wider range of commercially funded channels. Although public service broadcasting undoubtedly has certain weaknesses, particularly in the sense that it cannot ever be truly representative of a diverse civil society, there is little evidence that a purely commercially driven media would offer any improvement on the current situation. In addition, the increasing ability of broadcasts to cross national frontiers and the potential for an increased range of European channels to be carried offer a clear opportunity for the development of a 'European public sphere.' This development is likely to present opportunities for greater cohesion among European citizens and is likely to be led by the public service broadcasters.

Along with the strong tradition of public service broadcasting in the European Union there has generally been a tradition of other forms of state regulation of commercial broadcasters in order to ensure quality is met and also to ensure that output meets nationally accepted cultural standards for such matters as taste and decency and the protection of pluralism and diversity within national media markets. The restrictions which have been adopted relate to a number of different issues, many of which are featured in the following discussion. These measures

---

[14] Keane, J., *Civil Society: Old Images, New Visions* (London: Polity Press, 1998) at page 165.

[15] The BBC has recently launched a range of new channels, commencing with BBC News 24 in November 1997, followed by the launch of BBC Choice and BBC Parliament in 1998. These services have now been complemented by the launch of three new channels in 2001/2002 – CBBC and CBeebies, which are both childrens' channels and BBC Four – a documentary channel. See British Broadcasting Corporation, *BBC Annual Report and Accounts 2001/2002* London: British Broadcasting Corporation at pp. 13-14 and 22-23.

[16] The BBC have launched a range of new digital radio services including BBC Five Live Sports Extra, BBC 6 Music – Radio 1 XTRA, designed to play music which may appeal more strongly to black listeners, BBC Asian Network and BBC Radio 7 – a service dedicated to comedy and drama.

[17] The BBC states that 5.6 million users accessed its online services in 2001/2002 – it suggests that this comprises 33% of adult internet users in the UK over the year. See BBC Annual Report and Accounts 2001/2002 above, note 15 at page 11.

for a significant part of most legal systems of the Member States of the European Union and often have great constitutional significance.[18]

III. Freedom to Provide Services and Broadcasting

The European Court of Justice first decided that broadcasting should be considered as a service for the purposes of Article 49 EC in *Saachi*.[19] This has two significant effects for any Member State regulation of broadcasting activity. The first is that any Member State measure adopted either to support public service broadcasting or to regulate the activities of broadcasters should not have an effect on inter-state trade unless it can be justified under one of the exceptions in Article 46 EC[20] or, alternatively, under the 'mandatory requirements' test adopted under the now famous 'rule of reason' case law.[21] It must be noted at the outset that measures which discriminate on the grounds of nationality *can only* be justified by one of the exceptions under Article 46 EC. A somewhat wider range of measures which impose conditions on the freedom to provide services can be justified if the mandatory requirements are in the general interest under the 'rule of reason' test.

The EU has also moved to legislate in the area, using articles 47(2) and 55 EC as a legislative basis.[22] The choice of these Articles as a legislative base demonstrates that the institutions see broadcasting as an area which must be harmonized in some way in order to ensure some form of freedom of movement for those carrying on a business in the sector. In the same instance, there is a clear recognition by the institutions that little can be done to legislate for the regulation of broadcasting under the cultural provisions of the Treaty in Article 151 EC. This places limitations upon the potential for Community action in the broadcasting sector and places any action to regulate broadcasting firmly within the context of the market. The approach of

---

[18]   See *e.g.* Barendt, E.M. above, note 1, chapters 1, 4, 5 and 9.

[19]   Case 155/73 *Italy* v. *Sacchi* [1974] 2 CMLR 177.

[20]   Article 46 states that 'The provisions of this chapter and measures taken in pursuance thereof shall not prejudice the applicability of provisions laid down by law, regulation or administrative action providing for special treatment for foreign nationals on grounds of public policy, public security or public health'.

[21]   This test was most famously outlined in the Cassis de Dijon case – Case 120/78 *Rewe-Zentrale AG* v. *Bundesmonopollverwaltung für Branntwein* [1979] ECR 649, which was a case concerning free movement of goods under Article 30 EC. The case had, however, been predated in the field of services by Case 33/74 *Van Binsbergen* v. *Bestuur van de Bedrijfsvereniging voor de Metaalnijverheid* [1974] ECR 1299. The 'rule of reason' test essentially allows certain measures which regulate the provision of goods and services, but which are non-discriminatory, to stand if the court is satisfied that the justification offered by the Member State is satisfactory.

[22]   The *Television Without Frontiers Directive* (89/552) [1989] OJ L 298/23 as amended by Directive 97/36/EC [1997] OJ L 202/60.

this section will be to take each potential restriction in turn. First, there will be an examination of the approach under Article 46 EC, then the 'rule of reason' case law before a brief examination of the pertinent areas of the 'Television Without Frontiers' Directive are examined.

Discriminatory Measures under Article 46 EC

The application of Article 46 to national measures which regulate the media illustrate two limitations which will be placed on national legislatures when enacting discriminatory measures. In the first case to be considered the Spanish government passed a measure which linked the granting of a licence to dub foreign films to a requirement that the company must also be involved in the filming and distribution of Spanish films. The court considered that the regulation had an economic aim, and that as a result it should be found to be unjustifiable under Article 46 EC as

> ... objectives of an economic nature cannot constitute grounds of public policy within the meaning of that article.[23]

As a result of this case it is clear that no national measure which is looking to lend economic support to its media industries will be acceptable if it seeks to impose a discriminatory barrier to the provision of services. The second branch to this case illustrates the point that discriminatory measures which a member state seeks to justify on cultural grounds will not be successful either. The court stated that

> Apart from the fact that cultural policy is not one of the justifications set out in Article 56 [now 46], it is important to note that the Decree-Law promotes the distribution of national films whatever their content or quality.[24]

From this it becomes apparent that most national measures concerned with regulation of the media, or promotion of national broadcasting at the expense of those broadcasters who seek to broadcast from another jurisdiction and therefore discriminate on grounds of nationality, will not be justifiable before the court.[25]

If one is to consider the proportionality test as it has been applied to discriminatory measures, then it is clear that the court's approach will be strict, as the court sees a national measure under Article 46 as an interference with the right granted under Article 49. In the two media cases that will be examined here, *Bond van*

---

[23] Case C-17/92 *Federacion de Distribuidores Cinematograficos* v. *Estado Español et Union de Productores de Cine y Television* [1993] ECR I-2239 at para. 16.

[24] *Ibid.* at para. 20.

[25] It may be that measures which are designed to protect taste and decency or public morals could potentially be justified, although this is unlikely as the measures would surely have to be non-discriminatory and apply to those broadcasting or printing within the Member State as well.

Adverteerders[26] and *Commission* v. *Belgium*,[27] both show that the ECJ will apply a strict proportionality test to any measures that seek to be justified under Article 46.

In the *Bond van Adverteerders* case the Netherlands authorities sought to ban any radio or television broadcasts emanating from other Member States containing advertisements which were intended for members of the public in that Member State or which were subtitled in Dutch. Although the court accepted that the main aim of this measure was not economic but was aimed to safeguard the non-commercial and pluralistic nature of the Netherlands broadcasting system, the court ruled that the measure was disproportionate to the aim pursued. The court stated that

> It is sufficient to observe in that regard that the measures taken by virtue of that Article must not be disproportionate to the intended objective. As an exception to a fundamental principle of the Treaty, Article 56 [now 46] of the Treaty must be interpreted in such a way that its effects are limited to that which is necessary in order to protect the interests which it seeks to safeguard.[28]

It therefore rejected the complete ban on broadcasts from other Member States which contained advertising as disproportionate, as other measures, such as making the advertising restrictions imposed on national broadcasters applicable to all, whether national or non national, would have been less onerous.[29]

If the measure had been non-discriminatory, then the result of the case may have been different. The court stated that

> in the absence of harmonization of the national rules applicable to broadcasting and television, each Member State has the power to regulate, restrict or even totally prohibit television advertising on its territory on grounds of the public interest, provided that it treats all services in that field identically whatever their origin or the nationality or place of establishment of the persons providing them.[30]

The second case, that of *Commission* v. *Belgium*[31] was a case decided after the enactment of the 'Television without Frontiers' directive and may therefore be more

---

[26] Case 352/85 *Bond van Adverteerders* v. *The State (Netherlands)* [1989] 3 CMLR 113.

[27] Case C-11/95 *E.C. Commission* v. *Belgium (Re Cable Television Broadcasts)* [1997] 2 CMLR 289.

[28] Case 352/85 *Bond van Adverteerders* above, note 26 at para. 36.

[29] For more on this see Lenaerts, K, Van Nuffel, P. and Bray, R. (ed.), *Constitutional Law of the European Union* (London: Sweet and Maxwell, 1999) at para. 4-152.

[30] Case 352/85 *Bond van Adverteerders* above, note 26 at para. 38. Note, however, that this statement from the Court must now be considered in the light of the 'Television Without Frontiers' Directive, note 22 above. See the more detailed discussion of the effects of that directive below.

[31] Case C-11/95 *Commission* v. *Belgium*, above, note 27.

EUROPEAN CONTROLS ON PROMOTION AND REGULATION OF PSB   511

indicative of the court's approach at the present time. In this case the Belgian government had retained a system of prior authorisation before television programmes from other Member States could be retransmitted via cable. The court stated that

> It may be concluded from the case law that the maintenance and safeguarding of pluralism in the television sector or in the media in general is an objective of general interest which may justify restrictions on the freedom to provide services which is protected by Articles 59 [now 49] *et seq.* of the Treaty ... Those rules [in the 'Television Without Frontiers' directive] are, however, provisions of a rather technical nature which are only very indirectly related to diversity of opinion in the media.[32]

Despite these findings the court held that the requirement of a system of prior authorisation was excessively onerous and the Member State had failed to put forward any satisfactory justification for the prior approval regime so therefore the measure was disproportionate to the aim pursued.[33] From the above it is fairly clear that national measures which are discriminatory will be difficult to justify before the ECJ in any circumstances and will be subject to an intense proportionality test.

From the foregoing discussion it seems likely that any measures introduced by a Member State to support public service broadcasting through applying discriminatory measures will not be allowed to stand. Restrictions like the ones contained in the measures which led to the *Bond van Adverteerders*[34] case will no longer be acceptable due to the minimum harmonisation that has taken place under the 'Television Without Frontiers' directive which will be discussed below. The potential for national authorities to impose measures which expressly favour national broadcasters at the expense of those established overseas will generally not be tolerated. Examples of measures which will probably be impugned include: a reservation of the market for advertising to broadcasters which are established in the home state,[35] a requirement of prior authorisation before broadcast of foreign made programmes is permitted,[36] or any requirement that national firms which

---

[32] *Ibid.*

[33] *Ibid.* at para. 65.

[34] Case 352/85 *Bond van Adverteerders* above, note 26.

[35] *Ibid.* and see also Case T-266/97 *Vlaamse Televisie Maatschapij NV* v. *Commission of the European Communities* [1999] ECR II-2329.

[36] Case C-11/95 *Commission* v. *Belgium*, above, note 27. The recent case rejecting a Spanish administrative measure which required equipment used for decoding digital television signals is a further illustration that prior authorisation will not generally be acceptable, see Case C-390/99 *Canal Satélite Digital SL* v. *Administracíon General del Estado* [2002] ECR I-607 and Pooschke, S. 'ECJ – Judgment on Canal Satélite Digital', (2003) 29 *Legal Issues of European Integration* 267. The situation which arose in this case is unlikely to arise again, given the shift towards harmonisation of such technical standards in Articles 17, 18 and 19 of the Framework Directive

are involved solely in dealing with programming made in other states should also have to fund production of broadcasting content in their home state[37] will not be permitted under EC law.

The approach of the European Court of Justice in these cases is interesting because upon first examination the cases which are decided appear to permit Member States to take significant action to ensure diversity and pluralism in national media markets. The restrictive measures which were adopted by the Netherlands government were impermissible insofar as they were discriminatory, yet the court was willing to accept that restrictions could have been applied to all broadcasters, regardless of nationality, without difficulty. The developments since that case was decided render this decision somewhat obsolete, as Article 3 of the 'Television Without Frontiers' Directive permits Member States to apply more restrictive measures than those outlined in the Directive only to those broadcasters which fall within its jurisdiction. This could potentially make a significant difference to the ability of Member States to place restrictions on advertising which would traditionally be considered to be undesirable within the national media market.

Application to Measures which are non-discriminatory under the 'rule of reason' test

Prior to the discussion of restrictions put in place under the 'rule of reason' test it seems wise to highlight one substantial caveat: any measure adopted which conflicts with the minimum harmonization provisions of the 'Television Without Frontiers' directive will not stand, unless that measure applies only to those broadcasters under the jurisdiction of that Member State for the purposes of the directive. In *Leclerc-Siplec*[38] the ECJ argued that

> the attainment of the Directive's objective of ensuring freedom to provide broadcasting services complying with the minimum rules it lays down is in no way affected where Member States impose stricter rules on the television broadcasters under their jurisdiction in circumstances other than those set out in Article 19 [now subsumed into Article 3 of the Directive].[39]

This illustrates one of the main difficulties faced by Member States which are seeking to impose public service obligations on broadcasters, or which seek to maintain

---

– Directive 2002/21/EC of the European Parliament and of the Council on a common regulatory framework for electronic communications networks and services [2002] OJ L 108/33.

[37] Case C-17/92 *Federacion de Distribuidores Cinematograficos* v. *Estado Español et Union de Productores de Cine y Television* above, note 23.

[38] Case C-412/93 *Société d'Importation Edouard Leclerc-Siplec* v. *TF1 Publicité SA and M6 Publicité SA* [1995] ECR I-179.

[39] *Ibid.* at para. 44.

EUROPEAN CONTROLS ON PROMOTION AND REGULATION OF PSB   513

particular standards in programming. In other than the most limited circumstances,[40] where a broadcaster falls within the jurisdiction of another Member State, there is little that a government can do to regulate that output provided that the minimum standards outlined in the 'Television Without Frontiers' directive are met.[41] This statement only applies in the limited fields that are harmonized. It is important to note that only a relatively limited range of fields are actually harmonized by the directive, although the rulings of the European Court of Justice have rendered the grip of the directive to be very expansive.

The ECJ has generally been far more permissive to measures which are non-discriminatory and are based on the 'rule of reason.' The rule of reason test requires that three fundamental conditions are met before it is possible that the restrictive measure will be acceptable to the court:

(i) The rule must be non-discriminatory, *i.e.* it must apply to all providers of services without reference to the Member State in which they are established.[42]

(ii) The restrictions must be justified in the public interest. This justification can come in a huge number of ways.[43]

(iii) Finally the restrictions must be justified in the sense that they must not be rendered superfluous by the fact that the same protection is already present in

---

[40] Art. 22 of the Directive provides that 'Member States shall take appropriate measures to ensure that television broadcasts by broadcasters under their jurisdiction do not include programmes which might seriously impair the physical, mental or moral development of minors, in particular those that involve pornography or gratuitous violence. This provision shall extend to other programmes which are likely to impair the physical, mental or moral development of minors, except where it is ensured, by selecting the time of the broadcast or by any technical measure, that minors in the area of transmission will not normally hear or see such broadcasts.

Member States shall also ensure that broadcasts do not contain any incitement to hatred on grounds of race, sex, religion or nationality.' There is some debate over whether if Member States do not meet their obligations under this article that the receiving Member State may ban or prevent transmission of a channel into their territory. See *R* v. *Secretary of State for National Heritage, ex parte Continental Television Bvio* [1993] 2 CMLR 387 (CA) See also Coleman, F. and McMurtrie, S., 'Red Hot Television: Domestic and international Legal Aspects of the Regulation of Satellite Television', (1995) 1(2) *European Public Law* 201 and Robertson, G. and Nicol, A., *Robertson and Nicol on Media Law* , 4th Edition (London: Sweet and Maxwell, 2002) page 832.

[41] Certain caveats to this statement are necessary, see the discussion of *De Agostini infra.*

[42] See Lenaerts and Van Nuffel, above, note 29 at para. 4-154.

[43] The salient ones for the purposes of this chapter can be considered to be conservation of artistic and historical heritage – Case C-180/89 *Commission* v. *Italy* [1991] ECR I-709, measures to ensure the widest dissemination and publicity for items of national cultural and historical value – Case C-154/89 *Commission* v. *France* and measures of cultural policy introduced as an attempt to safeguard freedom of expression – Case C-288/89 *Collective Antennevoorziening Gouda* [1991] ECR I-4069, Case C-353/89 *Commission* v. *Netherlands* and Case C-23/93 *TV10* [1994] ECR I-4795. See also Lenaerts and Van Nuffel, above, note 29 at paras. 4-154 – 4-156.

the Member State where the service provider is established. The restrictions should also be proportionate to the aim pursued, *i.e.* they should be the least restrictive means possible.[44]

Non-discriminatory measures which have sought to regulate the media in the interests of freedom of expression or plurality of sources and which have been restrictive under the tests in Article 49 have still been allowed to stand in certain cases. In *TV10*[45] the court stated that

> The provisions of the EEC Treaty on freedom to provide services are to be interpreted as not precluding a Member State from treating as a domestic broadcaster . a broadcasting body constituted under the law of another Member State and established in that State but whose activities are wholly or principally directed towards the territory of the first Member State, if that broadcasting body was established there in order to enable it to avoid the rules which would be applicable to it if it were established within the first State.[46]

The proportionality test will be applied to any measure with the objective of maintaining diversity in the media, although it will generally be for the national court to decide whether the measure is proportionate to the objective pursued. The ECJ stated in *Familiapress*,[47] a case where the Austrian authorities had prohibited the sale of newspapers or periodicals which contained prize competitions in the interests of press diversity, that

> provided that that prohibition is proportionate to maintenance of press diversity and that that objective cannot be achieved by less restrictive means.[48]

Then the restriction would be allowed to stand. The court also argued that it was

> for the national court to determine whether those conditions are satisfied on the basis of a study of the national press market concerned.[49]

It is therefore quite possible that certain national measures that regulate the media which are non-discriminatory but restrict the freedom to provide services as expounded in Article 49 EC could indeed be justified under the rule of reason test,

---

[44] Lenaerts and Van Nuffel, above, note 29 at para. 4-155 and Case 154/89 *Commission* v. *France* [1991] ECR I-659.

[45] Case C-23/93 *TV10* [1994] ECR I-4795.

[46] *Ibid.* at para. 27.

[47] Case C-368/95 *Vereinigte Familiapress Zeitungsverlags- und vertriebs GmbH* v. *Heinrich Bauer Verlag* [1997] ECR I-3689.

[48] *Ibid.* at para. 34.

[49] *Ibid.*

providing that they do not interfere with any of the areas subject to the minimum harmonisation provisions in the 'Television Without Frontiers' directive. It is also quite likely that the national court will be left to apply the proportionality test to the measure concerned, although the measure may be impugned by the ECJ if it clearly fails to meet the 'least restrictive alternative' proportionality test.[50]

Restrictions under the 'Television Without Frontiers' Directive

The directive places a range of restrictions on the potential regulatory actions which a Member State might apply to broadcasters which come from outwith its jurisdiction. The directive only creates minimum harmonisation – Member States are free to apply stricter criteria to those broadcasters which fall within its jurisdiction.[51] Those broadcasters which do not fall within the jurisdiction of the Member States, however, must only meet the standards provided for in the laws of the host state. These provisions have created a range of controversy, particularly in relation to the decision over jurisdiction.

These restrictions and controversies may cause significant problems for Member States which aim to impose obligations upon all broadcasters which have access to viewers within its territory. A particular issue of concern has been exactly how jurisdiction is to be established. In *Commission* v. *United Kingdom*[52] the ECJ decided that the only state which would have jurisdiction for the purposes of the Directive was the state in which the broadcaster was established. It should be noted, however, that the European Court of Justice had decided previously, in *TV10*[53] that a broadcasting company could not take advantage of the provisions of the Directive to establish in a Member State with weaker controls in order to broadcast solely into another Member State and yet avoid more stringent controls on broadcasting activities in the law of the recipient state. This position in the case law clearly strengthens the potential for Member States to be able to place strict controls upon broadcasters and to impose obligations upon them if their aim is to transmit solely to one recipient Member State.

The recent developments in the case law have, however, called this position into question. The decisions of the Court in two later cases, those of *Commission* v.

---

[50] *Ibid* at paras. 31-33.

[51] Dougan, M. 'Minimum Harmonization and the Single Market', (2000) 37 *Common Market Law Review* 853 esp. at page 867.

[52] Case C-222/94 *Commission* v. *United Kingdom* [1996] ECR I-4025.

[53] See Case C-23/93 *TV10* and accompanying quotation above, note 45.

Belgium, where the Court stated that its rulings in *Van Binsbergen*[54] and *TV10*[55]

> do not in any event authorize a Member State generally to exclude provision of certain services by operators established in other Member States, since that would entail abolition of the freedom to provide services.[56]

There instead appears to be an increasing likelihood that the potential for Member States to claim jurisdiction over a broadcaster who is, to all intents and purposes, purely providing services to their jurisdiction and yet is broadcasting from another Member State is increasingly limited. The Court's decision in *VT4*[57] interpreted the jurisdiction provisions in the 'Television Without Frontiers' Directive in a similar manner to the 'real seat' doctrine of company law.[58] The Court has argued that

> Where a television broadcaster has more than one establishment, the competent Member State is the State in which the broadcaster has the centre of its activities. It is therefore for the national court to determine, applying that criteria, which Member State has jurisdiction over VT4's activities, taking into account in particular the place where decisions concerning programme policy are taken and the programmes to be broadcast are finally put together.[59]

This approach is useful in preventing the potential abuse of the Directive in order for broadcasters which might be considered to be purely domestic to one Member State from establishing in another Member State to avoid stricter laws in the recipient Member State. It should also be noted that since the decision in *VT4*[60] the text of the Directive has, at least to a certain extent, been altered to adopt the approach of the Court in legislation.[61] The European Court of Justice, in its recent case law on

---

[54] Case 33/74 *Van Binsbergen v. Bestuur van de Bedrijfsvereniging voor de Metaalnijverheid* above, note 21.

[55] Case C-23/93 *TV10* above, note 45.

[56] Case C-11/95 *E.C. Commission v. Belgium (Re Cable Television Broadcasts)* above, note 27 at para. 67.

[57] Case C-56/96 *VT4 Ltd v. Vlaamse Gemeenschap* [1997] ECR I-3143.

[58] The 'real seat' doctrine in company law provides that a company is actually established in 'the country where its administration or central place of business is located'. See Cheffins, B.R., *Company Law: Theory, Structure and Operation* (Oxford: Clarendon Press, 1997) at page 429. For a useful introduction to the nuances of the doctrine see pages 429-432 of this book.

[59] *Ibid.* at para. 19.

[60] Case C-56/96 *VT4 Ltd* above, note 57.

[61] Art. 2 of the Directive, as amended by Directive 97/36/EC provides for a complex array of tests based first on editorial control and the location of the head office in Art. 2(3)(a) before moving on to a range of assessments based on where the majority of the workforce associated with the production of television content is based in Article 2(3)(b). The final decision, if none of the other tests outlined in Art. 2(3) and (4) are satisfied is one based on country of establishment for the purposes of Art. 52 EC.

EUROPEAN CONTROLS ON PROMOTION AND REGULATION OF PSB   517

Article 52 of the Treaty has suggested that the concept of 'abuse' of the freedoms outlined in the Treaty is becoming increasingly narrow, with the likelihood that the ECJ will generally look little further than whether a company is lawfully established through whatever provisions exist in the laws of the particular Member State where establishment is claimed to have taken place.[62] This recent approach of the ECJ, linked with the dicta in *Commission* v. *Belgium*[63] above, will render it unlikely that the Court will go beyond a simple test of the country of lawful establishment in any cases where there is controversy over where a broadcaster is established for the purposes of the Directive.

This approach of the Community legislature and the Court may have a significant impact upon measures imposed by Member States on fields coordinated within the Directive. This would, as a most obvious point, seriously limit the ability of any Member State to be restrictive on advertising content which is legal in another Member State, as this is one of the areas which is specifically harmonized by the Directive. Member States are unlikely to wish to impose stricter regulation than that imposed within the directive to national broadcasters based within their jurisdiction for fear of placing those broadcasters at a competitive disadvantage in the market for advertising or, alternatively, encouraging broadcasters to shift to an alternative jurisdiction from which to carry out their activities. If Member States are driven not to regulate by this motive, then it may be that the directive, along with the interpretation of the Court, will lead to a 'race to the bottom' in the regulation of advertisements within the EU.[64]

A further question raised by the case law on the Directive is the extent to which Member States might regulate in areas which have been harmonised by the Directive.

---

[62] Case C-212/97, *Centros Ltd* v. *Erhvervs-og Selskabsstyrelsen* [2000] 2 W.L.R. 1048, [1999] ECR I-1459, where the court said that the failure to recognise an incorporation in the UK (which does not subscribe to the real seat doctrine) was incompatible with Arts. 52 and 58 EC. See also Siems, M. 'Convergence, Competition, *Centros* and Conflicts of Law: European Company Law in the 21st Century', (2002) 27:1, *European Law Review* 47 and Xanthaki, H., '*Centros*: Is this really the end for the Siège Réel Doctrine?', (2001) 22:1 *The Company Lawyer* 2

[63] C-11/95 *E.C. Commission* v. *Belgium (Re Cable Television Broadcasts)* above, note 56 and accompanying quotation.

[64] Examples of some recent discussions of regulatory competition and the 'race to the bottom' can be found in Sykes, A.O. 'Regulatory Competition or Regulatory Harmonization? A Silly Question?', (2000) 3:2 *Journal of International Economic Law* 257, Trachtman, J.P. 'Regulatory Competition and Regulatory Jurisdiction', (2000) 3:2 *Journal of International Economic Law*, 331, Revesz, R.L. 'Federalism and Regulation: Some Generalisations' in Esty, D.C. and Geradin, D., *Regulatory Competition and Economic Integration: Comparative Perspectives* (Oxford: Oxford University Press, 2001). A particular example of the arguments applied to the German model for broadcasting regulation can be found in Humphreys, P.J. and Lang, M. 'Regulating for Media Pluralism and the Pitfalls of *Standortpolitik*: The Re-Regulation of German Broadcasting Ownership Rules', (1998) 7:2 *German Politics* 176.

In the *De Agostini*[65] case, the European Court of Justice has laid down its clearest guidelines up to the present time on the interpretation of the harmonisation provisions within the 'Television Without Frontiers Directive.' The facts of the *De Agostini* case concerned, for the purposes of this discussion, a provision in Swedish law which aimed to protect minors by preventing television advertising aimed at children under 12 and a further provision which permitted the prohibition of the broadcast of other television advertisements which had the potential to be unfair to consumers or to other traders. The Swedish authorities issued injunctions against broadcasters in order to prevent the transmission of certain advertisements, which it seemed to be in breach of the law protecting minors. A company based in Britain involved in broadcasting certain channels into Sweden complained that such injunctions were a restriction on the freedom to provide services protected by Article 59 EC and also constituted a breach of the 'Television Without Frontiers' Directive. The reasons for this argument were that restrictions on television advertising were harmonised by the Directive and all the adverts which were broadcast were in compliance with UK law.

The Court's approach was somewhat contradictory, suggesting on the one hand that

> Although the Directive provides that the Member States are to ensure freedom of reception and are not to impede retransmission on their territory of television broadcasts coming from other Member States on grounds relating to television advertising and sponsorship, it does not have the effect of excluding completely and automatically the application of rules other than those specifically concerning the broadcasting and distribution of programmes.[66]

While, on the other hand, stating that

> If provisions of the receiving State regulating the content of television broadcasts for reasons relating to the protection of minors against advertising were applied to broadcasts from other Member States, this would add a secondary control to the control which the broadcasting Member State must exercise under the Directive ... It follows that the Directive is to be interpreted as precluding the application to television broadcasts from other Member States of a provision of a domestic broadcasting law which provides that advertisements broadcast in commercial breaks on television must not be designed to attract the attention of children under 12 years of age.[67]

---

[65] Cases C-34 – 36/95 *Konsumentombudsmannen (KO)* v. *De Agostini (Svenska) Forlag AB and TV-Shop i Sverige AB* [1998] 1 CMLR 32. For comment on this case see *e.g.* Greaves, R. 'Advertising Restrictions and Free Movement of Goods and Services', (1998) *European Law Review* 305 and Criscuolo, A. 'The "TV Without Frontiers Directive" and the Legal Regulation of Publicity in the European Community', (1998) *European Law Review* 357.

[66] *Ibid.* at para. 33.

[67] *Ibid.* at paras. 61-62.

EUROPEAN CONTROLS ON PROMOTION AND REGULATION OF PSB   519

The decision of the Court does not offer any clear indication of whether Member States are likely to be able to place additional restrictions on received programming content in areas which are harmonized by the Directive. The ECJ is rather unspecific about the types of measures which would not be considered to be 'secondary controls' in those areas which are harmonized and it seems likely that in general no further regulation of programming will be permitted on grounds which are covered in the Directive, providing that the provisions of the Directive are sufficiently specific.

A decision of the EFTA Court has suggested that where the Directive is not specific it may be that there is a greater margin of discretion afforded to measures which could otherwise be considered to be 'secondary controls.' In *TV 1000*[68] the EFTA Court opined that Article 22 of the 'Television Without Frontiers' Directive does not define what types of programming content could be considered to "seriously impair physical, mental or moral development of minors." The facts of the case concerned Norwegian measures to prevent the broadcast of certain pornographic programmes which were in breach of the Norwegian Penal Code through use of the justification provided in Article 22 of the Directive. An examination of the text of Article 22[69] reveals, as the Court argued, that

> The Court notes that, as pointed out by *inter alia* the EFTA Surveillance Authority and the Commission of the European Communities, the provision does not purport to lay down any standards for what might have such detrimental effects, leaving it up to the Member States to define these terms, as well as the term 'pornography', in accordance with their national legislation and moral standards.[70]

It is still the case, however, that the receiving Member State may only take measures to restrict the broadcasts from other Member States where the requirements in

---

[68] Case E-8/97 *TV 1000 Sverige AB* v. *Norwegian Government* [1998] 3 CMLR 318.

[69] Article 22 provides that:

> 1. Member States shall take appropriate measures to ensure that television broadcasts by broadcasters under their jurisdiction do not include any programmes which might seriously impair the physical, mental or moral development of minors, in particular programmes that involve pornography or gratuitous violence.
>
> 2. The measures provided for in paragraph 1 shall also extend to other programmes which are likely to impair the physical, mental or moral development of minors, except where it is ensured, by selecting the time of the broadcast or by any technical measure, that minors in the area of transmission will not normally hear or see such broadcasts.
>
> 3. Furthermore, when such programmes are broadcast in unencoded form Member States shall ensure that they are preceded by an acoustic warning or are identified by the presence of a visual symbol throughout their duration. N.B. Paragraph 3 was added by Directive 97/36/EC and was not considered by the Court in *TV 1000*.

[70] Case E-8/97 *TV 1000 Sverige AB* v. *Norwegian Government* above, note 68 at para. 24.

Article 2a of the Directive are met and only where the provisions of Article 22 or 22a are infringed. Any measures which are taken to prohibit broadcasting or retransmission must, of course, be compatible with the principle of proportionality. If one draws a parallel between the position under the Directive and the position with regard to free movement of goods under Article 30 EC. The Court has interpreted the provisions here in a similar light, stating that

> However, although Community law leaves the Member States free to make their own assessments of the indecent or obscene character of certain Articles, it must be pointed out that the fact that goods cause offence cannot be regarded as sufficiently serious to justify restrictions on the free movement of goods where the Member State concerned does not adopt, with respect to the same goods manufactured or marketed within its territory, penal measures or other serious and effective measures intended to prevent the distribution of such goods in its territory.[71]

It appears, therefore, that national measures restricting broadcasts under the justifications in Article 22[72] will be unable to attempt to ban such retransmission or broadcasting should domestic broadcasters be permitted to broadcast such material. It is, however, largely a matter for a domestic court to make the decision whether the material to be broadcast is really indecent according to domestic legal and moral standards.[73] This is significant, as many states have a strong set of constitutional and legal traditions surrounding the regulation of broadcasting which need to have some form of recognition in Community law.

IV. State Aids

Given that public service broadcasting usually requires some form of state support the position with regard to state aids in EC law is likely to be crucial to the public service mission.[74] The general position under Community law is that any form

---

[71] Case 121/85 *Conegate Limited* v. *HM Customs & Excise* [1986] ECR 1007.

[72] One of the more controversial cases in the UK concerning the attempted banning of a particular channel is that of the 'Red Hot TV' case – see the discussion above, note 40.

[73] For two recent discussions of the ECJ's approach to differing national constitutional, legal and cultural traditions see Dougan, M. 'Minimum Harmonization and the Internal Market', (2000) 37 *Common Market Law Review* 853 and Hatzopoulous, V., 'Recent Developments in the Case Law of the European Court of Justice in the Field of Services', (2000) 37 *Common Market Law Review* 43.

[74] There have been a number of recent discussions of state aids in relation to public service broadcasting, the most notable being Craufurd Smith, R. 'State Support for Public Service Broadcasting: The Position under European Community Law', (2001) 28 *Legal Issues of European Integration* 3, Bartosch, A. 'The Financing of Public Broadcasting and EC State Aid Law: An Interim Balance', (1999) *European Competition Law Review* 197 and Bavasso, A.F. 'Public Service Broadcasting and State Aid Rules: Between a Rock and a Hard Place', (2002) *European Law Review* 340.

EUROPEAN CONTROLS ON PROMOTION AND REGULATION OF PSB 521

of financial support provided to a public service broadcaster has the potential to be treated as 'state aid' for the purposes of Article 87 EC. The areas of particular significance at the present time will be the way in which the Commission and the ECJ treat the development of Public Service Broadcasting, particularly in terms of the development of a presence on the internet and the development of a greater number of themed channels for broadcast on digital networks. A further issue of interest will be the approach of Community law to 'must carry' obligations.

Article 87 EC provides that

> Save as otherwise provided in this Treaty, any aid granted by a Member State or through State resources in any form whatsoever which distorts or threatens to distort competition by favouring certain undertakings or the production of certain goods shall, insofar as it affects trade between Member States, be incompatible with the common market.

As Craufurd Smith has argued,

> The principal reason for excluding the financing of public service broadcasting from this definition is that it does not 'favour' the recipients, and thus cannot be held to distort competition.[75]

The Commission has recently produced a range of reports, along with decisions in a number of 'state aid' cases in relation to public service broadcasters. In a recent communication the Commission has stated that

> Public service broadcasting, although having a clear economic relevance, is not comparable to a public service in any other economic sector. There is no other service that at the same time has access to such a wide sector of the population, provides it with so much information and content, and by doing so conveys and influences both individual and public opinion.[76]

In the Communication the Commission also pointed out the relevance and importance of Article 86(2) EC and Article 16 EC. Article 86(2) EC offers a justification for state aid insofar as it allows for the performance of a service of general economic interest providing that it does not interfere with the interests of the community, whereas Article 16[77] offers a more general interpretative principle to be applied to

---

[75] Craufurd Smith above, note 74 at page 8.

[76] *Communication from the Commission on the Application of State Aid Rules to Public Service Broadcasting* [2001] OJ C 320/05. See also European Commission *Non Paper: Services of General Economic Interest and State Aid* (Brussels: Commission of the European Communities) available at: http://www.europa.eu.int/comm/competition/state_aid/others/1759_sieg_en.pdf (last accessed 28 April 2003).

[77] Art. 16 states 'Without prejudice to Arts. 73, 86 and 87, and given the place occupied by services of general economic interest in the shared values of the Union as well as their role in promoting

all Member State measures. The Commission has considered in some cases that state financing could be considered to be 'state aid' for the purposes of Article 87 EC[78] and, in others, that such financing could not be considered to be aid for the purposes of Article 87 EC.[79] This has been supported by the approach of the Court of First Instance in *Portuguese Television*, which has suggested that

> ... even where an advantage is granted in order to set off burdens arising from tasks undertaken in the public interest, that does not affect the classification of the measure in question as State aid, without prejudice to Article 90(2) of the Treaty.[80]

This approach rendered it likely that all types of funding for public service broadcasting would have to be subject to Commission scrutiny, which, in the first instance, had the potential to place additional pressure on states to justify their methods of funding public service broadcasting. However, in *Ferring*[81] the European Court of Justice appears to have redrawn the boundaries in state aid cases, deciding that where state funding of a particular activity offers no more than consideration for the public service obligations imposed upon the undertaking then the sums paid by the state to the provider would not constitute state aid for the purposes of Article 87 EC. The case concerned tax breaks offered by the French government to wholesale distributors of medicines in exchange for obligations imposed upon them to maintain stocks of a wide range of medicines. The ECJ's approach considered that measures such as the ones adopted by the French government

> [amount] to State aid to wholesale distributors only to the extent that the advantage in not being assessed to the tax on direct sales of medicines exceeds the additional costs that they bear in discharging the public service obligations imposed on them by national law.[82]

---

social and territorial cohesion, the Community and the Member States, each within their respective powers and within the scope of application of this Treaty, shall take care that such services operate on the basis of principles and conditions which enable them to fulfil their missions'. For commentary on the addition of Art. 16 EC see Ross, M. 'Article 16 EC and Services of General Interest: from Derogation to Obligation?', (2000) 25 *European Law Review* 22 and Prosser, T. 'Public Service Law: Privatisation's Unexpected Offspring', (2000) 63 *Law and Contemporary Problems* 63.

[78] Case NN 88/98 *BBC News 24* Available at: http://europa.eu.int/comm/secretariat_general/sgb/state_aids/industrie/nn088-98.pdf (Last accessed 28 April 2003).

[79] Case NN 141/95 *SIC* [1997] OJ C 67/10.

[80] Case T-46/97 *SIC – Sociedade Independente de Comunicaçao SA* v. *Commission of the European Communities* [2002] ECR II-2125 at para. 56. See also Case T-106/95 *FFSA* v. *Commission* [1997] ECR II-229.

[81] Case C-53/00 *Ferring SA* v. *Agence Centrale des Organismes de Securite Sociale (ACOSS)* [2001] ECR I-9067.

[82] *Ibid.* at para. 29.

EUROPEAN CONTROLS ON PROMOTION AND REGULATION OF PSB 523

Ferring is a decision which has proved to be highly controversial, provoking a range of comment in academic circles.[83] It is undeniable that the decision is likely to cause difficulties, potentially risking an excessive limitation on the scope of Article 87. For public service broadcasting the decision in *Ferring* might be good news. On the face of the decision it appears that PSBs might benefit, in the sense that providing that they can show any state aid is only recompense for fulfilling a public service mandate then the Commission's scrutiny of such aid is likely to be curtailed. However, it may be that the outcome is more likely to shift the question that the Commission is considering, in the sense that the Commission will shift its focus onto whether the public service mandate is outlined with sufficient clarity.[84] While the benefits for public service broadcasting should not be ignored the decision may have caused wider ranging consequences. As Lindner has argued

> The danger of *Ferring* is that Article 86(2) loses its significance. Furthermore, there is the danger that even the prohibition of Article 87(1) will become meaningless in cases of public service obligations. It is far from clear what benefit is derived from removing the Commission's control over state financing of public service obligations.[85]

These are difficulties which should not be ignored. While the public service broadcaster will potentially see benefit from the decision in *Ferring*, it may be that a more principled approach could be adopted. The significance of the Protocol on Public Service Broadcasting,[86] annexed to the Amsterdam Treaty offers interpretive principles which would have allowed the Commission to find justification for the state funding of public service broadcasting under Article 86(2), rather than excluding a raft of public service funding agreements from the scope of the state aid provisions in their entirety.

---

[83] See *e.g.* Bartosch, A. 'The Relationship between Public Procurement and State Aid Surveillance – The Toughest Standard Applies?', (2002) 39 *Common Market Law Review* 551, Nicolaides, P. 'Distortive Effects of Compensatory Aid Measures: A Note on the Economics of the *Ferring* Judgment', (2002) *European Competition Law Review* 313, Bacon, K. 'The Concept of State Aid: The Developing Jurisprudence in the European and UK Courts',(2003) *European Competition Law Review* 54 and Lindner, N. 'The Impact of the Decision of the European Court of Justice in *Ferring* on European State Aid Law', (2003) 9 *European Public Law* 359.

[84] Some support for this approach might be garnered from the response of Commissioner Monti to written question E-3475/02 where he stated that 'The definition of public service in the service contract between the Italian Government and RAI appears to be at variance with the requirements set out by the Commission in its Communication on State aid for public service broadcasting, in that it is excessively general and much broader than is considered acceptable in the communication'. See [2003] OJ C 280 E/18.

[85] Lindner, N. *ibid.* at 367.

[86] [1997] OJ C 340/109.

Despite these criticisms, including critical opinions of the *Ferring* case by Jacobs A-G in *GEMO*[87] and the critical opinion of Léger A-G in *Altmark*,[88] the European Court of Justice has not altered the interpretation of the law. In its ruling in the *Altmark* case, the Court of Justice followed *Ferring*, stating that

> ... where a State measure must be regarded as compensation for the services provided by the recipient undertakings in order to discharge public service obligations, so that those undertakings do not enjoy a real financial advantage and the measure thus does not have the effect of putting them in a more favourable competitive position than the undertakings competing with them, such a measure is not caught by Article 92(1) [now 87(1)] of the Treaty.[89]

While the decision in *Altmark* changes little from the approach in *Ferring*, it should be noted that the Court did make two issues abundantly clear. First, it is now without doubt that one of the key issues when deciding whether a measure is caught by Article 87 will be whether the public service obligations are sufficiently clearly defined. The court argued that there were two key issues to be considered in this situation.

> First, the recipient undertaking must actually have public service obligations to discharge, and the obligations must be clearly defined ... Second, the parameters on the basis of which the compensation is calculated must be calculated in advance in an objective and transparent manner, to avoid it conferring an economic advantage which may favour the recipient undertaking over competing undertakings.[90]

The Commission has been forced to alter its approach on the funding of public service broadcasting somewhat, following the approach taken in the European Court of Justice. As a result the Commission's position on this as expounded in the recent communication on the issue may be somewhat outdated, as it still considers the old case law as being the basis of the approach to be taken.[91] The approach of the European Court of Justice in *Ferring* and *Altmark* seems to render many types of state funding for public service broadcasting outside of the ambit of the state

---

[87] Case C-126/01 *Ministre de l'Economie, des Finances et de l'Industrie* v. *GEMO SA* [2004] 1 CMLR 9.

[88] C-280/00 *Altmark* [2003] 3 CMLR 12.

[89] *Ibid.* at para. 87.

[90] *Ibid.* at paras. 89-90.

[91] See paras. 17-20 of the Commission's Communication on the Application of State Aid Rules to Public Service Broadcasting above, note 73, 'State financing of public service broadcasters is normally to be regarded as State aid ... any transfer of State resources to a certain undertaking – also when covering net costs of public service obligations – has to be regarded as state aid ...".

aid provisions. The Commission's recent decision in the *BBC Licence Fee*[92] case shows the adoption of the new approach. In this case the Commission examined the compatibility of licence fee funding of the BBC's new thematic digital services. The Commission concluded that in the circumstances the grant of licence fee support to the BBC for the transmission of these new thematic channels could not be considered to be state aid after the recent decisions of the Court of Justice.

It seems that the new area of likely conflict between the Commission and the Member States is likely to lie not over whether the state's support for a public service broadcaster is actually state aid for the purposes of the treaty but, instead: whether the entrustment of the public service functions is done in a sufficiently specific manner. As the Commission noted in the licence fee case

> ... the Commission regrets that the conditions of entrustment of the new digital channels have not been precisely and clearly defined in the relevant legal documents, being the Agreement and the Charter, which describe the public service obligations of the BBC. The Commission considers that a clear and precise identification of the activities covered by the public service remit, and the conditions under which these have to be performed, is important for non-public service operators, so they can plan their activities.[93]

This aspect of the Commission's approach is also likely to be due to the need for them to assess the proportionality of the funding, which is unlikely to be possible should the definition of the public service goals not be sufficiently specific and succinct. In the recent statement in relation to the case brought against the Danish public service broadcaster[94] the Commission has suggested that the

> ... rather qualitative and broadly defined public service obligation has been properly entrusted to TV2 by means of a legislative act. However ... the Commission has come to the conclusion that the Danish authorities overcompensated the net public service costs of TV2, thereby risking to cross subsidise TV2's commercial activities and to distort competition.[95]

The general problem which is faced by the public service mandate is that it is necessarily open textured in order to leave the public service broadcaster the freedom to develop its services in such a manner as to preserve the diversity and pluralism that many of the systems of public service broadcasting in the European

---

[92] Case NN 631/01 *BBC Licence Fee*, notified in document number C (2002) 1886 available at: http://europa.eu.int/comm/secretariat_general/sgb/state_aids/industrie/n631-01.pdf (last Accessed 28 April 2003).

[93] *Ibid.* at para. 36.

[94] Aid C 2/03 *State Financing of Danish public service broadcaster TV2 by means of licence fee and other measures* [2003] OJ C 59/02.

[95] *Ibid.*

Union have achieved. This can clearly have difficulties in certain cases and the Danish situation is one such example. The real issue here, which would not be faced by a number of other public service broadcasters, is that the Danish public service broadcaster is also active in the market for television advertising and there are always likely to be difficulties in determining whether the state assistance granted to the broadcaster is allowing it to abuse its position in the advertising market. Although this is clearly a problem it seems to be somewhat undesirable that the Commission could look for the solution by requiring very highly specified mandates for public service broadcasters which would have the potential to damage the very flexibility and freedom which have allowed the public service broadcaster to develop such a strong tradition of independence and freedom within the European Union's broadcasting system.[96]

The entire issue of 'overcompensation' for the performance of public service broadcasting is a difficult one in any case. Most public service broadcasters merely work within the boundaries of the resources that are granted to them and, as such, could expand and improve their output should they be given additional resources. This would not necessarily have any impact on competitors because much of what the public service broadcaster offers is not standard commercial output and thus does not directly compete with the material offered via pay-TV.[97] It is undeniable that in certain cases where public service broadcasters have the opportunity to take advertising in competition with other providers of free to air television there are potentially issues where the public service broadcaster uses the financing received from the state to subsidise its advertising operations. Despite this fact it seems somewhat undesirable to allow this difficulty, which will only arise in a very limited number of cases, to require increasingly highly specified public service mandates.

V. Conclusions

The mass media in modern society play an increasingly crucial role, offering what Habermas has described as

---

[96] The Protocol on Public Service broadcasting, which is annexed to the Treaty of Amsterdam emphasises 'that the system of public broadcasting in the Member States is directly related to the democratic, social and cultural needs of each society and to the need to preserve media pluralism'. The significance and strength of the European public service broadcasting model has been outlined in a number of sources. See *e.g.* Hoffman-Riem, Barendt and Humphreys, all cited above, note 1.

[97] See Camasasca, P.D. 'Mayday or Heyday? Dynamic Competition Meets Media Ownership Rules after *Premiere*', (2000) *European Competition Law Review*, 76 at 78-79 where the author cites a German study which demonstrates that the current subscribers to digital pay TV devote 90% of their viewing time to free to air and public service broadcasting and only 10% to the subscription services.

EUROPEAN CONTROLS ON PROMOTION AND REGULATION OF PSB 527

... the abstract public sphere of isolated readers, listeners and viewers scattered across large geographic areas, or even around the globe, and brought together only through the mass media.[98]

This development of the mass media, particularly in the form of broadcast media has been considered to be likely to have a significant effect within the European Union. The importance of a vibrant media for democratic society and freedom of expression has not gone overlooked within the European Union[99] with a considerable amount of effort being expended by the various institutions within the Union's infrastructure stating their support for public service broadcasting. It was noted above that many PSBs within the Union are currently striving to improve the range of services that they provide by introducing a range of new channels which are more directly in competition with the services offered by private broadcasters. This has been controversial under Community law, particularly in relation to state aid; the current approach of the European Court of Justice adopted in *Ferring* is to be welcomed.

The existence of public service broadcasters is pivotal for the broadcast media's role in society for two reasons. First, one can argue that the obligations placed upon public service broadcasters to produce a wide range of diverse, quality programming and make it available as widely as possible aids the inclusion of all citizens within the media revolution and the cohesion which exists within society.[100] Most public service broadcasters are obliged to ensure that the content that is offered should be available on all systems of delivery, whether digital or analogue and is generally available regardless of the citizen's ability to pay. A second argument for the continued support of public service broadcasting is that it offers a means through which the shift toward digital technology can be promoted, as the free availability of a range of quality channels which are unavailable through traditional analogue broadcasting systems offers an incentive for a greater number of those who are currently receiving broadcasts through analogue technologies to make the shift to digital broadcasting technologies via one of the delivery mechanisms available.[101]

---

[98] Habermas, J., *Between Facts and Norms* (Cambridge, MA: The MIT Press, 1997) at page 374.

[99] The recent Charter of Fundamental Rights in the European Union [2000] OJ C 364/01 states in Art. 11 that 'The freedom and pluralism of the media shall be respected'.

[100] For comments on the potential for broadcasting to add to the notion of European citizenship, see Harrison, J. and Woods, L., 'European Citizenship: Can Audio-Visual Policy Make a Difference?', (2000) 38:3 *Journal of Common Market Studies* 471 and Habermas, J., 'Remarks on Dieter Grimm's "Does Europe Need a Constitution"', (1995) 1 *European Law Journal*, 303.

[101] It may be that the inclusion of the 'must carry' requirements in Art. 31 of the Universal Service Directive, *Directive 2002/22/EC of the European Parliament and of the Council of 7 March 2002 on universal service and users' rights relating to electronic communications networks and services* [2002] OJ L 108/51.

This growth in the services offered by public service broadcasters will not be possible without funding being made available. A number of the traditional mechanisms for the funding of high quality public service broadcasting through commercial means, such as the reservation of national broadcasting market to a limited number of national broadcasting companies,[102] or preventing the transmission of advertisements from other Member States without prior authorisation[103] are no longer permissible due to the interpretation of the free movement provisions in Community law. Instead, any further funding of public service broadcasting will have to be undertaken via more obvious means by the Member State concerned.

The Court's approach in *Ferring* is to be welcomed for a further reason. It is clear that one key attraction of PSB is that it ensures that all citizens have access to some form of high quality, pluralistic and reasonably diverse content that may be otherwise unavailable. In this sense the decision in *Ferring* could be considered to be a further expression of the development of public service law – what Prosser defines as

> ... law designed to make basic public services available to all citizens without discrimination.[104]

The development of public service is undoubtedly furthered by the decision in this case, given that there is now general acceptance from the Court of Justice that in many cases provision of remuneration for the performance of a public service or other such social obligations will no longer constitute state aid for the purposes of the EC Treaty, allowing Member States somewhat greater leeway when considering the expansion of public service obligations on a particular service provider.

The discussion in this article has also aimed to raise the issue of the effects of the concept of 'European public law' on the regulatory endeavours of Member States. According to Birkinshaw the concept

> ... is concerned with the development of the public law of European states, and their influence upon, and their influence in turn by, the developing law of the European Community or European Union as it is increasingly called.[105]

It has been suggested in this article that although certain elements of present EU law, such as the protocol on public service broadcasting and Article 16 EC reflect and strengthen the position of the concept of public service broadcasting, there are also causes for concern. Many Member States within the Union will seek to support public service broadcasting even in the face of developing technologies of

---

[102] Case T-266/97 *Vlaamse Televisie Maatschapij NV* above, note 35 and accompanying discussion.

[103] Case 352/85 *Bond van Adverteerders* above, note 26 and accompanying discussion.

[104] Prosser, T. 'Public Service Law: Privatisation's Unexpected Offspring' above, note 77 at 63-64.

[105] Birkinshaw, P.J., *European Public Law* (London: Butterworths LexisNexis, 2003) 1.

EUROPEAN CONTROLS ON PROMOTION AND REGULATION OF PSB   529

digitalisation which place strain upon many of the traditional justifications for the support of public service broadcasting. Many Member States will also seek to restrict certain types of broadcast or certain areas of content due to specific national cultural concerns. The potential for measures to be taken in order to support public service broadcasting or restrict certain broadcast services or types of content are becoming increasingly shaped and limited by the contours of Community law in this area. This will correspondingly close down the potential for individual Member States to take action to regulate in those areas which are subject to minimum harmonisation under Community law or, alternatively, will reduce the potential for public service broadcasters to extend their range of services or to gain further funding from the state without fear of potential state aid investigations.

The current approach of the Court of Justice in *Ferring*[106] and *Altmark*[107] appears to reduce the pressure on state funding of public service broadcasting. Uncertainties do, however, remain. As noted above, a key issue will be the degree of specificity which is required of a public service mandate to ensure that it falls within the protection of the decision in *Altmark* and is not considered as state aid. It may be that even if the current position regarding state financing of public services is ultimately reversed, or it is found that public service mandates are not sufficiently clearly defined to fall within the protection of the case law then the financing of public service broadcasting is not placed under significant threat. The reason for this is that even if state funding is considered to be state aid for the purposes of Article 87(1) then it is likely that the Commission will consider the aid to be justified under Article 86(2). If one considers the recent case law of the Commission prior to the decision in *Ferring* it is clear that the Commission considered it interpretive role outlined in the Protocol on Public Service Broadcasting to be of considerable importance. In the *BBC Licence Fee*[108] decision stated that

> In view of the interpretive provisions of the Protocol and given the specific nature of the broadcasting sector, the rather qualitative definition of the public service remit ... under which the new digital channels are to be provided, can be considered as legitimate services of general economic interest within the meaning of Article 86(2) EC.[109]

Although this element of the operation of Community law is not unexpected it may limit the potential for Member States to act to protect their own public service broadcaster to some degree, thus compromising what is often a key element of

---

[106] Case C-53/00 above, note 81.

[107] Case C-280/00 above, note 88.

[108] Case NN 631/01 above, note 92.

[109] *Ibid.* at para. 34. The treatment given to the Protocol in its interpretive role is covered relatively comprehensively in the *Communication from the Commission on the Application of State Aid Rules to Public Service Broadcasting* [2001] OJ C 320/05.

national culture. The limitation of restrictions on certain broadcasting activities by the law on freedom to provide services is also an obvious and legitimate development, although it is also one which can restrict the ability of Member States to protect their citizens in accordance with national preferences and traditions.[110] The current uncertainty over whether Member State measures which go further than the minimum harmonisation in the 'Television Without Frontiers Directive' will be allowed to stand by the ECJ adds to the difficulties which might be faced by Member States when creating national media regulation regimes.

This uncertainty, combined with closer restrictions on national measures which support national broadcasters leads one to believe that the current trend in media markets in the EU is likely to be toward increasing liberalisation, with decreasing scope for Member States to intervene to protect national traditions. While this is not necessarily a disaster in the making for European media markets it is clear that there is potential for pluralism and diversity to be threatened should Member States' scope to intervene be curtailed further without agreement at the supranational level to ensure the maintenance of some of the key traditions. This article has aimed to demonstrate that European public law clearly exists within the sphere of media regulation and, that at the present time, the effects on that sphere are profound.

---

[110] Harlow sees this as one of the key difficulties of European public law, see Harlow, C., 'Voices of Difference in a Plural Community', in Beaumont, P. Lyons, C. and Walker, N. (eds.), *Convergence and Divergence in European Public Law* (Oxford: Hart Publishing, 2002).

[8]

A Marketplace Approach to Broadcast Regulation

Mark S. Fowler* and Daniel L. Brenner**

Chairman Mark S. Fowler and Daniel L. Brenner argue that the time is long overdue for a national communications policy that will account for market forces in radio and television and accommodate the first amendment rights of those who operate commercial stations. The authors propose that the trusteeship model of broadcast regulation by which the Federal Communications Commission has regulated program content yield to a deregulated marketplace approach. New program responsibilities could then be assigned to noncommercial broadcasting in a deregulated environment for commercial radio and television.

I. Introduction

Regulation of radio and television by the Federal Communications Commission remains a frequent target for administrative law reformers. The vague licensing criterion provided by Congress—the standard of "public convenience, interest, or necessity"[1]—has provided a starting point for critics dissatisfied with the last fifty-five years of regulatory performance in this area. In applying this criterion, the Commission has built a series of legal fictions into a regulatory environment altogether different from that faced by the media ventures that preceded radio and television, or those that are now being introduced.

The Commission's world of regulation is not without intricacy. To be sanctioned as a licensee, an applicant has to prove it has investigated its community through "ascertainment."[2] Having adduced the needs

* Chairman, Federal Communications Commission. A.B. 1966, J.D. 1969, University of Florida.
** Legal Assistant to the Chairman, Federal Communications Commission. B.A., A.M. 1973, J.D. 1976, Stanford University.

The views expressed are those of the authors and do not necessarily reflect Commission views. It is not the intent of the authors to express any conclusions about the merits of specific actions currently before the Commission or decided during their tenure.

1. 47 U.S.C. §§ 303, 307(a) (1976).

2. *See* Ascertainment of Community Problems by Broadcast Applicants, 57 F.C.C.2d 418 (1975), *modified*, 61 F.C.C.2d 1 (1976); Primer on Ascertainment of Community Problems by Broadcast Applicants, 27 F.C.C.2d 650 (1971). The ascertainment process includes interviews with community leaders, general public opinion surveys, and demographic studies. Compliance with the Commission's engineering, ownership, and financial requirements must also be shown.

208   Texas Law Review   Vol. 60:207, 1982

and interests of the community, the applicant is expected to propose
programming that meets those needs and interests. If the applicant
seeks a television license, the Commission's guidelines also require the
programming to include a dose of news and public affairs.[3] A further
maze of rules details the procedures to be followed[4] if the applicant
owns more than one broadcast outlet or is involved in the cable television business,[5] employs more than four people,[6] happens to be an
alien,[7] or believes that partisanship, not objectivity, should characterize
station programming.[8]

Broadcasting in the United States conforms little to the model contemplated in the Commission's licensing philosophy. Most television
stations affiliate with one of the three major commercial networks and
delegate many programming decisions to the networks.[9] Acceptable
ascertainment by applicants for license renewal or new licenses can
amount to five-minute interviews with community leaders and a generic summary of community demographics prepared by a commercial

3. *See* 47 C.F.R. § 0.281(a)(8)(i) (1981).

4. *See, e.g., id.* § 73.642(a)(3), (f)(3) (1981); *id.* § 73.643(a). Deregulation of over-the-air pay
television has been underway since 1977, *see, e.g.,* Second Report and Order in Docket No.
21,502, 85 F.C.C.2d 631 (1981) (establishing comparative criteria for subscription television proposals in mutually exclusive application proceedings). The Commission's lease-only policy regarding decoders for subscription television and other restrictions, *see* Further Notice of Proposed
Rule Making in Docket No. 21,502, Subscription Television Service, 88 F.C.C.2d 213 (1981), have
recently been eliminated. *See* FCC News, Mimeo No. 4684 (June 18, 1982).

5. *See* OFFICE OF PLANS AND POLICY, FCC, POLICY ON CABLE OWNERSHIP (1981).

6. The Commission has required a broadcast station having more than four full-time employees to file an equal employment opportunities (EEO) program consistent with the policy set
forth at 47 C.F.R. § 73.2080 (1981) (adopted in 1976, Nondiscrimination in the Employment Policies and Practices of Broadcast Licensees, 60 F.C.C.2d 226 (1976)), and annual EEO reports, FCC
Form 395, 98 RAD. REG. (P & F) 395-1. The Commission first adopted formal regulations requiring nondiscrimination and affirmative action in 1969, *see* Petition for Rulemaking to Require
Broadcast Licensees to Show Nondiscrimination in Their Employment Practices, 18 F.C.C.2d 240
(1969), and extended these protections to women in 1971, Equal Employment Program, 32
F.C.C.2d 831 (1971). This Article does not specifically address the Commission's EEO efforts.
However, we do note that racial discrimination distorts ownership and employment opportunities
in the marketplace and that EEO efforts attempt to remedy this distortion. Commission programs
to promote equal treatment of all potential participants in broadcasting, both in employment and
ownership, are consistent with a marketplace approach because they ensure that all have an opportunity to compete.

7. 47 U.S.C. § 310(b) (1976). *See generally* Watkins, *Alien Ownership and the Communications Act*, 33 FED. COM. L.J. 1 (1981).

8. *See* 47 U.S.C. § 315(a) (1976); 47 C.F.R. § 73.1910 (1981); Brandywine-Main Line Radio,
Inc. v. FCC, 473 F.2d 16 (D.C. Cir. 1972), *cert. denied*, 412 U.S. 922 (1973).

9. *See* En Banc Programming Inquiry, 44 F.C.C. 2303, 2314 (1960); 2 OFFICE OF NETWORK
STUDY, FCC, SECOND INTERIM REPORT, TELEVISION NETWORK PROGRAM PROCUREMENT 199
(1965) ("[T]he composition of the network schedule, as a real matter, becomes a highly limiting
factor in the licensee's ability to serve his community."); *see also* 1 NETWORK INQUIRY SPECIAL
STAFF, FCC, NEW TELEVISION NETWORKS: ENTRY, JURISDICTION, OWNERSHIP AND REGULA-
TION 298 (1980) ("[E]ach of the network forms considered in this chapter that use interstate facilities to distribute programs appears to have, or likely may have, a substantial impact on the
broadcast service delivered to viewers.").

A Marketplace Approach to Broadcast Regulation **209**

research firm. The ascertainment process typically produces a perfunctory listing of community needs and of standard programs to fulfill those needs, often compiled in Washington by the broadcaster's attorney or the attorney's paralegal. The process also borders on the unseemly from a constitutional standpoint, since the Commission's zeal in reviewing program proposals treads on the editorial independence guaranteed by the first amendment to broadcasters. But year in, year out, the Commission has urged broadcasters to conduct these exercises and to carry public affairs programs that broadcasters may not want to carry and, apparently, few viewers elect to watch. Both the license renewal rate and the profits for most of the broadcasting business have been so high that neither the regulated nor the regulators have been anxious to challenge the system.[10]

The Commission's fiduciary approach to broadcast regulation may be ending at last. Competition to over-the-air broadcasting from new media has led to an awareness that traditional broadcasting is just one of many information delivery systems.[11] Technological plenty is forcing a widespread reconsideration of the role competition can play in broadcast regulation. And regulators and others have become increasingly aware that regulatory processes have infringed the first amendment rights of broadcasters without a sufficiently compelling constitutional justification.

This Article proposes a new direction for governmental regulation of broadcasting in the United States. The ideas raised are not entirely new, but they have been ignored by those who have been busy raising and lowering the drawbridge of licensing. Our thesis is that the perception of broadcasters as community trustees should be replaced by a view of broadcasters as marketplace participants. Communications policy should be directed toward maximizing the services the public desires. Instead of defining public demand and specifying categories of

---

10. *See generally* B. COLE & M. OETTINGER, RELUCTANT REGULATORS 36-49 (1978). The industry's renewal record is nearly perfect, standing at about 99%. In the last 40 years, only two licensees have lost licenses as a result of petitions to deny, *see* Office of Communication of United Church of Christ v. FCC, 425 F.2d 543 (D.C. Cir. 1969); Alabama Educ. Television Comm'n, 50 F.C.C.2d 461 (1975). These cases provide slim precedent for predicting renewal activity because the offending practices in both cases involved overt racial discrimination. Since the advent of television, only two licensees have been denied renewal in favor of a competing applicant on a purely comparative basis. *See* Greater Boston Television Corp. v. FCC (WHDH-TV), 444 F.2d 841 (D.C. Cir. 1970), *cert. denied*, 403 U.S. 923, *reopening denied*, 463 F.2d 268 (D.C. Cir. 1971); Simon Geller (WVCA-FM, Gloucester, Mass.), FCC Report No. 17,007, Mimeo No. 4193 (May 21, 1982).

11. *See* Report and Order on Direct Broadcast Satellite Service, FCC News, Mimeo No. 4775 (June 23, 1982). *See generally* NATIONAL ASS'N OF BROADCASTERS, NEW TECHNOLOGIES AFFECTING RADIO AND TELEVISION (1981).

210   Texas Law Review   Vol. 60:207, 1982

programming to serve this demand, the Commission should rely on the broadcasters' ability to determine the wants of their audiences through the normal mechanisms of the marketplace. The public's interest, then, defines the public interest. And in light of the first amendment's heavy presumption against content control, the Commission should refrain from insinuating itself into program decisions made by licensees.

A. Economics and Broadcasting

The proposition that consumers are best off when society's economic resources are allocated in a manner that enables people to satisfy their wants as fully as possible permeates all sectors of our economy.[12] Depending on what goods or services are involved, consumer satisfaction is enhanced by freedom of choice in the price, quality, or variety of products. We increase social utility by promoting competition, removing artificial barriers to entry, preventing any one firm from controlling price or eliminating its competitors, and in general establishing conditions that allow the price of goods to be as close as possible to their cost of production.[13]

Although we have relied on free markets to provide most of the goods and services in our society for over 200 years, this has not been the case in the broadcast industry. For a variety of reasons, the Commission has traditionally refused to recognize the undeniable fact that commercial broadcasting is a business. But it is a business, one that faces increasing competition in the years ahead for the eyes and ears of its audience.[14] The first step in a marketplace approach to broadcast regulation, then, is to focus on broadcasters not as fiduciaries of the public, as their regulators have historically perceived them, but as marketplace competitors.

B. Spectrum Markets

A threshold difficulty in applying a marketplace approach to commercial broadcasting lies in the definition of the market. Broadcasters differ from some other information providers because they receive exclusive use of an assigned frequency; the frequencies reserved for broadcasters are not available for nonbroadcasting uses regardless of

---

12. *See* A. SMITH, AN INQUIRY INTO THE NATURE AND CAUSES OF THE WEALTH OF NATIONS, (1st ed. Edinburgh 1776), *reprinted in* ADAM SMITH (R. Hutchins ed. 1952); *see also* R. BORK, ANTITRUST THEORY AND PRACTICE 92-106 (1981); B. OWEN, ECONOMICS AND FREEDOM OF EXPRESSION 26-31 (1975).

13. *See* R. BORK, *supra* note 12, at 93-94.

14. "Glamour and social influence not withstanding [sic], television is a business." B. OWEN, J. BEEBE & W. MANNING, JR., TELEVISION ECONOMICS 3 (1974).

A Marketplace Approach to Broadcast Regulation **211**

demand. In a true marketplace, broadcasters would compete with all potential users of the airwaves for the exclusive right to use a particular frequency, just as they must compete with other businesses for land, labor, buildings, equipment, and other factors of production. The spectrum market would consist of those buying and selling rights to use frequencies on an exclusive, protected basis.

It is difficult to define frequency rights in familiar terms. Those who hold rights to occupy a plot of land or to mine the minerals beneath its surface can establish precisely the dimensions of their claims, but broadcast frequencies are intangibles that exist only in conjunction with the technical apparatus for transmission and reception. The difficulty in defining the right to a frequency has led, on the one hand, to nearly mystical assertions about particulate flowing in the "ether"[15] and, on the other hand, to an unproductive debate over who "owns" the airwaves, the public or the broadcaster.[16]

Yet the Commission has allocated radio frequencies for a long time and spectrum users have accepted the system. The user's right is based in the government's provision of exclusivity to a patch of spectrum with sanctions, both civil and criminal, meted out to those who "trespass" with the user's exclusive enjoyment. Having said this, the broadcasting marketplace comes into focus: it consists of those seeking government-granted *exclusivities*.

A marketplace approach to exclusive use of radio frequencies would open all positions in the electromagnetic spectrum to bidding by those who want them. As with the allocation of other goods in society,[17] the highest bidder would acquire exclusive rights to a particular frequency. In the fully deregulated marketplace, the highest bidder would make the best and highest use of the resource.[18] R.H. Coase set forth the contours of this approach to the electromagnetic spectrum,

---

15. This point of view appears in discussions of the legal status of airspace, *see, e.g.,* C. ALEX-ANDROWICZ, THE LAW OF GLOBAL COMMUNICATIONS 27-28 (1971) (citing author's translation of SIBERT, 1 TRAITE DE DROIT INTERNATIONAL PUBLIC 848 (1951) ("Can a State which is between the two above States (i.e., between the State of origin of waves and the State of their destination) stop the passage of radio waves which are in transit above its territory?").

16. *Broadcast Reform Proposals: Hearings on H.R. 4726, H.R. 4780, and H.R. 4781 Before the Subcomm. on Telecommunications of the House Comm. on Energy and Communications,* 97th Cong., 1st Sess. 63 (1981) (remarks of Rep. Dingell). *Contra* Jaffe, *The Editorial Responsibility of the Broadcaster: Reflections on Fairness and Access,* 85 HARV. L. REV. 768, 783 (1972).

17. Such arrangements should not seem peculiar. Putting aside zoning considerations, a plot of land theoretically will be purchased by whichever user can make the highest and best use of it. If the land is twice as valuable when used for a six-story apartment building than for a gasoline station, the apartment builder will pay more for it in a competitive economy. Similarly, if a particular radio frequency is more valuable to a company offering car phone service than to an independent UHF television outlet, the former would outbid the latter in a deregulated market.

18. R. BORK, *supra* note 12, at 98.

212 Texas Law Review Vol. 60:207, 1982

and broadcasting in particular, in 1959.[19] Professor Coase observed that producers generally obtain more of a desired resource when buying it on the open market. If forced to bid for unused frequencies or to buy them from existing users, broadcasters would draw the frequencies away from other industries only if they paid more for them, and vice versa.[20] The pricing mechanism would bring the costs of spectrum use in line with those of other factors of production used in broadcasting or any other business.[21]

Commenting on Coase's argument, Professor Harry Kalven concluded that "the perspective is so radical by today's views that although I am persuaded of its correctness, I am not clear how it can be used in public discussion."[22] More than fifty years of regulatory precedent, now compounded by the settled expectations of the public and the broadcasting industry, would make it difficult to conduct an auction of the entire electromagnetic spectrum. And to its credit, the system of centralized grants probably contributes to the development of more efficient uses of frequency bands, forcing users to develop better tuners and transmitters to enhance their signal rather than consume more spectrum on the perimeter.[23]

In any event, Congress early on decided to abandon market forces in determining grants of exclusivity to the spectrum. Probably because commercial radio had already established squatter's rights to some frequencies, Congress reserved a portion of the spectrum (and, in fact, not a very large portion in terms of the frequencies that could be used for broadcasting) for radio and later television. This was the original electromagnetic sin. Regardless of what the marketplace would have man-

---

19. Coase, *The Federal Communications Commission*, 2 J.L. & ECON. 1 (1959). Some of the ideas presented in Coase's article first appeared in Note, *Old Standards in a New Context: A Comparative Analysis of FCC Regulation*, 18 U. CHI. L. REV. 78 (1950); *see also* Herzel, *Public Interest and the Market in Color Television Regulation*, 18 U. CHI. L. REV. 802 (1951).

20. Adoption of a pricing mechanism for exclusive use might require the government, a heavy user of the radio spectrum for military and civilian purposes, to pay its way, although such uses could remain exempt from such market forces. *See* M. MUELLER, PROPERTY RIGHTS IN RADIO COMMUNICATION: THE KEY TO THE REFORM OF TELECOMMUNICATIONS REGULATION 38 (Cato Institute Policy Analysis Series, 1982).

21. Coase, *supra* note 19, at 20-22.

22. Kalven, *Broadcasting, Public Policy, and The First Amendment*, 10 J.L. & ECON. 15, 30 (1967).

23. Spectrum-saving techniques have been particularly adapted to land mobile radio. One system, amplitude compandered single sideband transmission (ACSB), enables two-way radio to transmit over channels five kilohertz wide. Voice channels have traditionally been five or six times as wide. The number of channels could increase in that part of the spectrum—from low band through 800 megahertz—from 1,600 to 8,313. *See* Wilmotte, *ACSB: Spectrum Efficiency for the Future?*, TELOCATOR, June 1980, at 20. Cellular radio, which provides a service similar to land mobile radio, primarily through car telephones, also employs spectrum-saving technology.

A Marketplace Approach to Broadcast Regulation **213**

dated, broadcasting was to be entitled, as of right, to a number of exclusive channels.

II. The Trusteeship Model

Instead of being exchanged as a property right, exclusivity to a radio frequency has been assigned by the Commission on the amorphous "public interest" standard. Broadcaster responsibility officially runs to the viewing public as defined by the Commission, not to shareholders, sponsors,[24] or even the users of the sponsors' products or services who indirectly finance the stations. Two considerable evils have come from this arrangement: "broadcasters take advantage of the public-interest myth to promote a variety of protectionist policies, motivated in fact by economic self-interest . . . [and] . . . the public at large is misled in its perception of the role and function of broadcasting in America."[25] In short, by abandoning a marketplace approach in the determination of spectrum utilization, the government created a tension, in both first amendment and economic terms, that haunts communications policy to this day.

A. The Origins of the Model

The trusteeship model of broadcast regulation can be traced to the beginning of radio regulation in the United States in the early part of the twentieth century. Federal regulation of radio broadcasting emerged in the early part of the century out of the congestion in ship-to-shore and ship-to-ship communications, which the Department of the Navy described as an "etheric bedlam produced by numerous stations all trying to communicate at once."[26] Congress perceived spectrum scarcity to be a significant enough problem to justify federal oversight and abandonment of market techniques in spectrum management, and enacted the Radio Act of 1912,[27] which forbade operation of a radio apparatus without a license from the Secretary of Commerce and Labor. The limited regulatory power of the Commerce Department, however, did not extend beyond the role of nondiscriminating

---

24. The role of the sponsor's influence on program decisionmaking is detailed in E. BARNOUW, THE SPONSOR (1978).

25. B. OWEN, J. BEEBE & W. MANNING, JR., *supra* note 14, at 12.

26. "Mischievous and irresponsible operators seem to take great delight in impersonating other stations and sending out false calls. It is not putting the case too strongly to state that the situation is intolerable, and is continually growing worse." S. REP. No. 659, 61st Cong., 2d Sess. 4 (1910).

27. Ch. 287, 37 Stat. 302 (1912), *repealed by* Communications Act of 1934, ch. 652; § 602(a), 48 Stat. 1064, 1102.

registrar,[28] and the result was a frequency free-for-all in the mid-1920's, that doomed the 1912 scheme.[29]

The Radio Act of 1927[30] represented Congress' response to fifteen years of inadequate regulation. The Act was largely replicated in the Communications Act of 1934,[31] which transferred the powers of broadcasting regulation to a new federal agency, the Federal Communications Commission. The Act empowered the Commission to license radio stations in the "public convenience, interest, or necessity," providing for a "fair, efficient, and equitable distribution of radio service" to all communities.[32] The licensing scheme, with its inquiries into program service, received broad approval from the Supreme Court in the 1943 decision, *NBC v. United States*.[33] As Justice Frankfurter viewed it, the "confusion and chaos" existing prior to 1927

> was attributable to certain basic facts about radio as a means of communication—its facilities are limited; they are not available to all who may wish to use them; the radio spectrum simply is not large enough to accommodate everybody. There is a fixed natural limitation upon the number of stations that can operate without interfering with one another.[34]

The Supreme Court has described the "public convenience, interest, or necessity" standard as a "supple instrument for the exercise of discretion by the expert body which Congress has charged to carry out its legislative policy."[35] In reality, the meaning of this standard may be closer to the views of a commentator who concluded in 1930 that it meant "about as little as any phrase that the drafters of the Act could have used and still comply with the constitutional requirement that there be some standard to guide the administrative wisdom of the li-

---

28. Secretary of Commerce Herbert Hoover attempted to limit the number of radio licenses by using his authority under the Act of 1912. The courts, however, held that the Secretary lacked the power to refuse license applications or to choose the wavelength that a licensee could use. *See* Hoover v. Intercity Radio Co., 286 F. 1003 (D.C. Cir. 1923), *appeal dismissed*, 266 U.S. 636 (1924); United States v. Zenith Radio Corp., 12 F.2d 614 (N.D. Ill. 1926).

29. Judicial limitations imposed on the Commerce Department led to a rush for radio licenses. In the nine months following United States v. Zenith Radio Corp., 12 F.2d 614 (N.D. Ill. 1926), *discussed in* note 28 *supra*, more than 200 stations went on the air. The result was widespread signal interference. *See* Coase, *supra* note 19, at 51. *See generally* 1 E. BARNOUW, A HISTORY OF BROADCASTING IN THE UNITED STATES: A TOWER IN BABEL 94-122 (1966). At least one state court delineated private property rights in radio frequencies during this period. *See* Tribune Co. v. Oak Leaves Broadcasting Station (Cir. Ct., Cook County, Ill. 1926), *reprinted in* 68 CONG. REC. 216 (1926).

30. Ch. 169, 44 Stat. 1162, *repealed by* Communications Act of 1934, ch. 652, § 602(a), 48 Stat. 1064, 1102.

31. Ch. 652, 48 Stat. 1064 (codified in scattered sections of 47 U.S.C.).

32. 47 U.S.C. §§ 303, 307(a), 307(b) (1976).

33. 319 U.S. 190 (1943).

34. *Id*. at 213 (footnote omitted).

35. FCC v. Pottsville Broadcasting Co., 309 U.S. 134, 138 (1940).

A Marketplace Approach to Broadcast Regulation   **215**

censing authority."[36]

Over the years the Commission has gradually developed the trusteeship approach, fleshing out the programming obligations of broadcasters under the "public convenience, interest, or necessity" standard. In 1946 the Commission published the so-called "Blue Book," named after the hue of its cover, entitled *Public Service Responsibility of Broadcast Licensees*.[37] Although never actively enforced, the Blue Book stated that the Commission "proposes to give particular consideration" to four types of programming: (1) local and network programs that were carried on a sustaining (i.e., noncommercial) basis; (2) local live programs; (3) programs devoted to discussion of public issues; and (4) station efforts to limit the amount of time it devoted to hourly advertising.[38]

The Commission's next major effort to influence broadcaster service appeared in the *Report and Statement of Policy* in its *En Banc Programming Inquiry*,[39] which it issued in 1960 in the wake of the quiz show scandals on network television.[40] The 1960 *Statement* emphasized the importance of broadcaster service to the community: "The principal ingredient of such obligation consists of a diligent, positive and continuing effort by the licensee to discover and fulfill the tastes, needs and desires of his service area. If he has accomplished this he has met his public responsibility."[41] The *Statement* recognized that the

---

36. Caldwell, *The Standard of Public Interest, Convenience or Necessity as Used in the Radio Act of 1927*, 1 AIR L. REV. 295, 296 (1930).

37. FCC, PUBLIC SERVICE RESPONSIBILITY OF BROADCAST LICENSEES (1946). The Commission invoked this policy statement in several renewal decisions, *see, e.g.*, Eugene J. Roth (Mission Broadcasting Co.), 12 F.C.C. 102 (1947); Howard W. Davis, 12 F.C.C. 91 (1947); Community Broadcasting Co., 12 F.C.C. 85 (1947). The Blue Book is discussed in Deregulation of Radio, 84 F.C.C.2d 960, 994-95 (1981).

38. In 1949, the Commission issued an additional content pronouncement, which encouraged stations to express their editorial viewpoints on the air. Editorializing by Broadcast Licensees, 13 F.C.C. 1246 (1949). At that time, the Commission created the two-pronged "fairness doctrine," which obligated licensees to cover controversial issues of public importance and afford coverage for contrasting viewpoints. Congress subsequently codified the doctrine in 47 U.S.C. § 315(a) (1976). *See generally* Note, *The Future of Content Regulation in Broadcasting*, 69 CALIF. L. REV. 555, 561-66 (1981). Until 1981 the right to editorialize applied only to commercial broadcasters. Under 1981 amendments to the Communications Act, a noncommercial educational broadcast station may engage in editorializing if it does not receive a grant from the Corporation for Public Broadcasting. Omnibus Budget Reconciliation Act, Pub. L. No. 97-35, § 1229, 95 Stat. 357, 730 (1981) (amending 47 U.S.C. § 399 (1976)).

39. 44 F.C.C. 2303 (1960).

40. The scandals resulted from the proliferation of prime-time quiz programs offering large financial prizes. Some of these were rigged in order to prolong the appearances of the most intriguing contestants. Curiously, the only alleged "crimes" involved charges of perjury before the House of Representatives and New York City investigators. *See Hearings on Television Quiz Shows Before A Special Subcomm. on Legislative Oversight of the House Comm. on Interstate and Foreign Commerce* (pt. 1), 86th Cong., 1st Sess. (1959).

41. 44 F.C.C. at 2312.

216　　Texas Law Review　　　　　　　　　　　　　Vol. 60:207, 1982

Commission "may not condition the grant, denial or revocation of a broadcast license upon its own subjective determination of what is or is not a good program."[42] Yet, because the broadcaster is required to act in the public interest, the Commission did not view itself as "barred by the Constitution or by statute from exercising any responsibility with respect to programming."[43]

The *Statement* articulates fourteen "major elements [of programming] usually necessary to meet the public interest, needs and desires of the community . . . ."[44] The major change established by the *Statement* was the insertion of the ascertainment exercise into the application process.[45] Ascertainment was supposed to be the way for a station to factor the fourteen major elements into its program service. In order to enable broadcasters and their lawyers to prepare initial and renewal applications with adequate specificity, the Commission has issued a series of primers that articulate an acceptable scheme for determining community needs.[46] Since 1960, the Commission has adopted percentage guidelines for news and public affairs programs, which were eliminated for radio but remain in effect for television.[47]

---

42. *Id.* at 2308.

43. *Id.* at 2309. The schizophrenic tone of these introductory remarks characterizes the response of the 1960 *Statement* to the problem of regulating programming content without doing so directly. This on-again, off-again approach also appeared in the discussion of licensee responsibility for broadcasts. Thus, the Commission initially stated, "This duty is personal to the licensee and may not be delegated." *Id.* at 2313. But in the next paragraph it observed that licensees place " 'practical reliance' on networks for the selection and supervision of network programs which, of course, are the principal broadcast fare of the vast majority of television stations throughout the country." *Id.* at 2314.

44. *Id.* These major elements are: (1) opportunity for local self-expression, (2) development and use of local talent, (3) programs for children, (4) religious programs, (5) educational programs, (6) public affairs programs, (7) editorials by licensees, (8) political broadcasts, (9) agricultural programs, (10) news programs, (11) weather and market reports, (12) sports programs, (13) service to minority groups, and (14) entertainment programs. *Id.*

45. *Id.* at 2316. The 1960 *Statement* provided generalized requirements for stations for the determination of tastes, needs, and desires, and the manner in which the licensees could propose to meet them. Subsequent efforts to articulate with specificity the steps necessary to perfect this generalized ascertainment requirement have led to overregulation. *See supra* notes 2-8 and accompanying text.

46. The 1981 radio deregulation order eliminated this scheme for AM and FM licensees, but it remains in force for television licensees. 84 F.C.C.2d 960 (1981).

47. Television deregulation has been proposed along the lines of radio deregulation. *See infra* note 155.

The other major content-related pronouncements, both issued in 1974, avoid specific content obligations for broadcasters. *See* Children's Television Report and Policy Statement, 50 F.C.C.2d 1 (1974), *aff'd sub nom.* Action for Children's Television v. FCC, 564 F.2d 458 (D.C. Cir. 1977); Handling of Public Issues Under the Fairness Doctrine and the Public Interest Standards of the Communications Act, 48 F.C.C.2d 1 (1974), *reconsideration denied*, 58 F.C.C.2d 691 (1976), *aff'd sub nom.* National Citizens Comm. for Broadcasting v. FCC, 567 F.2d 1095 (D.C. Cir. 1977). A 1979 report criticized commercial broadcasters for failing to make a meaningful effort to air programs for children, and explored a myriad of regulatory alternatives. OFFICE OF PLANS AND

A Marketplace Approach to Broadcast Regulation **217**

The Commission thus has not hesitated to consider program content and prescribe categories of desirable programming when defining the duties of licensees. Governmental guidance in broadcast decision-making, the fundamental characteristic of the trusteeship model, sets it apart from a marketplace approach.

B. *The First Amendment and the Model*

The first amendment to the Constitution and section 326 of the Communications Act[48] both forbid censorship of broadcasters. There is a tension between these prohibitions and the Commission's examination of past or proposed programming to determine which of several competing applicants should receive a license.[49] The Commission does employ noncontent criteria to distinguish among applicants, e.g., in considering whether an applicant already has media properties in the community,[50] whether station owners will be involved in the daily management of the station,[51] and whether the applicant's record in providing equal employment opportunity is adequate.[52] But if all other

POLICY, FCC, TELEVISION PROGRAMMING FOR CHILDREN: A REPORT OF THE CHILDREN'S TELEVISION TASK FORCE (1979).

48. 47 U.S.C. § 326 (1976).

49. 47 C.F.R. § 0.281(a)(10) (1981). The Commission's policies concerning the weight to be given past or proposed programming in renewal proceedings have been vexing. The Policy Statement on Comparative Broadcast Hearings, 1 F.C.C.2d 393 (1965), established criteria for initial licensing. The Commission subsequently held that this statement governed the introduction of evidence in comparative renewal hearings, Seven (7) League Productions, Inc. (WIII), 1 F.C.C.2d 1597, 1598 (1965), but the criteria to be used and the weight to be accorded each criterion has remained in a state of flux. The Commission unsuccessfully attempted to establish a policy to assure renewal to incumbent licensees whose past program performance was deemed "superior." Policy Statement Concerning Comparative Hearings Involving Regular Renewal Applicants, 22 F.C.C.2d 424 (1970). Under this scheme, renewal would be guaranteed:

> if the applicant for renewal of license shows in a hearing with a competing applicant that its program service during the preceding license term has been substantially attuned to meeting the needs and interests of its area, and that the operation of the station has not otherwise been characterized by serious deficiencies . . . .

Id. at 425 (footnotes omitted). This statement was nullified in Citizens Communications Center v. FCC, 447 F.2d 1201 (D.C. Cir. 1971), on the ground that it violated § 309(e) of the Communications Act of 1934, 47 U.S.C. § 309(e) (1976), which requires a hearing by anyone seeking to compete for an application. *See* Brenner, *Toward A New Balance in License Renewals,* 17 J. BROADCASTING 63, 71 (1972-1973). The Commission has clarified with ardor the weight to be given past program service in a comparative proceeding for renewal. *See* Cowles Broadcasting, Inc., 60 F.C.C.2d 372 (1976), *clarified,* 62 F.C.C.2d 953 (1977), *vacated and remanded sub nom.* Central Fla. Enters., Inc. v. FCC, 598 F.2d 37 (D.C. Cir. 1978), *decided on remand,* Cowles Broadcasting, Inc., 86 F.C.C.2d 993 (1981), *aff'd sub nom.* Central Fla. Enters., Inc. v. FCC, No. 81-1795 (D.C. Cir. July 13, 1982). The Commission recently began a review of its renewal policies. *See* Formulation of Policies Relating to the Broadcast Renewal Applicant Stemming from the Comparative Hearing Process, 88 F.C.C.2d 21 (1981).

50. 47 C.F.R. § 0.281(a)(1) (1981); Policy Statement on Comparative Broadcast Hearings, 1 F.C.C.2d 393, 394 (1965).

51. Policy Statement on Comparative Broadcast Hearings, 1 F.C.C.2d 393, 395-98 (1965).

52. 47 C.F.R. § 0.281(a)(5) (1981); *see supra* note 6.

criteria are equal, the Commission looks at the content of proposed programs. Historically, the Commission has attempted to avoid content criteria. Nevertheless, because these criteria most directly predict what service to expect from an applicant, the Commission cannot avoid considering such criteria under the judgmental directive of the "public interest."

The mandate for intrusion into program service of a licensee under the public interest standard was best formulated, and legitimated, by Justice Frankfurter in *NBC v. United States*.[53] Justice Frankfurter stated that the Commission is more than a "traffic officer, policing the wave lengths to prevent stations from interfering with each other. . . . [T]he Act does not restrict the Commission merely to supervision of the traffic. It puts upon the Commission the burden of determining the composition of that traffic."[54] As Justice Frankfurter explained, the Commission's licensing function goes beyond finding an absence of technical objection to the granting of a license: "If the criterion of 'public interest' were limited to such matters, how could the Commission choose between two applicants for the same facilities, each of whom is financially and technically qualified to operate a station?"[55]

The times were perhaps different when Justice Frankfurter considered these matters. A Supreme Court Justice in the 1940's could not ignore the importance of a news service during wartime, nor could he easily dispute the public policy of mandating broadcaster "responsibility" in such times. Then, too, Justice Frankfurter was asked in *NBC v. United States* to consider the first amendment rights of broadcasters in a case having nothing to do with broadcasters as journalists. At issue instead were the Commission's "chain broadcasting" rules, which restricted what were perceived to be anticompetitive practices of the radio networks.[56]

The first amendment implications of governmental inquiry into broadcast service are evident today, even if they were obscure in 1943. For example, the Commission compares a television station's programming with "guidelines" about the percentage of news, public affairs, and other nonentertainment programs a station should carry, although the Commission does not consider the content and scheduling of these

---

53. 319 U.S. 190 (1943). Known as the "Network Case," the decision caused NBC to divest itself of one of its two radio networks, which in turn paved the way for creation of ABC.

54. *Id.* at 215-16.

55. *Id.* at 216-17.

56. For a discussion of these rules in the early days of network broadcasting, see 2 NETWORK INQUIRY SPECIAL STAFF, *supra* note 9, at 60-63.

A Marketplace Approach to Broadcast Regulation 219

programs.[57] A similar review would be forbidden if made of column inches in a newspaper or magazine to determine whether to grant newsrack or newsstand space, or permission to publish. So long as program review is part of the licensing process—and, under the Frankfurter formulation of public interest, it will remain so—first amendment problems will persist.

C. Economic Implications of the Trusteeship Model

Besides undermining the first amendment rights of broadcasters, the trusteeship role of the Commission has also distorted competition in the broadcasting marketplace. On the ground that advertiser support of over-the-air broadcasting is essential, courts have ordered the Commission to consider the competitive consequences of market entry. Despite the Supreme Court's admonition in 1940 in *FCC v. Sanders Brothers Radio Station*[58] that competition, not regulation, should characterize broadcasting, the D.C. Court of Appeals in *Carroll Broadcasting Co. v. FCC* held that the Commission should engage in limited vigilantism against newcomers to a local market.[59]

Under the *Carroll* doctrine, when an existing licensee offers proof of the detrimental economic impact of a new station, the Commission must consider such evidence and, if substantial, deny the competitor's license. The application of this formula to another industry would seem ludicrous. Imagine a city council attempting to bar the addition of a second motion picture theater on the basis of an existing theater's claim that the town was not big enough for both. But in effect this is how the court of appeals insisted that the Commission oversee entry into broadcasting. Although the Commission has never used the *Carroll* doctrine to foreclose issuance of a new license, it remains part of the arsenal used by existing licensees to forestall competition.

Other efforts to protect existing broadcasters from competition turned up in the Commission's policies to stunt the development of cable and subscription television. These policies raised barriers to entry and discouraged rather than encouraged more service offerings.[60]

57. 47 C.F.R. § 0.281(a)(8) (1981). The Commission declined to adopt percentage standards as a condition for renewal, but proceeded instead on a case-by-case basis. Formulation of Policies Relating to the Broadcast Renewal Applicant Stemming from the Comparative Hearing Process, 66 F.C.C.2d 419 (1977), *aff'd sub nom.* National Black Media Coalition v. FCC, 589 F.2d 578 (D.C. Cir. 1978).
58. 309 U.S. 470, 474 (1940); *see infra* text accompanying note 115.
59. 258 F.2d 440 (D.C. Cir. 1958). The Department of Justice rejected the Commission's request to appeal this decision to the Supreme Court.
60. *See* HOUSE SUBCOMM. ON COMMUNICATIONS OF THE COMM. ON INTERSTATE AND FOR-

Their misguided premise was that trustees could carry out their stewardship only in an environment protected from "ruinous" competition. Abandoned by the Commission in the late 1970's,[61] these policies evidence yet another downside to the trusteeship model.

The responsibilities imposed under the trusteeship model turn an operator into a super-citizen, with obligations that go beyond providing goods and services that the public wants. The system promotes "taxation by regulation," as one commentator called it.[62] The incidental costs of licensure would vanish if there were no program-tied licensing criteria. Furthermore, because the licenses have become imbued with a "community service" character, they have lost some of their marketplace attributes. Consequently, broadcast licensees have been subjected to restrictions that bear no relation to the marketplace. For instance, even though the Communications Act authorizes the President to shut down a radio frequency during a national emergency or the threat of one,[63] aliens have always been denied the right to become licensees.[64] No similar condition attaches to other important forms of mass communication.[65] Most significantly, broadcasting stations cannot be bought and sold freely. Licensees who acquire broadcast properties solely for quick resale can be accused of "trafficking" in the properties and the Commission can set aside their transfer of ownership.[66] The Commission must also approve a transfer before a new owner can assume control, again thwarting efficient management. This insistence on voluntary transfers, comparable to equerries exchanging stud horses for the betterment of the sport, has deflated prices for some broadcast properties. Unlike other business entities, broadcast stations cannot be the objects of unfriendly takeovers.

EIGN COMMERCE, 94TH CONG., 2D SESS., CABLE TELEVISION: PROMISE VERSUS REGULATORY PERFORMANCE (Subcomm. Print 1976).

61. Cable Television Syndicated Program Exclusivity Rules, 71 F.C.C.2d 951 (1979); Inquiry Into the Economic Relationship Between Television Broadcasting and Cable Television, 71 F.C.C.2d 632 (1979). These reports led the Commission to eliminate its distant signal and syndicated exclusivity rules, which had restricted the types of programs cable systems could carry. Cable Television Syndicated Program Exclusivity Rules, 79 F.C.C.2d 652 (1980), *affirmed sub nom.* Malrite T.V. v. FCC, 652 F.2d 1140 (2d Cir. 1981).

62. Posner, *Taxation by Regulation*, 2 BELL J. ECON. & MGMT. SCI. 22, 23 (1971).

63. 47 U.S.C. § 606(c) (1976).

64. *Id.* § 310(b) (1976).

65. *See* K. CROWE, AMERICA FOR SALE (1978). Efforts by foreigners to control the American press range from the short-lived attempt to buy the *New York Trib.*, which was the object of an aborted takeover by the South African government as part of a plan to gain influence abroad, Wash. Post, Apr. 3, 1979, at A1; *id.* Apr. 8, 1979, at A19, to the much-publicized endeavors of Australian Rupert Murdoch, currently owner of the *New York Post*.

66. The Commission has authorized its staff to deny licenses to those accused of having a history of short-term buying and selling of broadcast properties. 47 C.F.R. § 0.281(a)(2) (1981). *But see infra* note 164.

A Marketplace Approach to Broadcast Regulation   **221**

The grandest myth of the trusteeship concept is the belief that the value of licenses has remained unchanged since their granting. The Commission has ignored the fact that tremendous wealth attaches to the most desirable licenses, whose value far exceeds the tangible assets of the stations holding them.[67] Instead of adopting regulations that would reflect the actual value of these licenses, the Commission has buried its head deeper into the regulation books and considered additional behavioral rules. Such efforts have merely produced more obligations for these special public stewards who, in turn, are usually willing to comply with whatever the Commission asks, as long as the cost of compliance is slight.

D.   *The Flawed Rationales Supporting the Model*

1. Defects of the Scarcity Rationale.—Spectrum scarcity always has been the cornerstone of the justification for abandoning the marketplace approach and reducing first amendment protection for broadcasters. The Supreme Court pointed to spectrum scarcity in its ratification of the trusteeship model in *NBC*, and the Court has cited scarcity in some of its other, although not in all, pronouncements supporting Commission content regulation.[68] But the use of spectrum scarcity to justify "public interest" determinations over licensees is fraught with serious logical and empirical infirmities.

First, virtually all goods in society are scarce. In most sectors of the economy, the interplay of supply and demand regulates the distribution of goods. If a good becomes especially scarce, its price is bid up. Ideally the highest bidder will make the best use of the resource. The application of the trusteeship model to broadcasting is a substantial deviation from the ordinary allocation of scarce goods and services in society.[69]

One might argue, however, that deviations from the market should occur with regard to communications media. For instance, in wartime the government might be justified in regulating the amount of newsprint any one paper received. The supply of newsprint could be re-

---

67. *See* 47 C.F.R. § 0.281(a)(2) (1981). This provision curiously calls attention to sellers who will "realize" a profit on the sale of their broadcast station. *See generally* H. LEVIN, THE INVISIBLE RESOURCE: USE AND REGULATION OF THE RADIO SPECTRUM (1971); Greenberg, *Television Station Profitability and FCC Regulatory Policy*, 17 J. INDUS. ECON. 210 (1969).

68. *See, e.g.*, Red Lion Broadcasting Co. v. FCC, 395 U.S. 367, 399 (1969). *Contra* FCC v. Pacifica Found., 438 U.S. 726 (1978); *cf. id.* at 770 n.4 (Brennan, J., dissenting) ("The opinions of my Brothers POWELL and STEVENS rightly refrain from relying on the notion of 'spectrum scarcity' to support their result.").

69. *See supra* text accompanying notes 17-23.

222   Texas Law Review   Vol. 60:207, 1982

duced for newspapers intending to print only comics or other purely entertainment features. But no factors remotely comparable exist in broadcasting today. Yet the trusteeship model results in broadcast regulation that resembles this hypothetical.

Apart from this basic misunderstanding of scarcity, other factors should lead to a rejection of the belief that a condition of true scarcity prevails in broadcasting. Scarcity is a relative concept even when applied to the limited spectrum earmarked for broadcast use. Additional channels can be added, without increasing the portion reserved for broadcast, by decreasing the bandwidth of each channel.[70] Technology is an independent variable that makes scarcity a relative concept. At some point, quality becomes so reduced or costs so great that new channels should not be added. But until that point is reached, saturation of the spectrum has not occurred. The continued evolution of spectrum efficiency techniques makes it difficult to say with certainty that saturation of channels will ever be permanent in any market.

Channels can also be added by revising the interference rules. The Commission has traditionally shied away from this solution because of concerns about the risk of degrading signal quality.[71] Under the pres-

---

70. For instance, FM bandwidth could be narrowed, although a narrower channel could affect the quality of the FM signal. Bandwidth reduction techniques might be available that would not reduce quality significantly. Single sideband and amplitude companding have been suggested for use in land mobile communications. *See supra* note 23. Application of these techniques to broadcasting could increase the number of FM channels five- or seven-fold. These techniques, however, would require more expensive tuners and massive investments by existing broadcasters.

In television, bandwidth could be reduced from six to four megahertz without impairing quality significantly, thereby allowing more signals in markets with channel saturation under existing allocations. OFFICE OF PLANS AND POLICY, FCC, UHF TASK FORCE REPORT, TELEVISION BANDWIDTH REDUCTION 2 (1978). Bandwidth compression has been achieved through digital techniques and has been commercially used in video conferencing. One system permits up to 30 simultaneous color video links to be established on a single satellite transponder. Com. Daily, Dec. 29, 1981, at 2, 2-3. Bandwidth reduction would require consumers to acquire new receivers, an investment whose aggregate cost may exceed the benefits from new service. Still, cost considerations do not alone make the broadcast band ineluctably "saturated."

Additional channels could also, if desired, have been created in AM service. It has been proposed (but rejected by the Commission) to reduce channels on the AM band from 10 to 9 kHz, creating an additional 12 channels on the band. 9 kHz Channel Spacing for AM Broadcasting, 88 F.C.C.2d 290 (1981). One of the reasons for rejecting the shift was the expense that the change-over would have entailed to broadcasters and listeners.

The Commission could also consider reassigning portions of the spectrum neighboring the broadcast frequencies now used for other civilian or military uses. For example, the AM band could be expanded in this way, and the 1979 World Administrative Radio Conference has urged this change. *See* F.C.C. Public Notice, Mimeo No. 25,215, at 5-6 (Jan. 15, 1980).

71. The Commission could turn the question of interference over to the marketplace. A party suffering interference from another would be able to pay to terminate objectionable interference. This, of course, could lead to nuisance interference for purposes of extortion, but it is reasonable to assume that the marketplace would allow a spectrum user to pay to clear a frequency. Resolution of interference problems resembles the settlement process among competing

A Marketplace Approach to Broadcast Regulation 223

ent allocation scheme, the Commission assigns frequencies for television and FM radio to localities throughout the United States. The Commission created a master "table of allocations" to accomplish this purpose.[72] New assignments are added to the tables quite frequently in FM and occasionally in television. In addition, less than full strength service, such as low-power television, which radiates in an area as small as one-tenth of the typical television service area, can be added to the existing allocation scheme without creating destructive interference.[73]

The Commission's approach to AM radio has been to allow new stations to "shoe-horn" in, based on predicted levels of interference with existing stations.[74] By allowing this expansion of AM service, the Commission has acknowledged that new outlets can be brought to the market without the need for finite limits. The stream of new AM stations is proof of the dubiety of scarcity in that band. Indeed, the Commission is considering a similar demand-based approach to the FM band.[75] In short, the theoretically scarce airwaves continue to absorb more and more new channels and could accommodate additional channels. The only major factor limiting expansion—other than unacceptable levels of interference—is the cost of accommodating those new channels.

The scarcity rationale focuses on the wrong scarce resource, megahertz, instead of advertising dollars. Even in the indirect marketplace of over-the-air commercial broadcasting, the number of stations depends on the amount of advertising dollars or on other funding sources in the community. Except in the largest cities, where the Commission's allocation policies have limited the number of outlets, advertising support or subscriber dollars restrict broadcast opportunities more than does the number of channels.

applicants for a broadcast frequency, in which applications are mutually exclusive to each other. *See* 47 U.S.C. § 311(c) (1976); 47 C.F.R. § 73.3525 (1981); NBC, Inc., 26 RAD. REG. 2d (P & F) 951 (1964). Often during the application process all parties except one will drop out, content to receive reimbursement for costs incurred in seeking the license. Similarly, unauthorized interference could be "solved" by paying the offending broadcaster an amount equal to the expense of shielding the signal.

72. The Commission created the table in order to comply with the mandate of the Communications Act, 47 U.S.C. §§ 151, 307(b) (1976). The objectives of Congress were to provide television service as far as possible to all people in the United States and to establish a fair, efficient, and equitable distribution of stations throughout the country. *See* Television Assignments Amendment of § 3.606 of the Commission Rules and Regulations (Sixth Report and Order), 41 F.C.C. 148 (1952).

73. *See* Inquiry into the Future Role of Low-Power Television Broadcasting and Television Translators in the National Telecommunications System, 47 Fed. Reg. 21,468 (1982).

74. 4 C.F.R. § 73.37 (1981).

75. Modification of FM Broadcast Station Rules to Increase the Availability of Commercial FM Broadcast Assignments, 78 F.C.C.2d 1232 (1980).

224 Texas Law Review Vol. 60:207, 1982

In addition, scarcity is not the only reason behind the present limited number of VHF television stations (channels 2-13), which are the most profitable outlets. The Commission's allocation of only three VHF commercial outlets in most communities is hardly an unavoidable product of the limited ether; rather, it derives from the Commission's landmark allocation scheme for television, the _Sixth Report and Order._[76] The goal of the _Sixth Report_ was to ensure as far as possible that most communities in the United States would have at least one local television channel, preferably VHF.[77] The arrangement, however, has resulted in a national distribution system in which at most only three VHF commercial outlets prevail in most markets.[78] As Commission studies have found, this "three to a market" approach of the _Sixth Report_ assures the dominant position of the commercial television networks.[79] At the very least, one can hardly explain the availability of only the three VHF television outlets carrying the three commercial networks as a force of nature caused by a limited spectrum.[80] It should serve instead as a basis for authorizing more outlets, not for regulating those that already exist.

The scarcity upon which the trusteeship model relies exists only in some, not all, markets. Even under the current allocation scheme,

---

76. 41 F.C.C. 148 (1952). _See generally_ Schuessler, _Structural Barriers to the Entry of Additional Television Networks: The Federal Communications Commission's Spectrum Management Policies_, 54 S. CAL. L. REV. 875 (1981).

77. _See_ 41 F.C.C. at 151 (citing 47 U.S.C. 307(b) (1976)).

78. The 1952 allocation scheme issued four or more VHF assignments in only 7 of the top 50 markets; 20 markets received three VHF assignments, 16 received two VHF assignments, and 2 received only one VHF assignment. Five of the top 50 markets had only UHF assignments. One network could reach 45 of these markets with VHF stations, and the second network could reach 43 markets. A third network could reach only 27 and a fourth network had access to VHF stations in only 7 of the top 50 markets. MAJORITY STAFF OF THE SUBCOMM. ON TELECOMMUNICATIONS, CONSUMER PROTECTION, AND FINANCE OF THE HOUSE COMM. ON ENERGY AND COMMERCE, 97TH CONG., 1ST SESS., TELECOMMUNICATIONS IN TRANSITION: THE STATUS OF COMPETITION IN THE TELECOMMUNICATIONS INDUSTRY 247 (Comm. Print 1981) [hereinafter cited as TELECOMMUNICATIONS REPORT].

79. _See_ 2 NETWORK INQUIRY SPECIAL STAFF, _supra_ note 9, at 27-30; HOUSE COMM. ON INTERSTATE AND FOREIGN COMMERCE, NETWORK BROADCASTING, H.R. REP. No. 1297, 85th Cong., 2d Sess. 195 (1958) [hereinafter cited as the Barrow Report].

80. The Commission could have chosen a scheme that did not emphasize the concept of a local VHF outlet quite so much. Indeed, the Commission had before it the Dumont plan, which would have used regional stations to allow more than three outlets to service larger areas. AD HOC ADVISORY COMM. ON ALLOCATIONS TO THE SENATE COMM. ON INTERSTATE AND FOREIGN COMMERCE, 85TH CONG., 2D SESS., ALLOCATION OF TELEVISION CHANNELS 98-101 (Comm. Print 1958). _See generally_ Schuessler, _supra_ note 76, at 921-26. The Commission could have allocated television frequencies exclusively in the more plentiful UHF band (channels 14-83) or prohibited the mixing of UHF and VHF channels in the same market. _See id._ at 886-930. Perhaps the most interesting wrinkle to the Commission's choice is that both CBS and ABC had stressed the undesirability of any extended operation in the VHF band. ABC urged the Commission to move all commercial television to UHF, with VHF frequencies to be used for technical development directed at improving television on the UHF frequencies. _See_ Barrow Report, _supra_ note 79, at 20.

A Marketplace Approach to Broadcast Regulation **225**

which assigns fewer channels than could be accommodated on the available spectrum, channels outside larger cities go wanting for lack of a taker.[81] This situation is especially true for allocations in the UHF band, where some channels have remained unclaimed for decades. It is capricious to justify regulation of broadcasters in nonsaturated markets by claiming that their operation employs a scarce resource unavailable to potential entrants in other markets.

Scarcity does exist in the sense that there is no more room for additional full-power VHF stations in the largest markets under current levels of permitted interference. Yet one can always buy an existing station, just as one may be likelier to consider buying an existing newspaper operation than trying to launch a new one. Furthermore, the current complement of VHF stations exceeds the number of daily newspapers in large cities, and the total number of broadcast outlets far exceeds the number of daily circulated newspapers.[82] So a relatively low number of outlets in one medium should not lead to content-based rules in another.[83]

Finally, the scarcity notion also fails to recognize the substitutes for over-the-air distribution. In audio service, cassette and phono disc recordings vie with AM and FM channels and their subcarrier services like Muzak. Cable television, low-power television, multipoint distribution service, cassette and disc, and, in the future, direct broadcast satellites provide substitutes for over-the-air video service in many

81. The Commission periodically issues a report listing channels allocated in the UHF and VHF bands that have not been applied for or assigned. FCC Public Notice, Mimeo No. 3331 (Apr. 16, 1982).

82. Only 35 cities are served by two or more competing daily newspapers. In contrast, very few American communities have only one radio or television station. TELECOMMUNICATIONS REPORT, *supra* note 78, at 263; *see also* OFFICE OF PLANS AND POLICY, *supra* note 5, at 62 (citing data from ARBITRON, TELEVISION MARKETS AND RANKINGS GUIDE 1979-1980 (1979)). Yet no one has seriously suggested that the relative scarcity of newspapers justifies the regulations that have been imposed on broadcasters. Contrary to daily newspaper trends, the number of broadcast outlets is steadily rising; since the Court decided *Red Lion* in 1969, the number of radio outlets has increased by 38% and the number of television outlets by 21%. By 1981, there were 9060 radio and 1035 television stations. FCC News, Mimeo No. 3510 (Sept. 22, 1981). In contrast, the number of daily newspapers, which currently totals about 1750, has remained fairly constant over the past 35 years. TELECOMMUNICATIONS REPORT, *supra* note 78, at 263-64.

83. Professor Emerson argues that the significant comparison among media is the number of printing presses versus the number of persons who wish to use broadcast facilities, not the number of newspapers versus the number of stations. T. EMERSON, THE SYSTEM OF FREEDOM OF EX-PRESSION 662 (1970). Because the number of printing presses or copying machines is not limited by spectrum slots, television is the "scarcer" medium. But this distinction fails to distinguish between a medium of individual communication and a medium of mass communication. The distribution available by mimeograph and paper pales next to the circulation of a major daily paper; it is not an adequate substitute for the reach of a daily. Just because anyone has access to a copier does not mean that he can start a successful daily paper. The limiting factor in broadcast-ing is the same as in print: economic support.

226 Texas Law Review Vol. 60:207, 1982

markets. A five-meter backyard satellite dish can, for those who can afford them, bring in more channels "off the air" than a television antenna picks up in a city with the greatest number of stations on the air.

Nonspectrum-utilizing distribution modes like cable and video cassette provide virtually limitless diversity of scheduling and content. Where new high-capacity cable systems are in place, no scarcity exists with respect to the television spectrum. What may inhibit the number of cable channels, is again, a scarcity of dollars to support advertiser-based or subscription channels. Similarly, choice in video cassette programming is completely determined by what the consumer is willing to spend for software.[84] Thus, the scarcity rationale, as used to justify the regulation of broadcasting in a different manner than other media, misperceives what scarcity is in a free economy. Moreover, it ignores the practical realities that go a long way toward explaining the limited number of channels in some markets.

Even if one assumes that the absence of more television channel space in the largest markets justifies a licensing policy in those markets, this assumption establishes nothing about the form the regulations should take.[85] The trusteeship model endorsed the giant leap from scarcity to the current panoply of federal regulation over all broadcasters, not just those in saturated markets. Logic, however, does not support the assumption that the trusteeship scheme is more likely to maximize consumer welfare, even in markets without available outlets, than would a system relying on the judgment of marketplace players.[86]

2. *Other Justifications*

(a) *The "prior grant" theory.*—A more rational justification for continued government regulation is the bootstrap argument that rests on broadcasters' enjoyment of "the fruits of a prior government

84. In evaluating the "scarcity" of outlets for information, it is important to consider all information providers, from broadcast outlets and newspapers to magazines, paperback books, direct mail fliers, billboards, posters, handbills, sound trucks, and tee shirts. All of these provide some form of expression and each undercuts the significance of broadcast stations as necessary outlets for expression.

85. Judge Bazelon has suggested that when regulations are required, they should be structural regulations, such as cross-ownership limitations and content-neutral access requirements. *See* Bazelon, *The First Amendment and "The New Media"—New Directions in Regulating Telecommunications*, 31 F. Com. L.J. 201, 209-13 (1979).

86. *See* C. SCHULTZE, THE PUBLIC USE OF PRIVATE INTEREST 6 (1977):

Finally, and perhaps most important, we usually tend to see only one way of intervening [in the marketplace]—namely, removing a set of decisions from the decentralized and incentive-oriented private market and transferring them to the command-and-control techniques of government bureaucracy. . . . Instead of creating incentives so that public goals become private interests, private interests are left unchanged and obedience to the public goals is commanded.

A Marketplace Approach to Broadcast Regulation **227**

grant." The Supreme Court advanced this rationale in *Red Lion Broad-casting Co. v. FCC*[87] after acknowledging "gaps in spectrum utilization." The Court stated that "the fact remains that existing broadcasters have often attained their present positions because of their initial government selection in competition with others before new technological advances opened new opportunities for further uses."[88] Since the government has aided the market strength of incumbent licensees, it may under the "prior grant" rationale regulate some aspects of the conduct of those licensees in order to guarantee the best service to the public.[89]

This reasoning leads equally well to a market approach as to the trusteeship model, because it does not follow from licensing that the government also must affirmatively regulate licensee conduct. Once the Commission concludes that the best service for the public lies with a market system, where licensees can air programs designed to attract the largest audiences for advertisers or the largest subscriber base, it can refrain from reviewing programming and other licensee decisions. Moreover, now that broadcasting outlets face more competition from new media delivery outlets, activistic "grandfathering" of early licensed stations with trusteeship duties makes even less sense.

(b) FCC v. Pacifica Foundation: *"impact" theories.*—The Supreme Court has identified other reasons for regulating broadcast content under the public interest standard, and they appear most strikingly in *FCC v. Pacifica Foundation*.[90] The Court was confronted with a Commission policy statement prohibiting indecent broadcasting that allegedly applied to the airing of a comedy monologue by George Carlin on an FM nonprofit station in New York City. *Pacifica* upheld the Commission's determination that "indecent" broadcasts, as identified in congressional statutes and defined by the agency, could be punished.[91] The Court minimized the relative first amendment claims of broadcasters as compared to the right of the audience, particularly chil-

---

87. 395 U.S. 367, 400 (1969).

88. *Id.; see also* Office of Communication of United Church of Christ v. FCC, 359 F.2d 994, 1003 (D.C. Cir. 1966).

89. The "prior grants" especially benefit the networks with ownership of radio and television stations in the largest markets. ABC, NBC, and CBS each own AM, FM, and VHF-TV outlets in the three largest markets, New York, Los Angeles, and Chicago. These three markets alone comprise 16.6% of all television households. *See* 1982 BROADCASTING CABLECASTING YEAR BOOK, at B-76.

90. 438 U.S. 726 (1978); *see also* CBS v. Democratic Nat'l Comm., 412 U.S. 94, 116 (1973); Brandywine-Main Line Radio, Inc. v. FCC, 473 F.2d 16, 49 (D.C. Cir. 1972), *cert. denied*, 412 U.S. 922 (1973).

91. 438 U.S. at 731-32, 735-41.

228   Texas Law Review   Vol. 60:207, 1982

dren, to avoid exposure to offensive materials. The Court noted that "the broadcast media have established a uniquely pervasive presence in the lives of all Americans."[92] Likening reception of offensive broadcast signals to an indecent phone call, the Court surmised that listeners and viewers cannot insulate themselves from offensive program content. Second, the Court concluded that regulation of broadcasting content was justified because broadcasting is "uniquely accessible to children, even those too young to read."[93]

Neither argument, however, adequately distinguishes broadcasting from other mass media. Broadcasting may have a pervasive presence in the "lives of all Americans," but that says very little about the operation of a particular station, which is, after all, the unit of regulation under the licensing scheme. Under the Court's rationale, program producers have a "presence"—measured, for example, by having two or more network series on the air at the same time—far more "pervasive" than the operator of an individual station. Furthermore, it is unlikely that any viewer watches a single station's entire daily broadcast. The assertion of the pervasive influence of individual licensees is a gross exaggeration of the licensees' real impact.

Moreover, other media are also "pervasive." One can hardly argue that a one-newspaper town is not "pervaded," "uniquely," by the orientation of its paper. A blockbuster motion picture, unlike a typical television or radio broadcast, is repeated for weeks on end in a community. Its exhibition is also more likely to pervade the community's consciousness than a single television (or, as in *Pacifica*, a nonprofit FM afternoon) broadcast.

The fact that broadcasting is usually received in the home adds no support to the continued application of the trusteeship model to broadcasting. A large number of television programs probably offend some portion of the home audience. For example, evangelical programs may offend those whose faith is grounded in a different theological perspective,[94] but the annoyance caused to some viewers by these programs

---

92. *Id*. at 748.
93. *Id*. at 749.
94. The Commission's inclusion of religious broadcasters among groups eligible for noncommercial, reserved licenses was questioned in a petition requesting rulemaking to explore the entire matter of religious broadcasting in America. This petition, which the Commission declined to adopt for rulemaking, led to an avalanche of mail from listeners of religious broadcasting. Revision of Rules Permitting Multiple Ownership of Non-Commercial Educational Radio and Television Stations in Single Markets, 54 F.C.C.2d 941 (1975). Controversy has long surrounded religious broadcasting, starting with the Federal Radio Commission's refusal to renew the license of Reverend Shuler because of defamatory and otherwise objectionable utterances made over his Los Angeles radio station. *See* Trinity Methodist Church, S. v. Federal Radio Comm'n, 62 F.2d 850 (D.C. Cir. 1932), *cert. denied*, 288 U.S. 599 (1933).

A Marketplace Approach to Broadcast Regulation 229

hardly justifies government intervention to ascertain where the public interest lies in such matters. The viewer always retains ultimate control over what enters his home; he may choose to turn the channel.

In fact, religious programming is market-oriented, since only religious broadcasters who can afford to purchase time for their messages appear regularly on the air. There is every reason to believe that the marketplace, speaking through advertisers, critics, and self-selection by viewers, provides an adequate substitute for Commission involvement in protecting children and adults from television's "captive" quality.[95]

Indeed, those who would justify regulation by pointing to a program's potential to offend viewers stand the first amendment on its head. Those who deliver popular, acceptable speech have little reason to fear the rebuke of the majority. Only words and ideas that trouble or confound need the special aid of constitutional protection.[96] A licensing scheme justified by the avoidance of offensive programs is inconsistent with a society dedicated to free inquiry and expression.

Undoubtedly many children below the age of literacy watch television. This situation may justify regulation of indecent materials carried over the air. Indecent material can be withheld from distribution to children if it is in the form of print or film,[97] and scheduling of adult programs for late-night viewing can and does give parents more control over what their children watch. But these narrow restrictions do not justify a broad-scale trusteeship approach with its power to grant and revoke licenses based on content, any more than a trusteeship approach should be sustained over bookstores because they might at some point carry indecent materials on their shelves.[98]

In a separate opinion in *Pacifica*, Justice Powell argued that the different treatment of broadcast media for first amendment purposes is justified because children and adults have equal access to whatever is

95. Under *Pacifica*, the Commission can establish time of day standards for programs that might be inappropriate for children. Furthermore, the Commission can mandate warnings to advise parents of the potential offensiveness of a broadcast. *See* Pacifica Found., 56 F.C.C.2d 94, 98 (1975), *reconsideration granted*, 59 F.C.C.2d 892 (1976), *rev'd*, 556 F.2d 9 (D.C. Cir. 1977), *rev'd*, 438 U.S. 726 (1978). Curiously, the broadcast in *Pacifica* was carried early in the afternoon on a school day on a noncommercial station unlikely to attract a large audience of children.

96. *See* Kingsley Int'l Pictures Corp. v. Regents of the Univ. of New York, 360 U.S. 684 (1959); Pacifica Found., 36 F.C.C. 147 (1964).

97. *See* Ginsberg v. New York, 390 U.S. 629 (1968).

98. No one has ever seriously argued that broadcasters should air only what is fit for the youngest viewer. The child audience argument must give way to the realities of a pluralistic society. *See Pacifica*, 438 U.S. at 768-69 (Brennan, J., dissenting); Butler v. Michigan, 352 U.S. 380, 383 (1957). Justice Brennan observed in *Pacifica*: "As surprising as it may be to individual Members of this Court, some parents may actually find Mr. Carlin's unabashed attitude towards the seven 'dirty words' healthy and deem it desirable to expose their children to the manner in which Mr. Carlin defuses the taboo surrounding the words." 438 U.S. at 770 (Brennan, J., dissenting).

230   Texas Law Review   Vol. 60:207, 1982

broadcast.[99] This differs from a bookstore where access to store shelves can be monitored by a clerk. Yet Justice Powell's lament applies equally well to other materials in the home, such as the pictorials carried in Sunday newspapers, advertising circulars received through the mail,[100] and weekly or monthly subscription magazines, which do not depend upon literacy or access to a television set for their influence. Cause for alarm about either these materials or television is unjustified. In a free marketplace, whether broadcast or print, advertisers and subscribers will not eagerly support materials, whether delivered on the air or on the doorstep, that are as likely to offend as to attract potential customers. Similarly, there is no reason to assume that the Commission is a better clearinghouse for passing judgment on programs than advertisers or the subscribers who support them or the viewers who ultimately decide whether to watch their programs.

III.   The Marketplace Approach in Broadcasting

The reasons articulated by the Commission and the courts for the trusteeship model are hardly convincing, let alone compelling, when poised in a constitutional balance against the rights of broadcasters.[101] Scarcity analysis is theoretically misguided and, in many cases, factually erroneous. Other facets of broadcasting, such as intrusiveness, failure to segregate child and adult audiences, and "captiveness," do not call for government involvement. There is reason to believe that marketplace forces can, and indeed do, affect the success or failure of television programming, just as they affect the content of nonbroadcast media.

A scheme that empowers the Commission to judge content on these speculative rationales should be rejected, for the consequence has been and continues to be a level of first amendment protection for broadcasters that is not simply "different"[102] but substantially weaker than the protection given other media. In the meantime it has led to

---

99. 438 U.S. at 757-59.

100. "When I was a boy the sight of a girl's knee occasioned lewd thoughts, and *La Vie Parisienne*, a long-dead precursor of *Penthouse* and similar magazines, drove young males mad with pictures a good deal less explicit than today's department store advertisements of brassieres and bikinis." Gellhorn, *Dirty Books, Disgusting Pictures, and Dreadful Laws*, 8 GA. L. REV. 291, 298 (1974).

101. "[O]nly a compelling state interest in the regulation of a subject within the State's constitutional power to regulate can justify limiting First Amendment freedoms." NAACP v. Button, 371 U.S. 415, 438 (1963). The inadequacy of the trusteeship approach is especially glaring in light of Professor Kalven's admonition that the starting place in this analysis should be the constitutional rights of broadcasters. *See* Kalven, *supra* note 22, at 37.

102. *See* Joseph Burstyn, Inc. v. Wilson, 343 U.S. 495, 503 (1952).

A Marketplace Approach to Broadcast Regulation   **231**

the exclusion of new entrants who might have met unserved communications needs. A marketplace approach to broadcast regulation, on the other hand, emphasizes the role of new competitors, and new competition among existing firms, to ensure service in the public interest.

A. The Current Marketplace in Broadcasting

Market forces have not been totally absent under the trusteeship approach. Nor has the trusteeship philosophy had a devastating effect on broadcasting in America. First, despite the deviation from the marketplace approach that has occurred in broadcast regulation, the American system of broadcast service generally compares well with those of other nations.[103] Entertainment programming produced for domestic television, while not always aimed at the highest of brows, enjoys enormous audiences at home, and overseas demand for these shows is substantial. Network and local news departments have pioneered techniques of electronic news gathering and news coverage. Anyone proposing changes in our licensing system must concede the comparatively high quality of our domestic productions.[104]

Second, despite its content-oriented rules and the not-infrequent protest against its rulings, the Commission's actual impact on programming has probably been slight. There have been some close calls, but the Commission's bark has been worse than its bite.[105] The Commission has shown little desire to censor programming. This is not to give a ringing endorsement to the broadcast industry's less than strident defense of its first amendment rights, or to the Commission's ability to shut its regulatory jaw. Nevertheless, broadcasting has generally enjoyed widespread, sustained consumer acceptance and the Commission's regulation has rarely been overbearing.

Third, we must emphasize the twin idiosyncrasies of a market analysis applied to a business like broadcasting. The first has already

---

103. The average American household watches 6 hours and 45 minutes of television per day, according to Nielsen statistics. Recent public opinion surveys indicate that 51% of the public think that television is the most believable news source. *See* 1982 Broadcasting Cablecasting Year Book, *supra* note 89, at A-2.

104. An informal comparison with the television service provided by other nations indicates that, with the exception of teletext services, the United States provides the greatest number of distribution channels of television programming. *See* R. Neustadt, The Birth of Electronic Publishing 19 (1982).

105. "One embarrassment in attacking seriously the topic of free speech in broadcasting is that the admitted benignity of the FCC has made it difficult to mount appropriate indignation." Kalven, *supra* note 22, at 19. Yet broadcasters are subject to news and other nonentertainment program guidelines, the fairness doctrine, access rights for federal candidates, and other regulations that would be impermissible if imposed on newspapers. *See infra* notes 129-30 and accompanying text.

232   Texas Law Review   Vol. 60:207, 1982

been noted: a key resource in broadcasting, exclusivity of radio spectrum, is allocated by governmental decision, not by price. Prices, therefore, are not allowed to allocate frequencies in the same way they allocate other resources in the marketplace.[106] The second crucial idiosyncrasy of commercial broadcasting is that with the exception of subscription television, consumers cannot vote with dollars to get the programs they want.[107] With over-the-air, advertiser-supported broadcasting, it is impossible to measure directly the intensity of demand individual consumers feel for the programs they watch. Competitive markets easily determine what people want and how much they are willing to pay for it: consumers with the most intense demand for a scarce good outbid those with less desire for that good. But in the broadcasting market, where viewer or listener intensity cannot be measured accurately, this process cannot occur. Broadcasting, therefore, is an atypical market from the point of view of both the broadcaster as supplier and the viewer as consumer.[108]

Over-the-air broadcasting relies on an indirect market mechanism. Advertisers sponsor programs that they expect to appeal to the viewers they want to reach with their messages. In a sense, the advertiser acts as the representative for consumers, sometimes for all consumers, sometimes for demographic subgroups. This representative form of program selection is well served—but further distanced from traditional pricing mechanisms—by the fact that a program, once broadcast, is available to additional consumers without cost.[109] The broadcaster cannot collect fees from additional consumers who watch the program.[110]

Thus, the broadcasting marketplace is indirect and imperfect, but

---

106. B. OWEN, THE ECONOMICS OF DIVERSITY IN BROADCASTING (Studies in Industry Economics No. 60, 1976); Owen, *Regulating Diversity: The Case of Radio Formats*, 21 J. BROADCASTING 315 (1977); *cf.* M. FRIEDMAN & R. FRIEDMAN, FREE TO CHOOSE 13-24 (1980) (describing the role of price in the marketplace).

107. Owen, *supra* note 106, at 316-17; *see* Brenner, *Government Regulation of Radio Program Format Changes*, 127 U. PA. L. REV. 56, 69-72 (1978); Parkman, *The FCC's Allocation of Television Licenses: Regulation with Inadequate Information*, 46 ALB. L. REV. 22, 39 (1981).

108. In this instance, the "market" refers to programming that listeners desire. Because broadcasting is advertiser-supported, the product in the market consists of listeners. The buyer in this instance is the advertiser, the seller the broadcaster, with programming serving as the largest factor of production needed to generate an audience.

109. Products with this characteristic are called "public goods." *See* B. OWEN, J. BEEBE & W. MANNING, JR., *supra* note 14, at 15-16.

110. As a practical matter, advertisers pay either a fixed rate to broadcasters for each spot they run or receive guaranteed minimum numbers of audience exposures, with additional viewers coming as a bonus. A program that generates a larger audience than anticipated creates a windfall for the advertiser. On the bright side, from an efficiency viewpoint the broadcaster's marginal cost for serving that extra customer is zero. Owen, *supra* note 106, at 316-17.

we know that it generally works. The stations and networks that carry programs with the highest viewing ratings can charge the highest rates for advertising. Producers with programs that are in demand by the public can charge networks and stations the most for their productions.[111] Actors engaged in hit television series can, or at least can try to, obtain higher salaries. Although the advertiser, rather than the consumer, pays for the program, market forces still move the key resource—time on an exclusive broadcasting frequency—toward its highest and best use. The real issue is not whether the marketplace is fully efficient; rather it is whether the Commission, by ignoring until recently the realities of the broadcasting business, has substituted a system of regulation by trusteeship that has caused more harm than good.

B. Legal Basis For a Marketplace Approach

The Commission, as much as possible, should rely on market forces rather than its judgments on program service or other licensee decisions to determine where the public interest lies in broadcasting. The Supreme Court has interpreted the Commission's broad statutory mandate as granting wide discretion to the Commission for determining the public interest.[112]

Approval of the market approach first appeared in the Supreme Court's 1940 review of the Commission's decision in *FCC v. Sanders Brothers Radio Station*.[113] A station operator had protested that licensing an additional radio station in its community would cause it economic harm. The Court upheld the Commission's denial of the protest on the ground that such injury to a rival station was not "in and of itself" an element that had to be considered when passing on a broad-

---

111. All of this is necessarily imprecise. Even though a program generates the largest number of viewers for a particular period of time, its success says nothing about the intensity with which viewers prefer it over a competing program or whether they would prefer a type of programming not offered at all. Furthermore, the amounts advertisers pay do not represent income that might be collected directly from viewers if they could pay. Still, popular programs do receive advertiser support regardless of the intensity of their popularity. Less popular programs tend to fail to achieve adequate advertiser support and other programs are substituted to make better use of the time period. *See* Note, *supra* note 38, at 558; *see also* Deregulation of Radio, 84 F.C.C.2d 968, 983 (1981).

Another important factor in a program's success is its placement on the network schedule. Networks juggle series into different time slots in order to place a program within the overall flow that suits it best. This process helps a program "find" its audience or, conversely, prevents it from getting a regular following. Sometimes critical acclaim or viewer writing campaigns can influence a network to give a program a longer time to develop an audience. CBS may have retained "The Waltons" despite weak ratings in part because of a sustained write-in campaign. The show subsequently became a ratings leader.

112. *See, e.g.,* FCC v. National Citizens Comm'n for Broadcasting, 436 U.S. 775, 795 (1978); NBC v. United States, 319 U.S. 190, 218 (1943).

113. 309 U.S. 470 (1940).

cast license application.[114]   The Court found that the 1934 Act recognized:

> that the field of broadcasting is one of free competition. . . . *The Commission is given no supervisory control of the programs, of business management or of policy.* In short, the broadcasting field is open to anyone, provided there be an available frequency over which he can broadcast without interference to others, if he shows his competency, the adequacy of his equipment, and financial ability to make good use of the assigned channel.[115]

This is surely strong language in support of the free market approach, especially considering that Justice Frankfurter's *NBC* decision, which validated the broad regulatory powers of the Commission, would emerge three years later. *Sanders Brothers* does backpedal following this portion of the opinion and suggest that the Commission could consider whether the addition of a new station would cause both an existing and the proposed outlet to go under, or whether dividing the field among two stations would result in inadequate service by each.[116]   But the Court rejected the licensee's claim of too much competition.

The Court's concern with the effect of a new station on existing stations and service now appears myopic.[117]   The market that a new station enters comprises not simply existing broadcast facilities, but all competitors for the advertising dollar, from newspapers to billboards. Consistently applied, the Court's rationale would lead the Commission to be equally concerned that an additional newspaper in a community might lead to ruinous competition between existing broadcast properties and the newspaper. More generally, a policy of preserving existing service arbitrarily favors established editorial voices over new ones, an approach never sanctioned by the Supreme Court.

If competition, not entry control, is to determine the provision of mass communications service in the United States, as it already does in all media save broadcasting, the FCC should not worry about either of the possibilities identified in *Sanders Brothers*. The case reveals the heavy emphasis the Court and the Commission placed on the role of open competition in broadcasting and the scant authority they found for Commission supervision of programming or station business policies.

---

114. *Id.* at 473.
115. *Id.* at 474-75 (emphasis added).
116. *Id.*
117. The D.C. Circuit resurrected this view in 1958. *See* Carroll Broadcasting Co. v. FCC, 258 F.2d 440 (D.C. Cir. 1958); *see supra* text accompanying note 59.

A Marketplace Approach to Broadcast Regulation 235

In *FCC v. WNCN Listeners Guild*,[118] decided in 1981, the Supreme Court expressly sanctioned the Commission's discretion to invoke market forces in its regulatory mission. In *WNCN* the Court found no inconsistency between the first amendment and the Commission's decision that the public interest in radio is best served by promoting diversity in entertainment formats through market forces and competition among broadcasters. The Court noted that the Commission had admitted that the marketplace would not necessarily achieve a perfect correlation between listener preferences and available entertainment programs.[119] But given the choice of regulating format changes or leaving those decisions to the marketplace, the Court concluded that the Commission acted reasonably in adopting the latter. The Court recognized that the Commission was within its range of discretion in preferring a market approach to achieve the Communication Act's goal of providing "the maximum benefits of radio to all the people of the United States."[120]

The Supreme Court admittedly did not express any enthusiasm for open competition in broadcasting in the forty-one years between *Sanders Brothers* and *WNCN*. Instead, in 1969 in *Red Lion Broadcasting Co. v. FCC*[121] and, most recently, in 1981 in *CBS v. FCC*,[122] the Court reaffirmed the viewpoint of Justice Frankfurter in *NBC v. United States* that the Commission bears the "burden of determining the composition of . . . traffic" over broadcast frequencies.[123] None of these three cases, *NBC*, *Red Lion*, or *CBS*, directly involved the conflict between the marketplace and trusteeship approaches to broadcasting. Only in *WNCN* did these policies collide.[124] Presented with the question, the Supreme Court held that the Commission could rely on marketplace forces to ensure that licensees satisfy the public interest.

Under the Supreme Court's view of the Communications Act, then, the Commission can apply a free market model to broadcasting, particularly where it finds that the costs of content-oriented regulations outweigh their benefits. This approach differs from a trusteeship model, under which the Commission would require broadcasters to air programs—from public affairs shows to responses to station editorials—that might not be aired voluntarily, and that consumers, insofar as

---

118. 450 U.S. 582 (1981).
119. *Id.* at 596.
120. *Id.* at 593-94 (quoting NBC v. United States, 319 U.S. 190, 217 (1943)).
121. 395 U.S. 367 (1969).
122. 453 U.S. 267 (1981).
123. 319 U.S. 190, 216 (1943).
124. *See* 450 U.S. at 604.

236 Texas Law Review Vol. 60:207, 1982

they can be heard in the advertiser-supported marketplace, do not demand.

The market perspective diminishes the importance of the Commission's past efforts to define affirmatively the elements of operation "in the public interest." It recognizes as valid communications policy, well within Commission discretion, reliance on voluntary broadcaster efforts to attract audiences—whether by specialized formats, as in the case of major market radio, or with a mix of programs, as in the case of television—and to provide the best practicable programming service to the public. It concludes that governmental efforts to improve the broadcast market have led to distortions of programming that have merely yielded a different programming mix, not a better one, and that the costs of government intrusion into the marketplace outweigh the benefits. Important first amendment interests support this conclusion as well.

C. The First Amendment and the Marketplace Approach

1. The First Amendment Rights of Listeners and Viewers Under the Speech Clause. —The Supreme Court's recently repeated formulation of the hierarchy of values in broadcasting—that "the right of the viewers and listeners, not the right of the broadcasters . . . is *paramount*"[125]—is central to a first amendment analysis of broadcast regulation. Under this hierarchy, initially set forth in *Red Lion*, the rights of listeners "to receive suitable access to social, political, esthetic, moral and other ideas and experiences"[126] outweigh the first amendment claims of broadcasters when the two conflict. This ranking does not, however, create an individual right of access to broadcast time in any single listener or viewer.[127]

Even before *Red Lion*, the Court had subordinated broadcaster claims of first amendment rights to the public's interest in access to ideas and information and to rules designed to enhance that interest. In *NBC*, where the issue was the independence of station owners from network control, the Court rejected the broadcasters' claim that the licensing criteria established in the chain broadcasting rules offended their freedom of speech.[128]

The *Red Lion* decision addressed the first amendment question

---

125. *Red Lion*, 395 U.S. at 390 (emphasis added).
126. *Id.*
127. *See* CBS v. Democratic Nat'l Comm., 412 U.S. 94 (1973).
128. The Court described the broadcasters' first amendment claim as a "sort of last resort" argument. 319 U.S. at 226.

more directly. The Court endorsed a right of access to ideas and upheld the Commission's requirement that a radio or television station give an individual time to reply to personal attacks and political editorials. Five years later, in *Miami Herald Publishing Co. v. Tornillo*,[129] the Supreme Court unanimously rejected a similar regulation when applied to a daily newspaper. But the Court in *Tornillo* did not attempt to harmonize the disparate holdings of the two cases.[130]

In *CBS v. FCC*,[131] the Court, relying on *Red Lion*, again concluded that the public interest in access to particular communications outweighed the impact on the editorial functions of the broadcaster. The Court faced a conflict between the broadcaster's first amendment claim and a Commission interpretation concerning presentation of the viewpoints of candidates for federal office under a congressionally created right of "reasonable" paid access. The Court noted that a statutory right of access did not preclude broadcasters from presenting any particular viewpoint or program and sustained the Commission's mandate of air time for the Carter-Mondale reelection committee under the reasonable access provisions.

A divided Supreme Court subordinated the broadcaster's constitutional rights in a different manner in *FCC v. Pacifica Foundation*.[132] *Pacifica* has little to commend its constitutional analysis. The majority lacked support both for its claim that broadcasting "has received the most limited first amendment protection,"[133] and also for maintaining that a sound basis for more regulation is the pervasive "power" of the electronic media. Yet like the other broadcasting cases, *Pacifica* indicated that the Commission can, indeed should, subordinate a broadcaster's claim to editorial freedom to the perceived needs of the general public for access to expression over the airwaves or (as in *Pacifica*) for protection against harm from such expression.

What do the Supreme Court's repeated holdings on the hierarchy of first amendment interests tell us about a marketplace approach to broadcasting? First, it should be noted that the language of the first amendment protects the right of speech, not the right of access to ideas or even the right to listen. The direct concern of the first amendment is

---

129. 418 U.S. 241 (1974).

130. *See* Note, *Reconciling* Red Lion *and* Tornillo: *A Consistent Theory of Media Regulation*, 28 STAN. L. REV. 563 (1976).

131. 453 U.S. 367 (1981).

132. 438 U.S. 726 (1978); *see supra* text accompanying notes 90-100.

133. *Id.* at 748. For a critical assessment of the Court's approach in this case, see Brenner, *Censoring the Airwaves: The Supreme Court's* Pacifica *Decision*, ABA BARRISTER, Fall 1978, at 10.

with the active speaker, not the passive receiver. The listener's interest is certainly enhanced by the exercise of the right of free speech, especially where the first amendment is viewed as a tool for self-governance.[134] But listener rights are not the same as the individual's right to speak, and no such rights exist in broadcasting.[135] Thus, it remains unclear exactly what listener interests are protected under the first amendment, aside from the "values" spilling over from the exercise of free speech.

Even assuming the existence of a protected right of access to ideas under the first amendment, it is illogical to assume that broadcasting, and broadcasting alone, is the exclusive arena for the exercise of this right, as the language in *Red Lion* might suggest. "Crucial" access to ideas pertinent to self-governance or self-fulfillment can be provided by many sources other than the airwaves. Furthermore, broadcasters should not shoulder a broader responsibility for providing important information than other media. The argument that listener access to broadcasting is crucial may prove too much. For if listener rights are deemed "paramount" to broadcaster rights, so the rights of newspaper readers should be paramount to the rights of the publishers and editors and the rights of movie patrons superior to those of exhibitors, distributors, and producers. This is the logical result once one stops analyzing the issue in terms of the rights of individuals under the first amendment.

Finally, even assuming that the interest in access to ideas is more pronounced in radio and television than in other media, it does not follow that only governmental regulations can ensure this access. Again, *WNCN* provides the most instructive precedent, since in *WNCN* the Court confronted the free market approach and the *Red Lion* hierarchy for the first time.[136] The Court rejected the claim that the Commission's laissez-faire policy toward radio format changes[137] conflicted with the first amendment rights of listeners under *Red Lion*. It recognized that *Red Lion* provided individual listeners with no right to control the abandonment of a format and concluded that the Commission's reliance on market forces did not violate listeners' first amendment rights. Rather, the Court found that a station's format generally would reflect listener interests and therefore be consistent

---

134. A. MEIKLEJOHN, FREE SPEECH AND ITS RELATION TO SELF-GOVERNMENT 88-89 (1948).

135. The rights of listeners, in the form of paid editorial access, were trumped by broadcaster claims based on the first amendment protection of journalistic discretion in CBS v. Democratic Nat'l Comm., 412 U.S. 94, 114-21 (1973).

136. *See supra* text accompanying notes 118-24.

137. Changes in the Entertainment Formats of Broadcast Stations, 60 F.C.C.2d 858 (1976).

A Marketplace Approach to Broadcast Regulation   **239**

with the first amendment hierarchy in broadcasting.[138]

The Court did more than avoid a potential conflict between the rights of listeners and broadcasters in dismissing the *Red Lion* claim. It affirmed the importance of listener rights, regardless of broadcaster rights. But the Court agreed with the Commission that this "paramount" interest is best served when a broadcaster in the marketplace is free to respond to perceived listener demand. In this marketplace approach, the interests of listeners and broadcasters, in the past sometimes in conflict (such as over a right of individual access to the media), converge. The commercial broadcaster maximizes profits by providing the service it believes consumers most desire. In choosing a service that maximizes profit, the licensee serves listener interests because the choice of service is geared to attracting the most listeners. The market approach is superior to the alternatives because it does not put the government between the licensee and the listener it is wooing.[139]

Thus, a Commission policy that equates the functions of the marketplace in commercial broadcasting with satisfaction of listener interests finds support in the Court's analysis of the first amendment rights of listeners. Once the Commission concludes that market forces, rather than its own judgments, are most likely to produce programming that best serves the people, the paramount claims set forth in *Red Lion* are satisfied.

Admittedly, this conclusion reads much from the *WNCN* result, for the *Red Lion* claim is not analyzed at length in the decision. And one can characterize the recent *CBS* case, announced shortly after *WNCN*, as reducing the scope of licensee editorial discretion. But the 1981 *CBS* case dealt with a narrow access statute, itself an exception to the result in the Supreme Court's 1973 decision in *CBS v. Democratic National Committee*.[140] In denying a general right of individual access in the 1981 case, the Commission did not allow licensee discretion to override its own interpretation of the statute's purpose. Absent an express Commission finding that it cannot rely on licensee discretion to carry out its congressional mandate, however, *WNCN* suggests the

---

138. 450 U.S. at 604.

139. Some argue that if the government withdraws from an active licensing role, stations will become the province of the rich, who will use them to mold public opinion. These critics assume incorrectly that national media concentration will go unnoticed by the Commission or the Department of Justice. Moreover, daily newspapers can also affect public opinion and yet have not become the mouthpieces of rich individuals. Finally, media owners with strong views on some subjects can operate news organizations with little bias on the front page, as is shown by the *Christian Science Monitor*, and more recently the *Washington Times*.

140. 412 U.S. 94 (1973).

240 Texas Law Review   Vol. 60:207, 1982

compatibility of a marketplace approach and *Red Lion*'s emphasis on listeners' rights.

2. The First Amendment Rights of Broadcasters Under the Press Clause.—The marketplace approach emphasizes broadcaster discretion as a way to maximize listener welfare. An independent first amendment interest also protects broadcaster discretion from the dictates of the government. As Professor Kalven has sentiently observed:

> We have been beginning, so to speak, in the wrong corner. The question is not what does the need for licensing permit the Commission to do in the public interest; rather it is what does the mandate of the First Amendment inhibit the Commission from doing even though it is to license.[141]

Application of the first amendment to broadcasting largely dates from dictum in *United States v. Paramount Pictures, Inc.* [142] Justice Frankfurter's analysis in the 1943 *NBC* case, however, suggests that the Court already had recognized that broadcasters have a constitutional basis for objecting to overly intrusive regulation.[143] Despite later dictum in *Pacifica* devaluing the first amendment interests of broadcasters,[144] the Court in *CBS v. Democratic National Committee* championed the editorial freedom of broadcasters. It rejected a claim that the first amendment and the "public interest" standard required licensees to sell time for editorial advertisements. "For better or worse," the Court stated, "editing is what editors are for; and editing is selection and choice of material."[145]

The belated recognition of the first amendment rights of broadcasters may be due to the relatively late development of broadcast journalism as a serious professional calling. News and interpretation have

---

141. Kalven, *supra* note 22, at 37.

142. 334 U.S. 131, 166 (1948). Justice Douglas argued that broadcasting enjoyed the same first amendment protection as newspapers and magazines, CBS v. Democratic Nat'l Comm., 412 U.S. at 148 (Douglas, J., concurring), as did Senator Proxmire in his efforts to repeal the fairness doctrine, *see, e.g.,* 120 CONG. REC. 36,514 (1974) (remarks of Sen. Proxmire). *See also* Robinson, *The FCC and the First Amendment: Observations on 40 Years of Radio and Television Regulation*, 52 MINN. L. REV. 67, 160-63 (1967). This Article assumes that broadcasters' free speech rights are included in those protected by the press clause.

143. "But Congress did not authorize the Commission to choose among applicants upon the basis of their political, economic or social views, or upon any other capricious basis. If it did, or if the Commission by these Regulations proposed a choice among applicants upon some such basis, the issue before us would be wholly different." NBC v. United States, 319 U.S. at 226.

144. *See supra* notes 132-33 and accompanying text.

145. 412 U.S. at 124. The Court equated the broadcaster's right to reject controversial paid advertising with the corresponding right of the printed media. It concluded that "[c]alculated risks of abuse of editorial power had to be taken in order to preserve higher values"—the right of editors to be free from governmental control. *Id.* at 125.

A Marketplace Approach to Broadcast Regulation   **241**

always been part of radio programming,[146] but both radio and television have remained primarily entertainment media. Until recently, investigative broadcast journalism was scheduled sporadically, and it remains the exception to the rule despite its sometimes significant impact.[147] Questions of entertainment program selection and scheduling, not newsroom judgments, dominate the broadcaster's first amendment activity.[148]

Yet these different activities do bring broadcasting within the rubric of the "press" for first amendment purposes. The constitutional privileges accorded the press in the areas of privacy[149] and defamation[150] apply equally to broadcasters and print journalists. So, too, do rules limiting protection of the secrecy of news sources[151] and reporter access to public facilities.[152] Even the courtroom, once thought to be off-limits to the tools of broadcast journalists, can now be entered.[153] Print and broadcast journalists share as co-venturers in the rights accorded the press by the first amendment.[154]

3. Summary.—The marketplace approach to broadcast regulation has two distinct advantages from a first amendment perspective. First, it does not conflict with *Red Lion*. In basing editorial and program judgments on their perceptions of popular demand, broadcasters enforce the paramount interests of listeners and viewers. Even if licen-

---

146. *See* 2 E. BARNOUW, A HISTORY OF BROADCASTING IN THE UNITED STATES: THE GOLDEN WEB 17-22 (1968). *See generally* A. KENDRICK, PRIME TIME (1969).

147. Among the most celebrated confrontations was a 1971 CBS documentary, "The Selling of the Pentagon," which covered the public relations efforts of the Defense Department. The program's airing led to a showdown between broadcasters and the congressional subpoena power when Congress unsuccessfully tried to obtain nonbroadcast outtakes from the network. *See* E. KRASNOW & L. LONGLEY, THE POLITICS OF BROADCAST REGULATION 82-83 (2d ed. 1978).

148. *See, e.g.,* Bazelou, *FCC Regulation of the Telecommunications Press*, 1975 DUKE L.J. 213, 219-20.

149. Cox Broadcasting Corp. v. Cohn, 420 U.S. 469 (1975) (challenge to television broadcast of the name of a rape victim from official court records) (described in Nixon v. Warner Communications, Inc., 435 U.S. 589, 608-09 (1978), as a case involving the "right of access of the press").

150. *See, e.g.,* Gertz v. Robert Welch, Inc., 418 U.S. 323 (1974), in which the Court used the conjunctive "publishers and broadcasters" to describe the class of potential defendants in defamation cases.

151. *See, e.g.,* Branzburg v. Hayes, 408 U.S. 665 (1972), in which the Court considered three appeals from reporters concerning demands upon them for information from grand juries. Two of the appeals involved newspaper reporters; the third appeal involved a Massachusetts television reporter. The Court did not distinguish among the three cases in determining the limits on the obligations of reporters to respond to grand jury subpoenas.

152. *See, e.g.,* Houchins v. KQED, Inc., 438 U.S. 1 (1978) (right of San Francisco television station to photograph prison facility). The Court referred to "the media" as having no special right of access without distinguishing between print and broadcast journalism.

153. *See, e.g.,* Chandler v. Florida, 449 U.S. 560 (1981).

154. *See The Supreme Court, 1980 Term,* 95 HARV. L. REV. 91, 227-28 (1981); Fowler, *Freedom of (Electronic) Speech,* Wash. Post, Sept. 20, 1981, at C7, col. 2.

242   Texas Law Review   Vol. 60:207, 1982

sees occasionally misperceive the wants of their audiences, the present
regulatory system, which is based upon the Commission's judgment of
the community's needs, does not ensure a better result. Second, the
marketplace approach accords protection to the distinct constitutional
status of broadcasters under the press clause. This first amendment
interest is, or should be, coextensive with the first amendment rights of
the print media, regardless of whether the public is best served by its
uninhibited exercise. A broadcaster's first amendment rights may differ from its listeners' rights to receive and hear suitable expression, but
once the call is close, deference to broadcaster judgment is preferable to
having a government agency mediate conflicts between broadcasters
and their listeners.

IV.   Toward a Transition From a Trusteeship Approach to a Marketplace Approach

This Article has discussed the trusteeship model, the consequences
of that model during its half-century of existence, and the marketplace
approach to broadcast regulation. We now examine new directions that
the Commission and Congress can pursue in forging a communications
policy that utilizes marketplace theory.[155]

A.   Level I: A Return to the Marketplace

1.   General Approach: Resale.—In light of the fifty-five years of
spectrum regulation under the trusteeship model, the problems of applying market techniques to spectrum use are more practical than theoretical. One approach would be to require all spectrum users to retire
their licenses. The Commission would hold an auction to select new
users and frequency rights would go to the highest bidders, who under
a market theory should put the frequencies to their best use.[156] If a
higher use for a frequency later emerged, the holder could resell the
frequency rights.

---

155. It is beyond the scope of this Article to propose model legislation to accomplish the deregulatory goals advocated here. Some reforms, however, could be accomplished without legislation, since certain offending policies were originally adopted within the discretion of the
Commission under the Communications Act. The Commission proposed a package of legislative
reforms in 1981, known as Track I and Track II, which addressed many of the problems raised in
this Article. Much of Track I, including lottery provisions and lessened financial incentives for
licensure, was introduced in H.R. 5008, 97th Cong., 1st Sess. (1982). Track II provisions eliminating the fairness doctrine and political speech rules were introduced in H.R. 5584 and H.R. 5585,
97th Cong., 2d Sess. (1982).

156. *See* De Vany, Eckert, Meyers, O'Hara & Scott, *A Property System for Market Allocation
of the Electromagnetic Spectrum: A Legal-Economic-Engineering Study*, 21 STAN. L. REV. 1499,
1512-22 (1969).

A Marketplace Approach to Broadcast Regulation   **243**

Although a good way to have started in the 1920's, an auction would substantially disrupt current service and frustrate the expectations of those who have long held spectrum rights and of their customers.[157] Another way to encourage optimum frequency use would be to allow licenses to be bought and sold freely after the initial grant, regardless of whether the initial grant is determined by auction, lottery, or under the old trusteeship approach. On resale, the seller, rather than the government, would capture the higher value of the frequency,[158] but the allocation of resale profit would not prevent the frequency from reaching its highest use, thereby achieving the market objective.

To some, the major objection to free resale would be the windfall to incumbent licensees. The windfall, to the extent that it actually occurred, would consist of the increased value of a deregulated license created by its release from content and ownership restrictions and its new, freely transferable character. The problem presented by the windfall of free transferability is not entirely novel. Except for distressed properties or those that have never been transferred, the price paid to a transferor under existing assignment rules already reflects the steadily increasing value of the exclusivity. It is almost always greater than the value of the nonlicense assets being transferred. Restricted resales under section 310(d) of the 1934 Act have already occurred several times with respect to many licenses, so that the windfall has been captured.[159]

---

157. Some portions of the reserved broadcast spectrum have been reassigned for land mobile uses. In Land Mobile Use of TV Channels 14 through 20, 23 F.C.C.2d 325 (1970), the Commission authorized a "sharing" that amounted to a shift of two of the lower seven (14 to 20) UHF frequencies from broadcasting to land mobile use in the top ten markets. The Commission later added three other congested markets. In An Inquiry Relating to the Future Use of the Frequency Band 806-960 MHz, 51 F.C.C.2d 945 (1975), *aff'd sub nom.* National Ass'n of Regulatory Utility Comm'rs v. FCC, 525 F.2d 630 (D.C. Cir. 1976), the Commission reallocated all of the upper 14 UHF channels (70 to 83) for a variety of new land mobile technologies, including trunked and cellular systems. The Sheriff's Office of Los Angeles County has petitioned for additional allocation of UHF frequencies in the lower seven for public safety and other land mobile operations. *See* FCC Public Notice, Petitions for Rule Making, Mimeo No. 3479 (Sept. 21, 1981).

158. The capital gains tax recaptures some of this value. The elimination of programs and paperwork associated with the trusteeship approach also undoubtedly would reduce costs and lead to increased revenues, but its dollar value, especially in a more competitive environment, is hard to determine.

159. Free transferability eliminates the extra costs associated with the Commission's transfer process. These costs primarily stem from litigation arising out of the petitions of competitors and public interest groups to deny new licenses and the delays associated with the resolution of the petitions. Adoption of a marketplace approach would eliminate the grounds for such petitions because the marketplace model assumes that resale is in the public interest, as it represents transfer of an asset to a higher use as contemplated by the new owner. *See generally* J. GRUNDFEST, CITIZEN PARTICIPATION IN BROADCAST LICENSING BEFORE THE FCC (Rand Corp. R-1896-MF 1976); Schneyer, *An Overview of Public Interest Law Activity in the Communications Field*, 1977 WIS. L. REV. 619; Volner, *Broadcast Regulation: Is There Too Much "Public" in the "Public Interest?"* 43 CIN. L. REV. 267, 280-82 (1974). Under the Communications Act, a competing applica-

244   Texas Law Review   Vol. 60:207, 1982

More generally, the marketplace approach could be most expeditiously introduced to broadcasting by granting existing licensees "squatter's rights" to their frequencies. These rights embody the reasonable expectation of renewal that licensees presently enjoy for satisfactory past performance.[160] The critical next step, from a market viewpoint, would be to deregulate fully the sale of licenses.

This approach to resale need not preclude the use of lotteries or auctions for new assignments to broadcasters or other spectrum users. Consider the Commission's handling of low-power television service. Announcement of this new service led to the submission of thousands of applications, many mutually exclusive, so that the Commission is faced with choosing among competing applicants. Although the Commission has approved a comparative process to license this new service,[161] initial grants using either a lottery and resale[162] or an auction could inject market incentives into the distribution of this service. Either technique would be likely to raise the frequency exclusivity to its highest use as a broadcast frequency.

   2. Eliminating Content and Business Restrictions.—In addition to promoting resale, the marketplace approach requires an end to program regulation. Government oversight of broadcast content arrogates editorial responsibilities protected by the first amendment and interferes with the functioning of market forces as well. The agenda for restoring competition to the television market should include scrapping

---

tion will not be considered at the time of a proposed license transfer. 47 U.S.C. § 310(d) (Supp. III 1979). The Commission, however, accepts petitions to deny at the time of transfer, since the Commission must make an affirmative public interest finding to authorize the reassignment. This ban on competing applications has been part of the Communications Act since 1952, and was designed to operate so that "in applying the test of public interest, convenience, and necessity, the Commission must do so as though the proposed transferee or assignee were applying for the construction permit or station license and as though no other person were interested in securing such permit or license." H.R. REP. No. 1750, 82d Cong., 2d Sess. 12 (1952). The ban foreclosed future efforts by the Commission under its "AVCO ruling," which it had announced prospectively in Powel Crosley, Jr., 11 F.C.C. 3, 26 (1945), to permit competing applications.

   160. *See generally* Note, *The Recognition of Legitimate Renewal Expectancies in Broadcast Licensing,* 58 WASH. U.L.Q. 409 (1980).

   161. *See* Inquiry into the Future Role of Low Power Television Broadcasting and Television Translators in the National Telecommunications System, 47 Fed. Reg. 21,468 (1982).

   162. The 1981 Omnibus Budget Reconciliation Act, Pub. L. No. 97-35, 95 Stat. 736 (1981) (to be codified at 47 U.S.C. § 309(i)), authorized the Commission to use lottery procedures to choose among mutually exclusive applications for initial telecommunications licenses, subject to criteria specified by Congress. The Commission declined to implement its lottery authority because the statute did not eliminate the administrative burden of examining each lottery applicant under 47 U.S.C. § 308(b) (1976), and because of obstacles to implementing the statutory preference for "groups or organizations, or members of groups or organizations, which are underrepresented in the ownership of telecommunications facilities or properties." Amendment of Part I of the Commission's Rules, 50 RAD. REG. 2d (P & F) 1503 (1982).

A Marketplace Approach to Broadcast Regulation **245**

the content-oriented regulations that prescribe minimum amounts of nonentertainment programs and limit advertising. Their elimination would allow broadcasters to satisfy consumer desires based on their reading of what viewers want, from all-news to all-entertainment programming. The Commission also should seek repeal of other content regulations, such as the fairness doctrine and the political speech rules, although it might assign access obligations for political candidates and referenda to public broadcasters.[163]

Restrictions that impede resale should be the first barriers abandoned in the move to a market environment. The rule on "trafficking" licenses, which require applications for license assignment or transfer of stock control to be designated for hearing unless the license has been held for at least three years, are particularly perverse.[164] The rule condemns licensees who acquire a station and dispose of it in less than three years. Yet such behavior is not restricted in other segments of the economy. To the contrary, we generally reward those who buy an ailing company and, having turned its fortunes around, sell it. Under a trusteeship approach it is conduct unbecoming a public steward; under a market approach it is conduct rewarded by profit on resale.

The Commission should also consider abolishing rules that restrict growth by existing players or limit entry of new players in any of the competitive video fields. It should place particular attention on its restrictions on ownership of media facilities.[165] For example, the Com-

---

163. In 1981 the Commission recommended that Congress repeal the fairness doctrine, 47 U.S.C. § 315 (1976), and the equal opportunity and equal access requirements for political candidates, *id*. § 312(a)(7) (1976). *See* BROADCASTING, Sept. 21, 1981, at 23. Public broadcasters might be required to provide candidates with opportunities for political speech as part of their mission in a marketplace approach to regulation. *See infra* notes 190-92 and accompanying text.

164. 47 C.F.R. § 73.3597(a)-(d) (1981). "Trafficking" in broadcast licenses and permits was defined as the licensee's acquisition of a station "for the purpose of reselling it at a profit rather than for the purpose of rendering a public service." Powel Crosley, Jr., 11 F.C.C. 3, 23 (1945). In the late 1950's and early 1960's, Congress focused on this issue, *see generally* SPECIAL SUBCOMM. ON LEGISLATIVE OVERSIGHT OF THE HOUSE COMM. ON INTERSTATE AND FOREIGN COMMERCE, 85TH CONG., 2D SESS., REGULATION OF BROADCASTING: HALF A CENTURY OF GOVERNMENT REGULATION OF BROADCASTING AND THE NEED FOR FURTHER LEGISLATIVE ACTION (Subcomm. Print 1958). In 1960 House Subcommittee Chairman Oren Harris proposed in H.R. 11,340 that broadcast license transfers be prohibited within the first three years after a grant unless a public hearing held in the station's service area determined that the transfer was due to "inadequacy of operating capital, death, or disability of key management personnel, or other changed circumstances." H.R. 11,340, 86th Cong., 2d Sess. (1960). The bill died in the 86th Congress, but was reintroduced the next term, H.R. 1165, 87th Cong., 1st Sess. (1961), and remained pending at the time the FCC adopted the trafficking rule. Procedures on Transfer and Assignment Applications, 32 F.C.C. 689 (1962). The Commission recently proposed deleting the trafficking rule. Amendment of § 73.3597 of the Commission's Rules, Applications for Voluntary Assignments or Transfers of Control, 47 Fed. Reg. 985 (1982).

165. *See generally* OFFICE OF PLANS AND POLICY, *supra* note 5; Howard, *Multiple Broadcast Ownership: Regulatory History*, 27 FED. COM. L.J. 1 (1974).

mission has long enforced a "7-7-7" rule, which restricts one licensee to seven AM, seven FM, and seven television outlets, no more than five of which can be VHF stations.[166] The rule stems from the Commission's desire to establish some limit on the number of stations a single licensee can operate. This arbitrary rule has almost certainly promoted inefficiency, for it does not measure a licensee's share of the homes using television nationwide. An operator with twenty-one stations in the bottom twenty-one markets possesses far less market control than the owner of three stations in the top three markets. If national concentration is a concern, the Commission could limit station ownership by the percentage of homes reached rather than by an arbitrary number of stations. But even a percentage approach should have to demonstrate that a limit on ownership bears a close relationship to preventing an identifiable harm.

In revising the 7-7-7 rule, the Commission should consider whether express limitations on concentration are warranted or whether they create undesirable barriers to entry in programming or distribution. Concentration of media outlets, particularly in a local market, can pose special problems. But this fact alone should not subject the media industries to limitations on the ownership rights freely permitted in other concentrated industries.

A less restrictive policy toward group ownership would also aid program diversity. The 1952 allocation scheme led to the development of only three full-time television networks.[167] Significant group ownership in broadcasting exists outside of stations licensed to the networks, but the Commission's regulations have prevented these groups from gaining access to important markets and establishing alternatives to the traditional three-network structure.[168] In its review of the 7-7-7 rule and other ownership limits, the Commission should be aware that the right of group owners to acquire additional stations might make alternative networks viable. It should also consider anew the scrutiny it gives to financial[169] and character qualifications[170] in transfers and at

---

166. *See* 47 C.F.R. §§ 73.240(a)(2), .35(b)(1), .636(a)(2) (1981). The Commission arrived at the 7-7-7 figure by taking as a ceiling the largest number of stations held by any one licensee at the time of the rule's adoption.

167. *See supra* note 78 and accompanying text.

168. "Under the Commission's present Table of Assignments, a potential fourth network could expect to reach only 35.8% of the nation's television households by means of technically comparable affiliates, assuming that all assignments were operational." Schuessler, *supra* note 76, at 998 (footnote omitted).

169. New Financial Qualifications for Broadcast Assignment and Transfer Applicants, 87 F.C.C.2d 200 (1981), lessened the showing required by the Commission in the transfer situation. Under the new standards, an applicant must only demonstrate sufficient capital to consummate the transaction on the closing of the sale and to meet expenses for three months. *Id.* Previously,

renewals. The governing principle in this hard look is whether any Commission rule fosters or undermines market forces, forces designed to discover and meet the public's interest.

B. Level II: A Cost of Asset Approach: The Spectrum License Fee

1. Charging for Spectrum Use.—The concept of property is essential to the functioning of a marketplace economy. In a deregulated communications marketplace, the right to a frequency exclusivity for an unlimited period of time would be an intangible property interest. Indeed, the reasonable expectation of license renewal enjoyed by broadcasters today comes close to a property right, in reality if not in name.

The broadcast license, however, had never been deemed a property right, in part because the Commission can take it away for gross misbehavior without compensation. Under a marketplace approach, the grounds for revoking a license would narrow drastically, if not disappear. Lying or other malfeasance toward the Commission or persistent technical violations would be among the few bases on which the Commission would be likely to strip a licensee of its exclusivity.[171] Under these circumstances, whether or not Congress explicitly recognized the proprietary aspects of a broadcast license, the question of its value as property would be inescapable. Who should receive the value? And through what mechanism should it be distributed?

To the extent that the government should receive part of the value of the exclusivity, it is worth considering whether the Commission should charge a spectrum usage fee. The Commission could base a fee

the Commission required applicants to demonstrate an ability to meet expenses for the first year, Ultravision Broadcasting Co., 1 F.C.C.2d 544, 547 (1965); Public Notice, 1 F.C.C.2d 550 (1965), rather than 90 days. The next deregulatory step would be to eliminate all financial qualifications, just as there is no required showing when a buyer seeks to acquire a newspaper by transfer of ownership.

170. The Commission has wrestled with the question of what constitutes sufficiently good character for a broadcast licensee. The Commission found RKO General, Inc. unqualified to be licensee of its television stations, in part because its nonbroadcast misconduct called into question its character qualifications, in part because of misrepresentations before the agency. RKO Gen., Inc., 78 F.C.C.2d 1, 4, 47-80 (1980), *rev'd in part*, 670 F.2d 215 (D.C. Cir. 1981). The Commission has launched an inquiry directed toward reducing the scope of its character test in broadcasting. *See* Policy Regarding Character Qualifications in Broadcast Licensing, 87 F.C.C.2d 836 (1981).

171. The Commission has denied license renewal for a station's abdication of control over programs, Trustees of the Univ. of Pa., 71 F.C.C.2d 416 (1979), persistent violation of operating rules, United Television Co., Inc., 55 F.C.C.2d 416 (1975), and clipping network programs to insert local advertising and thereafter misrepresenting this conduct to the agency, Western Communications, Inc., 59 F.C.C.2d 1441 (1976). Revocation has occurred for misrepresentations in connection with fraudulent billing practices. Sea Island Broadcasting Corp., 60 F.C.C.2d 146 (1976).

248   Texas Law Review   Vol. 60:207, 1982

on a small percentage of a station's profits,[172] or it could levy a flat charge based on bandwidth use.

Merely charging a usage fee for the spectrum admittedly does not instill significant incentives in the broadcasting market. A charge would not lead to the most efficient frequency use because it would not be levied according to each licensee's relative use. A flat charge imposed on an increasingly competitive industry, if set too high, could force marginal broadcasters out of business. Even a fee based on a percentage of royalties would not measure the comparative worth of broadcasting against other spectrum uses.

A spectrum fee is, however, economically attractive because it puts a price on a major input of doing business in broadcasting—the method of distribution. Such a fee would recognize that broadcasters receive something of value in the exclusivity that the government provides them, similar to government franchises for offshore oil rights or food concessions in public parks. Additionally, the fee would end the competitive advantage that broadcasting enjoys over such delivery systems as cable television, which pays a franchise fee to the licensing municipality,[173] a regulatory advantage distinct from the natural

---

172. Congressman Van Deerlin proposed the inclusion of a fee provision in the Communications Act of 1978. The fee would have been based on the costs of processing the license and the value of the spectrum and would have gone to a "telecommunications fund" to support federal regulation, public broadcasting, minority ownership of stations, and rural telecommunications. H.R. 13,015, 95th Cong., 2d Sess. § 413 (1978). The bill also proposed broadcast deregulation, extending television license terms from three to five years for a period of ten years (and becoming indefinite thereafter), and creating indefinite radio license terms. Congressman Van Deerlin viewed the license fee and broadcast deregulation as "trade-offs." *See* BROADCASTING, June 12, 1978, at 29.

An inquiry by the Library of Congress into whether there is a legally certain method to collect more than the costs of administration where radio frequency spectrum is concerned concluded that "if there is, we are not aware of it." Congressional Research Service, The Library of Congress, Memorandum, Legal Analysis of Radio Spectrum Use Charges (Apr. 20, 1979). In 1981 Henry Geller, former General Counsel of the Commission, renewed support for a spectrum fee. *Public Broadcasting Oversight of 1981, Hearings on H.R. 4726, H.R. 4780, and H.R. 4781 Before the Subcomm. on Telecommunications, Consumer Protection, and Finance of the House Comm. on Energy and Commerce*, 97th Cong., 1st Sess. 98-99 (1981). The president of the Public Broadcasting Service, Lawrence K. Grossman, has recommended that spectrum fees be used to support public television. BROADCASTING, Jan. 4, 1982, at 14. In an accompanying editorial, *Broadcasting* urged consideration of Grossman's proposal, although it criticized the size of the fee proposed in H.R. 13,015. *Id.* at 114. The political viability of a fee to support public television thus seems to depend on the amount of the fee. The National Radio Broadcasters Association has proposed fifty-year licenses for radio tied to a spectrum fee of one percent of station revenues. The fee would be earmarked for public radio and minority ownership. The larger rival trade group, the National Association of Broadcasters, opposes a spectrum fee but would support smaller "license" fees, *see, e.g.,* S. 1629, 97th Cong., 2d Sess. (1982). *See generally* BROADCASTING, July 5, 1982, at 60.

173. On the other hand, broadcasting seems to suffer a disadvantage where copyright is concerned. The 1976 Copyright Act required cable operators for the first time to reimburse proprietors of copyrighted works. 17 U.S.C. § 111(d)(2) (1976). Cable systems pay the compulsory fees

advantage it enjoys in avoiding cable's high fixed costs in wiring a community. To be equitable, the Commission would have to impose the fee on all spectrum uses, whether for cable television microwave hops, direct broadcasting satellites, or multipoint distribution operations.

The spectrum fee approach is not free of negative aspects. The right to collect a fee ultimately depends on the supposition that the airwaves belong to the public at large, a premise that has no logical place in determining the degree of regulation permitted over broadcasters. The value of the exclusivity depends on a licensee's investment and ingenuity. The exclusivity granted by the government to a broadcaster is similar to a patent or copyright, for which the holder pays only nominal registration fees. The key to the success of a broadcaster, unlike a concessionaire in a public park, is ingenuity.

Administering a spectrum fee raises other problems. The fee would account for the exclusive frequency received by the licensees to distribute programs and the right to transfer freely the exclusivity. The fee could also cover the services rendered by the Commission in enforcement and licensing.[174] This approach accords with the trend to have the users of government services pay their way. The Commission, however, could not determine the market-clearing price of the spectrum because the spectrum would not be subject to bidding by the full range of potential users. Any fee beyond the value of services rendered by the Commission is thus bound to be somewhat arbitrary and lead to new distortions in the market. Therefore, a spectrum fee would be an inexact method of capturing the perceived windfall. In addition, when stations have been transferred in the past, the sellers already have captured much of the windfall. Consequently, fees imposed on subsequent

---

for carriage of radio and television programs to the Copyright Royalty Tribunal, which disburses them to copyright owners. In 1981, three trade groups, the National Cable Television Association, the National Association of Broadcasters, and the Motion Picture Association of America, agreed on a "great compromise" to amend the 1976 Act. The compromise would have maintained the compulsory license as well as the current copyright fee schedule. The syndicated exclusivity rule, rescinded by the Commission in 1980, would have been reimposed and made applicable to all television markets. *See* BROADCASTING, Nov. 30, 1981, at 32-33; CABLEVISION, Nov. 9, 1981, at 14. The proposal failed to generate support among members of the associations and eventually broke down. Its failure may be explained by the madcap internal subsidization between broadcasters and cablecasters. Cable television incurs low copyright liability for the off-the-air programming it retransmits, but it has high distribution costs. Broadcasters pay little to distribute programs, but pay both for their own programming (reimbursed by advertisers, of course) and, some argue, for a share of cable's programming costs as well.

174. The Commission has the authority to charge fees, but it must base fees on the "value to the recipient." The Commission may not include fees based on the cost of services that inure to the benefit of the public generally. National Cable Television Ass'n v. United States, 415 U.S. 336 (1974).

250   Texas Law Review   Vol. 60:207, 1982

owners of these stations to recapture prior windfalls create new unfairness.

Justification for a spectrum fee, thus, depends less on its economic merit and more on how one weighs the relative equities of a deregulated broadcast environment against a spectrum fee that is likely to be somewhat arbitrary. Deregulation does not necessitate a spectrum fee, nor does it exclude it. Ultimately, Congress must decide whether to impose a fee based on its valuation of the interests affected by the grant of exclusivity.

    2. Disposition of the Spectrum Fee in the Public Interest.—A congressional decision to apply a spectrum fee would raise the separate question of the proper disposition of the funds collected. On the one hand, the government could collect fees and remit them to the general treasury in obedience to the oft-repeated, though unproductive, contention that the airwaves "belong to the people." On the other hand, the government could pursue the public interest directly and use the fees collected from commercial broadcasters to support a public broadcast service. This concept is not novel,[175] but it has applicability to the marketplace approach to regulation advanced here. This suggestion requires a short digression, one that moves away from the general approach advocated thus far.

After the Commission decided to reserve the broadcasting spectrum for radio and television, it created two classes of broadcasting: commercial and noncommercial.[176] The need for noncommercial broadcasting has been hotly debated.[177] Today's noncommercial service combines instructional radio and television, which originated in the 1950's with the establishment of the Public Broadcasting Service (PBS) by the Public Broadcasting Act of 1967.[178] Over the years public television has never escaped its identity crisis. Should it attempt to reach the broadest audience, on the theory that the tax dollar supporting the system requires an expansive approach? How "commercial" should this system be? Who should be involved in decisionmaking? How repre-

---

  175. *See supra* note 172.

  176. *See generally* Lindsey, *Public Broadcasting: Editorial Restraints and the First Amendment*, 28 FED. COM. L.J. 63, 64-75 (1975).

  177. *See generally* R. COASE & E. BARRETT, EDUCATIONAL TV: WHO SHOULD PAY? (1968).
Commercial broadcasting, with the rare exception of special programs, was devoted exclusively to light entertainment. . . . But the citizen, rich or poor, who wanted something more, who happened to be eager to use Sunday night to stretch his mind, to face up to some of the issues of the day or even to enjoy some fine music, had no opportunity to do so.
Id. at 39.

  178. Pub. L. No. 90-129, 81 Stat. 365 (codified at 47 U.S.C. §§ 390-399 (1976)).

A Marketplace Approach to Broadcast Regulation 251

sentative are the boards of local public broadcasting stations? What is the appropriate mix of funding for public television? And, most basically, should public broadcasting exist at all?

These issues stem from two congressional actions in 1967. First, acting on studies by the Carnegie Commission and the Ford Foundation, Congress almost unanimously passed the Public Broadcasting Act. Second, Congress deferred the determination of how to fund the system. It declined to adopt the Ford Foundation's plan to create a communications satellite system that would provide free interconnection to public stations and establish a profit center for revenues earned by carrying other satellite traffic.[179] It also rejected the Carnegie Commission's recommendation that an excise tax on the sale of television sets be imposed to support the system.[180] Over the years, the question of financing has remained unsettled. Public broadcasting has even faced the danger of being "punished" in the budget process for programs that offended an incumbent administration.[181]

The issue of what type of programming public television should carry has been joined in the marketplace. New cultural channels have been launched on cable on a subscriber or advertiser-supported basis (or a combination of both).[182] PBS, hoping to use its expertise in this segment of the programming market, has proposed its own pay cable service devoted to the cultural and arts field.[183] Revenues from a PBS pay cable channel would support the chronically underfunded system.

What does a marketplace scheme of broadcast regulation portend for this format in public broadcasting? The fundamental question is whether the Commission should continue to maintain two sets of licen-

179. *See* Letter from McGeorge Bundy, Ford Foundation, to Rosel Hyde, Chairman, Federal Communications Commission (Aug. 1, 1966), *reprinted in* DOCUMENTS OF AMERICAN BROADCASTING 570 (F. Kahn ed. 1972).

180. CARNEGIE COMM'N ON EDUCATIONAL TELEVISION, PUBLIC TELEVISION: A PROGRAM FOR ACTION (1967), *portions reprinted in* DOCUMENTS OF AMERICAN BROADCASTING, *supra* note 179, at 576.

181. For a discussion of the role of public television before and during the Watergate hearings, see E. BARNOUW, TUBE OF PLENTY 454-55 (1975); *see also* C. STERLING & J. KITTROSS, STAY TUNED 457 (1978).

182. CBS Cable, offered generally as a basic (non-pay) cable service, serves three million homes on over 250 cable systems. Other cultural services, such as Bravo Pay Cable Service, which currently serves 120,000 homes, are offered on a pay basis. *See* CABLEVISION, Nov. 23, 1981, at 191.

183. S. MAHONY, N. DeMARTINO & R. STENGEL, KEEPING PACE WITH THE NEW TELEVISION (1980), reported on the status of pay cable ventures in the cultural sector and advocated a new, nonprofit corporation to provide a pay cable network independent of public television to program for "an elite with specialized tastes." *Id.* at 45. PBS rejected the recommendation to stay out of pay cable and has proposed a public subscriber network to provide additional revenues for over-the-air public television. *See* TELEVISION/RADIO AGE, Feb. 9, 1981, at 49. *See generally* Ginsburg, Book Review, 33 FED. COM. L.J. 309 (1981).

sees. Reserving frequencies, including valuable VHF frequencies, for noncommercial activity distorts the marketplace and deprives noncommercial operators of even the indirect reverberations of consumer demand that advertisers provide.[184] Despite efforts by public television to broaden its circle of decisionmakers, programming choices remain an insulated judgment call by those in power.

Yet as public broadcasters begin to look more like commercial operators, aiming programming at wider audiences and adding limited advertising,[185] new problems emerge. Why should a commercial enterprise be denied a chance to compete for their frequencies? One solution would be to end protection for noncommercial licensing and expose existing licenses, or at least unclaimed channels reserved for noncommercial broadcasting, to commercial licensure by lottery, auction, or traditional comparative hearing.

A differing viewpoint, however, assumes that noncommercial television will remain viable. The reservation of certain broadcast frequencies reflects a social value beyond market efficiency. Economists have long recognized the existence of "merit goods," which society values although the marketplace cannot explain or justify their retention.[186] Reservation of valuable real estate for public parks, public support for museums and libraries, the special tax treatment accorded religious and eleemosynary institutions, and the system of public education are all services shielded, to a greater or lesser extent, from marketplace forces. So, too, public television, in spite of the deficiencies in its method of program selection, has been a merit good.

Having distorted the market at the outset by reserving a number of spectrum exclusivities for broadcasting, the Commission can make some provision for programs that might not find their way on the air through market mechanisms. The Commission's long-standing policy of encouraging locally originated programming illustrates this point.[187]

---

184. *See supra* notes 107-11 and accompanying text.
185. Under the Omnibus Budget Reconciliation Act, Pub. L. No. 97-35, § 1232(b), 95 Stat. 357, 732 (1981), Congress created the Temporary Commission on Alternative Financing for Public Telecommunications (TCAF) with a mandate to study the options for new revenue sources for public radio and television. The TCAF has since reported to Congress on new financing schemes, although it did not evaluate spectrum fees. TCAF, ALTERNATIVE FINANCING OPTIONS FOR PUBLIC BROADCASTING (1982). The TCAF has already authorized an advertising experiment on ten public television stations. FCC Public Notice, Mimeo No. 2746 (Mar. 11, 1982); *see* BROADCASTING, July 19, 1982, at 68.
186. *See* B. OWEN, J. BEEBE & W. MANNING, JR., *supra* note 14, at 158-59; Breimer, *supra* note 107, at 88-92.
187. *See, e.g.,* En Banc Programming Inquiry, 44 F.C.C. 2303 (1960):
   Under [§ 307(b) of the Communications Act] the Commission has consistently licensed stations with the end objective of either providing new or additional programming ser-

A Marketplace Approach to Broadcast Regulation **253**

The desire to weave the nation's broadcasting system into a community's infrastructure may not reflect the desires of a majority of the broadcast audience, but Congress may nonetheless find it desirable to preserve local service. This judgment, after all, undergirded the 1952 television allocation plan.[188] Unlike satellite-distributed cable or network broadcast service, only a local station can distribute a local program over the air. Locally oriented news, public affairs, and cultural programs will not be provided by the national arts or news channels, but they could be part of a public television or radio service.

Similarly, experimental programming may take longer to develop an audience than the marketplace usually permits, but it can be an enduring objective of public television. One can seriously question whether pay cable cultural and arts channels will support offbeat productions. Pay cable networks, whether public television's or one of the commercial enterprise's, are likely to skim the most popular cultural programs, leaving little support for emerging but less marketable talent.

Public television can also carry a pilot or ongoing basis age-specific programming that does not find sufficient support in the marketplace. Programming for children is a prime candidate. An advertiser-supported system may be unable to meet the demand for children's programs because of the limited range of advertisers wishing to sponsor these programs.[189] Although cable television provides a way for parents to subscribe to programs for children, this service will not be of-

---

vice *to* a community, area or state, or of providing a new or additional "outlet" for broadcasting *from* a community, area, or state. Implicit in the former alternative is increased radio reception; implicit in the latter alternative is increased radio transmission and, in this connection, appropriate attention to local live programming is required. *Id.* at 2311. The ascertainment exercise also directed the broadcaster to determine local problems and describe programs designed to meet those problems. *See supra* notes 44-47 and accompanying text. One Commissioner has defined localism "as the maintenance of a studio for the production of local news and public affairs." Amaturo Group, Inc., 74 F.C.C.2d 299, 315 (1979) (Ferris, Chmn., concurring). Another approach to the "localism" concept starts from the § 307(b) mandate of a "fair, efficient, and equitable distribution" of stations. Localism under this approach relates not to program origination but to local service. *See* Comment, *The Promising Future of Direct Broadcast Satellites in America: Truth or Consequences?*, 33 FED. COM. L.J. 221, 222-32 (1981).

188. *See supra* notes 76-80 and accompanying text. Curiously, though the Commission touts localism in its decisions, it has never required any fixed percentage of local programming despite the suitability of over-the-air television to distribute local programs. *See* Community Television of S. Cal., 72 F.C.C.2d 349 (1979) (noncommercial licensee has wide discretion in fulfilling obligations to serve community needs; complaint that station spent disproportionate amount of funds on nonlocal programming provided no basis for renewal hearing); WPIX, Inc., 68 F.C.C.2d 381, 402-03 (1978) (renewal challenge denied; premise that "local needs can be met only through programming produced by a local station has not only been rejected by the Commission . . . but it also lacks presumptive validity").

189. OFFICE OF PLANS AND POLICY, *supra* note 47, at 41-44.

254 Texas Law Review   Vol. 60:207, 1982

fered in many communities. For some time to come, some child audiences will remain without access to specialized cable services. Public television's mission could be to provide programming for these viewers. A need also may exist for specialized programs for the elderly, who may be neither economically attractive to advertisers nor wealthy enough to generate a significant quantity of subscription programs for their special needs and interests.

Public television can also become a forum for individual access denied by commercial outlets.[190] Because public broadcasters are government funded, it is more likely that their denial of access to individuals would constitute state action for first amendment purposes.[191] The decision of a government-funded broadcaster to deny access would trigger strict scrutiny under the speech clause.[192]

---

190. In CBS v. Democratic Nat'l Comm., 412 U.S. 94 (1973), the Supreme Court upheld the Commission's rejection of a claim that individual groups have a right to purchase advertising time to comment on public issues. The concept of an affirmative right of access in broadcasting was set forth in Barron, *Access to the Press—A New First Amendment Right*, 80 HARV. L. REV. 1641 (1967); *see also* Rosenbloom v. Metromedia, Inc., 403 U.S. 29, 47 n.15 (1971).

191. In CBS v. Democratic Nat'l Comm., 412 U.S. 94 (1973), Justice Douglas suggested in a concurring opinion that editorial activities by public broadcast stations did constitute state action. Justice Douglas also stated that a denial of access in such an instance would constitute an abridgment under the first amendment:

> If these cases involved [the Corporation for Public Broadcasting], we would have a situation comparable to that in which the United States owns and manages a prestigious newspaper like the New York Times, Washington Post, or Sacramento Bee. . . . [T]he programs tendered by the respondents in the present cases could not then be turned down.

Id. at 149-50 (Douglas, J., concurring). Justice Douglas' views at least suggest that there would be a smaller burden on proponents of an access scheme to public television than required under *CBS v. Democratic National Comm*. Public broadcasters, insofar as they originate programming, would not necessarily lose first amendment protection. But to the extent that programming decisions by a public broadcaster are state action, the licensee would be bound to disseminate all views within the limits of its time schedule, as Justice Douglas stated. *Id*. at 150. However, *CBS* held only that the 1934 Act and the first amendment do not require broadcasters to accept paid editorial advertisements. It did not hold that carrying the advertisements, in particular on public stations, violated the first amendment. *But see* FCC v. Midwest Video Corp., 440 U.S. 689 (1979) (Communications Act, which prohibits treating broadcasters as "common carriers," 47 U.S.C. § 153(h) (1976), foreclosed imposition of access requirements amounting to common carrier obligations upon licensees).

192. It is beyond the scope of this Article to determine whether there is an individual right of access over public channels, but the exercise of this right doubtless would increase the number of speakers on the air. Yet it does not offend the first amendment rights of broadcasters as much as in the commercial sector, since the government funds the broadcasters in question. Creation of a limited right of access during certain hours on television for individual speakers as well as documentary and entertainment program producers would bring the public forum, long a tradition in American society, to the medium of broadcasting, which has functioned in many ways as the modern equivalent of the soap box in the town square.

In 1979, the Commission rejected a proposal for an access alternative to fairness that, if undertaken by licensees, would be deemed presumptive compliance with the fairness doctrine. The Handling of Public Issues Under the Fairness Doctrine and the Public Interest Standards of the Communications Act, 74 F.C.C.2d 163 (1979). The Commission based its decision on its experience with access programs, particularly the fact that the issues raised in access experiments fre-

A Marketplace Approach to Broadcast Regulation **255**

This Article cannot discuss all the arguments for and against maintenance of public television. This is properly a question for Congress, which passed the Public Broadcasting Act of 1967 without ensuring the system's financial security, because it involves broader questions about public financing.[193] Maintenance of public television and radio through revenues from a spectrum fee might be part of an overall approach to the spectrum used for broadcasting. Like the national park concessionaire whose fee supports nonprofit park activities, the broadcaster would find his transmission fee used to fund worthwhile activities on adjacent channels.

It may seem somewhat incongruous to require broadcasters to finance a government-sanctioned competitor. Yet, in creating public television stations in the first instance, the government has always used tax revenues, including those from commercial broadcasters, to support public broadcasting. A bolstered public broadcast system operating within a marketplace approach would inject a "best use" strategy for most frequencies while still accommodating the nonmarket considerations that gave rise to the reservation of spectrum initially. Commercial broadcasters would be absolutely free to pursue commercial objectives without lingering trusteeship obligations. At the same time, noncommercial broadcasters would have a clear mandate to provide services as alternatives to, not duplicates of, the programming available over commercial channels.

C. Level III: Deregulation of Broadcasting: No Spectrum Fee

The failure of the spectrum fee concept to generate substantial support over the years may in large measure be due to the inertia of both the regulators and the regulated. From the inception of federal regulation, broadcasters have received their grants without direct fee. The suggestion of imposing a fee for something that has always been a free and renewable resource—an exclusivity granted by the government—generates considerable opposition. And the aggregate cost of the trusteeship form of regulation may be less than the fee charged. Given the choice, many broadcasters might prefer the security of current regulation to true competition and a charge for their frequency exclusivity.

---

quently fail to concern important public matters. *Id.* at 172-78. Although access in terms of free speech opportunities may be sometimes more valuable in theory than in practice, it offers a safety valve for our proposed broadcasting scheme. Furthermore, it provides a logical alternative to the representative form of broadcasting embodied in the trusteeship approach.

193. *See generally* J. BUCHANAN, THE PUBLIC FINANCES 465 (1970); A. SHARP & B. SLIGER, PUBLIC FINANCE 55 (1970).

Moreover, not all broadcast facilities are profitable.[194] Those who have recently turned the corner would probably find it unfair for the government to charge them for an exclusivity that became valuable only through their persistent efforts. These broadcasters undoubtedly would argue that substantial deregulation of commercial broadcasting should occur without a fee.

The most significant point about fees and public television, in economic terms, is that there should be no quid pro quo for adoption of a marketplace approach. Free resale and the elimination of content and business restrictions do not depend for their validity or effectiveness on the existence of a fee or of a protected public broadcasting system. Congress should separate the fate of the marketplace approach to broadcast regulation from questions of the collection of spectrum fees or the maintenance of public broadcasting. Congressional consideration of the latter notions should not forestall a transition to a marketplace approach.

V. Conclusion

The Communications Act provides the Commission with discretion to translate consumer wants into the programming decisions of broadcasters by invoking marketplace principles. The need for a fresh approach to broadcasting, now spurred by competitive challenges from cable and other video providers, is long overdue. This new approach concludes that broadcasters best serve the public by responding to market forces rather than governmental directives. It restores the broadcasting business to the unregulated status of American enterprise generally. In doing so, it also recognizes that content regulation of commercial radio and television is fundamentally at odds with the first amendment status of broadcasting.

The time has come for Congress and the Commission to recognize the role of broadcasting within overall spectrum usage and adopt a more rational approach to broadcast regulation. One possible, though inessential, approach would be to charge for the exclusivity provided by a government license. Congress must also clarify the purpose of the noncommercial licensing function. Congress should either ratify the mission of public broadcasting in the overall scheme for the reserved broadcast spectrum or instruct the Commission to return its frequencies for reassignment to face the rigors of the marketplace. The end result

---

194. *See, e.g.,* 1 NETWORK INQUIRY SPECIAL STAFF, *supra* note 9, at 77. In 1978, 93% of VHF affiliates and 83% of UHF affiliates were profitable; among independents, 80% of VHFs and 60% of UHFs were profitable. *Id.*

A Marketplace Approach to Broadcast Regulation **257**

should be a commercial broadcasting system in which market forces rather than trustee duties govern as far as possible the provision of broadcast serviee to the American people.

Part III
Content Standards

[9]

You Can't Say "God" on the Radio: Freedom of Expression, Religious Advertising and the Broadcast Media after *Murphy v Ireland*

Andrew Geddis

Cases: *Otto-Preminger Institute v Austria* (A/295-A) (1995) 19 E.H.R.R. 34 (ECHR)
             Murphy v Ireland (44179/98) (2004) 38 E.H.R.R. 13 (ECHR)
             Handyside v United Kingdom (A/24) (1979-80) 1 E.H.R.R. 737 (ECHR)
             VgT Verein gegen Tierfabriken v Switzerland (24699/94) (2002) 34 E.H.R.R. 4 (ECHR)
Legislation: European Convention on Human Rights 1950 Art.10
                       Radio and Television Act 1988 (Ireland) s.10(3)
Subject: HUMAN RIGHTS. Other related subjects: Arts and culture. Media and entertainment
Keywords: Advertisements; Christianity; Freedom of expression; Radio; Television

Abstract: Analyses the European Court of Human Rights' reasons for distinguishing between religious expression and political expression by comparing the European Court's judgments in *Murphy v Ireland* (44179/98) and *VgT Verein gegen Tierfabriken v Switzerland* (24699/94) involving two attempts to gain access to the broadcast media in order to communicate particular beliefs. Criticises as unsustainable the argument that the particular, culturally specific risk of harm arising from religious expression warrants giving contracting states a wider margin of appreciation when regulating this form of speech. Suggests that the rulings have effectively demeaned the value of religious expression in relation to political expression and questions the implied distrust of state authorities' capacity to regulate public political expression in an honest way.

*181 This article[1] examines the European Court of Human Rights' decision in *Murphy v Ireland*, and compares the outcome in this case with that reached in its earlier judgment in *Vgt Verein gegen Tierfabriken v Switzerland*. It uses these twin judgments as a basis for examining the reasons given by the European Court for treating religious expression in a different manner to political expression. It will be argued that the European Court's claim that the particular, culturally-specific risk of harm arising from religious expression justifies its decision to accord contracting states a wider margin of appreciation when regulating this type of speech cannot be sustained. Instead, the European Court's approach reflects a combination of the downgrading of the value of religious expression vis-à-vis political expression; as well as a suspicion of the motives of the regulating authorities within contracting states when it comes to imposing controls on public, political expression.

People – not all people, to be sure, but certainly many people – care deeply about the particular political beliefs that they happen to hold. Equally, people – again, by no means all people, but certainly many people – care deeply about the particular religious beliefs that they happen to hold. In both cases, those holding a belief which they care deeply about may

---

[1]   My thanks to Rex Ahdar for his comments.

feel compelled publicly to espouse that belief, with the aim of encouraging others to embrace it, and perhaps thereafter follow some particular course of action as a result of adopting the belief. In an attempt to achieve this end, those who hold a belief that they care deeply about may wish to engage a variety of means to communicate this belief to others, including utilising any electronic broadcast media a particular country may happen to possess. However, when they attempt to gain access to the broadcast media, they may find that some regulatory action by the state prevents them from doing so. Faced with such an impediment, they may then allege that there has been a breach of their individual right to communicate with others. Where such a claim is advanced, a basic question must be addressed: in determining whether some person's rights have been infringed through denying them the opportunity to access the broadcast media to espouse their belief, should *182 it make a difference whether the belief at issue is "political" or "religious" in nature?

At first sight it might appear that this question ought to be answered in the negative. From the point of view of the person wishing to communicate their particular belief, the same sort of personal autonomy interests are engaged; and so if some individual right to espouse one's belief via the broadcast media is going to be recognised, then prima facie that right ought to exist irrespective of the basic character of the belief at issue. Yet when applying the right to free expression under Art.10 of the European Convention on Human Rights, the European Court of Human Rights has repeatedly distinguished between expression which relates to issues of a religious (or "moral") nature, and expression which has a political (or "public interest")[2] component, through according the signatories to the Convention a greater "margin of appreciation" when they regulate the former type of expression, as compared with the latter.[3] Simply put, the European Court has allowed the contracting states to place restrictions on religious expression which it would not have permitted had the relevant expression been deemed political in character. And with the recent decision in *Murphy v Ireland*,[4] the European Court has now extended this distinction into the realm of broadcast advertising, by holding that a contracting state is to be accorded a wider margin of appreciation when it chooses to ban all religious advertising from the broadcast media than it possesses when choosing to ban all political advertising from the broadcast media.

This article examines the European Court of Human Rights' decision in Murphy, and compares the outcome in this case with that reached in its earlier judgment in *Vgt Verein gegen Tierfabriken v Switzerland*.[5] It uses these twin judgments as a basis for examining the

---

[2]   The European Court has made it clear that it regards expression about matters of "public interest" as encompassing far more than party political issues. See, e.g. *Thorgeirson v Iceland* (1992) 14 E.H.R.R. 843 at [63]; *Hertel v Switzerland* (1998) 28 E.H.R.R. 534 at [46]. Compare with *Tanner v Estonia* (App. No.41205/98, judgment of February 6, 2001).

[3]   See *Handyside v United Kingdom* (1976) 1 E.H.R.R. 737 at [49]; *Lingens v Austria* (1986) 8 E.H.R.R. 407 at [41]-[42]; *Kokkinakis v Greece* (1993) 17 E.H.R.R. 397 at [48]. Also compare *Otto Preminger Institute v Austria* (1994) 19 E.H.R.R. 34 with *Jersild v Denmark* (1994) 19 E.H.R.R. 1; and *Wingrove v United Kingdom* (1997) 24 E.H.R.R. 1 with *Goodwin v United Kingdom* (1996) 22 E.H.R.R. 123. See generally D. Feldman, Civil Liberties and Human Rights in England and Wales (Oxford University Press, 2002), pp.754-755, 906-907; Paul Mahoney, "Universality versus subsidiarity in the Strasbourg case law on free speech: explaining some recent judgments" [1997] E.H.R.L.R. 364.

[4]   App. No.44179/98, judgment of July 10, 2003.

[5]   App. No.24699/94, judgment of June 29, 2001.

reasons given by the Court for treating religious expression in a different manner to political expression. It will be argued that the Court's claim that the particular, culturally-specific risk of harm arising from religious expression justifies its decision to accord contracting states a wider margin of appreciation when regulating this type of speech cannot be sustained. Instead, the European Court's approach reflects a combination of the downgrading of the value of religious expression vis-à-vis political expression; as well as a suspicion of the motives of the regulating authorities within contracting states when it comes to imposing controls on public, political expression.

*183 An analysis of the Murphy decision

The Murphy case involved a Christian pastor's placement of an advertisement on a local radio station to coincide with Easter week, which asked listeners: "What think ye of Christ? Would you, like Peter, only say that he is the son of the living God? Have you ever exposed yourself to the historical facts about Christ?" The advertisement then invited the curious to attend a public screening of a video "on the evidence of the resurrection". The radio station accepted the advertisement for broadcast, but Ireland's Independent Radio and Television Commission (IRTC) subsequently barred its transmission on the grounds that it was directed towards a "religious end", and therefore breached s.10(3) of Ireland's Radio and Television Act 1988.[6] An application to have the High Court declare either that this particular decision by the IRTC was unlawful, or that s.10(3) was itself invalid because it imposed an unreasonable limit on the right to communicate guaranteed by the Irish Constitution,[7] proved to be unsuccessful. [8]Ireland's Supreme Court subsequently refused to overturn the High Court's decision,[9] and having exhausted all domestic remedies, the applicant turned to Strasbourg. In his submission to the European Court, the applicant alleged that the s.10(3) blanket ban on broadcast advertising "which is directly towards any religious end" infringed his rights under both Arts 9 and 10 ECHR.

The applicant might have had cause for optimism given the European Court's 2001 ruling in the Vgt Tierfabriken case.[10] This involved a complaint by a Swiss animal rights group that a law preventing the screening of any religious and political advertising on Swiss national television[11] – which inter alia blocked the group's proposed advertisement drawing attention to the conditions under which pigs are raised, and urging viewers to "eat less meat" – unjustifiably breached their rights under Art.10 ECHR. The European Court upheld the group's claim, ruling that the Swiss Government had failed to show that the infringement of the group's right to freedom of expression was "necessary in a democratic society". While accepting

---

[6]   The relevant section, which applies to all independent radio and television broadcasters, reads "No advertisement shall be broadcast which is directly towards any religious or political end or which has any relation to an industrial dispute". The same prohibition applies to RTE, the national radio and television broadcaster, through the Broadcasting Authority Act 1960, s.20(4).

[7]   Constitution, Arts 40, 44.

[8]   [1995] No.317 J.R. (April 25, 1997).

[9]   [1999] 1 I.R. 12.

[10]   See n.5 above.

[11]   Bundesgesetz über Radio und Fernhesen, s.18.

that it "cannot exclude that a prohibition of 'political advertising' may be compatible with the requirements of Article 10 of the Convention in certain situations",[12] and that some form of regulation of broadcast political advertising could be justified in order to prevent wealthy interests from "obtain[ing] competitive advantages in areas of commercial advertising",[13] the Court found that the Swiss Government had not proven that the applicant group posed *184 any such danger.[14] Therefore, the imposition of a blanket ban on broadcasting political advertising was deemed to be in breach of Art.10, as it was a disproportionate response to any legitimate aim on the Swiss Government's part. Equally, it might appear to follow, Ireland's prohibition on transmitting all religious advertising–including the applicant's message in the Murphy case – also constitutes a disproportionate response to any concerns raised by the public expression of religious belief in that country. After all, the message at issue in Murphy would seem to be even more innocuous in its content than that in the Vgt Tierfabriken case, being purely informational in nature, and without the component of express advocacy to be found in the advertisement at issue in the latter case.

However, the European Court proved to be of a rather different mind. It distinguished the expression at issue in Murphy from the expression in Vgt Tierfabriken on the basis that the former dealt with matters of "intimate personal convictions within the sphere of morals or ... religion",[15] as opposed to the "matter of public interest" raised by the latter.[16] In keeping with its previous rulings with respect to expression that touches on matters of religion or morals,[17] the European Court was prepared to accord Ireland a wider margin of appreciation in choosing how to deal with the issue of religious advertising on the broadcast media than had been recognised on the part of Switzerland in respect of regulating political broadcast advertising. It then followed that while the European Court retained a final say on whether the applicant's treatment under Irish law was in breach of the Convention,[18] the Irish Government's task in defending the impugned provision was made substantially less difficult by the European Court's decision to grant it a wide latitude when addressing the issue.

Turning to consider the justifiability of the blanket ban imposed by s.10(3), the European Court stated that the question to be answered was "whether a prohibition of a certain type (advertising) of expression (religious) through a particular means (the broadcast media) can be justifiably prohibited in the particular case".[19] Although the prohibition in s.10(3) did prima

---

[12] Vgt Tierfabriken, n.5 above, at [75].

[13] ibid. at [73]. The Swiss Government did not try and claim that the fact that political advertisements might prove provocative or disagreeable to viewers provided a reason for banning them from television screens; ibid. at [76]. However, even if this argument had been advanced, it seems unlikely that the European Court would have accepted it could justify the ban in question; see *Handyside v United Kingdom* (1976) 1 E.H.R.R. 737 at [48].

[14] Vgt Tierfabriken, n.5 above, at [75]

[15] Murphy, n.4 above, at [67].

[16] ibid.

[17] See n.3 above. See also *Müller v Switzerland* (1991) 13 E.H.R.R. 212; *United Christian Broadcasters Ltd v United Kingdom* (App.No.44802/98), judgment of November 7, 2000.

[18] Murphy, n.4 above, at [68]. See also *Open Door and Dublin Well Woman v Ireland* (1992) 15 E.H.R.R. 244 at [68].

[19] Murphy, n.4 above, at [71]

facie infringe the applicant's expressive rights under Art.10 ECHR,[20] the Irish Government claimed that this infringement could be justified under Art.10(2), as being necessary to "ensure respect for the religious doctrines and beliefs of others so that the aims of the impugned provision were public order and safety together with the protection of the rights and freedoms of others".[21] As a brief aside, while the European Court accepted that this object formed a legitimate aim for *185 the purposes of Art.10(2),[22] it is a little unclear just what "rights and freedoms of others" needed protecting in this case. At most, the individual interest at issue would seem to amount to not becoming disturbed or upset through exposure to the public espousal of a religious belief which conflicts with yours. Quite why this particular interest ought to be raised to the status of a "right" deserving of state protection is not adequately spelt out by the European Court: is it a part of the right to religious freedom under Art.9 ECHR (as the Otto Preminger Institute case seems to suggest[23]); or does it have some separate, more free-floating basis?[24]

That being said, the European Court proceeded to evaluate whether the Irish Government's complete ban on religious advertising formed a proportionate response to its (accepted) legitimate aim of protecting the rights and freedoms of other religious believers. In assessing this question, and in keeping with its conclusion that Ireland enjoyed a wide margin of appreciation in respect of this issue, the European Court gave a great deal of weight to the conclusions expressed by Ireland's Minister for Arts, Heritage, Gaeltacht and the Islands in a parliamentary debate on whether to remove the legislative ban–namely, that Ireland's particular history and current religious sensitivities required that it be kept in place.[25] This was also the conclusion reached in the judgments of Ireland's domestic courts on the issue.[26] The European Court then noted that the ban went no further than was necessary to serve the concerns noted by Ireland's national authorities; in that it only covered advertising (and so the broadcast of religious expression in the form of ordinary programming was still permitted), and was restricted to the broadcast media (enabling the applicant to use other forums to advertise the screening of the video).[27]

Finally, the European Court rejected the applicant's contention that even if some limited form of restrictions on broadcast religious advertising could be justified by these relevant reasons, they still were insufficient to support Ireland's complete ban on such communications. Ireland, the European Court held, was entitled to decide that "the exclusion of all religious groupings from broadcasting advertisements generates less discomfort than any filtering

---

[20]   . ibid. at [61]. The applicant also alleged an infringement of his right to manifest his religion under Art.9(1) ECHR. However, the European Court chose to treat this claim as basically synonymous with his allegation of a breach of Art.10 ECHR, and so analysed the issue in terms of that article alone. See ibid. at [60].

[21]   ibid. at [63].

[22]   ibid. at [64], citing Otto Preminger Institute, n.3 above, at [47]. See also United Christian Broadcasters Ltd, n.17 above.

[23]   Otto Preminger Institute, ibid. at [20]-[21].

[24]   See Carolyn Evans, Freedom of Religion Under the European Convention on Human Rights (Oxford University Press, 2001), pp.160-164

[25]   Murphy, n.4 above, at [73]. The Minister's comments were laid out at length at [27]-[28].

[26]   ibid. at [73]. See nn.8-9 above.

[27]   ibid. at [74].

of the amount and content of such expression by such groupings"[28] Such a blanket ban
also maintained a "level playing field" amongst differing religious groups,[29] and kept the
national and independent broadcasters on an equal footing.[30] Therefore, in light of the lack
of consistent practice with respect to this issue amongst the various contracting states,[31] and
given the margin of appreciation accorded to Ireland in respect of the matter, the European
Court concluded that Ireland *186 had demonstrated the existence of "relevant and sufficient
reasons" that justified the interference with the applicant's Art.10 rights.[32]

The differing application of the "proportionality" test in the Murphy and Vgt Tierfabriken decisions

I shall argue in more detail below that the key to the contrasting outcome in the Murphy and
Vgt Tierfabriken cases lies in the differing margin of appreciation accorded by the European
Court to the decisions of the Irish and Swiss Governments as to how each form of expression
should be regulated. This claim can be substantiated by a brief analysis of the European
Court's disparate treatment of the concrete reasons given by the two Governments to justify
the imposition of a blanket ban in each case. Both Governments sought to defend their
respective bans as a "proportionate" response to some legitimate aim. In Murphy, as has been
noted, the European Court found the fact that the Irish Government only chose to bar religious
advertising on the broadcast media, therefore allowing alternative means of communications
to still be used by the applicant, was evidence that the ban did constitute a proportionate
response to the pressing and legitimate aim of protecting the rights of others.[33] However,
in Vgt Tierfabriken, the fact that Switzerland only chose to bar political advertising on its
national television channel was said to be evidence that the purpose of the ban – preventing
powerful and wealthy social interests from dominating political discourse – was "not of a
particularly pressing nature",[34] while the availability of alternative, less widely accessible
means of communications was considered to be irrelevant in light of the applicant's desire to
put its message before the entire Swiss public.[35]

By the same token, the European Court reached different conclusions with respect to similar
arguments when assessing whether "sufficient" reasons had been given by each Government
to justify the blanket nature of the bans in question. In the Murphy case, the European
Court accepted that the Irish Government's desire to protect the "principle of neutrality in
the broadcast media" – through not distinguishing between the content of different religious
advertisements, and maintaining a "level playing field" between different religious groups

---

28   ibid. at [77].
29   ibid. at [78]. See also United Christian Broadcasters, n.17 above.
30   ibid. at [79]. The Irish Government had expressed concern that if even limited broadcast religious
advertising were allowed, RTE would be required to accept all such advertising, whilst the country's
private stations would remain free to reject it for commercial reasons.
31   ibid. at [81].
32   ibid. at [82].
33   ibid. at [74].
34   Vgt Tierfabriken, n.5 above, at [74].
35   ibid. at [77].

– could justify the imposition of a complete prohibition on all religious advertising.[36] Yet the European Court ruled in Vgt Tierfabriken that the Swiss Government's desire to prevent powerful financial groups from endangering the equality of opportunity between different forces of society was not a sufficient reason to completely ban all political advertising on the broadcast media, given that the individual applicant posed no such threat of dominating the airwaves.[37] Equally, the practical difficulty in drawing up rules to regulate the use of the broadcast media by those wishing to air political advertisements was brushed off by the European Court, as "[i]ts task is to determine whether the Contracting States have achieved the result called for by the Convention. Various possibilities are *187 conceivable as regards the organisation of broadcasting television commercials ..."[38] And finally, the lack of any clear consensus between contracting states on how to regulate religious advertising–accepted as a justification for Ireland's decision to ban all such broadcast advertising–also exists in relation to political advertising. Numerous European countries, Ireland included,[39] prohibit the broadcast of any advertisement that has a political purpose.[40] Yet the European Court did not even discuss this pluralism of approaches in the Vgt Tierfabriken case, whereas the lack of a "uniform conception of the requirements of the protection of the rights of others" in relation to religious advertising was considered relevant to the justifiability of the Irish Government's decision in the Murphy case.[41]

The point of the foregoing analysis is simply this: in the Murphy and Vgt Tierfabriken cases, the European Court treats in diametrically opposite ways the quite similar arguments put forward by the two Governments as justifying the particular, comprehensive bans on broadcasting the expression in question. The only explanation for this difference in outcome – aside from the rather unpalatable idea that there has been a flat inconsistency in the European Court's treatment of what are actually "like" cases – must lie in the fact that the European Court accorded the Irish Government a wider margin of appreciation than Switzerland when deciding how to regulate the particular expression at issue. Because of the application of this different margin, Ireland remained free to reach the conclusions it did as to the necessity of certain regulatory measures with respect to the broadcast of religious advertising; conclusions that the Swiss Government was not entitled to reach under Art.10 with respect to the broadcast of political advertising. Therefore, the core question that emerges from these two cases is as follows: why does the European Court accord a contracting state a different margin of appreciation when the expression being regulated is religious in nature, as opposed to political?

---

[36] Murphy, n.4 above, at [76]-[78].

[37] See n.5 above at [75].

[38] ibid. at [78].

[39] See n.6 above.

[40] See, e.g. the UK's recently enacted Communications Act 2003, s.309(3). For a comment on the compatibility of this measure with Art.10 ECHR, see A. Geddis, "If Thy Right Eye Offend Thee, Pluck It Out: R. v BBC Ex p. Prolife Alliance" (2003) 66 M.L.R. 885.

[41] Murphy, n.4 above, at [81].

Why such a malleable margin of appreciation?

As noted in the introduction to the article, any difference in the margin of appreciation accorded to contracting states when it comes to regulating religious (as opposed to political) expression cannot sensibly be based upon drawing a distinction between the autonomy interests of those wishing to speak. Both political and religious expression can be said to stem from "core" human values; and as such, each are equally valuable from the point of view of the individual, autonomy-based interests of the speaker.[42] However, the European Court accounts for the different margin of appreciation accorded to each type of expression on the basis that religious speech poses a particular risk of offending or disturbing the personal beliefs of other members of a given community, a risk which the authorities in that state are in the best position to assess *188 given their superior understanding of the circumstances within that society.[43] As Paul Mahoney puts it; "in the vast sphere of activity covered by speech it is inevitable that, because of varying local cultures and traditions, different communities will choose different approaches, so that a form of expression that is restricted in some countries may well be permitted in others".[44] The accordance of a wider margin of appreciation when it comes to regulating religious speech is thus justified by the European Court on process-based, institutional competency grounds: the potential harm that religious expression may cause within a society, combined with the particular, culturally specific nature of that potential harm, means that the government of each contracting state has a comparative advantage over the European Court when it comes to deciding how best to regulate religious expression.

However, this kind of analysis appears equally applicable to political expression. It is not self-evidently true that speech about religious matters, as compared with political expression, always poses more of a risk of causing "harm",[45] whether in the sense of seriously offending the "deepest feelings and convictions" of others within the context of a particular community,[46] or otherwise. Indeed, deciding how harmful some given political expression might be calls for just the kind of contingent, situation-sensitive judgment that national authorities apparently are best placed to deliver, "by reason of their direct and continuous contact with the vital forces of their countries".[47] Nevertheless, while the European Court accepted in the Handyside case that political expression can, as a matter of fact, be offensive or disturbing

---

[42]   As opposed to, for instance, commercial advertising. See C. Edwin Baker, Human Liberty and Freedom of Speech (Oxford University Press, 1989).

[43]   Wingrove, n.3 above, at [58]; Murphy, n.4 above, at [67].

[44]   Mahoney, n.3 above, at 369. See also P. Mahoney, "Marvellous Richness of Diversity or Invidious Cultural Relativism?" (1998) 19 Human Rights Law Journal 1 at 3.

[45]   It may be that the European Court believes, as Ovey and White put it: "History--and, sadly, very recent history at that--shows that differences in religious belief are a potent source of conflict and bloodshed", C. Ovey and R. White, European Convention on Human Rights (Oxford University Press, 2002), p.274. My point is that substituting the word "political" for "religious" in this sentence does not appreciably alter its truth. For a discussion of this issue compare W. Marshall, "The Other Side of Religion" (1993) 44 Hastings Law Journal 843, with M. Schwarzschild, "Religion and Public Debate: Always Oil and Water or Sometimes More Like Rum and Coca-Cola?" (1993) 30 San Diego Law Review 903.

[46]   Wingrove, n.3 above, at [58]; Murphy, n.4 above, at [67].

[47]   Wingrove, ibid. at [58].

to those exposed to it within a particular community,[48] it proceeded to say that the European Court will not accord a state much of a margin when it decides how to respond to this fact.[49] Subsequent judgments have affirmed the European Court's stance: individual state authorities have only the narrowest of room to decide for themselves whether the potential harms that may result from political expression justify the suppression of that speech.[50] Therefore, it would appear that the difference in the European Court's approach to the margin accorded to contracting states when deciding how to regulate the two forms of expression cannot convincingly be explained by reference to the different possible harms that might arise from each. The difference must instead lie in *189 a combination of two further, background rationales which are not consciously articulated by the European Court, but rather serve as unvoiced assumptions that allow it to draw the distinction that it does between political and religious speech.

The first such assumption relates to the different potential benefits the European Court attributes to the two kinds of speech. Political expression is perceived by the European Court as (almost) always contributing towards a net positive outcome for a democratic society as a whole, even if it should happen to offend some members of that society, or threaten some other form of immediate harm, when it is heard/viewed. As the matter is expressed in the Handyside case; "[f]reedom of expression constitutes one of the essential foundations of such a society, one of the basic conditions for its progress and the development of every man".[51] Therefore, the contracting states are placed on a much tighter leash by the European Court when they attempt to block or restrict this type of speech, as the "base-line" presumption is that the overall benefits gained from having such expression in the public domain will outweigh any harm caused, and only in precisely and narrowly justified circumstances can this presumption be overturned.[52] In comparison, religious speech is viewed as producing fewer generally positive outcomes for society as a whole, above and beyond satisfying the interests of those who feel compelled to engage in the expression.[53] Therefore, the individual interests of these speakers legitimately can be traded off against the interests of those who may be offended by the message being communicated, with a far weaker "baseline" presumption operating in favour of allowing such expression.[54] Simply put, because religious expression is

---

[48] Handyside, n.3 above, at [48] ("[Art.10] is applicable not only to 'information' or 'ideas' that are favourably received or regarded as inoffensive or as a matter of indifference, but also those that offend, shock or disturb the State or any sector of the population").

[49] ibid. at [49]-[50].

[50] *Lingens v Austria* (1986) 8 E.H.R.R. 407; *Castells v Spain* (1992) 14 E.H.R.R. 445; Hertel, n.2 above.

[51] Handyside, n.3 above, at [49]. See also A. Mowbray, "The role of the European Court of Human Rights in the Promotion of Democracy" [1999] P.L. 703

[52] Consider, for example, the European Court's preparedness routinely to overturn Turkey's assessment of the risk of violence resulting from public criticism of its treatment of the Kurdish people. See *Incal v Turkey* (1998) 29 E.H.R.R. 449; *Ceylan v Turkey* (1999) 30 E.H.R.R. 73; *Erdogdu and Ince v Turkey* (App.No.25067/94, judgment of July 8, 1999).

[53] *Kokkinakis v Greece* (1993) 17 E.H.R.R. 397 at [31]; *Otto-Preminger Institute v Austria* (1994) 19 E.H.R.R. 34 at [47].

[54] The European Court does allow that there is some presumption in favour of allowing religious expression, on the grounds that such freedom is necessary to protect the general pluralism required for democracy is to flourish, see Kokkinakis, ibid. at [31]; *Manoussakis v Greece* (1997) 23 E.H.R.R. 387.

not thought to generate as great an externalised benefit for society as a whole when compared to political expression, there is less of a "thumb on the scale" when it comes to weighing the value of the speech against the possible harms it may engender.

In taking this position, the European Court treats the right to free expression under the Convention as having the primary purpose of allowing the political discourse which is necessary in any country that aspires to democracy.[55] Thus, political expression enjoys a privileged position due to the public consensus – or, at least, fair compromises amongst differing points of view – that can result from a free, open dialogue on matters of common interest.[56] The flip-side to this privileging of political expression then is that competing social values are discounted accordingly, providing *190 state authorities with less scope to use these values to trump the expressive rights of the speaker. (Hence, the European Court's preparedness to step in and override the Swiss Government's decision to ban all televised political advertising, no matter how smallscale, in order to prevent this medium from being dominated by the wealthy.)[57] Religious expression, by comparison, is viewed by the European Court as being, in Richard Rorty's words, a "conversation stopper".[58] Because it is not well suited to the furtherance of an open public dialogue on how to resolve the public issues facing a society, it is a form of communication which is of reduced value. At the most, such expression serves the private interests of the believer who feels compelled to speak out, or the private interest of anyone who comes to embrace the beliefs in question after hearing the message expressed.[59] While a diversity in private beliefs is considered by the European Court to be a healthy and desirable phenomena in a democratic society, and so these private interests can support some measure of free speech protection, the potential that religious expression has to harm the private interests of others – by upsetting or annoying others of competing belief systems, and possibly resulting in social unrest – means that the expressive rights of a believer may be trumped by these others' interests in the particular circumstances of a given society. (Hence, the European Court's preparedness to accept the Irish Government's decision to ban all broadcast religious advertising, no matter how innocuous and inoffensive, on the grounds that any such messages might cause Irish listeners/viewers to become upset.)

This reasoning on the part of the European Court can be criticised both for reflecting a particular, secular bias; and for failing to take seriously the Court's own claim to be concerned with protecting democracy. To begin with, the distinction drawn by the European Court appears to deny that the discussion of "religious" issues can ever have any bearing upon "political" matters.[60] Hence, at least in so far as it affirms that contracting states may decide to

---

As such, freedom of religious expression only has second order value, in so far as it can promote the first order commitment to democratic values

[55]   A. Meicklejohn, Political Freedom: The Constitutional Powers of the People (Oxford University Press, 1965); see also Mowbray, n.51 above.

[56]   J. Rawls, Political Liberalism (Columbia University Press, New York, 1993); J. Habermas, Between Facts and Norms (MIT Press, Cambridge Mass., 1995).

[57]   See also *Bowman v United Kingdom* (1998) 26 E.H.R.R. 1.

[58]   Richard Rorty, "Religion as Conversation-Stopper" (1994) 3 Common Knowledge 1 at 3.

[59]   See R. Moon, "Liberty, Neutrality, and Inclusion: Religious Freedom Under the Canadian Charter of Rights and Freedoms" (2003) 41 Brandeis Law Journal 563 at 569-570.

[60]   A claim which raises the obvious problem of "line drawing". How, for instance, would the European Court categorise an advertisement that states: "God loves all his children--so tell your elected

bar religious believers from directly accessing their national broadcast facilities, the European Court colludes in the exclusion of religiously inspired claims from a society's public sphere.⁶¹ Secondly, it can be argued that the European Court's approach fails to recognise the importance of tolerating the expression of differing religious viewpoints for a properly functioning democratic society. As Jürgen Habermas has argued recently:

"While religious toleration is basic to a democratic state, in this way religious consciousness itself undergoes a learning process. With the introduction of a right to freedom of religious expression, all religious communities must adopt the constitutional principle of the equal inclusion of everyone. They cannot merely **191* benefit from the toleration of the others, but must themselves face up to the generalized expectation of tolerance, with all the consequences this entails."⁶²

Hence, recognising a right to express publicly one's religious beliefs to others does not merely acknowledge the autonomy interests of the individual believer. Allowing such freedom is rather a part of a generalised message sent by the state to all its citizens – religious believers and otherwise – that they must be prepared to accept within their community even those beliefs and dogmas that they find offensive. The inculcation of such a broad attitude, arguably, is as essential to the flourishing of a democratic ordering as protecting the right to participate in a defined public, political discourse.

The second unvoiced assumption that underlies the European Court's differing approach to the two forms of expression is the Court's understanding of the disparate interests held not by those speaking, but by those national decision-makers who choose what regulations to put on each kind of speech. National regulators will be elected – or, at least, be subject to the control of those who are elected – and will have command of governmental power within the contracting state. This status might give them a personal, position-entrenching reason to try to block out the voices of those who disagree with them, and who may seek to challenge their actions or position. In an effort to achieve this end, national regulators might attempt to impose restrictions on political speech under the guise of somehow protecting the interests of the wider public. And even if some regulatory measure is not consciously intended to be selfserving in this fashion, there is still a risk that national authorities– as those most likely to be the target of political speech–might systematically over-estimate the potential for immediate "harm" resulting from political expression, and under-estimate the long term, net benefits provided by such speech. In light of this temptation to write the rules in their own favour, and recognising the likely bias in any risk-benefit analysis undertaken by national authorities in this field, the European Court ought to be particularly suspicious of a state's attempt to regulate political speech.⁶³ Religious speech, by comparison, is likely to be less immediately connected to the interests of individual regulators – or, at least, is less likely to

---

representative that God wants no more abortions in your country"?

⁶¹ See Stephen L. Carter's criticism of similar claims made in the US context; Stephen L. Carter, *The Culture of Disbelief: How American Law and Politics Trivialize Religious Devotion* (Basic Books, New York, 1993).

⁶² Jürgen Habermas, "Intolerance and Discrimination" (2003) 1 I.J.C.L. 2 at 6.

⁶³ John Hart Ely gives the classic account of this sort of "process based" judicial review, J.H. Ely, *Democracy and Distrust* (Harvard University Press, Cambridge Mass., 1980), Chs 4-6. See also C.A. Gearty, "The European Court of Human Rights and the Protection of Civil Liberties: An Overview" (1993) 52 C.L.J. 89 at 116-117.

be connected with the interests of the individual regulators in a uniform fashion. Therefore, there is less reason for the European Court to be suspicious of any particular balance that the regulator strikes as between the right to speak and the interests of those who may hear the speech. The regulations produced are more likely to be the product of a genuine reading of the situation in the particular society, rather than a self-interested move by the political "ins" designed to keep the political "outs" from challenging their position in power.

Conclusion

The European Court claims that the difference in the margin of appreciation it accords to states when regulating the two forms of expression is simply a matter of the European Court paying proper attention to the contracting states' judgment in those *192 areas where their national authorities have greater expertise. But what is not explained is why the national authorities are seen by the European Court as having "greater expertise" in respect of regulating religious expression, as opposed to political expression. It cannot be because of any difference in the autonomy interests of the speakers in each case. Nor can the difference in the national authorities' expertise convincingly be attributed to the nature or degree of the potential "harm" caused by each kind of speech – even though this is what the European Court uses as its surface justification for the different margin accorded in each case. Instead, it would appear that the European Court is prepared to relax its scrutiny of state regulation of religious speech – at least as compared with political speech – because:

1. The issue is not regarded as being as important, for religious expression is viewed as a less socially valuable form of speech than political expression. The former fails to produce the same kind of externalised benefits for society that occur in respect of the latter, meaning that a state's authorities have much more scope to conclude that the harms caused by some religious speaker outweigh the right of the speaker to espouse his or her beliefs.

2. Any decision that a state's authorities makes in regard to regulating religious expression can be assumed to be a response to a genuine estimation of the harms that may be caused by that speech, at least to a greater degree than is the case in respect of political expression. There is not the same degree of self-interest, or likely bias, involved in regulating the former type of expression as compared with the latter.

Therefore, two rather controversial assumptions lurk beneath the European Court's apparent willingness to defer to national and cultural particularities when reviewing how a contracting state chooses to regulate religious expression. It is the questionable nature of these premises that may account for why the European Court has not been more open about advancing them as reasons for the different margin accorded in respect of each type of expression. The former assumption appears to demean religious values by implying that the very nature of religious expression means it has less to offer society in general than does political expression. In practice, it means that the rights of those opposing cruelty to pigs are to be accorded a higher status under the Convention than those who are seeking to save the souls of men. This ordering draws on a particular, secularised view of the purpose of public discourse, one which has been the subject of some quite sustained criticism.[64] The second assumption implies a basic distrust on the part of the European Court of the capacity of state authorities to regulate honestly the

---

[64]   See, e.g. Moon, n.59 above, at 570-572.

field of political discourse within their own society. It also means that, in practice, a particular national choice with respect to how that society's political discourse will be regulated will only be allowed to stand if the choice accords with how the European Court thinks political discourse should be structured.[65]

---

[65] Bowman, n.57 above. For criticism of this position, see C.A. Gearty, "Democracy and Human Rights in the European Court of Human Rights: A Critical Appraisal" (2000) 51 N.I.L.Q. 381 at 394-395.

[10]

'A Monstrous and Unjustifiable Infringement'?: Political Expression and the Broadcasting Ban on Advocacy Advertising

Andrew Scott*

This paper considers the legality of the broadcasting prohibition on 'advocacy advertising' – the use of advertising space to communicate social, political and moral arguments to a wider public – in the light of the growing jurisprudence on the freedom of political expression. The prohibition is currently found in the Broadcasting Act 1990, and the Government has proposed its reiteration in the forthcoming Communications Bill to fall within the regulatory ambit of OFCOM. The paper begins by introducing and illustrating advocacy advertising and the restrictions upon it. It proceeds to review the relevant jurisprudence on political expression, to analyse the familiar arguments in favour of retention of the prohibition, and to weigh the counter-arguments. The paper concludes that the purported justifications sit ill against existing legal rulings, and evidence a poor understanding of the critical sophistication of the public as a broadcasting audience. It suggests that a continuation of the prohibition would be unlawful.

A notable feature of the British public sphere is the dearth of privately sponsored political representations made through the broadcast media. This absence of 'advocacy advertising' on television and radio can be attributed to a restriction imposed by statute. Ostensibly, the prohibition is designed to prevent the garnering of influence over elected government by affluent interests that might flow from the financing of party-political advertising. It is also said to limit the prospect of a public sphere inundated and overwhelmed by the ideas and values of privileged groups. The continuing value of the measure is currently under review as part of the wider proposal to create a single regulator for the communications sector.[1] The Government envisages that the restriction will be maintained, albeit transferred into the ambit of the new regulator.

At first glance, however, the prohibition sits at odds with the growing respect accorded by the courts to the freedom of political expression. Indeed, it has been described as 'a monstrous and unjustifiable infringement'.[2] Recent decisions – such as that of the Court of Appeal in the *ProLife Alliance* case and that of the European Court of Human Rights (ECtHR) in *VGT* v *Switzerland* – suggest that the measure would be unlikely to withstand a rights-based legal challenge.[3] The

* Norwich Law School, University of East Anglia. I would like to extend my warmest thanks to Michael Harker, Brigid Hadfield, David Mead, Noel Scott and the journal referees who each offered valuable comments on earlier drafts of this paper. Errors and inconsistencies remain my own.

1 DTI/DCMS, *A New Future for Communications* Cm 5010 (2000). A draft Communications Bill was published in May 2002. Moreover, the new body – OFCOM – has already been established in skeleton form by the Office of Communications Act 2002.

2 Professor Eric Barendt, in evidence to the Joint Committee on the Draft Communications Bill, 17 June 2002.

3 The first case involved a decision by the BBC and other terrestrial broadcasters to refuse on grounds of 'taste and decency' to air a party election broadcast recorded by the group. Although in no way sensationalised, the proposed broadcast included footage of dismembered foetuses that might have been expected to be deeply harrowing to a large number of viewers – see: *R*

aim of this paper is to consider further this quandary. The paper proceeds in four parts. First, the phenomenon of advocacy advertising is described, and its political orientation illustrated. Secondly, the restrictions imposed on the broadcasting of advocacy advertising are outlined. In light of these restrictions, recent developments in the jurisprudence concerning parallel limitations on political expression, at both the Strasbourg and domestic levels, are reviewed. The final, most substantial, part of the paper then offers an analysis of the balancing of interests required by this jurisprudence in order to assess the continuing legality of this ban. The paper concludes that aspects of the current prohibition are unsustainable, and that there may be alternative, more justifiable means of securing the remaining objects.

Advocacy advertising in the UK

Advocacy advertising is a form of publicity that evidences a predominantly political intent; political representations made through paid media. It is unusual in that it focuses not on the promotion of specific products, but rather on the advancement of some partisan opinion or social cause. Although certainly a related genre, it is distinct from both public information campaigns and party-political broadcasts: the former because it sets out to convey contentious opinions rather than an educational message,[4] and the latter due to the absence of any immediate association with formal, electoral politics. At its margins, advocacy advertising melds into two further forms of representation. On one hand, 'cause-related marketing' involves private companies in seeking directly to enhance the corporate brand through association with specific social causes.[5] On the other hand, 'electoral advocacy' comprises representations that, although issued by some third party, exhort voters to support a particular candidate or party in electoral contests.[6] At its core, however, advocacy advertising is issue-based; it is concerned with consciousness-raising regarding specific matters deemed by its sponsors to be of wider public concern. The viewpoints expressed through advocacy advertising can range from the mainstream to the unusual, alarming, or offensive. The agendas pursued are both non-commercial, in that they are not

---

(*On the application of ProLife Alliance*) v *British Broadcasting Corporation*, unreported, Court of Appeal, 14 March 2002. The second case saw an animal welfare pressure group attempt to broadcast an advocacy advertisement on Swiss television in response to meat industry commercials. The advertisement first showed footage of a wild sow building a nest for its piglets in a forest. It then depicted a noisy hall in which pigs, corralled in small individual pens, gnawed on the iron bars of their cages. The advertisement had been refused airtime on account of its 'clear political character' – see *VGT Verein gegen Tierfabriken* v *Switzerland* (2002) 34 EHRR 4.

4 The Government has recently come under fire for politicising such information campaigns – see BBC Panorama, *Tony in Adland*, 26 May 2002.

5 S. Adkins, *Cause Related Marketing: Who Cares Wins* (London: Butterworth Heinemann, 2000). The early decision by Iceland Frozen Foods plc to oppose GM foods, to source non-GM ingredients, and to make consumers aware of this practice can be cited as an illustration. It hoped to gain a commercial advantage by 'linking efficiency with a social conscience and profitability with good business ethics' – see J. Vidal, 'Genetic Engineering: Ethics Man', *The Guardian* 1 April 1998. Similarly, the Benetton company has long been associated with such marketing.

6 Contested examples can be seen *Walker* v *Unison* [1995] SLT 1226, and *R* v *Tronoh Mines Ltd* [1952] 1 All ER 697. The latter involved an advertised plea to voters by a company disgruntled at the socialist policies of the incumbent government to elect 'a new and strong government with ministers who may be relied upon to encourage business enterprise and initiative' (698).

associated with trade in products, and political in a sense beyond that associated with the formal party-political process.[7]

The proponents of advocacy advertising might be any interest grouping able to pay the requisite fees. Perhaps unsurprisingly, the American experience has seen the approach deployed most heavily by business corporations.[8] The business management, marketing and communications literatures are replete with the description and prescription of successful campaigns. Moreover, a recent survey suggests that around a third of the thousand largest corporations in the United States regularly deploy some form of advocacy advertising in the hope of fostering a broader cultural environment conducive to more directly commercial aims.[9] For some commentators, advocacy advertising is 'the Trojan horse of consumerism',[10] an aspect of the constitutionalisation of a particular socio-political outlook.[11] Others are more prosaic in considering it merely a standard component of 'corporate communications'.[12] Recognising the emphatic use of the mode by private corporations, however, does not deny that non-profit organisations have also made meaningful and influential use of the communicative mode.[13]

Although advocacy advertising has become a recognised phenomenon in the British context, the extent of its use is not comparable to that in the United States.[14] In particular, it is virtually absent from the broadcast media. None of three notable recent instances of the phenomenon in the UK involved broadcast advertising *per se*. First, having conducted a research project into the most effective medium,[15] the multinational corporation Monsanto preferred to place its series of advertisements lauding the prospective benefits of biotechnology in the weekend supplements of the broadsheet newspapers.[16] The company sought to promulgate the idea that biotechnology can be a positive benefit to society. Secondly, it is arguable that in fielding the requisite number of candidates in a succession of recent elections, the primary aim of the ProLife Alliance has been to gain the right to a party election broadcast. By doing so it has sought not to achieve electoral success, but rather to gain a platform through which it might

---

7 The relevant, albeit meagre, political science canon includes Brown et al, 'Daring To Be Heard: Advertorials by Organized Interests on the Op-Ed Page of *The New York Times*, 1985–1998' (2001) 18 *Political Communication* 23; W. Browne, 'Lobbying the Public: All-Directional Advocacy' in Cigler and Loomis (eds), *Interest Group Politics* (Washington: CQ Press, 5th ed, 1998); K. Kollman, *Outside Lobbying: Public Opinion and Interest Group Strategies* (Princeton: Princeton Univ Press, 1998).
8 Brown et al, *ibid*, 28.
9 M. Lord, 'Corporate Political Strategy and Legislative Decision-Making' (2000) 39 *Business and Society* 76 table 1.
10 S. Armstrong, 'You Say Tomato, We Say Genetically Altered Food Product That's Good for the Planet' *The Guardian* 6 July 1998.
11 D. Schneiderman, 'Constitutionalising the Culture-Ideology of Consumerism' (1998) 7 *Social and Legal Studies* 213.
12 S. Prakesh Sethi, *Handbook of Advocacy Advertising: Concepts, Strategies and Applications* (Cambridge MA: Ballinger, 1987).
13 For a review of its users in the United States, see the web pages of the Annenburg Public Policy Center of the University of Pennsylvania at *http://www.appcpenn.org/issueads/* (accessed 7 April 2002).
14 I. Ramsay, *Advertising, Culture and the Law: Beyond Lies, Ignorance and Manipulation* (London: Sweet & Maxwell, 1996) 92.
15 Alison Maitland, 'US Group in Drive to Popularise Biotech' *Financial Times* 16 September 1997.
16 The advertisements, which ran over a three-month period beginning in June 1998, have been reproduced on the company's UK website – see *http://www.monsanto.co.uk/highlights/ads/ad_biotech2.html* (accessed 4 April 2002). Besides the print advertisements, Monsanto produced information leaflets for distribution in supermarkets, operated a free telephone enquiry service, and designed a complementary web-based information site that included an 'on-line comments and questions' section.

proselytise its opposition to abortion.[17] Thirdly, when designing a further wave to its campaign against British adoption of the Euro currency, the 'no campaign' plumped for a combination of a series of cinema advertisements featuring a range of celebrity figures, a direct mail campaign, and a highly developed Internet presence.[18] Earlier missives had taken the form of billboard advertisements, leaflets and beer mats.[19] In each instance, the approach adopted was no doubt occasioned, at least in part, by the relatively caustic regulatory regime that covers broadcast advertising.

The strictures of broadcast advertising regulation

The form of regulation to which advocacy advertisements are subjected depends upon the medium by which they are communicated. For the present time, the schemes governing broadcast advertisements are elaborated under the Broadcasting Act 1990, and operated by the Independent Television Commission (ITC) and the Radio Authority (RA) as appropriate.[20] The regime covering most other forms of advertisement – including print, cinema and Internet-based representations – is self-regulatory, and is overseen by the Advertising Standards Authority (ASA).[21] It has been suggested that the regulation of broadcast advertising could be transferred into the domain of the self-regulatory scheme, with only scheduling issues remaining in the hands of the statutory authority.[22] This prospect was countenanced in the recent White Paper and the Government has professed itself 'keen to see further developments', but for the immediate future any emergent regulator is likely to find this remit unchanged among its new responsibilities.[23]

Whereas the bulk of the rules relating to broadcast advertising are elaborated only in codes of practice,[24] those focused on advocacy advertising are made explicit by the 1990 Act itself. They are peculiarly onerous: section 8(2) precludes political advertising on commercial television altogether, while section 92(2) does the same as regards radio broadcasts. These measures enjoy a substantial provenance having been instituted in the 1920s as part of the general exclusion of

---

17 Under s 36 Broadcasting Act 1990, the ITC, BBC and S4C make arrangements as to the entitlement to party political broadcasts.

18 The initial advertisement became embroiled in controversy on account of a portrayal of Adolf Hitler by comedian Rik Mayall – see A. Rawnsley, 'Adolf Hitler Would Hate the Euro' *The Observer* 7 July 2002; N. Watt, 'Anger at Video Spoof of Hitler Backing Euro', *The Guardian* 3 July 2002; J. Murphy, 'Geldof Leads Stars in 'No to Euro' Campaign' *Evening Standard* 2 July 2002.

19 Further details of these advertisements and the campaign more generally are available at: *http://www.no-euro.com* (accessed 9 July 2002)

20 The ITC and the RA were established by ss 1 and 83 of the 1990 Act respectively. The main functions of each concern the allocation and qualification of licences to commercial broadcasting companies. Self-regulatory, pre-transmission guidance is also offered by the Broadcast Advertising Clearance Centre (BACC).

21 C. Munro, 'Self-Regulation in the Media' [1997] *Public Law* 6.

22 See the submissions of the ASA, the CAP, and the Advertising Association to an initial DCMS consultation: *http://www.culture.gov.uk/creative/dti-dcms_comms-reform_submissions.html* (accessed 8 April 2002).

23 DTI/DCMS, n 1 above, paras 6.8.3–6.8.5. The further developments might consist of moves towards co-regulation based on the models of the ASA and the pre-broadcast clearing system that are currently in operation – see DTI/DCMS, *The Draft Communications Bill: The Policy* Cm 5508-III (2002) para 8.5.4.3.

24 In accordance with duties imposed on the ITC and the RA by s 9 and s 93 respectively.

advertising on the BBC, and extended to independent television some thirty years later.[25]

Sections 8(2) and 92(2) each include two prohibitions: (i) on advertising 'on behalf of any body whose objects are wholly or mainly of a political nature', and (ii) on 'any advertisement which is directed towards any political end'.[26] Ostensibly, the former aims to preclude all advertising by political parties, for whom the restriction is mitigated through access to party political broadcasts. The latter restriction is broader and extends to any political representation irrespective of the character of its proponent. Evidently, the breadth of interpretation accorded to the word 'political' will determine the question of precisely what advertising is covered by these limitations.

In policing their respective codes of practice, the ITC and the RA interpret the term as being wider than 'party political', so as to include more general matters of public controversy. The strictures of this approach can be seen in a decision concerning a television advertisement produced by Christian Aid. This sought to highlight the fact that financial obligations owed to the developed world often negate attempts to alleviate squalor in developing countries.[27] It depicted bailiffs taking a dummy from the mouth of an African child and a syringe from the hands of a doctor while intoning 'a debt is a debt is a debt'. Despite engaging with a pressing social issue that traversed party-political boundaries, the advertisement was deemed to fall foul of the restrictions.

Although the ITC and RA are amenable to the supervisory jurisdiction of the Administrative Court, judges have rarely been called upon to offer guidance on the meaning of 'political' in this context. Rather, litigation embroiling the ITC or RA has centred almost invariably on disputed licensing decisions.[28] The one case that did involve a contentious advertisement was *R v Radio Authority, ex parte Bull*.[29] This arose out of an altercation between Amnesty International and the Radio Authority, and saw the Court of Appeal consider section 92(2)(a)(i). Amnesty had recorded a radio broadcast that sought to question purported Western intransigence to suffering unfolding in Rwanda.[30] In assessing whether the objects of the organisation were 'wholly or mainly political in nature', the judges were agreed that there was nothing to warrant any divergence from the ordinary meaning of the word. Lord Woolf indicated that it should be understood to extend not only to designs that aimed to further the interests of a particular party, but also to those that sought to procure changes in the law or policy of this or any other country.[31] This definition extends the ambit of the first restriction significantly. Moreover, applied to section 92(2)(a)(ii) or its section 8 equivalent, it could be expected to encompass almost every non-commercial representation

---

25 Television Act 1954, Sched 2.

26 These requirements are then reflected in respective codes of practice of the ITC and the RA.

27 C. Midgeley, 'Charity Stunned by Ban on Third World TV Ad' *The Times* 16 December 1997; J. Rentoul, 'Now For a Short Break From Free Speech' *The Independent* 15 December 1997. In this instance, the BACC indicated the impending bar to the charity's plans.

28 T. Jones, 'Judicial Review of the Independent Television Commission' [1992] *Public Law* 372.

29 [1998] QB 294. See further, J. Stevens and D. Feldman, 'Broadcasting Advertisements by Bodies with Political Objects, Judicial Review, and the Influence of Charities Law' [1997] *Public Law* 615.

30 P. Vallely, 'You Can't Show That, Its Political' *The Independent* 20 June 1995.

31 n 29 above, 306. In this he drew support from the judgement of Slade J in *McGovern v Attorney General* [1982] Ch 321 340.

oriented to a public audience.[32] Thus, as they stand, the restrictions in the 1990 Act effectively preclude advocacy advertising by corporate and civil society organisations, alongside their prevention of party-political advertising.

This position regarding broadcast advocacy advertising has been reviewed, both inside and outside Government, on a number of recent occasions. Following a public consultation on its *Advertising Code*, the ITC mooted only minor changes to the rules on advocacy advertising.[33] The Puttnam Committee also declared its support for the principles underlying the composite ban.[34] In its *Fifth Report*, the Committee on Standards in Public Life (then the Neill Committee) argued for an extension of the regulatory regime to cover new media.[35] While suggesting that such a widening of the ban would not be appropriate,[36] the Government continues to endorse the broadcasting prohibition.[37] It envisages that OFCOM will exercise the combined functions of the ITC and RA in this as in other areas.[38] This is a questionable intent. At first glance, such consolidation would appear to sit ill with the increasingly high regard paid by the courts to the principle of freedom of expression.

Veneration of political expression: the convention and the common law

The individual right to freedom of expression forms an indispensable part of the rhetoric of the liberal democratic tradition.[39] Indeed, it has been ascribed a place 'at the very core of the concept of a democratic society'.[40] The extent to which it is afforded respect in practice, however, is a separate question. The guarantee of the right to freedom of expression lies in the willingness of judges to see it outbalance the variety of competing interests that are reined against it. The recent British experience is that the courts have increasingly been willing to offer openness of communication a primacy over other values. While a string of recent decisions have been founded explicitly on domestic jurisprudence, this movement has no doubt been accentuated by the domestication of the European Convention catalogue of rights. The trend has been most obvious in cases concerning freedom of 'political expression'.

A number of judges have sought to illuminate the indigenous foundations of the burgeoning value placed on freedom of expression in the UK. Prior to the

---

32 There has been no direct jurisprudence on the s 92(2)(a)(ii) provision or its s 8 equivalent. Subsequent to the Amnesty litigation, the relevant authorities have been willing to accept advertising by such bodies, providing that they cast their message in apolitical terms; that is, insofar as they present their appeals as an offer of a 'product' to be purchased by concerned consumers.

33 The new draft *Code* and related documents can be found at: *http://www.itc.org.uk/public_consultations/index.asp* (accessed 10 April 2002).

34 Joint Committee on the Draft Communications Bill, *The Draft Communications Bill* HL169-I/ HC876-I (2001–02) para 301.

35 Committee on Standards in Public Life, *Fifth Report: The Funding of Political Parties in the United Kingdom* Cm 4057 (1998), recommendation 94.

36 DTI/DCMS, n 1 above, para 6.6.7.

37 Home Office, *The Funding of Political Parties in the United Kingdom: The Government's Proposals for Legislation in Response to the Fifth Report of the Committee on Standards in Public Life* Cm 4413 (1999) para 9.2.

38 DTI/DCMS, n 1 above, para 6.6.

39 See generally, the essays collated in J. Beatson and Y. Cripps, *Freedom of Expression and Freedom of Information: Essays in Honour of Sir David Williams* (Oxford: OUP, 2000).

40 *Handyside* v *UK* [1976] 1 EHRR 737 para 42.

domestication of the Convention catalogue, a series of extra-curial ruminations lauded the liberality of the common law.[41] This view was also iterated by Lord Keith in *Derbyshire County Council* v *Times Newspapers*.[42] Such effusive commendation of the potential of the common law is not universally endorsed. For example, one commentator has lamented a supposed litany of judicial failure in cases involving political expression, and called for a 'thorough-going change in judicial attitude'.[43] The criticism is an unfair one, however, and sits ill with the overwhelming tenor of developments in the 1990s following Lord Bridge's celebrated dissent in the *Spycatcher* litigation.[44] These developments include Lord Hoffman's stout defence of the principle in *R* v *Central Independent Television plc*,[45] Lord Steyn's recognition that freedom of speech 'is the lifeblood of democracy' and 'a brake on the abuse of power',[46] and Lord Justice Sedley's remonstrance that expression rights include 'not only the inoffensive but the irritating, the contentious, the eccentric, the heretical, the unwelcome and the provocative... freedom only to speak inoffensively is not worth having'.[47] It seems fair to conclude that the common law principle had 'attained the status of a constitutional right with attendant high normative force'.[48]

This confidence in the common law is palpable in a series of decisions delivered subsequent to October 2000, in which the courts have politely continued to refute the need to rely on Strasbourg jurisprudence directly.[49] Indeed, Lord Justice Laws has gone so far as to present any strict recourse to the standard tripartite test employed by the Strasbourg court as tantamount to invoking the 'austerity of tabulated legalism'.[50] He would prefer to proceed immediately to the balancing of the right in question against the relevant competing interests; to focus on whether action fulfils a 'pressing social need' to the detriment of the other elements of the tripartite test. In contrast, Lord Steyn has maintained that 'the new landscape is of great importance inasmuch as it provides the taxonomy against which... question[s] before the [courts] must be considered'.[51] The Human Rights Act 1998 also makes clear that it would be wrong for the British courts simply to ignore the Strasbourg jurisprudence in their desire to foster a peculiarly British

---

41 Lord Browne-Wilkinson, 'The Infiltration of a Bill of Rights' [1992] *Public Law* 397; J. Laws, 'Is the High Court the Guardian of Fundamental Constitutional Rights?' [1993] *Public Law* 59.

42 [1993] AC 534 551. He cited similar comments offered by Lord Goff in *Attorney-General* v *Guardian Newspapers Ltd (No 2)* [1990] 1 AC 109 283.

43 B. Sheldrick, 'Judicial Review and Judicial Reticence: The Protection of Political Expression Under the Common Law' (1998) 3 *Journal of Civil Liberties* 191 192. Specific cases can be highlighted to bolster this position, notably *R* v *Secretary of State for the Home Department, ex parte Brind* [1990] 1 All ER 469.

44 *Attorney-General* v *Guardian Newspapers Ltd (No 1)* [1987] 3 All ER 316 342–346. Lord Bridge argued that 'freedom of speech is always the first casualty under a totalitarian regime' (345) and that its unwarranted limitation will invariably occasion 'condemn[ation]' at the bar of public opinion in the free world' (346).

45 [1994] 3 All ER 641 651.

46 *R* v *Secretary of State for the Home Department, ex parte Simms* [1999] 3 All ER 400 407.

47 *Redmond-Bate* v *DPP* [2000] HRLR 249 260.

48 Lord Steyn, *McCartan Turkington Breen* v *Times Newspapers Ltd* [2000] 4 All ER 913 927.

49 I. Loveland, 'Freedom of Political Expression: Who Needs the Human Rights Act?' [2001] *Public Law* 233.

50 n 3 above, para 34. The tripartite test involves questions as to whether the impugned restriction was first, 'prescribed by law', secondly, 'necessary in a democratic society' in the sense of fulfilling a 'pressing social need', and finally in service of one of the purposes articulated exhaustively in the second paragraph of Article 10(2)ECHR.

51 *Reynolds* v *Times Newspapers Ltd* [1999] 4 All ER 609 627.

approach.[52] Convention jurisprudence on the substantive content of rights should continue to inform domestic law, even as the latter corpus expands.

Even if tacit only, the influence of Strasbourg jurisprudence on domestic law has already been significant. Arguably, it is the confidence born of the new rights culture that has fostered the ready invocation of the 'elasticity of the common law principle',[53] and the judicial capacity to achieve desired results using 'ordinary principles of reasonably liberal and purposive contemporary interpretation'.[54] The signature of the international law can be discerned readily in the broadening scope of the concept of political expression. In determining the boundaries of political speech, Strasbourg case law has tended to focus on the restriction of commentary regarding the state or individual politicians, that is, upon matters in some way connected with the formal political process. The category has, however, also been held to include matters of more general public interest.[55]

This breadth and depth of protection offered to political expression has been emulated recently in seminal domestic case law. In his Court of Appeal judgment in the *Reynolds* case, Lord Bingham offered what was received as 'a liberal and modern interpretation' in determining what issues might be considered of public interest to the community.[56] He appeared to preclude only discussion of matters which, being entirely 'personal and private', give rise to 'no public interest in their disclosure'.[57] In the House of Lords, Lord Nicholls affirmed this approach, indicating that 'it would be unsound in principle to distinguish political discussion from discussion of other matters of serious public concern'.[58] Lord Cooke concurred that 'the rights and interests of citizens in democracies are not restricted to the casting of votes... matters other than those pertaining to government and politics may be just as important in the community'.[59] While this broad understanding of the ambit of the political is not accepted by all commentators,[60] it reflects the emergence of multi-focal, issue-based activism in modern society. It is also striking in its close tally with the definition employed to determine the category of advertisements that is denied broadcast time under the Broadcasting Act 1990.

Where Lord Justice Laws' ruminations on the peripheral importance of the Convention do hold substantial weight is in the rejection of any ready assimilation of the 'margin of appreciation' doctrine into domestic law. He has been emphatic in recording that, 'we are not... bidden to accord a "margin of appreciation"

---

52 ss 2 and 6.
53 Lord Nicholls, n 51 above, 625.
54 Lord Cooke, n 48 above, 932, 929.
55 *Thorgeirson* v *Iceland (1992)* 14 EHRR 843 (allegations of police brutality); *Fressoz* v *France* (2001) 31 EHRR 2 (publication of an individual's tax returns in a satirical paper).
56 K. Rimell, 'A New Public Interest Defence for the Media?: The House of Lords' Decision in *Reynolds* v *Times Newspapers Ltd*' (2000) 11 *Entertainment Law Review* 36, 37; K. Williams, 'Defaming Politicians: The Not So Common Law' (2000) 63 MLR 748; I. Loveland, '*Reynolds* v *Times Newspapers* in the House of Lords' [2000] *Public Law* 351; 'A New Legal Landscape: Libel Law and Freedom of Political Expression in the United Kingdom' [2000] EHRLR 476; F. Trindade, 'Defamatory Statements and Political Discussion' (2000) 116 LQR 185.
57 *Reynolds* v *Times Newspapers Ltd & others (CA)* [1998] 3 All ER 961 1004.
58 n 51 above, 625.
59 *ibid* 640.
60 Speaking of the *GKR Karate* case ([2000] 2 All ER 931), Professor Ian Loveland offered the highly disputable observation that 'the audience interest in the sale of sub-standard goods and services is not remotely comparable to that in knowing whether politicians are dishonest or corrupt' – see n 49 above, 234.

properly so called... and we should fall into confusion and error if we did so'.[61] The doctrine is used by the international court to allow recognition of national particularities, with the effective result that decision-takers are accorded a higher degree of latitude than might otherwise be the case.[62] It is for this reason that Lord Justice Laws has insisted that domestic courts should not become 'a Strasbourg surrogate'.[63] Rather, they should seek to avoid the 'devaluation' of basic rights that would accompany such deference.[64] Their decisions should confirm that 'we are... long the point when interference with fundamental rights by public authorities can be justified by a bare demonstration of rationality or reasonableness'.[65] Adopting this approach, the courts would continue to foster a system of rights protection that supersedes, on grounds of utility to individual litigants, the limited protection offered by the Strasbourg court.[66]

The demonstrated willingness of the courts to award a degree of primacy to political expression is important even in the context of limitations imposed by statute. It suggests that while judges will not be able simply to 'develop' apposite solutions as with the common law, they will be ready to utilise the mechanisms allotted by the Human Rights Act 1998. It might be expected that the interpretative obligation imposed by section 3 will be rigorously exercised, and that in the remainder the section 4 declaration will be wielded as necessary.

The price of free expression: the subversion of democracy by private wealth?

In light of this high constitutional regard for political expression, the tenability of the broadcasting prohibition on advocacy advertising would appear to be far from secure. Its legality must be assessed against the new jurisprudential landscape. Interestingly, the Neill Committee envisaged the possibility of a legal challenge.[67] Indeed, following its lack of success in *ex parte Bull*, Amnesty International did seek to have the European Court of Human Rights (ECtHR) rule on the question of whether the impugned decision abridged its right to freedom of expression. It eventually settled the case on the Government's promise both to compensate it, and to consider the question of political advertising further.[68] Pertinent guidance on the lawfulness of the restrictions can be gleaned, however, from more recent

---

61 n 3 above, para 31. This position has also been adopted by the House of Lords – see *R v DPP, ex parte Kebilene* [2000] 2 AC 326.
62 N. Lavender, 'The Problem of the Margin of Appreciation' [1997] EHRLR 380.
63 n 3 above, para 33.
64 T. Jones, 'The Devaluation of Human Rights Under the European Convention' [1995] *Public Law* 430. There is some debate as to how far a measure of deference should be accorded by the courts in recognition of the democratic legitimacy of Parliament – see P. Craig, 'The Courts, the Human Rights Act, and Judicial Review' (2001) 117 LQR 589; R. Singh, 'Is There a Role for the "Margin of Appreciation" in National Law After the Human Rights Act?' [1999] *EHRLR* 15; D. Pannick, 'Principles of Interpretation of Convention Rights Under the Human Rights Act and the Discretionary Area of Judgment' [1998] *Public Law* 545. At root, this discussion avers to the wider debate as to whether *ultra vires* provides the foundation of judicial review – see C. Forsyth (ed), *Judicial Review and the Constitution* (Oxford: Hart, 2000).
65 n 3 above, para 36. The *Wednesbury* approach had been considered apposite both at first instance by Scott Baker J, and in an earlier parallel: *R v British Broadcasting Corporation, ex parte Quintavelle*, unreported, Court of Appeal, 20 October 1997.
66 Loveland, n 49 above, 242.
67 Committee on Standards in Public Life, n 35 above, para 13.11.
68 DCMS, 'The Government and Amnesty International: Joint Statement', *Press release*, 8 December 1999.

jurisprudence of both the domestic and Strasbourg courts. Of particular importance are the decisions of the Court of Appeal in the *ProLife Alliance* case,[69] and of the ECtHR in the case of *VGT v Switzerland*.[70] If it were recognised that the statutory rule was in conflict with Convention principles, the occasion of its prospective reiteration in a forthcoming Communications Bill would offer the Government an opportunity to renege. Should it not do so, it may be left to judges to compensate. This might involve the courts in interpreting the statute restrictively so as to facilitate advocacy advertising, or failing this, in issuing a declaration of incompatibility.

As evident from the above discussion, the central issue in determining the legality of the prohibition on advocacy advertising would be whether the arguments in support of purported restrictions are such as to outweigh the right to non-interference. This is essentially a question of balance in which 'the nature of the expression which is restrained or interfered with by the State will determine the strength and the cogency of the justification for the interference required by the court'.[71] The political tenor of advocacy advertising should require the courts to insist upon the most persuasive of justifications.[72] In addition, the relevant authority would be called upon to show that the contrary ends pursued by the restrictions could not be secured by any other less intrusive means.

The justifications for the ban that successive governments have relied upon are fourfold. First, it has been stated that the aim of the ban is to prevent controversial viewpoints from being 'unexpectedly and unwelcomely injected into unsuspecting households';[73] 'to protect viewers and listeners from intrusive political or politically motivated and campaigning advertising'.[74] The current Government has recently affirmed that a principle of regulating communications is that 'audiences should be aware of when they might hear views and opinion and when they will receive, say, advertising or entertainment'.[75] Secondly, it has been argued that 'the provision of a forum for a wide range of views falls within the general duties of the media', and that given this, prospective advertisers 'should [already] have ample opportunity to express their views'.[76] Thirdly, there is the perceived risk that 'if political advertising were allowed, the overall broadcast output would be skewed by those best able to fund advertising'.[77] A purported aversion towards selling the public sphere to the highest bidder has been a long-standing concern in government.[78] This last concern melds into a fourth issue: that any lifting of the prohibition would leave the main political parties under a perceived obligation to broadcast advertisements and would therefore have an inopportune impact on questions of party-political funding.[79] In light of these

---

69 n 3 above.
70 n 3 above.
71 A. Lester and D. Pannick, *Human Rights Law and Practice* (London: Butterworths, 1999) para. 4.10.8.
72 This would remain the case even where such missives could be said to contain an amalgam of commercial elements and political representations – see *Barthold v Federal Republic of Germany* (1985) 7 EHRR 383.
73 Lord Inglewood, HL Deb vol 570 col 482 7 March 1996.
74 Iain Sproat MP, HC Deb vol 287 col 192 10 December 1996.
75 DTI/DCMS, n 1 above, para. 6.6.6.
76 *ibid*
77 *ibid* para 6.6.3.
78 Indeed, it was argued by the British Government before the European Commission of Human Rights in *X and the Association of Z v United Kingdom unreported*, although the Commission made no comment on this point when declaring the application inadmissible – see Committee on Standards in Public Life, n 35 above, para 13.9.
79 Home Office, n 37 above, para 9.2.

four concerns, government has long drawn succour in its maintenance of the ban from an apparent consensus on the question across the party-political spectrum.[80] Such support does not equate automatically, however, to an affirmation of the lawfulness of the prohibition; the legal weight of the purported justifications must be reviewed in turn.

Protecting audiences from intrusive political comment

The first justification offered is the supposed desire of successive Governments to protect broadcasting audiences from the interruption of their placid repose by 'intrusive sentiments'. This is a misconceived objective. On one hand, there is a striking absence of any analogous concern over the interjection of commercial advertising into viewers and listeners programme choices. On the other hand, any willingness to refuse access to the public sphere sits ill with the discursive principles that underpin democratic society. Moreover, it is not clear why audiences are thought incapable of choosing for themselves not to receive any political messages.

That the degree of intrusiveness of an unsolicited message varies according to its content is a curious contention. Yet, while overtly political representations are proscribed, commercial entities are both able to advertise and to include subtle political representations in the course of the promotion of specific products. They remain free to promulgate without remark a cauterised vision of a society,[81] subjecting the public to 'the soft compulsion of constant consumption training'.[82] This is despite the description of such advertising by one MP as 'mendacious' in its 'tend[ency] to abuse every decent human emotion'.[83] Indeed, the Frankfurt School critique of mass culture has long informed of how the primary aim of publicity has shifted from the provision of accurate information to the selling of goods.[84] Controversial material, often political in nature, is culled from broadcasts and publications to be supplanted by more agreeable representations. Moreover, insofar as tacit messaging interred within ostensibly apolitical advertising remains unnoticed it might acquire a subtle power. This instrumental use of the broadcast media attempts to coax the public into receiving information as a body of consumers and not citizens, and thereby threatens the depoliticisation of the public sphere.[85] Whether or not such prognoses are accurate, the level of 'intrusiveness' as a criterion of acceptability does not appear to offer a sufficient basis to differentiate between categories of speech.

The willingness to permit commercial speech to the exclusion of its political equivalent inverts the normal Strasbourg approach. Under Convention jurispru-

---

80 DTI/DCMS, n 1 above, para 6.6.4.
81 N. Klein, *No Logo* (London: Flamingo Press, 2000).
82 J. Habermas, *The Structural Transformation of the Public Sphere: An Inquiry into a Category of Bourgeois Society* (Cambridge: Polity Press, Eng tr, 1992) 192.
83 Bob Cryer MP, HC Deb vol 172 col 201 9 May 1990.
84 M. Horkheimer and T. Adorno, *The Dialectic of Enlightenment* (London: Allen Lane, 1973); A. Arato and E. Gebhardt (eds), *The Essential Frankfurt School Reader* (New York: Continuum, 1998); Habermas, n 82 above.
85 S. Benhabib, 'Models of Public Space: Hannah Arendt, the Liberal Tradition and Jürgen Habermas' in Calhoun (ed), *Habermas and the Public Sphere* (London: MIT Press, 1992) 93. For reasons discussed further below, this threat may have subsided somewhat in recent years. Certainly, the pessimism inherent in Habermas' early work (*ibid*) has been somewhat displaced in more recent contributions – see, for example, *Between Facts and Norms: Contributions to a Discourse Theory of Law and Democracy* (Cambride: Polity Press, Eng tr, 1996).

dence, political expression is uppermost of three categories differentiated and afforded protection on a sliding scale of stringency. Commercial speech is thought least worthy of protection.[86] The justification of the broadcasting ban on political advertising on this first ground is thus arguably anachronistic given the lack of concern in these other areas.

More generally, it must be a principle of every democratic state that censorship of speech should be undertaken only as a last resort. This principle is well illustrated by the recent decision of the Court of Appeal in the *ProLife Alliance* case, with its focus on the protection of viewers' sensibilities against offensive – as opposed to merely intrusive – content. The case involved a decision by the BBC and other terrestrial broadcasters to refuse to air a party election broadcast recorded by the group.[87] This action was taken pursuant to the relevant codes and guidelines on taste and decency. The images in question, including footage of dismembered foetuses, were in no way sensationalised. There is no doubt, however, that they could be considered deeply harrowing, and would be likely to be shocking or offensive to a very large number of viewers. Indeed, such an impact comprised a large part of their intended effect.

Impugning the decision, Lord Justice Laws was forthright in rejecting the broadcasters' contentions on this score. He characterised the decision as 'censorship' of political discussion, and refuted any 'implicit plea for the comfort of a euphemism'.[88] The broadcasters' dilemma was that they faced perhaps the extreme instance of a perceived imperative to protect the public from inappropriate content. In the circumstances, however, any judicial desire to accommodate this aim was outbalanced by the 'special responsibility' invoked by the courts 'as the constitutional guardian of freedom of political debate'.[89] Lords Justice Parker and Laws did each suggest that it remained possible for a recording to be considered too offensive to air, particularly were it 'gratuitous' or 'sensational', with the former citing a parallel recording made by the ProLife Alliance in 1997.[90]

The *ProLife* judgment concerned offensive output: the desire to protect viewers from merely 'intrusive' comment cannot found, *a fortiori*, the broadcasting ban on advocacy advertising. Furthermore, given the contrasting approach adopted toward commercial representations, it is possible to be sceptical as to the degree with which this purported conviction is held. At most, a proportionate response might be to require a message pre-empting the advertisement akin to those that introduce party-political broadcasts. This would facilitate members of the public in exercising their own right to choose not to watch or listen. An outright ban appears an overly draconian measure to deploy.

---

86 The intermediate form is 'artistic' expression.
87 Further information on the organisation's campaign, including a range of stills from the disputed broadcast, can be gleaned from its web pages at *http://www.prolife.org.uk* (accessed 20 May 2002).
88 n 3 above, para 38.
89 *ibid* para 36. Notably, the fact that the circumstances of this case arose 'in the rancour and asperity of a general election' was said to leave the need to protect political expression pristine (para 34). Nevertheless, as the discussion in the previous section indicates, it would be wrong to infer any significant reduction in the importance attached to freedom of political expression more generally.
90 *ibid* paras 62 and 42 respectively.

The existence of alternative outlets for political expression

The second justification raised to found the broadcasting ban, that media channels more generally offer adequate scope to communicate political messages, is plainly a *non sequitur*. First, it stands to reason that every prospective advertiser has already determined that the product or idea in question is not communicated adequately through the available media outlets. The purchase of additional exposure would otherwise be a wholly uneconomic choice. More importantly, as a matter of principle it is hard to explain why the right to freedom of expression should be contingent on the editorial decisions of some third party. In the wake of Marshall McLuhan's analyses,[91] few would argue that the manner in which a representation is delivered does not affect the substance of the message.[92]

Insulating the public sphere against over-powerful interests

The third justification offered by Government conjures the spectre of wealthy advertisers taking advantage of any more open regime to skew public sphere discourse by the incessant reiteration of their own agenda. The vision is that of a democracy sold to the highest bidder.[93] This argument advances from the knowledge that communication through the mass media is primarily monological; that it does not involve rational debate on issues, but rather the agonistic representation of fixed perspectives.[94] Due to this capacity to communicate information uninterrupted to citizen-consumers, broadcast representation is considered profound in its power to influence individual choices. This argument aspires to dignify the prohibition as a bastion of democratic fairness and equality. Its purported purpose is to deny wealthy groups a disproportionate access to such an important communicative vehicle. It can draw some support from a recent indication offered by the ECtHR that a desire to safeguard 'the formation of public opinion... from the pressures of powerful financial groups' might indeed fall within the 'protection of the rights of others' rubric of Article 10(2)ECHR.[95]

This intuition is not unimpeachable. There are two counter-arguments that can be raised against this purported justification. The first concedes that advertising might allow its proponents to garner influence over the public sphere, but only when it is sustained over time. Thus, the justification cannot found a generalised prohibition on all advocacy advertising. The second argument sees the content of a representation as all-important, given that it must persuade an intelligent and critical public. From this perspective, advocacy is only likely to be persuasive when well-founded, and all advocacy is to be welcomed for its contribution to a functioning public sphere.

---

91 M. McLuhan, *Understanding Media: The Extensions of Man* (London: Routledge, 1964); (with Quentin Fiore), *The Medium is the Massage* (London: Allen Lane, 1967).

92 Indeed, so much was acknowledged by Lord Justice Laws when he expressed 'profound disagreement with the very suggestion that the appellant's freedom to put its case in words somehow mitigates, no excuses, this censorship of its case in pictures' – see n 3 above, para 42.

93 Carlton Television, which serves around 5.5m households in Greater London area, charges in the region of £30,500 for a 30-second weekday evening peak time spot (figures supplied by the Advertising Association).

94 J. Cohen, 'Deliberation and Democratic Legitimacy' in Hamin and Pettit (eds), *The Good Polity: Normative Analysis of the State* (Oxford: Blackwell, 1991) 33.

95 n 3 above, paras 59–62.

The first rebuttal sees the justification as premised on too-ready an association between the ability to advertise even fleetingly and the attainment of leverage in the public sphere. It is well illustrated by the reasoning of the ECtHR in the *VGT* case.[96] This involved an attempt by an animal welfare pressure group to broadcast an advocacy advertisement on Swiss television in response to meat industry commercials. The advertisement first showed footage of a wild sow building a nest for its piglets in a forest while an accompanying voice referred to such zoological facts as the strong sense of community sustained by the animals. The second scene depicted a noisy hall wherein pigs, corralled in small individual pens, gnawed on the iron bars of their cages. The accompanying voice drew a parallel with concentration camps before exhorting, 'eat less meat, for the sake of your health, the animals, and the environment'. Under an analogous prohibition to those in the Broadcasting Act 1990, the advertisement had been refused airtime on account of its 'clear political character'. While the court accepted as conceivable that such a ban might be justified under Article 10(2)ECHR, it asserted that the relevant authority must also show 'why the grounds advanced in support of the prohibition... also served to justify the interference in the particular circumstances of [any given] case'.[97] It proceeded to reject any suggestion that VGT 'constituted a powerful financial group which, with its proposed commercial, aimed at undermining the independence of the broadcaster'.[98]

The decision suggests that the courts would insist on a demonstration that a particular advertiser enjoyed some form of structural power over the broadcaster's output before any restriction on its political expression could be justified through the third argument. The capacity to afford a single advertisement does not meet this criterion. Indeed, the requisite degree of commercial influence is patently not enjoyed by even the most affluent pressure groups. Yet, the strictures of the broadcasting prohibitions entail that 'most pressure groups no longer bother to try to advertise'.[99] This attitude ensues from a number of controversial altercations with regulators in the mid-1990s that included those surrounding a television advertisement on Third World debt relief produced by Christian Aid, and a radio broadcast recorded by Amnesty International.[100] It has been grudgingly accepted by pressure groups that advocacy advertising on television or radio is to all intents impossible.

In contrast, many major commercial enterprises do have the capacity to gain structural power over the public sphere. On one hand, the imperative of attracting revenues from commercial advertising can see editors become loath to offend the sensibilities of advertising interests.[101] On the other hand, major corporations enjoy the capacity to purchase control in media channels outright.[102] In light of this, it may be justifiable to devise some mechanism that would continue to restrict the capacity of such powerful groups to subvert the public sphere. A blanket ban, however, remains too blunt an instrument.

---

96 *ibid.*
97 *ibid* para 75.
98 *ibid.*
99 G. Monbiot, *Captive State: The Corporate Takeover of Britain* (London: MacMillan, 2000) 341.
100 See text accompanying notes 26–29.
101 Perhaps, this result is less likely in respect of television companies than with magazine publishers. However, illustrative examples of the 'capture' of television companies can be cited: see *http://www.foxbghsuit.com* (accessed 20 July 2002).
102 Indeed, alleviating the strictures on media ownership will comprise one of the main objectives of the forthcoming Communications Bill.

The second counter-argument to the phantasm of a public sphere subverted by wealth questions the supposed link between advertising and automatic public subscription to represented viewpoints. It maintains that such justifications of the exclusion of advocacy advertising ignore the critical sophistication of the public as the audience of the mass media. They invoke a 'hypodermic model of influence',[103] and assume that individuals can simply be programmed like the obedient automaton to ascribe to messages delivered. This proposition flies in the face of a substantial body of research, growing since the 1940s, which attests to the astuteness of audiences.[104] The public does not receive mass mediated messages passively. Their circumspection draws succour from a widespread cultural presumption – fomented by such disparate harbingers as Noam Chomsky and James Bond – of the likely partiality of representations made through the mass media.[105] Individuals collate information from a variety of sources, and assess it against their existing understandings and value-orientations before reaching conclusions accordingly. While it can be accepted that television in particular offers perhaps the most powerful communicative media, this is a matter of degree and not of principle. Such knowledge helps found the view of the Strasbourg court that 'a prohibition of political advertising which applies only to certain media and not to others, does not appear to be of a particularly pressing nature'.[106] It has also caused some commentators to recommend an extension of the ban to all advertising media.[107]

It is in this context that ongoing technological developments can be seen as crucial: the world-wide web, electronic mail, and other Internet-based functions promise an efficient and immediate virtual public sphere.[108] In particular, the growth of web-logs and associated databases allow for ready association between like-minded individuals whatever their common interest.[109] It is increasingly possible to divert frustrated cynicism at broadcasting output perceived as tendentious into more productive inquiry. Indeed, the development of the Internet has entailed that 'anyone with a modem is potentially a global pamphleteer'.[110] This possibility serves to undermine substantially the oft-voiced fears of a public denuded of critical faculties by a bowdlerising mass-media.[111] Civil society organisations and concerned individuals are able to gain immediate access to politically important news and views that would

---

103 D. Morley, 'Changing Paradigms in Audience Studies' in Seiter et al (eds), *Remote Control* (London: Routledge, 1989) 17.

104 K. Schoenbach, 'Myths of Media and Audiences' (2001) 16 *European Journal of Communication* 361 366–367.

105 N. Chomsky, *Deterring Democracy* (London: Vintage Books, 1992); (with Edward Herman), *Manufacturing Consent: The Political Economy of the Mass Media* (London: Vintage Books, 1994). A megalomanic media baron featured as the arch enemy in the 1997 James Bond episode, *Tomorrow Never Dies*.

106 n 3 above, para 74.

107 Committee on Standards in Public Life, *Fifth Report: The Funding of Political Parties in the United Kingdom – vol.II* Cm 4057-II (1998) para 497 *et seq*.

108 A. Gimmler, 'Deliberative Democracy, the Public Sphere and the Internet' (2001) 27 *Philosophy and Social Criticism* 21; Michael Froomkın (2001), *Habermas@discourse.net: Towards a Critical Theory of Cyberspace*. Available at: *http://www.discourse.net/* (accessed 20 September 2001); Mark Poster (1995) *CyberDemocracy: Internet and the Public Sphere*. Available at: *http://www.hnet.uci.edu/mposter/writings/democ.html* (accessed 20 September 2001).

109 For examples, see *http://blogdex.media.mit.edu* (accessed 18 July 2002); *http://www.blogger.com* (accessed 18 July 2002).

110 J. Markoff, 'If the Medium is the Message the Message is the Web', *New York Times* 20 November 1995.

111 R. Newman, 'Keeping Us Stupid: The Worst Aspects of Corporate Colonisation are Filtered Out by the Media and Politicians' *The Guardian* 7 August 1999; Schoenbach, n 104 above, 364.

formerly have seeped only slowly into the public consciousness. It seems fair to suggest that, 'the Internet represents the real information revolution... one that removes the governmental and corporate filters that have so long been in place with the traditional mass media'.[112] Certainly, it holds the prospect of a functioning alternative media freed from the practical constraints imposed by insufficient funding,[113] and offers the necessary tools to foster a less focused, more spontaneous, and eclectic network of civil society associations.[114]

The vastly augmented availability of readily accessible alternative sources of information, commentary and discussion has already begun to enervate the broadcasting paradigm that fostered a top-down, 'command and control' attitude amongst elite institutions, both public and private.[115] Perhaps revealingly, leading figures in the public-relations industry have begun to recognise and accept this trend. They warn colleagues and clients of the growing imperative of full engagement above didactic messaging: 'manipulating the message and the audience... will no longer be so possible, because the general public can access source material so much more easily'.[116] The risk that even the most subtle and sophisticated representations might be somewhere deconstructed and their manipulative aspirations then widely communicated is thought increasingly to be unacceptable.

An illustration of this changing social paradigm was the public excoriation suffered by Monsanto following its foray into advocacy advertising.[117] The company suffered derogatory comment from a range of elite respondents. Its campaign was described as a 'disgrace',[118] as 'folly, misrepresentation and exploitation',[119] and as a 'masterpiece of Machiavellian subterfuge'.[120] In particular, the philanthropic subtext of much of the corporate contribution to the public sphere was challenged as inconsistent with the practical reality of commercial activity in the area.[121] These high level ripostes were not the only manifestation of dissatisfaction; the episode also stands as testimony to the inaccuracy of the view that sees citizens as members of a passive audience unable adequately to recognise or respond to controversial missives. The editorial style of Monsanto's campaign did not appeal to a public that is suspicious of any corporate agenda.[122] The company's own research indicated that the purchasing

---

112 F. Beacham, 'Questioning Technology: Tools for the Revolution' (1995) 4 *Media Culture Review* 18.
113 One illustration of this is the emergence of alternative media web-sites – see, for example, that of IndyMedia: *http://www.indymedia.org/* (accessed 20 September 2001).
114 This is not to argue that the Internet is a communicative space entirely free from surveillance – see D. Brandt, 'Big Brother Covets the Internet' (1995) 12 *Flatland* 44. Indeed, the Regulation of Investigatory Powers Act 2000 allows government to monitor and intercept all e-mail messages.
115 C. Locke, *Gonzo Marketing: Winning Through Worst Practices* (Oxford: Capstone Publishing, 2001).
116 L. Stuart, 'The Netiquette of Cyber-Spin' *The Guardian* 17 June 2000; Public Relations E-Commission, *The Death of Spin: How the Internet Radically Changes the Way Corporations Will Communicate* (London: Institute of Public Relations, 2000).
117 See text accompanying notes 14–15.
118 Dr Sue Mayer, cited in GeneWatch UK, 'ASA Rules that Monsanto Adverts were Misleading: Genewatch UK Complaints Upheld' *Press release* 10 August 1999.
119 R. Page, 'Breeding Trouble in our Fields' *Daily Telegraph* 13 June 1998. See also Liz Hosken and Eric Brunner, 'Big Brother is Good for You?' (1998) 4(6) *Splice* 8.
120 G. Monbiot, 'Gene Prince' *The Guardian* 9 June 1998.
121 Professor Marion Nestle, cited in Editorial, 'European Consumer Opposition to GM Foods Remains Strong' *World Food Chemical News* 8 July 1998.
122 Nick Band, Chief Executive of PR firm Band and Brown, cited in Scott Hughes, 'Altering our Genetic Cynicism' *The Independent* 25 August 1998.

of a platform of advertising space stood as a metaphor in the public mind for its intention to impose products through commercial power.[123] It was parodied online and in the alternative media as both 'Nonsanto' and 'Mutanto'.[124] Monsanto had miscalculated the depth of public feeling, and having raised issues in a high profile manner suffered a backlash in the discursive arena.

In sum, the argument that relaxation of the broadcasting prohibition would see the subversion of the public sphere is unconvincing. On one hand, few advertisers are sufficiently powerful to warrant concern. On the other hand, members of the public possess sufficient critical faculties to identify and disparage attempts 'from above' to delude them into some errant consciousness.

Avoiding an arms race: advertising and the funding of political parties

The foregoing discussions suggest that a fourth justification is necessary better to explain the intended retention of the restriction on advocacy advertising. Such is often found in the perceived need to avoid an inexorable escalation in the expenditure on electoral advertising committed by political parties and others.[125] The existence of the ban, and the compensatory scheme of guaranteed party political broadcasts, is thought to secure a relatively fair distribution of available broadcast time among the major parties. The composite mechanism is considered almost universally to be an important foundation of British public life. Were the ban to be lifted, the two main parties would likely feel compelled to raise additional funds in order to advertise on television: 'no party chairman wants to be accused, after the event, of having lost an election because he or she did not spend 'that extra £500,000' shortly before polling day'.[126]

It is understandable on purely pragmatic grounds that this incessant accumulative obligation is one in which political luminaries are loath to engage. Of greater potential concern is the notion that donors of the funds that would sustain such a scheme, or advertise themselves on behalf of preferred parties, might come to expect 'government in their favour'. In addition to benefiting from a privileged access to the public sphere secured by wealth, such third parties might seek to gain a structural influence over the implementation of governmental policy.

The apocalyptic vision is that of minority parties effectively excluded from the public sphere, while their more established contemporaries become enthralled to private interests. Any relaxation of the prohibition matched by a withdrawal of free broadcast time for political parties would be likely to polarise political representations in the public sphere, and increase the strain on public trust in the integrity of government. The byword for this concern is 'Americanisation': 'the American model of political advertising is decidedly not something that we want

---

123 S. Greenburg, *Re: The British Test – The Fall 1998 Research* Research paper (1998). Extracts from the leaked document were printed in national newspapers, see 'Genetic Engineering: Root of the Matter' *The Guardian* 25 November 1998.

124 See (1998) 4(6) *Splice* 1, *http://www.mutanto.de* (accessed 18 July 2002).

125 Interestingly, during the 1997 general election the main contenders, the Conservatives and Labour, spent £14.4m and £5.75m respectively on non-broadcast advertising, whereas the Liberal Democrats spent only £80k - Committee on Standards in Public Life, n 35 above, table 13.1.

126 *ibid*, para 13.3. Smaller parties also favour retention of the prohibition. They appreciate that the improbability of their gaining power leaves them less able to raise substantial sums from private sources, and so fear the prospect of a concomitant loss of free-to-air election broadcasts.

to witness in the United Kingdom, given its risk of diluting the quality of political debate'.[127] Notwithstanding that this notion of 'quality' is a somewhat nebulous concept, equivalent explanations are reiterated with regularity.[128] The derided American experience does see political parties and candidates advertising their views directly to voters on television, often in concert with similar electoral advocacy sponsored by third party corporations and interest groups. The potential influence over elected representatives implicitly garnered by this devotion of 'soft money' has become a significant focus for public concern in the United States as it has in Britain.[129]

In terms of the balancing required by Article 10(2) ECHR, arguments that aver to the sustenance of the democratic ethic are immediately persuasive. The ECtHR has confirmed on numerous occasions that democracy and the enunciated rights are to be considered as mutually supportive.[130] This is not to say, however, that such arguments are compelling. Eminent commentators have still maintained that the outright ban on paid political advertising is likely to suffer under any analysis against the Convention catalogue.[131] Further consideration of the issue must proceed after recollection of the distinction between different forms of advocacy: first, 'pure' advocacy advertising, secondly, third-party electoral advocacy, and finally, party-political representations.

As regards pure advocacy advertising – that focused on social issues generally – the fourth argument justifying the broadcasting prohibition is simply not pertinent. Indeed, such representations should arguably be positively encouraged for their contribution to the vitality of public discourse. While their promulgation is most definitely designed to influence citizens, this is not in the first instance in their capacity as voters; the advertisements bear no relation to electoral contests. Any attempt to retain the restriction on advertising of this nature is liable to be impugned by the courts as contrary to the Human Rights Act 1998 if and when it is challenged. At least in this regard, the restriction should be lifted. Notably, a proposed movement in this direction has been mooted in the past. An amendment that would have seen the words 'party-political' replace 'political' in sections 8(2)(a)(i) and 92(2)(a)(i) of the 1990 Act was rejected by the Government during the passage of the Broadcasting Act 1996.[132] This decision should now be rethought in the deliberations on the Communications Bill.

It is only where advertising pursued by private organisations strays into electoral advocacy that it might engage the fourth justification for the restriction on broadcast representation. The apparent result is that in order to relieve the prohibition on pure advocacy advertising it becomes vital to distinguish it from electoral advocacy: 'unless you can cope with... third party expenditure... then there is a coach and horses that can run through any system you can invent'.[133] It might sometimes be difficult, however, to determine whether a specific missive is

---

127 Iain Sproat MP, HC Deb vol 287 col 192 10 December 1996.
128 David Mellor MP, HC Deb vol 172 col 203 9 May 1990; Committee on Standards in Public Life, n 35 above, para 13.11; Committee on Standards in Public Life, n 107 above, para 15 (*per* Peter Riddell), para 1439 (*per* Lord Parkinson).
129 N. Cohen, 'Ecclestone, Enron, Desmond: Is There a Pattern Here?' *The Observer* 19 May 2002.
130 See, for example, *UCPT v Turkey* (1998) 26 EHRR 121 para 41 *et seq.* Indeed, the Preamble to the Convention itself establishes a clear connection between the catalogue and democracy.
131 Electoral Commission, *Party Political Broadcasting*, Consultation Paper (2002) para 2.10, citing the opinion of Professor Eric Barendt.
132 HL Deb vol 570 col 482 7 March 1996.
133 Committee on Standards in Public Life, n 107 above, para 1442 (per Michael Trend)

aimed at promoting a particular perspective on some given issue, or rather at encouraging voters to elect one candidate over another.

It would be overly pessimistic to argue that such distinctions are beyond the wit of the legislature to enact. Indeed, an attempt to do precisely this can be seen in the delineation of 'election material' located in Part VI of the Political Parties, Elections and Referendums Act 2000, and overseen by the Electoral Commission.[134] The purpose of this part of the Act is to register third parties interested in campaigning towards particular electoral outcomes, and thereby to facilitate the regulation of their expenditure against established limits.[135] In essence, it provides for the identification of material that can reasonably be regarded as 'intended to promote or procure electoral success... or otherwise enhance the standing [of particular parties]' even though it might serve some additional purpose as well.[136] The period of the electoral campaign is deemed to be the entire year prior to the actual vote.[137] Expenditure on such material is then set against the cash limits.[138] This regime should also cater for the circumstance where, assuming that a restriction on advertising by political parties is maintained, hollow and transient interest groups are established merely to act as a 'front' for partisan advertising.[139] Necessarily, such election materials will not take the form of television or radio broadcasts.

Similarly, in the United States an attempt to regulate the inflow of soft money to political parties in the form of privately sponsored electoral advertising has recently been legislated.[140] The Bipartisan Campaign Reform Act 2002 seeks to compensate for the failure of an earlier attempt to preclude such tacit support that subsequently was deemed to be unconstitutional by the Supreme Court due to its lack of precision.[141] It does this by establishing a 'bright-line' determinant: 'broadcast ads that refer to a... candidate and that are run in the period right before an election... will be treated as campaign ads, rather than issue ads'.[142]

There is no reason why a suitable variant of these rules could not be applied to broadcast advocacy advertising. If unrelated to any impending election, a political representation should be allowed to proceed unhindered. This conclusion might be reached either where the substance of the advertisement did not align with the proposed policies of any political party, or importantly, where it surpassed party politics by gaining support or opprobrium from proponents of all formalised persuasions. Conceivably, the Government could make a correction during the

---

134 On the regulatory regime installed by the 2000 Act and overseen by the Electoral Commission, see K. Ewing, 'Transparency, Accountability and Equality: The Political Parties, Elections and Referendums Act 2000' [2001] *Public Law* 542; Paul Webb, 'Parties and Party Systems: Modernisation, Regulation and Diversity' (2001) 54 *Parliamentary Affairs* 308.

135 In respect of national elections in England, this controlled expenditure is capped at around £750K (Sched 10). Non-registered parties commit an offence if they expend more than £10K in similar circumstances (s 94).

136 s 85.

137 Sched 9 para 3(7).

138 This includes 'notional expenditure', or payments in kind (s 86).

139 Notably, in *FEC* v *Massachusetts Citizens for Life* (1986) 479 US 238 264, the US Supreme Court noted that non-profit organizations could not simply act as 'conduits' for otherwise forbidden spending in federal elections.

140 An information site on 'Campaign Finance' hosted by the Brookings Institute – see *http://www.brook.edu/dybdocroot/gs/cf/cf_hp.htm* (accessed 18 July 2002)

141 *Buckley* v *Valeo* (1976) 424 US 1 44. The impugned provisions had been contained in the Federal Election Campaign Act 1974.

142 T. Potter, 'New Law Follows Supreme Court Rulings' *BNA Daily Report for Executives* 22 April 2002. Reproduced at: *http://www.brook.edu/dybdocroot/gs/cf/debate/Potter.pdf* (accessed 10 July 2002).

passage of the Communications Bill. Failing this, the courts may in future be motivated by their high regard for political expression to achieve a propitious result. They may deploy a restrictive interpretation of the term 'political' in the existing or any reiterated proscription to allow Convention-compliance as required by section 3 of the Human Rights Act. In any event, the continued justification of the broadcasting ban, at least insofar as it applies to pure advocacy, cannot be sustained on this fourth ground.

Third – and political party broadcast electoral advocacy

The foregoing discussion has been premised on the assumption that for the reasons stated broadcast electoral advocacy, whether promulgated by political parties or their supporters, will continue to be considered a proscribed activity. While it lies at the fringe of the focus of this paper, a number of reflections can be offered on this point.

First, it is arguable that the dubious legality of the broadcasting ban as it impacts specifically on political parties is likely to remain merely an academic issue. The Electoral Commission has suggested that maintenance of the prohibition is possible primarily on account of the existence of the regime of party-political broadcasts.[143] As noted above, the overwhelming weight of opinion among political parties is to concur. This apparent unanimity is important in that it dilutes the likelihood that any challenge to this arm of the prohibition will be brought.

It is possible to conceive of a potential litigant, for example, the minority party not allocated a broadcast on account of its diminutive size. Such a party might be motivated to object to its inability to advertise through paid channels. It is likely, however, that such groups would consist of either single-issue campaigners akin to the ProLife Alliance, or of independent candidates motivated by some local controversy. For a group in the former category, the strategy of standing candidates in numerous constituencies with its attendant costs simply in order only to gain access to electoral broadcasts would become unnecessary. They could mitigate their inability to broadcast as a political party simply by de-registering, and instead redirecting their resources towards accessing the public sphere through paid airtime. As regards the locally oriented candidate, national or regional broadcasting would seem a wholly inappropriate communicative vehicle, both in terms of effectiveness and because of the much more tight controls on local electoral expenditure. Thus, they would be more likely to direct their resources to other means.

It is less easy to dismiss the prospect of a challenge mounted by a disgruntled third party advertiser. Notably, for such a litigant the attempt to justify the ban by reference to a desire to avoid the garnering of excessive degrees of influence over elected politicians would sit awkwardly against the relatively generous limits allowed in respect of other forms of advertising.[144] Rather than engage in hypothesising the propensity of litigants to take action, it is more attractive to recognise that even these arms of the broadcasting ban serve a limited purpose and would be better repealed.

---

143 Electoral Commission, n 131 above, para 5.16.
144 n 126 above.

This would not be to leave the field of broadcast airtime open to abuse. Any tendency towards exuberant political broadcasting occasioned by the removal of the ban could be curtailed by the maintenance of existing election expenditure limits. To the extent that this mechanism still involves an effective restriction on the freedom of expression of supporting organisations, this is more likely to be considered proportionate to the general interest in avoiding the subversion of the democratic process by wealthy interests. The recent Strasbourg decision in the case of *Bowman* implicitly suggested that the retention of some expenditure limit, if not overly restrictive, could be justifiable under Article 10(2) ECHR.[145] Any perceived need to further restrict or permit broadcast electoral advertising could then be addressed by amending the relevant expenditure limits.

Conclusions

The four standard justifications that support the broadcasting ban on advocacy advertising are insufficient to found its legality. At best, the arguments deployed warrant only a much less proscriptive interference, at least insofar as there is little evident relation to party politics. On one hand, they could justify minor restrictions and embellishments on representations that would facilitate the citizen-consumer in his or her viewing choices. On the other hand, they might coalesce in some form of regulatory watchfulness for anti-democratic conglomeration in the advertising market. At worst, however, the purported justifications misapprehend the vitality, plurality, and ingenuity of the public sphere, and condescend towards a general populace conceived as a semi-cognisant mass.

A lifting of the ban on advocacy advertising may have a significant impact on the character of the public sphere. It is possible, however, that major advertisers will not rush into adopting the method. The prevailing view among professionals in the public relations industry is that the public is increasingly resistant to the imposition of ideas by powerful entities. Perhaps only consciousness-raising communication by groups concerned with marginal issues would be effective in such a new environment. Of course, such missives may be accompanied by much representation that is commonly considered to be misguided and irresponsible. Thus, it would be vital under a more open regime that individuals develop and maintain the capacity to discriminate between arguments presented to them. If the Internet is to continue to offer a fillip to this aim, then measures to bolster further levels of IT literacy, Internet access and evaluative skills must be pursued as part of a wider commitment to citizenship education.

---

145 *Bowman* v *United Kingdom* (1998) 26 EHRR 1. The language used was that a limit on expenditure of £5 was 'disproportionate' (para 47).

[11]

THE NEWNESS OF NEW TECHNOLOGY

Monroe E. Price*

Every new technology transforms the world around it. A century ago, in a gentle preface to his novel *Under the Greenwood Tree*,[1] Thomas Hardy wrote of the transformation of little church orchestras in village England. Humble and amateur community instrumentalists were being displaced by an "isolated organist" employing a newly manufactured and more cheaply distributed technology, the harmonium or barrel organ. The new device presented certain advantages in control and accomplishment, but, he suggested, the change caused the stultification of the clergy's aims and resulted in loss of interest among parishioners. In these tiny hamlets the technology of musical development had consequences for participation, organization of the institution, the nature of the music that was played, and, Hardy seemed to be saying, for country life as well. Of these multiple and small transformations major changes in society take place.

Newness, a preoccupation with the unknown, a twinning of heralded benefits and fears of danger is one trope of restructuring that is evident throughout the process of legal and policy transformation. Every candidate for new information technology has invited a super-heated rhetoric of millennial social change, a balloon of Hardy's modest and precise description of the effect of the harmonium. When wireless radio technology was introduced in the first decades of the twentieth century, world peace was said to be only a turn of the dial away.[2] The *New York Times* wrote: "Nothing so fosters and promotes a mutual understanding and a community of sentiment and interests as cheap, speedy, and

---

* Sadie and Joseph Dancyger Professor of Law, Cardozo School of Law, Yeshiva University and co-director, Programme in Comparative Media Law and Policy, University of Oxford, LLB Yale Law School, 1964. This Essay is adapted from a forthcoming book tentatively titled *Journeys in Media Space: Law, Identity and Technology in a Global Environment*. I presented this paper at the Institute for Advanced Study (information technology and society group) in fall 2000 as a Member in the School of Social Science.

[1] THOMAS HARDY, UNDER THE GREENWOOD TREE (Tim Dolin ed., Penguin Putnam 1999) (1872).

[2] *See* Susan J. Douglas, *Amateur Operators and American Broadcasting: Shaping the Future of Radio, in* IMAGINING TOMORROW: HISTORY, TECHNOLOGY, AND THE AMERICAN FUTURE 35 (Joseph J. Corn ed., 1986).

convenient communication."[3] Promised riches by hawkers of the new technology, investors poured enormous amounts of money into fledgling, often nearly bankrupt, wireless companies. As a guide to restructuring, newness in information technologies is almost always packaged with a stated capability for fulfilling dreams and, simultaneously, challenging existing institutions and mores.

It is possible that the satellite, the Internet, and other information technologies will lead to the greatest revolution in information since the invention of the printing press.[4] The extent to which this will be the case is not the point of this Article. Rather, it is to ask how change in technology is conceptualized, evaluated, and manifested in the process of reshaping institutions and laws. Governments try to divine how the newness of information technology affects the porousness of boundaries, capacities of old institutions to regulate new realities, the cultural horizons that result from altered patterns of data and image flows. Then, based on inadequate information, states probe ways to manage what they think are the consequences.

Elsewhere, I have explored examples of the threat of the new: its articulation as a carrier of illegal and harmful content and the capacity of new information technologies to present or intensify potential mischief and dangers.[5] Legislation to reshape modes of access and surveillance can be seen as an effort to deflect the use of new media for such purposes. In 1996, President Clinton established the President's Commission on Critical Infrastructure Protection to investigate the potential for terrorism on the Internet and legislation ensued from that.[6] A President's Working Group on Unlawful Conduct on the Internet called for restrictions on anonymity in cyberspace, citing law enforcement's inability to trace online fraud, hacking, and trafficking in child pornography, firearms, and drugs.[7] A society that fears revolutionary,

---

[3] *Id.* at 39 (quoting N.Y. TIMES, Aug. 15, 1899, at 6).

[4] *See* Jonathan Wallace & Michael Green, *Bridging the Analogy Gap: The Internet, the Printing Press and Freedom of Speech*, 20 SEATTLE U. L. REV. 711 (1997); Michael Hauben, *The Expanding Commonwealth of Learning: Printing and the Net, in* NETIZENS: ON THE HISTORY AND IMPACT OF USENET AND THE INTERNET (1994), *at* http://www.columbia.edu/~rh120/ch106.x16 (last visited Feb. 18, 2001).

[5] THE V-CHIP DEBATE: CONTENT FILTERING FROM TELEVISION TO THE INTERNET xiv (Monroe E. Price ed., 1998).

[6] *See* CRITICAL INFRASTRUCTURE ASSURANCE OFFICE, DEP'T OF JUSTICE, WHITE PAPER: THE CLINTON ADMINISTRATION'S POLICY ON CRITICAL INFRASTRUCTURE PROTECTION: PRESIDENTIAL DECISION DIRECTIVE 63 (1998); PRESIDENT'S COMM'N ON CRITICAL INFRASTRUCTURE PROTECTION, CRITICAL FOUNDATIONS: PROTECTING AMERICA'S INFRASTRUCTURE (1997). The Commission's website may be found at http://www.pccip.ncr.gov.

[7] *See* PRESIDENT'S WORKING GROUP ON UNLAWFUL CONDUCT ON THE INTERNET,

destabilizing, and dangerous dissent is prepared to vest in its government extended powers to defend the status quo. Terrorism or radicalism of dissent becomes another trope that justifies greater state authority.[8]

Another quality of newness is how we describe the social organization by which information comes from those who originate content to those who consume it. New media technology famously disintermediates, or is said to, altering the power of traditional entities such as department stores, political parties, and television networks.[9] Policymakers who hope for a technology that destroys existing mediators—creating a freer path between consumer and producer of information—might be more tolerant of implementing problems than those who think that the new technology merely remediates (yielding different institutional arrangements in place of the old). Legislative and judicial doctrines often build on a static concept of mediators or gatekeepers, dependent on actors who can be held responsible.[10]

Media technologies, as they are implemented, scotch the snake of power but do not destroy it. The language of technological determinism, as a descriptor of what constitutes the new, is overblown in this regard. Of course it is true that states will lose some capacity for control as a result of the spread of communications technologies. There is no reason to privilege the existing arrangements of states and the distribution of power among them. Some states, however, will increase their capacity to monitor and control as a result of their means of marshalling the new technology. And there will be other, as yet unknown, shifts as well.[11] States where information is produced may gain power over states where information is consumed. It may be a hallmark of increased power to be a state where information is processed or uplinked to satellite. Power may come from control over vital elements of the hardware, such as the capacity to build microchips,

---

THE ELEC. FRONTIER: THE CHALLENGE OF UNLAWFUL CONDUCT INVOLVING USE OF THE INTERNET (2000).

8 *See* ELEC. PRIVACY INFO. CTR., CRITICAL INFRASTRUCTURE PROTECTION AND THE ENDANGERMENT OF CIVIL LIBERTIES: AN ASSESSMENT OF THE PRESIDENT'S COMMISSION ON CRITICAL INFRASTRUCTURE PROTECTION (PCCIP) (1998), *available at* http://www.epic.org/security/infowar/cip.pdf (last visited Jan. 15, 2001).

9 *See* Charles Firestone, *Digital Culture and Civil Society: A New Role for Intermediaries?*, INTERMEDIA, 22 no.6 (Dec.-Jan. 1994-95); *see also* Symposium, *Financial Services: Security, Privacy, and Encryption*, 3 B.U. J. SCI. & TECH. L. 4 (1997) (comments of Valerie McNevin noting the Internet's potential to disintermediate financial services).

10 *See* Kathleen M. Sullivan, *First Amendment Intermediaries in the Age of Cyberspace*, 45 UCLA L. REV. 1653 (1998).

11 *See* James Boyle, *Foucault in Cyberspace: Surveillance, Sovereignty, and Hardwired Censors*, 66 U. CIN. L. REV. 177 (1997).

or control of software, as in encryption or filtering. States gain money and power when industries—gaming, pornography, or adventurous sale of pharmaceuticals—for various reasons, though often taking advantage of technology that allows new zones of immunity, relocate or establish themselves under the state's jurisdiction.

Throughout the global debate over new forms of producing and distributing information, the consistent and haunting question is whether technology overwhelms law and the capacity of a state to regulate. It is hardly ever that easy. New technology changes the frame for negotiation, for making decisions and for the formation and application of policy. It is much less the case that technological change eliminates either the need for law or reduces the capacity for establishing and enforcing norms to nothingness. What occurs, almost always, is a process of adjustment: norms and institutions that were created for one set of technologies adjust or erode. Where basic values and social needs are at stake, alternative modes of governance and standards emerge.

At the outset, the transformation appears radical. An entire construct seems dependent on an old form of industrial organization and assumptions about the structure of the media. Or even if that is not the case, then the capacity of the governing authority to enforce is, itself, dependent on assumptions that are in the process of being undermined. But even before the question of possibility arises, there is the issue of whether a technology is "new" in the sense that it calls for such a law-transformative moment. We need to be able to tell when a technological advance allows us to address a traditional problem in a new fashion, and, increasingly, we search for ways to maintain (or appear to maintain) traditional customs notwithstanding the introduction of technological change.

It is, however, popular to question the capacity of the state to engage in lawmaking and law enforcement, especially as technology advances and the implications of the Internet stagger the statist imagination. Jack Goldsmith has challenged those who ridicule the possibility of law:

> The skeptics make three basic errors. First, they overstate the differences between cyberspace transactions and other transnational transactions. Both involve people in real space in one territorial jurisdiction transacting with people in real space in another territorial jurisdiction in a way that sometimes causes real-world harms. In both contexts, the state in which the harms are suffered has a legitimate interest in regulating the activity that produces the harms. Second, the skeptics do not attend to the distinction between default laws and mandatory

laws. Their ultimate normative claim that cyberspace should be self-regulated makes sense with respect to default laws that, by definition, private parties can modify to fit their needs. It makes much less sense with respect to mandatory or regulatory laws that, for paternalistic reasons or in order to protect third parties, place limits on private legal ordering. Third, the skeptics underestimate the potential of traditional legal tools and technology to resolve the multijurisdictional regulatory problems implicated by cyberspace. Cyberspace transactions do not inherently warrant any more deference by national regulators, and are not significantly less resistant to the tools of conflict of laws, than other transnational transactions.[12]

Newness, then, has many faces; it can be newness within technology (as in the design of the interface or shifts in control over computational processes). Newness can be found in the impact on altering notions of distance or altering the speed of processes that in a slower environment could not be accomplished. Newness can mean altered institutional arrangements, as when states lose power or intermediating institutions lose force. Newness can have epistemological consequences, as when technology changes a person's idea of self or of collectivity and when it challenges existing ethical norms. We could speak of newness if technology brought to bear new narratives, new apocalyptic stories, and new ideas of perfection or immortality. The newness of new technology can be measured by whether its introduction alters, profoundly, human behavior. These broader senses of the new are important even as we turn to the narrow sense of introduction of technology that is the focus here.

I.   CAUTION AND PATIENCE

To look at this trope of newness in depth, I focus on a single judicial decision where a court was obliged to integrate new media technologies into its existing patterns of thinking. The opinions in the 1997 decision of the United States Supreme Court in *Reno v. ACLU*,[13] taken together with opinions in related cases, furnish a bouquet of opportunities for understanding. In their opinions, the Justices see themselves as obliged to determine whether a new technology is such a departure from what has gone before that it demands new forms of conceptualization. The Justices also explore how to ride change—to make and define law while the technology to be regulated is still indeterminate and there is

---

12 Jack L. Goldsmith, *Against Cyberanarchy*, 65 U. CHI. L. REV. 1199, 1200-01 (1998).
13 521 U.S. 844 (1997). Other related cases include *United States v. Playboy Entertainment Group*, 529 U.S. 803 (2000) and *Denver Area Educational Telecommunications Consortium, Inc. v. FCC*, 518 U.S. 727 (1996).

insufficient experience or knowledge to understand its actual impact and consequences. Examining this one example—in which the United States assessed the regulatory framework for the Internet so as to control indecency—has its analytic perils. Each society has its own distinct pattern of determining whether innovation in media technologies requires altered policies. Different societies have different mechanisms for rendering this judgment just as different societies have varied grids for determining which variables are significant. And in the United States, more than in many other countries, judges are instrumental in the defining process.

In the U.S. debate over media technologies and indecency, there is a specific rhetoric (not replicated in Europe) relating to the distinction between old media and new. As a consequence of constitutional tradition and judicial interpretation, every "new" media technology has to be dissected to see the way it functions measured against the template of the First Amendment.[14] One question often asked is, does the newness of the medium differentiate it from, or make it similar to, newspapers, broadcasting, or cable? By so assessing the characteristics of the technology (and its surrounding social arrangements), its newness is tested to determine what features call forth doctrinal differences. This includes asking whether or how a technology can be "zoned," establishing specific geographical or time areas for one form of programming or another. It also includes questions about whether the technology, coupled with the structure of distribution, renders the images on the screen more "invasive," or, rather, more subject to informed choice and selection.

The technology models for the Internet in the 1996 Communications Decency Act ("CDA") are the telephone as well as radio and television.[15] However, the Internet poses no obvious opportunity, as radio and television familiarly do, to establish parts of the program day, safe parts and "freer" parts, watersheds or so-called safe harbors for protecting children from inappropriate content. Such devices, familiar from European practice and earlier efforts in the United States, divide the schedule into spans when indecent programming can be broadcast for adults under the somewhat old-fashioned assumption that children would not be so predominantly in the audience. Given global access, this approach

---

[14] This process is superbly described in Jonathan Weinberg, *Broadcasting and Speech*, 81 CAL. L. REV. 1103 (1993).

[15] For an excellent discussion of questions concerning the constitutionality of regulations protecting children as discussed in *Reno*, see Eugene Volokh, *Freedom of Speech, Shielding Children, and Transcending Balancing*, 1997 SUP. CT. REV. 141 (1998).

would not work for the Internet. The architecture of the Net precludes the comforting notion that society can protect itself by having family viewing times, or times of lower brutality and reduced sexual programming. The new qualities of the Internet (its global quality) require constraints that do not distinguish by time period. On this score, much of the CDA is patterned after existing legislation prohibiting harassing calls on the telephone.[16]

A significant issue, in the U.S. framing of the question, was whether anything new or different occurs with the interaction of child and image on the screen in the newer technology as opposed to older technologies. Could it be the case, for example, that for all the complexity of distribution, for all the newness of new technology, there is little basis for distinguishing between what a minor saw on a computer screen and what he or she saw on a television screen?[17] The psychological or cultural implications could be roughly the same. Qualities of technological newness might not be sufficient to change the standard of what should be permitted or banned from what had been present in legislative treatment of other similarly received images.

It was in the context of this conflict between the old and continuous or new and differentiated that the CDA came to the United States Supreme Court. Assessing newness requires knowledge of context, but the Court made remarkably clear that too little is reliably known about the behavioral assumptions or legislative rationale concerning the Internet to determine how to conceptualize the new technology. In a footnote to his opinion for the Court, Justice John Paul Stevens sternly points out that no hearings were held in the Congress on the provisions at issue in the case until after their passage. He quotes at length one senator's dismay at Congress's "willy-nilly" intervention in the Internet.[18] Justice Stevens concludes his opinion by driving home the Court's dissatisfaction with "the absence of any detailed findings by the Congress, or even hearings addressing the special problems of the CDA."[19]

The Court thus found it difficult to rule decisively; its efforts were like a powerful automobile moving in a confusing dusk, forced to do something, but not necessarily in custody of all the relevant information. The Justices had to assess the nature of newness at a

---

[16] *See, e.g.,* Glen O. Robinson, *The Electronic First Amendment: An Essay for the New Age,* 47 DUKE L.J. 899 (1998).

[17] As it happens, the post-1996 technology meant that individuals would often view the Internet on their television screens, received through their cable.

[18] *Reno,* 521 U.S. at 858 n.24 (1997) (quoting Senator Leahy).

[19] *Id.* at 879.

time when the potential for change was great, but not yet realized, or even if realized did not exist in a manner that had an institutional filter. The Court was asked to furnish constitutional standards to guide Congress, but the governmental mechanisms for clarifying basic assumptions were still unclear. Fervent was the wish, among many in the technology world, for a recognition that the Internet was new in such a radical way as to call for a totally new jurisprudence that was wholly liberating. The forces for the new sought a ruling that would sweepingly defend the Internet from the hands of those inclined to regulate. Though the Court struck down the CDA, an impulse to the categorically new was deflected by the ordinary notion of deference, or perhaps of deferral, to the legislative branch and to the pull of the constitutionally familiar.

Because these decisions came before a judicial tribunal, one with limited expertise in media effects (though often called upon to make assumptions about such effects), one way to read the Court's decision in *Reno* may be in terms of the rhythm of decision making. The proper rhythm or pace can be formulated by asking when, or under what circumstances, is it appropriate to evaluate the implications of a technology. The provocative writings of Lawrence Lessig, especially his views on postponement and readiness, have addressed this issue. Two articles, *The Path of Cyberlaw*, and *Reading the Constitution in Cyberspace*, both written before *Reno*, proved unusually influential in this then-young constitutional field.[20] Several ideas basic to Lessig's scholarship seem to haunt the Justices' opinions. One is a plea for caution before policymakers impose a standard decision-making grid on the use of new technologies. Professor Lessig states, "if we had to decide today . . . just what the First Amendment should mean in cyberspace, . . . we would get it fundamentally wrong."[21]

In a second suggestion, Lessig cautions that one must be careful not to be swept away by metaphors from the physical world when thinking about cyberspace.[22] Constitutional doctrine adapted from our preexisting environment may not be fully suitable in the brave, new context.[23] Circumstances, facts, and technologies change.

---

[20] Lawrence Lessig, *The Path of Cyberlaw*, 104 YALE L.J. 1743 (1995) [hereinafter Lessig, *Cyberlaw*]; Lawrence Lessig, *Reading the Constitution in Cyberspace*, 45 EMORY L.J. 869 (1996) [hereinafter Lessig, *Reading the Constitution*].

[21] Denver Area Educ. Telecomm. Consortium, Inc. v. FCC, 518 U.S. 727, 777 (1996) (Souter J., concurring) (quoting Lessig, *Cyberlaw, supra* note 20, at 1745).

[22] *See* Lessig, *Reading the Constitution, supra* note 20, at 886. This idea is a source for Justice O'Connor in *Reno*, 521 U.S. at 889 (1997) (O'Connor, J., concurring in part and dissenting in part) (citing Lessig, *Reading the Constitution, supra* note 20, at 886).

[23] *See* Lessig, *Reading the Constitution, supra* note 20, at 902-03 ("We come from a tradition of translation in constitutional interpretation; in a wide range of cases, the aim has been to preserve founding values as interpretive contexts have changed. . . . But

Existing conceptualizations (often based on metaphor) arise and may be necessary for day-to-day life. But transfer of category may be the mind's lazy approach to analysis. Taken together, these cautionary ideas suggest that the Court (or *a* court), muddling through, must wait and see before it prescribes solutions.[24]

Indeed these notions have transcending and complex implications not only for jurisprudence in the Internet era but for all decisionmakers dealing with new media technologies. The idea that doctrine turns on timing means that there are moments in which insecurity about power ought to lead to its nonexercise or to a fuzzy outcome. Yet that conflicts with strongly held views about how constitutional determinations ought to be articulated by an entity like the Supreme Court consistent with obligations to communicate clearly and decisively to the public, the Congress, and other judicial tribunals.

Doubt and caution may be reasons for the Supreme Court not to take a case, but once taken, it is hard to accept the notion of the Court saying "we don't know yet, but here's the best we can say." When the plurality in *Denver Area Educational Telecommunications Consortium, Inc. v. FCC,*[25] a First Amendment case from the cable television medium, came close to saying just that, Justice Kennedy responded angrily in dissent:

> This is why comparisons and analogies to other areas of our First Amendment case law become a responsibility, rather than the luxury the plurality considers them to be. The comparisons provide discipline to the Court and guidance for others, and give clear content to our standards—all the things I find missing in the plurality's opinion.... We have before us an urgent claim for relief against content-based discrimination, not a dry run.[26]

Furthermore, a position of doubt can conflict, as occurred in *Reno*, with an extraordinary pressure to categorize the new technology, *now*, as a technology of freedom, unhinged from the ambivalent and government-justifying history of the regulation of broadcasting. The publishing industry, library associations, colleges and universities— an enormously impressive list of plaintiffs—urged (unsuccessfully

---

translations in cyberspace will not always be clear.").

[24] *See* Lessig, *Cyberlaw, supra* note 20, at 1754. Lessig states:

> Cyberspace is elsewhere, and before carving the First Amendment into its silicon, we should give the culture a chance to understand it.... If there is sanction to intervene, then it is simply to assure that the revolution continue, not to assure that every step conforms with the First Amendment as now understood.
> *Id.*

[25] 518 U.S. 727 (1996).

[26] *Id.* at 787 (Kennedy, J., concurring in part and dissenting in part).

on this narrow ground) that certainty was necessary and that the proclivity to regulate by Congress should be nipped in the bud by a clear decision applying the greatest possible protection to Internet communications. As the Court states in a different context, "liberty finds no refuge in a jurisprudence of doubt."[27]

The second important *Reno*-related contribution of Professor Lessig—his articulation of a tentativeness about facts and about how to capture and reduce the array of facts available—tends to the poetic. His arguments suggest how complicated it is to adapt the metaphors and analogies that have influenced the constitutional doctrine of the physical world to the world of cyberspace, particularly when that world is itself still being constructed, both physically and conceptually.[28] Time may be necessary to transcend metaphor. This, then, is a further challenge: to acknowledge that many legal systems depend on metaphors that are fragile and limited and that misportray evolving circumstances. Implicit in this suggestion is a critique of the standard process of extending law, suggesting that shifting to cyberspace from more physical counterparts requires a rethinking of how categories are established, and who determines the character of the real world (in the U.S. case, the respective role of Congress, administrative agencies, and the courts).

The opinion of Justice O'Connor in *Reno* illustrates the problem of adjusting to metaphors while assessing a new technology. She relates a wish to think of the Internet as a land, inhabited by a number of institutions, some of whom are purveyors of indecent material. For her, the relevant ways of thinking about the law are to consider the applicability of legal analogies. In her opinion she looks, especially, toward decisions concerning the more physical world of bookstores and their locations. There, the Court has endorsed the establishment of "adult zones," specified physical sites that deal in pornographic materials and that can be segregated to particular parts of towns and cities, thus removed from children. By relying on the notion that this is a "zoning case"[29]—which is itself a vision of cyberspace—she makes her own leap, coping with the new but well within existing modes of fashioning principles.[30]

---

[27] Planned Parenthood v. Casey, 505 U.S. 833, 844 (1992).

[28] *See* Lessig, *Cyberlaw, supra* note 20, at 1753 ("[N]o court should purport to decide these questions finally or even firmly. Here especially should be the beginning of a dialogue, which perhaps more than others is meant to construct its subject more than reflect it.").

[29] Reno v. ACLU, 521 U.S. 844, 886 (1997) (O'Connor, J., concurring in part and dissenting in part).

[30] *See* Lessig, *Reading the Constitution, supra* note 20, at 886-95.

But Justice O'Connor demonstrates that she cannot be sure the analogy would work. Is zoning in cyberspace the same as zoning in the physical world? Justice O'Connor expresses doubts whether the received doctrine respecting speech-related zoning—rules that she finds acceptable in their traditional application to street corners in cities—should apply in cyberspace.[31] The image of the adult bookshop, with its masked windows, the forbidden entry, the lonely monitor working into the night, translates into cyberspace only with difficulty. "Before today," Justice O'Connor writes, there was no reason to question the approach of zoning, for before the Internet case "the Court has previously only considered law that operated in the physical world, a world with two characteristics that make it possible to create 'adult zones': geography and identity."[32] This new layer of abstraction is what forces the rethinking of the Constitution and basic principles in the world of cyberspace.[33] Thus, Justice O'Connor retains her commitment to the architecture of her past constitutional doctrine, but recognizes the complexity of extending it to the new technologies.

How does a decision maker act in such a moment of indecision—a moment when it is unclear whether the judicially accepted verities of a physical world exist in the cyberspace counterpart? Justice O'Connor concludes,

> Although the prospects for the eventual zoning of the Internet appear promising, I agree with the Court that we must evaluate the constitutionality of the CDA as it applies to the Internet as it exists today. Given the present state of cyberspace . . . the [statute's] 'display' provision could not pass muster.[34]

However, she justifies her belief that it will pass eventually by saying, "Cyberspace is malleable. Thus, it is possible to construct barriers in cyberspace and use them to screen for identity, making cyberspace more like the physical world and, consequently, more amenable to zoning laws. This transformation of cyberspace is already underway."[35]

II. ASSESSING NEW TECHNOLOGY

To determine the newness of a media technology one must have a description of it, fixing the points for a factual assessment. To achieve such a description involves notions of relevance. It may be important, for example, that new satellite dish technology

---

31 *See Reno*, 521 U.S. at 888-91.
32 *Id*. at 889.
33 *See* Lessig, *Reading the Constitution, supra* note 20, at 885-88.
34 *Reno*, 521 U.S. at 891 (citation omitted).
35 *Id*. at 890.

is handkerchief-sized, but the relevant question is whether a reduction of diameter has legal and constitutional consequences. In societies where the state seeks to monitor or control the viewing habits of its citizens, the largeness or smallness of satellite dishes may be of great significance. What makes a new technology new for purposes of legal or constitutional analysis may often be a matter of the extent to which the new technology threatens, sustains, or even enhances a particular state's position in the marketplace for loyalties.[36] In this respect, the concept of technological newness may function as cover for very traditional state concerns. What is new in a new technology may simply be those aspects of the technology that challenge state control or render current legal doctrine untenable.

Assembling facts to evaluate which attributes of significance have become realized or are likely to exist within a period relevant to a societal decision is central, then, to the project of deciding what is paradigm-shifting about a technology. Almost by definition, however, newness is often a series of claims, a series of promises, and a series of hopes. The questions of changing constitutionality or paradigm-shift arise during times of aspiration, before industry structure and performance in the world are fully realized. The potential for stalemate is obvious. Financial investment in the industry may not be maximized until a reliable legal environment is established, yet the decisions concerning norms cannot take place until there is sufficient information.

Let us turn to *Reno* again for an example of the relevance of a factual base. One background issue of significance was whether circumstances existed that allowed parents easily to control what their children saw on the Internet.[37] Danger to children, after all, was the big fear (justified or not) motivating Congress, the dark omen confounding the Internet's benefits. The CDA put the onus of keeping the Internet clean largely on the senders of information. Providers or senders had to ensure, more or less, that only material "not indecent" flowed through the wires if young people would have access to it. Online providers were immune from responsibility only if they took specifically designated steps to assure that the recipient was not a minor. However, because of the shape of American First Amendment jurisprudence, this congressional approach would not be constitutional if less

---

[36] *See* Monroe E. Price, *The Market for Loyalties: Electronic Media and the Global Competition for Allegiances*, 104 YALE L.J. 667 (1994).

[37] For a full discussion of these questions, see Mark S. Nadel, *The First Amendment's Limitations on the Use of Internet Filtering in Public and School Libraries: What Content Can Librarians Exclude?*, 78 TEX. L. REV. 1117 (2000).

restrictive alternatives were available to meet the legitimate goals of Congress.

Thus, in the *Reno* litigation, one of the major questions was whether or not such solutions—less restrictive alternatives that would allow speakers to be unfettered (or less fettered)—are truly available. One of the revolutionary ways of thinking about "alternatives" was technology similar to the V-chip, software-filtering systems that would allow screening by the user, rather than restrictions on the sender.[38] But a determination that a technology provides a "less restrictive alternative" is necessarily based on an assumption that the technology actually exists (or is very likely to exist). The evaluation of which alternatives are viable or restrictive are questions concerning what the world is really like. Justices must determine what the world of technology and behavior can do or reliably promises to do at the moment in question and how to integrate a desired or imagined future into current constitutional doctrine.

In *Reno*, Justice Stevens, desirous of invalidating the burdens Congress imposed on the senders of information, had to stretch to make his point on the utility of alternatives. Outlining the anticipated types of devices available through the Internet, he writes, in carefully chosen words:

> Systems have been developed to help parents control the material that may be available .... A system may either limit a computer's access to an approved list of sources that have been identified as containing no adult material, it may block designated inappropriate sites, or it may attempt to block messages containing identifiable objectionable features.[39]

Justice Stevens notes that current technologies include parental control software that can screen for suggestive words or for known sexually explicit sites, though there is no software that can screen for sexually explicit images.[40]

The passive voice suggests the distance Justice Stevens places between his convictions and the description of reality that he presses into service. He also employs a device available to reviewing courts like the Supreme Court. On a "matter of fact" (like whether these devices are available), a Justice of the Supreme Court can rely on the trial court as a "finder of fact." Here, the

---

[38] For a review of these issues in advance of the Supreme Court's 2000 decision in *United States v. Playboy Entertainment Group*, 529 U.S. 803 (2000), see the perceptive student Note by Barton Beebe, *Parental Initiative in the Age of Signal Bleed*, 109 YALE L.J. 627 (1999).

[39] *Reno*, 521 U.S. at 854-55.

[40] *See id.* (relying on finding 72 of the trial court, citing ACLU v. Reno, 929 F. Supp. 824, 842 (E.D.Pa. 1996)).

District Court had, according to Justice Stevens, determined from the evidence that "a reasonably effective method by which parents can prevent their children from accessing material which parents believe is inappropriate will soon be widely available."[41] Note that the method is not yet available, and the "evidence" is probably a self-serving declaration by those who hope to introduce such software that it will be available.[42]

This technological meliorism has been criticized. One year after the Court handed down *Reno*, Professor Lessig published an influential law review article, *What Things Regulate Speech: CDA 2.0 vs. Filtering*.[43] In the article, he warns that even if the less restrictive means relied on by the Court became available in the form of effective filtering software, this technology would be more intrusive on speech than the provisions rejected in *Reno*. He states,

> My sense is that this first major victory—in *Reno v. ACLU*—has set us in a direction that we will later regret .... The "less restrictive means" touted by free speech activists in *Reno* are, in my view, far more restrictive of free speech interests than a properly crafted CDA would be. And unless we quickly shift ground, we will see Congress embracing these less protective (of speech) means, or worse, we will see the success of the President in bullying industry into accepting them.[44]

Professor Eugene Volokh was also dissatisfied with the reasoning.[45] In his view, the most troubling aspect of Justice Stevens's opinion was the statement that the CDA's burden on free speech "is unacceptable if less restrictive alternatives would be at least as effective in achieving the legitimate purpose that the statute was enacted to serve."[46] The important phrase, to Volokh, is "at least as effective."[47] To him, no alternative could reach this standard. "None of the Court's proposed alternatives to the CDA—or any other alternatives I can imagine—would have been

---

[41] *Reno*, 521 U.S. at 846 (emphases omitted).

[42] The Court also made much of the fact that "existing technology did not include any effective method for a sender to prevent minors from obtaining access to its communications on the Internet without also denying access to adults." *Id.* at 876. In contrast, "[d]espite its limitations, currently available *user-based* software suggests that a reasonably effective method by which *parents* can prevent their children from accessing sexually explicit and other material which parents may believe is inappropriate for their children will soon be widely available." *Id.* at 877.

[43] Lawrence Lessig, *What Things Regulate Speech: CDA 2.0 vs. Filtering*, 38 JURIMETRICS J. 629 (1998).

[44] *Id.* at 632.

[45] *See* Volokh, *supra* note 15.

[46] *Id.* at 148 (quoting *Reno*, 521 U.S. at 874).

[47] *Id.* at 148-60.

as effective as the CDA's more or less total ban."[48] Volokh continues, "The pregnant negative in the Court's reasoning is that, had there really been no equally effective alternatives (as in fact there are not), the CDA should have been upheld."[49]

There are a few other areas, lurking in *Reno,* where decision makers have to decide what dignity to accord to those things that pass as "facts." What assumptions, for example, exist about the nature and functioning of the family that inform evaluations of the role of new technology? Since so much of the social concern over the Internet seems to be about the child, and so many of the remedies deal with interactions between that child and his or her family, one would think the empirical grounding for difficult decisions would be abundant, even if not wholly adequate.

There are normative questions such as whether a parent ought to be able to determine that his or her child should watch images that the state considers inappropriate. But there are factual questions that underlie proposals for change. Are filters useful? How do parents influence the viewing habits of children? In *Reno,* Justice Stevens visits, glancingly, the issue of whether Congress can protect children from indecent programming regardless of the desire of their parents. The United States, in its argument, had contended that the First Amendment does not preclude "a blanket prohibition on all 'indecent' and 'patently offensive' messages communicated" to a minor "regardless of parental approval."[50] The Court demurred, but in doing so, it seemed to raise a new kind of test. It is true, Justice Stevens writes, that protection of children is a "compelling interest" that, in some instances, justifies regulation. But a regulation that potentially overrules parental preferences, or even covers parental speech to children, "imposes an especially heavy burden" on Congress to demonstrate why less restrictive provisions would not be suitable.[51]

This "parent-protecting" test and the context in which this debate arises is intriguing. For just as moralistic as Congress (and perhaps the Court) seems to be in terms of limiting the access of children to indecent material, it is similarly concerned about

---

[48] *Id.* at 149.

[49] *Id.* at 157.

[50] *Reno,* 521 U.S. at 878. A dispute, really a skirmish, within this discussion is whether or not "minor" should include individuals under eighteen or under seventeen years of age.

[51] *Id.* at 879. In dealing with this question, Justice O'Connor concluded that the record did not show that "many E-mail transmissions from an adult to a minor are conversations between family members"; but more important, she finds "no support for the legal proposition that such speech is absolutely immune from regulation." *Id.* at 896. Perhaps both the Court and Justice O'Connor agree that such speech is not "absolutely immune," since the Court holds that such speech might be regulable if Congress were to meet an especially heavy burden. *Id.*

trenching on parent-child relationships. And this conflict drives Congress and the Court to make unfounded, sometimes silly, but almost always sweeping, statements about parents and their relationship to children. The Court cites earlier decisions for the "consistent" principle that "the parents' claim to authority in their own household to direct the rearing of their children is basic in the structure of our society."[52] This principle rests on the earlier pronouncement (having to do with foreign-language education) that, "[i]t is cardinal with us that the custody, care, and nurture of the child reside *first* in the parents, whose primary function and freedom include preparation for obligations the state can neither supply nor hinder."[53]

Having decided that the CDA covers e-mail, Justice Stevens engaged in an elaborate conceit to indicate the constitutional infirmity of the legislation. "[M]any e-mail transmissions from an adult to a minor are conversations between family members," he says, setting a predicate for their special protection.[54] Under the CDA, Justice Stevens contends, "a parent who sent his 17-year-old college freshman information on birth control via e-mail could be incarcerated even though neither he, his child, nor anyone in their home community found the material 'indecent' or 'patently offensive,' if the college town's community thought otherwise."[55] To be fair, Justice Stevens's concern goes beyond e-mail. It seems wrong to him that under the CDA, a parent "could face a lengthy prison term" for "allowing her 17-year-old to use the family computer to obtain information on the Internet that she, in her parental judgment, deems appropriate."[56]

Here again, as with so much in *Reno*, it is a dependence on a specific and possible empty understanding of the facts of the world that virtually controls how the new media technology is judged. The present state is such that the relationship between conclusions and available facts is dismal. Take just the vision of what we mean by "parents," what relationship there is (much less ought to be) between parents and children, and how, in fact, decisions are made to deploy sites that are considered "indecent" by Congress. To make a decision, Justice Stevens must have a mental picture of how decisions to deploy indecent sites are made so he can tell whether there is a problem serious enough to warrant

---

[52] *Id.* at 865 (citation omitted).

[53] Prince v. Massachusetts, 321 U.S. 158, 166 (1943) (emphasis added) (holding constitutional a statute barring the teaching of German language in public schools).

[54] *Reno,* 521 U.S. at 865 n.32. *But see Reno,* 521 U.S. at 886-97 (O'Conner, J., dissenting).

[55] *Id.* at 878.

[56] *Id.*

congressional intervention, and his examples are somewhat class-biased, to use an old-fashioned term that seems relevant here. The image that must be in the mind of the lawmaker is of the fractured, possibly "dysfunctional" family, what the government in its brief for *Denver Area* described as the condition of "absence, distraction, indifference, inertia, or insufficient information" that besets "innumerable parents" in America.[57] A view of the family that supports intervention includes the imagined nonparent parent, incapable or unwilling to establish standards, "consenting" not in the active mode of reviewing and approving material, but acquiescing in an environment where the imposition of standards is impossible (for reasons of time, will, or culture).[58]

Another one of the most interesting debates about the Internet concerns the utility of national law given the extraordinarily international and cross-border nature of modern communications, especially in new media. Justice Stevens's opinion in *Reno* is not centrally about this subject, but there is some passing mention of a possible constitutional test. The issue is nestled in a footnote, ruminating within the Supreme Court decision. Justice Stevens cites an argument made by one of the plaintiffs, the American Library Association, that "[b]ecause so much sexually explicit content originates overseas," the Association argued, "the CDA cannot be 'effective.'"[59] as that term is precisely used in American jurisprudence. Justice Stevens fends off the argument, saying that it "raises difficult issues regarding the intended, as well as the permissible scope of, extraterritorial application of the CDA."[60] This is the Court's first careful encounter with an issue widely anticipated in legal literature on the Internet.[61] Because the Act could be condemned

---

[57] Respondent's Brief at 37, Denver Area Educ. Telecomms. Consortium v. FCC, 518 U.S. 727 (1996) (Nos. 95-124, 95-227).

[58] Implicit is the problem, addressed in *Butler v. Michigan*, 352 U.S. 380 (1957), of assuring sufficient adult access to speech while also protecting children. How does one tell what the profile of impact is of a congressional proscription—whether it depletes speech available to adults while protecting children? Of course, every congressional proscription or even channeling must have that impact; what constitutes too much, what constitutes adequate alternative availability of information is a matter that has never been adequately addressed by the Court, nor has it been clear what factual bases should underlie a conclusion. *See id.* (finding that Michigan Penal Code section providing that selling to a police officer a book found to have a potential effect of corrupting the morals of a youth violates the Due Process Clause).

[59] *Reno*, 521 U.S. at 878 n.45.

[60] *Id.*

[61] *See, e.g.*, David R. Johnson & David Post, *Law and Borders: The Rise of Law in Cyberspace*, 48 STAN. L. REV. 1367, 1367 (1996). Johnson and Post state:
    While these electronic communications play havoc with geographic boundaries, a new boundary, made up of the screens and passwords that separate the virtual

on other grounds, the Court suggests, it does not have to deal with it.

Still, there is much within these few words worthy of comment. Let us assume that "so much sexually explicit content originates overseas."[62] It is unclear, from this terse discussion, what it is in the foreign origin of some pornographic material that can limit Congress's capacity to devise a set of satisfactory statutory prohibitions for indecent programming that originates in the United States. Justice Stevens suggests that, perhaps the CDA was not intended to apply extraterritorially, though it is highly likely that almost every prohibited set of images or digits passes through a domestic telecommunications facility.[63] Much more interesting is the question of "effectiveness." A law is not "effective" if it can only be enforced against domestic violators *and* much of the damage, unremediated, will be caused by those seemingly beyond the law's reach. And here, the argument seems to be that these "overseas" violators are incapable of being prosecuted because of the special nature of Internet technology. Even if Congress had the power to enact legislation that is extraterritorial in its reach, technology and practicalities would render such a law ineffective. In a world of incapacity to stop one source of illegal conduct, focusing on another might be discriminatory and therefore unconstitutional.

It is clear why the American Library Association would make this argument. Its members are among the possible available defendants to be singled out, though they are small instruments in a world in which the massive "real" wrongdoers are "overseas" entrepreneurs, clever commercial pornographers, largely beyond the nation's enforcement capacity. The Association has been at the forefront of efforts to fight local regulation of Internet speech, both as a matter of principle and because, in an irony of the "post-

---

world from the "real world" of atoms, emerges. This new boundary defines a distinct Cyberspace that needs and can create its own law and legal institutions. Territorially based law-makers and law-enforcers find this new environment deeply threatening.

Id.

[62] Even the term "overseas" has a certain charm as an anachronistic way of conceiving the relationship between space and jurisdiction.

[63] Note that both 47 U.S.C.A. § 223(a) and (d) apply to both "interstate and foreign communications." 47 U.S.C.A. § 223(a), (d) (West Supp. 1991). Justice Stevens also suggested that there might be questions about the "permissible scope" of extraterritorial application of the CDA. *Reno*, 521 U.S. at 878 n.45. Does that mean that Congress could not make it a crime for a company in France to send an obscene book to an American address, that only those parts of a stream of action that touched American soil could be subject to criminal sanctions? *See generally* Henry H. Perritt, Jr., *Jurisdiction in Cyberspace*, 41 VILL. L. REV. 1 (1996).

Gutenberg" age, public libraries are often the institutions that are sued.[64]

But the argument is extremely suggestive, perhaps disturbing, in its implications for the limits of law in a digital world and in a world of increasing cross-border mobility of capital. Law will tend to be increasingly incapable of perfect enforcement where transactions and performances can so easily be moved "overseas." Here, the laws that are putatively discriminatory because of difficulties of enforcement are disagreeable images, and the argument could well be made that they should not be sanctioned at all. In the future, however, an argument based on inherent discrimination could be far more encompassing, including the disallowance of laws applying to electronic commercial transactions and possibly other areas, for example, aspects of family law, areas where enforcement might be thwarted if activities were moved offshore.

Could it be that U.S. law becomes "impossible," or difficult, to enforce because of the structure of the Internet and the relationship between extraterritorial actors and U.S. users? Certainly that argument is in the air, and it is one product of the facially attractive idea of preserving the Internet as a "regulation-free" zone.[65] At any rate, it is not hard to image that the result of such incapacity or difficulty would be discriminatory enforcement against "those poor blokes" who, for reasons of lack of imagination, willpower, or other place-related reasons stayed within the power of the state.

How to think about these questions is not yet clear. Making law disappear is one answer, but not necessarily one that seems to have many institutional proponents or broad public support. In November 2000, a French court took issue with the question of practicality of enforcement. It gave Yahoo Inc. three months to find a technological means to prevent Web surfers in France from gaining access to some Web pages on its U.S.-based auction site that featured over 1,200 Nazi-related items. After the deadline,

---

[64] *See* Nadel, *supra* note 37. In an important early case dealing with online censorship in the context of public library access, *Mainstream Loudon v. Board of Trustees*, 24 F. Supp.2d 552 (E.D. Va. 1998), a public library was forced to discontinue its use of restrictive Internet screening software. *See generally* Julia M. Tedjeske, Note, Mainstream Loudon *and Access to Internet Resources in Public Libraries*, 60 U. PITT. L. REV. 1265 (1999). In another closely watched case, *Kathleen R. v. City of Livermore*, No. A086349, 2001 WL 216719 (Cal. Ct. App. March 6, 2001), http://www.techlawjournal.com/censor/19990115.htm, a state court refused to force a public library to abandon its open access policy regarding Internet use.

[65] *See generally* Gary W. Glisson, *A Practitioner's Defense of the White Paper*, 75 OR. L. REV. 277 (1996); *see also* Vikas Arora, Note, *The Communications Decency Act: Congressional Repudiation of the "Right Stuff,"* 34 HARV. J. ON LEGIS. 473 (1997).

1904   *CARDOZO LAW REVIEW*   [Vol. 22:1885

Yahoo would be fined $13,000 for each day it did not comply with the order. Of course, unlike the invisible pornographic providers, Yahoo had a French office and, also, could be easily located for litigation purposes in the United States.

Taxation, copyright, and defamation law are all areas where, if care is not taken, discrimination may be the consequence of patterns of capacity of law enforcement. There will be suggestions that certain prohibitions that have been taken for granted within a society are no longer available. More likely, it may mean that a different form of extraterritorial as well as domestic enforcement pattern must be devised.[66] What it certainly means is that, as Justice Stevens indicated, these are "difficult issues" indeed, and may sometime come, in a ripe manner, before the Court.

III.   BROADCASTING, RADIO, AND FILM REGULATION V. INTERNET REGULATION

I have sought in this Article to identify several areas where, using *Reno* as an example, new media technology is evaluated according to its relationship to existing constitutional standards. The *Reno* case is part of the Supreme Court's ongoing debate over the qualities in film, traditional television and radio broadcasting, cable, and the Internet that render their regulation subject to different degrees or kinds of constitutional scrutiny. In this last section, I want to examine another facet of the decision: the way the Court, as revisionist historian, uses its evaluation of new media technologies to replay and reorganize its justifications for the treatment of the technology's predecessors. All government agents are, to some extent, revisionists as they try to understand the power of the new in the context of the old. How the Court engages in revision helps us understand what it is about technology that is emerging as significant—from this constitutional perspective.

For example, in *Reno* Justice Stevens asserts a novel reading of past doctrine, namely, that the "history of extensive government regulation of the broadcast medium"[67] serves, itself, as a "special justification" for treating one technology (broadcasters) in

---

[66] Does it mean, for example, that even though transmission or display of "obscene" material might ordinarily be prosecuted under the CDA, even after the Court's decision, the necessarily discriminatory aspect of such a prosecution (given the putative invulnerability of massive foreign purveyors) would be a defense? *Cf.* Lawrence Lessig, *Zones of Cyberspace*, 48 STAN. L. REV. 1403 (1996). Invoking Coase, Lessig argues that "[a] regulation need not be absolutely effective to be sufficiently effective. It need not raise the cost of the prohibited activity to infinity in order to reduce the level of that activity quite substantially." *Id.* at 1405.

[67] *Reno*, 521 U.S. at 845.

restrictive ways not applicable to other speakers. In his discussion he cited, *Red Lion Broadcasting Co. v. FCC*,[68] a case that is so out of fashion that it had gone virtually unmentioned by the Court for years. Another precedent, *Turner Broadcasting, Inc. v. FCC*,[69] is cited for the novel observation that scarcity of available frequencies, where such scarcity existed for an information technology "*at its inception*,"[70] is a further justification for lower scrutiny of broadcasting regulation. Justice Stevens also renews a somewhat controversial ground for justifying regulation and distinguishing broadcasting from other media, namely its "invasive" nature.[71]

What is interesting about Justice Stevens's citation of *Red Lion* is the subtle shift in the meaning that is implied. The previous standard understanding of *Red Lion* had been that broadcasting was more readily subject to regulation because scarcity of available frequencies made some form of rationing necessary and that necessity allowed the imposition of public interest standards. Because it is supposed that it is impossible for everyone who so wishes to get on the airwaves, government has to pick and choose. Almost from the beginning this reading of the First Amendment, this prong of *Red Lion*, endured attack.[72] Economists argue that any scarcity shortage is government-imposed, in that it was always possible to allocate more spectrum to broadcasting and technically possible to make spectrum accommodate more voices. This argument gained emotive power when cable television and other technologies made channels plentiful. In a world of abundance, there seems no reason to pitch constitutional reasoning on a scarcity that, according to some

---

[68] 369 U.S. 367 (1969). For a thorough and useful history and discussion of *Red Lion*, see CASS R. SUNSTEIN, DEMOCRACY AND THE PROBLEM OF FREE SPEECH 49 (1993) (arguing that the scarcity rationale in *Red Lion* is based on the need to ensure "broad diversity of views").

[69] 512 U.S. 622 (1994) [hereinafter *Turner I*]. The citation of *Turner I* is unusual. *Turner I*, after all, recites the history of regulatory distinctions only to hold that hierarchies of constitutional concern do not encompass both broadcasting and cable television. *Turner I* was primarily about the weaknesses of congressional lawmaking. *Turner Broadcasting Systems, Inc. v. FCC*, 520 U.S. 180 (1997) [hereinafter *Turner II*], specifically rejected *Red Lion*'s application of spectrum-scarcity as a ground for regulation in favor of some new "bottleneck" theory of regulation.

[70] *Reno*, 521 U.S. at 845 (emphasis added).

[71] *See* Sable Comm., Inc. v. FCC, 492 U.S. 115 (1989) (prohibiting provider of sexually oriented prerecorded telephone messages from participating in obscene interstate telephone communications for commercial purposes but enjoining statutory enforcement applying to indecent messages).

[72] *See* Monroe E. Price & John F. Duffy, *Technological Change and Doctrinal Persistence: Telecommunications Reform in Congress and the Court*, 97 COLUM. L. REV. 976 (1997); *see also* Thomas W. Hazlett, *Physical Scarcity, Rent Seeking, and the First Amendment*, 97 COLUM. L. REV. 905 (1997).

versions, simply does not exist.

Over the years, the Court, itself contested its *Red Lion*-based justification in a variety of cases suggesting that subsequent information and emerging technology might one day require abandonment of the doctrine. Its survival hung by a hair (or a vote or two). Now, however, after *Reno*, the justification may have changed. Now *Red Lion* seems to stand for the proposition that the status of broadcasting as a more regulable medium is historically contingent, rather than solely technologically based. A medium that has had significant attention from the government from the outset will be treated differently from one that has not. Since most media technologies have close relationships to government in their development—and the Internet is certainly no exception—this reading of judicial history is important.

The Court could be saying that traditional television and radio broadcasting meet three conditions, each of which is necessary for its peculiar susceptibility to regulation. These are: its history of extensive government regulation, the spectrum scarcity at its founding, and its special quality of invasiveness. A medium that does not have all of these qualities cannot be successfully compared with broadcasting so as to determine the category of constitutional analysis in which it fits. On the other hand, the Court could be arguing that these are relevant factors, not an ensemble of required conditions. Invasiveness alone, a history of extensive regulation, early shortages of frequencies, or their equivalents alone (or some combination of them) in this reading would be sufficient to justify a lower threshold for congressional regulation. The relevance of these factors to the Internet and to Justice Stevens's analysis in *Reno* therefore bears further analysis.

Justice Stevens recreates the jurisprudence of the broadcasting cases precisely so as to differentiate the historical electronic media from this new form of using wires and ether. His very explanation of cyberspace consists of facts designed to fit into a reinterpretation of the constitutional basis for regulation in broadcasting. The qualities of broadcasting that permit greater regulation, according to Justice Stevens, "are not present in cyberspace."[73]

But is Justice Stevens correct, not in terms of his retrospective interpretation of the broadcasting cases, but in terms of the way he differentiates broadcasting from cyberspace? The first area for differentiation is "history." Justice Stevens makes the claim that broadcasting had a history of extensive regulation while the "vast

---

[73] *Reno*, 521 U.S. at 868.

democratic forums" of the Internet has not been subject to similar government supervision and regulation.[74] In one sense, of course, this is a false statement. The Internet, as the Court's decision traces, has a history rooted in federal supervision and largesse. It is an outgrowth of what began in 1969 as a military program to enable computers operated by the military defense contractors and universities conducting defense-related research to communicate with one another by redundant channels. The Advance Research Project Association Network ("ARPANET") is much more firmly rooted in a history of government involvement than were the early days of spectrum usage when radio broadcasting was relatively wild and open.[75]

Besides, the relationship between the Internet and Congress can be likened to the relationship between radio and the federal government at the time of the Radio Conference that led to the 1927 Act. In the early days of radio, as in the 1990s with the Internet, there was dynamism, ingenuity, and a period of unregulated innovation. With radio, explosive growth led to concern (though on different issues), federal study, and eventually legislation. Despite Justice Stevens's apparent desire, history cannot begin when the historian wants it to. What has become the Internet originated with the Pentagon and involved an almost exclusively federally authorized network. Also, it is hard to understand how one characterizes a medium by its history when it is the very nature of that history that is being fashioned.[76]

We also know, now that we have *Reno,* that the Internet is not invasive. Why? Because the district court told us so, and the Supreme Court accepts that finding. Justice Stevens concludes, "the risk of encountering indecent material by accident is remote."[77] This is, as is said, a "constitutional fact."[78] Perhaps a constitutional fact is different from a garden-variety fact. To conclude, as Stevens does, that the Internet is distinguishable from broadcasting with respect to invasiveness, is a complicated matter.

---

[74] *Id.*

[75] True, it was ARPANET, not the vast democratic fora of the Internet, that was so regulated, but in some respects it is the same medium. *Cf.* Hazlett, *supra* note 72, at 908.

[76] There is something here of Bollinger's interesting, but never fully judicially embraced, theory that it was possible to regulate some parts of the media so long as there was at least one unregulated one, like newspapers or the Internet. *See* Lee C. Bollinger, Jr., *Freedom of the Press and Public Access: Toward a Theory of Partial Regulation of the Mass Media,* 75 MICH. L. REV. 1 (1976).

[77] *Reno,* 521 U.S. at 867.

[78] *See* Martin B. Louis, *Allocating Adjudicative Decision Making Authority Between the Trial and Appellate Levels: A Unified View of the Scope of Review, the Judge/Jury Question, and Procedural Discretion,* 64 N.C. L. REV. 993 (1986); Henry P. Monaghan, *Constitutional Fact Review,* 85 COLUM. L. REV. 229 (1985).

"Unlike communications received by radio or television," Justice Stevens writes, "'the Internet requires a series of affirmative steps more deliberate and directed than merely turning a dial. A child requires some sophistication and some ability to read to retrieve material and thereby to use the Internet unattended.'"[79]

First meaningfully formulated in the dial-a-porn case *Sable Communications of California, Inc. v. FCC,* the notion of "affirmative steps" represents a patina on "invasiveness." Affirmative steps certainly enable a more accurate analysis of the emerging "interactive media model" in U.S. telecommunications, in which most content will be accessed rather than broadcast, pulled rather than pushed.[80] Yet even for current Internet technology, there are problems with this innovative approach. It is true, for example, that, at least the first time, a child has to do more in a more directed and deliberate way, than turn the dial to get access to some particularly outrageous or erotic material. But once the place is saved, or "bookmarked," there is very little functional difference between turning a dial and gaining access to a website.

Odder still is the supposed distinction between those children with some "ability to read" and those without the ability. Invasiveness and uninvitedness may have to do with a child's sophistication, but in no previous case did this issue turn on actual literacy or its absence. Who are we talking about: the seventeen-year-old deemed to be a computer wizard, or the five-year-old who stumbles onto the satiric-erotic false-Disney program? How does the society make this decision? Can it? Are these questions about which we do not know the answer or is the district court finding in this case sufficient, even against a congressional finding to the contrary? Where does Justice Stevens arrive at his factual understanding of a world that is interacting with the computer and how that world differs from or is similar to the world that interacts with radio and television? For constitutional analysis to be careful, we must know how contingent doctrine is on factual understandings and what constitutes adequate information supporting a notion of invasiveness or to the contrary.[81]

---

[79] *Reno,* 521 U.S. at 854 (citing finding 89 of the District Court decision in *ACLU v. Reno,* 929 F. Supp. 824, 845 (E.D. Pa. 1996)).

[80] For an early First Amendment analysis of this model, see Jerry Berman & Daniel J. Weitzner, *Abundance and User Control: Renewing the Democratic Heart of the First Amendment in the Age of Interactive Media,* 104 YALE L.J. 1619 (1995).

[81] In *Denver Area Educ. Telecomms. Consortium v. FCC,* 518 U.S. 727 (1996), Justice Breyer relied on only a few books and articles to conclude that cable television was invasive in the *Pacifica* sense. *See* FCC v. Pacifica Found., 438 U.S. 726, 748-49 (1978) (asserting that the broadcast media is invasive because of its "pervasive presence in the

The third and most convincing difference between broadcasting and Internet questions whether spectrum scarcity exists. It is now almost an article of faith that whatever scarcity existed in the bad old days of analog spectrum no longer exists. In *Reno*, Justice Stevens puts a new and unexamined spin on the question, asking, for the first time in the Court's treatment of this subject, whether the Internet is a "'scarce' expressive commodity."[82] He seemed to be inviting a refocus from an older, economic analysis of spectrum availability to a broader focus on the element of "expressiveness." Justice Stevens reveled in the Internet's plenty: "It provides relatively unlimited, low-cost capacity for communication of all kinds. . . . Through the use of chat rooms, any person with a phone line can become a town crier with a voice that resonates farther than it could from any soapbox."[83] All the magic elements are there: pamphleteer, town crier, and soapbox. No wonder this is Justice Stevens's clinching point before concluding that "our cases provide no basis for qualifying the level of First Amendment scrutiny that should be applied to this medium."[84]

Yet there are some factors to consider. We are at a stage in the development of the Internet—perhaps like early radio—where entry is certainly easy, inexpensive, and nondiscriminatory. But, as with radio, it was later developments in industrial organization and government action that made entry more difficult and a broadly democratic means of becoming a town crier, almost impossible. Radio spectrum was not really "scarce," though radio spectrum as an "expressive commodity" may have been. It would be wonderful if the Internet were to retain its capacity for expressiveness, as nonscarce as it seems currently to be, but we do not know yet whether that will be the case or whether the Court's limitations on congressional action will expand or restrict that zone. Certainly, the history of radio would have been different if the Court had held the earliest forays into regulation and licensing unconstitutional because of the heady, egalitarian patterns of entry that characterized the time of basement radio transmission and ease of speaker entry.

The Court's decision also raises interesting questions about which numbers—what kinds of abundance—are relevant to the issue of scarcity, or scarcity of "an expressive commodity," to

---

lives of Americans" and because "it is uniquely accessible" to children). Compare the role of the district court's fact findings in *A CLU v. Reno*, 929 F. Supp. 824 (E.D. Pa. 1996).

[82] *Reno*, 521 U.S. at 870.

[83] *Id.*

[84] *Id.*

repeat again Justice Stevens's novel and stunning phrase.[85] There are millions of radio receivers just as there are millions of computers. Penetration is obviously not the same, but moving in the same direction of universality. The important point for Justice Stevens, however, is that computers, unlike radios, are interactive. What is being compared is access or entry by *speakers*, not *receivers*. The end of scarcity with respect to "expressiveness" comes precisely because of the radical transformation of access to convey or impart as opposed to receive information.

Here the Court is committing to a particular conception of the Internet. Justice Stevens is assuming that the number of subscribers to the Internet is equivalent to the number of speakers, i.e., like the telephone, and that subscribing is a mark of entry as speaker. At the moment, that may be a valid assumption. But the structure and custom of usage of the Internet could change. The behavior in the future might be that, other than for an e-mail function, ninety-nine percent of subscribers act like passive receivers or dial turners: selectors at best but never, otherwise, as communicators. Information may come in packaged channels, with a market structure dominated by three or four giants. Then the question might be whether bottlenecks to entry exist, and whether analysis of the Internet (in terms of congressional power) should be assimilated to cases that justified regulation not on spectrum scarcity, but on the difficulty of access by those who program channels and distribute them over cable.[86]

In one respect, this hypothetical future of packaged channels and a market dominated by oligopolistic producers has already come into existence, and the implications for "scarcity" have already begun to take shape. The abundance of the Internet has produced a new form of scarcity, one described by Jack Balkin:

> All communications media produce too much information. So in that sense, all media have a problem of scarcity. But the scarcity is not a scarcity of bandwidth. It is a scarcity of audience. There is only so much time for individuals to assimilate information. And not only is there too much information, some of it is positively undesirable. As a result, all media give rise to filtering by their audience, or, more importantly, by people to whom the audience delegates the task

---

[85] *Id.* This is interesting because of the history of the "scarcity" rationale and its tie to limitations on spectrum. This was thought to be a physical limitation, as compared to shortages of printing presses or limitations on the number of newspaper dailies in a market that could survive, both of which were considered economic. By shifting the phrase from spectrum scarcity to scarcity of an expressive commodity, Justice Stevens might be opening the way for a reconsideration of this long-held distinction.

[86] *See Turner II*, 520 U.S. 180 (1997).

of filtering.[87]

Information overproduction creates a problem not merely of unwanted offensiveness greeting an Internet user, but also of unwanted irrelevance. Portals to the Internet, such as Yahoo or Excite, exist to remedy this problem. Their home pages form some of the most expensive "real estate" in cyberspace. These portals provide free search engine technology to aid the user in finding desired websites. They also advertise websites. If a website is not listed by these search engines, it effectively does not exist. The search portals have become the dominant brokers in the "expressive commodity" of the Internet.[88]

Justice Stevens, in *Reno,* reopens questions of definition, exploring considerations that make one information technology more sensitive than another, more susceptible to regulation. He identifies history, scarcity, and invasiveness as criteria for decision. But his treatment of broadcasting and the Internet are not necessarily convincing, even as his own grid of analysis is applied. This is not surprising. "We are not the first generation," as Carolyn Marvin has written, "to wonder at the rapid and extraordinary shifts in the dimension of the world and the human relationships it contains as a result of new forms of communication, or be surprised by the changes those shifts occasion in the regular pattern of our lives."[89]

Technology has the potential to alter every institution, to provide even more access to education, to jobs, and to opportunities.[90] But things are new from a particular perspective. A new technology may be one that replaces or substantially augments a predecessor or establishes difference of a kind that must cross a hurdle of significance. We might reserve the notion

---

[87] J.M. Balkin, *Media Filters, the V-chip, and the Foundations of Broadcast Regulation,* 45 DUKE L.J. 1131 (1996).

[88] The idea that scarcity no longer exists because of the Internet and various other technologies of abundance has been challenged by other comparative analysts of media law and policy. *See* Stefaan Verhulst, *About Scarcities and Intermediaries: The Regulatory Paradigm Shift of Digital Content Reviewed, in* NEW MEDIA HANDBOOK (Leah Lievrouw & Sonia Livingstone eds., forthcoming 2001). Verhulst proposes that the very abundance of content has caused a need for new intermediaries that can navigate, contextualize, filter, decode, customize, and authenticate the information and its source for the user. He states, a "phenomenon of re-intermediation is emerging, [that] in many ways creates new (artificial) scarcities." *Id.* at 32.

[89] CAROLYN MARVIN, WHEN OLD TECHNOLOGIES WERE NEW: THINKING ABOUT ELECTRIC COMMUNICATIONS IN THE LATE NINETEENTH CENTURY 3 (1988); *see also* TECHNOLOGICAL REVOLUTIONS IN EUROPE: HISTORICAL PERSPECTIVES (Maxine Berg & Kristine Bruland eds., 1998).

[90] *See, e.g.,* GEORGE GILDER, TELECOSM: HOW INFINITE BANDWIDTH WILL REVOLUTIONIZE OUR WORLD (2000); JOEL KOTKIN, THE NEW GEOGRAPHY: HOW THE DIGITAL REVOLUTION IS RESHAPING THE AMERICAN LANDSCAPE (2000).

of newness for innovations that have major significance for cultural developments, the distribution of power in society, the organization of the polity, or the recognition of new consumer markets.[91] Altered flows of information, resulting from new technologies, change in almost every case the balances that previously existed in a legal framework.[92]

The point of this Article, as I noted at the outset, is not to take sides in the grueling debate over whether new information technologies are truly revolutionary.[93] Anthony Smith established a fairly elevated test for the "newness" of new technology: "An age in which a new transforming technology is taking hold must, almost self-evidently, express its most profound social, economic, and political changes in terms of that technology—so closely and completely that historians try, but fail, to disentangle the resulting skeins of cause and effect."[94] The task, rather, has been to ask how these transformations interact with the processes of law-making and adjudication. As electronic technologies capture our time, our lives, our imagination, they socially and culturally overwhelm our older modes of thinking about the legal regulation of data, speech, imagery. As Ethan Katsh has noted, the new technologies create "shifts in the value of information, in the language used to describe information, in customs used to employ information, in expectations about how information will be used, and in norms that are applied to information and communication."[95] Katsh likens technology changes to changes in fundamental tools and hastens to indicate how significant such transitions might be. "The new media enable us to expand in rather extraordinary ways our capabilities for processing, storing, organizing, representing, and communicating information."[96] In the early period of the technology's use, the prevailing attitude might be that all that is occurring is the development of new methods, techniques to do existing tasks more efficiently. But in certain circumstances, tools become virtually autonomous engines for change. Like the

---

[91] For a study of the scope of newness of the printing press, see ELIZABETH EISENSTEIN, THE PRINTING REVOLUTION IN EARLY MODERN EUROPE (1993). The Rand Corporation established a project, partly based on Eisenstein's model of change, to look at parallels between the coming of the Internet and the coming of the printing press. *See New Paradigms and Parallels: The Printing Press and the Internet, at* http://www.rand.org/parallels/ (Oct. 2000).

[92] *See* M. Ethan Katsh, *Cybertime, Cyberspace, and Cyberlaw,* J. ONLINE L. (1995), *at* http://warthog.cc.wm.edu/law/ publications/jol/Katsh.html (last visited Jan. 15, 2001).

[93] *See, e.g.,* GILDER, *supra* note 90; KOTKIN, *supra* note 90.

[94] ANTHONY SMITH, FROM BOOKS TO BYTES 3 (1993).

[95] M. Ethan Katsh, *Law Reviews and the Migration to Cyberspace,* 29 AKRON L. REV. 115, 120 (1996).

[96] *Id.* at 120.

process-changing harmonium in Hardy's modest village church, "a plow may compel its users to arrange their agricultural activity, and perhaps also other parts of their lives, in a way that conforms to its own logic" in ways neither intended nor foreseen by those who originally devised the innovation.[97]

Law moves more slowly than its external impacts and not always or immediately in parallel with them. The development of law is imprisoned in the rhetoric of its prior existence. That is the weakness, certainly of courts, but of legislatures as well. Altered flows of information, resulting from new technologies, change the balances that previously existed in a legal framework. But it is hard to know when those changes undo the preexisting formulaic approaches to a task. *Reno* is an example of striving to move outside of existing formulae, but still being bound by them, of pushing at categorical boundaries, but functioning within the boundaries themselves. Throughout the law, this process of adjustment takes place. Disputes over the power and effect of images on children are no different. Something is changing, changing markedly (as has always been the case) in the interaction between the staggering symbolic output of the society and the development of its children. Courts and legislatures try to mediate this interaction, as happened in the CDA, its descendants and the court opinions (like *Reno)* interpreting and evaluating them. In the flood of novelty captured by the new technology, it is difficult to determine what attributes of change yield revolutionary consequences and what attributes merely expedites distribution. Newness is a quality that fits uneasily with law.

---

[97] PETER L. BERGER, THE SACRED CANOPY 9 (1969).

[12]

Beyond Madison? The U.S. Supreme Court and the Regulation of Sexually Explicit Expression

Ian Cram

Subject: HUMAN RIGHTS. Other related subjects: Information technology

Keywords: Freedom of expression; Internet; Pornography; United States

Abstract: Argues that Sup Ct treatment of sexually explicit expression fails to reflect settled principles underpinning First Amendment discourse based on over protection of virtual pornography and under protection of adult theatres and clubs.

*743 The purpose of this article is to consider how, if at all, the U.S. Supreme Court's treatment of restrictions impacting directly on sexually explicit expression (as in the case of laws which prohibit the production, distribution, sale or possession of actual or virtual child pornography) or more obliquely (as occurs in the case of zoning restrictions imposed on adult theatres) upholds a Madisonian account of the First Amendment in which primacy is accorded to political speech forms. The central argument which is developed below is that, in each context, the court has failed to reflect the settled principles underpinning First Amendment discourse. I argue that this failure is apparent not only in the overprotection afforded to virtual pornography from federal rulemaking but also in the under-protection of adult theatres and nude-dancing clubs where the court has been unwilling to recognise that local authorities' regulatory stances may frequently reflect an element of official disapproval of particular expressive activities.

One indicator of the changed nature of expression disputes in advanced liberal democracies is provided by the U.S. Supreme Court's First Amendment caseload. Whereas the required reading of earlier generations of American free speech lawyers comprised in the main classic political dissent cases such as *Schenck v. United States*, *Bridges v. California* and *Dennis v. United States*,[1] recent decades have seen a qualitative shift across speech categories. The court has had to grapple with the constitutionality of rules regulating race-hate speech, the use of private funds to influence the outcome of electoral contests and misleading advertisements.[2] Within the newer categories of First Amendment dispute, the freedom to engage in sexually explicit expression figures prominently, whether at establishments where customers are

---

[1] Respectively 249 U.S. 47 (1919), 314 U.S. 252 (1941) and 341 U.S. 494 (1951)

[2] *RAV v. City of St Paul, Minnesota* 120 L.Ed. 2d 305 (1992); *Buckley v. Valeo* 424 U.S. 1 (1976); *Colorado Republican Federal Campaign Committee v. Federal Election Commission* 518 U.S. 604 (1996); *Virginia State Board of Pharmacy v. Virginia Citizens Consumer Council* 425 U.S. 748 (1976). See further C. Sunstein, Democracy and the Problem of Free Speech (Macmillan, New York 1993), p. 4.

entertained by nude dancing,[3] or in the privacy of people's homes via cable television,[4] or, as has ***744*** occurred most recently, through the internet. In 1997, the Supreme Court ruled in *Reno v. A.C.L.U.* that two provisions of the Communications Decency Act 1996 ("CDA") which criminalised both the "knowing" transmission of "indecent" or "patently offensive" materials on the Internet to recipients under 18 years and allowing minors to access such materials concluded that these constituted impermissibly vague and overbroad contents-based restrictions upon speech.[5] In response, Congress drafted a more tightly defined set of provisions in the Child Online Protection Act 1997 ("COPA"). The new statute made it an offence for a person to transmit for commercial purposes material over the World Wide Web that is "harmful to minors".[6] This latter phrase is defined by reference to the three pronged obscenity test from *Miller v. California*,[7] which requires jurors to apply a contemporary community standards test when assessing with respect to minors whether the material in question appeals to the prurient interest and whether it depicts or describes in a patently offensive way sexual conduct specifically defined by the applicable state law.[8] Excluded from the ambit of COPA are materials which, objectively judged, possess serious literary, artistic, political or scientific value. Web publishers challenged the application of the contemporary community standards test on overbreadth grounds claiming that, in the absence of technological means to control the geographic location of recipients, COPA effectively forced all Web speakers to abide by the most puritan community's standards, thereby curtailing some constitutionally protected speech. In May 2002, the court in *Ashcroft v. A.C.L.U.* upheld COPA's reliance upon community standards with varying degrees of enthusiasm. The strongest defence of variable community standards is to be found in the plurality opinion of Thomas J.[9] He emphasised the relatively narrow class of materials prohibited by Congress, citing the fact that COPA applied to web-based material communicated for commercial purposes only. CDA had, by contrast, caught all internet material including e-mail messages and was not limited to those communications sent for purely commercial purposes. COPA's narrow reach was also evident from the incorporation of both "prurient interest" and "serious value" prongs from Miller, neither of which had found their way into CDA. When these narrowing features were taken into account, the obligation on a speaker who wished to address a national audience to observe varying community standards could not, in itself, be said to violate the First Amendment. As Thomas J. pointed out, the court had already upheld resort to community standards in the context of statutes regulating the mailing of obscene material[10] and the use of telephones

---

[3]   *City of Erie et al. v. Pap's A.M., tdba "Kandyland"* 527 U.S. 277 (2000), see further P. Rumney, "*City of Erie et al v. Pap's A.M., tdba 'Kandyland'*: Low-Value Speech and the First Amendment" [2001] P.L. 158; *Barnes v. Glen Theatre Inc.* 501 U.S. 560 (1991).

[4]   *U.S. v. Playboy Entertainment Group Inc.* 529 U.S. 803 (2000).

[5]   21 U.S. 844 (1997).

[6]   COPA, s. 1405 also establishes a Commission to identify and report on technological or other means of reducing young persons' access to harmful material on the internet.

[7]   413 U.S. 15 (1973). The other prong of the test is that the material, taken as a whole, lacks serious literary, artistic, political, or scientific value.

[8]   See further *Pope v. Illinios* 481 U.S. 497, 500 (1987).

[9]   Comprising Rehnquist C.J. and Scalia J.

[10]   *Hamling v. U.S.* 418 U.S. 87 (1974).

to make obscene or indecent communications for commercial purposes.[11] O'Connor J. for her part agreed *745 that A.C.L.U. had failed to show on the facts that the variation in local community standards would be so great as to render COPA substantially overbroad.[12] However, she suggested that the technical burden placed on internet speakers of controlling the geographic locations in which the speech is received might well permit a future litigant to make a more convincing case for substantial overbreadth.[13] In these circumstances, the court should be prepared to consider the adoption of a national, uniform standard of 'patent offensiveness" and "prurient interest".[14]

Of course, *Ashcroft v. A.C.L.U.* was concerned with a narrow point about the constitutionality of the contemporary community standards test in webbased speech cases. Other issues of First Amendment compliance (principally COPA's alleged vagueness and the application of strict scrutiny analysis) were not argued before the Supreme Court. At the time of writing, these matters are now pending before the Third Circuit Court of Appeals. Whether COPA will ultimately emerge intact is difficult to say.

In separate legislative moves post-Reno, Congress also made federal subsidies for schools and libraries' internet access conditional upon the adoption of filtering software that screens out material deemed harmful to minors,[15] and, in an effort to curtail paedophiles' use of internet images of children, passed the Child Pornography Prevention Act 1996 ("CPPA"). The latter measure prohibits the distribution, receipt or possession of an image that "appears to be of a minor engaged in sexually explicit conduct"[16] or "conveys" that impression.[17] In conflicting rulings from the lower courts, CPPA was held by the First Circuit Court of Appeals not to infringe the First Amendment,[18] whilst the Ninth Circuit reached the contrary conclusion.[19] The Supreme Court has now pronounced upon the constitutionality of these criminal offences. An analysis of the court's regulation of sexually explicit speech here and in earlier decisions follows shortly. To begin with however, the Madisonian account of speech protection will be set down.

---

[11]   *Sable Communications of California., Inc. v. F.C.C.* 492 U.S.115 (1989).

[12]   Kennedy, Souter and Ginsburg JJ. separately doubted that A.C.L.U. had established overbreadth.

[13]   For O'Connor, Kennedy, Souter and Ginsburg JJ., the lack of control over the recipients of speech in the present case meant that the earlier cases of Hamling and Sable could be distinguished.

[14]   She envisaged juries across Maine, Mississippi, Las Vegas and New York City being asked to decided whether the "nationwide community of adults" would find the charged material to appeal to the prurient interest and patently offensive.

[15]   Children's Internet Protection Act 2000, s.97

[16]   s.2256(8)(B).

[17]   s.2256(8)(D). For a domestic comparison see the Protection of Children Act 1978, s.7 as amended by Criminal Justice and Public Order Act 1994, s.84(3)(c) and *R. v. Fellows, R v. Arnold* [1997] 2 All E.R. 548; *Atkins v. DPP, Goodland v. DPP* [2000] 2 All E.R. 425.

[18]   *U.S. v. Hilton* 167 F..3d. 61 (1st Cir. 1999).

[19]   *Free Speech Coalition v. Reno* 68 Law Week 1381 (9th Cir. 2000). See further T. L. Tedford and D. A. Herbeck, 2000 Update--Freedom of Speech in the United States (Strata Publishing, 2000).

The First Amendment--some enduring themes and an analytical framework

A common theme in the work of judges and free speech scholars from diverse theoretical perspectives is that the abstract or open-textured nature of the First *746 Amendment obliges each generation of Supreme Court judges to look beyond the terms of the written Constitution to have an understanding of the central themes or settled values which underpin the corpus of First Amendment jurisprudence and then to apply that understanding to the individual cases that come before them.[20]

Unsurprisingly, judicial and academic attempts to distil these themes/values have generated much controversy. Nonetheless, over time Supreme Court jurisprudence has yielded up a body of basic principles that can lay claim to general acceptance. One principle commanding widespread support maintains that not all speech forms enjoy the same level of protection from state interference.[21] On this view, the First Amendment is predicated upon a tiered system of speech forms in which "political" speech is accorded greater protection than lower value speech forms such as pure commercial or artistic expression.[22] Significantly however in the context of sexually explicit expression, obscene speech and child pornography involving the use of actual children have been cast outside the protective ambit of the First Amendment altogether on the basis that the value of the expressive conduct to society is de minimis.[23] This hierarchy of speech protection may be traced back to the Constitution's distinctive emphasis upon popular sovereignty. James Madison, the author of the First Amendment, famously contrasted the British system of government where sovereignty rested with the King in Parliament to that established under the U.S. Constitution where "the People, not the

---

[20]   Sometimes referred to as the "non-interpretivist" approach to constitutional adjudication. For justification see, e.g. W. Brennan, "The Constitution of the United States: Contemporary Ratification" (1986) S. Texas L. Rev. 433; A.M. Bickel, The Least Dangerous Branch--The Supreme Court at the Bar of Politics (Bobbs-Merrill, Indianapolis 1962) R. Dworkin, Freedom's Law The Moral Reading of the American Constitution (Oxford University Press, 1996) esp. Introduction; J. Hart Ely, Democracy and Distrust--A Theory of Judicial Review (Harvard University Press, 1980), Chap. 2. For a statement of the "interpretivist" counter-view that judicial interpretation to be legitimate must be based upon the actual language and original meaning of the framers, see R. Bork, The Tempting of America: The Political Seduction of the Law (1990). See further D. Barnum, The Supreme Court and American Democracy (St Martin's Press, New York, 1993), Chap. 14.

[21]   See thus the Supreme Court rulings in *Chaplinksy v. New Hampshire* 315 U.S. 568 (1942); *Dennis v. U.S.* 341 U.S. 494 (1951); *Gertz v. Robert Welch Inc.* 418 U.S. 323 (1974); *Virginia Pharmacy Board v. Virginia Consumer Council* 425 U.S. 748 (1976); *Dun & Bradstreet Inc. v. Greenmoss Builders Inc.* 472 U.S. 749 (1985). See further C. Sunstein, Democracy and the Problem of Free Speech (Macmillan, New York, 1993); G. Stone, "Content-Neutral Restrictions" (1987) 54 Univ. Chic. L. Rev. 46.

[22]   Of course, attempts at line drawing between "political" and "commercial" or "artistic" speech forms may not always be convincing or command universal agreement but this fact alone does not mean that the distinction is without force.

[23]   This is despite the fact that the categorisation of obscene speech as morally offensive or corrosive is plainly contents-based. See respectively *Miller v. California* 413 U.S. 15 (1973) and *New York v. Ferber* 458 U.S. 747 (1982). Other examples of unprotected contents-based categories of expression include defamation of private figures (*Gertz v. Robert Welch* 418 US 323 (1974)) and "fighting words" (*Chaplinsky v. New Hampshire* 315 US 568 (1942)).

Government, possess the absolute sovereignty".[24] To function effectively, popular sovereignty requires public access to information and opinions so as to make informed decisions. If this is granted, it would seem to follow that political speech – that is speech "intended and received as a contribution to public *747 deliberation about some issue"[25] – ought to be the central concern of the First Amendment and accorded the highest level of protection from governmental interference. The self-interested motives of government for suppressing such speech forms provide a supporting reason to uphold strict judicial oversight.[26] Accordingly, restrictions on political speech must satisfy an especially heavy burden of proof--namely clear and compelling evidence of substantial and imminent harm to a legitimate state interest.[27] Moreover, they must not be overbroad and strike at otherwise protected expression.[28]

Consistent with this view, speech falling outside the definition of political speech such as commercial advertising, artistic expression or non-obscene sexually explicit speech belongs to the lower tier of protected expression. However, even this lower value speech is deemed worthy of some protection and may be regulated only where the restriction advances a substantial government interest in a proportionate manner and does not inadvertently chill political speech.[29] This degree of protection is usually justified on two grounds, although, as will be argued, the second of these offers a comparatively weak basis for protecting speech claims against competing state and individual interests. The first defence of lower level speech claims can be traced back to Madison. In essence, it argues that contents-based restrictions prompted by official disagreement with the message contained in the material are contrary to the Madisonian ideal of protecting speech at odds with the view of the state. Non-obscene sexually explicit speech for example, whilst falling short of an intentional contribution to public deliberation about some issue, might nonetheless be considered to convey a message about forms of sexual conduct at odds with, and therefore challenging to, prevailing norms. On these lines, the Supreme Court struck down an Indianapolis anti-pornography ordinance in *American Booksellers Association v. Hudnut*,[30] on the basis that it attempted to establish and enforce an approved view of women and relations between the sexes which violated the First Amendment.[31]

---

[24] Report on the Virginia Resolution, January 1800 6 Papers of James Madison 385.

[25] This is the definition preferred by C. Sunstein, Democracy and the Problem of Free Speech (Macmillan, New York, 1993), at p. 130

[26] See, e.g. *New York Times v. Sullivan* 376 U.S. 254 (1964); *New York Times v. U.S.* (Pentagon Papers case) 403 U.S. 713 (1971) see the academic work of F. Schauer, Free Speech--a philosophical enquiry (Cambridge University Press, 1982) and T. M. Scanlon, "A Theory of Freedom of Expression" (1972) 1 Philosophy and Public Affairs 204 on this point.

[27] See, e.g. the test of "clear and present danger of imminent and serious evil" adopted by the court in *Bridges v. California* 314 U.S. 252 (1941) applied to restrictions on speech pertaining to court proceedings.

[28] *Broadrick v. Oklahoma* 413 U.S. 601 (1973).

[29] *Central Hudson Gas & Electricity v. Public Service Commission* 447 U.S. 557 (1980).

[30] 475 U.S. 1001 (1986), upholding the Seventh Circuit of Appeals

[31] The rap artist Dr Dre recently successfully invoked his First Amendment rights against the cities of Detroit and Auburn Hills which had prevented him showing a video at his concerts which included scenes of a gunfight in a liquor store as well as some shots of topless women. Without having to go to court, the cities agreed to pay his legal fees and instructed their respective police forces to undergo First

Secondly, regulations which are motivated by a concern that people may be influenced or offended by the messages contained within communications undermine other core precepts in First Amendment thinking--the linked *748 notions of listener autonomy and the self-fulfilment of individuals.[32] The emotional and intellectual maturation of individuals requires them to have access to a wide variety of ideas and information. The cogency of the connection between self-fulfilment and expressive freedom is however questionable.[33] It is apparent for example that if autonomy is taken to include making the most of oneself, it is difficult to see why speech in particular ought to be singled out for especial protection. After all, values such as equal respect, individual privacy, religious freedom and freedom of association might also seem relevant to individual development and flourishing. In the case of child pornography, the weakness of the self-fulfilment rationale is compounded by the fact that arguments for restrictions on speech rest on broader claims to privacy and equal respect which enjoy constitutional status. Accordingly, in the case of legislative restrictions on speech intended to further a conflicting constitutional value, the Court might be justified in adopting a less hostile stance than might be appropriate in cases of other majoritarian restrictions of political speech.[34] This deferential approach to federal and state restrictions on sexually explicit imagery of children commended itself to the court in *New York v. Ferber*.[35] New York's compelling interest in the well-being of its youth and the particular vulnerability of children was held to confer some leeway on the state to regulate pornographic material. More recent support for an attenuated standard of review in respect of the regulation of sexually explicit expression is evident in the dissenting opinions in *United States v. Playboy Entertainment Group Ltd*. A challenge was taken in respect of a statute designed to shield children from "signal bleed"– the phenomenon whereby audio and/or visual portions of programmes scrambled for paying audiences may be heard/seen by non-payers.[36] Section 505 of the Telecommunications Act 1996 required cable television operators either to "fully scramble or otherwise fully block" programming consisting of primarily sexually explicit material or to limit transmission of the same to the period between 10 p.m. and 6 a.m. unless a subscriber asked to receive it. Most cable operators chose to limit the transmission to the late evening/early morning period. Given that some 30-50 per cent of all adult programming was apparently viewed in households before 10 p.m., a significant reduction in communicative activity (and, hence, Playboy's revenues) resulted from section 505. The majority applied a strict scrutiny standard to the 1996 Act and held that the state had failed to show that section 505 represented the least restrictive means

---

Amendment sensitivity training. See further http:// news.bbc.co.uk/hi/english/entertainment/music/newsid_1953000/1953026.stm.

[32] See Brandeis J. in *Whitney v. California* 274 U.S. 357, 374 (1927): "[t] hose who won our independence believed that the final end of the state was to make men free to develop their faculties ...". For an instance of offensive political speech see *Cohen v. California* 403 U.S. 15 (1971). See further T. M. Scanlon, "A Theory of Freedom of Expression" (1972) 1 Philosophy and Public Affairs 204.

[33] Christopher Manfredi has argued that self-fulfilment is the purpose "furthest from the essential objectives of expressive freedom" in Judicial Power and the Charter, (2nd ed., (Oxford University Press, Ontario, 2001), p. 64.

[34] See also I. Cram, "Criminalizing Child Pornography--A Canadian Study in Freedom of Expression and Charter-led Judicial Review of Legislative Policy Making" (2002) 66 Jo. Crim Law 359.

[35] 458 U.S. 747 (1982).

[36] 529 U.S. 803 (2000).

of shielding children when *749 parents could expressly request cable operators to be opted out of sexually explicit programming under section 504 of the same Act. In a dissenting opinion which can be read as essentially Madisonian in approach,[37] Breyer J. faulted the majority's adoption of a strict scrutiny standard. Noting that the statute regulated commercial actors broadcasting "virtually 100% sexually explicit material", and that it required cable operators to use better scrambling technology or confine broadcasting between 10 p.m. and 6 a.m. (thereby not prohibiting sexually explicit expression altogether), he concluded that the narrow tailoring concerns presented in other cases were absent here. In particular, the material could not be said to have an obvious informational character (such as in Reno where non-commercial material including birth control advice was caught by Communications Decency Act 1996). Nor, unlike Reno, did the statute purport to impose an absolute ban on the communicative activity. Viewed in this light, the proper question for the court was whether, allowing a degree of leeway to the legislature in deciding among regulatory strategies, section 505 constituted an excessive means of ensuring that children did not have access to sexually explicit programmes. Finding that it did not, Breyer J. relied on recent empirical evidence which showed that at least 5 million children were left at home without parental supervision each week. The opt-out provision in section 504 could not be construed to be a "less restrictive but similarly practical and effective means" of pursuing the same objective because it only worked when several preconditions were in place; namely parental awareness of section 504 rights, parental knowledge or suspicion that their children were watching sexually explicit programmes and, finally, a prompt response from a cable operator to a blocking request.[38]

The incidental restriction of sexually explicit expression?

Not all restrictions upon expressive activity target the particular message which is being conveyed. Content-neutral restrictions (such as time, manner, place restrictions which regulate noisy gatherings outside hospitals or the distribution of leaflets at airports) have typically been subject to a less strict standard of review, surviving constitutional scrutiny provided both that a substantial governmental interest is served and that the measure is narrowly tailored to allow the speaker alternative avenues of communication.[39]

Somewhere between contents-based and contents-neutral restraints on expression lies a hybrid type of speech curb of a sort commonly used to limit sexually explicit expression. This is found where the communicative activity is *750 regulated by reference to subject-matter (in common with contents-based restrictions) but without regard to the actual viewpoint of

---

[37]   Joined by Rehnquist C.J., O'Connor and Scalia JJ.

[38]   There was evidence before the court that parents experienced difficulties in getting cable operators to act on blocking requests.

[39]   *Cox v. Louisiana* 379 U.S. 536, 554 (1965); *Ward v. Rock Against Racism* 491 U.S. 781 (1989). For criticism of the practice of submitting contents-neutral restrictions to less strict scrutiny, see M. Redish, "The Content Distinction in First Amendment Analysis" (1981) 34 Stan. L. Rev. 113 who argues that the values behind the constitutional protection of speech are undermined by any limitation on speech, whether contents-based or not. For a response, see G. Stone, "Content-Neutral Restrictions" (1987) 54 Univ. Chic. L. Rev. 46, 54- 57. See further "Restrictions of Speech Because of its Content: The Peculiar Case of Subject-Matter Restrictions" (1978) 46 Univ. Chic. L. Rev. 81

the speaker or its effects upon listeners/viewers (as with contents-neutral restrictions). Where a speech restriction is classed as contents-based/viewpoint neutral, the Supreme Court has tended to apply a relatively relaxed standard of constitutional review which allows a measure of latitude to rule-makers to regulate the undesirable secondary effects that are associated with the expressive activity.[40] Thus, some incidental interference with communicative activity will be First Amendmentcompliant provided that the regulation is within the state's constitutional powers, advances a substantial governmental interest unrelated to the suppression of free expression and restricts First Amendment freedoms no more than is essential to the furtherance of the governmental interest.[41] For example, a prohibition on any sign or public display within 500 feet of a foreign embassy concerning the affairs of that country might be permitted if narrowly tailored to maintain the security of embassies or to prevent serious traffic congestion.[42] The application of this category to the sexual expression cases has however proved problematic (and controversial, as reflected in Supreme Court majority decisions) – a point evident in challenges both to zoning laws which restrict the location of adult cinemas and to public decency ordinances affecting nude dancing clubs.[43] Here, the court has tended to underplay the contents-based aspects of state restrictions, preferring instead to view local regulations as legitimate attempts to deal with the adverse secondary effects of the expression on public morality, communities, crime rates and property values. Take, for example, zoning regulations which aim to preserve the quality of neighbourhoods and urban life by preventing adult cinemas locating within a specified distance of residential areas, schools, parks and churches. The court has declared these zoning rules to be "justified without reference to the content of the regulated speech"[44] and hence treated them as contents-based/viewpoint neutral means of minimising the undesirable secondary effects associated with the zoned activity. As a result, city authorities have merely to show that regulations advance a substantial governmental interest (such as preserving the quality of urban life) and do so using means which are narrowly tailored to that end.[45] For example, the majority in *City of Renton v. Playtime Theatres Inc.* held that a zoning restriction did not suppress protected speech altogether, but rather controlled the location where such speech might occur. So categorised, the ordinance was subject to a less intense level of scrutiny than a contentsbased ***751*** restriction, an aspect of which emerged in the majority's view that the ordinance need not be based upon local empirical studies relating to the activity's harmful secondary effects on the community but could properly rely on earlier studies conducted in other U.S. cities.[46] The categorisation of

---

[40]   *Young v. American Mini-Theatres Inc.* 427 U.S. 50 (1976); *City of Renton v. Playtime Theatres Inc.* 475 U.S. 41(1986).

[41]   *U.S. v. O'Brien* 391 U.S. 367, 376-77 (1968).

[42]   cf. *Boos v. Barry* 485 U.S. 312 (1988) where the prohibition on public displays near foreign embassies was limited to displays tending to bring foreign governments into public odium or disrepute. The court treated this restriction as contents-based since it sought to protect the dignity of foreign diplomatic personnel by shielding them only from that speech which was critical of their governments.

[43]   See further Rumney at n.3 above.

[44]   Or by reference to listeners reactions to it, see further *Boos v. Barry* 485 U.S. 312 (1988).

[45]   *Young v. American Mini-Theatres Inc.* (1976) 427 U.S. 50 (1976); *City of Renton v. Playtime Theatres Inc.* 475 U.S. 41(1986).

[46]   "The First Amendment does not require a city before enacting such an ordinance to conduct new studies or produce evidence independent of that already generated by other cities, so long as whatever

place restrictions on adult cinemas as viewpoint-neutral did not however command universal support. In his forceful dissent, Brennan J. argued that Renton's ordinance was viewpoint-based since it imposed limitations on cinema location according to the type of film shown.[47] Indeed, the films did carry an implicit message in favour of more relaxed sexual mores.

The secondary effects doctrine has also been invoked by the court to resolve the constitutionality of ordinances prohibiting public nudity in challenges brought by nude dancing clubs. In *City of Erie v. Pap's AM tdba "Kandyland"*[48] a majority of the court refused to strike down an ordinance banning public nudity. Although it was conceded that the full erotic message conveyed by nude dancing would be muted when a dancer was required to retain her G-string, this was characterised as an "incidental" limitation on expressive activity since the perceived "evil" addressed by Indiana's law was public nudity, not the erotic message conveyed by nude dancing. Thus characterised, the ordinance could be seen as arising from the state's legitimate powers to pass regulations which furthered important governmental interests, namely public health, safety and morals.[49] As for the analysis of the negative secondary effects aimed at by the measure, Erie, like Renton before it, was allowed to rely on evidence of associated harms generated by previous studies in other localities. By way of comment, it may be thought difficult to disentangle the various motives which are at play in such cases. Brennan J. expressed himself concerned that the secondary effects doctrine created "a possible avenue for governmental censorship whenever censors can concoct 'secondary' rationalizations for regulating the content of political speech".[50] Laws passed to protect public morals and the avoidance of offence clearly do rest in part on some view of prevailing moral standards. The regulatory stances taken towards adult cinemas/nude dancing clubs may frequently reflect both official disapproval of the contents of sexually explicit expression and a genuine desire to safeguard vulnerable members of the community from criminal and other anti-social activities as well as to protect property values. This motivational inquiry required of the courts under the secondary effects doctrine suggests a subtle supplanting of the contents-based category. Statutes which, in practice, have the effect of restricting speech by reference to content, are thus able to evade *752 more rigorous constitutional scrutiny. City of Erie shows that the clear distinction between the secondary and direct effects of speech which seems to underpin these cases will not always be workable. The concession implicit in the majority ruling that the erotic message conveyed by fully/partially clothed dancing is less intense than that conveyed in nude dancing even if the same dance is performed appears to support the conclusion that the ordinance impacts on the expressive content of the dance.[51] The Erie ordinance is also problematic from a proportionality perspective when reflecting upon the extent to which the substantial governmental interests were advanced by the minimal clothing rule. How much healthier, safer, morally decent did the citizens of Indiana become as a result of the requirement to wear G-strings? This difficulty might point to the lack of a rational connection between the

---

evidence the city relies upon is reasonably believed to be relevant to the problem the city addresses." (Rehnquist C.J. in Renton) ibid.

[47]   Joined by Marshall J.

[48]   527 U.S. 277 (2000). Similar reasoning is to be found in *Barnes v. Glen Theatre* 501 U.S. 560 (1991).

[49]   The Indiana law was treated as legitimately falling within the traditional legislative power of the state to protect morals and public order recognised previously in *Paris Adult Theatre v. Slaton* 413 U.S. 49 (1973).

[50]   *Boos v. Barry* 485 U.S. 312, 335 (1988).

[51]   This was the position of the dissenting judgment of White J.

state's objectives and the means chosen to secure those ends. A final aspect of the under-protection of speech in Erie is evident in the court's disinclination to evaluate the council's claims of a causal link between nude dancing and a host of social evils. By permitting Erie to rely on earlier empirical studies of adverse impacts in other localities, it may be argued that, even in respect of lower tier speech forms, the evidential burden on the state was set at an inappropriately low level.[52]

In view of the above difficulties, it may be thought preferable to treat these controls as contents-based restrictions of lower tier speech. Essentially, this would require the court to determine whether the restrictions advance a substantial government interest in a proportionate manner without inadvertently chilling political speech. Recalling the weaknesses of the selffulfilment rationale on which the case for sexually explicit expression is usually grounded, the application of this less strict standard of judicial scrutiny would permit the state a margin of discretion in deciding how to regulate such speech. As a result, a range of regulatory stances would be considered First Amendment-compliant. At the same time, given that erotic expression is entitled to some protection, the need to show a proportionate restriction could be read as obliging the state to furnish some localised evidence of a causal link between the expressive activity and the deleterious impact on the community and, also that the measures adopted were both a rational response to that impact and narrowly tailored to counter it.

Sexually explicit internet speech

Recent legislative efforts to combat computerised forms of child pornography and internet-based transmission of material judged harmful to minors for commercial purposes constitute more clearly contents-based regulations. Unsurprisingly then, the efforts of Congress have run into choppy constitutional waters. Despite being presented with opportunities to signal the lesser value which the Madisonian two-tier approach attaches to sexually explicit speech, the court's intervention in *Ashcroft v. Free Speech Coalition* may come to *753 be seen as extending an unwarranted level of protection to sexually explicit speech, serving in the process to raise questions about the legitimacy of judicial intervention with legislative policy choices.

In *Ashcroft v. Free Speech Coalition*, the court considered the constitutionality of two provisions of the Child Pornography Prevention Act 1996. The first of these prohibited any visual depiction including computer-generated images that "is or appears to be of a minor engaged in sexually explicit conduct".[53] The latter phrase was defined to include both actual and simulated sexual conduct. The Act also contained a separate prohibition on the production or distribution of material which conveys the impression that it depicts a minor engaged in sexually explicit conduct (otherwise the "pandering" provision).[54]

Writing the majority opinion, Kennedy J. declared both provisions to be overbroad and unconstitutional. The reach of the first prohibition extended beyond the Miller obscenity standard (namely, materials that appealed to the prurient interest, and were patently offensive

---

[52]   See the opinion of Souter J. and also Rumney at n.3 above.
[53]   18 U.S.C. s.2256(8)(B).
[54]   18 U.S.C. s. 2256(8)(D).

and lacking in serious literary, artistic, political or scientific value).[55] The court's earlier recognition in Ferber of the state's interest in the well-being of its youth could not be pleaded in support of the present restriction since the New York statute targeted expressive conduct which was intrinsically related to sexual abuse of children and which constituted a record of that abuse. Conversely, the present prohibition on virtual child pornography caught expressive conduct which did not directly cause harm to children, even if the government maintained that virtual images played some subsequent role in the sexual abuse of children:

The argument that virtual child pornography whets paedophiles' appetites and encourages them to engage in illegal conduct is unavailing because the mere tendency of speech to encourage unlawful acts is not a sufficient reason for banning it, *Stanley v. Georgia*, absent some showing of a direct connection between the speech and imminent illegal conduct, see e.g. *Brandenburg v. Ohio*. [56]

Aside from computer-generated imagery of children, the provision's reference to simulated sexual activity was said by the majority to catch youthful looking adult actors depicted as engaged in suggestive sexual activity. This might criminalise a production of Shakespeare's "Romeo and Juliet" and more recent cinematic works such as "Traffic" and "American Beauty". This conclusion suggested a separate basis for upholding the finding of overbreadth since, once *754 more, no children might actually be harmed in the production of the material.

The "pandering" provision also failed the overbreadth test. The reference to "conveys the impression" meant that film titles and trailers which gave the false impression that the film's contents contained sexually explicit scenes involving young persons would be treated as child pornography with the result that possessors were in breach of the criminal law even if they did not actually intend to possess materials containing depictions of real minors engaged in sexually explicit activity.

The failure of the CPPA's provisions to survive constitutional scrutiny is nonetheless controversial on a number of counts. The court's intervention may be considered to lack a properly contextualised approach to review of legislative policy-making in what is a complex and fast-developing area. At issue here is the appropriate level of judicial protection for sexually explicit expression which, far from advancing a core constitutional value, contributes in an uncertain way to the self-fulfilment of individual possessors (in its most innocent form perhaps a masturbatory aid)--a rationale somewhat removed from the essential objectives of expressive freedom. In these circumstances, it is doubtful whether Kennedy J. was right to apply the *Brandenburg v. Ohio* standard requiring some direct connection between virtual child pornography and imminent illegal conduct. Brandenburg was above all else a political speech case in which the speaker – a Ku Klux Klan leader – advocated the forcible repatriation of Jews and Blacks and warned that "there might have to be some revengeance taken" if the white Caucasian race continued to be suppressed. His conviction under an Ohio Criminal Syndicalism statute for advocating "the duty, necessity, or propriety of crime, sabotage, violence, or unlawful methods of terrorism as a means of accomplishing industrial or political

---

[55] 413 U.S. 15 (1973).

[56] As confirmed in *American Booksellers Association v. Hudnut* (above) the tendency of published materials to give rise to 'bad' attitudes per se does not afford a basis for regulating such materials. By contrast, the Canadian Supreme Court has recently accepted that private viewing of child pornography may be regulated on the basis that it gives rise to a reasoned apprehension of harm to children by means of cognitive distortion, suggesting as normal adult-child sexual relations. *R. v. Sharpe* [2001] 1 S.C.R. 45

reform" was reversed as his speech did not incite imminent unlawful action. Apart from the fact that child pornography falls outside the definition of political speech (it is neither intended nor received as a contribution to public deliberation about some issue), it is doubtful whether 'imminence' is an appropriate standard in child pornography where the available expert evidence indicates that the material is used in part to whet the appetite of child abusers and in part to break down children's inhibitions over time and condition them to accept the normality of adult/child sex. A further factor pointing towards an attenuated standard of judicial scrutiny is the fact that the legislature's restrictions upon expression were intended to promote constitutionally recognised interests of a vulnerable section of society-- namely the inherent dignity of each child. A more deferential approach to legislative policy choices in this arena is provided by the earlier ruling in Ferber. The leeway afforded to the state there upon recognition of its compelling interest in the well-being of the young could, it is suggested, have been stretched without too much difficulty across to the more recent category of virtual child pornography. Indeed, Justice O'Connor in her partial dissent found the expert evidence presented to Congress to support claims of appetite whetting and conditioning in conjunction with "the rapid pace of advances in computer-graphics technology" *755 sufficient to defer to Congressional judgment and rejected the claim of overbreadth in respect of the ban on virtual child pornography.[57] The majority's willingness to canvass unusual applications of the law in order to discover overbreadth would also appear to fly in the face of established jurisprudence. Recognised to be "strong medicine" in its prevention of any enforcement of provisions impacting on constitutionally protected expression (even where the person challenging the statute cannot point to interference with his/her rights to expression), the doctrine of overbreadth has been employed sparingly by the courts and only as a last resort.[58] Thus, overbreadth challenges have failed when a limiting construction has been or could be placed on the impugned statute which is consistent with its legislative purpose.[59] Equally, the court has been reluctant in the past to strike down a statute on finding that there are a substantial number of situations to which it might validly be applied.[60] A survey of congressional debates during the passage of the CPPA reveals that the legislation's real target was an extension of an existing federal ban on actual child pornography across to the newer category of virtual child pornography. The new provisions did not seek to ban film portrayals of Shakespeare, rather they aimed instead at a narrow class of images, namely those visual depictions "which are

---

[57]   Citing Congressional findings at ss. 121, 110 Stat. 3009-26. Joined by Rehnquist C.J. and Scalia J. The existence of expert testimony on this point provides a means of distinguishing the court's previous striking down of Georgia's obscenity laws in *Stanley v. Georgia* 394 U.S. 557 (1969). "Georgia asserts that exposure to obscene materials may lead to deviant sexual behavior or crimes of sexual violence. There appears to be little empirical basis for that assertion ... Given the present state of knowledge, the State may no more prohibit mere possession of obscene matter on the ground that it may lead to antisocial conduct than it may prohibit possession of chemistry books on the ground that they may lead to the manufacture of homemade spirits."

[58]   *Broadrick v. Oklahoma* 413 U.S. 601 (1973). As Blackmun J. observed in *Illinois Board of Elections v. Socialist Workers Party* 440 U.S. 173 at 188 (1979), all but the most unimaginative judges can find an alternative, slightly less restrictive rule in almost any situation which enables them to strike almost any legislation down.

[59]   *U.S. v. Thirty-Seven Photographs* 402 U.S. 363 (1971).

[60]   *Parker v. Levy* 417 U.S. 733 (1974).

virtually indistinguishable to unsuspecting viewers from unretouched photographs of actual children engaging in identical sexual conduct".[61]

Judicial intervention in legislative policy choices

Mark Tushnet has argued that contemporary constitutional theorists tend to urge minimal judicial review and vigorous democratic dialogue on those issues which it is believed that the latter are likely to yield a favoured substantive policy outcome whilst endorsing more-than-minimal review on matters where the political process is likely to produce a disfavoured outcome.[62] It is this article's contention that a more principled approach to the intensity of judicial scrutiny in speech cases may be possible which is in keeping with established *756 First Amendment thinking. The case for allowing federal and state legislatures a certain leeway to regulate sexually explicit speech can now be stated. Viewed against the central concerns of the First Amendment, the freedom to disseminate and acquire pornography is of peripheral importance only. In respect of child pornography, any benefits to individual self-fulfilment of this lesser value expression are countered by the undisputed empirical evidence of its role in the sexual abuse of children. Statutory regulation of virtual sexually explicit imagery of children seeks to address new technological means available to those wishing to harm children and uphold this vulnerable group's constitutional entitlements to privacy, dignity and non-violence. Of course, deference to elected bodies' rule-making must not be carried over to the extent that it relieves the state of the burden of demonstrating that the limits placed on expressive freedom advance a substantial government interest in a proportionate manner. However, the recent decision in *Ashcroft v. Free Speech Coalition* does not suggest that a majority among the current members of the Supreme Court are prone to excessive deference. In a fast developing area such as virtual child pornography, judicial intervention in legislative policy making must surely be carefully thought through. After all, the First Amendment has never required Congress to wait for harm to occur before legislating against it. As the court noted in *Turner v. FCC*:

Even in the realm of First Amendment questions where Congress must base its conclusions upon substantial evidence, deference must be accorded to its findings as to the harm to be avoided and to the remedial measures adopted for that end, lest we infringe on traditional legislative authority to make predictive judgments when enacting nationwide regulatory policy.[63]

Where in contrast intense scrutiny is mistakenly applied, a risk of distorted policy-making arises in one of two ways. In the first, legislators concerned to offer the judges little or no basis for taking constitutional offence, shy away from enacting what is considered to be best policy, adopting instead a least riskladen alternative.[64] Conversely, the very likelihood of judicial

---

[61]   Senate Reports No. 104-358 pt.I, p. 7 (1996). The court has had regard to the legislative history of previous child pornography statutes which have been considered when construing the ambit of particular provisions, see *U.S. v. X-Citement Video, Inc.* 513 U.S. 64 (1994).

[62]   "Policy Distortion and Democratic Debilitation: Comparative Illumination of the Counter-Majoritarian Difficulty" (1995) 94 Mich. L. Rev. 245.

[63]   *Turner Broadcasting System Inc. v F.C.C.* 520 U.S. 180, 212 (1997).

[64]   For a more sanguine account of judicial intervention in a Canadian context, see the discussion of Charter Dialogue in the work of P. Hogg and A. Bushell, "The Charter Dialogue Between the Courts

intervention may influence the legislature to disregard constitutional norms altogether in the knowledge that the judges will simply strike down those aspects of the new law which infringe the Constitution. The latter process in which the legislature does not take its own view of the Constitution's meaning seriously enough has been described as one of "democratic debilitation".[65] Either way, the processes of democratic politics and traditional legislative authority are weakened.

*757 Conclusion

On the Madisonian approach to the First Amendment outlined here, laws restricting speech advocating the legalisation of paedophilia will rarely be justified, even where the majority find this viewpoint repulsive. This is political speech par excellence, intended to change people's attitudes towards current laws and thus worthy of the highest protection from state interference. Much sexually explicit expression involving actual/apparent imagery of children does not however attempt to engage in social deliberation.

The main argument in this article has been that the Supreme Court has achieved the dubious feat of both under-protecting and over-protecting sexually explicit expression. The under-protection is evident in the artificial treatment of city ordinances regulating nude-dancing clubs and adult theatres as contents-neutral and, as such, subject to low intensity review under the secondary effects doctrine. This approach was seen to lack credibility. A more plausible response was proposed in which the official disapproval element was recognised, requiring local regulations to be a proportionate response in defence of a compelling state interest. Specifically, some localised evidence of deleterious impact on community interests could properly be demanded.

In the case of more straightforwardly contents-based restrictions, I have argued that the Supreme Court's reluctance to recognise the lesser importance of sexually explicit speech in the hierarchy of First Amendment speech types has resulted in an inappropriately strict level of scrutiny being brought to bear on legislative activity. As *Ashcroft v. Free Speech Coalition* demonstrates, features of this strict scrutiny standard have included the requirement on the state to show some direct connection between virtual pornography and imminent illegal conduct, a willingness to canvass unusual or peripheral applications of statutory provisions in order to find overbreadth and the discarding of expert empirical evidence regarding the uses to which sexually explicit imagery of children is put. In these circumstances, it is difficult to see how the claims to individual autonomy of either the producers of child pornography or their audience can trump the interests of children, their parents/guardians and the state in the well-being of young persons. The latter, after all, has a particularly vital interest in the mental and emotional maturing of children so that in later life they participate constructively in community affairs as adult citizens.

---

and Legislatures" (1997) 35 Osgoode Hall Law Journal 75; B. McLachlin, "Charter Myths" (1999) 33 University of British Columbia Law Review 23.

   [65] Policy Distortion and Democratic Debilitation: Comparative Illumination of the Counter-Majoritarian Difficulty" (1995) 94 Mich. L. Rev. 245.UKPL 2002, Win, 743-757

[13]

THE REVISED TELEVISION WITHOUT FRONTIERS DIRECTIVE: IS IT FIT FOR THE NEXT CENTURY?

BEREND JAN DRIJBER *

1. Introduction

Few things have become so self-evident nowadays as the possibility of watching foreign television channels. It was, however, not until 1989 that a common legal framework necessary to ensure cross-border broadcasting was created when the Council of Ministers adopted Directive 89/552, commonly referred to as the "Television Without Frontiers Directive".[1] That Directive has established[2] the principle of free flow of television programmes within the Community, while harmonizing the broadcasting laws of the Member States in a number of crucial areas. However, like other high technology industries, the broadcasting sector is being revolutionized by the digital compression technology. Consequently, since 1989 the audiovisual landscape has undergone some profound changes.

Faced with the challenge to ensure that the rules keep pace with those technological developments, the European Commission took the view that the Television Without Frontiers Directive needed updating and revising.[3] Like the original Directive, the amending Directive is based on Articles 57(2) and 66 EC, since its primary objective is to further the free provision of broadcasting services within a single market. It was adopted in June 1997, in accordance with the the co-decision procedure referred to in Article 189b EC.[4]

---

* The opinions expressed are personal to the author.
1. O.J. 1989, L 298/23.
2. The country of origin principle is not something flowing automatically from Art. 59 EC. It is based on a choice by the legislator. See Case C-233/94, *Germany* v. *European Parliament and Council,* [1997] ECR I-2405, at 64, annotated by Roth in CML Rev. 1998, p. 459 et seq.
3. Art. 26 of Directive 89/552 requires the Commission to submit to the Council and the Parliament a report on the application of that Directive, accompanied if necessary by proposals to adapt it to developments in the field of television broadcasting, within 5 years from the date of adoption.
4. Directive 97/36 of the European Parliament and the Council of 30 June 1997 amending Council Directive 89/552/EEC (O.J. 1997, L 202/60). For another overview see Chabrit, "Une nouvelle Télévision sans Frontière", *Editions du Juris-Classeur*, Novembre 1997, p. 3 et seq.

This article provides an evaluation of the reforms which the new Directive has introduced. In that connection, the essence of the discussions on the most salient issues will be highlighted, even if they have not always resulted in changes in the text of the Directive. A number of Court cases concerning the interpretation of the existing Directive were decided while the proposal was being negotiated. In general those rulings gave strong backing to several of the amendments proposed. It is therefore necessary to expand the analysis of the new Directive to those judgments as well. Below, the expression "the Directive" will refer to the consolidated text of Directive 89/552 following its amendment by Directive 97/36.

2. Sequence of events

The revision of the Directive was preceded by a Green Paper on the European programme industry.[5] The consultation procedure that was launched by the Green Paper prompted the Commission to prepare a partial revision of the 1989 Directive. During those preparations two controversial issues heavily dominated the internal discussions which were fuelled by numerous lobby papers submitted by the industries most directly affected.

The first lively debated topic concerned the scope of the Directive. In its original version, the Directive applies to broadcasting services, i.e. all services that consist of pre-determined programme schedules broadcast simultaneously to more than one receiver. This also covers newer services such as near-video-on-demand or pay-per-view multiplexed services. Initially, it was envisaged to extend the scope of the Directive to interactive teleservices, such as video-on-demand. Two arguments spoke in favour of such an extension: (a) competition between providers of largely interchangeable services from a consumers' perspective would be distorted if content related rules[6] were to vary according to the mode of transmission and (b) disparities between national legislations were likely to occur if these new services were not regulated at a Community level. However, the discussions ended up by not including point-to-point services in the framework of the Directive, essentially because of the specific problems these new services were likely to present in both tech-

---

5. COM(94)96 final of 6 April 1994. The Green Paper drew amongst other things on the report by the Think-Tank on the audiovisual policy in the European Union.

6. In particular, advertising restrictions and rules designed to protect minors. It has never been seriously proposed to impose quotas on inter-active services.

nological and regulatory terms.[7] A separate legal framework for "information society services" was seen as a preferable option.[8]

The second controversial issue concerned the rules on the promotion of European works through broadcasting quotas. Pursuant to Article 4, Member States shall ensure "where practicable and by appropriate means", that broadcasters reserve for European works[9] a majority proportion of their transmission time, excluding the time appointed to news, sports events, games and advertising. The flexible language used – the result of a delicate political compromise – had caused uncertainty about the nature and the meaning of these provisions. It was therefore felt necessary to clarify them. Initially, it was proposed to suppress the words "where practicable", while incorporating sufficient elements of flexibility, and to enhance the effectiveness of the quotas by excluding studio productions (talk shows, games etc.) from the "base" for calculating the transmission time to be devoted to European programmes. The latter idea was abandoned following protests from, in particular, commercial broadcasters who were facing the perspective of having to invest in comparatively expensive European cinematographic programmes. In the end, as regards the quotas the following compromise was agreed upon: on the one hand, the words "where practicable" were suppressed in order to dispel doubts as to the legally binding nature of the obligations provided for in Articles 4 and 5; on the other hand, there was the option to choose, for thematic channels, an investment quota, as an alternative to broadcasting quotas based on transmission time. In addition, a "phase out" after 10 years was proposed,[10] indicating that the quota system was perceived as a measure of a transitional nature.

After lengthy discussions the Commission adopted its proposal for a directive on 23 March 1995.[11] Apart from the unchanged scope and the compromise on the quotas, the main features of that proposal were: (a) clarifying and adding detail to "establishment" as the sole criterion determining jurisdiction; (b) introducing an obligation to establish penalties and means of redress in case of non-compliance with the minimum standards; (c) modernizing the

---

7. In some respects the discussion held early 1995 anticipated the current debate on convergence between the audiovisual and the telecommunications sector. Cf. the Commission's Green paper on Convergence (COM(97) 623 final of 3 Dec. 1997).

8. Recital 7 to the preamble of Directive 97/36 stipulates that "any legislative framework concerning new audiovisual services must be compatible with the primary objective of this Directive." It is unclear, however, what is exactly meant by "new audiovisual services".

9. As defined in Art. 6 of the Directive.

10. See Art. 3, second sentence, of the Commission's original proposal.

11. The proposal was published in O.J. 1995, C 185/4.

provisions on teleshopping;[12] and (d) clarifying and adding detail to a number of definitions. The proposal was combined with a detailed report on the application of Directive 89/552.[13]

During the negotiations that followed in the Council of Ministers, a majority of delegations was in favour neither of extending the scope of the Directive to point-to-point services nor of strengthening the quotas in whatever manner. A number of Member States even expressed a preference for abolishing the quotas altogether, considering them either as economically ineffective or as unduly encroaching on domestic cultural policy.[14] A majority of the European Parliament, on the contrary, followed the "French line": widening the scope of the Directive and strengthening the quotas.

Shortly before the Parliament delivered its opinion[15] in first reading, the Council had reached, under Spanish Presidency, a global compromise on the most controversial parts of the Directive. That compromise turned out to become the blue-print of the final text known as Directive 97/36. Key element of the Council compromise was not to touch upon the 1989 text of the quota provisions. As an extra safeguard, a Contact Committee of national experts had to be created whose task it should be to ensure a smooth functioning of the Directive. After other miscellaneous issues had been settled, a political agreement in view of a common position was reached in June 1996. Sweden was the only Member State to vote against the compromise, since it wished the rules on television advertising intended for children to be more stringent.[16] The Commission accepted the Council's text in spite of substantial differences with its own proposal. Consequently, the Swedish vote did not prevent the Council from adopting the common position.[17]

---

12. Under Art. 18(3) of Directive 89/552 teleshopping is subject to a daily limit of one hour only. This limit was no longer tenable given the number of channels devoted to teleshopping services that had emerged.

13. COM(95) 86 final of 31 May 1995.

14. One should not forget that the legislation of most if not all Member States (including those which objected to European quotas) provides for programming restrictions, among which language quotas. Under Dutch law for instance, 40% of transmission time must consist of programmes in the Dutch or the Frisian(!) language (See Art. 52L of the *Mediabesluit, Staatscourant* 1987, 573, amended since).

15. Opinion of 14 Feb. 1996 (O.J. 1996 C 65/113).

16. In an attempt to accomodate the Swedish requests, the Commission made the following declaration when the common position was adopted: "The Commission states that it will make a study of the impact of television advertising and teleshopping on minors, with a view to reexamination of the subject in the next revision of the Directive."

17. A common position can only be the basis for the remainder of the legislative process if it replaces the proposal of the Commission. This will be the case in either of the two situations: either the Commission accepts the common position (normally the responsible Commissioner has received a mandate to do so at the Council meeting at which the political agreement is reached) or the common position is adopted by unanimity (Art. 189a(1)). In the first situation, the Commission in fact voluntarily aligns its own proposal with the text of the common

Most observers expected the remainder of the legislative procedure to be difficult because of the diverging views of Council and Parliament. However, in second reading the Parliament rather unexpectedly accepted the essentials of the Council's common position, when several amendments tabled by the Committee for Culture failed to get sufficient support in the Plenary.[18] The Parliament moreover adopted unanimously two new amendments designed to ensure that the viewing public may continue to have access to major (sports) events on in-the-clear-television. The Ministers of Culture generally shared the concerns underlying these amendments, but a conciliation procedure as provided for in Article 189b(4) was needed for the fine-tuning of the text. The constructive discussions under Dutch Presidency in the framework of the "trilogue" preceding the opening of the conciliation procedure resulted in a balanced compromise text. On 16 April 1997, the Conciliation Committee, composed of Members of the Council or their representatives and an equal number of representatives of the Parliament, reached an agreement on a joint text. On 30 June 1997, Directive 97/36 was formally adopted. It was published in the Official Journal one month later and it must be transposed into national law by 30 December 1998.

3. Jurisdiction (Article 2)

3.1. *Introductory remarks*

The Directive provides the legal reference framework needed to ensure the free circulation of television broadcasts within the Community. Like other "Internal Market directives", the Directive is based upon the country of origin principle, while laying down minimum standards where necessary in a certain number of areas. In the 1989 Directive, there are four such "coordinated fields":[19] promotion of distribution and production of European television programmes (Chapter III), television advertising and sponsorship (Chapter IV), protection of minors (Chapter V) and the right of reply (Chapter VI). In the new version, Chapter IV has been extended to teleshopping, whereas Chapter V has been rearranged. Directive 97/36 has added one coordinated

---

position. The common position in this case was formally adopted on 8 July 1996 (O.J. 1996, C 264/52).

18. Resolution of the Parliament of 12 Nov. 1996 (O.J. 1996, C 362/56).

19. (Old) Art. 2(1) has the effect of harmonizing the jurisdictional criteria applied by the Member States. That does not mean, however, that this provision constitutes another "coordinated field". These terms must be understood as referring to areas in which general interests enjoying protection in national legislations (but not necessarily in all Member States) have been recognized as overriding reasons relating to the public interest.

field, i.e. the accessibility of events of major importance for society on free to air television.

Certain core subjects, such as pluralism of the media, are not coordinated at all, whereas other matters, for instance advertising, are harmonized but not in an exhaustive manner. The Directive therefore provides for *a partial harmonization* of the broadcasting laws of the Member States. Moreover, Article 3(1) permits Member States to lay down more stringent rules in the areas covered by the Directive with regard to television broadcasters under their jurisdiction. This indicates that the Directive provides for *minimum harmonization* only. Directive 97/36 has not changed any of these basic principles.

3.2. *The place of establishment determines jurisdiction*

Article 2(1) of Directive 89/552 stipulates that each Member State shall ensure that all television broadcasts transmitted by broadcasters under its jurisdiction comply with the law applicable to broadcasts intended for the public in that Member State. That text failed, however, to indicate a criterion determining which Member State has jurisdiction regarding a given broadcaster. In borderline cases, this absence of a clear rule could give rise to Member States applying differing criteria so that, potentially, a channel was under no State's jurisdiction (conflicting renvoi of jurisdiction) or under several States' jurisdiction (conflicting claim of jurisdiction).

In *Commission* v. *United Kingdom*,[20] the Court decided that the Member State on whose territory the broadcaster is established is the only State to have jurisdiction for the purposes of the Directive, thus upholding the interpretation defended by the Commission and shared by several Member States amongst which France and Germany. While noting that the wording of the Directive left room for doubt, the Court held that establishment within the meaning of Article 59 EC was the most effective criterion for defining jurisdiction *ratione personae*. The outcome of this case must be welcomed: if the location of the up-link were to be decisive (as the UK had argued), it would be easy for a broadcaster to change jurisdiction whenever convenient simply by moving the up-link to another Member State. Moreover, the actual operation of the up-link is normally entrusted to a telecom operator not having any editorial responsibility for the television programmes.

3.3. *The criteria defining establishment*

In accordance with this case law, the new Article 2(2) clearly stipulates that for the purposes of the Directive the broadcasters under the jurisdiction of a

---

20. Case C-222/94, [1996] ECR I-4025.

Member State are "those established in that Member State in accordance with paragraph 3." Another helpful clarification is the definition of broadcaster given in new Article 1(b): "the natural or legal person who has editorial responsibility for the composition of schedules of television programmes ... and who transmits them or has them transmitted by third parties." The absence of such a definition in the original version of the Directive was felt as an omission.

Article 2(3), to which the second paragraph refers, sets out hierarchical rules for determining the place of establishment. If the broadcaster has its head office in Member State A and the editorial decisions about programme schedules are taken in that same State it is deemed to be established in that State. That obviously is the easiest of all situations. If a broadcaster has its head office in Member State A but editorial decisions are taken in Member State B, it shall be deemed to be established in the Member State "where a significant part of the workforce involved in the pursuit of the television broadcasting activity operates."[21] This workforce requirement is of great practical importance, in particular for broadcasters whose head office is located in a Member State other than the one they target with their programmes, because it is usually in the latter State that programmes are produced and that acquisition takes place.

These clarifications are extremely helpful: it is one thing to retain "establishment" as the unique criterion determining jurisdiction; but it is another to determine the place of establishment in the specific context of television broadcasting. The Court had to deal with the latter question under the text of the 1989 Directive in *VT4*[22] with regard to a broadcaster having more than one place of establishment. In such a situation, "... the competent Member State is the State in which the broadcaster has the centre of its activities. It is therefore for the national court to determine, applying that criterion, which Member State has jurisdiction over VT4's activities, taking into account in particular the place where decisions concerning programme policy are taken and the programmes to be broadcast are finally put together."[23]

Throughout the proceedings the Flemish Community, defendant in the main proceedings, argued that the undertaking VT4 had established its corporate seat in London for the sole purpose of escaping the Flemish broadcasting

---

21. If a significant part of that workforce operates *in each of those Member States*, the broadcaster shall be deemed to be established in the Member State where it has its head office. If, on the contrary, a significant part of the workforce operates *in neither of those Member States*, the broadcaster shall be deemed to be established in the Member State where it first began broadcasting in accordance with the system of law of that Member State, provided that it maintains a stable and effective link with the economy of that Member State. The last criterion (genuine link) stems from the 1962 General Programme on free provision of services.

22. Case C-55/96, *VT4 Ltd* v. *Vlaamse Gemeenschap*, [1997] ECR I-3143.

23. Ibid. para 19.

rules. In *Van Binsbergen*,[24] as confirmed in *Veronica*[25] and particularly in *TV 10*,[26] the Court held that "... a Member State cannot be denied the right to take measures to prevent the exercise by a person providing services whose activity is entirely or principally directed towards its territory, of the freedoms guaranteed by the Treaty for the purpose of avoiding the rules which would be applicable to him if he were established within that State; such a situation may be subject to judicial control under the provisions of the chapter relating to the right of establishment and not the provisions of services." Relying on this case law, the Flemish Community claimed that VT4 had to be treated as a domestic broadcaster. While leaving to the national court the ultimate decision on the question whether or not VT4 had circumvented the Flemish rules, the Court stated very clearly: "The Treaty does not prohibit an undertaking from exercising the freedom to provide services if it does not offer services in the Member State in which it is established."[27]

In this connection one may raise the more general question whether it should not be seen as incompatible with the very essence of harmonization if Member States are still allowed to plead circumvention within the internal market. It is submitted that there is no such incompatibility. The possibility of imposing stricter rules on domestic broadcasters in areas covered by the Directive, as expressly recognized in Article 3(1), would become practically meaningless if Member States were not entitled to enforce such stricter rules by combating circumvention. In *Commission* v. *Belgium*,[28] the Court, however, expressly left open whether, in the light of the Directive, a Member State is still entitled to rely on the *Van Binsbergen* case law.[29]

Depending on particular sensitivities and traditions, several Member States have indeed enacted stricter rules than the ones laid down in the Directive,[30] thus taking the risk that "competition" from other legal systems cause broad-

---

24. Case 33/74, *Van Binsbergen* v. *Bedrijfsvereniging voor de metaalnijverheid*, [1974] ECR 1299.

25. Case C-148/91, *Veronica Omroep Organisatie* v. *Commissariaat voor de Media*, [1993] ECR I-487.

26. Case C-23/93, *TV 10 SA* v. *Commissariaat voor de Media*, [1994] ECR I-4795; 32 CML Rev., 1257, annotated by Wattel.

27. Para 22 of the judgment. There is no indication that in *VT4* the Court overruled *TV10*. A specific feature of the latter case was that the referring court, the Dutch Council of State, had established that TV10 had circumvented the Dutch legislation. That is why the first (and most interesting) question raised was to know whether Art. 59 is applicable at all in situations where a broadcaster seeks to avoid the application to it of the rules of the Member State to which it directs its programmes. A similar finding had not been made by the Belgian courts when the Belgian Council of State referred the VT4 case to Luxembourg. The Court rightly leaves the decision on that question of fact to the referring judge.

28. Case C-11/95, *Commission* v. *Belgium*, [1996] ECR I-4117.

29. See para 65.

30. Well known examples are the quota rules in France (60% European content during the hours of the day when there is a significant audience), the Swedish ban on all television

casters to establish their principal centre of activities elsewhere in the Community. In the course of the negotiations in the Council, a minority of Member States was keen to see the *"Van Binsbergen* rule" enshrined in the body of the Directive. Similarly, the Parliament proposed in first reading to retain the "destination" of a television programme as an additional criterion for allocating jurisdiction.[31] That amendment could only have the effect of increasing legal uncertainty. By way of compromise, it was decided to insert a recital in which the *Van Binsbergen* case law is mentioned (recital 14).

It emerges from that case law that only in exceptional circumstances may a *"Van Binsbergen* defence" be successfully invoked by the receiving State. First, a Member State cannot generally and *a priori* exclude the provision of certain services by operators established in other Member States.[32] In other words, circumvention cannot be presumed; it must be established on a case-by-case basis. Moreover, circumvention involves an element of abuse.[33] There is only abuse of right if the broadcaster has been acting "wrongfully" or "improperly".[34] To that effect, it is not in itself sufficient that all programmes and advertisements transmitted are intended for the public of one Member State. Finally, there can only be circumvention within the meaning of the Court's case law if the rules purportedly circumvented are themselves compatible with Community law.[35] .3

3.4. *Giving effect to the new rules of conflict*

It is inherent in any law-shaping activity that new solutions, whether legislative or judicial, are liable to give rise to new problems of interpretation. In spite of the substantial improvements they entail, the amendments made to Article 2 of the Directive will probably not escape that fate. With regard to the new rules on jurisdiction, it is uncertain, for example, how one is to determine the place where editorial decisions on the programme schedules are taken.

---

advertising aimed at children under 12 years and the Greek ban on toy advertising which seeks to preserve "peaceful family life".

31. Amendment proposed by Mr Philippe De Coene. See doc PE 213.974 of 26 Jan. 1996, amendment 23, at c).

32. See *Commission* v. *Belgium*, para 65.

33. As was convincingly argued by A.G. Lenz in *Commission* v. *Belgium* (C-11/95), paras. 71 et seq. of his Opinion.

34. See in that sense also A.G. Jacobs' Opinion in *De Agostini*, at p. 3859.

35. That is another key element in the discussion about VT4. Indeed, VT4 has been accused of withdrawing from the application of a national rule (namely VTM's advertising monopoly on commercial television destined for the entire Flemish territory) which the Commission later held to be contrary to Art. 90(1) juncto 52 in its decision of 26 June 1997 (O.J. 1997, L 244/18). Further details on the status of VT4 are given by Valcke, "VT4: van verboden Britse naar erkende Vlaamse zender", (1998) *Mediaforum*, 2 et seq. and, "Het nieuwe juridische kader voor de Vlaamse omroep", (1998) *Mediaforum*, 102 et seq.

For the purposes of applying the Directive, internal corporate arrangements should not be decisive. What matters is the location of the centre of gravity regarding the editorial content of the programme schedules.[36]

Although the criteria laid down in Article 2(3) are essentially meant to consolidate the situation prevailing under the 1989 text, it may happen that the new criteria cause jurisdiction to shift from one Member State to another Member State. Thus, the Dutch broadcasting authority *Commissariaat voor de Media* now claims jurisdiction[37] over channels RTL4 and RTL5, so far under Luxembourg jurisdiction. Article 4 of the Dutch *Mediawet* defines jurisdiction of the Netherlands by direct reference to Directive 89/552. The *Commissariaat* contends that under (new) Article 2(3) both channels must be deemed to be established in the Netherlands, the underlying presumption being that the direct reference to Directive 89/552 constitutes a sufficient implementation of Directive 97/36.

It is submitted that this presumption is questionable. A direct reference to a rule of conflict contained in a directive is as such an appropriate method of implementation. Where such a reference is "dynamic" (i.e. refers to the relevant provisions as subsequently amended), modifications in the directive need not be transposed into national law. However, unless stated otherwise in the directive, such a provision will become applicable *in the national legal order only* from the date on which the amending directive enters into force. In the present context, the new rules defining the place of establishment will become applicable only when the national law transposing Directive 97/36 enters into force (in principle 30 December 1998 at the latest[38]), and not from the day on which the Directive entered into force (30 July 1997). In addition, the reference in the *Mediawet* is formulated in such a way that it is not properly speaking a "dynamic reference". It is therefore hardly surprising that meanwhile the decision of the *Commissariaat* has been suspended by an administrative court pending the main proceedings.[39]

By their very nature, rules of conflict should be capable of being directly applied. One would therefore expect to find such rules in a regulation rather than in a directive. The obvious risk of their becoming effective at different dates in the various Member States can be an extra argument for not incorporating rules of conflict in a directive. Such disparities can nevertheless be avoided if a directive fixes not only a date for transposition but also a date as

---

36. It is no coincidence that the words "editorial responsibility" are a core element of the definition of broadcaster contained in Art. 1(b).

37. *Staatscourant* 226 of 24 Nov. 1997. See also Van den Beukel, (1997) *Mediaforum*, 116–117.

38. See Art. 2(1) of Directive 97/36.

39. President District Court Amsterdam, 20 May 1998, published in (1998) *Mediaforum*, 239.

from which the implementing rules shall become applicable. This system has been followed in a number of directives,[40] but not in Directive 97/36.

3.5. *Rules applicable to domestic broadcasters*

Article 2(1) of the Directive provides that each Member State shall ensure that all television broadcasts transmitted by broadcasters under its jurisdiction comply with the rules applicable to broadcasts intended for the public in that Member State. The imperative language ("shall ensure") shows that the rules of conflict laid down in the Directive are designed to be cogent and complete. Consequently, jurisdiction cannot be declined on the ground, for example, that the programmes of a particular broadcaster are transmitted in a foreign language. However, there is nothing in the Directive to oblige the Member States to exercise their jurisdiction through a system of broadcasting licences.

It follows from the words "intended for the public in that Member State" that all broadcasters coming under the jurisdiction of a Member State should in principle be subject to identical rules. Obviously, this does not go as far as meaning that constraints imposed on public broadcasters by reason of their public service remit must also be applied to, for instance, thematic satellite channels. What the Directive seeks to avoid is that Member States apply more lenient rules to broadcasters whose programmes are intended for foreign audiences (typically satellite channels). Indeed, a preferential "export regime" is not in keeping with the concept of a single market.

This was precisely one of the objections raised by the Commission in Case C-222/94 against the *United Kingdom*. The reason for raising this issue was that in comparison to other categories of broadcasters under British jurisdiction "non-domestic satellite services"[41] benefited from a more lenient regime as far as the implementation of Articles 4 and 5 was concerned. This favourable treatment might have acted as an incentive for television stations, both from inside and from outside the Community, to choose the UK as springboard for their European operations.[42] The Court needed only one

---

40. For a random example see Directive 91/439/EEC of the Council on the driving licence (O.J. 1991, L 237, p. 1). See also Timmermans, "Community Directives", *Rapport communautaire* for the FIDE Congress held in Stockholm on 3–6 June 1998, at paras. 10 et seq.

41. For a definition see *Commission v. United Kingdom*, para 10, quoting Art. 43(2) of the Broadcasting Act 1990.

42. In 1994, the overwhelming majority of satellite channels operating in the Community had been licensed by the British ITC as non-domestic satellite services. Several of them have given rise to litigation (e.g. TNT Cartoon, VT4 and TV3). Comprehensive lists of all satellite channels operating in the EU are attached to the Commission's monitoring reports on the application of Arts. 4 and 5 of the Directive. See for the period 1991–1992: COM(94) 57 final of 3 March 1994; for 1993–1994: COM(96) 302 final of 15 July 1996; and for 1995–1996:

paragraph to uphold the Commission's claim[43] and, consequently, to confirm the illegal character of this loophole.[44] This somewhat laconic passage of the judgment gives support to the argument that Member States are restrained from organizing more favourable regimes for the benefit of broadcasters whose programmes are exclusively or principally directed at other Member States.

4. Transmission State principle (Article 2a)

4.1. *Introductory remarks*

Directive 97/36 has split the old Article 2 in two separate articles, with the (old) paragraphs 2 and 3 having become a new Article 2a. The key principle is still the same: Member States shall ensure freedom of reception and shall not restrict retransmission on their territory of television broadcasts from other Member States for reasons which fall within the fields coordinated by the Directive. Although these principles have not changed, it is necessary to examine the precise meaning of some of the terms that are used. For the remainder, some minor amendments were made to the sole exception to the rule, i.e. the possibility of derogating provisionally from the transmission State principle when a television broadcast coming from another Member State "manifestly, seriously and gravely" infringes the provisions regarding the protection of minors and public order.

4.2. *Restricting retransmission*

In *Commission* v. *Belgium*, the Court notes that the Directive does not draw a distinction between primary and secondary broadcasting. It must therefore be interpreted as applying to the distribution of television programmes by cable.[45] The Court prohibited a system requiring prior authorization for the retransmission by cable of television broadcasts emanating from other Member States. Such a system was applied by both the Flemish and the French

---

COM(1998) 199 final of 3 April 1998. The last report also includes an overall assessment of the application of the quota rules over the whole period 1991–96.

43. Para 74.

44. Following the Court ruling, the British authorities made a serious effort to improve compliance with Art. 4 through what they call "a milestones approach". This positive development led the Commission to suspend the infringement procedure it had opened against the UK for having failed to give effect to the Arts. 4 and 5 in relation to non-domestic satellite services.

45. See paras. 20 to 23.

Community. The numerous arguments to justify a second control[46] were one by one rejected, either because they referred to matters coordinated by the Directive or because the means chosen (a general system of prior authorization) were disproportionate to the objective(s) pursued. The judgment unambiguously confirms that it is only for the Member State of establishment to monitor compliance with the standards laid down by the Directive.

The Court also made it clear that, even where there is evidence that a particular broadcaster does not abide by the rules fixed by the Directive, it is not for the State of reception to adopt unilaterally, on its own authority, corrective or protective measures designed to obviate any breach by another Member State of rules of Community law. This case law was confirmed in *Denuit*.[47] The prohibition of prior authorization by means of agreements does not augur well for the *politique de conventionnement* practiced by the French *Conseil supérieur de l'audiovisuel*. The Court's decision should, however, not be understood as obliging the authorities of the State of reception to refrain from exercising any form of control. Those authorities may legitimately ascertain that the broadcaster whose programmes are up for distribution by cable is a Community broadcaster. Indeed, the transmitting State principle does not apply to programmes transmitted by broadcasters not falling under the jurisdiction of any Member State.[48] Consequently, cable operators may be asked to make a plausible case that the programmes they intend to distribute fall within the scope of the Directive.

An entirely different question is whether the terms "restriction of retransmission" must be understood as covering national measures or actions by the authorities of the State of reception which may affect the retransmission only indirectly. That issue was at the heart of *Konsumentombudsmannen* v. *De Agostini and TV Shop*. The Swedish Consumer Ombudsman brought an action against two Swedish advertisers for respectively misleading advertising and infringement of a Swedish rule prohibiting all television advertising

46. Involving as broad a spectrum as Art. 10(2) of the ECHR, Art. 128 EC (culture), Art. 3b EC (subsidiarity), the preservation of pluralism in the media and the protection of copyright.

47. Case C-14/96, [1997] ECR I-2729. Following a Ministerial Decree the Belgian authorities had refused permission to the cable distributor Coditel Brabant to distribute the programmes of the British broadcasting service "Turner Network Television Limited" and "The Cartoon Limited Network" on the ground that they did not comply with Arts. 4 and 5 of the Directive. The Brussels *Tribunal de Commerce* referred the matter to the Court (Case C-316/94). That referral was withdrawn, after the Brussels Court of Appeal had overturned the reference order. In spite of the Ministerial Decree having been annulled by the domestic courts, criminal proceedings were brought against Mr Denuit, the Director of Coditel, for having infringed domestic law by distributing the above programmes during the period in which the prohibition was in force.

48. The Directive not only applies to all broadcasters established on the territory on one of the Member States, but also to broadcasters using a frequency, a satellite capacity, or a satellite up-link of or in a Member State. This follows from Art. 2(4), formerly Art. 2(1), 2nd indent.

designed to attract the attention of children under 12 years of age.[49] The Court was above all asked to define the scope of the Directive.

As regards *misleading advertising*, the receiving State may take measures intended to protect consumers with regard to (national) advertisers but not introduce a second control of the television programmes broadcast by (non-national) broadcasters, as these programmes must be controlled by the trans-mitting State. On the issue of *advertising directed at children*, the level of harmonization attained is considered sufficient by the Court for the Directive to prevent the receiving State from applying measures of protection of minors provided in a broadcasting law, whoever the operators concerned might be.[50]

The Court's reasoning unfortunately raises more questions than it answers. It is unclear what is meant under the first heading by "prevent the retransmis-sion, as such," and under the second heading by "the application to television broadcasts". In both instances, the Consumer Ombudsman relied on a nation-al rule against a national advertiser, its action did not involve any technical of legal interference with the retransmission, and the two sets of national law were "applied to" the broadcasts in exactly the same manner. On a closer look, the Court has construed a link between two wholly distinct matters, i.e. the question which categories of operators can rely on the transmitting State principle and the question what general interests have been harmonized by the Directive.[51] In so doing, the Court gave a narrow interpretation of the first part of (old) Article 2(2) ("Member States shall not restrict retransmissions on their territories of television broadcasts from other Member States ... ") and an ostensibly broad interpretation of the second part of that same paragraph ("... for reasons which fall within the fields coordinated by the Directive"). The approach chosen by the Court might have the effect of narrowing the scope of (new) Article 2a(1), since only interference with the retransmission as such is covered.

4.3. *What is a coordinated field?*

Much of the confusion characterizing the *De Agostini* judgment results from the unclear meaning of the terms "the fields coordinated by this Directive".

---

49. Joined Cases C-34/95, C-35/95 and C-36/95, [1997] ECR I-3843 annotated by Stuyck in 34 CML Rev., 1445 et seq. See also the elucidatory comments by Temmink in (1998) SEW, 255.

50. Summary given in the Commission's 2nd "Report on the Application of Directive 89/552/EEC 'Television Without Frontiers'"; COM (97) 523 final of 24 Oct. 1997.

51. One gets the impression that in the second part of the judgment (on protection of minors) the Court had some difficulty in being consistent with its findings in the first part of the judgment (on misleading advertising) in which it had held that advertisers cannot rely on the Directive (paras. 36 to 38).

In inviting the national court to examine whether any form of second control has taken place, the Court did not feel the need to clarify that expression. On the contrary, Advocate General Jacobs extensively addressed the issue in his Opinion preceding the judgment. With regard to the relation between the Directive and Directive 84/450/EEC on misleading advertising, he defended the view that the Directive encompasses misleading advertising and that, in general, two issues had to be distinguished, "namely the fields coordinated by the [D]irective and the specific matters regulated by it". According to the Advocate General, "it is the former concept which is crucial in determining whether Article 2(2) applies."

On this particular issue the Advocate General's Opinion calls for some critical comments. In the system of the Directive the free circulation of television programmes is the corollary of the coordination of national laws. Since none of the provisions of the Directive (neither in its original nor in its new version) deals specifically with misleading advertising, it would be logical to accept that unrestricted transmission cannot be warranted by the Directive.[52] In addition, the country of origin principle, the cornerstone of the Directive, is difficult to carry over to misleading advertising since in consumer law it is normally the law of the Host State that should be applicable. Indeed, a commercial considered as appropriate for the public in one Member State might still be considered misleading in another State.

A strong argument in support of the opposite view can however be inferred from the provision permitting Member States to lay down more detailed or stricter rules in the "areas covered by this Directive" (Article 3(1)). In *Leclerc-Siplec*,[53] the Court emphasized the breadth of that provision: a law prohibiting televised advertising in the distribution sector, the stated purpose of which was to protect the (regional) written press, was held to be covered by this provision. It is plain, however, that the Directive neither contains specific rules on advertising by the distribution sector nor coordinates national laws designed to protect media pluralism. Those circumstances did not prevent the Court from refusing to limit the grounds on which a Member State is entitled to enact stricter rules in accordance with Article 3.[54]

Even more explicitly, recital 44 to the preamble of Directive 97/36 recalls that "Member States remain free to apply to broadcasters under their jurisdiction more detailed or stricter rules in the *fields coordinated by this Directive, including, inter alia,* rules concerning the achievement of language policy goals, protection of the public interest in terms of television's role as a provider of information, education, culture and entertainment, the need to

52. It follows that the legality of such restrictions falls to be assessed on the basis of Arts. 30 and/or 59 EC.
53. Case C-412/93, [1995] ECR I-179.
54. See in particular at para 47 of the judgment.

safeguard pluralism in the information industry and the media, and the protection of competition with a view to avoiding the abuse of dominant positions ... " (emphasis added). Arguably, the emphasized passage confirms that the "areas covered by this Directive" mentioned in Article 3(1) and the terms "fields coordinated by this Directive" referred to in Article 2a(1) have exactly the same meaning. If that view is correct, the scope of the coordinated fields is not determined by the sort of interest pursued (e.g. pluralism), but by the matter actually affected (e.g. television advertising).

4.4. *Exceptions to the transmitting State principle (Article 2a(2))*

Stricter rules may only be applied in relation to domestic broadcasters. For broadcasts from other Member States, the transmitting State principle applies unconditionally. There is only one exception to that rule, namely the faculty of a Member State to suspend provisionally broadcasts emanating from another Member State if these broadcasts manifestly, seriously and gravely infringe one of the rules on protection of minors (Article 22). Even then, this possibility is subject to a number of strict conditions of a procedural nature.

Article 22 of the Directive makes a distinction between programmes that might *seriously* impair the physical, mental or moral development of minors and those programmes that are *likely* to impair the physical, mental and moral development of minors. Programmes belonging to the first category shall not be transmitted at all. The mere risk of serious impairment of minors is sufficient to justify a total transmission ban irrespective of the way in which the programme can be accessed. Even encrypted programmes broadcast at night time are therefore prohibited if they have the stated effect. Programmes belonging to the second category are prohibited as well, "except where it is ensured, by selecting the time of the broadcast or by a technical measure, that minors in the area of transmission will not normally hear or see the broadcasts." In other words, this is a conditional prohibition only.

The difference between the two categories of programmes is one of degree. For systematic reasons, the two sentences of (old) Article 22 have now been rearranged in two separate paragraphs.[55] By virtue of a third paragraph, Member States shall ensure that each time when "such programmes[56] are broadcast in unencoded form they are preceded by an acoustic warning or are identified by the presence of a visual symbol throughout their duration". The compulsory use of a V-chip, an electronic device designed to filter harmful content, was not seen as the magic solution to the problem of ensuring effective

---

55. Moreover, Art. 22(3) has become new Art. 22a.
56. Necessarily referring to the second category, since the former category of broadcasts is banned altogether.

protection of minors against harmful television programmes. However, a new article was added (Article 22b) requiring the Commission "to carry out a study on the possible advantages and drawbacks of further measures with a view to facilitating the control exercised by parents or guardians over the programmes that minors may watch."

Article 22 gives a non-exhaustive list of types of programmes that may qualify as seriously impairing the development of minors. It mentions "in particular those that involve pornography or gratuitous violence". Pornography does not fall automatically under the absolute transmission ban of paragraph 1. It must be shown that a programme involving pornography may have the effects on minors referred to. This interpretation was recently confirmed by the EFTA Court in proceedings brought by *TV 1000 Sverige,* a Swedish channel which had transmitted to Norway programmes containing sexually explicit material.[57] The EFTA Court also confirmed that it is for the national authorities of the receiving State to determine, in accordance with that State's values and national legislation, which programmes might seriously impair the development of minors. Thus the moral assessment of the content of a particular programme is left to the judgment of the Member States. This approach is fully in keeping with the case law of the European Court of Human Rights in relation to the interpretation of Article 10 ECHR.[58] It anyhow makes a lot of sense: if even the Norwegian standards are substantially different from those prevailing in neighbouring country Sweden, any attempt to harmonize the concept of pornography will be doomed to fail – quite independently of the institutional question whether or not the Community is at all competent to set any standards in this area.

Pursuant to Article 22, the *Member State of origin* shall ensure that its national law prohibits the transmission of programmes covered by the first paragraph of Article 22. For the reasons stated in section 3.5 above, a Member State shall not apply discriminatory moral criteria to the broadcasters under their jurisdiction: a stricter attitude to programmes to be received in their territory and a more lenient attitude to programmes destined to be broadcast abroad would not be acceptable.[59] Under certain procedural conditions (which have not been changed) the *receiving State* "may, provisionally, derogate" from the transmission State principle. This formulation is slightly more open than the original text which specifically mentioned "suspension". That small innovation finds its likely explanation in the experience gained with this special procedure. At several instances, the British authorities adopted a proscription order against foreign pornographic channels transmitting their

57. Case E-8/97, Advisory Opinion of 12 June 1998 (not yet published).
58. See *Handyside* v. *UK*, ECHR of 7 Dec. 1976, Series A Vol. 24.
59. Cf. 2nd report on the application of the Directive (cited above), at 4.2 on p. 8.

programmes in the UK. Such orders did not normally involve the suspension of the programme itself but proved to be equally effective.[60]

In exercising its duty to "ensure that the suspension is compatible with Community law", the Commission adopted on a number of occasions an "opinion" which it notified to both the receiving State (invariably the UK) and the transmitting State. Under the new text of the Directive, the Commission shall, "within two months following notification of the measures taken by the Member State [of reception], take a *decision* on whether the measures are compatible with Community law." This tightening up of the procedure must be welcomed, since there can be little doubt that a broadcaster's interests are directly affected by a Commission decision upholding a national measure banning its programmes. One may indeed wonder how "provisional" such a measure actually is.

5. Monitoring and enforcement of the Directive (Article 3(2) and (3) and Article 23a)

Although it is addressed to the Member States, the Directive provides for a whole series of obligations that must be fulfilled by broadcasters. For that reason, Article 3(2) of the Directive obliges the Member States to ensure "that television broadcasters under their jurisdiction effectively[61] comply with the provisions of this Directive". Far from being superfluous,[62] this provision confirms the idea that full implementation of a directive not only involves the transposition of its contents into national law, but also the correct application of those national measures by their addressees as well as the enforcement of those measures by the competent authorities.

Several complaints from consumer organizations report that the quantitative ceilings on transmission time devoted to advertising are systematically exceeded, particularly by broadcasters in Spain, Portugal and Greece. In those circumstances, Article 3(2) may be the correct legal basis for an Article 169 action. It will then be for the Commission to gather and verify the information needed to assess the extent to which such excesses actually take place and to

---

60. E.g. a prohibition to sell the decoders that are needed to have access to the programme in question or a ban on purchasing air time for commercials. The likely consequence of such an order is that the channel in question will no longer be commercially viable. Cf. Commission opinions C(96) 3933 final in case *Rendez-Vous Télévision* and C(95) 2678 final in the *XXXTV* case.

61. The word "effectively" has been added. Otherwise the provision is unchanged.

62. Notwithstanding the fact that the obligation to ensure correct application of a Community directive already arises from Arts. 189(3) jo 5 EC. See e.g. Case C-287/91, *Commission* v. *Italy*, [1992] ECR I-3515 and Case C-341/94, *Allain*, [1996] ECR I-4631.

establish that the competent authorities of the Member State in question have failed to take the necessary corrective measures.

At the time of the 1994 Green Paper, the relatively poor state of compliance with the Directive had led some observers, including certain Member States, to call for the State of reception to be given a right of enforcement. Meeting such a request would, however, have seriously detracted from the fundamental principle of free movement of services. Mindful of the concerns expressed, the Commission recognized the need to have more detailed provisions on national enforcement. It proposed that Member States determine penalties that shall be sufficient to enforce compliance. It also proposed a provision aimed at facilitating private enforcement, by ensuring that judicial access in the country of origin be available to interested parties.

The first of those provisions expressed in a slightly different wording the general obligation incumbent upon the Member States to provide for effective, proportionate and dissuasive sanctions.[63] However, it was dropped during the negotiations in the Council, not because of its limited added value but, surprisingly, on the ground that an obligation to impose penalties might be seen as conflicting with the independent status of broadcasters. The second provision proposed by the Commission did survive the negotiations albeit in a somewhat attenuated form: "The measures shall include the appropriate procedures for third parties directly affected, including nationals of other Member States, to apply to the competent judicial or other authorities to seek effective compliance according to national provisions."[64]

A more informal instrument designed to contribute to a better compliance with the Directive is the creation of a so-called Contact Committee composed of experts of Member States under the aegis of the Commission (Article 23a). This Committee formalizes the pre-existing ad hoc Group and is clearly not a committee assisting the Commission in deciding implementing measures.[65] Although the Contact Committee was part of the compromise on the quotas, its remit encompasses a much wider range of topics. The Contact Committee is likely to become a very useful forum for Member States and the Commission to have exchanges of view while benefiting from each others expertise and experience.[66]

63. See e.g. Case C-382/92, *Commission v. United Kingdom*, [1994] ECR I-2435, para 55 and Joined Cases C-58/95 etc., *Gallotti*, [1996] ECR I-4345, para 14.

64. On top of this, Directive 98/27/EC of the European Parliament and the Council of 19 May 1998 grants consumer organizations access to justice in the State of origin in the case of transborder infringements of one of the Community directives which are listed in the Annex to that Directive. Directive 89/552, as amended by Directive 97/36, is on the list.

65. Cf. "Comitology Decision" 87/373/EEC of 13 July 1987 (O.J. 1987, L 197/33).

66. There are precedents of a Contact Committee in other areas characterized by a high degree of technicality and/or a great amount of political sensitivity. See e.g. Art. 52 of the Fourth company law Directive on annual accounts (Directive 78/660/EEC, O.J. 1978, L 222/11,

6. Promotion of distribution and production of European works (Chapter III – Articles 4 to 9)

6.1. *Introductory comments*

In maintaining the words "where practical and by appropriate means" in the Articles 4 and 5, the Community legislature accepted that the obligation provided for is to behave in a certain manner (*une obligation de comportement*)[67] rather than to produce a specific result. The definition of the relevant transmission time for the purposes of calculating the required proportions is virtually unchanged.[68] It is left to the Member States to define the notion of "independent producer" for the purposes of giving effect to Article 5.[69] Both Articles 4 and 5 must be observed by all channels falling under the jurisdiction of a Member State, "taking economic realities into account".[70] With the number of specialized channels rapidly growing, it may be foreseen that "economic realities" will more and more often prevent channels from attaining the majority proportion lacking sufficiently available European content. Channels broadcasting entirely in a language other than those of the Member States are the only category to be formally exempted from the provisions of Articles 4 and 5.[71]

The notion of "European works" is defined in Article 6. Under the 1989 text, it already covered certain works originating in European States other than Community Member States. A newly added paragraph 4 has widened that definition even further. It now includes works that are produced within the framework of bilateral co-production treaties concluded between Member States and third countries, provided the Community co-producers supply

amended since) and Art. 13 of Council Directive 91/308 of 10 June 1991 on the prevention of the utilization of the financial system for the purposes of money laundering (O.J. 1991, L 166/77). In the same spirit, the process of implementing Directive 96/92/EC of 19 Dec. 1996 concerning common rules for the internal market in electricity (O.J. 1997, L 27/20) is discussed and scrutinized in an informal setting of national experts chaired by a Commission representative. That is another example of the Commission and national experts getting together with a view to solving existing problems and preventing new ones from occurring, rather than wait for Court litigation.

67. See, in that sense, already the answer given by Commissioner Bangemann to Written Question 758/89 by Mr Kenneth Collins (O.J. 1990, C 97/22).

68. The only modification is that teletext services and teleshopping are now also expressly excluded from the relevant transmission time.

69. Recital 31 to the preamble of Directive 97/36 gives, however, some guidance: "whereas Member States, in defining the notion of 'independent producer', should take appropriate account of criteria such as the ownership of the production company, the amount of programmes supplied to the same broadcaster and the ownership of secondary rights."

70. See recital 30.

71. See recital 29.

a majority share of the total costs of the production and production is not controlled by one or more producers established outside the territory of the Community.[72] The inclusion of works originating from European third countries is conditional on works originating from Member States not being the subject of discriminatory measures in the third countries concerned.[73]

Article 9 stipulates that Chapter III is not applicable to broadcasts that are intended for local audiences *and* do not form part of a national network. It follows from the use of the conjunction "and" that channels whose programmes cover an entire region must comply with Articles 4 and 5. Finally, the Commission shall continue drawing up its bi-annual reports on the application of the system (Article 4(3)), whereas a further review of the quota system shall take place before 30 June 2002 (Article 25a). That last provision is a concession of limited importance to the opponents of the system.

In conclusion, very little has changed. Even the "non-slip back clause" of Article 4(2) is still in force. Consequently, the average level of European works attained in 1988 per Member State is theoretically still the bottom line. At that time, however, the audiovisual landscape was still largely dominated by public broadcasters most of whom easily attained the proportions required. The same will not be true of the numerous commercial channels that have been launched since. It is not surprising that the initial ideas of stiffening the language of Articles 4 and 5 caused commercial broadcasters, besides other interested circles such as the US entertainment industry, to challenge the effectiveness and even the legality of those provisions.

A number of economic circumstances, however, speak in favour of European origin requirements. The huge domestic market allows American programmes more easily a return on investment. Paradoxically, the creation of a European-wide single market cannot but enhance this comparative cost advantage. It was therefore reasonable to set up, precisely in the framework of a single market directive, a system helping improving the competitiveness of the European programme industry. In addition, the significant growth in the number of broadcasters has substantially enhanced competition for attractive programme content, directing broadcasters towards the most cost advantage solution. That will often mean purchasing American series. Apart from those economic aspects, one has to recognize the existence of a cultural interest in taking measures aimed at supporting the audiovisual industry, given the undeniable importance of television in defining a cultural identity and in preserving the cultural and linguistic diversity of Europe.

---

72. This extension may have practical relevance for *interalia* films produced under bilateral conventions between Spain and one of the Latin American countries.

73. See Art. 6(1), last paragraph.

Admittedly, there are some weaker sides too. First, by defining European works on the basis of residence, the Directive does not guarantee that the programmes covered express or further any better the European cultural identity than do many American productions.[74] Secondly, there is nothing to guarantee that broadcasters will incorporate in their programming a growing proportion of works originating from other Member States, since the majority proportion can be attained with national programmes too. Thirdly, one may wonder whether there is really something like a European cultural identity or integrity, unless that identity is precisely the expression of Europe's diversity. Finally, the application and monitoring of the system is becoming increasingly cumbersome. As the Commission conceded in its latest Report on the application of Articles 4 and 5: " . . . current developments, in particular digital television, will . . . pose challenges to the monitoring system based on the concept of television channel."[75]

Be that as it may, the possible weaknesses of the system in terms of its effectiveness might well be its strength under the angle of proportionality. An important element to take into account is that Articles 4 and 5 put limits as to the geographic origin of the programmes only; they do not limit the overall quantity or value of audiovisual works from outside Europe. It is therefore more correct to speak of "European content requirements".[76]

6.2. *The legality of the European content requirements*[77]

In academic writing as well as in numerous lobby papers, the legality of the Articles 4 and 5 of the Directive has been challenged on essentially three grounds: (a) lack of legal basis in the Treaty; (b) violation of Article 10 ECHR; and (c) breach of international obligations. The first argument is the

---

74. The extension of "European works" to films produced under bilateral conventions between a Member State and a non Member State also detracts from the idea that "a" European identity needs to be protected.

75. Doc. COM(1998) 199 final of 3 April 1998, p. 62. As a result of the digitalization, the number of channels has dramatically increased, the very concept of channel is becoming increasingly blurred and channels are becoming more and more specialized, particularly the new ones coming on the market.

76. See De Witte, "The European content requirements in the EC Television Directive – Five years after", in (1995) *Yearbook of Media and Entertainment Law*, p. 101.

77. For a comprehensive analysis, see De Witte, op. cit., p. 115 et seq. A superb analysis from an American perspective is given by Donaldson, "Television without frontiers: continuing tension between liberal free trade and European cultural integrity", (1996) *Fordham International Law Journal*, 90 et seq. For the main arguments put forward by the American entertainment industry at the time that Commission was preparing its proposal for revision see Dolmans, "Quotas without content: The questionable legality of European contents quotas under the TVWF Directive", (1995) *Entertainment Law Review*, 329 et seq.

most interesting, the second the least convincing, and the third may become the most problematic.

6.2.1. *Legal basis of the Directive*

It has been argued that the Articles 57(2) and 66 EC are not a sufficient legal basis to introduce a new EC-wide requirement that at least 50% of television broadcasts must be works of European origin, because this requirement goes further than merely abolishing pre-existing barriers to the freedom to provide broadcasting services and because the Community has no competence to regulate on cultural matters. Article 128(5) EC now even expressly excludes harmonization of laws for cultural objectives. In reply to these arguments, which found a lot of support in Germany in particular, the following can be observed.

At the time that the Commission proposed the 1989 Directive, the legislation of at least three Member States (France, Italy and Spain) provided for quota rules. Although applicable to domestic programmes only, it could not be excluded that those rules would also affect transborder broadcasting. More importantly, a level playing field for Community broadcasters requires the existence of common rules in order to prevent distortions of competition. It is true that the content requirements constitute a restriction on the provision of broadcasting services, but such a restriction can be seen as justified by an overriding objective relating to the public interest, namely the improvement of knowledge and of dissemination of European culture. The Court has recognized that cultural considerations may permit derogations by a Member State from the rules on free movement.[78] That should also hold true for Community measures. In accordance with the case law of the Court,[79] it was not necessary to have recourse to other provisions of the EC Treaty to "cover" specifically this cultural objective of Chapter III, as the main objective of the Directive is neither cultural nor industrial, but to achieve the internal market for broadcasting.[80]

Furthermore, harmonization inevitably results in Community-wide rules affecting States whose legislation did not previously provide for similar rules. Otherwise even minimum harmonization could not be achieved, obstacles would remain and competitive relationships between companies in the various Member States would be distorted. By the same token, harmonization should extend to broadcasters operating on a purely national level. Thus a Member State is inhibited from fixing for its own broadcasters standards

---

78. See e.g. Cases 60 and 61/84, *Cinéthèque*, [1986] ECR 2605 and *TV10*, cited above.

79. See e.g. Case C-155/91, *Commission* v. *Council*, [1993] I-939.

80. If in 1989 the Council had considered that one of the main objectives of the Directive was cultural, in addition to the objective of the establishment of the internal market, it should have added Art. 235 EC as a legal basis.

below the Community level resulting in a competitive disadvantage for foreign broadcasters. It is anyhow not unusual for harmonization measures to "spill over" into domestic situations or to affect areas belonging to national competence, such as culture or education. There are even various examples of harmonization measures impacting on trade with third countries.[81] This is a consequence of the functional way in which Community competence is defined. It is therefore submitted that the Articles 57(2) and 66 EC are correct and sufficient legal bases for Directive 89/559 as well as for amending Directive 97/36.

The proposition that Articles 4 and 5 are necessary to protect an overriding objective relating to the public interest calls nonetheless for some further comments. Since one of their objectives is to strengthen the competitive position of the European audiovisual industry, Articles 4 and 5 appear to pursue an economic aim, whereas it is traditionally accepted that mandatory requirements should be limited to non-economic considerations. In answer to that possible objection, it is worthwhile reminding that improving the competitiveness of the European programme industry[82] is not meant to be an aim in itself, but rather a means to achieve another – and indeed non-economic – objective, i.e. improving the knowledge and the dissemination of European culture.[83] Neither does Chapter III pertain to harmonization in one of the areas mentioned in Article 128(2) EC. Since the quota requirements only relate to the geographic origin of television programmes, and not to their contents, the cultural policy of the Member States remains entirely unfettered.[84]

One may wonder whether submitting the quotas to a time limit of 10 years, as the Commission proposed back in 1995, would not have called into question the validity of the above line of argument. Admittedly there is some contradiction in, on the one hand, holding that quotas are the best means

81. A recent illustration of the last phenomenon is given by the Court's judgment of 16 July 1998 in Case C-355/96, *Silhouette*, nyr. The most striking example is probably Directive 95/45/EEC on Data Protection and, in particular, Art. 25 thereof (O.J. 1995, L 281).

82. Cf. recital 28 to the preamble of Directive 97/36.

83. Similarly, rules putting a maximum on the transmission time to be devoted to television advertising are designed to help safeguarding media pluralism. Inevitably, they also protect the economic interests of publishers of print media. This example shows that economic and non-economic considerations cannot easily be dissociated. In the context of applying Art. 90(2) EC, the Court appears to have recognized that economic aspects (f.e. allowing a company to recover its costs) are a prerequisite to that company fulfilling its public service obligations (see e.g. Case C-393/92, *Almelo*, [1994] ECR I-1477). In other cases, the Court rejected a justification as being of a purely economic nature. For two recent (but not necessarily convincing) examples see Case C-398/95, *SETTG v. Ypourgas Ergasias*, [1997] ECR I-3091, para 23 and Case C-203/96, *Dusseldorp*, judgment of 25 June 1998, nyr, para 44.

84. As recital 25 to the preamble of Directive 97/36 rightly recalls, Art. 128(4) precisely requires the Community to take cultural aspects into account in its action under other provisions of the Treaty.

to achieve an overriding objective relating to the public interest and, on the other hand, considering that quotas will no longer be necessary once a certain period of time has lapsed. In a "phase out scenario", it would also have been unclear whether after the ten years period European quotas would have been prohibited[85] or whether Member States would have been allowed to maintain such rules. In other words, there would have been considerable unclarity as to whether promotion of European works was still "a field coordinated by the Directive".

6.2.2. *Article 10 ECHR*
It has also been contended that Article 4 restricts freedom of expression and is therefore in breach of Article 10(1) ECHR. It is submitted that the Court (or, where appropriate, the ECHR in Strasbourg) should give short shrift to this argument, should it ever be raised in court proceedings. It is difficult to see how the quota system, based on the origin of works, could affect the content of the programmes and thereby restrict freedom of expression. Quite significantly, Article 10(1) of the European Convention on Transfrontier Broadcasting contains provisions which are comparable (if not identical) to those of Article 4(1) of the Directive. Since the very purpose of that Convention is to give effect to Article 10 ECHR, the argument that quotas breach that same provision is hardly sustainable.

6.2.3. *International obligations*
Ever since the Commission adopted its proposal for the 1989 Directive, American interests have not stopped alleging that the European content requirements are incompatible with, in particular, two key principles of the GATT Agreement, i.e. the most favoured nation principle ("MFN") and the national treatment principle. For the purposes of the present article, there is no need to

---

85. Prohibiting a certain activity can also be an appropriate way of harmonizing national laws (cf. the prohibition of television advertising for cigarettes laid down in Art. 13 of the Directive). The controversial Directive on tobacco advertising (Directive 98/43/EC of the European Parliament and the Council of 6 July 1997, O.J. 1998, L 213/9) raises similar questions. It obliges the Member State to introduce a ban on tobacco advertising on most forms of tobacco advertising within three years. Germany challenged this Directive (Case C-376/98) and so did a number of private companies and associations. The latter applications are likely to be dismissed as inadmissible, because the applicants would not appear to be individually concerned by the Directive. Compared to the Television Directive, the transborder dimension is perhaps less clear, but probably sufficient to justify recourse to Art. 100a. At first view, a total prohibition appears to be an overbroad measure. However, Art. 3(5) of the Directive provides for important exceptions, whereas Art. 6 allows for transitional periods. The print media will enjoy an extra year's respite, while sponsorship involving cigarettes will be granted a further year's grace period. Major events such as Formula One motor racing will have until 2006 to find alternative sponsorship. The Tobacco advertising Directive is accordingly not necessarily disproportionate.

rehearse the main arguments of both sides in this trade dispute. Rather should one examine briefly the legal situation following the Agreements concluding the Uruguay Round, more particularly the General Agreement on Trade in Services ("GATS").[86]

It cannot be denied that GATS applies to measures affecting the cable or broadcast distribution of radio or television programmes,[87] since the proposal for a general "Cultural exception" ended up by being rejected. Article II(1) GATS lays down the principle of MFN treatment as a general commitment. It is undisputed that the quota system provided for by Articles 4 and 5 of the Directive is as such incompatible with that general commitment. That does not mean that it is illegal. Indeed, under paragraph 2 of the same Article, a Member may maintain a national discriminatory measure provided that such a measure is listed in the "Annex on Article II Exemptions". To that effect, the Community and its Member States have notified the WTO of an exemption (of unlimited duration) for the Articles 4 and 5 of the Directive.

As regards national treatment, the provisions of GATS leave the Members a certain amount of leeway. According to Part III (Specific Commitments) and Part IV (Gradual Liberalization) of GATS and the Annexes concerning Specific Commitments, Members may undertake to accord national treatment both on market access and on conditions governing the provision of services. Those specific commitments must then be recorded in national "schedules". Such a schedule was lodged by the Community and its Member States. However, no notification has been given of specific commitments in the field covered by the Directive.[88] In essence, the obligation to accord national treatment has therefore been deferred.

It follows that, for the time being, the quota provisions are not in breach of GATS. It may be expected, however, that in a relatively near future the Community cannot escape entering into bilateral negotiations with the United States with a view to finding a resolution of the longstanding dispute on the quotas. In that respect, it is also relevant that in principle a MFN exemption should not exceed ten years and that it shall be reviewed at any subsequent round on trade liberalization.[89]

86. By Decision 94/800/EC of the Council of 22 Dec. 1994, the Community concluded, as regards matters within its competence, the Agreement establishing the World Trade Organization including various multilateral agreements, such as GATS and TRIPS. GATS is attached as Annex IB (O.J. 1994, L 336/190).

87. Art. 2b) of the Annex on Telecommunications expressly excludes those services from the scope of that Annex.

88. In the field of basic telecommunication services the Community and the Member States meanwhile entered into specific commitments. (see Decision 97/838/EC of 28 Nov. 1997, O.J. 1997, L 347/45).

89. See the "Annex on Article II Exemptions."

Finally, one may highlight the link between the discussion on the scope of the Directive (in particular the question whether it was necessary to include video-on-demand services) and the scope of the areas covered by MFN exemptions. The borderline between audiovisual services and telecommunications services will be a core element in the discussions, precisely where this distinction is becoming increasingly blurred as a result of the convergence between these two sectors and that of information technology. Reportedly, the US entertainment industry is now primarily interested in securing unrestricted access for programmes transmitted by satellite and fibre optics, particularly video-on-demand channels.[90]

7. Television advertising, sponsorship and teleshopping (Chapter IV)

7.1. *Introductory observations*

The rules on television advertising and sponsoring belong to the core matters regulated by the Directive because advertising was one of the areas where transborder obstacles were most notable.[91] In today's economy, new products often pass through a sophisticated marketing process before reaching the consumer. In this process, advertising funded television channels play a key role. But they are far from being the only players: marketing departments of large corporations, publishing houses and other media, all sorts of intermediaries and specialized sub-contractors, outside legal counsel and communication advisors, consultants and lobbyists, – they all seek to get their share out of the silver "food chain" generated by the marketing of goods and services. With so many urban professionals making their living out of commercial communications related activities, it becomes understandable why national advertising restrictions easily give rise to a lot of outcry,[92] particularly in advertising and lobby capitals as London and Brussels.[93]

---

90. See for further details, Donaldson, op. cit. *supra* note 77, p. 140.

91. See Case 52/79, Debauve, [1980] ECR 833.

92. Three measures have been particularly criticized: the French prohibition of advertising for alcoholic beverages and tobacco products (Loi Evin), the Greek prohibition of television advertising for toys between 7 a.m. and 10 p.m., and the German rules prohibiting most forms of rebates (*Rabattgesetz* and *Zugabeverordnung*).

93. One of the common features of the intensive lobby campaigns against national advertising restrictions is to create the impression that, from a legal point of view, a given advertising restriction is a "clear-cut infringement" of Art. 59, the only "problem" being that certain decision-makers lack the courage to act accordingly. Such a suggestion is often entirely misleading: far from being straightforward, the national measures most fiercely criticized (see previous footnote) all raise particularly complex legal questions.

Against this background, it is not very surprising either that when the work on revising the Directive was taken up there was a certain amount of pressure from the industry to increase the transmission time that may be devoted to television advertising. With numerous channels having entered the market since 1989 and many others expected to be launched in a forseeable future (in particular digital bouquets) the "captive viewer" was said to exist no longer, so that accordingly there was not the same need (if any) to protect the consumer against an overkill of advertising. That line of argument seems to be based on the presumption that quantitative limits on television advertising are exclusively designed to protect the "captive viewer". In reality, the objectives sought are wider: the protection of pluralism of the media, including the written press, with a view to preserving diversity of opinion, is equally if not more important. In any event, the Community legislature has resisted the pressure to liberalize substantially the advertising rules.

7.2. *Main innovations*

Directive 97/36 has clarified the distinction between advertising and teleshopping. "Television advertising" now includes announcements for self-promotional purposes.[94] "Teleshopping" covers "direct offers broadcast to the public with a view to the supply of goods and services, including immovable property, rights and obligations, in return for payment". The text of (old) Article 18(1) had caused a certain amount of confusion where it stipulated that the authorized amount of daily transmission time to be devoted to advertising "may be increased to 20% to include forms of advertising such as direct offers to the public for sale . . . ". The words "such as" wrongly suggested that teleshopping is a form of advertising whereas in reality it is a wholly different activity.

Three forms of *advertising* are now being distinguished: (a) advertising spots, (b) other forms of advertising, such as telepromotions (television promotions of products or services by means of games or studio shows) and (c) self-promotional activities. The distinction is relevant for the maximum permissible volume of advertising. Article 18(1) sets a ceiling of 20% of the daily transmission time for advertising spots and other forms of advertising. Article 18(2) sets an additional hourly limit applicable to advertising spots only. For the purpose of applying Article 18, "advertising" does not include "announcements made by the broadcaster in connection with its own programmes and ancillary products directly derived from those products." This means that trailers consisting of extracts from programmes should be treated

---

94. Art. 1(c).

as programmes, not as advertising.[95] By the same token, advertising does not include public service announcements and charity appeals broadcast free of charge.[96] Finally, channels exclusively devoted to self-promotion should comply with the quantitative limits set by Articles 18(1) and(2).[97]

A major innovation are the rules governing *teleshopping*. The Directive makes a distinction between (a) teleshopping spots, (b) teleshopping windows on generalist channels and (c) channels exclusively devoted to teleshopping.[98] In recognizing the existence of the last category of channels, the Community legislature could obviously not maintain the daily limit of one hour of teleshopping.[99] However, the other two categories of teleshopping programmes are subject to certain quantitative limits: for spots, those limits are identical to those applicable to advertising spots,[100] whereas the maximum number of teleshopping windows shall be eight per day of a minimum uninterrupted duration of 15 minutes each.[101]

The other rules applicable to teleshopping are largely aligned with the rules on content and presentation that apply to advertising. For teleshopping windows and teleshopping spots, this follows from Articles 12, 13, 15 and 16. For teleshopping spots this follows moreover from Article 10 concerning the presentation and perceptibility of advertising and from Article 11 concerning the interruption of programmes by advertising breaks. By virtue of Article 19a, the whole of the Directive, including Article 18(2) (but with the obvious exception of Chapter III on quotas), applies *mutatis mutandis* to teleshopping channels.[102] There are also two special rules on teleshopping: the prohibition of teleshopping for medicinal products which are subject to a marketing authorization[103] as well as for medical treatment, and an obligation not to exhort minors to contract for the sale or rental of goods and services.[104]

The other provisions on advertising have not been changed. Sweden pro-

95. Cf. recital 39 to the preamble of Directive 97/36.

96. See Art. 18(3).

97. This is a rather obscure provision: if a "channel exclusively devoted to self-promotion" carries "other forms of advertising" it is no longer exclusively devoted to self-promotion.

98. In order to help the public distinguish between the various forms of advertising, Art. 18a(2) provides that each window shall be clearly identified by optical and acoustic means at least at the beginning and the end of the window (see also recital 37).

99. See (old) Art. 18(3).

100. Arts. 18(1) and (2).

101. Art. 18a.

102. Art. 19a provides for a similar general reference in relation to channels exclusively devoted to self-promotion.

103. Art. 14(2). This issue proved to be controversial. As recital 33 recalls, advertising for medicinal products for human use is subject to the provisions of Directive 92/28/EEC (O.J. 1992, L 113/1).

104. Art. 16(2).

posed to make Article 16 on the protection of minors more stringent[105] but failed to get sufficient support for its proposals. Sweden and Finland both had wished to reinforce Article 15 on advertising for alcoholic beverages but again negotiations ended up by leaving the text unchanged. The rules on interruption of feature films by advertising breaks[106] have not been changed in any substantial manner, in spite of calls for further liberalization. Admittedly, the drafting could have been clarified, but perhaps this was so sensitive a matter that the better option was not to change anything at all.

Article 17 provides for rules on sponsoring of television programmes. The parameters on content and presentation of sponsored programmes have not been changed. In *Reti Televisive Italiane (RTI)*,[107] a dispute between the media group controlled by the then Italian Prime Minister and the Italian State, the Court accepted that the Directive does not prohibit references to the name and/or the logo of the sponsor at moments other than the beginning and/or the end of the sponsored programme. However, such mentioning of the sponsor's name shall not amount to circumventing the prohibition of surreptitious advertising.[108] This case law is still relevant under the Directive as amended.

Two minor innovations must be mentioned. Article 17(2) extends the prohibition of television advertising for tobacco products to sponsoring of television programmes by undertakings whose principal activity is the manufacture or sale of cigarettes and other tobacco products. Paragraph 3 on the contrary introduces an element of slight liberalization: companies whose activities "include" the manufacture or sale of medicinal products are allowed to sponsor programmes and may, in that connection, promote their name or their image. Under the old text of Article 17(2), companies "whose principal activity"[109] was the manufacture or sale of those goods, were not allowed to engage in sponsoring. It is expressly stated in the new text that the faculty of sponsoring television programmes should not amount to circumvention of the prohibition of advertising laid down in Article 14.

---

105. After having mooted the idea of prohibiting all television advertising directed at minors, Sweden subsequently insisted on the deletion of the word "directly" in Art. 16(1)(a): "Television advertising shall not directly exhort minors to buy a product or a service by exploiting their inexperience or credulity." Interestingly, the word "directly" does not appear in Art. 16(2) concerning teleshopping directed at minors, presumably because the legislator considered this to be a more intruding way of addressing viewers which accordingly justifies a slightly higher standard of protection.

106. Arts. 11(3) and (4).

107. Joined cases C-320/94 a.o., [1996] ECR I-6471.

108. Prohibited by Art. 10(4).

109. This condition could create unwarranted discrimination *vis-à-vis* other companies effectively in the same position but with the sole difference that activities devoted to the manufacture or sales of these products do not exceed 49% of their total operations.

The possibility given to Member States to impose stricter rules on broadcasters under their jurisdiction (Article 3(1)) is of particular relevance in the field of advertising. This is illustrated by the case law of the Court, in particular *Leclerc-Siplec* and *RTI*. Thus, in the latter case, the Court gave a liberal interpretation of Article 17 (see above) and of (old) Article 18, to the extent that the lucrative *telepromozioni* were considered to be "other forms of advertising" for the purposes of extending from 15% to 20% the daily limit devoted to television advertising. However, the Court also pointed out that this increase was an option left to the Member States, which can choose not to avail themselves of it. It followed that, contrary to RTI's submissions, the Italian law was not in breach of the Directive.

Pending case *Bruto/Netto*[110] could be decided along the same lines. It raises the question how one has to define the programmed duration which must be taken into account for calculating the permitted advertising breaks (Article 11(3)). On an earlier occasion, the Commission stated that in its view "gross" time (i.e. including the duration of advertising spots) constitutes the minimum level required for the purposes of the Directive, but it also admitted that the Member States retain the power to regulate broadcasters within their jurisdiction in a stricter or more detailed fashion.[111] If that view is correct, it follows that Germany is free to impose the "nett system" and that compliance with that system can be enforced through the court actions provided for by the applicable national law.

8. Transmission of major (sporting) events on free-to-air television (Article 3a)

8.1. *Introductory observations*

Like the rules on advertising, sponsoring and teleshopping, the wholly new regime on television broadcasting of major events on free-to-air television concerns an area where considerable financial interests are at stake. The new provisions enable Member States to take measures to protect the right of information and to ensure wide access by the public to television coverage of national or non-national events of major importance for society, such as the Olympic Games or the Football World Cup. They strike a delicate balance between the entrepreneurial freedom of owners of pay TV channels and the overriding interest in ensuring the general public adequate access to major televised events.

---

110. Case C-6/98, *ARD* v. *PRO Sieben Media AG*, pending.
111. See the first report on the application of Directive 89/552 of 31 May 1995, p. 22.

In several Member States, similar rules are in force. For example, under the Broadcasting Act 1996, the United Kingdom has drawn up a list of protected events. Likewise, in France, the *Conseil supérieur de l'audiovisuel* agreed, in 1995, with *Canal Plus* a list of non-exclusive events.[112] However, such lists can only be enforced against broadcasters coming under the jurisdiction of the Member State in question. That is precisely the reason why there was a need to establish a Community system that allows to prevent the possibility of circumventing such national measures. The system operates in three phases:

(1) Member States may draw up lists of major events and take measures to ensure that a "substantial proportion of the public" is not deprived of the possibility of following such events via live coverage or deferred coverage on free television.

(2) These measures must be notified to the Commission which must verify that they are compatible with Community law and seek the opinion of the Contact Committee; each set of national measures – if judged compatible with Community law – is then communicated to all the other Member States and published in the Official Journal.

(3) Member States are obliged to ensure that broadcasters under their jurisdiction do not circumvent national lists of events drawn up by other Member States in accordance with this procedure.

8.2. *Legal basis*

Although Article 3a definitely presents an important innovation, one may have some conceptual difficulties in fitting it into the framework of a directive whose primary objective is to ensure the free movement of broadcasts. Putting limitations on the feedom of pay TV channels to broadcast major sporting events would appear to have the opposite effect. On a proper construction, however, it becomes clear that national laws securing certain events for free-to-air television will normally constitute a restriction to the free provision of services by pay TV channels. These obstacles are, however, justified, provided certain conditions are met. Since it is not feasible to draw up a single and exhaustive list of common heritage events for the whole of the Community, one has to accept the existence of national lists. Such lists can only have a useful meaning if on the basis of a Community mechanism their circumvention can be prevented.

This analysis is not entirely free from ambiguities. Whereas the purpose of the system is to help combating overbroad restrictions to information arising out of commercial practices (in essence: giving access to subscribers only) it

---

112. Art. 18 of the *cahier de charges* of Canal Plus.

is the regulatory response to such restrictions which accounts for the "obstacles" that justify the matter being brought within the scope of this Directive. Likewise, whereas a single market is supposed to involve the freedom to carry out business operations from the most attractive location – also in regulatory terms – and where it is only in very exceptional circumstances that circumvention of national legislation can be successfully combated, in the present set-up, companies must observe the rules of the receiving State, even if formally the legal basis for such a legal duty is enshrined in the law of the State in which they are established.[113]

8.3. *The first phase*

Member States are not under a legal duty to draw up a list of major events; the Directive merely recognizes that they have the right to take measures which shall ensure that *events of major importance for society* are not broadcast on an exclusive basis in such a way as to deprive *a substantial proportion of the public of that Member State* of the possibility of following such events via live or deferred coverage on *free television*. However, if a Member State decides to take such measures, it shall draw up a list in a clear and transparent manner in due and effective time. Such a list may also include events other than sporting events. It is for each Member State to decide what are major events. Depending on national traditions, the lists are likely to vary,[114] even if a tournament like the Football World Final will presumably be on everyone's list. The discretion of the Member State in defining events is not unlimited: for the purposes of the Directive, such events should be of interest to the general public in the European Union or in a given Member State or in an important component part of a given Member State and they must be recognized in advance by an event organizer who is legally entitled to sell the rights pertaining to that event.[115] For reasons of legal certainty, it is necessary that events are designated by reference to a single event (e.g. the Tour de France) or by reference to objectively defined criteria.

The way in which one defines the terms "a substantial proportion of the public" may have far-reaching consequences. It has been argued that "a substantial proportion" must be understood as meaning "nearly the whole

---

113. Recital 19 to the preamble of Directive 97/36 puts it as follows: "Whereas it is necessary to make arrangements within a Community framework, in order to avoid potential legal uncertainty and market distortions and to reconcile the free circulation of television services with the need to prevent the possibility of circumvention of national measures protecting a legitimate general interest."

114. E.g. the Derby may be selected by the UK and not by France, whereas for the Tour de France that may be the other way round.

115. Recital 21.

population". There is some logic in that proposition: if an event is considered to be of such utmost importance that it needs to be put on the list, it makes sense that nearly the whole population must be given access. This interpretation also carries a danger with it: if near universal coverage is required, there is a serious risk that channels having a lower coverage are precluded in advance from transmitting major events. This is likely to be to the detriment of foreign channels, whose coverage will normally be substantially below that of domestic channels. It is not excluded either that this circumstance may also have an adverse knock-on effect on foreign channels' chances to acquire the rights to top events. What should be avoided, however, is that a regime designed to ensure wide access to television coverage is turned into an instrument directly or indirectly favouring domestic generalist channels.

The position of satellite channels also needs careful consideration. It has been argued that households that do not dispose of satellite TV equipment are part of the public that is "deprived of" the event if that were to be transmitted on a satellite channel only. That proposition implies that the more successful a satellite channel is in obtaining subscribers the better chances it has to satisfy the "substantial proportion criterion". The real question is whether satellite channels can at all be covered by the expression "free television" which is defined in recital 22 as follows: "Broadcasting on a channel, either public or commercial, of programmes which are accessible to the public without payment in addition to the modes of funding of broadcasting that are widely prevailing in each Member State (such as licence fee and/or the basic tier subscription fee to a cable network)." If that definition were to mean that it does not encompass television services requiring for their access the payment of a subscription fee going above these reference sums, and/or the acquisition of special technical equipment, such as a decoder or a satellite dish, then satellite channels would *a priori* be excluded, with the possible exception of advertising funded satellite channels distributed by cable. Such an interpretation may, however, be source of distortions of competition that are hardly capable of being justified by reference to the need to ensure wide access by the public to television coverage.

8.4. *Second phase*

The notification of measures to the Commission does not have a suspensive effect. In practice, however, Member States may be expected to contact the Commission beforehand and try to get its approval informally, before formally adopting and notifying the measures. The notification entails important legal consequences. Indeed, Member States are requested to apply the "mutual recognition rule" provided for in the third paragraph only if (a) they know exactly what measures have been taken by other States and (b) those measures have been found to be in conformity with EC law. The Commission is likely to verify notified measures on their compatibility with the obligations resulting from in particular Articles 59 and 90 EC. A key element will be the proportionality of the measure: its impact on the free marketing of broadcasting rights (through restrictions as to the exercise of such rights) set against the public interest sought.

Clearly, a Member State cannot put any random sports event on its list; it shall state reasons why an event is to be considered as being of major importance for society. The possibility of distinguishing between live coverage or deferred coverage adds a further element that may be taken into consideration when assessing the proportionality of a measure. Yet it will not be easy for the Commission to establish clear-cut criteria on the basis of which to approve event A and to disapprove event B. Another question is whether the Commission will merely issue an opinion or whether it will adopt a decision that may be challenged in the Court of First Instance. On this issue, there is some analogy with the special procedure laid down in Article 2a(2) of the Directive.

8.5. *Third phase*

The obligation on Member States to ensure that broadcasters under their jurisdiction do not exercise the exclusive rights purchased by those broadcasters in such a way that a substantial proportion of the public in another Member State is deprived of the possibility of following events which are on that other State's list constitutes the core of the system. It must be feared, however, that its practical application will raise all sorts of difficulties. For example, how do the competent authorities know what are precisely the rights broadcasters under their jurisdiction have acquired to events taking place in other Member States? What happens if a pay TV operator has not found a free to air broadcaster willing to pay a reasonable fee for a sub-licence to the broadcasting of a given event? Who should arbitrate?

The obligation to observe the list of the receiving State mentioned in paragraph 3 applies to events for which the exclusive rights have been purchased following the *date of publication* of the Directive, i.e. after 30 July 1997, *and* concerning events taking place after the *date of implementation*, i.e. 30 December 1998. It was decided to use the date of publication as cut-off date for the purchasing of rights, on the one hand, "to avoid speculatative rights purchases with a view to circumventing national measures" and, on the other hand, to respect the principles of legal certainty and legitimate expectations by not upsetting agreements concluded before that date. The reference to the date of implementation raises the question what happens if a Member State belatedly transposes the Directive into national law. Does that mean that for so long, events taking place after December 1998 are not covered? It would be unacceptable if certain operators were to benefit from a delay incurred by a Member State in implementing the Directive. That does not alter the fact that in those circumstances there will not be a basis in national law for giving effect to the "mutual recognition mechanism" established by paragraph 3 of Article 3a. On few occasions have Member States so clearly had a mutual interest in ensuring timely implementation of a Community directive!

9. Conclusions

The revision of the Television Without Frontiers Directive is first of all a success from an institutional point of view, since the Council and the European Parliament succeeded in agreeing on a text within a relatively short period of time. Moreover, a number of crucial matters have been clarified whereas outdated rules have been modernized. Yet the rapidly changing broadcasting market and the expected shift of consumer preferences to services on individual demand may have the effect of either reducing the importance of the Directive or calling for a further revision relatively soon. For example, the substantial liberalization of the teleshopping rules may not have so much of an impact where in a forseeable future "traditional" teleshopping channels may be more and more replaced by interactive internet-based services using a television set. It is therefore doubtful whether the Directive will in its present form survive much of the next century. The most important innovation brought about by the revision is undoubtedly the regime on events of major importance for society. While being an appropriate regulatory response to what has become a genuine political problem, the day-to-day application of this regime may be source of disputes, putting the Commission (and the Contact Committee) before a delicate task. In that environment, the competition rules may have a corrective role.

[14]

Media Convergence and the Regulation of Audiovisual Content: Is the European Community's Audiovisual Media Services Directive Fit for Purpose?

*Rachael Craufurd Smith**

In sum, the objective of the Commission's proposal is to modernise and simplify the regulatory framework for broadcasting or linear services and introduce minimum rules for non-linear audiovisual media services.[1]

This article examines how technological developments are currently destabilizing established regulatory regimes in the media sector and the response of one particular political institution, the European Community, to these developments. In particular, it considers the European Commission's proposal for a new 'Audiovisual Media Services Directive' (AVMS), designed to extend Community content regulation beyond traditional broadcasting to audiovisual services relayed over the Internet and mobile telephone networks.[2] Political agreement on a common position on the AVMS was reached by the European Parliament and

---

* I would like to thank Mónica Ariño Gutierrez and Sandra Keegan for helpful discussions on the issues raised by this article. This article was presented as a lecture at University College London, 16 November 2006.

[1] European Commission, *Proposal for a Directive of the European Parliament and of the Council amending Council Directive 89/552/EEC on the coordination of certain provisions laid down by law, regulation or administrative action in Member States concerning the pursuit of television broadcasting activities*, COM(2005) 646 final ('Commission initial AVMS proposal'), at 3.

[2] Commission initial AVMS proposal, n1 above. This proposal was published by the Commission in a consolidated version ('initial draft consolidated AVMS') incorporating the proposal's provisions into the existing Television Without Frontiers Directive ('TVWF'), see n 15 below. This consolidated version has been removed from the Commission's audiovisual website. The Commission revised its initial text in March 2007 in the light of amendments put forward by the European Parliament in December 2006. Both the European Parliament's 2006 legislative resolution on the Commission's initial proposal, P6_TA-PROV(2006)0559, together with a consolidated version of the Commission's March proposal ('revised draft consolidated AVMS'), COM(2007) 170

Council of Ministers in May 2007 and it is anticipated that the Directive will be adopted in this form later in 2007, leaving Member States two years to bring it into force.[3] References to the AVMS in the text of this article therefore refer to the May 2007 text.

The technological developments at issue here are of essentially three kinds.[4] Firstly, it is now possible to access audiovisual material over a diverse range of delivery platforms: via the Internet and mobile phones, as well as established terrestrial, cable, and satellite networks. Viewers can already watch the same programme at home on the television, at work on their computer, or when on the move, using their mobile phone. The ability to transmit audiovisual material over a range of networks does not simply enable viewers to watch programmes wherever they want; it has also greatly expanded the range of services and programmes that are on offer. The second related point is that an increasing number of viewers are now able to control not only where and what they watch but also when they watch it. The development of digital video recorders and sophisticated programme recording and retrieval systems, such as TiVo in the United States ('US') and Sky + in the United Kingdom ('UK'), enable viewers to record and time-shift programmes to suit their own schedules.[5] Video-on-demand services, accessible over cable networks and the Internet, also offer considerable choice and flexibility for viewers. Thirdly, the popularity of digital cameras and recording equipment has stimulated an extraordinary growth in user-generated audiovisual content, with the potential blurring of professional and amateur services.

The need to review regulation in response to technological innovation is, of course, not a new phenomenon in the communications sector. The

final, can be found at: <http://ec.europa.eu/comm/avpolicy/reg/tvwf/modernisation/proposal_2005/index_en.htm>. All websites were last accessed on 30 May 2007.

[3] The modifications agreed in May 2007 have been consolidated, for ease of reference, with the existing TVWF. Citation of AVMS article numbers in the following text refer to those in this consolidated document, available on the Europa website at: <http://ec.europa.eu/information_society/newsroom/cf/itemlongdetail.cfm?item_id=3430>.

[4] For detailed discussion of the regulatory implications of digital technology see C Marsden and M Ariño, 'From Analogue to Digital' in A Brown and R G Picard (eds) *Digital Terrestrial Television in Europe* (London: Lawrence Erlbaum Associates, 2005) 1–34.

[5] Carat and Koan, *Comparative study on the impact of control measures on the television advertising markets in European Member States and certain other countries*, 2005, 70, at: <http://ec.europa.eu/comm/avpolicy/info_centre/library/studies/index_en.htm>. For details of the Sky+ system, see the Sky 2007 press release, which estimates the facility is now in over 2 million households in the UK, at: <http://phx.corporate-ir.net/phoenix.zhtml?c=104016&p=irol-newsArticle_Print&ID=945710&highlight>.

Internet is just one in a long line of developments, ranging from the printing press to radio broadcasting, that have repeatedly expanded the capacity of both individuals and organizations to communicate. The Internet is, however, particularly destabilizing, in that it highlights the need for a fundamental reappraisal of the technological compartmentalization that has been a characteristic of media regulation in the past. From the end of the Second World War, when television broadcasting became a commercial venture, media regulation in much of Western Europe and North America has been medium specific.[6] On the one hand, content regulation of fixed line telephony and mail services, used for private correspondence, has been limited.[7] Similarly, the printed press, a mass rather than private communications medium, but one that has successfully asserted its freedom from government intervention on democratic grounds, has been largely free from direct state regulation.[8] Although states have undoubtedly regulated what are considered to be the more damaging forms of printed content, such as obscene or defamatory material, considerable reliance is placed on industry self-regulation.[9] On the other hand, terrestrial radio and television services were, from their origin, and continue to this day, to be subject to extensive state regulation in pursuit of a number of social, cultural, and political ends.[10]

Heightened regulation of the audio and video media has variously been justified on the limited availability of radio spectrum, leading to the categorization of broadcasters as public trustees,[11] and the greater public

---

[6] During the Second World War most countries suspended television production and transmissions, though there were exceptions, notably German broadcasts from the Eiffel Tower in occupied Paris. Television broadcasting in the UK recommenced in 1946. See A Abramson, 'The Invention of Television' in A Smith (ed), *Television: an International History* (Oxford: Oxford University Press, 1995), 13–34.

[7] Some states, such as the UK, prohibit the transmission by post of particular types of 'damaging' material, for example, material that is obscene or could harm children. See, for example, s 85 of the Postal Services Act 2000 and s 1 of the Protection of Children Act 1978. The latter act was used to prosecute the recipient of an email containing an attachment showing a photograph of a naked child in *R v Smith and R v Jayson* [2002] EWCA Crim 683.

[8] R Craufurd Smith, *Broadcasting and Fundamental Rights* (Oxford: Clarendon Press, 1997).

[9] See, for example, the 1881 French Law on the Freedom of the Press, as amended, which seeks to balance the interests of the press with other collective and individual interests in one document: <http://www.legifrance.gouv.fr/texteconsolide/PCEAA.htm>. By contrast, in the UK the press is subject to general legislation or common law rules in these areas rather than specific press regulation.

[10] E M Barendt, *Broadcasting Law, A Comparative Study* (Oxford: Clarendon Press, 1993) at 96–120.

[11] See, in particular, *Red Lion Broadcasting Co v FCC*, 395 US 367 (1969).

Media Convergence and the Regulation of Audiovisual Content 241

impact of audiovisual communications in contrast to the print media.[12] Regulatory obligations thus mapped technological transmission lines and the system was relatively clear in practice, if less clear in terms of underlying principle.[13] With the capacity of the Internet to offer, among other things, private telephone and email services; online versions of the printed press; streamed radio and television programmes; film, sport, and music downloads; not to mention a host of user-generated content, both text and audiovisual—the means of delivery no longer provides, if it ever did, a coherent basis for determining the level of regulatory intervention in relation to media content.

The European Community has responded to these developments by regulating electronic communication networks separately from the content of services relayed over them, and by seeking to realize the principle of 'technological neutrality'.[14] Technological neutrality requires the same service to be regulated in the same manner whatever its mode of transmission. Thus, it should make no difference from a regulatory perspective, whether a television programme is relayed on terrestrial, satellite, or cable networks, accessed over a mobile telephone or downloaded from the Internet. In order to give effect to this principle and ensure a level playing field for audiovisual media service providers, the Commission has proposed the new AVMS. The AVMS will extend the reach of the existing 1989 Television Without Frontiers Directive (TVWF), which presently covers traditional, scheduled, television broadcasts, to include audiovisual services provided on an on-demand basis.[15] A greatly expanded range of Internet, cable, and mobile audiovisual services will thus be brought within the scope of Community content rules.

---

[12] E M Barendt, n10 above, at 2–9.

[13] ibid and see also L C Bollinger, 'Freedom of the Press and Public Access: Towards a Theory of Partial Regulation' (1976) 75 *Michigan Law Review* 1–42.

[14] Commission, initial AVMS proposal, n1 above, at 3. For details of the five Directives that make up the European Community's regulatory framework for electronic communications and which came into force in July 2003 see: <http://ec.europa.eu/information_society/policy/ecomm/todays_framework/overview/index_en.htm>.

[15] Council Directive 89/552/EEC on the coordination of certain provisions laid down by law, regulation or administrative action in Member States concerning the pursuit of television broadcasting activities, [1989] OJ L298/23–30, as amended by European Parliament and Council Directive 97/36/EC, [1997] OJ L202/60–70. For commentary on the proposed AVMS see H Lutz, 'The distinction between linear and non-linear services in the new proposal for an audiovisual media directive' (2006) 12 *Computer and Telecommunications Law Review*, 141–5 and K Böttcher and O Castendyk, 'The Commission proposal for a new directive on audiovisual content—a feasible solution?' (2006) 17 *Entertainment Law Review* 174–80.

There is, however, another key motivation behind the Commission's proposal and that is to relax some of the restrictions currently placed on television advertising by the TVWF. The Internet is now a serious competitor to broadcast television for advertising revenues and the ability of viewers to skip advertisements using digital video recorders could ultimately eat away at the price that broadcasters can charge for advertising space on their channels.[16] The AVMS is thus intended to assist television broadcasters financially by opening the way to limited product placement and removing many of the current restrictions on the frequency and timing of advertising breaks.[17]

This article focuses on the AVMS's extension of Community content regulation to the on-demand sector; that is, on its regulatory rather than deregulatory aspects. On the one hand, it argues that the practical impact of the directive on on-demand audiovisual services is likely to be limited. This is primarily because of the nature of the rules that the AVMS extends into the on-demand field. These rules are not only framed in very general terms, allowing Member States considerable scope to adapt them to their domestic circumstances, but states retain competence to restrict foreign on-demand services on a wide range of general interest grounds. In addition, in many Member States there are already in place cross-cutting state and/or industry measures to protect the important public interests at stake. On the other, it suggests that the directive's incremental and partial response to media convergence is inadequate, given the scale of developments. Thus, the AVMS continues to apply different rules, for example, in relation to child protection and the right of reply, to scheduled and on-demand services that are difficult to rationalize from a viewer perspective. Moreover, it establishes a number of new demarcation lines, for example, in relation to text-based and user-generated content, that are similarly problematic. Ultimately, the directive may prove to be more important for its deregulation of broadcast advertising than for its extension of Community content regulation into the Internet and mobile domains.

---

[16] Carat and Koan, n.5 above, 69–71; E O'Neill and M Barrett, 'TiVO—The Next Big Thing? DVRs and Television Advertising Models', paper presented at the 6th World Media Economics Conference, Montreal, Canada, May 2004, available at: <http://66.102.9.104/search?q=cache:cMSB9hVx0ekJ:www.cem.ulaval.ca/6thwmec/oneill_barrett.pdf+TiVO-The+Next+Big+Thing%3F&hl=en&ct=clnk&cd=1>. Neil and Barrett, at 26, suggest that broadcasters are only likely to be significantly affected once accurate data becomes available as to whether viewers actually watch the advertisements they transmit.

[17] See the explanatory memorandum accompanying the Commission's initial AVMS proposal, n 1 above.

European Community Regulation of Audiovisual Content: The Present Position

At present, two European Community directives have a bearing on the content of audiovisual services: the Electronic Commerce Directive[18] and the TVWF. Although these measures superficially adopt similar approaches, with an emphasis on regulation by the country of origin, in practice they operate in quite different ways.

The Electronic Commerce Directive applies to 'information society services'. These are defined as services 'normally provided for remuneration, at a distance, by means of electronic equipment for the processing . . . and storage of data, at the individual request of a recipient of a service'.[19] It thus covers video-on-demand services, or services providing information for a fee, and is broad enough to cover text and audio, as well as video, services. The definition does not cover scheduled radio or television services, broadcast to the general public, or near video-on-demand services, which involve repeatedly broadcasting a programme at short intervals to give viewers enhanced flexibility as to when they watch it.

As indicated above, the Electronic Commerce Directive adopts a 'country of origin' or 'home state control' principle, which sets up the presumption that information society services are to be regulated solely by the country from which they originate.[20] A service provider does not, therefore, need to comply with the various rules in place in all the EU countries where its service can be received. The Directive establishes very few rules relating to the content of information society services. Its main focus is on ensuring that consumers receive certain basic information about who is providing a given service, on protecting Internet service providers from liability for material they merely relay on behalf of others, and on facilitating online contracting. Each state can impose more exacting requirements on information society service providers within their jurisdiction than the minimum rules set out in the Directive but must let in services from other countries, even if those countries impose less exacting requirements, provided the basic requirements of the Directive are met.[21]

---

[18] European Parliament and Council Directive 2000/31/EC on certain legal aspects of information society services, in particular electronic commerce, in the Internal Market, [2000] OJ L178/1–16.

[19] Recital 17, further explained at Recital 18, Electronic Commerce Directive, n 18 above.

[20] Article 3.2, Electronic Commerce Directive, n 18 above.

[21] Article 3.1 and 2, Electronic Commerce Directive, n 18 above.

The system is not, however, quite this simple, in that it also allows Member States to derogate from the country of origin/home state control principle where important general interests are at stake.[22] Thus, it is possible for a state to restrict access to an information society service from another country on the basis that this is necessary for public policy reasons. These reasons are expressly stated to include the protection of minors, public health, security, and consumers, and the prevention of incitement to hatred on grounds of race, sex, religion, or nationality and violations of human dignity.[23] The state is required to demonstrate to the Commission that the foreign service prejudices these interests or poses a 'serious and grave risk' of such prejudice and that any measures it proposes to restrict the service are proportionate.[24] Thus, Member States retain considerable freedom under the Electronic Commerce Directive to regulate not only their own information society services but also services offered by providers established in other Member States.

The TVWF, adopted in 1989 and revised once in 1997, relates to 'television broadcasting'. 'Television broadcasting' is defined as 'the initial transmission by wire or over the air, including that by satellite, in unencoded or encoded form, of television programmes intended for reception by the public... It does not include communication services providing items of information or other messages on individual demand such as telecopying, electronic data banks or other similar services.'[25] The TVWF does not, therefore, cover radio, largely unregulated by the European Community, private communications or programmes provided on-demand. The European Community has thus sought to draw a bright line between those services covered by the TVWF and those by the Electronic Commerce directive. Television broadcasting is, however, defined widely enough to cover the streaming of audiovisual programmes at scheduled times over the Internet, so that a limited category of Internet services are covered by the TVWF.

Although the TVWF adopts a country of origin approach, it differs from the Electronic Commerce Directive in establishing a significant body of harmonised content rules. It includes, for example, provisions relating to events of major importance; European and independent programmes; the content, amount, and timing of advertising; sponsorship and teleshopping; child protection; hate speech and the right of reply. Member States are required to enforce these provisions in relation to

---

[22] Article 3.4, Electronic Commerce Directive, n 18 above.
[23] ibid.
[24] ibid.
[25] Article 1(a), TVWF, n 15 above.

broadcasters under their jurisdiction and are not allowed to restrict broadcasts from other Member States in the areas covered by the Directive.[26] A limited exception to this rule is provided where a foreign broadcast contravenes the Directive's rules concerning child protection and hate speech. In such circumstances the receiving state can take direct action against the service having first notified the broadcaster and consulted with the Commission and transmitting Member State.[27] The TVWF consequently constrains the ability of Member States to regulate foreign television broadcasts considerably more than the Electronic Commerce constrains their ability to regulate foreign information society services.

Why has the Commission Proposed a New Audiovisual Media Services Directive?

There are three main reasons why the Commission has sought to overhaul the existing system of Community audiovisual regulation. The first is that it has become apparent that the distinction drawn between broadcast and information society services in the TVWF and Electronic Commerce Directive can have decidedly arbitrary consequences. Similar services can now be offered on an on-demand or broadcast basis but are subject to very different content requirements under the two directives.

This importance of a service being classified under the TVWF or Electronic Commerce Directive is illustrated by the *Mediakabel* case, which came before the Court of Justice in 2004.[28] The case concerned a pay-per-view film service, provided by Mediakabel, called Filmtime. Films were broadcast at frequent intervals and subscribers could order a film by telephone or their remote control and pay by direct debit. They would then receive a key that enabled them to decrypt and watch their chosen film. Mediakabel argued that its service was provided 'on individual request' within the terms of the Electronic Commerce Directive. It therefore did not need to comply with the standards set out in the TVWF, notably the requirement that a majority of transmission time be filled with European programmes.[29] The Court concluded that the Filmtime

---

[26] Articles 2 and 2a, TVWF, n 15 above.

[27] Article 2a, TVWF, n 15 above.

[28] C-89/04, *Mediakabel BV v Commissariaat voor de Media* (2005) ECR I-4891.

[29] Although the quota provisions in Article 4 of the TVWF afford states considerable latitude in their implementation, the quota has in practice been widely enforced: Commission,

service did fall within the scope of the TVWF: although individuals could decide whether to access and pay for particular films, the films were selected by Mediakabel and offered to all subscribers simultaneously at times determined by the company. Moreover, since the films were broadcast it was technically possible for Mediakabel to ensure that a majority of its transmission time was taken-up by European films.

Although this ruling ensured that traditional, scheduled broadcast services and near video-on-demand services were treated in the same way, true video-on-demand services remain subject to the Electronic Commerce Directive and thus escape the more exacting requirements in the TVWF, notably the advertising restrictions and European and independent programme quotas.[30] The AVMS is consequently intended to level the uneven playing field on which on-demand and broadcast/near video-on-demand services currently compete, by extending a number of key provisions in the TVWF to certain on-demand services.

The second reason for intervention is that under the Electronic Commerce Directive there remains considerable scope for Member States to restrict the transmission of foreign information society services on public interest grounds, relying on the derogation clause in Article 3.4.[31] Member States thus have the potential to create barriers to the developing European market for on-demand audiovisual services.[32] The AVMS was intended to prevent such barriers by extending the regulatory approach adopted in the TVWF: harmonisation of basic standards and rigorous application of the country of origin principle. Thus, the Commission's initial proposal for the AVMS explicitly envisaged only very limited derogations in relation to on-demand services from the country of origin principle, notably where the service provider deliberately established itself in one Member State in order to evade the more exacting rules in another, and also where fundamental concerns were raised concerning hate speech.[33] This aspect of the proposal was, however, radically amended in the revised March text after the European Parliament's first reading, enabling Member States to restrict foreign on-demand services, provided that they first notified the Commission and

---

Seventh Report on the application of articles 4 and 5 of the TWF Directive for the period 2003–2004, COM(2006) 459.

[30] Albeit leaving considerable scope for regulation at the domestic level.

[31] See text accompanying n 22 above.

[32] Commission, initial AVMS proposal, n1 above, 5.

[33] See proposed Article 2.7–10 of the Commission's initial AVMS proposal and Article 3.2–5 of the revised consolidated proposal, detailed at nn 1 and 2 respectively above.

host Member State of their intention to take such action.[34] The proposal did not spell out the basis on which foreign services could be restricted but could be understood as permitting only those grounds already recognised as legitimate in the jurisprudence of the Court of Justice. The final text of the AVMS retains this approach but also explicitly sets out the basis on which foreign on-demand services can be restricted.[35] These are: public policy, which is stated to include the detection of crime, protection of minors, fight against incitement to hatred and violations of human dignity; public security; public health; and consumer protection.[36] The internal market basis for the AVMS has thus been significantly undercut by modifications made to the directive during the legislative process.

Finally, as indicated above, the existing rules in the TVWF were considered to need updating in the light of market developments.[37] In particular, the proposal seeks to enable broadcasters to compete more effectively for revenues by relaxing some of the advertising restrictions in the TVWF. The proposal also opens the way to the introduction of limited product placement. The legality of product placement under the TVWF has remained unclear, with the majority of Member States, including the UK, considering it a form of surreptitious advertising contrary to Article 10.4.[38] Product placement is, however, an established feature of the American media landscape and the amount spent on product placement on television grew from 709 to 1,878 million dollars between 1999 and 2004.[39] Although it constituted only 1.7 per cent of total free-to-air broadcasting revenues in the US, it is seen as a potentially valuable addition to the income of European broadcasters.[40]

---

[34] Article 2a.3 revised consolidated AVMS, n 2 above.

[35] Article 2a.4 AVMS, n 3 above.

[36] ibid.

[37] See text accompanying n 6 above.

[38] See OFCOM, *Summary of responses to consultation on issues relating to product placement*, October 2006 at: <http://www.ofcom.org.uk/consult/condocs/product_placement/statement/>, and Commission, *Interpretative Communication · on Certain Aspects of the Provisions on Televised Advertising in the Television Without Frontiers Directive*, C(2004)1450, [2004] OJ C102/2, available at: <http://eur-lex.europa.eu/LexUriServ/LexUriServ.do?uri=CELEX:52004XC0428(01):EN:HTML>. The Commission communication rather confusingly suggested 'undue prominence' as a defining characteristic of surreptitious advertising.

[39] Commission, 'The Modernisation of the Television Without Frontiers Directive: Frequently Asked Questions', November 2006, MEMO/06/208, at 4, available at: <http://europa.eu/rapid/pressReleasesAction.do?reference=MEMO/06/419&format=HTML&aged=0&language=EN&guiLanguage=en>.

[40] Carat and Koan, n 5 above, 59.

The Audiovisual Media Services Directive and the Linear/Non-linear Divide

A level playing field?

The AVMS establishes a new category of 'audiovisual media services'. An audiovisual media service is defined as one that falls within the scope of 'Articles 49 and 50 of the EC Treaty which is under the editorial responsibility of a media service provider and the principal purpose of which is the provision of programmes in order to inform, entertain or educate the general public by electronic communications networks...'.[41] The category of audiovisual media services encompasses both 'television broadcasts' or 'linear' and 'on-demand' or 'non-linear' services. Television broadcasting, as under the original TVWF, takes place where the service provider decides when a particular programme is to be transmitted for simultaneous viewing by incorporating it into a fixed schedule. Such services therefore include traditional broadcasting services, near video-on-demand services of the type at issue in the *Mediakabel* case, as well as scheduled services streamed over the Internet, which fall within the scope of the current TVWF.[42] On-demand services are those where the user determines the time at which a programme is transmitted by selecting it from a catalogue offered by a media company.[43] Services of this type, such as video-on-demand services obtained over the Internet or via cable, are at present covered by the Electronic Commerce Directive. By imposing on all audiovisual media services a basic tier of fundamental obligations, the AVMS seeks, as noted above, to level the playing field for providers of linear and non-linear services.

The basic tier of obligations in the AVMS includes requirements in five main areas: consumer information, hate speech, commercial speech, the accessibility of services to those with disabilities, and the protection of cinematographic works.[44] Member States must ensure that audiovisual media service providers under their jurisdiction make available to recipients details of their name, address, how they can be contacted, and the relevant regulatory or supervisory institution that governs their activities.[45] They

---

[41] Article 1(a), AVMS, n 3 above.

[42] Article 1(c), AVMS, n 3 above, and for explanatory note see Commission initial AVMS proposal, n 1 above, 10.

[43] Article 1(e), AVMS, n 3 above, and for explanatory note see Commission initial AVMS proposal, n 1 above, 10.

[44] Article 3a–3f, AVMS, n 3 above.

[45] Article 3a, AVMS, n 3, above.

Media Convergence and the Regulation of Audiovisual Content 249

must also ensure that audiovisual media services do not contain programmes that incite to hatred on grounds of race, sex, religion, or nationality.[46] The AVMS includes a number of fundamental requirements relating to the content of advertising. Advertising must not, for example, be surreptitious and advertising for tobacco products and drugs available only on prescription in the country where the media service provider is established is prohibited.[47] The Directive also seeks to limit the impact of sponsorship on audiovisual programmes, in particular, the sponsorship of news and current affairs programmes is prohibited.[48] After much controversy, the final text of the Directive states that product placement is in principle prohibited but Member States can choose to allow product placement in films, television series, light entertainment, and sports programmes, provided certain standards are met.[49] Product placement is not permitted in children's programmes. Although this allows a certain relaxation of the rules applicable to broadcasting services, where product placement has been prohibited, it also imposes new restrictions in the field of on-demand services where there has previously been no such European ban. In relation to all these fundamental obligations, it will consequently make no difference whether a programme is transmitted as part of a scheduled television service or offered on an on-demand basis over a cable network or on the Internet.

A number of requirements are imposed specifically on non-linear services that are similar, but not identical, to those applicable to linear services. These rules are rather less exacting in the non-linear field and relate to child protection and the promotion of European works.[50] The AVMS does not, therefore, level the playing field completely, and linear services continue to be subject to an additional, more exacting, tier of requirements than non-linear services based on the remaining requirements in the TVWF.[51] Linear services are thus subject to additional rules relating to the amount and placement of advertisements, independent productions, the right of reply and transmission of events of major importance. Alongside these additional restrictions, the AVMS also introduces a new provision that grants to linear broadcasters a right of access 'on fair, reasonable and non-discriminatory terms' to short news reports of events of high interest to the public transmitted by broadcasters in other Member States.[52] So, although there is a move towards 'technological

---

[46] Article 3a and b, AVMS, n 3 above.
[47] Article3d, AVMS, n 3 above.
[48] Article 3e, AVMS, n 3 above.
[49] Article 3f, AVMS, n 3 above.
[50] Article 3g–h, AVMS, n 3 above.
[51] Articles 5, 10–20, 23 and 3i, AVMS, n 3 above.
[52] Article 3j, AVMS, n 3 above.

250 *Rachael Craufurd Smith*

neutrality' and greater convergence in the rules applicable to linear and non-linear services, these rules are by no means equivalent. The disparity in treatment shown up by the *Mediakabel* case has not, therefore, been entirely removed.

Three rationales for continuing differentiation

Why does the AVMS not seek to level the playing field between linear and non-linear services completely? The Commission gives two reasons in Recital 28 of its initial proposal: the first is that viewers exercise more control over linear than non-linear services; the second is that linear services have a greater impact on the public than non-linear services.[53] Thus, the Commission states that it 'sees no justification for regulating audiovisual content supplied at the viewer's request ("pull content"), beyond safeguarding essential public interests such as protecting minors and preventing incitement to hatred. The differing degrees of regulation ... therefore reflects differences in user choice and control and in the likely impact on society.'[54] A third reason for differential regulation is an economic one. The non-linear sector is still at an early stage of development, with numerous small and medium-sized businesses; heightened regulation could consequently damage growth and encourage companies to relocate outside the EU.[55]

The concept of 'user control' requires some unpacking. Unless the service is interactive, viewers have no control over the actual content of programmes, and, even then, control may extend simply to selecting one feed over another. User control is, in most contexts, no more than the power to select programmes: to decide what to watch, when to watch it, and when to turn off. Two factors are particularly relevant in relation to programme selection: how audiences interact with particular media services and the quality and accessibility of programme information. In relation to the first, viewers of traditional linear television services are sometimes

[53] Recital 28, Commission initial draft AVMS proposal, n 1 above. See also the report for the Council of Europe Standing Committee on Transfrontier Television by A Grünwald, 'Possible options for review of the European Convention on Transfrontier Television', T-TT(2003) 2 of 24 April 2003, which considers possible ways of distinguishing broadcasting from other audiovisual services: <http://www.coe.int/t/e/human%5Frights/media/2%5Ftransfrontier%5Ftelevision/Texts%5Fand%5Fdocuments/>.

[54] Commission, n 39 above, at 7.

[55] Detailed discussion of the potential impact of further regulation on new media, in particular IPTV, online games and mobile media, is contained in the study by C Marsden, J Cave, E Nason, A Parkinson, C Blackman, and J Rutter, *Assessing Indirect Impacts of the EC Proposals for Video Regulation* (Cambridge: Rand Europe, 2006).

Media Convergence and the Regulation of Audiovisual Content 251

characterized as 'passive', merely reacting to programmes that are 'pushed' upon them.[56] At most they 'surf' between linear channels using a remote control, but careful scheduling can keep them watching a particular channel over the course of an evening. By contrast, on-demand services require a heightened degree of deliberate selection on the part of viewers, who actively research what is available and 'pull down' material from their chosen sites.

This active/passive distinction fails, however, to track exactly the non-linear/linear divide; at best it can be a rough proxy. Rather, viewers can be placed on a spectrum, depending on how active they are in determining what they watch. Although the most 'passive' viewers constitute a distinct sub-set of those who watch solely linear channels, the larger set of linear viewers also contains many who are considerably more pro-active. Even those equipped with only a basic remote control can be highly selective in what they watch, while those with the resources to invest in digital video recorders ('DVRs') or broadband Internet access have greatly enhanced opportunities to record both linear and non-linear programmes and to re-configure their own schedules.

The broadcaster Sky estimates, for example, that in those households that subscribe to Sky+, 22 per cent of viewers of programmes originally broadcast between 9 and 10pm watch those programmes on a time-shifted basis.[57] In a small scale study of early adopters of DVRs and Internet downloaders, Barry Brown and Louise Barkhuus found that virtually all the households they monitored that subscribed to Sky+ had 'moved almost entirely to watching pre-recorded shows from the PVR. Some even struggled to name the last show they had watched on live TV.'[58] In relation to the viewers in their study who downloaded programmes from the Internet, Brown and Barkuus found that these were split between 'supplementors' and 'replacers'. Supplementors continued to watch broadcast television channels but supplemented these with programmes from the Internet, in particular US programmes that were not yet available in the UK. Replacers, on the other hand, relied entirely on programmes that they had downloaded from the Internet. Active control over viewing

---

[56] See, for example, Andersen, *Outlook of the development of technologies and markets for the European Audiovisual sector up to 2010*, June 2002, 123 at: <http://ec.europa.eu/comm/avpolicy/info_centre/library/studies/index_en.htm>.

[57] Sky 2007 press release, n 5 above.

[58] B Brown and L Barkhuus, 'The Television Will Be Revolutionized: Effect of PVRs and Filesharing on Television Watching' , paper given at the SIGCHI conference, April 2006, Montreal , Canada, at: <http://portal.acm.org/citation.cfm?id=1124772. 1124870>. Early empirical research is also discussed in the Andersen report, n 56 above at 222.

is undoubtedly occurring in all these instances and at least these 'early adopters', with the exception of the replacers, appear to be building their schedules from linear services, or a combination of broadcast and on-demand services. Viewers consequently exercise varying degrees of control over what they watch, whether or not they have access solely to linear or a combination of linear and non-linear services.

A linked concern is that viewers of linear services may more easily 'stumble' across potentially disturbing material than viewers of on-demand services, the latter requiring an additional two or three clicks of a remote control or computer mouse to access. Thus, one of the considerations that the UK Communications Act 2003 requires OFCOM, the UK communications regulator, to bear in mind when drawing up its programme code is 'the likelihood of persons who are unaware of the nature of a programme's content being unintentionally exposed, by their own actions, to that content'.[59] This is, however, a risk that the adult linear surfer arguably chooses to bear, in that newspapers and specialized television guides, both print and electronic variants, offer considerable information on linear television services. Nevertheless, it would clearly be unreasonable to ascribe a similar assumption of risk to children and some countries have taken steps to alert viewers as to broadcast programmes that could be unsuitable for children. In France, for example, television programmes are classified according to their suitability for children aged less than 10, 12, 16, and 18, and, for programmes that contain more challenging material, the relevant age recommendation must be indicated by a pictogram displayed on screen throughout the whole of the transmission.[60] Similar guidance for viewers is provided in the Netherlands through the 'Kijkwijzer' system, which applies to television films and has been expanded to some mobile content.[61]

User control, meaning here the ability of the provider, as opposed to the consumer, of the service to determine who can gain access, can be a convincing basis for differential regulation in certain contexts. For example, the transmission of programmes considered unsuitable for children might reasonably be prohibited on freely accessible services but allowed

[59] Communications Act 2003, s 319(4)(d).

[60] Conseil supérieur de l'audiovisuel, 'Les conditions d'application de la signalétique jeunesse', available at: <http://www.csa.fr/infos/controle/television_signaletique_ C.php>.

[61] Discussed by Paulzer, C., 'Horizontal Rating of Audiovisual Content in Europe. An Alternative to Multi-Level Classification?' (2003) 10 *Iris Plus* 2–8 at: <http://www.obs.coe.int/medium/law.html.en#menu71>. The Parliament in its 2006 legislative resolution, Amendment 103, called for consideration of the development of a harmonised system of content symbols that could be used regardless of the delivery platform, n 2 above.

on encrypted services that require a password to decrypt. Once again, however, this draws a rather different distinction to the linear/non-linear one, in that many linear services are encrypted, while many non-linear services are unencrypted and readily accessible by anyone with the relevant equipment and basic technical knowledge.

The second basis for distinguishing linear from non-linear services mentioned by the Commission relates to their impact, in that linear services are seen as having a greater impact on the public than non-linear services. The special capacity of the moving image to shock or disturb has been relied on to justify regulating the audiovisual media more heavily than the print media, but here we are using impact to distinguish between two different types of audiovisual services.[62] Nor can the distinction turn on the type of programmes made available on linear and non-linear services in that increasingly almost everything available on a scheduled basis is also available for downloading on an on-demand basis over the Internet or cable networks.[63] Rather, it appears to be the scale and reach of audiences that continue to be attracted by the main linear television channels that underpins the distinction.[64] Certain linear services have also acquired a reputation for reliability and impartiality. But only a few of the many linear services on offer in each country are sufficiently authoritative to be able to 'speak to' the nation in this way, while the number of viewers who access on-demand services is steadily increasing.[65] The linear/non-linear distinction is thus a rather blunt mechanism for determining audience impact and is liable to be undermined by future developments in audience behaviour.

---

[62] See discussion by Barendt, n 10 above.

[63] Consider for example the BBC's iMP facility, which allows viewers to download, using peer-to-peer technology, programmes broadcast during the preceding seven days. Details provided by the BBC on iMP are available at: <http://www.bbc.co.uk/imp/>.

[64] Impact is a criterion used in Germany to distinguish broadcasting from other media services, subject to different regulatory regimes. A broadcasting service is considered to be typically one where, inter alia, it is capable of broad and simultaneous public reception and contains content capable of significant public impact, which is realistic and is subject to strong editorial control. See Directors' Conference of the German State Regulatory Authorities for Broadcasting, 'Third Structural Paper on the Distinction of Broadcast Services and Media Services' (2004) at: <http://66.102.9.104/search?q=cache: SJW9dTtLt2UJ:www.alm.de/fileadmin/Download/Positionen/3.Strukturpapier_ english.pdf+third+structural+paper&hl=en&ct=clnk&cd=2>.

[65] The speed with which consumers move to access on-demand services will depend on a number of factors, in particular, the cost of the services themselves: see Carat and Koan, n 5 above, at 67–68. For forecasts relating to PVR take up and on-demand revenue growth to 2010 see Screen Digest Limited, CMS Hasche Sigle, Goldmedia Gmbh, Rightscom Ltd, *Interactive Content and Convergence: Implications for the Information Society*, (London: Screen Digest, 2006), 73–75, at: <http://ec.europa.eu/information_society/eeurope/ i2010/ studies/index_en.htm>.

254   *Rachael Craufurd Smith*

The third reason for regulating non-linear less intensively than linear services relates to the relative stage of development of the underlying industries. Although non-linear services are still at an early stage of development, the Commission expects the video-on-demand market in Western Europe to grow to €235 million by 2008, with 57 million mobile TV subscribers by 2010.[66] Over-regulation could damage the sector and, as indicated above, drive some companies to relocate outside the EU. A recent report by RAND Europe suggests that new technology industries are 'more complex and dynamic than the traditional industries of broadcasting or telecoms' and may find it more difficult to internalize the costs of additional regulation than the larger, established media companies.[67] An increase in regulatory risk could consequently lead to market consolidation and a reduction in overall competition.

Areas where differential regulation remains justified: quantitative advertising limits, European programming, and events of major importance to society

In certain areas, the AVMS's differential regulation of linear and non-linear services can be justified on one or more of the grounds identified above. Thus, the additional advertising restrictions that are imposed on linear services can be explained on viewer control grounds. These restrictions relate to the amount of advertising that can be shown in any hour; the placement of advertisements in news, children's programmes, and films; and the prohibition on all advertising during religious services.[68] Although, as noted above, many viewers of linear services have time-shifting capabilities, and can thus fast forward through unwanted advertisements, there remains a category of viewers that do not have such facilities. Among this group one might expect to find significant numbers of elderly or less well-off viewers.[69] Since the capacity to time-shift linear services is determined by the user, not the producer of the service, the only way to continue to offer protection to this sub-group of linear viewers from

---

[66] Commissioner V Reding, 'Audiovisual media services directive: the right instrument to provide legal certainty for Europe's media businesses in the next decade', speech given in Brussels, 7 June 2006, SPEECH/06/352 available at: <http://ec.europa.eu/information_society/newsroom/cf/news.cfm?redirection=1&item_type=speech&tpa_id=123>.

[67] C Marsden *et al*, n 55 above, at xi.

[68] Commission, revised consolidated draft AVMS, Articles 10.2, 11 and 18, n 2 above.

[69] Commission Staff Working Document, Impact Assessment—Draft Audiovisual Media Services Directive, SEC (2005) 1625/2, 10, at: <http://ec.europa.eu/comm/avpolicy/reg/tvwf/modernisation/proposal_2005/index_en.htm>.

excessive advertising is to impose restrictions across the linear domain. As more and more viewers gain access to time-shifting facilities, however, the linear/non-linear distinction will become a less convincing basis for differential regulation in the advertising field. Increasing pressure from the broadcast industry for removal of the additional advertising constraints can consequently be expected in the future.

Viewer control also helps to explain why the AVMS adopts different provisions in relation to the transmission of European programmes.[70] In the linear context, it is proposed that the existing rules in the TVWF continue to apply: Member States will thus be required to ensure that broadcasters under their jurisdiction allocate, 'where practicable and by appropriate means', a majority of their transmission time to European programmes.[71] In the non-linear sector it is not practical to impose a quota based on transmission time, as the service provider has no control over which programmes are actually selected by viewers.

There are, however, a number of alternative approaches to stimulating the transmission of European works in the non-linear context. For example, on-demand service providers might be required to include a certain percentage of European works in their programme catalogues or to invest a certain proportion of their income in the production of European/independent programmes. Article 3h of the AVMS does in fact leave scope for these alternative measures by requiring simply that Member States 'ensure that media service providers . . . promote, where practicable and by appropriate means, production of and access to European works'.[72] The European Parliament had sought to clarify this further by noting that in the non-linear context this might take the form of 'a minimum number of European works proportionate to economic performance, a minimum share of European works and of European works created by producers who are independent of broadcasters in video-on-demand catalogues, or the attractive presentation of European and works created by such independent producers in electronic programme guides'.[73]

But technical differences alone cannot explain the diverse approach to European and independent programme requirements in the linear and non-linear contexts. The TVWF establishes a relatively high quota of over 50 per cent of transmission time for European programmes and 10 per cent

---

[70] Commission, Frequently Asked Questions, n 39 above.

[71] TVWF, n 15 above, Articles 4–6.

[72] Article 3h, AVMS, n 3 above.

[73] European Parliament, legislative resolution on the Commission's initial proposal, n 2 above, Amendment 104. Some, but not all, of these suggestions are now reflected in Article 3H, AVMS, n 3 above, on which see text below.

256   *Rachael Craufurd Smith*

for European works created by producers who are independent of broadcasters. In contrast, the AVMS does not suggest even minimum percentages
for catalogue content or investment in European production, nor does it
include any reference at all to independent works, though, as noted above,
independent works had been mentioned in the European Parliament's
gloss on the original proposal. One of the objectives behind the existing
European programme quota was to ensure that a significant proportion of
European programmes gain access to European television screens, faced
with highly competitive programmes from the US.[74] Many of the new
on-demand services, such as Filmflex in the UK, are film services and it has
been estimated that online movie revenues in Europe will exceed a billion
euros by 2010, growing from a mere 1.4 million euros in 2004.[75] But the
European film industries are equally, if not more, challenged by US imports
than the television industry and there is a real risk that only a small proportion of the revenue realised by online film services will be recouped by
European producers.[76] In its concern not to overburden the developing
on-demand market, the Commission has sidestepped an opportunity to
provide meaningful support for the European film industry. That it is
possible to balance the various competing interests rather differently is illustrated by a French inter-professional agreement, entered into in December
2005, between film producer associations, French screenwriters and
directors, ISPs, and companies providing feature-length films on a video-
on-demand basis, in particular over the Internet. The agreement requires
such video-on-demand service providers to make a financial contribution,
dependent on their gross annual turnover, to the production and development of French and European films.[77]

The reporting rules are also considerably less demanding than those
that apply to the existing European programme quota in the TVWF.[78] In
particular, there is no requirement that Member States provide detailed
information regarding the proportion of European programmes in non-
linear service catalogues or the extent to which non-linear services actually
fund the production of European programmes. Member States have merely

[74] I Katsirea, 'Why the European Broadcasting Quota Should be Abolished', (2003) 28
European Law Review, 190–209.

[75] Figures taken from Screen Digest Limited *et al*, n 65 above, 34.

[76] Independent European distributors and investors are, however, involved in the
development of these services and there is scope for European film to benefit in the longer
term: Screen Digest Limited *et al*, n 65 above, at 62. See also Commission comments at
Frequently Asked Questions, n 35 above.

[77] Screen Digest Limited *et al*, n 65 above, at 69 and N D Dalton, France- News Section
(2006) *Entertainment Law Review* nn 33–4.

[78] Article 4.3 of the TVWF, n 15 above.

to report every four years on how they have sought to implement the measure. Framed so weakly, it is doubtful whether the new programme provisions will either provide useful information or have any significant impact on Member State regulation in this area.

The major event rules are rather different to the provisions discussed above in that they grant linear broadcasters special privileges rather than impose additional burdens. They seek to ensure that major public events are widely covered, on social and democratic grounds.[79] The major event provisions in the AVMS, which replicate those in the TVWF, do this by enabling Member States to designate certain socially important events and to take measures to ensure that a significant proportion of their population can gain access to those events 'via live or deferred coverage on *free television*'.[80] The restriction of these provisions to *freely accessible* linear services can be explained by the fact that this particular category of linear services still has the capacity to attract the largest audiences and consequently be the most inclusive.

Areas where differential regulation of linear and non-linear services remains problematic: short reporting, child protection, and the right of reply

There are three areas where the AVMS applies different rules to linear and non-linear services that are difficult to rationalize on any of the grounds discussed above. The first concerns the right to 'short reports' set out in Article 3j of the AVMS. This entitles linear broadcasters to request a programme feed from a foreign broadcaster in relation to 'an event of high public interest' transmitted by that broadcaster on an exclusive basis. The excerpt can be used solely to provide a short news report. Given that providers of subscription and pay-per-view linear services are entitled to short reports, however small or large their audience, one might have expected a similar facility for the providers of on-demand services. Although major free-to-air broadcasters will tend to have a wider reach and impact than on-demand services, smaller subscription linear and on-demand services can contribute meaningfully to the citizens' right to information.[81] Ultimately, the provision helps to consolidate the position

---

[79] Article 3i of AVMS, n 3 above. For commentary on the listed event provisions in the TVWF see S Weatherill, 'Sport as Culture in EC Law' in R Craufurd Smith (ed), *Culture and EU Law* (Oxford: Oxford University Press, 2004), 112–52, and B Böttcher and R Craufurd Smith, 'Football and Fundamental Rights: Regulating Access to Major Sporting Events on Television' (2002) 8 *European Public Law* 107–33.   [80] Italics added.

[81] See Recital 27 of the AVMS, n 3 above.

of established linear news broadcasters in the face of competition from a developing on-demand sector.

The second area relates to child protection. This might seem surprising, given indications that a common approach would be adopted in this field.[82] In practice, however, important differences remain. In the linear sector, the existing provisions in the TVWF will continue to apply. These require Member States to take action to prohibit the inclusion of programmes on non-domestic services that 'might seriously impair' the development of minors, even when these services are encrypted and require user verification. Programmes that are merely 'likely to impair', as opposed to 'seriously impair', child development must be made available in such a way that children will not normally see them.[83] Where foreign services contravene these provisions Member States are exceptionally permitted, under Article 2a, to take direct action to prevent their reception, provided they follow certain notification procedures.[84]

In the non-linear context, however, Member States are required to take action against programmes that 'might seriously impair' child development offered by service providers under their jurisdiction only where the service provider has not taken adequate steps to prevent children gaining access by, for example, installing age verification or credit card checks.[85] The prohibition focuses, therefore, on the impact of the transmission in practice, rather than simply on its content. Although Article 2a.4 of the AVMS affords Member States scope to restrict foreign non-linear services under the jurisdiction of another Member State on public interest grounds, including child protection, this is subject to a number of constraints. Thus, before taking such action, the state of reception must notify the Commission and host state of its intention to impose restrictions, the foreign service must actually prejudice the public interest at stake or pose a 'serious and grave risk' of causing such prejudice, and the measures taken must be proportionate.[86] Where a foreign non-linear service containing explicit sexual or violent material takes effective steps to prevent child access it will be difficult for a Member State to establish that the service might seriously impair child development, or that restrictive

[82] See, for example, the Commission's initial AVMS proposal, n 1 above, at 5 and 11, and Recital 31 of the revised consolidated draft AVMS, n 2 above.

[83] Article 22, TVWF, n 15 above.

[84] Article 2a, TVWF, n 15 above.

[85] Article 3g, AVMS, n 3 above. Absent biometric facilities built into one's television, computer, or mobile phone, no age verification system is completely failsafe but a number of systems, for example, iAC (interactive Age Check), are available, see: <http://www.citizencard.com/iAC/index.htm>.

[86] Article 2a.4, AVMS, n 3 above.

measures are proportionate, given that Member States are not required to take action against similar domestic services. Only where a Member State exercises its power under Article 3.1 of the AVMS to impose more exacting rules on domestic service providers than those set out in the Directive, and thus prohibits domestic encrypted services of this type, might similar action against foreign services be found proportionate.

There is no separate provision in the AVMS relating to programmes that are merely 'likely to impair' child development relayed over non-linear services. Member States are thus not bound to require such material to be subject to access controls on domestic non-linear services, though they remain free to do so under Article 3.1 of the directive. Once again, therefore, Member States may only be able to justify restricting foreign non-linear services on this basis, relying on Article 2a.4 of the AVMS, where they impose similar restrictions on their own non-linear service providers.

There is thus a significant shift in regulatory approach towards 'zoning' and access controls in the non-linear sector. But if it is acceptable for programmes that might seriously impair child development to be transmitted on an on-demand basis provided children can be prevented from gaining access, why should the same approach not be adopted in the linear domain? One is left with a situation where the basis for regulation in the linear field rests on the contentious distinction between programmes that 'might seriously impair' child development and those merely 'likely' to cause impairment, while in the on-demand field it rests on the effectiveness of child prevention technology.[87] A consistent approach is clearly required for both linear and non-linear services.

In contrast, the fact that the AVMS imposes solely on linear service providers a requirement to put in place measures to prevent children from 'normally obtaining access' to programmes that are likely to impair their development can be explained on the basis of the service provider's control over scheduling. Linear broadcasters are able to time the transmission of programmes in such a way that the risk of exposure to an unsuitable audience is reduced. This is clearly not possible in the non-linear sector, where the user determines when to watch the programmes on offer. Extending to non-linear services a requirement similar to that applicable to linear broadcasters would result in standards being dictated by the very youngest member of the audience. Thus, with the exception of programmes considered

---

[87] For discussion of the position under the TVWF see R Craufurd Smith, 'Sex and Violence in the Internal Market: The Impact of European Community Law on Television Programme Standards' (1998) 3 *Contemporary Issues in Law* 135–153.

suitable for very young children, access to all non-linear programmes would have to to be dependent on age verification procedures or alternative methods, such as prior credit card payment, to prevent children gaining access. This could have the unfortunate effect of excluding particular categories of adults from accessing services—around thirty-five per cent of over eighteens, for example, do not have credit cards—as well as imposing additional costs on at least some non-linear service providers.[88]

Although a concern not to overburden the on-demand industry largely explains the different treatment of linear and non-linear services in this area, the result is that children may be exposed to unsuitable material relayed by non-linear services. In the non-linear environment considerable reliance is thus placed on parents and guardians to ensure that children do not gain access to unsuitable material by activating relevant filtering services.[89] Inevitably, the level of protection this provides will vary, depending both on the views and commitment of individual parents and the technological abilities of their children. In an attempt to address this concern, the European Parliament proposed an amendment requiring all audiovisual media service providers to offer their customers filtering systems for content 'damaging to the physical, mental or moral development of minors', but this was not taken up by the Commission in its revised draft or in the final version of the AVMS.[90] The (far from clear) dividing line between programmes that 'might seriously impair' child development and those that are otherwise likely to damage their development is thus important in the non-linear, as well as in the linear, context. It is only in relation to programmes that might seriously impair child development that the AVMS places the onus on the provider of a non-linear service to prevent child access.

[88] 'Online ID scheme to target paedophiles', Guardian Unlimited, 23 April 2003, at: <http://technology.guardian.co.uk/online/news/0,12597,941955,00.html>. Credit card verification systems also exclude all children under 18 even though the programme at issue might be suitable for children over, say, 16.

[89] Although parental content control systems are now well developed for Internet access via computers, they are still being developed in relation to mobile phones. The voluntary code of conduct for mobile phone operators in the UK provides that parents are to be offered the option of applying a filter that will filter out content deemed unsuitable for children under 18: UK Code of Practice for the self-regulation of new forms of content on mobiles, January 2004 at: <http://www.imcb.org.uk/assets/documents/10000109 Codeofpractice.pdf>

[90] European Parliament 2006 legislative resolution, n 2 above, Amendment 101, creating a new Article 3d, para 1a. This would have brought the EU into line with the approach adopted by Australia, which requires ISPs to offer parents filters at cost or below cost. The take-up among users, after a concerted government educational campaign, was estimated at around only 35 per cent, see comments by Senator Helen Coonan, Senate Hansard, 1 December 2005 at: <http://libertus.net/censor/aboutdcita.html#DCITA05>.

The third area where there remains a marked difference in the regulation of linear and non-linear services is that of the right of reply. A right of reply for persons whose 'legitimate interests, in particular reputation and good name, have been damaged by an assertion of incorrect facts in a television programme' was included in the original TVWF but the Commission's initial proposal for the AVMS did not extend this to on-demand audiovisual services.[91] Certain on-demand services, such as YouTube, can, however, attract many millions of viewers and have the capacity to cause considerable damage if they transmit incorrect information. The right of reply is intended to provide an alternative to defamation proceedings, which are too costly, time-consuming and unpredictable for most individuals to wish to pursue, and there appears to be no reason in principle why a similar alternative should not be available where a person has been damaged by a programme on a non-linear service.

The failure to extend the right of reply is even more surprising given that, prior to adopting its 2005 proposal, the Commission had noted that such a move was 'widely supported by the consulted experts'.[92] Moreover, the 2006 European Parliament and Council Recommendation on the protection of minors and human dignity and on the right of reply, calls for Member States to consider introducing a right of reply in relation to all on-line media.[93] The European Parliament amended the proposed AVMS by extending the right of reply to all those affected by 'transmissions', but failed to define 'transmission', thereby leaving the scope of its modification unclear.[94] Article 23 of the AVMS maintains the Commission's initial position and limits the right to linear audiovisual services.

Inevitably, one might expect that the fact that one is dealing with an on-demand rather than scheduled service would influence how the right of reply could be exercised and it may be that the most effective place to include the reply would here be on the initial page of the service provider's site. As with linear services, however, where the programme forms part of a series, an effective way of reaching those who have seen the contested transmission could be to place the reply before a subsequent programme in the series. Although a major objective of those whose interests have

---

[91] Article 23, TVWF, n 15 above.

[92] Commission, Issues Paper for the Liverpool Audiovisual Conference: Protection of Human Dignity and Right of Reply, July 2005, available at: <http://ec.europa.eu/comm/avpolicy/reg/tvwf/modernisation/consultation_2005/index_en.htm>.

[93] Para I.1, European Parliament and Council Recommendation on the protection of minors and human dignity and on the right of reply in relation to the competitiveness of the European audiovisual and on-line information services industry, [2006] OJ L378, 72–77.

[94] European Parliament, 2006 legislative resolution, n 2 above, Amendment 136.

been affected will be to ensure that the programme is either corrected or removed altogether from a catalogue of programmes, the right of reply can perform a useful function in correcting misunderstandings created by prior access to the programme.

It will be apparent from the above discussion that although the rules applicable to linear and non-linear services will be broadly similar under the AVMS, they will not be identical. Certain differences, for example, in relation to advertising time limits or the major event provisions, can be justified on the degree of user control or the public reach of the service. In other areas, however, these justifications appear less convincing, notably in relation to the right of reply and to a certain extent also in relation to child protection and European programming. Here, the central concern has been to avoid unduly burdening a developing industry and to ensure that as far as possible domestic barriers to an internal market in audiovisual services are removed. Viewers consequently need to be aware that different standards will continue to apply in the linear and non-linear environments. In particular, there is greater reliance on the viewer to put suitable child protection measures in place.

Reaching the Outer Boundaries of Control? The Print/Audiovisual and Amateur/Professional Divide

In seeking to address one boundary, that between linear and non-linear services, the Commission has thrown up another, potentially even more contentious, dividing line—that between audiovisual media services and other forms of online content. The Commission has emphasized that the AVMS is not intended to extend content regulation generally into the Internet field and has defined audiovisual media services as those, the 'principal purpose' of which is to provide 'programmes in order to inform, entertain or educate, to the general public'.[95] A 'programme' refers to a set of moving images with or without sound, so that online radio and text-based services such as newspapers, as well as private forms of communication such as e-mail, are excluded.[96] But the boundary here is a fluid one, leaving considerable scope for interpretation and dispute.

Two areas in particular are likely to prove problematic in the future. Firstly, services that combine text with a video feed and, secondly, user-generated

[95] Article 1a, AVMS, n 3 above.
[96] Article 1(aa) AVMS, n 3 above. See also recital 15 of the AVMS which provides that the Directive does not cover 'electronic versions of newspapers and magazines'.

services. In relation to the former, Commissioner Reding has stated that a short video included in an online newspaper, as in the SUN newspaper's website, should be regarded as merely ancillary to the text-based service and thus outside the reach of the AVMS.[97] But at what point do video components cease to be merely ancillary and when does their transmission become the principal purpose of the overall service? Is purpose to be assessed using a subjective or objective test? If the former, it would be open to a company that included extensive video coverage in its website to argue that its principal purpose remained the provision of a text-based service. Consumers would then lose the guarantee of the basic level of protection set out in the AVMS in relation to the video component. On the other hand, to bring all elements of such services within the scope of the AVMS would subject text services to what, at least in some countries, would be seen as an unacceptable level of state regulation, given the hard-won tradition of press freedom from government control.[98]

Convergence is thus facilitating the combination of two forms of communication that have traditionally been subject to different regulatory approaches, direct state regulation, and self-regulation. The Commission's response to these developments, which focuses on whether a service is composed primarily of text or video, is both uncertain in its operation and could lead, for the reasons indicated above, to either over or under regulation of parts of the service. There are two alternatives to this approach. Firstly, one could recognize the hybrid nature of the service and include within the scope of the AVMS the video, but not text, elements of the service regardless of its centrality to the overall service. Although this could lead to a number of regulatory bodies being responsible for different parts of the same service, this is not a new phenomenon. The print sector in the UK, for example, is subject to oversight by the Press Complaints Commission (PCC), in relation to matters such as privacy and accuracy of content,[99] and by the Advertising Standards Authority (ASA), in relation to advertising.[100] Secondly, one could break with

[97] Reding, n 66 above. The SUN website is at: <http://www.thesun.co.uk/>.

[98] Though, as indicated at n 9 above, Member States have been prepared to tolerate varying degrees of state intervention in the press field. In countries such as France, for example, a right of reply is mandated by law in Articles 12 and 13 of the 1881 Freedom of the Press Act, while in Britain it is left to self regulation. See the MediaWise briefing by M Jempson, 'Right of Reply in Europe', February 2005, at: <http://66.102.9.104/search? q =cache:glO8mOcC2DAJ:www.mediawise. org.uk/display_page. zphp%3Fid%3D841 + MediaWise+briefing+Mike+Jempson+right+of+reply&hl=en&ct=clnk&cd=2>.

[99] Press Complaints Commission (PCC) Code of Practice: <http://www.pcc.org.uk/ cop/practice.html>.

[100] For details of the ASA and the various codes of practice that it administers see: <http://www.asa.org.uk/asa/>.

tradition and extend certain of the basic requirements in the AVMS applicable to non-linear audiovisual media services to all commercial text, audio and video services offered to the public on an on-demand basis over electronic communications networks.[101] These requirements could include those relating to consumer information, child protection, hate speech, and advertising standards, but one might also consider extending the right of reply to such services for the reasons indicated above.

This latter option would guarantee consumers a consistent level of minimum protection across all non-linear online services but it would also be fiercely opposed by the newspaper sector, which would regard this as a significant step towards European Community regulation of 'offline' printed newspapers and magazines.[102] It is, nevertheless, worth noting that the basic requirements in the AVMS reflect standards that are already widely recognized in the print sector across Europe.[103] In the UK, for example, the Code of Practice adopted by the newspaper and periodical industry, enforced by the PCC, establishes a right of reply to inaccurate facts and to the prompt correction of significant inaccuracies.[104] It also calls on editors and publishers to avoid any 'prejudicial or pejorative reference to an individual's race, colour, religion, gender, sexual orientation or to any physical or mental illness or disability'.[105] In addition, there are statutory measures designed to prevent hate speech. Thus, the Public Order Act 1986 establishes an offence of publishing or distributing 'threatening, abusive or insulting' written material where there is an intention, or the material is likely, to stir up racial hatred.[106] In 2006 the Act was amended to include further offences, including that of publishing or distributing 'threatening' written material, where the disseminator intends to stir up religious hatred.[107]

---

[101] For the Community to have competence to harmonize under Articles 47(2) and 55 EC, the basis of both the TVWF and AVMS, the services would need to be commercial in scope. The Commission has, however, proposed general cross-media measures relating to child protection, hate speech and the right of reply in the form of a non-binding recommendation, adopted by the Parliament and Council in 2006, under Article 157 EC, the industry article. See n 93 above.

[102] It would also significantly extend Community regulation of the content of audio services where there has not to date been considered a need for harmonisation.

[103] D Leonardi, 'Self-Regulation and the Print Media: Codes and Analysis of Codes in Use by Press Councils in Countries of the EU', 30 April 2004, at: <http://www.selfregulation.info/iapcoda/0405-press-report-dl.html>.

[104] PCC, n 99 above, at paras 1 and 2.

[105] PCC, n 99 above, at paras 1 and 12.

[106] Public Order Act 1986, s 19.

[107] Public Order Act 1986, Part 3A. The offences relating to incitement to racial and religious hatred in the Act extend beyond written publication to the use of words, distribution of recordings, public performance and broadcasting, see Articles 17–22 and 29A–F.

Media Convergence and the Regulation of Audiovisual Content 265

Press and periodical advertising is covered by the British Code of Advertising, Sales Promotion and Direct Marketing, and the provisions in the Code map, if not go beyond, those contained in the basic tier of obligations in the AVMS.[108] In particular, the paragraphs relating to advertising aimed at children and alcoholic drinks are considerably more detailed than those in the directive.[109] In the offline environment, a range of statutory and self-regulatory measures also make it more difficult for children to gain access to printed pornographic material. Thus, section 85 of the Postal Services Act 2000 prohibits the mailing of any 'indecent or obscene... written communication', while shops that sell 'to a significant degree' sexually oriented books and magazines require a local authority licence and must exclude children.[110] Newsagents do, however, continue to stock what are loosely termed 'lad's magazines' so that, as in the online field, considerable reliance is placed on parental supervision to ensure that children do not gain access to inappropriate material.[111]

In substantive terms it would be difficult, therefore, for the print media to object to the application of the basic requirements included in the AVMS to online text services. In answer to the argument that inclusion of such services within the scope of the AVMS would expose the press to undue governmental influence one may thus note that the print media are already subject to a number of statutory controls in the UK and across Europe; self-regulation has never been a comprehensive approach.[112] Moreover, state involvement in the further elaboration and implementation of standards set out in directives can be relatively 'light touch': it is sufficient for the state to be ultimately responsible for the Directive's effective implementation.[113] In 2004, for example, OFCOM, the UK national communications regulator, sub-contracted oversight of broadcast advertising, an area covered by the TVWF, to the ASA, a body that

---

[108] British Code of Advertising, Sales Promotion and Direct Marketing, 2003, at: <http://www.asa.org.uk/asa/codes/cap_code/ >.

[109] ibid, at paras 47 and 56.

[110] G Robertson and A Nicol, *Media Law* (London: Penguin, 2002) 216–217.

[111] The National Federation of Retail Newsagents recently adopted guidelines which recommend that magazines with 'sexually graphic' covers should not be displayed at children's eye level or below, or adjacent to children's titles and comics: BBC News, 'Newspapers and magazines with sexual content are to be moved to higher shelves under new guidelines', 25 March 2006, at: <http://news.bbc.co.uk/1/hi/uk/4843808.stm >.

[112] See n 98 above. Self-regulatory bodies are also aware that if they do not operate effectively the state may step in and impose centralized regulation, on which see s 361(7) of the Communications Act 2003, which enables the Secretary to State to intervene in the field of on-demand audiovisual services, currently regulated by ATVOD.

[113] Hans-Bredow-Institut, *Study on Co-Regulation Measures in the Media Sector*, June 2006, 157–60 at:<http://ec.europa.eu/comm/avpolicy/info_centre/library/studies/index_en.htm >. Note also Recital 25 of the AVMS, n 3 above.

266   *Rachael Craufurd Smith*

had previously operated solely on a self-regulatory basis. Although this necessitated significant changes to the way in which the ASA was organized in order to leave final authority in the hands of OFCOM, OFCOM has undertaken to use its powers 'only in exceptional circumstances'.[114] If the Community were to include online text services within the scope of the Directive there would still remain, therefore, considerable scope for the newspaper and magazine industries to be involved in the fleshing out and enforcement of the standards set.

Finally, Recital 46c of the AVMS emphasizes that independent national regulatory bodies and institutions should be able to exercise their powers 'impartially and transparently'.[115] This falls short of the more specific requirement of regulatory independence that had been included in the revised draft of the Directive after the European Parliament's first reading. Article 23b in the main body of the draft Directive had called on Member States to 'guarantee' the independence of their regulatory bodies, while Recital 47 had indicated that this would entail independence not only from national governments but also from the industry being regulated.[116] These provisions could have affected the way in which co- and self-regulatory initiatives, of the sort envisaged in the AVMS, are implemented.[117] On this basis it would have been unacceptable for industry alone to determine the content of codes of conduct for a particular sector or to have a decisive role in their enforcement. Within the UK this principle is widely, though by no means universally, respected. For example, although a majority of members of the PCC and the ASA Council, which adjudicate on press and advertising complaints respectively, have no connection with the press or advertising industries, only three of the eleven members of ATVOD, which regulates on-demand television services, are reserved for independent members. Retention of the proposed Article 23b was inevitably going to prove contentious and the provision was deleted from the final version of the AVMS.

The Commission's narrow focus in the AVMS on ensuring a level playing field for linear and non-linear audiovisual services consequently prevented

[114] Memorandum of Understanding between OFCOM, ASA(B), BCAP, and BASBOF, May 2004, at: <http://www.ofcom.org.uk/consult/condocs/reg_broad_ad/update/mou/ >. See, in particular, paras 8–9. A new body, the Broadcast Committee of Advertising Practice (BCAP), was established to set and monitor compliance with the advertising codes.

[115] Article 23b revised consolidated draft AVMS, n 2 above.

[116] Recital 47 and Article 23b of the revised consolidated draft AVMS, n 2 above. By contrast Article 3.3 of the AVMS provides that co- and self-regulatory regimes should be 'broadly accepted by the main stakeholders . . . and provide for effective enforcement', n 3 above.

[117] See Recital 25, AVMS, n 3 above.

it from addressing the broader implications of convergence. But if basic consumer protection standards are important in the audiovisual sector, they are important also in relation to online services consisting of text as well as pictures. Although Member States and industry groupings have stepped in to provide protection in certain areas, the degree of intervention varies from one state to another. Thus, the PCC in the UK regulates versions of newspapers and magazines that subscribe to the Editors' Code of Practice, and will even consider complaints regarding certain types of audiovisual material on those websites, but it does not regulate online newspapers that have no offline counterparts.[118] These observations suggest that a better way forward could have been to amend the Electronic Commerce Directive, to include a basic tier of consumer protection provisions applicable across all on-demand services whether text, radio or audiovisual, rather than to enact a limited extension of the TVWF.

Nor is the Community unaware that there is a case for the uniform application of basic standards across all online services. The 2006 European Parliament and Council Recommendation on the protection of minors and human dignity and the right of reply provides that the European Union should 'gear its political action to preventing any form of violation of the principle of respect for human dignity'; it then notes that 'legislative measures need to be enacted at Union level on the protection of the physical, mental and moral development of minors *in relation to the content of all audiovisual and information services* and the protection of minors from access to inappropriate adult programmes or services'.[119] The Recommendation, which is non-binding, and based on the industry article in the EC Treaty, seeks merely to encourage Member States, industry and interested parties to work together to ensure that consumers are adequately protected across all online services.[120]

Given these observations, how can the Community's fragmented approach be justified? In relation to the 2006 Recommendation on the protection of minors and human dignity, the Commission notes that '[g]iven that the harmonisation of laws of the Member States is excluded from industrial and cultural policies, the Community is bound to use

---

[118] Press Industry Guidance Note on the extension of the PCC's remit to include editorial audiovisual material on newspaper and magazine websites, available at: <http://www.pcc.org.uk/news/index.html?article=NDMyMQ>. Leonardi, n.103 above, notes that a number of other press councils, such as the German, Swedish, and Catalan councils, have similarly extended their remit to online versions of newspapers and magazines that fall within their remit.

[119] European Parliament and Council Recommendation on the protection of minors and human dignity and on the right of reply, n 93 above, at Recitals 2 and 3, italics added.

[120] Article 157 EC Treaty.

non-binding instruments, such as recommendations, to fulfill the tasks and obligations enshrined in the Treaty'.[121] But if harmonization is inappropriate, and intervention in these areas is motivated by cultural and industrial concerns, why are provisions on child protection, human dignity and, at least for linear services, a right of reply, included in the AVMS, a harmonising directive? The answer may simply be that the Commission considers it can currently make out a convincing case that domestic regulations in the audiovisual sector genuinely impede, or could impede in the future, the provision of cross border services but is less sure in relation to other media.[122] Ultimately, continuing sensitivity over state regulation of the print media may have led the Commission to work through recommendations rather than seek to impose binding European standards in the field of online text services. By avoiding the use of a directive the Community affords Member States scope to build around existing self-regulatory systems and to adapt basic requirements in the light of domestic social and cultural expectations.

In addition to text-based online services, the AVMS also excludes most user-generated material from its ambit. Recital 13 explicitly states that the Directive does not cover 'activities that are primarily non-economic and which are not in competition with television broadcasting, such as private websites and services consisting of the provision or distribution of audiovisual content generated by private users for the purposes of sharing and exchange within communities of interest'. Audiovisual media services must be under the 'editorial responsibility' of a media service provider and although Recital 17 now leaves the determination of what constitutes editorial responsibility to the Member States, earlier drafts of the directive had indicated that this would require involvement in a 'professional capacity'.[123] It is probable that this latter phrase was introduced to distinguish those who are editors by profession, in the sense that this is their main occupation, from those who aggregate content merely on an amateur basis. But the professional/amateur divide may also focus on whether the activity is a remunerated one and increasingly services carrying user-generated content have the potential to realise revenues through advertising

[121] Commission, Proposal for a Recommendation of the European Parliament and of the Council on the protection of minors and human dignity and the right of reply in relation to the competitiveness of the European audiovisual and information services industry, COM/2004/0341 final, para. 4.

[122] In Case C-376/98, *Germany v European Parliament and Council* [2000] ECR I-8419, the Court of Justice at para 84, held that Community measures must genuinely pursue the objectives set out in the Treaty article on which they are based.

[123] Article 1(kd), revised consolidated draft AVMS, n 2 above.

or sponsorship.[124] The term 'professional' was consequently far from clear and has been removed from the text of the Directive. The way in which editorial responsibility is defined does, however, leave scope for modification to the reach of the Directive.

Article 1(a) of the AVMS also defines an audiovisual media service as one that has as its principal purpose 'the provision of programmes'. A 'programme' is further defined as one 'whose form and content is comparable to the form and content of television broadcasting'.[125] Examples of programmes given in Article 1(aa) are 'feature-length films, sports events, situation comedy, documentary, children's programmes and original drama'. Although this would appear to exclude most user-generated material, user-generated material is now being incorporated in some broadcast channels, an example being Al Gore's 'Current TV', which recently launched in the UK.[126] About a third of Current TV's content is made up of short videos, or 'pods', of three to eight minutes in length submitted by viewers.

One conclusion that might be drawn from this is that broadcast channels containing a significant proportion of user-generated content are not covered by the AVMS. There will thus be two categories of broadcast channels: those that contain traditional 'programmes', subject to both the basic and enhanced tier of obligations in the AVMS, and channels that contain principally user-generated content that fall outwith the scope of both the AVMS and the Electronic Commerce Directive, regulated in accordance with domestic law. It is, however, more likely that Current TV, as a broadcast television channel, would be regarded as establishing what can now constitute the 'form and content of television broadcasting'.

This then opens the door for on-demand services that incorporate user-generated audiovisual content to fall within the scope of the AVMS, provided they meet the other criteria for classification as an 'audiovisual media service'. Sites such as YouTube exercise a degree of editorial control over the content posted,[127] incorporate advertising, and can attract many thousands of viewers. Their capacity to influence the public, particularly

---

[124] It is increasingly easy for user-generated websites to incorporate commercial elements, by using, for example, the Google AdSense facility, or allowing sponsored links, on which see: <http://www.google.com/services/adsense_tour/index.html>.

[125] Article 1(aa), revised consolidated draft AVMS, n 2 above.

[126] O Gibson, 'Al Gore brings DIY television 'revolution' to Britain', *Guardian Unlimited*, 13 March 2007, at: <http://www.guardian.co.uk/frontpage/story/ 0,2032528,00.html>.

[127] See YouTube's Code of Conduct at: <http://www.youtube.com/t/community_ guidelines>. YouTube relies on members to 'flag-up' videos they consider in breach of the code and then reviews them.

the young, is thus considerable. Moreover, YouTube has recently agreed to carry material generated by the BBC, so that, as with Current TV, it offers a mix of user-generated and professional material.[128] It is therefore possible that the more successful, commercially oriented, on-demand sites carrying user-generated content will be covered by the AVMS. Drawing regulatory boundaries on the basis of the type of service offered by a particular sector at any given time certainly creates a degree of flexibility, enabling regulators to respond to changing market conditions. But, for the reasons given above, it is also likely to cause considerable uncertainty as to exactly which services fall within the scope of the directive and which do not.

To What Extent is the AVMS a Harmonizing Measure and is Further European Harmonization of Audiovisual Content Desirable?

One of the Commission's stated objectives in putting forward the AVMS was to introduce harmonized European rules in those areas where divergent domestic regulations are most likely to impede the development of cross-border audiovisual media services. In a background memo on the directive the Commission noted that '[m]ost Member States already have rules protecting minors from harmful content and outlawing incitement to hatred. However, these are now to be harmonised EU-wide, so that audiovisual media service suppliers need only comply with the rules of the Member State in which they are established, and not with the disparate rules of all 25 Member States potentially receiving their services.'[129] The explanation is clear enough, but does it accurately reflect how the AVMS, in its final form, is likely to operate in practice?

Some articles in the AVMS do establish standards that can be consistently applied, for example, Article 3a, which requires the publication of basic information in relation to who is providing a service and how they can be contacted. Other provisions, such as those relating to child protection and hate speech are considerably more open-ended. Thus, the directive does not elaborate on the kind of programmes that 'might seriously impair the physical, mental or moral development of minors', a category

---

[128] M Sweney, 'BBC makes deal with YouTube', The Guardian, 2 March 2007, at: <http://technology.guardian.co.uk/news/story/0,2025233,00.html>.

[129] Commission, Frequently Asked Questions, n 39 above, at 6. See also Recital 5 of the AVMS, n 3 above.

Media Convergence and the Regulation of Audiovisual Content 271

that triggers either prohibition or the imposition of access controls depending on whether the service is linear or non-linear.[130] Nor does the directive define what constitutes 'incitement to hatred based on race, sex, religion or nationality' within the terms of Article 3b.[131] It would be plausible, given statements such as that of the Commission in its memo noted above, to conclude that these provisions establish Community standards, to be ultimately interpreted by the Court of Justice.[132] But is this realistic?

There are a number of possible explanations as to how the child protection and hate speech provisions might operate in practice. The first is that they do indeed establish harmonised European standards and, given the importance of the interests at stake, offer a high level of protection.[133] But in both these areas Member States currently apply divergent standards at the domestic level, balancing the competing interests in freedom of expression and protection from mental or physical harm differently.[134] With regard to hate speech, for example, the UK has not, unlike many Member States, criminalised Holocaust denial, and the passage of the Racial and Religious Hatred Act 2006 met with considerable opposition both within and outside Parliament.[135] Under the Act an offence of incitement to religious hatred arises only where the words or behaviour at issue are 'threatening', as opposed to 'abusive or insulting', and it is not sufficient that such acts or behaviour are likely to stir up religious hatred, there must actually be an intention to do so.[136]

If Article 3b of the AVMS is intended to establish common Community standards regarding 'incitement to hatred on grounds of race, sex, religion and nationality', one would have expected a rather more carefully elaborated provision, along the lines, for example, of the Protocol to the Council of

---

[130] See text accompanying n 82 above.

[131] The European Parliament proposed extending what was then Article 3e even further to include incitement to hatred on grounds of 'belief' and to require state action against material that would 'offend against human dignity in any other manner'. Perhaps not surprisingly, these proposals were not incorporated by the Commission in its revised proposal and the current Article 3b merely extends Article 22a of the TVWF to non-linear services.

[132] Recital 11a of the Commission's revised AVMS proposal, n 2 above, referred to 'minimum standards' in relation to the protection of minors, while Recital 30 stated that the Directive 'must promote a high level of protection of objectives of general interest, in particular the protection of minors, the rights of persons with disabilities and human dignity'. On which see further the discussion below.

[133] For support see Recital 30 AVMS, n 3 above.

[134] On variations in rating practices regarding child protection see Paulzer, n 56 above.

[135] BBC News, 'Controversial plans to make incitement to religious hatred illegal have been unveiled by the government', 11 June 2005 at: <http://news.bbc.co.uk/1/hi/uk_politics/4075442.stm>.

[136] The religious hatred offences are thus more limited in scope than those relating to racial hatred in the Public Order Act 1986, on which see text accompanying n 100 above.

Europe Cybercrime Convention.[137] To date, however, only five Member States have ratified the Protocol and the proposed EU Council Framework Decision on combating racism and xenophobia has made little progress since it was put forward in 2001.[138] Agreement on common standards in these sensitive areas is clearly far from easy and the suspicion that the AVMS does not seek to establish such standards finds support in Recital 9, which states that the directive 'does not in any way prevent Member States from applying their constitutional rules relating to freedom of the press and freedom of expression in the media'.

Is it more plausible for the AVMS to be construed as establishing minimum standards in these areas? Minimum standards, after all, underpin the regulatory approach adopted in the AVMS, which allows states to impose more exacting standards on domestic service providers, but requires them to allow in services from other Member States provided these comply with the minimum standards in the directive.[139] Minimum harmonization should in principle, therefore, offer considerable certainty for traders and greatly facilitate free movement. But the AVMS fails to clarify what these minimum standards entail and even if the nature of these minimum standards can be established over time by, for example, recourse to the Court of Justice, Member States will be reluctant, given political sensitivities in these areas, to allow reception of foreign services that fail to comply with more exacting domestic standards they impose. For this reason Member States have retained competence under the AVMS to restrict foreign linear and non-linear services that contravene their domestic rules on child protection and hate speech.[140] A company based in the UK offering video-on-demand services in the UK, France, and Germany could consequently still be prosecuted in France and Germany if it relayed material that denied the Holocaust, even though its service might be perfectly lawful in the UK.[141]

---

[137] The Protocol itself permits states not to apply certain provisions, for example, the requirement to criminalise racist insults in Article 5. The Protocol can be accessed at: <http://conventions.coe.int/Treaty/Commun/QueVoulezVous.asp?NT=189&CM=2&DF=3/29/2007&CL=ENG>.

[138] ibid and Commission, Proposal for a Council Framework Decision on combating racism and xenophobia, COM(2001) 664. The German Presidency has more recently sought to push this forward.

[139] Recital 5, articles 2a.1 and 3.1 AVMS, n 3 above.

[140] Albeit subject to various notifications and Commission scrutiny, see Articles 2a.2 and 2a.4 AVMS, n 3 above. Note that in relation to on-demand services Member States remain competent to restrict foreign services on a wider range of grounds, including consumer protection.

[141] See, for example, *LICRA and UEJFA v Yahoo! Inc and Yahoo France*, Tribunal de Grande Instance de Paris, 20 Nov 2000. Detailed discussion of the application of the country of

Media Convergence and the Regulation of Audiovisual Content 273

Without clearly defined minimum standards, the AVMS may, in reality, do no more than require Member States to take action in these areas, leaving them to determine what standards should be applied in light of their specific cultural and constitutional traditions. This was the approach taken by the EFTA Court in a case referred to it in 1997 by the Oslo City Court concerning the interpretation of the child protection provisions in the TVWF.[142] Although Norway is not a member of the EU, its membership of EFTA means that it is bound to comply with the terms of the TVWF in its relations with other EFTA and EU countries. The dispute concerned the prohibition by the Norwegian authorities of the carriage by Norwegian cable networks of a Swedish television channel called FilmMax. FilmMax contained 'hard core' adult programming but was transmitted in encrypted form and was legal in Sweden. The European Commission, together with the EFTA Surveillance Authority, Norway, the UK, and Sweden all argued that the child protection provisions in Article 22 of the TVWF did not establish a Community standard. The Commission observed that it was 'very difficult to determine objectively what programmes are covered by Article 22, first sentence' as there were legitimate 'differences of interpretation from one country to another, depending on different traditions and value systems'.[143] The EFTA Court accepted the Commission's arguments, ruling that it was for each state to decide what was detrimental to minors and to define the terms of Article 22 TVWF, including the word 'pornography', 'in accordance with their national legislation and moral standards'.[144] Dual regulation by both the transmitting and receiving state was thus held to be legitimate on child protection grounds.

Although the approach adopted by the EFTA Court has not to date been endorsed by the Court of Justice, it is probable that the child protection and hate speech provisions in the AVMS would be construed in a similar way. Member States will thus retain a wide margin of discretion in shaping their domestic rules in these areas.[145] Where important competing

origin principle under the existing TVWF is provided by J Hörnle, 'Country of Origin Regulation in Cross-Border Media: One Step Beyond the Freedom to Provide Services?' (2005) 54 *ICLQ* 89–126.

[142] Case E-8/97, *TV1000 Sverige AB v Norwegian Government* [1998] EFTA Court Reports 68. For commentary see Craufurd Smith, n 82 above.

[143] Report for the hearing, *TV1000 Sverige AB*, n 134 above, at paras 49–50.

[144] *TV1000 Sverige AB*, n 134 above, at para 24.

[145] Deference to the Member States in these contexts would be in line with Article 151(4) EC which provides that the Community 'shall take cultural aspects into account in its action under other provisions of this Treaty, in particular in order to respect and to promote the diversity of its cultures'.

interests are at stake and Member States choose to resolve the tensions between these interests in quite different ways then the Community should be wary, if not about intervention generally, then about harmonization in particular.[146] One cannot entirely discount the possibility, however, that the Court of Justice might take recital 30 of the AVMS at face value and construe the child protection and hate speech provisions as establishing 'a high level of protection', to be determined at European level. But if European harmonization is the intended outcome, whether at maximum or minimum levels, this should be made explicit in the legislative measure and the standards formulated clearly, allowing for proper democratic scrutiny. Matters of such importance should not be devolved to the Court of Justice because agreement proves difficult between the Member States.

Were the hate speech and child protection provisions in the AVMS to be construed along the lines adopted by the EFTA Court in the *TV1000* case, the rationale for Community regulation would be seriously undermined. This is because the AVMS would not significantly advance market liberalization beyond the position already established in the Electronic Commerce Directive. Although, as noted above, the AVMS would then require, rather than permit, states to take action in these areas, it would not only not dictate the nature of this action but would also allow domestic barriers to cross-border trade to remain in place. Even were the AVMS to be construed as establishing minimum standards, the licence afforded Member States to require that foreign service providers comply with more exacting domestic rules will limit the Directive's capacity to integrate domestic markets.

Conclusion

The above discussion leads to the conclusion that the AVMS is both an unduly limited response to convergence in the communications sector and, paradoxically, also an overambitious one. Unduly limited, in that the main focus of the Directive is simply on levelling the playing field between linear and non-linear services. By excluding text and user-generated material from its scope, it curtails discussion of the need for consumer protection measures more generally across the online and mobile fields.

---

[146] A more incremental, soft law, approach is envisaged in the European Parliament and Council Recommendation on the protection of minors and human dignity and on the right of reply, n 90 above.

Media Convergence and the Regulation of Audiovisual Content 275

And the linear/non-linear playing field looks set to remain decidedly bumpy even after this levelling process, with disparate rules on, among other things, child protection, advertising, short news reports, European and independent programming, and the right of reply.

A major objective of the Commission in drafting the Directive was to avoid over-regulating and thus stifling the developing, and potentially highly dynamic, on-demand industry in Europe. Inspection of the draft AVMS suggests that there is, in fact, little chance of this concern being realized in practice. Of those areas where regulation is imposed on on-demand services—the information requirements replicate those that already exist under the Electronic Commerce Directive; the hate speech and child protection provisions may well enable Member States to continue to apply their own disparate standards; the adverting rules can at best be described as skeletal and are widely enforced under self-and co-regulatory regimes in place across the Member States; while the European programme provisions are purely aspirational in nature. Regulation of non-linear services under the AVMS could consequently prove tó be something of a chimera, and the real centre of gravity of the proposal rests with its deregulation of the existing linear advertising rules under the TVWF.

Minimal harmonization has, of course, significant repercussions when linked to a strong country of origin principle. This was the approach adopted by the Commission in its original proposal. Thus, the limited advertising rules established for on-demand services would have prevented a Member States from imposing its own more exacting domestic rules on foreign services in this area. The AVMS would have taken a significant step beyond the Electronic Commerce Directive towards the creation of a single market for on-demand audiovisual services. As finally agreed, however, the AVMS affords Member States continuing scope to restrict foreign on-demand services on general interest grounds, which include child and consumer protection.[147]

The AVMS also seeks to create new boundaries between audiovisual media services and other text and user-generated services. Although key concepts that mark out these boundaries, such as 'programmes', may inject a degree of flexibility, allowing the directive to evolve with the services it regulates, they also create uncertainty for business, something the AVMS was deliberately designed to reduce. Terms such as 'editorial responsibility' are also open to varying interpretations and, if the child protection and

---

[147] Albeit subject to the notification requirements and tests of proportionality and necessity in Article 2a.4 AVMS, n 3 above.

hate speech provisions are considered to establish Community standards, then they lack necessary elaboration.

Ultimately, there may be a case for extending some of the basic obligations in the AVMS more widely across the online and mobile fields, where regulation, by both state and industry, remains patchy. Online, the old regulatory barriers begin to dissipate and consumers should be assured of a certain level of protection whether they are accessing an online newspaper, downloading a film, or listening to their favourite foreign radio station from another Member State. Basic consumer information requirements and the right of reply should arguably be extended across all online media, and a common European code of advertising content could be developed that is technology neutral. There seems little basis, for example, in applying, as does the AVMS, different rules to linear and non-linear services in relation to alcohol advertising.[148] In the short term, greater horizontality might have been achieved by amending the Electronic Commerce Directive, rather than the TVWF. This is not to say that the Community is unaware of these arguments, as the recent Council and Parliament recommendation on the protection of minors and human dignity illustrates, but there appears to be a dissipation of energies leading to a fragmented approach.[149]

The AVMS may be considered overambitious to the extent that it appears to incorporate harmonized Community standards on child protection and hate speech, areas where the Member States continue to apply divergent rules consequent on their different cultural and constitutional histories. If the Directive does indeed establish common standards, these should have been set out in detail to enable proper scrutiny in the legislative process. But it is not even clear that this is what the AVMS intends to do and, given the uncertainty that persists in relation to the existing child protection measures in the TVWF, the operation of these provisions should have been clarified.

On the one hand, therefore, the AVMS has limited ambitions in relation to consumer protection and support for the European programme industry in the on-demand sector; on the other, it pursues harmonization on internal market grounds in areas, such as child protection and hate speech, where it may not be able, politically, to deliver concrete results. The perception that the directive is here pushing the boundaries of Community law to its limit is supported by the explicit incorporation not

---

[148] Contrast Articles 3d and 15 AVMS, n 3 above.

[149] A more global perspective has been taken by the Commission in its public consultation on content online in the Single Market, detailed at the europa webpage: <http://ec.europa.eu/avpolicy/other_actions/content_online/index_en.htm>.

Media Convergence and the Regulation of Audiovisual Content 277

only of general interest derogations but also the abuse of law principle into the final text.[150] All these concerns suggest that it would have been better for the Community to have undertaken a specific review of linear broadcasting under the TVWF, thereby bringing the implications of the advertising changes to the fore, and left for further reflection how best to regulate content in the converging communications field.

[150] Articles 2a.4 and 3 AVMS, n 3 above.

[15]

THE VALUE OF COMMERCIAL SPEECH

COLIN R. MUNRO*

I. INTRODUCTION

RECENT decisions in the courts have encouraged discussion of the extent to which the common law does or should place a high or higher value on political expression.[1] Some scholars argue for a more explicit recognition of the high value of political speech,[2] and would seek, for example, to "constitutionalise" defamation laws.[3] Others have adopted a more sceptical attitude to the desirability of importing American approaches to freedom of expression generally[4] or to the privileging of political speech as a category.[5]

The categorisation of different kinds of expression which is inherent in discussions of political speech is a tendency which is liable to have other applications. However, aside from some debate over political speech, the tendency has not been much explored in a British context. The relative absence of discussion may be explained, if rather circularly, by the observation that the area is under-theorised.[6] As against this, it might be suggested that, at least until recently, English law had no particular need to demonstrate a principled coherence, and apparent inconsistencies might even be interpreted as "a sign of the pragmatic genius of the common law in producing a workable solution to an important problem by paying scant regard to the theoretical and analytical issues that may arise".[7]

Be that as it may, it would seem that categorisation of expression cannot be entirely ignored. This much is shown by a

---

* Professor of Constitutional Law in the University of Edinburgh.
[1] See, for example, *Derbyshire C.C.* v. *Times Newspapers* [1993] A.C. 534; *Reynolds* v. *Times Newspapers Ltd.* [2001] 2 A.C. 127; *R. (on the application of ProLife Alliance)* v. *BBC* [2002] EWCA Civ 297, [2002] 2 All E.R. 756.
[2] The terms "speech" and "expression" may be distinguished for some purposes, but are here used interchangeably unless the context implies otherwise.
[3] See, for example, I.D. Loveland, *Political Libels: A Comparative Study* (Oxford 2000).
[4] S. Sedley, "The First Amendment: A Case for Import Controls", in I.D. Loveland (ed.), *Importing the First Amendment* (Oxford 1998).
[5] I. Hare, "Is the Privileged Position of Political Expression Justified?", in J. Beatson and Y. Cripps (eds.), *Freedom of Expression and Freedom of Information* (Oxford 2000).
[6] J. Gardner, "Freedom of Expression", in C. McCrudden and G. Chambers (eds.), *Individual Rights and the Law in Britain* (Oxford 1994).
[7] C. Forsyth, "The Protection of Political Discourse: Pragmatism or Incoherence?", in J. Beatson and Y. Cripps (eds.), *Freedom of Expression and Freedom of Information* (Oxford 2000), at p. 90.

discussion of the Strasbourg case law on Article 10 of the European Convention on Human Rights:

> The indications are that commercial expression is not regarded as so worthy of protection as political or even artistic expression and that some considerations which make expression valuable in the political context may not apply in quite the same way in the commercial environment.[8]

In this article, it is proposed to consider commercial speech. That category has not been much discussed on this side of the Atlantic Ocean.[9] However, at least to the extent that it features in ECHR law, it is clearly not without potential significance in domestic law, made more immediate through the passing of the Human Rights Act 1998.

The recognition of a category of commercial speech may be traced back earlier than the European Convention, to First Amendment case law in the United States. Indeed, it may not go too far to say that the categorisation approach to issues of freedom of expression may itself be attributed broadly to American origins. It may therefore be instructive to glance at the treatment of commercial speech in the United States, before considering the treatment of commercial speech at Strasbourg. Then the larger parts of this article are devoted to considering the position of commercial speech in domestic law, and exploring the difficulties of defining commercial speech.

United States Law

In the United States, the First Amendment to the Constitution provides (in part) that "Congress shall make no law ... abridging the freedom of speech, or of the press". With the adoption of the Fourteenth Amendment in 1868, the guarantee became applicable to the States.

Although the words may be framed as an apparently absolute guarantee, their interpretation has been critical, as always. In *Chaplinsky* v. *New Hampshire*,[10] a unanimous Supreme Court upheld the constitutionality of state legislation prohibiting offensive name calling in a public place. They did so by a categorisation: obscenity, profanity, libel, and "fighting words" were cited as

---

[8] D.J. Harris, M. O'Boyle and C. Warbrick, *Law of the European Convention on Human Rights* (London 1995), p. 402.
[9] An honourable exception is the paper by G. Quinn "Extending the Coverage of Freedom of Expression to Commercial Speech: A Comparative Perspective", in L. Heffernan (ed.), *Human Rights: A European Perspective* (Dublin 1994). See also A. Lester and D. Pannick, "Advertising and Freedom of Expression in Europe" [1985] P.L. 349; G. Marshall, "Taking Rights for an Override: Free Speech and Commercial Expression" [1989] P.L. 4.
[10] 315 U.S. 568 (1942).

examples of classes of speech which did not merit First Amendment protection.

The vogue for categorisation soon spread. Shortly after, in *Valentine* v. *Chrestensen*,[11] the Supreme Court had before it a First Amendment challenge to the validity of a New York City ordinance prohibiting distribution of advertising matter on the streets, which had been used to prosecute the owner of a submarine using handbills to promote its exhibition. The Court unanimously rejected the challenge, putting commercial speech entirely outside the realm of First Amendment concern. A decade later, the doctrine was reinforced by the upholding of another municipal ordinance prohibiting door-to-door solicitations, even though the merchandise involved was magazine subscriptions.[12]

The dissent of Douglas J. in a 1973 case[13] recorded his conversion from the doctrine, and in 1975 the Court came closer to abandoning it. In the aftermath of the abortion decision in *Roe* v. *Wade*,[14] there was still a patchwork of restrictions on information regarding the availability of services. *Bigelow* v. *Virginia*[15] involved the conviction, under a Virginia statute, of the editor of a newspaper for running an advertisement for an abortion clinic in New York. With two judges dissenting, the Supreme Court found the application of the state law to be in violation of the First Amendment. A year later, there was a case touching more squarely on typical commercial speech, with a challenge to a state statute that made the advertising of prescription drug prices "unprofessional conduct". Here, in *Virginia State Board of Pharmacy* v. *Virginia Citizens Consumers Council*,[16] a Supreme Court majority found that, because commercial speech often provided useful information to consumers, it was covered by the First Amendment guarantee.

However, the landmark decision extended only qualified protection to commercial speech. In *Central Hudson Gas and Electricity Corporation* v. *Public Service Commission*,[17] the courts were considering a ban on promotional advertising by a state's electricity companies, which a public agency had deemed requisite in order to conserve energy. In striking it down as too extensive, the majority of the Supreme Court acknowledged that restrictions on commercial speech were justifiable in some circumstances:

[11] 316 U.S. 52 (1942).
[12] *Breard* v. *Alexandria* 341 U.S. 622 (1951).
[13] *Pittsburgh* v. *Pittsburgh Commission on Human Relations* 413 U.S. 376 (1973).
[14] 410 U.S. 113 (1973).
[15] 421 U.S. 809 (1975).
[16] 425 U.S. 748 (1976).
[17] 447 U.S. 557 (1980).

At the outset, we must determine whether the expression is protected by the First Amendment. For commercial speech to come within that provision, it at least must concern lawful activity and not be misleading. Next, we ask whether the asserted governmental interest [in curbing it] is substantial. If both enquiries yield positive answers, we must determine whether the regulation directly advances the governmental interest asserted, and whether it is not more than is necessary to serve that interest.[18]

In a later case, the fourth prong was further refined as requiring "a fit that is not necessarily perfect, but reasonable ... that employs not necessarily the least restrictive means but ... a means narrowly tailored to achieve the desired objective".[19]

Thus, instead of the strict scrutiny which is applied, for example, to restrictions on political speech, intermediate scrutiny is applied to commercial speech regulation, consistently with what the Supreme Court has called its "subordinate position in the scale of First Amendment values".[20] The test does not only allow restrictions on the advertising of illegal activities and untruthful or misleading advertising. It also allows restrictions on the promotion of activities, which, while lawful, may be judged more or less harmful, such as gambling or alcohol or tobacco use, if the restrictions are justifiable and proportionate. In one case, therefore, a comprehensive ban on casino advertising targeted at Puerto Rico residents was upheld by the Supreme Court, albeit narrowly.[21] In others, the Court has invalidated a Rhode Island law which prohibited the advertisement of the prices of alcoholic drinks, and Massachusetts regulations which banned outdoor advertising of tobacco products in the neighbourhood of schools, as being too broad, when discouragement could have been accomplished by other methods less damaging to freedom of speech.[22] The latter case echoed a decision on the Canadian Charter of Rights and Freedoms, where a 5–4 majority in the Supreme Court sustained a challenge to legislation imposing a comprehensive ban on tobacco advertising as being an unwarranted infringement of rights to commercial expression.[23]

The position of commercial speech in the United States can scarcely be regarded as satisfactorily settled, however. At time of writing, the Supreme Court has in January 2003 agreed to hear an

---

[18] *Ibid.*, at pp. 565–566.
[19] *Board of Trustees of State University of New York (SUNY)* v. *Fox* 492 U.S. 469, 479 (1989).
[20] *Ohralik* v. *Ohio State Bar Association* 436 U.S. 447, 456 (1978).
[21] *Posadas De Puerto Rico Associates* v. *Tourism Company of Puerto Rico* 478 U.S. 328 (1986).
[22] *44 Liquormart Inc.* v. *Rhode Island* 517 U.S. 484 (1996); *Lorillard Tobacco Co.* v. *Reilly, A.G. of Massachusetts* 533 U.S. 525 (2001).
[23] *R.J.R. Macdonald* v. *Attorney-General of Canada* [1995] 3 S.C.R. 199.

appeal from the decision in *Kasky* v. *Nike Inc.*[24] There a narrow majority of the California Supreme Court decided that the corporation's statements in defence of its business practices did not enjoy First Amendment protection. When the appeal is heard, it is potentially important for clarification of the commercial speech doctrine.

ECHR Law

With its rather gnomic affirmation that "Everyone has the right to freedom of expression", Article 10 of the ECHR does not precisely specify what types and forms of expression it protects but, as the European Court of Human Rights noted in one case, "neither, on the other hand, does it distinguish between the various forms of expression".[25] The implication to be drawn is that all expression, whatever its content, is encompassed by the guarantee of Article 10(1), so that the key questions depend on scrutiny of the justification for interference under Article 10(2).[26] In this way the European Convention draftsmen sidestepped the issue of what is protected "speech", which has been troublesome in the experience of the First Amendment in the United States.

A restriction on advertising provided the European Commission of Human Rights with the first opportunity to fashion a stance on commercial speech, in its decision on admissibility in *X and Church of Scientology* v. *Sweden*.[27] There, the Swedish Consumer Ombudsman had secured an injunction relating to some passages in an advertisement issued by the Church of Scientology, which made various claims for a device called the "E-meter". Rejecting the complaint against the member state, the Commission indicated that it did not believe commercial speech lay outside the protection of Article 10(1), but did consider that the level of protection should be less than that accorded to the expression of political ideas, in the broadest sense.

The Commission's somewhat diffident double negative proved to be an accurate indicator of future attitudes. The case of *Barthold* v. *Germany*[28] involved German courts' injunctions against a veterinary surgeon who, in an interview with a newspaper, had incidentally promoted his own facilities amidst broader criticisms of the lack of

---

[24] 27 Cal. 4th 939 (2002)
[25] *Müller* v. *Switzerland* (1988) 13 E.H.R.R 212, para. 27.
[26] See generally D.J. Harris, M. O'Boyle and C. Warbrick, *Law of the European Convention on Human Rights* (London 1995), ch. 11; F.G. Jacobs and R.C.A. White, *The European Convention on Human Rights*, 2nd edn. (Oxford 1996), ch. 12; P. van Dijk and G. van Hoof, *Theory and Practice of the European Convention on Human Rights*, 3rd edn. (The Hague 1998), ch. 7.10; A. Nicol, G. Millar and A. Sharland, *Media Law and Human Rights* (London 2001), ch. 12.
[27] App. No. 7805/77, 16 D.R. 68 (1979).
[28] (1985) 7 E.H.R.R. 383.

all-night veterinary services. The German government argued that Article 10 was not engaged, because it did not extend to commercial speech. However, observing that the publication at issue was an article composed by a journalist, the European Court of Human Rights found it impossible to disassociate opinions, information and "publicity-like" elements in it, and by a majority of five to two found that there had been a violation of Article 10. The Court, therefore, did not have to confirm that commercial speech as such came within the protection of Article 10, although Judge Pettiti, in a separate concurring opinion, stated clearly that commercial speech was protected, "even if it were to be conceded that the State's power to regulate is capable of being more extensive in relation to commercial advertising", and incidentally remarked on its beneficial role in providing financial backing for media and communications.

Several other cases have concerned advertising by members of professions such as the legal or the medical, where traditionally there were prohibitions or severe restrictions on forms of advertisement.[29] In many European countries, these restrictions have been or are in the process of being relaxed, but in the meantime there is a wide divergence of practice. Accordingly, the Court has tended to take refuge in the margin of appreciation doctrine in cases of that type. A British application in the same area was resolved by a friendly settlement, which acknowledged that the rules were undergoing change.[30]

Absent such divergences of practice, the need for a margin of appreciation is perhaps more questionable, but the doctrine had been employed in the leading case of *Markt Intern. and Beermann v. Germany*.[31] The applicants were publishers of a trade bulletin, an issue of which had included an item about a customer's dissatisfaction with a mail-order firm's products, which also requested further feedback on the firm from readers. A court order under the German Unfair Competition Act 1909 was issued to restrain the applicants from repeating the statements, and became the subject of a petition to Strasbourg. The European Court was agreed that information "of a commercial nature" was included within the scope of Article 10, but was evenly divided (9–9) as to whether there was a violation. The President used his casting vote

---

[29] *Casado Coca* v. *Spain* (1994) 18 E.H.R.R. 1; *Lindner* v. *Germany* (App. No. 32813/96, 9 March 1999). For an attempt to explain the Court's disposition to subsidiary in Article 10 cases, see P. Mahoney, "Universality versus Subsidiary in Free Speech Cases" [1997] E.H.R.L.R. 364.

[30] *Colman* v. *United Kingdom* (1993) 18 E.H.R.R. 119. More recently, in *Stambuk* v. *Germany* (App. No. 37928/97), the Court found a violation of Article 10 in a professional disciplinary tribunal's punishment of an ophthalmologist who had been interviewed by a newspaper about his laser treatment practice.

[31] (1990) 12 E.H.R.R. 161.

to hold that the state was not in breach, supporting the view that states were permitted a wide margin of appreciation in the area of commercial matters, and in particular on unfair competition, since otherwise the Court would be put in the position of having to undertake re-examinations of all the facts and circumstances. The opposing view, lost on the casting vote, would have been less deferential to states.

However, the line of substantial deference to the state's laws on unfair competition was followed in another, somewhat similar, case, *Jacubowski* v. *Germany*.[32] There the national court had issued an injunction to restrain a dismissed news agency editor from sending to journalists a mailing with newspaper articles critical of his former employer along with a letter in which he offered to meet them. A majority (6–3) of the Court held that there was no violation of Article 10, on the view that the injunction was not disproportionate. In a forceful dissent, the minority warned: "To accept in this case a preponderance of the competitive element amounts to reducing the principle of freedom of expression to the level of an exception and to elevating the Unfair Competition Act to the status of a rule".

A more rigorous test of the necessity of the interference was applied by the Court in *Hertel* v. *Switzerland*,[33] where the publication in question was a journal article concerning the alleged effects of microwave cookery on the health of users. The applicant had been restrained from expressing his views by an injunction, granted by a Swiss court at the behest of a manufacturers' association. The Court characterised the issue as involving a debate which was of general interest, and not purely commercial statements. That being so, the margin of appreciation was less, and it was concluded that the injunction violated the applicant's right to freedom of expression because it was disproportionate.

Again, in *Vgt Verein Gegen Tierfabriken* v. *Switzerland*,[34] the Court found a violation. Swiss television companies, purportedly following a prohibition of political advertising, refused to broadcast an advertisement from an animal welfare group which would have advised viewers to "eat less meat, for the sake of your health, the animals and the environment". The Court held that the extent of the margin of appreciation was reduced, given that the filmed advertisement "fell outside the regular commercial context" and rather "reflected controversial opinions pertaining to modern society in general".

---

[32] (1994) 19 E.H.R.R. 64.
[33] (1998) 28 E.H.R.R. 534.
[34] (2002) 34 E.H.R.R. 4.

Several of the cases, therefore, indicate a willingness to classify instances of expression as being of general interest, even when they are colourably commercial or involve payment for advertising space. In one instance, the classification issue was simply avoided by being ignored. In *Open Door Counselling and Dublin Well Woman Centre* v. *Ireland*,[35] the Court ruled against Ireland, where injunctions had been issued to prevent the publication of advertisements or information relating to the availability of abortions in the United Kingdom. The Dublin clinics which were amongst the applicants charged for their provision of advice and the British abortion services operated commercially. However, in finding that there had been a violation of Article 10 because the restrictions were not "necessary", the Court did not categorise the speech involved at all, but seemed to proceed on an unarticulated assumption that it was political, if anything.

Along with the tendency to cross-classify, we may also notice that the Court has occasionally seemed to doubt whether distinctions between different types of expression are appropriate.[36] However, much more often it has employed a categorisation and, as the writers of a leading textbook conclude, "the categories of expression to which it has from time to time referred must relate to the different characteristics of each of them and, therefore, ... the necessity for interfering with any particular exercise of the freedom".[37] In the Strasbourg case law, it appears that the necessity of a legitimate interference is more readily accepted when the instance of expression is categorised as commercial speech. While restrictions on freedom of expression must normally be justified by demonstrating that they correspond to "a pressing social need",[38] it would seem that restrictions on commercial speech may be compatible with the Convention so long as a state reasonably views them as necessary. So, for example, a state's restrictions on tobacco advertising, with the aim of the protection of health, are likely to be compatible with Article 10, provided they are not disproportionate.[39]

---

[35] (1992) 15 E.H.R.R. 244.

[36] *Müller* v. *Switzerland* (1988) 13 E.H.R.R. 212, para. 27; *Thorgeirson* v. *Iceland* (1992) 14 E.H.R.R. 843, para. 64.

[37] D.J. Harris, M. O'Boyle and C. Warbrick, *Law of the European Convention on Human Rights* (London 1995), p. 396.

[38] *Handyside* v. *United Kingdom* (1976) 1 E.H.R.R. 737; *Sunday Times* v. *United Kingdom* (1979) 2 E.H.R.R. 245.

[39] As implied by *Germany* v. *European Parliament and European Union Council* [2000] 3 C.M.L.R. 1175. The European Court of Justice annulled the EC's Tobacco Advertising Directive 98/43 because the Community did not have powers to make it under the purported bases. Advocate-General Fennelly considered the alternative challenge of inconsistency with the ECHR and regarded the ban as compatible with Article 10, except for provisions which prohibited cross-branding. See E. Barendt, "Tobacco Advertising: The Last Puff?" [2002] P.L. 22.

II. COMMERCIAL SPEECH IN ENGLISH LAW

Other systems, rather than English law, have employed categorisations of speech. So when we consider the position of commercial speech, or what protection is given to it, in English law, the inquiry is novel, because it has not previously been called for. Moreover, the term "commercial speech" is relatively unfamiliar and (as discussed in the following section) ill-defined. Notwithstanding these difficulties, it may perhaps be of interest to make the attempt.

Neutrality

Unless there is an evident privileging of some category of speech on the one hand, or proscription or disfavouring of it on the other hand, it seems appropriate to describe the attitude of the law to it as one of neutrality. On that basis, it is submitted that the attitude to commercial speech in English law is a stance of neutrality.

As evidence of the neutrality to broad categories, consider the operation of criminal offences such as blasphemy or incitement to racial hatred[40] or a contempt of court under the strict liability rule,[41] all being examples of offences which may be committed by offending expression. In each instance, the essence of the offence lies in the publication of the matter defined as harmful or offensive. In the case of blasphemous libel, when a prosecution was brought in respect of a published poem, it was neither necessary nor relevant to consider whether the publication concerned might be classifiable as literary or artistic.[42] In the case of prosecutions for the offences of incitement to racial hatred, it has been neither necessary nor relevant to inquire whether provocative speakers or pamphleteers were indulging in "political speech", as many of them arguably were.[43] If a television broadcast is held to involve a substantial risk that it would seriously prejudice legal proceedings, it is immaterial whether the publisher is a public corporation (like the BBC)[44] or a "commercial" television company.[45] In all of these cases, if the material involved were classifiable as "commercial", it would not serve either to mitigate or to aggravate the commission of the offence.

---

[40] Public Order Act 1986, ss. 17–23.
[41] Contempt of Court Act 1981, ss. 1–7.
[42] *Whitehouse* v. *Lemon* [1979] A.C. 617.
[43] See A. Dickey, "Prosecutions under the Race Relation Act 1965, s. 6" [1968] Crim.L.R. 480; W.J. Wolffe, "Values in Conflict: Incitement to Racial Hatred and the Public Order Act 1986" [1987] P.L. 85.
[44] As, for example, in *A–G* v. *BBC* (1996) *The Times*, 26 July or *Muir* v. *BBC* 1996 S.C.C.R. 584.
[45] As, for example, in *Atkins* v. *London Weekend Television Ltd.* 1978 S.L.T. 76 or *A-G* v. *TVS Television Ltd.* (1989) *The Times*, 7 July.

Similarly, to take the most obvious example from the civil law, it makes no difference in the law of defamation whether a publication might be classified as being in some way commercial or not. Occasionally, defamation actions arise from the content of advertisements. A well known instance was *Tolley* v. *J.S. Fry and Sons Ltd.*,[46] where an advertisement for chocolate featured the caricature of the plaintiff, who was a famous amateur golfer, and was held to carry the innuendo that he had unworthily permitted his likeness to be used commercially for reward. More commonly, actions are based on imputations in the text of a book or newspaper or the words of a broadcast programme. Again, it is immaterial to consider whether it was or was not "commercial speech" in the setting.

Advertising Controls

The ordinary law of the land may treat commercial speech with neutrality. However, in respect of one type of commercial speech, it is evident that there are controls and restrictions over content. The practice of advertising is subject to a battery of legal requirements, supplemented by schemes of self-regulation.

Thus there is legislation to prohibit the misdescription of the qualities of goods or aspects of the provision of services, accommodation or facilities in the course of trade or business,[47] and further legislation makes it a criminal offence to give misleading price indications.[48] In implementation of EC Directives, there are regulations on misleading advertising and on comparative advertising.[49] There are besides more than a hundred statutes which prohibit, restrict, or affect advertising in specific ways, ranging from the Accommodation Agencies Act 1953 to the Wireless Telegraphy Act 1949, by way of the Firearms Act 1968 (which prohibits unregistered persons from offering a restricted firearm for sale)[50] and the Sex Discrimination Act 1975 (which makes unlawful the publication of an advertisement which indicates, or could reasonably be understood as indicating, an intention by anyone to do an act of unlawful discrimination),[51] for example.[52] In addition, under the broadcasting legislation broadcast advertising is subject to some statutory rules and codes provided

---

[46] [1931] A.C. 333.
[47] Trade Descriptions Act 1968. See R. Bragg, *Trade Descriptions* (Oxford 1991).
[48] Consumer Protection Act 1987, Part III.
[49] Control of Misleading Advertisements Regulations 1988, S.I. 1988/915; Control of Misleading Advertisements (Amendment) Regulations 2000, S.I. 2000/914.
[50] Firearms Act 1968, s. 3.
[51] Sex Discrimination Act 1975, s. 38.
[52] See generally G. Crown, *Advertising Law and Regulation* (London 1998). A recent example is found in the Tobacco Advertising and Promotion Act 2002.

for by these rules.[53] Non-broadcast advertising is subject to self-regulation, most importantly through the Committee of Advertising Practice and the Advertising Standards Authority.[54]

All of this may be conceded, but should also be put in context. The laws on trade descriptions and price indications and on misleading advertising may be viewed along with other areas of consumer law and competition law, as intended to provide protection for consumers along with fair trading for businesses.[55] The European Community approach faces both ways. On the one hand, there are aspirations to develop Community measures on advertising in furtherance of market integration, while on the other, given the objective of free trade (and respect for human rights), it is generally supportive of advertising as an ancillary informational right.[56] Some national restrictions on advertisements may be accepted by the European Court of Justice as not constituting measures having equivalent effect to quantitative restrictions, so as to be unlawful under Article 28, EC (previously Article 30).[57] However, if the restrictions are discriminatory in law or fact, or involve a ban which is liable to affect imports more than domestic goods or services, national restrictions would be unlawful unless they were justified by a permitted exception and were proportionate.[58]

As for the miscellany of specific restrictions on advertising found in domestic legislation, most are incidental or collateral to a particular mischief which is the subject matter: if restricted firearms are only to be sold lawfully by registered dealers, it is logical to seek to discourage preparations for unlawful activity. The relevant provisions are not meant to downgrade or disfavour commercial speech; they are merely incidents of legislation against perceived harms.

There is an extensive body of broadcasting law, much of it concerned with organisational structures, financing and regulation. Most of the requirements and rules regarding the content of broadcast output apply without distinction to the service as a whole because, for the purpose of the legislation, " 'programme'

---

[53] Broadcasting Acts 1990 and 1996. See N. Reville, *Broadcasting Law and Practice* (London 1997); E. Barendt and L. Hitchens, *Media Law: Cases and Materials* (Harlow 2000), ch. 6.

[54] See S. Spilsbury, *Guide to Advertising and Sales Promotion Law* (London 1998); C.R. Munro, "Self-Regulation in the Media" [1997] P.L. 6.

[55] See generally C. Scott and J. Black, *Cranston's Consumers and the Law*, 3rd edn. (London 2000).

[56] S. Weatherill, *EC Consumer Law and Policy* (London 1997), ch. 6; A.M. Collins, "Commercial Speech and the Free Movement of Goods and Services at Community Law", in J. O'Reilly (ed.), *Human Rights and Constitutional Law* (Dublin 1992).

[57] (C-267/91) *Criminal Proceedings against Keck and Mithouard* [1993] E.C.R. 1-6097, [1995] 1 C.M.L.R.101.

[58] (C-405/98) *Konsumentombudsmannen* v. *Gourmet International Products* [2001] 2 C.M.L.R. 31.

includes an advertisement and ... any item included in that service".[59] There are some additional provisions specific to advertisements, and there is provision for a code on this, as on some other matters. Generally, it may be thought that the regime of broadcasting law (contrasted with, say, the press) is explained by apprehensions of the greater influence and impact attributable to the broadcast media and residual perceptions that control lies in relatively few hands.[60]

A self-regulation system is applied to non-broadcast advertising, in order to protect consumers and to encourage responsibility in advertisers.[61] In many respects the system is comparable to the self-regulation of newspapers and magazines through the Press Complaints Commission or the vetting of films by the British Board of Film Classification. In all these cases, the industries concerned are aiming to enhance standards and to demonstrate a sense of responsibility to consumers and to society.

Positive Protection

If advertising controls are suggestive of a negative attitude to some forms of commercial speech, there are broad areas of English law which give positive protection to commercial speech and, therefore, may be thought to redress the balance somewhat.

It was noticed earlier that instances of actionable defamation may arise from commercial speech, such as advertisements. However, it must equally be remembered that business associations are able to bring actions for defamation. Trading companies can sue in respect of statements that affect their business or trading reputation. In some cases, malicious falsehood may be the appropriate cause of action.[62]

From such cases, we see that the law operates to protect businesses, as well as operating as a restraint. The commercial interests of businesses are protected through company and partnership law and in a variety of ways. The commercial speech engendered by businesses is most obviously protected by the laws

---

[59] Broadcasting Act 1990, s. 202.
[60] T. Gibbons, *Regulating the Media*, 2nd edn. (London 1998).
[61] The Advertising Standards Authority has been held subject to judicial review, and more recently has been held to be a public authority under the Human Rights Act 1998: *R.* v. *Advertising Standards Authority, ex p. The Insurance Service plc* [1990] C.O.D. 42; *R.* v. *Advertising Standards Authority, ex p. Matthias Rath* [2001] E.M.L.R. 581. In the latter case, Turner J. accepted that the Codes' rules on which the Authority adjudicated had an "underpinning of subordinate legislation". However, it has been submitted that doubts remain on the issues of whether the Codes are "prescribed by law" and whether all of their provisions are related to legitimate aims: see R.G. Lawson, "Challenging the Advertising Standards Authority" (2001) 151 N.L.J. 526.
[62] See, for example, *Compaq Computer Corporation* v. *Dell Computer Corporation Ltd.* [1992] F.S.R. 93, where an interlocutory injunction was granted in an instance of comparative advertising.

of intellectual property. These are not, of course, designed solely to afford protection to commercial speech, but it is submitted that they do extend substantial protection to this amongst other things. To the extent that they do, it may be inferred that the policy of the law is to value commercial speech as socially useful.

Often, intellectual property laws are liable to be something of a hindrance as well as a help, in practical terms, to someone who is formulating commercial speech. Take, for example, an advertising agency charged with the task of creating a television advertisement for a client's product. On the one hand, the law of copyright limits the material which can legitimately be used, by precluding unauthorised acts in relation to other creators' original works. So, for instance, when an advertisement created for a bus company involved a parody of the Rodgers and Hammerstein song, "There is Nothin' like a Dame", an injunction was granted to restrain its use as an arguable infringement of copyright in the music.[63] On the other hand, original works created by an advertising agency themselves enjoy copyright protection.[64] Many advertisements involve more than one copyright, as they are multiple works. Thus a filmed advertisement is a copyright work in its own right, but is also made up of separate copyright works such as, possibly, the script (a literary work), the sound track (a sound recording) and music or a jingle (as a musical work). Moreover, if it is broadcast on television, the broadcast has a separate copyright.

Similarly, other heads of intellectual property law may give protection to commercial speech within their purposes. Under the Trade Marks Act 1994, the law of trademarks protects those signs which have been registered in order to distinguish an undertaking's goods or services from others'. Trade marks may be non-verbal or may consist of words, including personal or brand names or signatures.[65] The common law action for passing off, in protecting a trader's goodwill, also includes verbal and non-verbal distinctive marks within its scope. Goodwill might, for example, consist in a title: in one case, an injunction was obtained to restrain the unauthorised use by another business of the name "Internet World", when it was used by the plaintiffs as the title for their magazine and in the promotion of their trade fairs.[66] The law of breach of confidence was largely developed in a commercial and industrial context, to protect trade secrets and the like. Its modern extension to areas such as government secrecy and personal

---

[63] *Williamson Music* v. *Pearson Partnership* [1987] F.S.R. 97.
[64] *Hutchison Personal Communications Ltd.* v. *Hook Advertising Ltd.* [1996] F.S.R. 549.
[65] *Wagamama Ltd.* v. *City Centre Restaurants plc* [1995] F.S.R. 713.
[66] *Mecklermedia Corporation* v. *DC Congress Gmbh* [1997] F.S.R. 627.

relations should not blind us to the fact that it may still be deployed in regard to commercial communications, such as a public relations consultancy's report for a client,[67] a company's internal documents,[68] or the development of a concept for a television series.[69]

Categorisations of Expression

Notwithstanding the general neutrality as between different types of expression, it is of interest to observe that there are at least a few areas identifiable in English law where some overt categorisation has been employed.

Thus in copyright law which, as has been observed, protects commercial speech in important ways, there are some distinctions depending on the category of "work" or on the medium in which expression is made.[70] However, the key definitions are sufficiently inclusive as to leave no doubt that advertisements and other instances of commercial speech fall within the ambit of protected categories. The Copyright, Design and Patents Act 1988 characterises literary works as "any work, other than a dramatic or musical work, which is written, spoken or sung",[71] a definition which has been judicially explained as extending to every "work which is expressed in print or writing, irrespective of the question whether the quality or style is high".[72] An "artistic work" is defined to include *inter alia* "a graphic work, photograph, sculpture or collage, irrespective of artistic quality".[73]

Beyond this, we find several other examples of categorisation. However, it is submitted that in each case commercial speech is not excluded from qualifying for the preferred categories, but actually cuts across them so as to be included in the named categories in at least some instances.

Take, for example, the Data Protection Act 1998. It incorporates exemptions when personal data is processed under certain conditions and with a view to publication for any of the "special purposes," these being "(a) the purposes of journalism; (b) artistic purposes; and (c) literary purposes".[74] These terms are left undefined, but the analogy of copyright law is persuasive, especially as in the parliamentary passage of the 1998 Act it was confirmed

---

[67] *Fraser* v. *Evans* [1969] 1 Q.B. 349.
[68] *British Steel Corporation* v. *Granada Television Ltd.* [1981] A.C. 1096.
[69] *Fraser* v. *Thames Television Ltd.* [1984] Q.B.44.
[70] Copyright, Designs and Patents Act 1988, ss. 1–8.
[71] Copyright, Design and Patents Act 1988, ss. 1 (1)(a), 3.
[72] *University of London Press* v. *University Tutorial Press* [1916] 2 Ch. 601, 608 *per* Peterson J.
[73] Copyright, Designs and Patents Act 1988, s. 4 (1).
[74] Data Protection Act 1998. s. 3. See R. Jay and A. Hamilton, *Data Protection Law and Practice* (London 1999), ch. 15.

that the categories were not intended to import qualitative criteria.[75]

The same categories recur in section 12(4) of the Human Rights Act 1998: courts are required to pay particular regard to the importance of the Convention right to freedom of expression, and additionally to some other considerations, such as the public interest, when "the proceedings relate to material which the respondent claims, or which appears to the court, to be journalistic, literary or artistic material (or to conduct connected with such material) ...". Again, the terms are left undefined, so analogies may be persuasive. Besides, on the face of it the provision treats a respondent's claim that material falls within one of the categories as conclusive, in the alternative to a court's so regarding it. On that basis, for example, a claim that an advertisement constituted "literary" or "artistic" material would apparently suffice to bring it into the category.

Finally, an older example of categorisation is found in the defence in the law of obscenity, where "it is proved that publication of the article in question is justified as being for the public good on the ground that it is in the interests of science, literature, art or learning, or of other objects of general concern".[76] Again, commercial speech seems to cut across these categories. Occasionally advertisements have been adjudged to be obscene.[77] However, notice that it is not the item itself which must be shown to be for the public good under the provision, but its publication. In the leading case, the House of Lords favoured a broad view of the innominate "other objects of general concern"[78] and, as a commentator observes, it has been "accepted that almost any kind of redeeming social value in a publication ... could be relied upon to support a public good defence".[79] Granting this, it seems entirely likely that many instances of advertising, and commercial speech more widely, could be justified on the basis that the publication was in the interests of a permitted object.

III. DEFINING COMMERCIAL SPEECH

It has been persuasively argued that there are considerable difficulties in defining political speech and distinguishing it from other kinds of expression, which are such that we should hesitate

[75] HC Standing Committee D col. 212 (21 May 1998).

[76] Obscene Publications Act 1959, s. 4(1).

[77] As in *Shaw* v. *DPP* [1962] A.C. 220, although the case is better remembered for the conviction on the alternative charge of conspiracy to corrupt public morals.

[78] *DPP* v. *Jordan* [1977] A.C. 699.

[79] J. Gardner, "Freedom of Expression", in C. McCrudden and G. Chambers (eds.), *Individual Rights and the Law in Britain* (Oxford 1994), at p. 215.

before adopting it as an organising concept.[80] Equally, from case law[81] and legal literature,[82] it is apparent that there are problems and uncertainties in the definition of "artistic" works or expression. In a broadly similar way, it is submitted that there are also significant difficulties in defining and distinguishing commercial speech.

Category Crossover

Some of the difficulties are exemplified by category crossover. Thus we might be put on guard immediately by noticing that some of the cases provoking discussion in the literature on "political" expression also represent, in some sense, instances of "commercial" activity. The English case of *R.* v. *Radio Authority, ex parte Bull*[83] concerned the regulatory authority's decision to refuse to allow the broadcast of an advertisement on commercial radio services. A section of Amnesty International had hoped to advertise, referring to genocide in Rwanda and Burundi. The pressure group was rejected on the group that its objects were "wholly or mainly of a political nature", which meant that the advertisement fell to be prohibited under primary legislation.[84] Another example is seen in the landmark decision of *New York Times* v. *Sullivan,*[85] where the United States Supreme Court held that a public official could not succeed in a defamation action unless he could prove that the untrue allegation against him was made with actual malice. The alleged libel was contained in an advertisement signed by Alabama clergymen, protesting against the Montgomery authorities' mishandling of civil rights demonstrations, paid for and published in the *New York Times*. Noting that it was an advertisement which "communicated information, expressed opinion, recited grievances, protested claimed abuses, and sought financial support on behalf of those whose existence and objectives are matters of the highest public interest and concern",[86] the Supreme Court did not treat it

[80] I. Hare, "Is the Privileged Position of Political Expression Justified?", in J. Beatson and Y. Cripps (eds.), *Freedom of Expression and Freedom of Information* (Oxford 2000). Christopher Forsyth's paper in the same book also has a sceptical tone.

[81] The leading decision on the meaning of "artistic craftsmanship" in the legislation on copyright is *Hensher* v. *Restawile* [1976] A.C. 64, in which the speeches notably lack uniformity of approach: see W.R. Cornish, *Intellectual Property: Patents, Copyright, Trade Marks and Allied Rights*, 4th edn. (London 1999), pp. 390–392.

[82] P.H. Karlen, "What is Art? A Sketch for a Legal Definition" (1978) 94 L.Q.R. 383; P. Kearns, *The Legal Concept of Art* (Oxford 1998), ch. 3.

[83] [1998] Q.B. 294. See J. Stevens and D. Feldman, "Broadcasting Advertisements by Bodies with Political Objects" [1997] P.L.615.

[84] Broadcasting Act 1990, s. 92. The decision of the European Court of Human Rights in *Vgt Verein Gegen Tierfabriken* v. *Switzerland* (2002) 34 E.H.R.R. 4 will have to be taken account of in this area.

[85] 376 U.S. 254 (1964).

[86] *Ibid.,* at p. 266 *per* Brennan J.

as commercial speech. As already noticed, in *Open Door Counselling and Dublin Well Woman Centre* v. *Ireland*,[87] the European Court of Human Rights simply evaded the question, when the relevant information was in some senses commercial, but the implications were political.

Of course, there are certain instances of expression which appear to come clearly within the category of commercial speech. The newspaper advertisements in the *Pall Mall Gazette* and elsewhere which justified the claim against the manufacturers of the Carbolic Smoke Ball provide an obvious illustration,[88] as do television advertisements for Nestlé's Gold Blend coffee.

However, even if we may say with some confidence that these types of advertisements are commercial and not political, we may not find it possible to deny that they are commercial and artistic. Some species of advertisement, such as the classified advertising typically found in local newspapers, cannot easily be viewed as artistic, but many others can and should be. Toulouse-Lautrec and Alphonse Mucha originated much of their art for commercial purposes. Guy Bourdin and Helmut Newton produced many of their most memorable images for fashion photography. Writers, including William Trevor and Fay Weldon, have worked as advertising copywriters, and film directors from Orson Welles to Ridley Scott have worked on television commercials. These examples remind us that creative endeavours lie behind the images and the words in many advertisements, even when the results are less distinguished or less celebrated. All in all, it is reasonable to conclude that, with many types of advertisements, the overlap between commercial expression and artistic expression is substantial.

The Wider Dimension

Besides, it should be emphasised that, while some types of advertisement may provide standard examples of the category of commercial speech, the categories of advertising and of commercial speech are not co-extensive. From a case such as *New York Times* v. *Sullivan*,[89] it may appear that the category of commercial speech is narrower than the category of advertisements, since not every advertisement was to be classified as commercial. Conversely, there are cases where facts and opinions have been treated as commercial speech, although not occurring in advertisements. In *Markt Intern. and Beermann* v. *Germany*,[90] the reporting of a consumer complaint

---

[87] (1992) 15 E.H.R.R. 244.
[88] *Carlill* v. *Carbolic Smoke Ball Co.* [1893] 1 Q.B. 256.
[89] 376 U.S. 254 (1964).
[90] (1990) 12 E.H.R.R. 161.

about a firm's products in a trade bulletin for pharmacies and beauty shops was treated by the European Court of Human Rights as being "of a commercial nature" and a court's interdict in connection with the publication considered accordingly.

Therefore, items such as are found in a newspaper's display advertising or "spot" advertisements on commercial television may be paradigms, but it is important to appreciate that the types and examples of communication which might properly or reasonably be designated as commercial speech are considerably wider. Business associations may advertise to the public at large or, in more restricted fashion, to the trade. But they and their employees also communicate in multifarious other ways. The employees often communicate to each other. They also communicate to shareholders and potential investors, to fund managers and financial journalists, to auditors, lawyers and advisers, to central government and local government, to allies and to rivals, to employers' organisations and to trade unions, to purchasers and to suppliers, amongst others. Some of these communications are made to meet, or to prepare for meeting, legally imposed requirements, such as are found in the Companies Act 1985 or the Income and Corporation Taxes Act 1988, for example.

Thus there is identifiable a universe of communications which are related to business activity, yet are quite different from the advertisement paradigms. According to one author, difficulties along these lines explain why the United States Supreme Court "for all it has said about commercial speech, has conspicuously avoided saying just what it is".[91]

Domestic Definitions

It might be wondered whether any assistance is to be gathered from definitions identified in domestic law, whether statutory or judicially worked. Courts in the United Kingdom have not as yet found it necessary to define what is to be counted as "commercial speech", although the concept has come close to surfacing, for example in cases which have involved challenges to Advertising Standards Authority decisions by reference to human rights arguments.[92]

The adjective "commercial" appears sometimes in legislation in tandem with other nouns, but these uses do not seem to afford any guidance. Often the use of the adjective is coloured by its adjacent noun. When the words form a composite phrase, such as

---

[91] S. Shiffrin, "The First Amendment and Economic Regulation : Away from a General Theory of the First Amendment" (1983) 78 Northwestern University Law Review 1212, 1213.
[92] *R. v. Advertising Standards Authority, ex p. Matthias Rath* [2001] E.M.L.R. 581; *R. (on the application of SmithKline Beecham)* v. *Advertising Standards Authority* [2001] EWHC Admin 6, [2001] E.M.L.R. 598.

"commercial traveller",[93] "commercial unit",[94] "commercial vehicle",[95] or "commercial rent",[96] the meaning attributed either in a statutory definition or by the courts' construction is so particular to the context as to be unilluminating outside that context.

There are other, more open, phrases such as "commercial basis"[97] and "commercial undertaking"[98] to be found in legislation where, however, the phrases are left undefined. There is a definition of "commercial transaction" for the purposes of the State Immunity Act 1978,[99] but it is neither free of prolixity nor of circularity, while it also offers courts an escape route: in litigation turning on the distinction between sovereign state activity and activity "for commercial purposes", the English courts have been content to devise tests for characterising the activity as sovereign or non-sovereign, and so have largely managed to avoid discussion of "commercial".[100]

Recently, in the Freedom of Information Act 2000, it has been provided that prejudice to "commercial interests" operates as one of the exemptions from the duty to disclose information, subject to the public interest test.[101] It may be thought significant that, again in this legislation, the decision was taken to provide no guidance as to the definition.

Approaches in the Literature

If little assistance is to be found in domestic legislation and case law, can any be found in the approaches to definition canvassed in the literature?

One approach could be to focus on subject-matter so that, let us say, facts or opinions concerning the qualities of goods or services offered for sale or purchase would be regarded as "commercial speech". However, this cannot be a satisfactory approach. The magazine *Which* and the online services of the Consumers'

---

[93] Used in the Finance Act 1915, s. 39. It was defined according to ordinary usage in *Findlay & Co.* v. *Inland Revenue* 1928 S.C. 218.

[94] Used in the Sale of Goods Act 1979, s. 39 (7), as substituted by the Sale and Supply of Goods Act 1994, s. 2.

[95] Used in the Public Passenger Vehicles Act 1981, s. 48.

[96] Used in the Finance Act 1994, s. 120 (3).

[97] Income and Corporation Taxes Act 1970, s. 170.

[98] Small Lotteries and Gaming Act 1956, s. 1(1).

[99] Section 3(3) defines it as: "(a) any contract for the supply of goods or services; (b) any loan or other transaction for the provision of finance and any guarantee or indemnity in respect of any such transaction or of any other financial obligation; and (c) any other transaction or activity (whether of a commercial, industrial, financial, professional or other similar character) into which a State enters or in which it engages otherwise than in the exercise of sovereign authority ...". By section 4, the phrase "commercial purposes" is defined by reference to section 3(3).

[100] *I Congreso del Partido* [1983] 1 A.C. 244; *Littrell* v. *United States of America (No. 2)* [1994] 4 All E.R. 203; *Arab Republic of Egypt* v. *Gamal-Eldin* [1996] 2 All E.R. 237.

[101] Freedom of Information Act 2000, s. 43.

Association are designed to inform readers and subscribers of the merits and demerits of competing products. The BBC television series *Watchdog* alerts viewers to dishonest and dubious business practices. These are surely examples of information published in the public interest which, if there were to be lesser protection for commercial speech, ought not to be included in the category.

A distinction may, of course, be drawn between a television programme and television advertisements or between a magazine's news and features and its display advertising. So it might be asked whether the medium or form of expression provides a way of distinguishing commercial speech. Some media, such as the BBC's "non-commercial" channels and services, on the one hand, or outdoor advertising in public places, on the other, may appear clearly to be one thing or the other.

However, other media are more heterogeneous in this respect. Obviously, advertisements are carried along with other material in newspapers and magazines, commercial radio and television broadcasting, cinema presentations, viewdata services and non-broadcast electronic media, for example. Therefore, any distinction along these lines would have to be more carefully refined, depending not only on the medium of expression, but also turning on secondary criteria such as the positioning of the item or whether third parties have made payment for its insertion. These refinements might cover standard cases of advertising adequately, but are undiscriminating at the margins. An announcement of a birth or a death typically appears amidst the "classified advertisements" in a newspaper and has to be paid for, but is surely not to be categorised as "commercial speech"? Some media, such as broadcasting regulated by the Independent Television Commission, operate under rules designed to effect a clear separation between advertising content and programme content, but other media are less insistent on separation and there are phenomena such as government advertising and announcements, party political broadcasts, sponsored programmes (in broadcasting) and advertising features (in newspapers and magazines) which straddle or blur the categories, often deliberately. Besides, as already noticed, advertising is not identical to, or co-extensive with the boundaries of, commercial speech. A definition of commercial speech which turns on the medium or form of expression seems to be unworkable, or at least irrational.[102]

---

[102] A United States decision which typified anomalies was *Koch* v. *FTC* 206 F. 2d 311 (1953). While upholding the Federal Trade Commission's finding that advertisements for pharmaceutical drugs contained falsities, the Sixth Circuit court conceded that the statutory provisions relied on could not have been applied to a book written by the drugs company's president (which made similar claims) without violation of the First Amendment.

Finally, another approach to definition would use as a criterion the intention or motives of the speaker, as suggested by Professor Thomas Scanlon:

> presumably "commercial speech" is to be defined with reference to participant intent: expression by a participant in the market for the purpose of attracting buyers or sellers. It is not identical with advertising, which can serve a variety of expressive purposes, and it cannot be defined by its subject matter.[103]

However, one immediately encounters the difficulty that intentions are often difficult to ascertain or verify. Another problem is that communications may involve a mixture of motivations. At first sight, an article in a newspaper might be categorised as commercial speech under this approach on the ground that the newspaper proprietor's motive is to profit from their business. However it would be too cynical to assume that newspaper proprietors, individual or corporate, are concerned solely with maximising profit without regard to the product involved. Those who founded *The Independent* might perhaps be credited with higher motives while, for example, the first Lord Beaverbrook owned newspapers not merely as a business but as a vehicle for the promotion of his political views.

Besides, when there are different participants responsible for a publication, the mixture of motivations becomes even richer. A freelance journalist may be motivated chiefly by reward. A staff writer or a salaried radio producer is doing his or her job, for remuneration certainly, with other aims and objectives probably. An unpaid contributor of an article or a letter cannot reasonably be classed as having a "commercial" motive.

On examination, a test of participant intent is not only difficult to apply, but is unsatisfactory. Politicians and political parties are not disinterested in their expression, even if (which would be debatable in some instances) the motivation is not economic. Authors and artists may often be motivated by the prospect of pecuniary reward. The point is well made by Frederick Schauer:

> The mistake made by those who talk of motives ... is that they fail to consider fully the nature of the interests being protected ... many great works have been produced for quite pedestrian reasons. *The Prince* was written not to provide the world with an important and controversial work, but to curry favour in the crassest sense. Much beneficial technology was developed for the original purpose of killing human beings

---

[103] T.M. Scanlon, "Freedom of Expression and Categories of Expression" (1979) 40 University of Pittsburgh Law Review 519, 540.

during time of war. And for every worthless occupant of the
pages of an academic journal that is written solely to gain
promotion or tenure, there is an important contribution to
knowledge published for precisely the same reason. In dealing
with free speech problems it is especially important that we
look to the value of the product more than we look to the
motives of the producer.[104]

IV. CONCLUSION

Professor Schauer's conclusion that we should look to "the value of
the product" invites some inquiry into the benefits or otherwise of
commercial speech as such.

   To be sure, some types of commercial speech have their critics.
Critics of capitalism or at least of its excesses are apt to see
"dystopian visions of a passive citizenry in a society dominated by
commercial interests where politics and the public sphere are
infected by the values of a promotional culture".[105] Critiques often
alight on advertising, with its high profile in consumer capitalism.
The journalist Vance Packard gained a large readership for his
thesis that the advertising industry was ready, willing and able to
use manipulative techniques to persuade defenceless consumers to
spend.[106] In more scholarly literature, the economist J.K. Galbraith
would suggest that when the majority of a state's citizens could be
considered affluent, markets would focus on creating demand for
non-essentials, and the trend would transfer excessive power to the
advertisers and the corporations that financed them.[107] From the
perspective of literature, writers such as Richard Hoggart and
Raymond Williams, anticipating later cultural theorists, dissected
the relationships between ideology and culture, and warned of the
dangers of the drift to a mass culture in a commercialised
society.[108]

   However, some of the accusations levelled at advertising have
not been borne out by empirical analysis. Of the contention that
advertising is anti-competitive, by creating barriers to entry and
inhibiting competitive processes, Veljanovski noted that "despite
four decades of intensive research by economists, it has not been
possible to find robust evidence to support this claim".[109] As for
the simplistic argument that advertising must increase prices

---

[104] F. Schauer, *Free Speech: A Philosophical Enquiry* (Cambridge 1982), p. 160.
[105] I. Ramsay, *Advertising, Culture and the Law* (London 1996), p. 2.
[106] V. Packard, *The Hidden Persuaders* (London 1957).
[107] J.K. Galbraith, *The Affluent Society* (London 1958).
[108] R. Hoggart, *The Uses of Literacy* (London 1957); R. Williams, *Television: Technology and Cultural Form* (London 1974); *Communications* (London 1965).
[109] C. Veljanovski (ed.), *Freedom in Broadcasting* (London 1989), p. 107.

because it costs money, the same author, citing research on branded products and on opticians' services, concluded that "the evidence points in the opposite direction—advertising reduces prices".[110] It is, of course, true that successful advertising increases demands, and to an extent artificially; however, in the society that we have, goods and services which Galbraith would have dismissed as frivolous are now deemed by many to be essentials. It is, no doubt, true that eternal vigilance is required to detect and to monitor the influence of commercial interests on mass communications. However, the development of a critical literacy which encourages such vigilance has arguably increased rather than declined in the population. It should also be remembered that commercial activity sustains, and adds to the diversity of, the mass communications media.

Granting acceptance of a market economy, there is a general acceptance that advertising necessarily has a place in it. More positively, it is reasonable to contend that advertising performs useful social and educational functions. Speaking for the majority of the United States Supreme Court in *Virginia State Board of Pharmacy* v. *Virginia Citizens Consumer Council*, Blackmun J. said:

> So long as we preserve a predominantly free enterprise economy, the allocation of our resources in large measure will be made through numerous private economic decisions. It is a matter of public interest that those decisions, in the aggregate, be intelligent and well informed. To this end, the free flow of commercial information is indispensable ...
>
> As to the particular consumer's interest in the free flow of commercial information, that interest may be as keen, if not keener by far, than his interest in the day's most urgent political debate.[111]

In the same opinion, Blackmun J. argued that there was a "listener's right to receive advertising".[112] The need for a political justification or rationale for constitutional protection is more pressing in the United States context.[113] A few writers, locating their justification for free speech narrowly in its instrumental role in democracy, would exclude commercial speech from protection.[114] However, when justification is found by other consequentialist

---

[110] *Ibid.*
[111] 425 U.S. 748, 763 (1976).
[112] 425 U.S. 748, 756–757 (1976).
[113] R.M. Dworkin, *Freedom's Law: The Moral Reading of the American Constitution* (Cambridge, USA 1996), ch. 8. For some discussion of theoretical justifications generally, see E.M. Barendt, *Freedom of Speech* (Oxford 1985); D. Feldman, *Civil Liberties and Human Rights in England and Wales*, 2nd edn. (Oxford 2002), ch. 13.
[114] A. Meiklejohn, *Political Freedom* (New York 1965); R. Bork, "Neutral Principles and Some First Amendment Problems" (1971) 47 Indiana Law Journal 1. Interestingly, both were later to retract their narrower views: Meiklejohn, "The First Amendment is an Absolute" 1961 Supreme Court Review 245, 263; Bork said that he had abandoned his view in the Senate hearings which considered his nomination to the Supreme Court.

arguments or through subscription to the value of personal autonomy, the case for inclusion is strong.[115] When the Supreme Court of Canada confirmed that commercial speech was included in the guarantee of freedom of expression in section 2(b) of the Canadian Charter of Rights and Freedoms, in *Ford* v. *A.G. Quebec*, they considered the rationales as based not only on the welfare enhancing argument that individuals were enabled to make improved economic choices, but also on the proposition that the making of market choices was "an important aspect of individual self fulfilment and personal autonomy".[116] These justifications view matters from the point of the recipient rather than the speaker, which is arguably the better way to proceed in general.[117] When advertising represents the artistic creations of individuals, there is also justification by the same arguments for self-expression as apply to other artistic works. There could even be constructed an argument that businesses have rights to self-expression, given that expression has economic as well as personal and political applications.[118]

If advertising may be justified on the basis of its social utility, there should be no difficulty in defending other types of commercial speech such as corporate communications. The activities of business and commerce are, in general, in the public interest, so commercial speech scarcely deserves to be treated as "low value" speech as if it involved criminality.

It may be wondered whether the issue of how commercial speech is to be treated need arise at all. It may arise, perhaps through litigation involving challenges to some of the restrictions or conditions which apply to some types of commercial speech. Suppose, for example, that a member of one of the professions, being restricted in their freedom to comment or in their freedom to advertise their services, suggests that the restriction violates Convention rights. Or suppose that a business, vexed by the censure of their advertisement by the Advertising Standards Authority, argues that the Code rule relied on by the Authority does not correspond to any of the legitimate aims which can justify interference with freedom under Article 10(2) of the ECHR. In

---

[115] M. Redish, "The First Amendment in the Marketplace: Commercial Speech and the Values of Free Expression" (1971) 39 George Washington Law Review 429; "The Value of Free Speech" (1982) 130 University of Pennsylvania Law Review 591; R.H. Coase, "Advertising and Free Speech" (1977) 6 Journal of Legal Studies 1; F.S. Haiman, *Speech and Law in a Free Society* (Chicago 1981).

[116] [1988] 2 S.C.R. 712, 767 (1989) 54 D.L.R. (4th) 577, 618.

[117] F. Schauer, *Free Speech: A Philosophical Enquiry* (Cambridge 1982), p. 159.

[118] G. Quinn, "Extending the Coverage of Freedom of Expression to Commercial Speech: A Comparative Perspective", in L. Heffernan (ed.), *Human Rights: A European Perspective* (Dublin 1994), at p. 231.

these situations, the court would be faced with the possibility of categorising the subject matter as commercial speech and allowing the categorisation to influence its approach.

However, it is perhaps a moot point whether English courts, which have been able to avoid employing the category in the past, need alter their practice in this regard now. Admittedly, the Strasbourg authorities' jurisprudence, which incorporates the "commercial" categorisation, must be taken account of when cases arise in connection with Convention rights.[119] However, importantly courts and tribunals in Britain are not bound by the case law from Strasbourg and, as Keith Ewing has observed, "the nature and extent of judicial power under the Act is greater than may be realised", so far as the interpretation and application of Convention rights is concerned.[120] Therefore, it is open to English courts to treat issues of freedom of expression on their merits *without* engaging in a classification of the subject matter as involving "commercial speech" or not and without, therefore, allowing anything to turn upon such a distinction. In view of the difficulties of defining "commercial speech" satisfactorily, and in the light of the social utility of commercial speech, it would be preferable for them to do so.

---

[119] Human Rights Act 1998, s. 2.
[120] K.D. Ewing, "The Human Rights Act and Parliamentary Democracy" (1999) 62 M.L.R. 79, 86.

Name Index